Children's Testimony

Wiley Series in

The Psychology of Crime, Policing and Law

Series Editors

Graham Davies and **Ray Bull**
University of Leicester, UK

The Wiley Series in the Psychology of Crime, Policing and Law publishes concise and integrative reviews on important emerging areas of contemporary research. The purpose of the series is not merely to present research findings in a clear and readable form, but also to bring out their implications for both practice and policy. In this way, it is hoped the series will not only be useful to psychologists but also to all those concerned with crime detection and prevention, policing, and the judicial process.

For other titles in this series please see www.wiley.com/go/pcpl

Children's Testimony

A Handbook of Psychological Research and Forensic Practice

Edited by

Michael E. Lamb, David J. La Rooy, Lindsay C. Malloy, and Carmit Katz

This second edition first published 2011

Edition history: John Wiley & Sons, Ltd. (1e, 2002)

Wiley-Blackwell is an imprint of John Wiley & Sons, formed by the merger of Wiley's global Scientific, Technical and Medical business with Blackwell Publishing.

Registered Office
John Wiley & Sons Ltd, The Atrium, Southern Gate, Chichester, West Sussex, PO19 8SQ, United Kingdom

Editorial Offices
350 Main Street, Malden, MA 02148-5020, USA
9600 Garsington Road, Oxford, OX4 2DQ, UK
The Atrium, Southern Gate, Chichester, West Sussex, PO19 8SQ, UK

For details of our global editorial offices, for customer services, and for information about how to apply for permission to reuse the copyright material in this book please see our website at www.wiley.com/wiley-blackwell.

Library of Congress Cataloging-in-Publication Data

Children's testimony : a handbook of psychological research and forensic practice / edited by Michael E. Lamb . . . [et al.]. – 2nd ed.
p. cm.
Includes index.
ISBN 978-0-470-68677-5 (cloth) – ISBN 978-0-470-68678-2 (pbk.)
1. Child witnesses. I. Lamb, Michael E., 1953–
K2271.5.C49 2011
347′.066083–dc22

2011002206

A catalogue record for this book is available from the British Library.

This book is published in the following electronic formats: ePDFs 9781119998501; Wiley Online Library 9781119998495; ePub 9781119996156

Typeset in 10/12pt Century Schoolbook by Aptara Inc., New Delhi, India
Printed in Singapore by Ho Printing Singapore Pte Ltd

1 2011

Contents

Contributors

Caroline Bettenay

Senior Lecturer, London South Bank University, London, United Kingdom
e-mail: bettenc2@lsbu.ac.uk

Rebecca Brigham

MSW graduate of School of Social Policy and Practice, University of Pennsylvania, Philadelphia, United States
e-mail: rbrigham@sp2.upenn.edu

Deirdre Brown

Lecturer in Clinical and Forensic Psychology, School of Psychology, Victoria University of Wellington, New Zealand
e-mail: deirdre.brown@vuw.ac.nz

Sonja P. Brubacher

PhD Student in Psychology, Wilfrid Laurier University, Canada
e-mail: sonja.brubacher@gmail.com

Daniel P.J. Carney

Graduate Teaching Assistant, London South Bank University, London, United Kingdom
e-mail: carneyd@lsbu.ac.uk

Mary Connell

Clinical and Forensic Psychologist, Independent Practice, Fort Worth, Texas, United States
e-mail: mary@maryconnell.com

Graham M. Davies

Professor Emeritus of Psychology, University of Leicester, Leicester, United Kingdom
e-mail: gmd@le.ac.uk

Richard J. Gelles

Dean, School of Social Policy and Practice, University of Pennsylvania, Philadelphia, United States
e-mail: gelles@sp2.upenn.edu

Lucy A. Henry

Professor of Psychology, London South Bank University, London, United Kingdom
e-mail: henrylc@lsbu.ac.uk

Irit Hershkowitz

Professor of Social Work, University of Haifa, Haifa, Israel
e-mail: irith@research.haifa.ac.il

Carmit Katz (Editor)

Research Associate, University of Cambridge, Cambridge, United Kingdom
e-mail: drckatz@gmail.com

Kathryn Kuehnle

Clinical and Forensic Psychologist, Independent Practice, Tampa, Florida, United States; Associate Professor of Psychology, University of South Florida, Tampa, Florida, United States
e-mail: kkuehnle@aol.com

Michael E. Lamb (Editor)

Professor of Social and Developmental Psychology, University of Cambridge, Cambridge, United Kingdom
e-mail: mel37@cam.ac.uk

David J. La Rooy (Editor)

Scottish Institute for Policing Research Lecturer, University of Abertay Dundee, Dundee, United Kingdom
e-mail: D.LaRooy@abertay.ac.uk

Thomas D. Lyon

Professor of Law & Psychology, University of Southern California, United States
e-mail: tlyon@law.usc.edu

Lindsay C. Malloy (Editor)

Assistant Professor of Psychology, Florida International University, Florida, United States
e-mail: lmalloy@fiu.com, lindsay.malloy@gmail.com

Rebecca Milne

Reader in Forensic Psychology, Institute of Criminal Justice Studies, University of Portsmouth, Portsmouth, United Kingdom
e-mail: becky.milne@port.ac.uk

John E. B. Myers

Professor of Law, University of the Pacific, California, United States
e-mail: jmyers@pacific.edu

Trond Myklebust

Detective Chief Superintendent, Norwegian Police University College, Oslo, Norway
e-mail: trond.myklebust@phs.no

Yael Orbach

Senior Scientist, US National Institute of Child Health and Human Development, United States
e-mail: yael_orbach@nih.gov

Gavin E. Oxburgh

Senior Lecturer in Forensic Psychology, Teesside University, Middlesbrough, United Kingdom
e-mail: G.Oxburgh@tees.ac.uk

Margaret-Ellen Pipe

Professor of Psychology, Brooklyn College, New York, United States
e-mail: MEPipe@brooklyn.cuny.edu

Martine B. Powell

Professor of Psychology, Deakin University, Melbourne Campus at Burwood, Victoria, Australia
e-mail: martine.powell@deakin.edu.au

Heather L. Price

Assistant Professor of Psychology, University of Regina, Regina, Canada
e-mail: heather.price@uregina.ca

Jodi A. Quas

Associate Professor, University of California, Irvine, California, United States
e-mail: jquas@uci.edu

Kim P. Roberts

Professor of Psychology, Wilfrid Laurier University, Waterloo, Ontario, Canada
e-mail: kroberts@wlu.ca

Kevin Smith

National Vulnerable Witness Adviser, Specialist Operations Centre, UK National Policing Improvement Agency, United Kingdom
e-mail: Kev.Smith@npia.pnn.police.uk

John R. Spencer

Professor of Law, University of Cambridge, Cambridge, United Kingdom
e-mail: jrs1000@cam.ac.uk

Heather Stewart

Assistant Program Manager, Salt Lake County Children's Justice Center, Salt Lake City, Utah, United States
e-mail: hstewart@slco.org

Mariya Sumaroka

PhD Student in Psychology, University of California, Irvine, Caliornia, United States
e-mail: msumarok@uci.edu

Bryan Tully

Registered Clinical and Forensic Psychologist, Chartered Neuropsychologist, Psychologists at Law Group, London, United Kingdom
e-mail: bryan.tully@btinternet.com

Series Preface

The Wiley Series in the Psychology of Crime, Policing, and the Law publishes both single and multi-authored monographs and edited reviews of emerging areas of contemporary research. The purpose of this series is not merely to present research findings in a clear and readable form, but also to bring out their implications for both practice and policy. Books in this series are useful not only to psychologists, but also to all those involved in crime detection and prevention, child protection, policing, and judicial processes.

Concerns over the gathering and giving of children's evidence have been a consistent theme of books in this series. The first, Dent and Flin's *Children as Witnesses* (1992) reviewed research that undermined the view that child witnesses were necessarily unreliable and suggestible, and highlighted the legal and procedural difficulties children faced in having their evidence heard under the adversarial system of justice operated in courts in Britain, the United States, and most Commonwealth countries. It foreshadowed legal changes designed to make it easier for children to have their evidence heard in court, including the use of the live television link and pre-recorded interviews conducted by specially trained police officers and social workers as a substitute for live examination at court. In the ensuing years, such innovations were rapidly adopted in the United Kingdom and spread rapidly to other Commonwealth countries (Davies, 1999). However, the consequent increase in children testifying at court in turn provoked a backlash in legal and psychological opinion, fuelled by actual or potential miscarriages of justice involving inappropriate or leading interview procedures being used with vulnerable witnesses (Ceci & Bruck, 1995).

How to resolve the conflict between the need for children to have their voice heard in court and the rights of an accused to a fair and balanced trial formed a central theme for the second book in the series: *Children's Testimony* (2002), edited by Westcott, Davies, and Bull. This first international handbook devoted to the evidence of children placed an emphasis upon accessible presentations and wide perspectives for a wide, non-specialist audience. A more recent volume in the series, *Tell Me What Happened* (2008) by Lamb, Hershkowitz, Orbach, and Esplin demonstrated from an analysis of actual interview transcripts that investigators overly rely upon closed or specific questions when interviewing children with a consequent risk of minimal or suggestive responding. The authors advocated the use of a new interview technique with a rigorous emphasis upon open-ended questions – the NICHD Protocol – which allows children more opportunity to express their own version of events and to provide the kind of detail that the courts require to reach safe verdicts.

A decade has passed since the chapters were written for Westcott *et al.*'s handbook and a great deal of research has been conducted in the interim on the characteristics of children's memory as well as developments in interviewing practice. Likewise, legislation and court procedure on hearing children's evidence in common law has also changed and progressed. It seemed timely to produce a second edition of *Children's Testimony* to bring the story up to date.

In seeking an editor for the new edition, I unhesitatingly turned to Michael Lamb and his colleagues. Since his return from the United States, where he led research on social and emotional development for the National Institute of Child Health and Human Development, Professor Lamb has headed the Department of Social and Developmental Psychology at Cambridge University, where he continues to conduct research on interviewing techniques as part of his wider concern for policy-related family issues.

Professor Lamb's international reputation as a scientist has ensured that the new edition of *Children's Testimony* contains contributions from leading researchers and practitioners from around the globe. As with the first edition, the focus is not merely on current research on interviewing and the characteristics of children's memory, but also the implications of that research for court practice and child protection policy. It is written and designed for the wider audience who are involved in policy and practice in the child forensic area, including investigators, lawyers, judges, expert witnesses, and legislators.

I am confident that this second edition will have the same positive impact upon the development of research and practice in the field as the first edition. My major concern is the changed economic climate into which the new volume emerges. The original *Children's Testimony* appeared at a time of relative economic prosperity in both public and private sectors in most leading industrial countries: there was finance available for training personnel, building dedicated interviewing facilities and funds for research. The second edition appears in more straightened times. As a sign of that changed climate, one need look no further than the policy on the fees charged to local authorities in England and Wales for bringing child protection cases to court. Originally, these were set at £150, but then rose to £4825 in 2008. Following public concern over sensational instances of child abuse, there were moves to abolish fees entirely, but in the light of current cutbacks in governmental expenditure, it has been announced that higher fees will be maintained, reducing still further the likelihood of care cases coming to court (Doward, 2010). Research and policy on child witnesses can never be divorced from wider economic considerations. It is to be hoped that the many positive messages emerging from this important new book may serve to convince governments everywhere that effective child protection and child witnesses are causes worthy of support.

Graham M. Davies
University of Leicester

REFERENCES

Ceci, S.J., & Bruck, M. (1995). *Jeopardy in the Courtroom: A Scientific Analysis of Children's Testimony*. Washington, DC: American Psychological Association.

Davies, G.M. (1999). The impact of television on the presentation and reception of children's evidence. *International Journal of Law and Psychiatry, 22*, 241–256.

Dent, H.R., & Flin, R.H. (1992). *Children as Witnesses*. Chichester: Wilcy.

Doward, J. (2010). Abused children 'at greater risk' after U-turn on court fees. *The Observer* (31 October 2010, p. 20).

Lamb, M.E., Hershkowitz, I., Orbach, Y., & Esplin, P.W. (2008) *Tell Me What Happened: Structured Investigative Interviews of Child Victims and Witnesses*. Chichester: Wiley.

Westcott, H., Davies, G.M., & Bull, R. (Eds). (2002). *Children's Testimony: A Handbook of Psychological Research and Forensic Practice*. Chichester: Wiley.

Acknowledgements

We were honoured and thrilled when the original editors of *Children's Testimony: A Handbook of Psychological and Forensic Practice* (2002) invited us to edit the second edition of this volume. Because we greatly admire Helen Westcott, Graham Davies, and Ray Bull's groundbreaking first edition of *Children's Testimony,* we would first like to thank them for entrusting us with preparation of this up-to-date revision. Secondly, we are grateful to our contributors for sharing their knowledge and expertise while working diligently to create a comprehensive and practical handbook. Thirdly, we appreciate the remarkable dedication and efforts of all who work in the field of children's testimony – investigative interviewers, law enforcement officers, social workers, lawyers, judges, psychologists, and more. This field (and this book) would not exist without the extensive efforts of this diverse group of professionals around the world. Although they are far too numerous to name, we would like to acknowledge their many contributions. Fourthly, we would like to extend a massive 'thank you' to all those legal, child protection, medical, and charity agencies that promote cooperation and collaboration with researchers. Fifthly, we thank Karen Shield, Maxim Shrestha, Andrew Peart, and the whole Wiley team who have supported our efforts cheerfully and efficiently. Finally, the research presented in this book would not have been possible without the help of countless children and families, many in very stressful and difficult circumstances. We thank them for their critical roles in advancing the science and practice of children's eyewitness testimony and dedicate this book to them.

1

Developmentally Sensitive Interviewing for Legal Purposes

LINDSAY C. MALLOY, DAVID J. LA ROOY, MICHAEL E. LAMB, AND CARMIT KATZ

Originally edited by Helen Westcott, Graham Davies, and Ray Bull and published in 2002, *Children's Testimony: A Handbook of Psychological and Forensic Practice* represented a significant collaborative achievement of researchers and practitioners. The book not only provided a comprehensive guide to the available research on children's testimony, but also called attention to unanswered questions and issues remaining to be resolved by researchers and practitioners striving to ensure that investigators elicited detailed and accurate testimony from child witnesses so that children and innocent suspects could be protected and guilty perpetrators prosecuted.

A comprehensive understanding of children's testimony requires expertise from a diverse group of professionals with knowledge of topics ranging from memory to language to law to mental health, with insights drawn from both practitioners and researchers. Not surprisingly perhaps, such interdisciplinary collaboration is, unfortunately, rare. Because the past decade has been marked by substantial progress and

Children's Testimony: A Handbook of Psychological Research and Forensic Practice, Second Edition.
Edited by Michael E. Lamb, David J. La Rooy, Lindsay C. Malloy, and Carmit Katz.

achievements, the time is ripe for a new and fully up-to-date edition of *Children's Testimony*.

Before providing an overview of the book and describing our goals, we begin by placing the field of children's testimony in context. A complete review of the social and historical context is beyond the scope of this chapter (for such discussions see Bruck, Ceci, & Principe, 2006; Poole & Lamb, 1998), but it is necessary to explain the development of the field – even since the first edition of this book was published almost a decade ago – in order to make sense of current issues and debates. Frankly, there is too much yet to be discovered to repeat the lessons and mistakes of the past.

When children are asked to testify, it is usually about maltreatment (Bruck *et al.*, 2006; Lamb, 2003; Lamb, Hershkowitz, Orbach, & Esplin, 2008); a body of knowledge about 'children's testimony' largely exists because a shocking number of children around the world do not live in safe and secure circumstances. In the United States, for example, about 3.5 million investigations or assessments are carried out annually in response to reports of suspected child maltreatment. Following these investigations, nearly 800 000 children were classified as victims of maltreatment in 2007 (US Department of Health and Human Services, Administration on Children, Youth, and Families, 2009). Similarly alarming situations exist in the United Kingdom, Canada, Australia, and elsewhere (Australian Institute of Health and Welfare, 2007; Creighton, 2004; Trocmé *et al.*, 2001). Increased awareness of child maltreatment beginning in the 1970s complemented by the reduction of barriers to children's participation in the legal system in the 1980s together ensured that increasing numbers of children have come to be viewed as potential witnesses (Lamb, 2003).

Each year, increasing numbers of children thus come into contact with the legal, social service, and child welfare systems around the world. As a result, children represent 'a large and growing legal constituency, one that possesses a special set of constraints involving basic developmental competencies, including cognitive, social, and emotional, that may constrain their effective participation' (Bruck *et al.*, 2006, p. 777). In response to these trends, the amount of research concerning children's testimony has grown rapidly; it remains one of the fastest-growing areas in all of developmental psychology (Bruck *et al.*, 2006).

Accurate identification of child maltreatment and its victims is crucial if we wish to end victimization, protect children, and provide children, families, and, potentially, perpetrators with appropriate services and treatment. This is particularly important given that maltreatment can profoundly affect children's cognitive, socio-emotional, and even physical, development (for a review see Cicchetti, 2010). Early identification is often difficult because (as we explain in this book) child maltreatment is a crime that is extremely difficult to investigate. Because corroborative evidence is often absent, especially when sexual abuse is involved, suspected victims may often be the sole sources of information about their experiences.

For this reason, investigative interviewers have vital roles in the investigation of child maltreatment. The investigative interview typically sets into motion criminal proceedings and/or a variety of other interventions for children and families. Information originating from investigative interviews may powerfully affect legal and administrative decisions that may profoundly affect the lives of children, families, and suspects, so it is imperative that children's reports are clear, consistent, detailed, and accurate.

Enough has been written about the McMartin and similar trials to make an extensive review unnecessary here, but it is worth noting how cases such as this highlighted the importance of careful interviewing and the profound need for empirical research on children's testimony. These highly publicized cases involving allegations of child sexual abuse in daycare centres occurred around the world (e.g., in the United States, Norway, New Zealand, and the United Kingdom) particularly underscored the counterproductive ways in which alleged victims were sometimes questioned, at times rendering their testimony flawed and inaccurate (Bruck *et al.*, 2006; Ceci & Bruck, 1995). In the McMartin case, for example, children made bizarre allegations (e.g., that they were taken into tunnels underneath the school, saw witches fly, went on hot-air balloon rides, and witnessed human and animal sacrifice), but the charges were eventually dropped after years of expensive investigation and litigation. Defendants in other cases similarly served long periods in jail before their convictions were overturned (Ceci & Bruck, 1995; Nathan & Snedeker, 1995).

As so often happens in child maltreatment cases, these daycare cases relied almost entirely on children's allegations, and it was the jury's task to determine whether the children could be believed. These decisions had to be made in the face of competing claims by prosecutors that children never lie about sexual abuse, and by defence lawyers that children could easily be led to provide false reports following repeated suggestive interviews by zealous therapists. Such competing claims were made about child witnesses' capabilities and limitations despite scant research on children's testimony and a strong need for empirical research on these issues.

Researchers responded to this need enthusiastically. In the last 30 years, literally hundreds, if not thousands, of studies have been conducted by an international and disciplinarily diverse group of researchers. These studies have revealed much about children's abilities, capacities, and limitations, and the factors that influence children's eyewitness testimony. Drawing upon the findings of laboratory research, researchers have developed (and continue to develop) creative ways to conduct more ecologically valid research – interviewing children about stressful medical procedures, and involving maltreated children as research participants, for example. By identifying children's strengths, weaknesses, and characteristics, investigative interviewing procedures and protocols have improved the quality of information elicited from children. We have learned quite a lot, therefore, even since the 2002 publication of the first edition of *Children's Testimony*.

What do we know and what have we accomplished? We now know that children – even very young children – can provide reliable and accurate testimony about experienced or witnessed events. We also know that children (like adults) are suggestible, and that we must be aware of ways in which suggestibility can be minimized. We further know that the level of accuracy and the amount of detail provided by young witnesses is largely dependent on the ways in which children are interviewed and that the role of the interviewer is thus paramount.

Close collaboration between researchers, interviewers, legal experts, and the police has been especially marked in this field, as exemplified by the achievements of the team who developed the National Institute of Child Health and Human Development (NICHD) Investigative Interview Protocol, a set of structured guidelines for interviewing children about experienced or witnessed events which has been validated extensively around the world (Bull, 2010; Lamb *et al.*, 2008). In fact, it has now been more than a decade since publication of the first field study validating the NICHD Investigative Interview Protocol (Orbach, Hershkowitz, Lamb, Esplin, & Horowitz, 2000). Many researchers have also tested a variety of techniques and procedures ostensibly designed to enhance children's testimony (e.g., dolls/props, CCTV, drawing). Growing confidence in scientific research is evident in the development of a professional organization that focuses specifically on investigative interviewing and facilitates meaningful interaction among a diverse group of researchers and practitioners from around the world – the International Investigative Interviewing Research Group (iIIRG). Research on child testimony also features prominently at the conferences organized by such organizations as the American Psychology–Law Society, the European Association of Psychology and Law, the Society for Applied Research in Memory and Cognition, and the Society for Research in Child Development. Professionals in many different fields have come to realize that there is much to gain – practically, theoretically, and methodologically – from studying children's eyewitness testimony in both laboratory and field contexts. Above all else, we have learned that, in this field, researchers and practitioners need and complement one another in unique and important ways and that the promotion and pursuit of children's welfare requires cooperation with and learning from each other.

Of course, there is much yet to learn. The willingness to learn and draw on new evidence characterizes good investigative interviewers and researchers alike. Research on children's testimony that is informative and helps to solve problems in the field needs to be implemented by practitioners, whose insights and experiences in the field should help in the formulation of new studies and in the interpretation of their findings. The NICHD Investigative Interview Protocol, described in detail throughout this volume, continually strives to accommodate the results of new research and changing needs. Recognition of its overall effectiveness has prompted other researchers and practitioners to consider ways in which it might be altered to address the differing needs of specific groups of individuals who need to be interviewed forensically, including those who are very young or especially reluctant to talk, those who are suspects rather than victims or witnesses, and those who have mental or intellectual difficulties.

Clearly, we have come a long way since the McMartin trials and the associated intense debates about what child witnesses can and cannot do, and we have come a long way since the first edition of *Children's Testimony* was published in 2002. Surely, the next decade promises to be as exciting and productive as the last.

WHAT WE SET OUT TO DO IN THIS UPDATED HANDBOOK

Our aim in preparing this handbook is to create a resource that will be valuable to all professionals working in the field of children's eyewitness testimony – academics and practitioners alike – because it provides a fully up-to-date review of the significant developments made in the last decade. This book contains valuable and practical information of direct relevance, not only to investigative interviewers, but also to lawyers, judges, expert witnesses, social workers, intermediaries, academics, and students. We believe that new advancements must be shared in accessible ways, and have thus asked both academic and practitioner contributors to write in a user-friendly style that make their conclusions available to a wide audience. The book comprises a collection of short focused chapters, organized to deal with the issues in the sequence with which they must often be addressed as investigations unfold and progress.

Whereas most comparable resources emphasize the research and issues of concern to scholars and practitioners in individual countries, we have invited authors from as diverse an array of national and disciplinary backgrounds as the consumers of the burgeoning literature on children's testimony. The editors themselves have experience working in the British, American, New Zealand, Canadian, and Israeli systems and we have included contributors from both these and other national backgrounds because it is so advantageous and important to learn from the experiences and diversity of other systems and practices. Knowledge of what is done elsewhere allows us to reflect on the procedures that characterize our own jurisdictions, helping us to generate new ideas for both research and implementation. Although it was not possible or desirable to address every concern in every jurisdiction, we have attempted to build a diverse knowledge base from which international researchers and practitioners can draw.

This book is also distinguished by our determination to include contributors from many different professional backgrounds. We are pleased to have secured contributions by psychologists, police officers, lawyers and legal scholars, clinicians, expert witnesses, and experienced investigative interviewers and trainers. This allows us to provide a truly comprehensive overview of children's testimony while ensuring that information is topical and directly relevant to practitioners.

WHAT TO EXPECT

The contributors consider all aspects and stages of the investigative process. First, we provide some critical foundational chapters and address issues pertaining to child development and memory. Second, we discuss the various phases of the investigation – from planning the interview to reviewing its value after the fact. Finally, other important issues (including the challenges of interviewing children with intellectual disabilities, the use of supplementary interview techniques and interviewer training) are discussed.

Authors were asked to provide short and focused chapters emphasizing information of direct relevance to practitioners in the field. Of course, relevant theory is discussed when applicable but the focus is on practical recommendations and solutions. In that sense, we asked authors to stress non-technical information and to present research findings in ways that could be readily applied by investigative interviewers and 'consumers' (e.g., decision makers) of the information provided in those interviews. We asked authors to avoid using jargon and highly technical language or providing unnecessary methodological details. Whenever possible, authors reference key resources (reviews and secondary sources) and provide examples directly from the field. To facilitate learning, each chapter begins with bullet points foreshadowing key concepts discussed in the chapter and their relevance for practice.

CHAPTER OVERVIEW

The first chapters (Chapters 2 and 3) provide essential background for those who study and work within the field of children's testimony, because interviewers and legal professionals need to understand the body of knowledge about children's developmental characteristics (Chapter 2) and memory capacities (Chapter 3) that has allowed development of the best-practice guidelines that shape their everyday work. Readers may find that this information helps them better understand why they need to behave (or not behave) in certain ways, and may also help them describe and defend their practices when they are challenged in court, or wish to challenge the behaviour of others. The developmental considerations chapter provides a brief overview of developmental concepts that are directly relevant to interviewing, including, for example, language, children's concept of time, and children's understanding of the word 'touch'. In the memory foundations chapter, we discuss key aspects of human memory and its developmental characteristics that must be taken into account when evaluating accounts of allegedly experienced events. These two chapters set the stage for the remainder of the book by reminding us that our expectations of children must be reasonable and that our demands must respect their developmental capacities and limitations. The field of children's testimony owes a tremendous debt to basic developmental and memory researchers, and this knowledge is summarized in these initial chapters.

Chapter 4, written by an American law professor/developmental psychologist, focuses on issues of testimonial competency, with distinctions made between basic competency and the ability to distinguish between truth and falsehood. In the chapter, Thomas Lyon shows how these competencies can be assessed in ways that are sensitive to children's developmental capacities and limitations. Furthermore, he reveals that truth–lie competency does not predict children's honesty, but that eliciting a developmentally appropriate promise to tell the truth does – an important consideration given the need to encourage truthful reports from victims/witnesses.

Chapters 5–10 take us through phases of the investigative process. Planning is a prerequisite for good interviewing and is thus the focus of Chapter 5 by Kevin Smith (UK police force) and Rebecca Milne (British forensic psychologist) in which detailed advice is provided about the planning process. Key tasks include collating relevant information, setting interview objectives, and making other key practical decisions, such as when the child should best be interviewed.

In Chapter 6, Irit Hershkowitz (an Israeli professor of social work) shows that rapport building is an essential part of the interview process, especially because children may be reluctant to disclose intimate and perhaps embarrassing details about their experiences (e.g., of sexual abuse) unless they feel comfortable with the interviewer. Hershkowitz also describes and provides easy-to-use examples of empirically based best-practice methods for developing rapport. As she shows, the NICHD Investigative Interview Protocol includes a sequence of prompts designed to build rapport with children in the pre-substantive part of the interview. For example, rapport building should involve open-ended invitations for children to talk about personally meaningful experiences. She also emphasizes that interviewers must evaluate how children are responding to rapport-building attempts, asking themselves whether the child is sufficiently engaged and cooperative for an effective interview to proceed.

In Chapter 7, Kim Roberts, Sonja Brubacher, Martine Powell, and Heather Price (a team of Canadian and Australian developmental forensic psychologists) describe the important role that a practice narrative can have in preparing children to talk. The practice interview involves asking children to describe an episodic event (e.g., their last birthday) so they can become familiar with an unusual task – providing a detailed narrative in response to open-ended invitations. As Roberts and her colleagues show, practice narratives have both cognitive and motivational benefits. Although research on the practice narrative is not as abundant as in some other areas addressed in this book, the authors show that practice leads children to later provide longer and more accurate reports of substantive issues. In a sense, children actually learn how to exploit their memories by practicing with interviewers. Practice helps interviewers, too. Practice interviews, which should adhere to the same best-practice guidelines as regular interviews, allow interviewers to practice asking open-ended questions, thereby reducing the total number of questions and the number of less desirable questions asked in the subsequent substantive phase of the interview.

Margaret-Ellen Pipe and Yael Orbach (respectively, New Zealand and Israeli cognitive psychologists now based in the United States) describe the desired hierarchical structure and sequential organization of the substantive portion of the interview in Chapter 8. They provide examples about the ways in which interviewers can maximize the amount of information obtained using open-ended prompts, while delaying the use of focused-recall directive prompts, minimizing focused-recognition prompts and eliminating suggestive prompts. These exemplary descriptions are accompanied with an invaluable description of the reasons why these strategies should be adopted.

However, after the interview has been conducted (ideally in accordance with best-practice guidelines), the job is not done. In Chapter 9, Trond Myklebust and Gavin Oxburgh (respectively, Norwegian and British academics with police backgrounds and responsibilities) describe how investigators must review the case after the interview is conducted and show in the process how and why some cases progress (or fail to progress) and how decisions concerning case progression are made. Of particular relevance to interviewers and other legal professionals, they describe steps (such as examining the crime scene or interviewing the child again) that can be taken if a case is not ready to progress. Thus, among other helpful recommendations, this chapter provides practical suggestions about what to do when it is not appropriate to close an investigation but additional information is needed.

While gathering and reviewing information about the alleged event, the clinical circumstances must also be considered. In Chapter 10, Kathryn Kuehnle and Mary Connell (US clinical and forensic psychologists) thoroughly discuss the risks associated with children's involvement in the legal system – particularly during the period between the abuse report and any possible judicial determination. This period can be very stressful for children, especially when, for example, they face or fear the loss of family members. Kuehnle and Connell discuss the delicate balance between the children's clinical needs and the requirements of the legal case. They advocate that abuse-specific therapy should not be provided for children involved in Family or Dependency court proceedings until their abuse status has been determined legally and remind forensic interviewers that they are uniquely placed to assess the stresses that children are experiencing and, where necessary, ensure that they get referred to appropriate services. As the authors point out, all children do not react similarly to abuse, and thus their vulnerabilities and strengths must be determined on an individual basis.

The remaining nine chapters discuss a number of important issues, techniques, and dilemmas.

We cannot say enough about the importance of interviewer training. It is imperative that those who deal with children's testimony – both on the front lines and behind the scenes – are trained in empirically based best practices. In Chapter 11, Heather Stewart (a US social worker), Carmit Katz (an Israeli social worker), and David La Rooy (a New Zealand-born Scotland-based forensic psychologist) focus on interviewer training. This chapter underscores the need for empirically based training methods and discusses the successful NICHD training model developed by teams involving researchers, practitioners, and expert witnesses. This model emphasizes the crucial importance of ongoing training for maintaining best practices, and Stewart *et al.* discuss studies showing considerable deterioration after the termination of ongoing feedback sessions. Interviewers, their managers or trainers, and policy makers will all find the chapter invaluable.

In Chapter 12, Deirdre Brown (a clinical and forensic psychologist from New Zealand) discusses the use of supplementary techniques that interviewers sometimes choose to help elicit testimony from children, with emphasis on what empirical research has (or has not) revealed about their effectiveness in enhancing children's reports. In her overview, Brown explains the issues (such as the developmental level of the child) that interviewers must consider before using supplementary techniques and draws attention to the potential risks associated with use and misuse of the techniques.

In Chapter 13, Lucy Henry, Caroline Bettenay, and Daniel Carney (British psychologists) discuss the special considerations that attend interviews with children and adults who have special needs or intellectual disabilities. As the authors point out, such children are at greater risk of maltreatment but have difficulty participating effectively in the legal system. Recent research shows that children with mild and moderate intellectual disabilities are capable of providing forensically relevant details about their experiences, however, and the authors of this chapter provide practical recommendations regarding interviewees with specific disabilities (e.g., Down syndrome, autistic spectrum disorder). Too often 'children with intellectual disabilities' are lumped together even though they do not comprise a homogeneous group with respect to either causes or presentation (e.g., severity, symptoms).

The next two chapters focus on the evaluation and utilization of children's testimony in court proceedings. In Chapter 14, British law professor John Spencer puts cross-examination in context by discussing different legal traditions and diverse attempts to elicit reliable testimony from witnesses in the course of criminal proceedings, noting the centrality of cross-examination in the Anglo-American legal tradition. Spencer also highlights the problems associated with cross examination, particularly when children are involved, and suggests how such problems might be mitigated. Spencer presents the legal theory and cases in a straightforward fashion, closing with a solid legal and practical argument in favour of fully implementing the 1989 Pigot Commission proposal that child witnesses should provide direct evidence and be cross-examined as soon as possible after the alleged crime, even when the trial itself is delayed.

In Chapter 15, an American law professor, John Myers, focuses on the special difficulties associated with hearsay evidence. Like John Spencer and Thomas Lyon, he discusses legal concepts clearly and concisely, beginning with definitions of hearsay and hearsay exceptions. The chapter documents the critical role hearsay testimony has in legal cases and calls for all professionals who interact on a regular basis with children (e.g., teachers, medical doctors, child care providers) to be trained in the importance of hearsay evidence as well as in the collection of hearsay evidence. Disclosures made by children need to be documented carefully and not followed up with suggestive questioning. Training should also explain the factors considered when determining whether children's statements qualify for one of the hearsay exemptions.

In Chapter 16, we learn about potential consequences of children's involvement in the legal system. Jodi Quas and Mariya Sumaroka (American developmental psychologists) begin by characterizing the children likely to be involved in the legal system. The authors emphasize aspects of legal involvement that may be particularly difficult and problematic for children, including, for example, multiple delays and continuances, testifying in open court and lacking support from non-offending family members. As they point out, it is not feasible to eliminate such stresses entirely, but some risks and consequences can be recognized and minimized.

In Chapter 17, Bryan Tully reflects on his years of experience providing expert testimony in British courtrooms. In this chapter, he discusses what the courts can expect from expert testimony. Of particular value to interviewers, he explains how they can avoid common pitfalls and attacks on children's testimony. Based on his extensive experience as an expert witness, Tully gives interviewers a snapshot of the expert witness's role and helps them to take the expert's perspective, thereby teaching interviewers how to evaluate children's evidence critically and how to anticipate challenges and criticism, perhaps by modifying their practices.

In Chapter 18, Graham Davies and Lindsay Malloy (a team of British and American forensic developmental psychologists) focus on the relationship between researchers and practitioners. Their chapter addresses the strengths and weaknesses of basic and applied research and touches on some of the important lessons and controversies in the field of children's testimony. As anyone who has worked in this field knows, there are many difficulties and complexities encountered when conducting research in the 'real world' and translating such research into practical guidelines. Davies and Malloy draw attention to areas in which researchers and practitioners collaborated productively (e.g., while studying how investigative interviews should be conducted, or how children's evidence is presented in court) and suggest ways in which communication and dissemination might be improved.

In Chapter 19, the penultimate chapter, Richard Gelles and Rebecca Brigham (American social work academics) shed light on the 'screening process' employed as child protective service workers try to determine whether children have been maltreated, helpfully represented by reference to a series of 'gates'. Surprisingly little attention is paid to these decision-making processes, even though child protection decisions are importantly influenced by the quality of investigative interviews. Gelles and Brigham recommend that the workers concerned be given training about the implications of their decisions and the frequency with which they serve as 'gate keepers' while systems are reformed to ensure that child protection workers get the information they need in a timely fashion so that they can make the best possible decisions.

In the final chapter, the editors bring the book to a close by highlighting key overall conclusions that can be drawn from the informative contributions provided by the diverse and knowledgeable authors involved in producing this volume. They also remind readers of current challenges and the work that lies ahead by emphasizing the continued need for practical and ecologically valid research in this broad and ever-changing field. Finally, the editors underscore the critical need for both academics and practitioners to keep abreast of new developments in the field.

The field of 'children's testimony' is broad and complex, requiring expertise from diverse groups of researchers and practitioners whose knowledge concerning a wide range of topics must be compiled in an accessible manner to facilitate comprehensive understanding and interdisciplinary communication. We must consider the 'child as a whole' – with attention paid to developmental, cognitive, and social capacities and limitations. We must bear in mind the normal workings of human memory. And, of course, we must work within the constraints of various legal and social service systems. It is a rewarding and challenging field peopled by an interdisciplinary group of researchers and practitioners all working toward a common goal – the elicitation of detailed and accurate testimony from child witnesses so that children and innocent suspects can be protected and guilty perpetrators prosecuted. By preparing this fully up-to-date review of the research on children's testimony, we hope to further that goal.

REFERENCES

Australian Institute of Health and Welfare (2007). *Child Protection Australia 2005–06*. Child Welfare Series no. 40, Cat. no. CWS 28. Canberra, Australia: AIHW.

Bruck, M., Ceci, S.J., & Principe, G.F. (2006). The child and the law. In K.A. Renninger, I.E. Sigel, W. Damon, & R.M. Lerner (Eds), *Handbook of Child Psychology* (6th ed., Vol. *4*, pp. 776–816). Hoboken, NJ: Wiley.

Bull, R. (2010). The investigative interviewing of children and other vulnerable witnesses: Psychological research and working/professional practice. *Legal and Criminological Psychology, 15*, 5–23.

Ceci, S.J., & Bruck, M. (1995). *Jeopardy in the Courtroom: A Scientific Analysis of Children's Testimony*. Washington, DC: APA Books.

Cicchetti, D. (2010). Developmental psychopathology. In R.M. Lerner (Gen Ed.), M.E. Lamb & A. Freund (Vol. Eds), *Handbook of Lifespan Development* (Vol. 2 Social and personality development). Hoboken, NJ: Wiley.

Creighton, S.J. (2004). Prevalence and incidence of child abuse: International comparisons. *National Society for the Prevention of Cruelty to Children*. Retrieved on September 5, 2009 from www.nspcc.org.uk/Inform/research/Briefings/prevalenceandincidenceofchildabuse_wda48217.html

Lamb, M.E. (2003). Child development and the law. In R.M. Lerner, M.A. Easterbrooks, & J. Mistry (Eds), *Handbook of Psychology: Developmental Psychology*, Vol. 6. (pp. 559–577). Hoboken, NJ: Wiley.

Lamb, M.E., Hershkowitz, I., Orbach, Y., & Esplin, P.W. (2008). *Tell Me What Happened: Structured Investigative Interviews of Child Victims and Witnesses*. Hoboken, NJ: Wiley.

Nathan, D., & Snedeker, M. (1995). *Satan's Silence: Ritual Abuse and the Making of a Modern American Witch Hunt*. New York: Basic Books.

Orbach, Y., Hershkowitz, I., Lamb, M.E., Esplin, P.W., & Horowitz, D. (2000). Assessing the value of structured protocols for forensic interviews of alleged child abuse victims. *Child Abuse and Neglect, 24*, 733–752.

Poole, D.A., & Lamb, M.E. (1998). *Investigative Interviews of Children: A Guide for Helping Professionals*. Washington, DC: American Psychological Association.

Trocmé, N., MacLaurin, B., Fallon, B., Daciuk, J., Billingsley, D., Tourigny, M., Mayer, M., Wright, J., Barter, K., Burford, G., Hornick, J., Sullivan, R., & McKenzie, B. (2001). *Canadian Incidence Study of Reported Child Abuse and Neglect: Final Report*. Ottawa, Ontario: Minister of Public Works and Government Services Canada.

US Department of Health and Human Services, Administration on Children, Youth and Families (2009). *Child Maltreatment 2007*. Washington, DC: US Government Printing Office.

2

Setting Realistic Expectations: Developmental Characteristics, Capacities and Limitations

MICHAEL E. LAMB, LINDSAY C. MALLOY, AND DAVID J. LA ROOY

Key Points

- Compared to adults, young children have more limited and idiosyncratic vocabularies; they interpret words more concretely and restrictedly, and they are less effective in coping with misunderstandings and understanding the concept of time.
- Even very young children can nonetheless provide temporally organized and coherent narratives if they are interviewed appropriately.
- Although preschool children are particularly suggestible, suggestibility is multiply determined by cognitive, social, and motivational variables.
- Fantasy and pretend play are normal aspects of childhood. Beliefs in imaginary characters (e.g., Tooth Fairy) do not mean that children cannot provide accurate and reliable reports of their experiences.

Because children are often crucial sources of information about the offences in which they have been involved as victims or witnesses, it is important to know how well children can remember and describe

Children's Testimony: A Handbook of Psychological Research and Forensic Practice, Second Edition.
Edited by Michael E. Lamb, David J. La Rooy, Lindsay C. Malloy, and Carmit Katz.

stressful experiences. Our goal in this chapter is to summarize what we currently know about the capacities and limitations of young witnesses, with the development of memory discussed in the next chapter. We first discuss research on children's abilities to communicate about their experiences before turning to some aspects of cognitive development, suggestibility and some social characteristics that affect their behaviour in interview contexts.

Both the amount and the reliability of information reported by children are affected by the children's developmental level, characteristics of the events in question, and the techniques used by interviewers to elicit testimony. Numerous studies have shown a developmental progression in the amount of information that children report, with younger children typically reporting less than older children, but there is also huge variability among children of similar ages, and differences can be minimized or maximized by changing the types of questions asked (for reviews see Bruck, Ceci, & Principe, 2006; Goodman, Quas, & Ogle, 2010; Lamb, Hershkowitz, Orbach, & Esplin, 2008). Age, it seems, does not determine children's ability to recount personal experiences but rather serves to encapsulate the influence of a number of interrelated factors.

DEVELOPMENT OF LANGUAGE AND COMMUNICATION

The clarity and completeness of children's testimony is clearly affected by their developing communicative abilities. Young children often do not articulate individual sounds consistently even after they seem to have mastered them (Reich, 1986), so it is quite common for interviewers to misunderstand children, especially preschoolers. In addition, although young children actually have large vocabularies (perhaps as many as 6–8 thousand words by the age of 6, according to Clark & Clark, 1977) the vocabularies of young children are more limited, less descriptive, and more idiosyncratic than those of adults (Brown, 1973; Dale, 1976; de Villiers & de Villiers, 1999), and their statements are likely to lack adjectival and adverbial modifiers (e.g., very, quickly). Misunderstandings between children and interviewers may also occur because children's rapid vocabulary growth often leads adults to overestimate their linguistic capacities and thus use words, sentence structures or concepts that are age-inappropriate and exceed the children's competencies (Evans, Lee, & Lyon, 2009; Saywitz & Camparo, 1998; Saywitz, Nathanson, & Snyder, 1993; Walker, 1999; Zajac & Hayne, 2003). Despite their apparent maturity, young children – especially preschoolers – frequently use words before they know their conventional adult meaning, may use words that they do not understand at all or only understand in certain contexts, and may understand poorly some apparently simple concepts, such as 'any', 'some', 'touch', 'yesterday', and 'before' (Harner, 1975; Orbach & Lamb, 2007; Walker, 1999). For example, Bruck's (2009) research demonstrates that young children have a narrow understanding of the word 'touch' and may fail to report touches in laboratory analogue studies because children classify the touching actions as, for example, 'rubbing' or 'scratching' instead.

The accuracy of children's accounts is greatly influenced by the linguistic style and the complexity of the language addressed to them by questioners, especially in legal contexts (Carter, Bottoms, & Levine, 1996; Imhoff & Baker-Ward, 1999; Perry *et al.*, 1995; Zajac, Gross, & Hayne, 2003). Children are often asked to negate adult statements or to confirm multifaceted 'summaries' of their accounts (e.g., 'Is it not true that...?'), and are expected to understand unfamiliar words and syntactically complex or ambiguous compound sentences (Dent, 1982; Evans *et al.*, 2009; Perry & Wrightsman, 1991; Saywitz, 1988; Walker, 1993; Walker & Hunt, 1998; Warren, Woodall, Hunt, & Perry, 1996). For example, consider the question, 'Did you say that when they were playing this game called Bingo that you knew that somebody was going to hurt people and when that happened you hid? Do you remember that?' asked of a 5-year-old girl who had allegedly witnessed a murder (Walker, 1993, p. 66). In a recent study of felony child sexual abuse cases (Evans *et al.*, 2009), neither defence *nor* prosecution attorneys varied the length or complexity of their sentences despite the fact that the age range of the alleged child victims varied widely (i.e., 5–15 years). Evidence reveals that lawyers are not the only professionals who fail to vary their language in accordance with children's developmental level. Even mental health professionals who specialize in children and trained investigative interviewers ask children developmentally inappropriate or complex questions in investigative interviews (Korkman, Santtila, Dzewiecki, & Sandnabba, 2008; Plotnikoff & Woolfson, 2009).

Certainly, empirical evidence shows that children struggle to answer complex questions. Brennan and Brennan (1988) showed that fewer than two-thirds of the questions addressed to 6- to 15-year-olds in court were comprehensible to their peers. Perry *et al.* (1995) similarly showed that kindergarten- to university-aged students had much more difficulty correctly answering complex questions than more simply phrased questions about the same witnessed event. More importantly, the kindergarteners did not even recognize that they misunderstood the complex questions. Such failures to recognize miscomprehension may help explain why children rarely ask for clarification (Saywitz, 1995; Saywitz, Snyder, & Nathanson, 1999).

Children's comprehension-monitoring skills and mechanisms for coping with misunderstandings likely develop gradually over time (Flavell, Speer, Green, & August, 1981; Saywitz, Jaenicke, & Camparo, 1990; Singer & Flavell, 1981). For instance, metacognitive and metalinguistic awareness and skills develop more fully after age 5 (Markman, 1977, 1979; Saywitz & Wilkinson, 1982), meaning that preschool children are seldom able to monitor their comprehension as effectively as older children or adults (Markman, 1977, 1979). Stress, challenging memory searches, difficult-to-comprehend questions as well as the complexity and unfamiliarity of the investigative interview may further tax the ability of young children to monitor their comprehension successfully.

The more impoverished children's language, the greater the likelihood that their statements will be misinterpreted or that they will misinterpret the interviewers' questions and purposes (King & Yuille, 1987; Perry & Wrightsman, 1991; Walker, 1993). When interviewers misrepresent what children say, furthermore, they tend not to be corrected, and thus the mistakes, rather than the correct information, may be reported by the children later in the interview (Roberts & Lamb, 1999). Hunt and Borgida (2001) confirmed that disagreement with mistaken assertions was uncommon, with adults significantly more likely than children to disagree when interviewers distorted their answers. In subsequent interviews, 4- and 5-year-old children were more likely than older children or adults to incorporate the interviewers' earlier distortions into their later reports about witnessed events, suggesting that their memories of the event might have been distorted. This further underscores the extent to which the interviewers' behaviour – particularly their vocabularies, the complexity of their utterances, their suggestiveness, and their success in motivating children to be informative and forthcoming – profoundly influences the course and outcome of the interviews they conduct with children.

In addition, children frequently interpret words very concretely and restrictedly (e.g., a child may not respond to a question about something that happened at 'home' if the child lives in an 'apartment'), or make references that fall outside of the listener's knowledge base (e.g., 'He looked like my English teacher'), thus making their accounts ambiguous (Hewitt, 1999; Saywitz *et al.*, 1999; Walker, 1999). Their vocabularies, of course, may also be very idiosyncratic, as indicated earlier.

Children also *learn* how to participate in conversations, and this learning is often still a work in progress at the time that children are interviewed forensically. Children must learn how to stay on topic, how to adapt their speech appropriately to different audiences (e.g., an unfamiliar interviewer who does not know their family members and was not present during the event in question) and how to structure coherent narratives about past events (Nelson & Fivush, 2004; Warren & McCloskey, 1997). The challenge confronting investigators is to obtain organized accounts that are sufficiently rich in descriptive detail to permit an understanding of the children's testimony. Unlike adults and older children, furthermore, young children cannot draw upon an array of past experiences to enrich and clarify their descriptive accounts.

The richness and usefulness of children's accounts of abusive experiences are also influenced by social or pragmatic aspects of communication. For example, when asked questions such as 'Do you remember his name?', 'Do you know why you are here today?', or 'Can you show me where he touched you?', older children usually read between the lines and provide the desired information, whereas younger children may simply answer literally 'Yes' or 'No' (Walker & Warren, 1995; Warren *et al.*, 1996). In addition, young witnesses are typically unaware of the amount and type of information being sought by forensic investigators and are unaccustomed to being viewed as informants rather than novices being tested about the quality of their knowledge. Children are used to being questioned by adults who are already knowledgeable about the topic of conversation (Lamb, Orbach, Warren, Esplin, & Hershkowitz, 2007). By contrast, alleged victims of abuse are often the sole sources of information about the suspected events. As a result, interviewers need to communicate their needs and expectations clearly, motivating children to provide as much information as they can. One of the goals of the 'pre-substantive' portions of forensic interviews is to ensure that children understand the unique demands of forensic interview contexts (e.g., see Chapter 6; Sternberg, Lamb, Esplin, Orbach, & Hershkowitz, 2002). If children fail to appreciate that the interviewer has little, if any, knowledge of the alleged events, or attribute superior knowledge to the adult interviewers (e.g., Ceci, Ross, & Toglia, 1987a,b), they may fail to report all they know. Children are cognizant of differences between knowledgeable and naïve adults and vary their responses accordingly (Welch-Ross, 1999).

Even when interviewers have attempted to communicate that they do not know what the children experienced, they may, by using the wrong sorts of questions, inadvertently encourage young children to respond as though they are being tested. For example, forensic interviewers frequently ask very specific questions (such as 'Did he touch you?'). Young children (those under 6) have special difficulty answering specific questions, and may exhibit a response bias (e.g., Ahern, Lyon, & Quas, in press; Fivush, Peterson, & Schwarzmeuller, 2002; Peterson, Dowdin, & Tobin, 1999), or a reluctance to give 'don't know' responses when they would be appropriate (Davies, Tarrant, & Flin,

1989; Saywitz & Snyder, 1993). Children rarely say 'don't know' in response to difficult questions or questions for which they do not know the answer (Bruck & Ceci, 1999; Lamb, Sternberg, & Esplin, 1998; Memon & Vartoukian, 1996; Poole & White, 1991) and do not provide more 'don't know' responses to complex as opposed to simple questions (Carter *et al.*, 1996). In fact, Waterman, Blades, and Spencer (2000, 2001, 2004) showed that children (5- to 9-year-olds) often attempt to answer impossible (nonsensical) or unanswerable questions (where the information has not been provided), especially if they are phrased as yes/no rather than wh- questions and even when they accurately judge that the questions are nonsensical. The type of questions asked and the context in which they are introduced thus determine whether they enhance or degrade the reliability of children's reports (Poole & Lamb, 1998; Saywitz & Lyon, 2002).

Increases in the amounts of information reported by children as they grow older may also reflect their increasingly sophisticated skills as narrators. Young children are still developing their metalinguistic abilities – coming to know what listeners want to know, and how to report information coherently, monitor the success of their communication and modify strategies as necessary to ensure that the listeners have understood (Lamb & Brown, 2006; Saywitz & Snyder, 1996). In addition, if children infer that interviewers would prefer particular responses, they may tailor their accounts in order to appear cooperative (Ceci & Bruck, 1993, 1995; Ceci, Kulkofsky, Klemfuss, Sweeney, & Bruck, 2007; Melnyk, Crossman, & Scullin, 2007). In the forensic context, therefore, interviewers must be sensitive to children's perceptions of their knowledge and status.

Early Accounts of Experienced Events

As children grow older, the length, informativeness and complexity of their narratives increase (for reviews see Fivush, 1997, Lamb *et al.*, 2008; Poole & Lamb, 1998; Saywitz & Camparo, 1998; Schneider & Pressley, 1997), but even very young children provide temporally organized and coherent narratives (e.g., Flin, Boon, Knox, & Bull, 1992; Lamb *et al.*, 2003). Nelson and her colleagues have argued that children start to form long-term memories only when they begin talking about their experiences with others, thereby creating meaningful and enduring autobiographical records of their experiences (Nelson & Fivush, 2004). This social construction of personal narratives influences the quantity and quality of children's narratives (Hudson, 1990; Ratner, 1984; Reese, Haden, & Fivush, 1993). In addition, the development of children's self-concepts (Howe & Courage, 1993; Howe, Courage, &

Edison, 2003) and their awareness of how memories were acquired (i.e., 'source' knowledge), affect the emergence of autobiographical memory (Howe *et al.*, 2003; Nelson & Fivush, 2004; Perner, 2000; Roberts & Blades, 2000).

Once children begin to recall and talk about their experiences, their abilities are often impressive, although significant developmental changes continue through early childhood. Young children typically recall significantly less information than older children, particularly in response to very general prompts such as 'Tell me what happened', and although their recall responses are not less accurate than those of older children they may omit much information that adults consider important (for reviews see Lamb *et al.*, 2008; Ornstein, Baker-Ward, Gordon, & Merritt, 1997). Thus, 4- and 5-year-olds typically receive more specific prompts from interviewers (Hamond & Fivush, 1991) to which they respond less accurately than older children (Bjorklund, Bjorklund, Brown, & Cassel, 1998; Goodman, Quas, Batterman-Faunce, Riddlesberger, & Kuhn, 1994). Nevertheless, field research shows that children as young as 4 years of age provide proportionally as much information in response to open-ended questions as older children, although the brevity of their responses makes it necessary for interviewers to prompt for additional information, preferably using the child's prior responses as cues to trigger further recall (Lamb *et al.*, 2003).

Types of Questions Used by Interviewers

Regardless of the types of experiences being remembered or reported, the methods used by interviewers to elicit children's accounts of their experiences affect both the quantity and quality of information obtained. As explained in the next chapter, the distinction between recall and recognition testing is crucial. When adults and children are asked to describe events with free-recall prompts ('Tell me everything you remember...'), their accounts may be brief and sketchy, but are more likely to be accurate. When provided with open-ended prompts like 'Tell me more about that' or 'And then what happened?', children often report additional details. When interviewers prompt with leading questions such as 'Did he have a beard?', 'Did he touch you with his private', or 'Did this happen in the day or in the night', however, they shift from recall to recognition testing, and the probability of error rises dramatically (e.g., Dent, 1982, 1986; Dent & Stephenson, 1979; Hutcheson, Baxter, Telfer, & Warden, 1995; Lamb & Fauchier, 2001; Orbach & Lamb, 2001). When open-ended prompts are used, respondents attempt to provide as much relevant information as they 'remember', whereas children may have to confirm or reject information provided by interviewers when focused questions tapping recognition memory are asked. Recognition questions or prompts refocus the child on domains of interest to the investigator and exert greater pressure to respond, whether or not the respondent is sure of the response. Recognition probes are more likely to elicit erroneous responses in eyewitness contexts because of response biases (i.e., tendencies to say 'yes' or 'no' without reflection) and false recognition of details that were only mentioned in previous interviews or are inferred from the gist of the experienced events (Brainerd & Reyna, 1996). Effective interviewers should thus maximize the reliance on free recall by offering open-ended prompts so as to minimize the risk of eliciting erroneous information. Free recall reports are not always accurate, of course, especially when the events occurred long before the interview or there have been opportunities for either pre- or post-event contamination (Bruck & Ceci, 2004; Leichtman & Ceci, 1995; London, Bruck, & Melnyk, 2009; Poole & Lindsay, 1995; Poole & White, 1993; Quas *et al.,* 2007; Warren & Lane, 1995) but they are likely to be much more accurate than reports elicited using recognition cues or prompts. The completeness of brief initial responses can be increased when interviewers use the information provided by children in their first spontaneous utterance as prompts for further elaboration (e.g., 'You said the man touched you; tell me more about that touching'; Lamb *et al.*, 2003).

When children are witnesses in criminal cases, one issue that poses special challenges is the need to establish *when* target events occurred. Although legal requirements are relaxed in cases involving young children (Poole & Lamb, 1998), the prosecution must generally specify alleged events that occurred at designated times in order to provide the defence with sufficient opportunity to challenge the allegations. Furthermore, when children's testimony includes temporal information such as the time of day when an offence occurred, investigators obtain valuable forensic information.

Unfortunately, as Piaget (1927/1971) commented long ago, children have difficulty conceptualizing time. The ability to make accurate temporal judgements improves gradually across development (e.g., Carni & French, 1984; Fivush & Mandler, 1985; Friedman, 1977, 1986, 2000), especially in middle childhood (i.e., 8–10 years; Friedman, 1986, 1992; Montangero, 1992; Tartas, 2001). However, even adolescents do not fully understand some temporal concepts.

Of course, not all judgements or concepts about time are equally difficult or develop at the same time. For instance, during the course of investigative interviews, children may be asked to locate particular events in time, to judge the relative recency of events or to sequence events. Children and adults alike struggle when asked to date autobiographical events – making inferences about their 'location' in time or when the event could have taken place (Friedman, 1987; Wright, Gaskell, & O'Muircheartaigh, 1997), even when temporal cues are provided (Friedman & Lyon, 2005). Such judgements require knowledge of conventional time patterns (e.g., days of the week, months, seasons), which are acquired gradually over many years (Friedman, 1991, 1993). The awareness of temporal distance develops earlier than the ability to locate events in time, and the ability to link events to a location on a long time scale increases with age (Friedman, 1991, 1992). Thus, children as young as 4 years can locate past events on the time-of-day scale (e.g., 'It happened at lunchtime') but are still unable to locate past events on a scale longer than a day (Friedman, 1991).

Although children have difficulty accurately locating events in time even in adolescence or adulthood, they are able to order or sequence events and to make judgements of relative recency at earlier ages (e.g., Which one happened a longer time ago?; e.g., Friedman, 1991; Friedman & Lyon, 2005). In one study (Friedman, 1991), children aged 4–8 years were asked to (a) make judgements about the relative recency of two stimulus events, one that occurred 1 week ago and another that occurred 7 weeks ago, and (b) report the season, month, day of the week and time of day of these events. The 4-year-old group could order the two events accurately when asked questions about relative recency, but they could only localize events in terms of time of day. By the age of 6 years, children demonstrated the ability to make accurate judgements using scales longer than a day. Friedman and Lyon (2005) asked 4- to 13-year-olds to reconstruct the time of past events based on temporal cues included in two in-class demonstrations. Children were asked to judge the order of the two events, as well as their proximity to a major holiday – Halloween. Children, even the oldest among them, rarely mentioned the planted temporal cues (e.g., sunglasses, leaves) in their free recall reports. By first grade (i.e., age 6), children were able to order the two staged events accurately. However, none of the children (even the oldest) were able to judge correctly whether 'the box demonstration' occurred before or after Halloween.

In sum, even very young children (i.e., 4 years old) can make some judgements relating to time. Children are able to make sequencing and relative recency judgements before location-based judgements. The ability to provide accurate reports about time develops gradually though, and is still incomplete by adolescence (Friedman, 1991).

Even when children have a firm grasp of time concepts, they must understand the questions that interviewers ask before they can answer accurately. Temporal terms are problematic for children, however, perhaps in part because words like 'before', 'after', 'first', and 'last' have both spatial and temporal meaning: Friedman and Seely (1976) reported that understanding of these terms improved between 3 and 5 years of age. The youngest children understood the terms as having either spatial or temporal meaning but not both. Context also matters. When placed in the context of familiar daily activities, children may be able to make temporal judgements that they are incapable of making in other contexts. For example, children can specify backward sequences of familiar daily activities ('Before we went to sleep, we watched TV') earlier than they can specify backward sequences of the months of the year ('November is the month before December'; Friedman, 1986, 1990). Although children as young as 3 years might know some time language and be able to recite the days of the week or months, this does not mean that they know how these things fit together into a temporal pattern or how to apply this knowledge in all contexts.

Field studies examining children's reports of temporal information are rare indeed. In a study examining young children's responses to open-ended prompts, sequencing was often referenced by 4- to 8-year-old children during forensic interviews, with children as young as 4 years structuring narrative accounts of allegedly experienced events and using the appropriate relational vocabulary (e.g., next, before, after; Lamb *et al.*, 2003). In another field study, Orbach and Lamb (2007) examined 250 forensic interviews of 4- to 10-year-old alleged victims of sexual abuse. There were age-related increases in children's references to temporal attributes using the appropriate relational terminology, both spontaneously and in response to temporal requests. Sequencing was the most commonly referenced temporal category. Although references to both sequences and temporal locations increased with age, there was a marked shift in the number of references to both temporal categories at age 10 as would be expected based on what we know about children's temporal understanding.

More field research is clearly needed. However, it is important for interviewers to be aware of children's incomplete understanding of temporal concepts and terminology and of their difficulties locating events in time. Awareness that some temporal skills are acquired late in development should invalidate attempts to challenge young witnesses' competence when they fail to provide the requested temporal information.

SUGGESTIBILITY OF CHILD WITNESSES

The enormous publicity accorded to allegations of multi-victim sexual abuse in child care centres in the 1980s and early 1990s (Bruck *et al.*,

2006; Ceci & Bruck, 1995; Kelley, 1996; Nathan & Snedeker, 1995) helped prompt many researchers to study the accuracy of children's recollections and the unreliability of their responses when questioned. In these high profile multi-victim cases, interviewers often appeared to have questioned children about their allegations suggestively or coercively, introducing details that had not been volunteered by the children, implying expected responses, and posing the same questions repeatedly.

In one particularly notorious case, members of the McMartin family were accused of abusing hundreds of children over a 10-year period (Reinhold, 1990). Interviewers and therapists confirmed that the children were asked suggestive questions, such as 'Can you remember the naked pictures?' when the children had not mentioned either photography or nakedness (Garven, Wood, Malpass, & Shaw, 1998, p. 348). In addition, Garven *et al.* (1998) noted that many questions were repeated even when the children had previously given unambiguous answers. For example, after a child responded that he/she did not remember any pictures of naked bodies, the interviewer repeated the question saying, 'Can't you remember that part?' Even after the child again responded 'no', the interviewer persisted saying 'Why don't you think about that for a while...Your memory might come back to you' (Garven *et al.*, 1998, p. 349). Such statements suggest that the event really happened and convey that the interviewer is dissatisfied with the child's response. Another questionable tactic involved inviting children to pretend or imagine that something had happened (e.g., 'Mr Ray might have done some of that touching? Do you think that's possible? Where do you think he would have touched her?'; Schreiber *et al.*, 2006, p. 29). Children asked to imagine that events occurred sometimes have difficulty when later asked to distinguish between events that 'really happened' and events that were just imagined (Foley & Johnson, 1985). In addition, children may later think that the interviewers are interested in reports of both experienced and imagined events.

Repeated suggestive questioning has characterized the investigation of other cases involving multiple alleged victims at child care centres. For instance, Kelly Michaels was accused of sexually abusing children at the Wee Care centre in New Jersey where she was a teacher (Ceci & Bruck, 1995; Schreiber *et al.*, 2006). Suspicions first arose when a child having his temperature checked rectally remarked to the paediatrician that his teacher 'does that' to him. When later questioned by an investigator, the child inserted his finger into the rectum of an anatomically detailed doll and indicated that other boys had their temperature taken too. Other children were repeatedly questioned about the alleged abuse in a series of interviews by police investigators and therapists; most of these children eventually alleged that Michaels had abused them. Similar techniques were used in other such cases in countries around the world (e.g., *Lillie and Reed v Newcastle City Council & Ors* as discussed in Bruck *et al.*, 2006). For example, when children made allegations of abuse by owners and workers at the Little Rascals daycare centre in Edenton, North Carolina, therapists and police officers began to interrogate all of the children who attended the centre. Some of the children disclosed abuse after 10 months of 'therapy' (Ceci & Bruck, 1995). In this case, none of the interviews were electronically recorded, but some of the coercive techniques were described to journalists or at trial.

Investigative interviewers in the Kelly Michaels case also capitalized on children's sensitivity to the high status of the interviewer, as when they commented, 'I'm a policeman; if you were a bad girl, I would punish you wouldn't I? Police can punish bad people' (Ceci & Bruck, 1995, p. 152). Furthermore, interviewers induced negative stereotypes about Kelly Michaels by telling the children that she was 'bad' or 'scary'. Interviewers in both the McMartin and Wee Care cases, among others, also used peer pressure in their attempts to elicit disclosures. For example, they would tell the children that their friends had already identified them as victims. In addition, interviewers promised the children rewards – such as snacks or the termination of the interview – if they would make allegations.

Analysis of these notorious cases helped draw attention to such potentially problematic investigative techniques as repeated questioning and suggestion, references to the interviewer's high status, peer pressure, promises of rewards and threats, requests that children pretend or imagine that something occurred and the use of anatomical dolls as interview aids. Such practices aroused alarm and helped stimulate a number of studies that clarified our understanding of suggestibility (Ceci & Bruck, 2006; Kuehnle, 1996; Lamb, Sternberg, Orbach, Hershkowitz, & Esplin, 1999; Malloy & Quas, 2009; Poole & Lamb, 1998), while fuelling intense controversy about the value of laboratory analogue studies (e.g., Ceci & Bruck, 1995; Ceci & Friedman, 2000; Lyon, 1999, 2002).

Both social factors, such as the superior status of the interviewer, and cognitive factors, including those relating to pretence or imagination, may influence children's susceptibility to misinformation (Ceci & Bruck, 2006). However, initial laboratory-based research appeared to produce inconsistent findings regarding the suggestibility of young children. Goodman and her colleagues showed that children as young as 3–4 years of age could successfully resist misleading questions suggesting actions that were very different from those that had occurred or been witnessed (Goodman & Aman, 1990; Goodman, Aman, & Hirschman, 1987; Goodman, Bottoms, Schwartz-Kenney, & Rudy, 1991; Goodman, Rudy, Bottoms, & Aman, 1990). In other early studies conducted in laboratory settings, however, preschoolers appeared especially susceptible to suggestion (e.g., Ceci *et al.*, 1987a,b; King & Yuille, 1987). Ceci and his colleagues found, for example, that preschoolers are less likely to accept false suggestions made by 7-year-old children rather than by adults. In addition, Leichtman and Ceci (1995) showed that preschoolers who were repeatedly led to believe that a person was very clumsy acquiesced more easily over a 10-week period to allegations about that person than children who were given neutral information about him. Indeed, children may, under certain conditions, come to provide elaborate accounts of entire events that have never been experienced (e.g., Bruck, Ceci, & Hembrooke, 2002; Ceci, Huffman, Smith, & Loftus, 1994; Ceci, Loftus, Leichtman, & Bruck, 1994; Quas *et al.*, 2007; Strange, Garry, & Sutherland, 2003). In a classic study, Ceci *et al.* (1994) asked 3- to 6-year-olds to repeatedly imagine experiencing a fictitious event (e.g., getting their fingers caught in a mousetrap and going to the hospital to have it removed). Many children later claimed to have experienced these events and, even after debriefing, some of the children refused to accept that the events were only imagined. Such findings suggest that young children may have difficulty distinguishing fantasy from reality, and are suggestible in part because they tend to confuse the sources or origins (fantasy vs. reality) of their knowledge (Ackil & Zaragoza, 1995; Roberts & Blades, 1999; Thierry, Spence, & Memon, 2001). When subjected to such suggestive techniques as repeated suggestion, instructions to imagine/pretend, and selective reinforcement in a series of interviews, preschool children assented to 95% of the false events (e.g., claiming that they witnessed the theft of food in their daycare centre) by the third interview session (Bruck, Hembrooke, & Ceci, 1997). Such findings are not limited to children, however, with several studies demonstrating that adults too may come to produce detailed 'memories' of entirely fictitious events (for reviews see Loftus, 1997, 2003).

In the experimental laboratory, information suggested by interviewers is often incorporated by eyewitnesses into their memories of experienced events (Ackil & Zaragoza, 1995; Ceci & Bruck, 1993, 1995) especially when preschool children are involved (Brady, Poole, Warren, & Jones, 1999; Cassel & Bjorklund, 1995; Ceci & Bruck, 1993; Ceci & Huffman, 1997; Leichtman & Ceci, 1995; Quas *et al.,* 1999) and the suggestions are repeated (Mitchell & Zaragoza, 1996). In addition, Endres, Poggenphol, and Erneb (1999) showed that suggestive prompts led preschoolers to contradict information that they had provided earlier in an interview.

The contaminating effects of option-posing and suggestive utterances are aggravated when they are repeated. Thus, children contradict themselves at a higher rate when option-posing questions are repeated (Bruck, Ceci, & Hembrook, 1998) while repeated exposure to yes/no and suggestive questions reduces children's overall accuracy (Memon & Vartoukian, 1996; Poole & White, 1991, 1993, 1995; but see Lyon, Malloy, Quas, & Talwar, 2008). Whereas repeated open-ended questions are often perceived as requests for additional information, suggested Poole and White (1991), repeated yes/no questions might be perceived as indications that the initial responses were unacceptable and thus should be changed, especially by younger children (4-year-olds).

It is clear that preschool-aged children are particularly suggestible, and this led researchers such as Ceci and Bruck to argue that jurists should view with skepticism the testimonies of children in the Wee Care, Little Rascals, and McMartin cases because interviewers had wittingly or unwittingly exploited children's vulnerabilities when eliciting accounts from them. Such conclusions implied, of course, that the results of laboratory analogue studies could and should be generalized to the interpretation of information provided by alleged victims in the course of forensic interviews.

For obvious ethical reasons, the events studied in these laboratory analogue studies lacked many characteristics of abusive incidents, leading to questions about their ecological validity. For example, getting a finger caught in a mousetrap and being sexually abused are quite different experiences with respect to both their nature and complexity. Additionally, some early analogue studies tested children's memory for events that the children merely watched on a video (Dale, Loftus, & Rathbun, 1978; Wells, Turtle, & Luus, 1989) or heard about in stories that were read to them (Ceci *et al.*, 1987a,b). Of course, children may not remember events depicted in videos they watched or stories they heard as well as they recall events in which they were active participants. In fact, Rudy and Goodman (1991) showed that 4- and 7-year-olds were more likely to accept suggestions when they were mere observers rather than participants in a real-life event. Similarly, Tobey and Goodman (1992) found that 4-year-olds who participated in a real-life event were more resistant to suggestion and provided more accurate free-recall reports than those who just watched the event on a video.

Children can also be led to make false reports about a medical exam when they are interviewed suggestively. For example, when Bruck, Ceci, Francoeur, and Barr (1995) interviewed 5-year-old children 1 week and 1 year after they had been inoculated in a paediatrician's office, children given repeated misleading information about the doctor's or research assistant's actions produced more false allegations (e.g., indicating that the research assistant had given the inoculation when, in fact, the paediatrician gave the inoculation) 1 year later than did children who were not misled. Quas *et al.* (1999) interviewed 40 children about a stressful medical procedure that children really experienced as well as about a fictitious medical procedure (nose surgery). Seventeen children assented to questions about the false surgery, and 13 of these children elaborated providing new false details.

Lyon (1999) questioned the value of such laboratory analogue studies, arguing that the interview techniques they employed do not represent typical forensic practices. He further noted that most sexual abuse cases involve a single victim whose abuser is a family member or relative, as opposed to the multiple alleged victims of daycare providers.

Lyon (1999) also criticized laboratory analogue research on the grounds that most real-world cases of sexual abuse do not involve the coercive and suggestive practices used in many of these studies. For instance, Ceci and Bruck's studies explored the highly suggestive techniques used in the controversial daycare cases, including stereotype induction, repeated questioning, suggestion and peer pressure (Bruck *et al.*, 1997; Ceci *et al.*, 1994; Leichtman & Ceci, 1995). Lyon argued that option-posing questions, which give children the option of denying potentially false information in response to yes/no questions or to select the correct option in response to forced choice questions, are less risky than questions that presuppose information not mentioned by the children. Most of the laboratory analogue studies revealing high levels of suggestibility involved 'highly misleading' suppositional-type questions. For example, Leichtman and Ceci (1995) asked children such questions as, 'When Sam Stone ripped the book, did he do it because he was angry, or by mistake?' which make it more difficult for children to deny the misinformation (e.g., that the book was ripped) than do questions like 'Did Sam Stone rip the book?' In particular, the former question requires children to correct the interviewer in resisting the misinformation, a problematic task for young children.

Bruck *et al.* (1997) misled children by telling them about the fictitious events in the context of reinforcement and pretend/imagine instructions. Lyon argued that the suggestibility effects found in this analogue study were 'likely the least generalizable to the real world' (p. 1038), because such techniques are seldom used by forensic investigators. By contrast, he argued that the types of option-posing questions that occur in the real world (e.g., 'Did he touch you there?') are not associated with high levels of error in analogue studies (Goodman *et al.*, 1987; Saywitz, Goodman, Nicholas, & Moan, 1991), and thus should not be as problematic as suppositional questions in forensic contexts.

Garven *et al.* (1998) showed that the exact techniques used in the McMartin preschool case quickly led children to respond inaccurately. These researchers first examined transcripts of interviews conducted with alleged victims in the McMartin case, identifying such techniques as offering positive (or negative) consequences for making (or not making) allegations of abuse, posing the same repeated questions and suggesting that other children had already disclosed. They then interviewed 3- to 6-year-old children about a staged event in which a male stranger visited children at their daycare centre, read them a story and handed out stickers and cupcakes. The children who were interviewed about the man's actions using a combination of highly suggestive techniques (e.g., repeated suggestive questions plus rewards for making allegations) produced significantly more false accusations than children who were interviewed using only one suggestive technique. In fact, after being interviewed with multiple suggestive questioning techniques for only 4.5 minutes, children acquiesced to the false accusations nearly 60% of the time, whereas those interviewed using only one suggestive technique acquiesced 17% of the time.

Garven, Wood, and Malpass (2000) further showed that children interviewed suggestively using reinforcement made false allegations about mundane events (e.g., that a man said a bad word) 35% of the time, whereas those interviewed without such reinforcement made false allegations 12% of the time. Children who were reinforced also alleged fantastic events (e.g., that a man took a child on a helicopter ride) more often than children in the control group. Taken together, the results of these studies show that poor interview practices are quite likely to elicit erroneous reports from young children.

The apparently contradictory findings regarding children's suggestibility may be resolved by examining methodological differences in both the manipulation and measurement of suggestibility and reliability. Suggestibility is multiply determined by cognitive, social, motivational, and individual difference variables. Suggestive techniques may include instructions from the interviewer to pretend or imagine what might have happened, introduction of information by the interviewer that has not been reported by the child, and pressure to provide a response or comply with propositions made by the interviewer (e.g., by telling children they will feel better if they tell, alluding to statements made by other children, introduction of stereotypes about the alleged perpetrator or descriptions of him/her as 'bad' and 'needing to be punished'), and repetitive questioning over a series of interviews with encouragement to speculate about what might have happened.

Children's sensitivity to the interviewers' status and knowledge may also foster compliance with suggestive techniques, because children misunderstand the purpose of the interviewers' statements, assume that interviewers have superior knowledge or simply want to be cooperative. When interviewers (a) adequately prepare children for their role as experts, empower them to correct interviewers, and admit that they 'don't know' some answers, (b) avoid asking children to pretend or imagine, (c) avoid being coercive, (d) do not repeat misleading questions within the interview, and (e) keep children focused on central details of personally experienced events, children are better able to resist misleading questions and provide meaningful and accurate accounts of their experiences (Pipe, Lamb, Orbach, & Esplin, 2004).

INDIVIDUAL CHARACTERISTICS

There are often marked individual differences in the amount and/or accuracy of the information children recall, even about 'non-substantive' or neutral events. Individual differences may be forensically relevant to the extent that they predict, for example, whether or not a child is likely to be suggestible or easily misled, to lie, or to benefit from a particular interview strategy (Blandon-Gitlin & Pezdek, 2009; Bruck & Melnyk, 2004; Gordon *et al.*, 1993; Pipe & Salmon, 2002). More generally, understanding sources of variation in children's recall may help place their testimony in context, and help interviewers understand why some children say less about their experiences than others do.

Most studies examining the role of individual differences among young witnesses have focused on identifying those children likely to be vulnerable to suggestive questioning (Bruck & Melnyk, 2004; Quas, Qin, Schaaf, & Goodman, 1997). As Bruck and Melnyk highlighted in their review, there are few consistent predictors of individual differences in children's suggestibility. A small, but growing, number of studies have also been concerned with both cognitive and personality variables that moderate children's recall. In addition to knowledge (see above), intelligence is positively correlated with event recall (Elischberger & Roebers, 2001; Geddie, Fradin, & Beer, 2000) although the relation may be stronger for older children (e.g., 8- to 10-year-old; Roebers & Schneider, 2001) and may also depend on how interviews are conducted (Brown & Pipe, 2003). Low IQ is associated with heightened suggestibility but only when children who have IQs falling in the 'normal' range are compared with children who have low IQs (Bruck & Melnyk, 2004).

Several researchers have investigated individual differences in language/narrative abilities, and such abilities are fairly consistently associated with suggestibility (Bruck & Melnyk, 2004). For example, Clarke-Stewart, Malloy, and Allhusen (2004) found that children who had better language abilities (assessed via several standardized measures) were less susceptible to suggestive questions and persuasive attempts to mislead children into making false reports, including false reports of bodily harm. Other studies have similarly found that more advanced language abilities are associated with increased resistance to misleading suggestions (Bruck & Melnyk, 2004; Kulkofsky & Klemfuss, 2008). Language or narrative skills are positively associated with recall in some studies (e.g., Gordon *et al.*, 1993; Salmon *et al.*, 2003) but not in others (Greenhoot, Ornstein, Gordon, & Baker-Ward, 1999; Quas, 1998). Brown and Pipe (2003) found that WISC-III vocabulary scores were related to event recall, but a measure of narrative ability was not (see also Kleinknecht, 2001). Interestingly, although language abilities appear to help children resist misleading questions or suggestions, narrative ability can also be associated with increased recall of false information (Kulkofsky, Wang, & Ceci, 2008). When these researchers interviewed 3- to 5-year-olds about playing a novel game, they found that children who provided more complex and lengthier narratives also provided proportionally more incorrect information.

Children are often reticent with strangers and most adults recognize the need to establish rapport when initiating conversations with unfamiliar children, especially when the topics are stressful or embarrassing. Forensic interviewers are thus routinely encouraged to establish rapport with alleged victims before seeking to elicit information about the suspected incidents of abuse. Despite this consensus, many forensic interviewers fail to make more than perfunctory efforts to establish rapport before broaching the substantive issue under investigation (Sternberg, Lamb, Esplin, & Baradaran, 1999; Warren *et al.*, 1996). Hershkowitz discusses what research has told us about effective rapport-building strategies in Chapter 6.

Social and emotional factors, in particular relating to attachment and temperament, may also affect children's event reports and help explain why some children may be more reticent with interviewers or take more time to talk about their experiences. Attachment and temperament may mediate the way in which children's experiences are appraised, encoded and organized in memory, and influence the ways in which they are subsequently retrieved. For example, Goodman, Quas, Batterman-Faunce, Riddlesberger, and Kuhn (1997) argued that attachment may influence children's accounts of emotionally laden experiences. In two studies, Goodman and colleagues found that parental attachment style accounted for the relation between stress and memory (Goodman *et al.*, 1994, 1997). Children whose parents reported insecure attachment were both more stressed during a painful and distressing medical procedure, and subsequently made more errors when recounting it than children whose parents reported secure attachment styles. In Bruck and Melnyk's review of the literature on individual differences, attachment was linked with suggestibility in several studies. Furthermore, attachment style may interact with interview style (Bottoms, Quas, & Davis, 2007).

With respect to children's temperament, findings have been mixed. Gordon *et al.* (1993) examined temperament in relation to event memory using the Temperament Assessment Battery (Martin, 1988) and found that three dimensions from the battery (approach–withdrawal, emotionality and adaptability) were related to recall of a medical examination by both 3- and 5-year-old children. Merritt, Ornstein, and Spickler (1994) likewise found that adaptability and approach–withdrawal were related to children's recall of the VCUG (voiding cystourethrogram – an unpleasant medical procedure that involves inserting a catherer into a child's urethra). However, Burgwyn-Bailes, Baker-Ward, Gordon, and Ornstein (2001) did not find any association between temperament and recall of minor surgery for facial lacerations, although coping style during the surgery was related to recall (for review see Pipe & Salmon, 2002; Quas, 1998; Quas *et al.*, 1997). Roebers and Schneider (2001) found that shy children answered specific questions less accurately than did children who were less shy, and manageability was positively related to the number of intrusions reported by 3-year-olds when re-enacting an event using dolls and props (Greenhoot *et al.*, 1999). Greenhoot *et al.* (1999) suggested that the more manageable or 'easy' children may be more compliant and eager to please, which, in turn, may have led them to produce more intrusion errors. Additionally, Greenhoot *et al.* (1999) found that less persistent 3-year-olds were more likely to produce errors than children who were more persistent and thus better able to attend to the tasks. When behaviourally re-enacting events, Salmon, Roncolato, and Gleitzman (2003) found that children with higher levels of 'effortful control' (i.e., the ability to shift and refocus attention in order to regulate behaviours and emotions) produced more details than children with lower levels of effortful control.

As Bruck and Melnyk (2004) highlight in their review, many researchers have investigated individual differences in children's suggestibility, and few consistent predictors have emerged. Although this line of research is important for understanding the mechanisms underlying suggestibility, it also signals that rather than attempting to identify 'suggestible' children, it is important for interviewers and other practitioners to recognize that children enter the forensic interview or courtroom with different abilities and characteristics and having had different experiences. Children will inevitably vary with respect to how much information they provide, how long it takes them to build rapport, and how shy they appear when talking with new adults, for example. Findings concerning individual differences underscore the need for interviewers to adhere to best practices with all children.

FANTASY

Like adults, children over 6 years of age can discriminate between imagined and experienced events (Johnson & Foley, 1984; Lindsay & Johnson, 1987; Roberts, 2000; Roberts & Blades, 1995, for a review see Carrick, Rush, & Quas, in press,), and the extent to which younger children have difficulty discriminating between fantasy and reality is more complex. Although young children may have some difficulty discerning fantasy from reality, studies show that even 3.5-year-olds can do so accurately in some contexts. For example, young preschool children understand various properties of imaginary objects (e.g., other people cannot see or touch them; imaginary objects cannot simply appear in real life; Estes, Wellman, & Woolley, 1989; Wellman & Estes, 1986; Woolley & Wellman, 1993). Although young children may 'play' with imaginary friends or cartoon television characters, when children are questioned about such characters, they rarely claim that the characters are 'real' (Skolnick & Bloom, 2006; Taylor, Shawber, & Mannering, 2009).

Children are more likely to claim that false positive events (e.g., hot-air balloon rides) rather than false negative events (e.g., getting stitches after a fall) have occurred (Ceci, Loftus, Leichtman, & Bruck, 1994), and are similarly sensitive to emotional valence when distinguishing between fantasy and reality. For instance, Carrick and Quas (2006) presented 3- to 5-year-old children with real versus fantastical emotional images (e.g., a mother yelling at a child versus a mother cat yelling at kittens; mice dancing in clothes versus people celebrating) and then asked, 'Can this happen in real life?' Regardless of how realistic the events were, children were more likely to say that the positive images were 'possible'. Of course, in many studies concerned with the discrimination of fantasy from reality, there were no consequences associated with endorsing fantasy. This is a critical point: children may 'play along' with fantasy-oriented questions and activities because they like pretend play or because they would like mice to dance. Carrick (2007) thus designed a clever study to determine whether expected consequences would affect children's discrimination between fantasy and reality. She presented children with images like those described above and again asked, 'Can this happen in real life?' Thereafter, however, children were motivated to be accurate: they were told that they would win a prize for every correct answer. Children were significantly less likely to endorse the fantastic events when they received prizes for making accurate judgements, showing that children *can* make accurate judgements concerning fantasy – they simply choose not to do so in some circumstances.

It is important to note that fantasy and pretend play are normative and developmentally appropriate behaviors for children. Furthermore, parents and other individuals (e.g., siblings, grandparents, the community) often go to great lengths to encourage and reinforce children's beliefs in fantasy and fantastical characters. Consider the 'Santa Claus' character known to children in many cultures: parents may read books about Santa Claus, remind children of him in efforts to modify children's behavior (e.g., 'Santa only brings toys to nice boys and girls'), provide children with false evidence (e.g., leaving a note to Santa that disappears, milk and cookies or biscuits that are eaten) and even take children to have their pictures taken with Santa Claus himself. Because parents have such an influence on children's beliefs more generally, it is no wonder that children often believe in Santa Claus and other fantastical characters, and that parents have been employed in several suggestibility studies to create false reports (e.g., Poole & Lindsay, 2001; Quas *et al.*, 2007).

Children are more likely to provide false information about a fantastical character when they believe in that character. For example, Principe and Smith (2008a,b) studied the event reports (losing a tooth and leaving it for the Tooth Fairy) of 5- to 6-year-olds who believed, did not believe, or were uncertain about the existence of the Tooth Fairy. Children who believed in the Tooth Fairy were more likely to elaborate on their experiences by including fantastical details (e.g., the presence of magic dust) and more often claimed to have actually heard or seen the Tooth Fairy than children who did not believe or were uncertain. However, in the second study (Principe & Smith, 2008b), children who were uncertain about their belief in the Tooth Fairy were more accurate when asked to answer the questions in a 'truthful' manner than in a 'fun' manner. Believers' fantastical reports did not change based on these instructions. It is worth noting that the false information provided was *about the Tooth Fairy character*, and believers, non-believers and uncertain children alike provided similar amounts of information about other aspects of the event and were similarly accurate.

It is important for interviewers and other legal professionals to understand that fantasy and pretend play are normal aspects of childhood. Beliefs in Santa Claus, the Tooth Fairy, or imaginary friends do not mean that children cannot provide accurate and reliable reports of witnessed or experienced events. Beliefs in fantasy or engaging in pretend play do not, in themselves, discredit children. Also, interviewers should know that the presence of fantastic elements in children's accounts of abuse is affected by the presence of props (such as toys or dolls) usually associated with fantasy (Thierry, Spence Orbach, & Pipe, 2005), or by interviewers prompting children to 'imagine' or 'pretend'. As a result, forensic investigators have been urged to avoid having such props present during investigative interviews and to avoid using such expressions (Lamb, Sternberg, & Esplin, 1995, Lamb *et al.*, 1998; Poole & Lamb, 1998). Interviewers should also avoid asking children to imagine what might have happened or to visualize events (e.g., 'picture in the head game') as these techniques have led to false reports in laboratory studies (e.g., Ceci, Loftus, Leichtman, & Bruck, 1994; Leichtman & Ceci, 1995; Schreiber & Parker, 2004).

CONCLUSIONS

Several decades of research on the frailties and competencies of young witnesses have demonstrated the advantages of a developmentally sensitive approach to interviewing. Although the quality of children's reports are influenced by a number of factors pertaining to the children themselves and the events they have experienced, the ways in which interviewers behave and attempt to elicit information are critical. Even quite young children are able to provide reliable testimony about abusive experiences when questioned appropriately. In addition to the child's age, a variety of factors (including the interviewer's skills) influence the quality of information provided. To be effective, interviewers need to be aware of children's capacities and tendencies and must recognize that children may need help retrieving, structuring and reporting their experiences in an elaborative manner. For example, even very young children are able to provide meaningful and accurate accounts of their experiences when: 1) They understand their role as informants, the naivety of the interviewer, the importance of only reporting what they know and not guessing, the permissibility of 'don't know" responses and of correcting an interviewer's mistakes; 2) they feel comfortable with the interviewer and have had an opportunity to practise talking about the past in a detailed manner; and 3) interviewers avoid relying on closed, leading, or misleading questions. The onus is therefore on interviewers to ensure that they establish the optimal conditions for children to provide accurate and detailed accounts, even of very distressing and traumatic, experiences.

REFERENCES

Ackil, J.K., & Zaragoza, M.S. (1995). Developmental differences in suggestibility and memory for source. *Journal of Experimental Child Psychology, 60*, 57–83.

Ahern, E.C., Lyon, T.D., & Quas, J.A. (in press). Young children's emerging ability to make false statements. *Developmental Psychology*.

Bjorklund, D.F., Bjorklund, B.R., Brown, R.D., & Cassel, W.S. (1998). Children's susceptibility to repeated questions: How misinformation changes children's answers and their minds. *Applied Developmental Science, 2*, 99–111.

Blandon-Gitlin, I., & Pezdek, K. (2009). Children's memory in forensic contexts: Suggestibility, false memory, and individual differences. In B.L. Bottoms, C.J. Najdowski, & G.S. Goodman (Eds), *Children as Victims, Witnesses, and Offenders: Psychological Science and the Law* (pp. 57–80). New York: Guilford.

Bottoms, B.L., Quas, J.A., & Davis, S.L. (2007). The influence of the interviewer-provided social support on children's suggestibility, memory, and disclosures. In M.E. Pipe, M.E. Lamb, Y. Orbach, & A.C. Cederborg (Eds), *Child Sexual Abuse: Disclosure, Delay, and Denial* (pp. 135–158). Mahwah, NJ: Erlbaum.

Brady, M., Poole, D.A., Warren, A., & Jones, D. (1999). Young children's responses to yes-or-no questions: Patterns and problems. *Applied Developmental Science, 3*, 47–57.

Brainerd, C.J., & Reyna, V.F. (1996). Mere testing creates false memories in children. *Developmental Psychology, 32*, 467–476.

Brennan, M., & Brennan, R.E. (1988). *Strange Language: Child Victims under Cross Examination* (3rd ed.). Wagga Wagga, NSW, Australia: Riverina Literacy Centre.

Brown, R. (1973). *A First Language*. Cambridge, MA: Harvard University Press.

Brown, D.A., & Pipe, M.E. (2003). Individual differences in children's event memory reports and the narrative elaboration technique. *Journal of Applied Psychology, 88*, 195–206.

Bruck, M. (2009). Human figure drawings and children's recall of touching. *Journal of Experimental Psychology: Applied, 15*, 361–374.

Bruck, M., & Ceci, S.J. (1999). The suggestibility of children's memory. *Annual Review of Psychology, 50*, 419–439.

Bruck, M., & Ceci, S. (2004). Forensic developmental psychology: Unveiling four common misconceptions. *Current Directions in Psychological Science, 13*, 229–232.

Bruck, M., Ceci, S.J., Francoeur, E., & Barr, R. (1995). "I hardly cried when I got my shot!": Influencing children's reports about a visit to their pediatrician. *Child Development, 66*, 193–208.

Bruck, M., Ceci, S.J., & Hembrooke, H. (1998). Reliability and credibility of young children's reports: From research to policy and practice. *American Psychologist, 53*, 136–151.

Bruck, M., Ceci, S.J., & Hembrooke, H. (2002). The nature of children's true and false narratives. *Developmental Review*, *22*, 520–554.
Bruck, M., Ceci, S.J., & Principe, G.F. (2006). The child and the law. In K.A. Renninger, I.E. Sigel, W. Damon, & R.M. Lerner (Eds), *Handbook of Child Psychology* (6th ed., Vol. *4*, pp. 776–816). Hoboken, NJ: Wiley.
Bruck, M., Hembrooke, H., & Ceci, S.J. (1997). Children's reports of pleasant and unpleasant events. In D. Read, & S. Lindsay (Eds), *Recollections of Trauma: Scientific Research and Clinical Practice* (pp. 199–219). New York: Plenum.
Bruck, M., & Melnyk, L. (2004). Individual differences in children's suggestibility: A review and synthesis. *Applied Cognitive Psychology*, *18*, 947–996.
Burgwyn-Bailes, E., Baker-Ward, L., Gordon, B.N., & Ornstein, P.A. (2001). Children's memory for emergency medical treatment after one year: The impact of individual difference variables on recall and suggestibility. *Applied Cognitive Psychology*, *15*, S25–S48.
Carter, C.A., Bottoms, B.L., & Levine, M. (1996). Linguistic and socioemotional influences on the accuracy of children's reports. *Law and Human Behavior*, *20*, 335–358.
Cassel, W.S., & Bjorklund, D.F. (1995). Developmental patterns of eyewitness memory and suggestibility: An ecologically based short-term longitudinal study. *Law and Human Behavior*, *19*, 507–532.
Carni, E., & French, L.A. (1984). The acquisition of before and after reconsidered: What develops? *Journal of Experimental Child Psychology*, *37*, 394–403.
Carrick, N. (2007, October). "Mice can't really dance": Reducing the effects of emotion on children's fantasy–reality distinctions. Poster presented at the meeting of the Cognitive Development Society, Santa Fe, NM.
Carrick, N., & Quas, J.A. (2006). The effects of discrete emotions on young children's ability to discern fantasy and reality. *Developmental Psychology*, *42*, 1278–1288.
Carrick, N., Rush, E., & Quas, J.A. (in press). Suggestibility and imagination in early childhood. Chapter to appear in M. Taylor (Ed.), *Oxford Handbook of the Development of Imagination*. NY: Oxford University Press.
Ceci, S.J., & Bruck, M. (1993). Suggestibility of the child witness: A historical review and synthesis. *Psychological Bulletin*, *113*, 403–439.
Ceci, S.J., & Bruck, M. (1995). *Jeopardy in the Courtroom: A Scientific Analysis of Children's Testimony*. Washington, D.C.: APA Books.
Ceci, S.J., & Bruck, M. (2006). Children's suggestibility: Characteristics and mechanisms. *Advances in Child Development and Behavior*, *34*, 247–281.
Ceci, S.J., & Friedman, R.D. (2000). The suggestibility of children: Scientific research and legal implications. *Cornell Law Review*, *86*, 34–108.
Ceci, S.J., & Huffman, M.L. (1997). How suggestible are preschool children? Cognitive and social factors. *Journal of the American Academy of Child and Adolescent Psychiatry*, *36*, 948–958.
Ceci, S.J., Huffman, M.L.C., Smith, E., & Loftus, E.F. (1994). Repeatedly thinking about a non-event: Source misattributions among preschoolers. *Consciousness and Cognition*, *3*, 388–407.
Ceci, S.J., Kulkofsky, S., Klemfuss, J.Z., Sweeney, C.D., & Bruck, M. (2007). Unwarranted assumptions about children's testimonial accuracy. *Annual Review of Clinical Psychology*, *3*, 311–328.

Ceci, S.J., Loftus, E.F., Leichtman, M.D., & Bruck, M. (1994). The possible role of source misattributions in the creation of false beliefs among preschoolers. *International Journal of Clinical and Experimental Hypnosis*, *42*, 304–320.
Ceci, S.J., Ross, D.F., & Toglia, M.P. (1987a). Suggestibility of children's memory: Psycholegal issues. *Journal of Experimental Psychology: General*, *116*, 38–49.
Ceci, S.J., Ross, D.F., & Toglia, M.P. (1987b). Age differences in suggestibility: Narrowing the uncertainties. In S.J. Ceci, M.P. Toglia & D.F. Ross (Eds), *Children's Eyewitness Memory* (pp. 79–91). New York: Springer-Verlag.
Clark, H.H., & Clark, E.V. (1977). *Psychology and Language*. New York: Harcourt Brace Jovanovich.
Clarke-Stewart, K.A., Malloy, L., & Allhusen, V. (2004). Verbal ability, self-control, and close relationships with parents protect children against misleading suggestions. *Applied Cognitive Psychology*, *18*, 1037–1058.
Dale, P.S. (1976). *Language Development: Structure and Function*. New York: Holt, Rinehart & Winston.
Dale, P.S., Loftus, E.F., & Rathbun, L. (1978). The influence of the form of the question on the eyewitness testimony of preschool children. *Journal of Psycholinguistic Research* *7*, 269–277.
Davies, G., Tarrant, A., & Flin, R. (1989). Close encounters of the witness kind: Children's memory for a simulated health inspection. *British Journal of Psychology*, *80*, 415–429.
de Villiers, J., & de Villiers, P. (1999). Language development. In M.H. Bornstein, & M.E. Lamb (Eds), *Developmental Psychology: An Advanced Textbook* (4th ed. pp. 313–373). Mahwah, NJ: Erlbaum.
Dent, H.R. (1982). The effects of interviewing strategies on the results of interviews with child witnesses. In A. Trankell (Ed.), *Reconstructing the Past: The Role of Psychologists in Criminal Trials* (pp. 279–297). Stockholm: Norstedt.
Dent, H.R. (1986). Experimental study of the effectiveness of different techniques of questioning child witnesses. *British Journal of Social and Clinical Psychology*, *18*, 41–51.
Dent, H.R., & Stephenson, G.M. (1979). An experimental study of the effectiveness of different techniques of questioning child witnesses. *British Journal of Social and Clinical Psychology*, *18*, 41–51.
Elischberger, H.B., & Roebers, C.M. (2001). Improving young children's free narratives about an observed event: The effects of nonspecific verbal prompts. *International Journal of Behavioral Development*, *25*, 160–166.
Endres, J., Poggenpohl, C., & Erneb, C. (1999). Repetitions, warnings and video: Cognitive and motivational components in preschool children's suggestibility. *Legal and Criminological Psychology*, *4*, 129–146.
Estes, D., Wellman, H.M., & Woolley, J.D. (1989). Children's understanding of mental phenomena. *Advances in Child Development and Behavior*, *22*, 41–86.
Evans, A.D., Lee, K., & Lyon, T.D. (2009). Complex questions asked by defense lawyers but not prosecutors predicts convictions in child abuse trials. *Law and Human Behavior*. *33*, 258–264.
Fivush, R. (1997). Event memory in early childhood. In C. Nelson (Ed.), *The Development of Memory in Childhood. Studies in Developmental Psychology* (pp. 139–161). Hove, UK: Psychology Press/Erlbaum (UK) Taylor & Francis.
Fivush, R. & Mandler, J.M. (1985). Developmental changes in the understanding of temporal sequence. *Child Development*, *56*, 1437–1446.

Fivush, R., Peterson, C., & Schwarzmueller, A. (2002). Questions and answers: The credibility of child witnesses in the context of specific questioning techniques. In M.L. Eisen, J.A. Quas, & G.S. Goodman (Eds), *Memory and Suggestibility in the Forensic Interview* (pp. 331–354). Mahwah, NJ: Erlbaum.

Flavell, J.H., Speer, J.R., Green, F.L., & August D.L. (1981). The development of comprehension monitoring and knowledge about communication. *Monographs of the Society for Research in Child Development*, *46*, 1–65.

Flin, R., Boon, J., Knox, A., & Bull, R. (1992). The effect of a five month delay on children's and adults' eyewitness memory. *British Journal of Psychology*, *83*, 323–336.

Foley, M.A., & Johnson, M.K. (1985). Confusions between memories for performed and imagined actions: A developmental comparison. *Child Development*, *56*, 1145–1155.

Friedman, W.J. (1977). The development of children's understanding of cyclic aspects of time. *Child Development*, *48*, 1593–1599.

Friedman, W.J. (1986). The development of children's knowledge of temporal structure. *Child Development*, *57*, 1386–1400.

Friedman, W.J. (1987). A follow-up to 'scale effects in memory for the time of events': The earthquake study. *Memory and Cognition*, *15*, 518–520.

Friedman, W.J. (1990). Children's representations of the pattern of daily activities. *Child Development*, *61*, 1399–1412.

Friedman, W.J. (1991). The development of children's memory for the time of past events. *Child Development*, *62*, 139–155.

Friedman, W. J. (1992). Children's time memory: The development of a differentiated past. *Cognitive Development*, *7*, 171–187.

Friedman, W.J. (1993). Memory for the time of past events. *Psychological Bulletin*, *113*, 44–66.

Friedman, W.J. (2000). The development of children's knowledge of the times of future events. *Child Development*, *71*, 913–932.

Friedman, W.J., & Lyon, T.D. (2005). Development of temporal-reconstructive abilities. *Child Development*, *76*, 1202–1216.

Friedman, W.J., & Seely, P.B. (1976). The child's acquisition of spatial and temporal word meanings. *Child Development*, *47*, 1103–1108.

Garven, S., Wood, J.M., & Malpass, R.S. (2000). Allegations of wrongdoing: The effects of reinforcement on children's mundane and fantastic claims. *Journal of Applied Psychology*, *85*, 38–49.

Garven, S., Wood, J.M., Malpass, R.S., & Shaw, J.S. III. (1998). More than suggestion: The effect of interviewing techniques from the McMartin preschool case. *Journal of Applied Psychology*, *83*, 347–359.

Geddie, L., Fradin, S., & Beer, J. (2000). Child characteristics which impact accuracy of recall and suggestibility in preschoolers: Is age the best predictor? *Child Abuse and Neglect*, *24*, 223–235.

Goodman, G.S., & Aman, C. (1990). Children's use of anatomically detailed dolls to recount an event. *Child Development*, *61*, 1859–1871.

Goodman, G.S., Aman, C., & Hirschman, J. (1987). Child sexual and physical abuse: Children's testimony. In S.J. Ceci, M.P. Toglia, & D.F. Ross (Eds), *Children's Eyewitness Memory* (pp. 1–23). New York: Springer-Verlag.

Goodman, G.S., Bottoms, B.L., Schwartz-Kenney, B.M., & Rudy, L. (1991). Children's testimony about a stressful event: Improving children's reports. *Journal of Narrative and Life History*, *1*, 69–99.

Goodman, G.S., Quas, J.A., Batterman-Faunce, J.M., Riddlesberger, M.M., & Kuhn, J. (1994). Predictors of accurate and inaccurate memories of traumatic events experienced in childhood. *Consciousness and Cognition*, *3*, 269–294.

Goodman, G.S., Quas, J.A., Batterman-Faunce, J.M., Riddlesberger, M.M., & Kuhn, J. (1997). Children's reactions to and memory for a stressful event: Influences of age, anatomical dolls, knowledge, and parental attachment. *Applied Developmental Science*, *1*, 54–75.

Goodman, G.S., Quas, J.A., & Ogle, C.M. (2010). Child maltreatment and memory. *Annual Review of Psychology*, *61*, 325–351.

Goodman, G.S., Rudy, L., Bottoms, B.L., & Aman, C. (1990). Children's concerns and memory: Issues of ecological validity on the study of children's eyewitness testimony. In R. Fivush, & J. Hudson (Eds), *Knowing and Remembering in Young Children* (pp. 249–284). New York: Cambridge University Press.

Gordon, B.N., Ornstein, P.A., Nida, R.E., Follmer, A., Crenshaw, M.C., & Albert, G. (1993). Does the use of dolls facilitate children's memory of visits to the doctor? *Applied Cognitive Psychology, 7*, 459–474.

Greenhoot, A.F., Ornstein, P.A., Gordon, B.N., & Baker-Ward, L. (1999). Acting out the details of a pediatric check-up: The impact of interview condition and behavioral style on children's memory report. *Child Development*, *70*, 363–380.

Hamond, N.R., & Fivush, R. (1991). Memories of Mickey Mouse: Young children recount their trip to Disney World. *Cognitive Development*, *6*, 433–448.

Harner, L. (1975). Yesterday and tomorrow: Development of early understanding of the terms. *Developmental Psychology*, *11*, 864–865.

Hewitt, S.D. (1999). *Assessing Allegations of Sexual Abuse in Preschool Children*. Thousand Oaks, CA: Sage.

Howe, M.L., & Courage, M.L. (1993). On resolving the enigma of infantile amnesia. *Psychological Bulletin*, *113*, 305–326.

Howe, M.L., Courage, M.L., & Edison, S.C. (2003). When autobiographical memory begins. *Developmental Review*, *23*, 471–494.

Hudson, J.A. (1990). The emergence of autobiographical memory in mother–child conversation. In R. Fivush, & J.A. Hudson (Eds), *Knowing and Remembering in Young Children* (pp. 166–196). New York: Cambridge University Press.

Hunt, J.S., & Borgida, E. (2001). Is that what I said? Witnesses' responses to interviewer modifications. *Law and Human Behavior*, *25*, 583–603.

Hutcheson, G.D., Baxter, J.S., Telfer, K., & Warden, D. (1995). Child witness statement quality: Question type and errors of omission. *Law and Human Behavior*, *19*, 631–648.

Imhoff, M.C., & Baker-Ward, L. (1999). Preschoolers' suggestibility: Effects of developmentally appropriate language and interviewer supportiveness. *Journal of Applied Developmental Psychology*, *20*, 407–429.

Johnson, M.K., & Foley, M.A. (1984). Differentiating fact from fantasy: The reliability of children's memory. *Journal of Social Issues*, *40*, 33–50.

Kelley, S.J. (1996). Ritualistic abuse of children. In J. Briere, L. Berliner, J. Bulkley, C. Jenny, & T. Reid (Eds), *The APSAC Handbook on Child Maltreatment* (pp. 90–99). Thousand Oaks, CA: Sage.

King, M.A., & Yuille, J.C. (1987). Suggestibility and the child witness. In S.J. Ceci, D.F. Ross, & M.P. Toglia (Eds), *Children's Eyewitness Memory* (pp. 24–35). New York: Springer-Verlag.

Kleinknecht, E. (2001). Emerging autobiographies: The role of social-cognition in the development of event memory skills. *Dissertation Abstracts International: Section B: the Sciences & Engineering*, *61*, 5019.

Korkman, J., Santtila, P., Drzewiecki, T., & Sandnabba, N.K. (2008). Failing to keep it simple: Language use in child sexual abuse interviews with 3–8-year-old children. *Psychology, Crime, and Law*, *14*, 41–60.

Kuehnle, K. (1996). *Assessing Allegations of Child Sexual Abuse*. Sarasota, FL: Professional Resource Exchange.

Kulkofsky, S., & Klemfuss, J.Z. (2008). What the stories children tell can tell about their memory: Narrative skill and young children's suggestibility. *Developmental Psychology*, *44*, 1442–1456.

Kulkofsky, S., Wang, Q., & Ceci, S.J. (2008). Do better stories make better memories? Narrative quality and memory accuracy in preschool children. *Applied Cognitive Psychology*, *22*, 21–38.

Lamb, M.E., & Brown, D.A. (2006). Conversational apprentices: Helping children become competent informants about their own experiences. *British Journal of Developmental Psychology*, *24*, 215–234.

Lamb, M.E., & Fauchier, A. (2001). The effects of question type on self-contradictions by children in the course of forensic interviews. *Applied Cognitive Psychology*, *15*, 483–491.

Lamb, M.E., Hershkowitz, I., Orbach, Y., & Esplin, P.W. (2008). *Tell Me What Happened: Structured Investigative Interviews of Child Victims and Witnesses*. Hoboken, NJ: Wiley.

Lamb, M.E., Orbach, Y., Warren, A.R., Esplin, P.W., & Hershkowitz, I. (2007). Getting the most out of children: Factors affecting the informativeness of young witnesses. In M.P. Toglia, J.D. Read, D.F. Ross, & R.C.L. Lindsay (Eds), *Handbook of Eyewitness Psychology. Vol 1: Memory for Events*. Mahwah, NJ: Erlbaum.

Lamb, M.E., Sternberg, K.J., & Esplin, P.W. (1995). Making children into competent witnesses: Reactions to the amicus brief In re Michaels. *Psychology, Public Policy, and the Law*, *1*, 438–449.

Lamb, M.E., Sternberg, K.J., & Esplin, P.W. (1998). Conducting investigative interviews of alleged sexual abuse victims. *Child Abuse and Neglect*, *22*, 813–823.

Lamb, M.E., Sternberg, K.J., Orbach, Y., Esplin, P.W., Stewart, H., & Mitchell, S. (2003). Age differences in young children's responses to open-ended invitations in the course of forensic interviews. *Journal of Consulting and Clinical Psychology*, *71*, 926–934.

Lamb, M.E., Sternberg, K.J., Orbach, Y., Hershkowitz, I., & Esplin, P.W. (1999). Forensic interviews of children. In A. Memon, & R. Bull (Eds), *Handbook of the Psychology of Interviewing* (pp. 253–277). NY: Wiley.

Leichtman, M.D., & Ceci, S.J. (1995). The effects of stereotypes and suggestion on preschoolers' reports. *Developmental Psychology*, *31*, 568–578.

Lillie and Reed v Newcastle City Council & Ors [2002] EWHC 1600 (QB)

Lindsay, D.S., & Johnson, M.K. (1987). Reality monitoring and suggestibility. In S.J. Ceci, M.P. Toglia, & D.F. Ross (Eds), *Children's Eyewitness Testimony* (pp. 79–91). New York: Springer-Verlag.

Loftus, E.F. (1997). Creating false memories. *Scientific American*, *277*, 70–75.

Loftus, EF. (2003). Make-believe memories. *American Psychologist*, *58*, 864–873.

London, K., Bruck, M., & Melnyk, L. (2009). Post-event information affects children's autobiographical memory after one year. *Law and Human Behavior*, *33*, 344–355.

Lyon, T.D. (1999). The new wave in children's suggestibility research: A critique. *Cornell Law Review*, *84*, 1004–1087.

Lyon, T.D. (2002). Expert testimony on the suggestibility of children: Does it fit? In B.L. Bottoms, M.B. Kouera, & B.D. McAuliff (Eds), *Children and the Law: Social Science and Policy* (pp. 378–411). New York: Cambridge University Press.

Lyon, T.D., Malloy, L.C., Quas, J.A., & Talwar, V. (2008). Coaching, truth induction, and young maltreated children's false allegations and false denials. *Child Development*, *79*, 914–929.

Malloy, L.C., & Quas, J.A. (2009). Children's suggestibility: Areas of consensus and controversy. In K. Kuehnle, & M. Connell (Eds), *The Evaluation of Child Sexual Abuse Allegations: A Comprehensive Guide to Assessment and Testimony* (pp. 267–297). New Jersey: John Wiley & Sons.

Markman, E.M. (1977). Realizing that you don't understand: A preliminary investigation. *Child Development*, *48*, 986–992.

Markman, E.M. (1979). Realizing that you don't understand: elementary-school children's awareness of inconsistencies. *Child Development*, *50*, 643–655.

Martin, M. (1988). Individual differences in everyday memory. In M.M. Gruneberg, P.E. Morris, & R.N. Sykes (Eds), *Practical Aspects of Memory: Current Research and Issues, Vol. 1: Memory in Everyday Life* (pp. 466–471). Oxford, UK: John Wiley & Sons.

Melnyk, L., Crossman, A.M., & Scullin, M.H. (2007). The suggestibility of children's memory. In D.F. Ross, R.C.L. Lindsay, M.P. Toglia, & J.D. Read (Eds), *The Handbook of Eyewitness Psychology, Vol 1: Memory for Events* (pp. 401–427). Mahwah, NJ: Erlbaum.

Memon, A., & Vartoukian, R. (1996). The effect of repeated questioning on young children's eyewitness testimony. *British Journal of Psychology*, *87*, 403–415.

Merritt, K.A., Ornstein, P.A., & Spicker, B. (1994). Children's memory for a salient medical procedure: Implications for testimony. *Pediatrics*, *94*, 17–23.

Mitchell, K.J., & Zaragoza, M.S. (1996). Repeated exposure to suggestion and false memory: The role of contextual variability. *Journal of Memory and Language*, *35*, 246–260.

Montangero, J. (1992). The development of a diachronic perspective in children. In F. Macar, V. Pouthas, & W.J. Friedman (Eds), *Time, Action, and Cognition: Towards Bridging the Gap* (pp. 55–65). Dordrecht, Netherlands: Kluwer.

Nathan, D., & Snedeker, M. (1995). *Satan's Silence*. New York: Basic Books.

Nelson, K., & Fivush, R. (2004). The emergence of autobiographical memory: A social cultural developmental model. *Psychological Review*, *111*, 486–511.

Orbach, Y., & Lamb, M.E. (2001). The relationship between within-interview contradictions and eliciting interviewer utterances. *Child Abuse and Neglect*, *25*, 323–333.

Orbach, Y., & Lamb, M.E. (2007). Young children's references to temporal attributes of allegedly experienced events in the course of forensic interviews. *Child Development*, *78*, 1100–1120.

Ornstein, P.A., Baker-Ward, L., Gordon, B.N., & Merritt, K.A. (1997). Children's memory for medical experiences: Implications for testimony. *Applied Cognitive Psychology*, *11*, 87–104.

Perner, J. (2000). Memory and theory of mind. In E. Tulving, & F.I.M. Craik (Eds), *The Oxford Handbook of Memory* (pp. 297–312). London, Oxford: Oxford University Press.

Perry, N.W., McAuliff, B.D., Tam, P., Claycomb, L., Dostal, C., & Flanagan, C. (1995). When lawyers question children: Is justice served? *Law and Human Behavior, 19*, 609–629.

Perry, N.W., & Wrightsman, L.S. (1991). *The Child Witness: Legal Issues and Dilemmas*. Newbery Park, CA: Sage.

Peterson, C., Dowden, C., & Tobin, J. (1999). Interviewing preschoolers: Comparisons of Yes/No and Wh- questions. *Law and Human Behavior, 23*, 539–555.

Piaget, J. (1971). *The child's conception of time* (A.J. Pomerans, Trans.). New York: Ballantine Books. (Original work published 1927.)

Pipe, M.E., Lamb, M.E., Orbach, Y., & Esplin, P.W. (2004). Recent research on children's testimony about experienced and witnessed events. *Developmental Review, 24*, 440–468.

Pipe, M.E., & Salmon, K. (2002). What children bring to the interview context: Individual differences in children's event reports. In M.L. Eisen, J.A. Quas, & G.S. Goodman (Eds), *Memory and Suggestibility in the Forensic Interview* (pp. 235–261). Mahwah, NJ: Erlbaum.

Plotnikoff, J., & Woolfson, R. (2009). *Measuring Up? Evaluating Implementation of Government Commitments to Young Witnesses in Criminal Proceedings*. NSPCC: London.

Poole, D.A., & Lamb, M.E. (1998). *Investigative Interviews of Children: A Guide for Helping Professionals*. Washington, DC: American Psychological Association.

Poole, D.A., & Lindsay, D.S. (1995). Interviewing preschoolers: Effects of nonsuggestive techniques, parental coaching, and leading questions on reports of nonexperienced events. *Journal of Experimental Child Psychology, 60*, 129–154.

Poole, D.A., & Lindsay, D.S. (2001). Children's eyewitness reports after exposure to misinformation from parents. *Journal of Experimental Psychology: Applied, 7*, 27–50.

Poole, D.A., & White, L.T. (1991). Effects of question repetition on the eyewitness testimony of children and adults. *Developmental Psychology, 27*, 975–986.

Poole, D.A., & White, L.T. (1993). Two years later: Effect of question repetition and retention interval on the eyewitness testimony of children and adults. *Developmental Psychology, 29*, 844–853.

Poole, D.A., & White, L.T. (1995). Tell me again and again: Stability and change in the repeated testimonies of children and adults. In M.S. Zaragoza, J.R. Graham, G.C.N. Hall, R. Hirschman, & Y.S. Ben Porath (Eds), *Memory and Testimony in the Child Witness* (pp. 24–43). Thousand Oaks, CA: Sage Publications.

Principe, G., & Smith, E. (2008a). Seeing things unseen: Fantasy beliefs and false reports. *Journal of Cognition and Development, 9*, 89–111.

Principe, G., & Smith, E. (2008b). The tooth, the whole tooth and nothing but the tooth: How belief in the tooth fairy can engender false memories. *Applied Cognitive Psychology, 22*, 625–642.

Quas, J.A. (1998). Children's memory of experienced and nonexperienced events across repeated interviews. Unpublished doctoral dissertation, University of California, Davis.

Quas, J.A., Goodman, G.S., Bidrose, S., Pipe, M.E., Craw, S., & Ablin, D.S. (1999). Emotion and memory: Children's long-term remembering, forgetting, and suggestibility. *Journal of Experimental Child Psychology*, *72*, 235–270.

Quas, J.A., Malloy, L., Melinder, A., Goodman, G., D'Mello, M., & Schaaf, J. (2007). Developmental differences in the effects of repeated interviews and interviewer bias on young children's event memory and false reports. *Developmental Psychology*, *43*, 823–837.

Quas, J.A., Qin, J.J., Schaaf, J.M., & Goodman, G.S. (1997). Individual differences in children's and adults' suggestibility and false event memory. *Learning and Individual Differences*, *9*, 359–390.

Ratner, H.H. (1984). Memory demands and the development of young children's memory. *Child Development*, *55*, 2173–2191.

Reese, E., Haden, C.A., & Fivush, R. (1993). Mother–child conversations about the past: Relationships of style and memory over time. *Cognitive Development*, *8*, 403–430.

Reich, P.A. (1986). *Language Development*. Englewood Cliffs, NJ: Prentice-Hall.

Reinhold, R. (1990). How lawyers and media turned the McMartin case into a tragic media circus. *New York Times* (January 25), p. 1D.

Roberts, K.P. (2000). An overview of theory and research on children's source monitoring. In K.P. Roberts, & M. Blades (Eds), *Children's Source Monitoring* (pp. 11–57). Mahwah, NJ: Erlbaum.

Roberts, K.P., & Blades, M. (1995). Children's discriminations of memories for actual and pretend actions in a hiding task. *British Journal of Developmental Psychology*, *13*, 321–333.

Roberts, K.P., & Blades, M. (1999). Children's memory and source monitoring of real-life and televised events. *Journal of Applied Developmental Psychology*, *20*, 575–596.

Roberts, K.P., & Blades, M. (2000). *Children's Source Monitoring*. Mahwah, NJ: Lawrence Erlbaum.

Roberts, K.P., & Lamb, M.E. (1999). Children's responses when interviewers distort details during investigative interviews. *Legal and Criminological Psychology*, *4*, 23–31.

Roebers, C.M., & Schneider, W. (2001). Individual differences in children's eyewitness recall: The influence of intelligence and shyness. *Applied Developmental Science*, *5*, 9–30.

Rudy, L., & Goodman, G.S. (1991). Effects of participation on children's reports: Implications for children's testimony. *Developmental Psychology*, *27*, 527–538.

Salmon, K., Roncolato, W., & Gleitzman, M. (2003). Children's report of emotionally laden events: Adapting the interview to the child. *Applied Cognitive Psychology*, *17*, 65–80.

Saywitz, K. (1995). Improving children's testimony: The question, the answer and the environment. In M. Zaragoza, G. Graham, G.N. Hall, R. Hirschman, & Y. Ben-Porath (Eds), *Memory and Testimony in the Child Witness* (pp. 113–140). Thousand Oaks, CA: Sage.

Saywitz, K., Jaenicke, C., & Camparo, L. (1990). Children's knowledge of legal terminology. *Law and Human Behavior*, *14*, 523–535.

Saywitz, K., & Wilkinson, L. (1982). Age-related differences in metalinguistic awareness. In S. Kuczaj (Ed.), *Language Development: Vol. 2: Language, Thought, and Culture* (pp. 229–250). Hillsdale, NJ: Erlbaum.

Saywitz, K.J. (1988). The credibility of the child witness. *Family Advocate, 10,* 38.

Saywitz, K.J., & Camparo, L. (1998) Interviewing child witnesses: A developmental perspective. *Child Abuse Neglect, 22,* 825–843.

Saywitz, K.J., Goodman, G.S., Nicholas, E., & Moan, S.F. (1991). Children's memories of a physical examination involving genital touch: Implication for reports of child sexual abuse. *Journal of Consulting and Clinical Psychology, 59,* 682–691.

Saywitz, K.J., & Lyon, T.D. (2002). Coming to grips with children's suggestibility. In M.L. Eisen, J.A. Quas, & G.S. Goodman (Eds), *Memory and Suggestibility in the Forensic Interview* (pp. 85–113). Mahwah, NJ: Erlbaum.

Saywitz, K.J., Nathanson, R., & Snyder, L.S., (1993). Credibility of child witnesses: The role of communicative competence. *Topics of Language Disorders, 13,* 59–78.

Saywitz, K.J., & Snyder, L. (1993). Improving children's testimony with preparation. In G.S. Goodman, & B.L. Bottoms (Eds), *Child Victims, Child Witnesses: Understanding and Improving Testimony* (pp. 117–146). New York: Guilford.

Saywitz, K.J., & Snyder, L. (1996). Narrative elaboration: Test of a new procedure for interviewing children. *Journal of Consulting and Clinical Psychology, 64,* 1347–1357.

Saywitz, K.J., Snyder, L., & Nathason, R. (1999). Facilitating the communicative competence of child witness. *Applied Developmental Science, 3,* 58–68.

Schneider, W., & Pressley, M. (1997). *Memory Development Between Two and Twenty* (2nd ed.). Mahwah, NJ: Erlbaum.

Schreiber, N., Bellah, L.D., Martinez, Y., McLaurin, K.A., Strok, R., Garven, S., & Wood, J.M. (2006). Suggestive interviewing in the McMartin Preschool and Kelly Michaels daycare abuse cases: A case study. *Social Influence, 1,* 16–47.

Schreiber, N., & Parker, J.F. (2004). Inviting witnesses to speculate: Effects of age and interaction on children's recall. *Journal of Experimental Child Psychology, 89,* 31–52.

Singer, J.B., & Flavell, J.H. (1981). Development of knowledge about communication: children's evaluations of explicitly ambiguous messages. *Child Development, 52,* 1211–1215.

Skolnick, D., & Bloom, P. (2006). What does Batman think about SpongeBob? Children's understanding of the fantasy/fantasy distinction. *Cognition, 101,* B9–B18.

Sternberg, K.J., Lamb, M.E., Esplin, P.W., & Baradaran, L. (1999). Using a scripted protocol to guide investigative interview: A pilot study. *Applied Developmental Science,* 70–76.

Sternberg, K.J., Lamb, M.E., Esplin, P.W., Orbach, Y., & Hershkowitz, I. (2002). Using a structured protocol to improve the quality of investigative interviews. In M. Eisen, G.S. Goodman, & J. Quas (Eds), *Memory and Suggestibility in the Forensic Interview* (pp. 409–436). Mahwah, NJ: Erlbaum.

Strange, D., Garry, M., & Sutherland, R. (2003). Drawing out children's false memories. *Applied Cognitive Psychology, 17,* 607–619.

Tartas, V. (2001). The development of systems of conventional time: A study of the appropriation of temporal locations by four-to-ten-year old children. *European Journal of Psychology of Education, 16,* 197–208.

Taylor, M., Shawber, A., & Mannering, A. (2009). Children's imaginary companions: What is it like to have an invisible friend? In K. Markman, W. Klein, & J. Suhr (Eds), *Handbook of Imagination and Mental Simulation* (pp. 211–224). NY: Psychology Press.

Thierry, K.L., Lamb, M.E., Orbach, Y., & Pipe, M.E. (2005). Developmental differences in the function and use of anatomical dolls during interviews with alleged sexual abuse victims. *Journal of Consulting and Clinical Psychology*, *73*, 1135–1134.

Thierry, K.L., Spence, M.J., & Memon, A. (2001). Before misinformation is encountered: Source monitoring decreases child witness suggestibility. *Journal of Cognition and Development*, *2*, 1–26.

Tobey, A.E., & Goodman, G.S. (1992). Children's eyewitness memory: Effects of participation and forensic context. *Child Abuse and Neglect*, *16*, 779–796.

Walker, A.G. (1993). Questioning young children in court: A linguistic case study. *Law and Human Behavior*, *17*, 59–81.

Walker, A.G. (1999) *Handbook on Questioning Children: A Linguistic Perspective* (2nd ed.). Washington, DC: American Bar Association Center on Children and the Law.

Walker, A.G., & Warren, A.R. (1995). The language of the child abuse interview: Asking the questions, understanding the answers. In T. Ney (Ed.), *True and False Allegations of Child Sexual Abuse: Assessment and Case Management* (pp. 153–162). New York: Brunner/Mazel.

Walker, N.E., & Hunt, J.S. (1998). Interviewing child victim-witnesses: How you ask is what you get. In C.R. Thompson, D. Herrman, J.D. Read, D. Bruce, D. Payne, & M.P. Toglia (Eds), *Eyewitness Memory: Theoretical and Applied Perspectives* (pp. 55–87). Mahwah, NJ: Erlbaum.

Warren, A.R., & Lane, P. (1995). Effects of timing and type of questioning on eyewitness accuracy and suggestibility. In M.S. Zaragoza, J.R. Graham, G.C.N. Hall, R. Hirschman, & Y.S. Ben-Porath (Eds), *Memory and Testimony in the Child Witness Applied Psychology: Individual, Social, and Community Issues* (pp. 44–60). Thousand Oaks, CA: Sage.

Warren, A.R., & McCloskey, L.A. (1997). Language in social contexts. In S.B. Gleason (Ed.), *The Development of Language* (4th ed., pp. 210–258). New York: Allyn & Bacon.

Warren, A.R., Woodall, C.E., Hunt, J.S., & Perry, N.W. (1996). 'It sounds good in theory, but': Do investigative interviewers follow guidelines based on memory research? *Child Maltreatment*, *1*, 231–245.

Waterman, A.H., Blades, M., & Spencer, C.P. (2000). Do children try to answer nonsensical questions? *British Journal of Developmental Psychology*, *18*, 211–226.

Waterman, A., Blades, M., & Spencer, C. (2001). Interviewing children and adults: The effect of question format on the tendency to speculate. *Applied Cognitive Psychology*, *15*, 521–531.

Waterman, A.H., Blades, M., & Spencer, C. (2004). Indicating when you do not know the answer: The effect of question format and interviewer knowledge on children's "don't know" responses. *British Journal of Developmental Psychology*, *22*, 335–348.

Welch-Ross, M.K. (1999). Interviewer knowledge and preschoolers' reasoning about knowledge states moderate suggestibility. *Cognitive Development*, *14*, 423–442.

Wellman, H.M., & Estes D. (1986). Early understanding of mental entities: A reexamination of childhood realism. *Child Development*, *57*, 910–923.
Wells, G.L., Turtle, J.W., & Luus, C.A.E. (1989). The perceived credibility of child eyewitnesses: What happens when they use their own words? In S.J. Ceci, D.F. Ross, & M.P. Toglia (Eds), *Perspectives on Children's Testimony* (pp. 23–46). New York: Springer-Verlag.
Woolley, J.D., & Wellman, H.M. (1993). Origin and truth: Young children's understanding of imaginary mental representations. *Child Development*, *64*, 1–17.
Wright, D.B., Gaskell, G.D., & O'Muircheartaigh, C.A. (1997). Temporal estimation of major news events: Reexamining the accessibility principle. *Applied Cognitive Psychology*, *11*, 35–46.
Zajac, R., Gross, J., & Hayne, H. (2003). Asked and answered: Questioning children in the courtroom. *Psychiatry, Psychology, and Law*, *10*, 199–209.
Zajac, R., & Hayne, H. (2003). I don't think that's what really happened: The effect of cross examination on the accuracy of children's reports. *Journal of Experimental Psychology: Applied*, *9*, 187–195.

3

The Development of Memory in Childhood

David J. La Rooy, Lindsay C. Malloy, and Michael E. Lamb

Key Points

- Interviewers need to take into account children's developing abilities to remember their experiences.
- Interviewers should not only follow guidelines, but also strive to understand the rationale for these recommendations.
- Features of memory development affect what we can expect children to remember.
- Although we keep learning more about memory, our knowledge of the fundamental mechanisms is unlikely to change.
- There are clear areas of consensus among memory researchers about basic memory issues.

After many decades of research, experimental psychologists have come to understand the strengths, weaknesses, and features of memory very well. It is important for investigative interviewers to appreciate the complexities of human memory given the critical implications of eyewitness testimony for the legal system and the need for interviewers to have reasonable expectations of children. So too must fact finders and other professionals who evaluate investigative interviews and the veracity of children's testimony.

Children's Testimony: A Handbook of Psychological Research and Forensic Practice, Second Edition.
Edited by Michael E. Lamb, David J. La Rooy, Lindsay C. Malloy, and Carmit Katz.

Information concerning basic memory processes has informed best-practice guidelines for interviewing child witnesses. Interviewers should not only follow these guidelines, but also strive to understand how our knowledge of basic memory processes informs what they are being asked to do. Furthermore, when interviewers are challenged (e.g., in the courtroom or by managers and peers), knowledge of basic memory principles and memory development can help them defend their practices or understand the implications of failures to follow best practices.

In this chapter, we focus on principles of memory about which memory researchers agree and which are important for interviewers to understand. Professionals who work with child witnesses can rely on these findings when interviewing children, evaluating their testimony, and making recommendations to the courts. Considerable amounts of research illustrate the superiority of eliciting information from free-recall memory as opposed to recognition memory, and other studies have shown how memory can be further enhanced. Research has helped develop an international consensus about the ways in which interviews should be conducted, revealing the conditions under which recall is likely to be accurate and the conditions in which it is likely to be inaccurate.

Before examining some of the specifics of memory research, it is worth considering some of the terms used by researchers when talking about memory for experienced events. Researchers use terms like 'eyewitness memory', 'event memory', 'autobiographical memory', and 'episodic memory'. These different terms can be confusing, leading readers to assume that these are very different types of memory. However, these terms can be used somewhat interchangeably to describe memory for our *experiences* (i.e., what happened on particular occasions), and research on all of these topics contributes to our understanding of investigative interviewing. In addition, research on other kinds of memory (e.g., memory for word lists) can inform our understanding of basic memory processes and thus contribute to our understanding of eyewitness memory.

Researchers have sought to understand memory as a three-stage process of *encoding, storage,* and *retrieval* (Melton, 1963). Encoding refers to the information transfer from our experiences into our memory (Atkinson & Shiffrin, 1971). How much attention we are able to pay to our experiences and the surrounding environment affects how much we are able to encode and this affects how much information about our experiences we actually store in memory (Tulving, 1974). Features of our experiences and surroundings 'capture' our attention so that we become consciously aware of things that are important to us; conscious mental processing, sometimes referred to as short-term memory, then allows some memories to become stored in long-term memory. Experiences are more likely to be remembered when they make sense, which limits younger children who may sometimes not store information because the events are inexplicable. Information about events is also more likely to be stored when there are ready associations to other experiences – experiences that share some features, or perhaps have contrasting features. Again, this places children at a disadvantage, because they have had fewer experiences with which to make associations. Information about our experiences and surroundings that has been successfully stored in long-term memory can be recalled into consciousness, allowing us to remember our past experiences (e.g., Atkinson & Shiffrin, 1968, 1971). The processes involved in encoding, storage and retrieval can operate independently and in complex ways. For example, information can be 'forgotten' (lost from conscious memory) and later remembered, memories can be confused with newer memories, and specific memories can be recalled on one occasion but not on others. Some of these complexities are discussed in the next section.

THE DEVELOPMENT OF MEMORY

When does memory development begin and how does memory develop over the lifespan? For a long time it was thought that the ability to remember our experiences was closely related to the development of language. This conclusion seemed plausible: when children learn to speak, they become able to store memories using words to name and describe their experiences, and to locate memories in 'time' by linking personal experiences to other events and concepts. Language would thus be necessary in order to fully remember our experiences and to communicate them in a coherent way to others. This view is consistent with the observation that, as adults, we have virtually no recollection of our very early years of life, and that the events we do remember tend to date from the age at which we learned to use language well. This is referred to as the paradox of infantile amnesia; paradoxical because we cannot remember our early experiences as well as we can remember later events whereas young children and infants nevertheless *can* and *do* remember their experiences. That is, 3-year-olds can recount details of an event that occurred 1 year earlier, but are likely to have forgotten the event by adulthood.

Although older children and adults cannot remember events that occurred in infancy or toddlerhood (Bauer, 2006a,b; Pillemer & White, 1989), many people nonetheless believe that they can and do remember. In a study of adults', including jurors', perceptions of children's abilities, almost two-thirds (64%) agreed with the statement, 'If a child has been repeatedly and painfully sexually abused as an infant, he or she can remember it' (Quas, Thompson, & Clarke-Stewart, 2005). In fact, evidence shows infantile amnesia with respect to non-emotional and positive events such as the birth of a sibling as well as negative or stressful experiences such as distressing medical procedures or emergency room visits (e.g., Peterson & Parsons, 2005; Quas *et al.*, 1999; Sheingold & Tenney, 1982; Usher & Neisser, 1993).For instance, Quas *et al.* (1999) tested children's memory for negative events – invasive medical procedures that occurred when the children were between 2 and 7 years of age. The procedure (voiding cystourethrogram, or VCUG) involves taking X-rays while the child urinates to identify potential kidney problems and infections after filling the bladder with fluid containing X-ray visible dye. In the study, children were interviewed between 1 and 5 years after experiencing this procedure. Not one of the nine children who had been 2 years old at the time of the procedure had any memory of what had happened; half of the eight children who had been 3 years old remembered it, and most of the 26 children aged 5 and older at the time of the procedure remembered some details about it. Thus, although the procedure involved invasive genital contact and was quite distressing for most children, those who were between 2 and 3 years of age when it took place simply could not remember it later.

What are the implications of these findings for interviewers? Importantly, if older children or adults are asked to report events that occurred prior to age 3 or 4 (i.e., during the phase of infantile amnesia), it is highly unlikely that their reports will be based on clear or detailed memories of the events in question. Instead, they may reconstruct what 'probably' happened based on conversations with others (e.g., parents), interviewer and therapist suggestions, photographs, or from vague memories that have been reinterpreted over time and mixed with their current knowledge and beliefs.

Of course, children between the ages of 2 and 3 years can and do remember many experiences (e.g., Bruck, Ceci, Francouer, & Renick, 1995; Fivush, Gray, & Fromhoff, 1987; Quas & Schaaf, 2002). In fact, even infants remember their experiences, although they are often unable to tell us about them verbally. Using a method to study memory using toy mobiles attached to infants' cots, researchers have showed that memory for experienced events actually begins to develop very early in life – before we can speak (Hayne, 2004). A mobile is placed above an infant's cot and researchers then connect the mobile with a ribbon to his/her foot. The infant soon learns to make the mobile move by kicking the foot. Because infants find watching a mobile juggling above them rather captivating, they maintain a 'kick rate' to keep the mobile moving. The 'memory test' involves re-installing the mobile sometime later and measuring how well infants remember their previous experience by seeing how enthusiastically they kick their feet.

Several studies using this procedure have shown that 2-month-olds remember the 'kick-to-make-the-mobile-move' experience for 1–3 days, 3-month-olds for 6–8 days, and 6-month-olds for 15–16 days (Hayne, 2004). However, when 3-month-olds are reminded about their mobile experience by being shown them again, their memories of the association can last for as long as 45 days. Older infants (who are no longer interested in mobiles) can be tested by seeing how long they remember that pressing a button makes a toy train move: by 18 months, toddlers can remember this association for up to 12 weeks (Hartshorn *et al.*, 1998).

Older children's memory can be studied more easily and their memories measured more directly once they can speak. Researchers studying children's memory usually 'stage' events about which the children are questioned sometime later. Because the events in question are preplanned and documented in detail, it is possible to compare what is later recalled with what actually happened and determine the accuracy of memory. Experimental findings using this basic procedure have been conducted using a variety of different events which have included stressful events (e.g., medical emergencies, vaccinations, and painful medical procedures), well child medical examinations during which children are touched by a doctor as part of the routine examination and interactive events in which children participate in or 'witness' a series of activities (e.g., play sessions, magic shows, pirate shows, science demonstrations). In other studies, children see short films or video presentations about which they are later questioned.

Taken together, these studies lead to one clear conclusion: the most important determinant of children's memory capacity is age. As children develop, they are progressively able to remember their experiences for longer and longer periods of time – from a few days in infancy to several years by the time children are 5 years old. For example, Goodman, Hirschman, Hepps, and Rudy (1991) studied children's memory for an inoculation at a medical clinic, finding that the 3- to 6-year old children were able to remember some details even a year later. Pipe, Sutherland, Webster, Jones, and La Rooy (2004) similarly showed that 5- and 6-year-old children could still report details of a visit to their school by a 'pirate' 2 years later when they were 7 and 8 years old. The basic finding that younger children forget more quickly than older children is also supported by the results of laboratory experiments in which children memorize and recall word lists (Brainerd, Reyna, Howe, & Kingma, 1990).

Just how much do we actually remember about our experiences and the relevant context and how quickly do we forget details about them? These important questions have direct implications for our expectations about how much children should be able to tell us about their experiences. Should we expect children to remember lots of details about interactions with abusers, especially if those interactions were brief, confusing and/or long ago?

Experiments suggest that we actually remember a lot less than we may realize. In one study, for example, La Rooy, Pipe, and Murray (2005) asked 5-year-old children about a 15-minute interaction with a 'friendly pirate' in a staged 'pirate show' during which the children performed a series of activities like 'feed the bird', 'paint the map', and 'finding the treasure', involving a total of 60 actions and associated objects. When the children were interviewed immediately after the pirate visit, at a time when recall is expected to be the best, they only recalled 15 pieces of information on average; this amounts to a mere 25% of the available details. When the children were interviewed again 6 months later they recalled 8 pieces of information, only 13% of the details.

How much we remember also depends on the salience and significance of our experiences. In another school-based experiment, 5- and 6-year-old children either directly experienced an event, observed another child in the event, or were told a story about it. The children's memory of their experiences was tested a few days later and showed that those with the direct experience of the event produced the most complete and accurate accounts of what happened compared with children who had only seen or heard what happened (Murachver, Pipe, Gordon, Owens, & Fivush, 1996). How well children remember their experiences at least partly depends on how well they comprehend these experiences and can associate or 'link' them with other experiences in their memory. For example, children's prior knowledge of medical experiences or what happens during a routine medical 'check up' facilitates children's recall of specific doctor office visits (for a review see Ornstein *et al.*, 1997). Prior knowledge may help children encode events because they are better able to process and understand the events at the time. This knowledge may be used subsequently to generate cues linking the events with other experiences, thus facilitating retrieval.

Jones and Pipe (2002) documented the rate at which memory declines over time by asking different groups of 5- and 6-year-old children about such visits to the 'friendly pirate', either immediately, or 1 day, 1 week, 1 month, or 6 months later. The children were asked to provide a free recall account of what they could recall before they were given open-ended cued prompts (e.g., 'I heard that you had to become a real pirate, tell me about that') to elicit further information. When the results were graphed, it became apparent that the average rate of forgetting was very similar to the rate of forgetting measured in other experimental contexts – including those derived from experiments conducted over 100 years ago (Ebbinghaus, 1964/1885). Specifically, forgetting is most rapid soon after the event; as more and more time passes, the amount of forgetting decreases, until there is very little further forgetting. To make matters worse, forgetting is accompanied by gradual increases in the number of errors made as people, including children, try to remember what happened (Bruck, Ceci, & Hembrooke, 2002; La Rooy, Pipe, & Murray, 2007; Melnyk & Bruck, 2004). Both because we forget and because our residual memories become increasingly fallible, memories are likely to be most accurate soon after our experiences.

This is not always the case, however. Several researchers have shown that the amount of correct information recalled about experienced events does not necessarily decrease dramatically as time goes by. Studies examining children's memory for medical treatments or procedures (Ornstein *et al.*, 1992; Peterson, 1999), and natural disasters (Ackil, Van Abbema, & Bauer, 2003; Fivush, McDermott Sales, Goldberg, Bahrick, & Parker, 2004) have shown relatively stable recall over time, for example. Perhaps because many of these events were important and personally significant for the children, their memories were kept 'alive' by opportunities to talk and think about the events. These opportunities to keep memory alive through discussion and reminders about what happened provide opportunities for memory 'rehearsal' whereby memories are hypothesized to become 'consolidated' or stronger over time and are therefore less likely to be forgotten. It is important to realize that opportunities for memory rehearsal may also provide opportunities for contamination. For example, if misinformation is introduced in a conversation with a friend about a past experience, it can be incorporated into future recollections (for a review see La Rooy, Lamb, & Pipe, 2009).

MEMORY CHANGES OVER TIME

How stable are memories? What changes may happen over time? The above discussion suggests that we can only recall a small amount about our experiences initially, and that what we do recall either decreases or remains stable as time goes by. This observation needs to be considered in light of the fact that we do not actually report everything stored in memory the first time we are questioned about it: more information is encoded into memory than we recognize, so that correct new details about events are sometimes remembered days, weeks or even years later. What we remember about our experiences is therefore dynamic (Erdelyi, 1996, 2010; La Rooy, Lamb, & Pipe, 2009).

In the study described earlier, La Rooy *et al.* (2005) re-interviewed the 5- and 6-year-old children about their visit to the pirate the following day. All of the 40 children tested reported new accurate information the next day. In another study, La Rooy *et al.* (2007) conducted repeated interviews after a 6-month delay and found that 81% of the children recalled additional information the second time they were questioned. Similarly, Hamond and Fivush (1991) re-interviewed preschoolers about a trip to Disneyworld and found that, although most of the information provided in the second interview was accurate, most of it (75%) was also new (i.e., not reported in the first interview). This phenomenon – called reminiscence – is also very common in adults. For example, Gilbert and Fisher (2006) asked adults who had witnessed a bank robbery to recall what they could remember immediately and then re-interviewed them 48 hours later; 98% reported new details that they had not reported earlier. This basic research finding in the area of eyewitness memory is consistent with findings from many studies, including some conducted a century ago (Ballard, 1913).

Such well-established features of memory are quite troublesome within the legal world and especially in the realm of investigative interviewing. When new information is not mentioned initially but recalled later in time, it is often greeted suspiciously because competing explanations appear plausible – perhaps the new information is fabricated or inaccurate. In fact, jurors often rely on consistency as an indicator of veracity, and inconsistencies (including the addition of new details to subsequent re-tellings) are commonly viewed as reflecting low accuracy (Leippe, Manion, & Romanczyk, 1992). In legal contexts, witnesses, including children, are often cross-examined about earlier statements that are inconsistent with later testimony in the hopes of impeaching witness credibility.

While the accuracy of later added information may vary for a variety of reasons, including the way that information is elicited (La Rooy *et al.*, 2009), the better remembered an event is, the more likely it is that the new details will be accurate (La Rooy *et al.*, 2005). Interviewers and fact finders should remember that inconsistencies (in the form of new information) are a normal function of memory and are not uncommon when children (or adults) recount true experiences (Fivush, Hamond, Harsch, Singer, & Wolf, 1991; Hamond & Fivush, 1991; Peterson, Moores, & White, 2001).

THE RECONSTRUCTIVE NATURE OF MEMORY AND SUGGESTIBILITY

We forget and recover details because memories *are* (re)constructed over time, a process that also makes them vulnerable to suggestive influence and distortion (for reviews see Loftus, 2005; Pezdek & Lam, 2005) and sometimes allows entirely false memories to be produced. Memory does not work like a video recorder that faithfully stores details completely, accurately and in chronological order so that they can be replayed at a later time. Instead, reconstructions allow the incorporation of errors, and reflect biases which affect the way a story is rationalized, elaborated, and made more concise (Bartlett, 1932).

An often-cited study illustrating how susceptible memory is to distortion was conducted by Leichtman and Ceci (1995). In this study, a children's daycare centre was visited during story time by 'Sam Stone' who commented on the story (saying it was one of his favourites), walked about the classroom, and then waved goodbye and left. The children were then interviewed about the visit once a week for 5 weeks. Some of the children were interviewed in a neutral manner and some were interviewed suggestively. In addition, half of the children were told that Sam Stone was clumsy (a negative stereotype) before he came into the classroom. The suggestive interviewing involved showing children a ripped book and a soiled teddy as evidence of 'bad deeds' by Sam Stone. In the final interviews all children were asked, 'Did you see him. . .[rip the book/soil the teddy] with your own eyes?' When children were interviewed non-suggestively almost no children made claims about the 'bad deeds' whether or not the negative stereotype (i.e., clumsiness) had been introduced beforehand. However, the combination of suggestive interviewing and negative stereotyping led 30% of the 5- to 6-year-olds and 46% of the 3- to 4-year olds to agree that they had seen Sam rip the book or soil the teddy. Clearly, pressure can lead children to report things incorrectly. It is important to recall, however, that the interviews were *highly* suggestive and that the interviewers used techniques that are not commonly encountered in investigative interviews, notably, falsifying physical 'evidence' before presenting it in the interview. Further, despite the extensive and repeated suggestive interviewing, over half of the youngest children did not acquiesce to the interviewer's suggestions.

It is also important to realize that *acquiescence* – the tendency for children to agree – describes how children answer *specific types of questions*. When children are asked leading questions about things about which they have little or no knowledge, perceived social pressure increases the tendency to acquiesce (e.g., Greenstock & Pipe, 1997; Pipe & Wilson, 1994). Acquiescence also increases when a power imbalance exists between the person asking the questions and the person answering them (Ceci, Ross & Toglai, 1987). It is therefore important not to introduce into the interview information that the child has not already mentioned in case the child simply goes along with what is said.

Re-asking the same questions is also suggestive because it re-focuses children on their previous responses instead of on the memory for what happened. When children are asked repeated questions they frequently change their answers (Fivush & Schwarzmueller, 1995; Fivush & Shukat, 1995; Lyon, 2002; Poole & White, 1993). In Poole and White's (1991) study, 4- to 8-year-old children were asked the same questions immediately after an event, and again 1 week later. When open prompts were repeated, children provided additional accurate information not reported earlier, a phenomenon discussed earlier in the chapter. When yes/no questions were repeated, however, children provided inconsistent responses 25% of the time, and when children were asked repeated questions that were actually unanswerable the majority expressed uncertainty, while some offered plausible educated guesses. Howie, Sheehan, Mojarrad, and Wrzesinska (2004) estimated that 88% of the children they studied changed at least one response to repeated questions.

TWO IMPORTANT WAYS WE REMEMBER: FREE RECALL VERSUS RECOGNITION

Free recall memory and recognition memory can be seen to be different ends of a memory continuum. Free recall memories are accessed in conditions where there is no specific memory cue. For example, asking someone to 'tell everything that happened' does not specify or cue particular aspects of memory. Exactly what is recalled in free recall depends on a search of memory directed by the person being questioned. By contrast, recognition memory is involved when an interviewee is asked using specific questions to select between alternatives offered by the interviewer ('Was the touch over or under your clothes?'). These multiple choice questions restrict the possible responses and increase the risk of inaccuracy because interviewees may choose one of the options even if they cannot recognize the correct answer. *What, when, where*, and *how* type questions fall somewhere in the middle of the continuum between free-recall and recognition memory. They do not typically force the respondent to choose between options provided by the interviewer, and instead ask for more details about something the interviewee has already mentioned, but they nonetheless require only short answers about an aspect of the event or object that may or may not be well encoded or remembered.

Focused questions vary greatly in complexity. For example, answers to questions about the timing of events – when things happened – may be important to investigators, but it is difficult (especially for children) to recall times and dates accurately (see Chapter 2). Because questions like these seem very reasonable, children often make educated guesses in response rather than recalling information from memory. By contrast, other focused questions (e.g., 'What is your brother's name?') are easier to answer because the requested information involves semantic general knowledge rather than memory of a specific event. Questions like 'How come he got away with it for so long?' may seem similarly reasonable but unfortunately invite speculation by the child, and do not direct him/her to search memory of an experienced event. Some questions (e.g., 'Why did he do that?') are simply impossible for children to answer even with the best of memory for an event and thus should be avoided.

Researchers have studied the accuracy of children's answers to these different types of questions. For example, Dent and Stephenson (1979) showed 10- and 11-year-old children a short film of a theft, capture, escape, and ensuing chase of offender. They compared the accuracy of answers to questions about the event and found that the children were 91% accurate when responding to open prompts but only 81% accurate when answering closed/specific questions. In a specific case study examining information obtained from a 5-year-old girl using open and closed prompts, Orbach and Lamb (2001) found that 90% of the contradictory details this alleged victim provided were elicited using closed/specific questions and suggestive questions whereas no contradictions came in response to open-ended prompts. Such dramatic differences in the quality of information elicited using different types of questions explain why interview guidelines universally emphasize the importance of getting as much information as possible using open-ended questions (see Chapter 7 on practice interview and Chapter 8 on investigating substantive issues).

CONTEXT REINSTATEMENT AND THE THEORY OF 'ENCODING SPECIFICITY'

According to the principle of encoding specificity (Tulving, 1983), what we remember depends crucially on what is stored in memory at the time of encoding; each encoded detail about the event and its context can serve as a cue that allows other details to be retrieved. This explains how information can be stored in memory, but at the same time not be recalled; the retrieval cue needed to 'open' the memory may be missing. However, as memories come into consciousness they themselves can act as further cues that help more details to be recalled. As we gradually recall information, we also mentally recreate the original context and that, in itself, becomes a possible retrieval cue.

Context reinstatement and encoding specificity have been examined extensively in studies of children's eyewitness memory in both experimental (Pipe & Wilson, 1994; Priestley, Roberts, & Pipe, 1999; Wilkinson, 1988) and field contexts (Hershkowitz, Orbach, Lamb, Sternberg, Horowitz, & Hovav, 1998; Orbach, Hershkowitz, Lamb, Sternberg, & Horowitz, 2000); all show that recall is facilitated when children are given reminders of the context in which the events occurred. For example, Hershkowitz *et al.* (1998) interviewed 4- to 13-year-old children about alleged abuse and then took the children to the scene of the alleged crime so as to reinstate the original context. When re-interviewed in that context, children reported additional forensically relevant new information that they had not reported in the interviewer's office. According to Tulving, encoding specificity facilitates recall because the task of recalling becomes simpler, benefiting from recognition cues rather than solely on retrieving information.

STRESS, TRAUMA AND MEMORY

The relations between stress and memory are inconsistent, with some studies indicating enhanced performance by children (e.g., Goodman *et al.*, 1991) and others showing detrimental effects of stress (e.g., Quas, Bauer, & Boyce, 2004), and may vary depending on whether one is talking about encoding or retrieving a memory. Importantly, however, memories of stressful or even traumatic experiences are subject to the same basic encoding, storage, and retrieval principles as are memories for more mundane events, meaning that we can forget traumatic events, just as we can forget other experiences, that traumatic or stressful experiences are not necessarily remembered in richer detail just because the events were traumatic and that *all* memories can be contaminated (e.g., Howe, Toth, & Cicchetti, 2006). People do *not* remember every detail about such experiences – even when they think they do.

Consider the phenomenon of 'flashbulb memories' – named for the vividness and perceptual clarity that people often report when recalling some salient experiences. Where were they and how did they react when President Kennedy was shot? When the Challenger Shuttle exploded? When the Twin Towers were hit on September 11? What characterizes these 'flashbulb memories' is the confidence with which people claim to remember exactly where they were, what they were doing, who they were with, and how they heard about these significant events, almost as though they were experiencing 'flashbacks' to the event. Interestingly, while these memories are associated with strong confidence in their accuracy, they are not often associated with actual accuracy (e.g., Neisser & Harsch, 1992), an important reminder to interviewers that confidence and accuracy do not necessarily go hand in hand.

Brown and Kulik (1977) proposed that a special mechanism accounts for flashbulb memories, which are, by definition, about events that are surprising, emotional and consequential. As expected, people interviewed about significant events, such as the assassinations of Martin Luther King and John F. Kennedy, vividly described what they were doing and who communicated the 'big news' but, unfortunately, these researchers could not determine how accurate these flashbulb memories were.

By testing people's memory for such events on multiple occasions, researchers have since revealed that, while flashbulb memories are characterized by confidence, they are often inconsistent or inaccurate (Neisser & Harsch, 1992; Talarico & Rubin, 2003; Weaver, 1993). For instance, Neisser and Harsch tested college students' memory for the Challenger Shuttle explosion by interviewing them soon after the event and again 2.5 years later. Participants were highly confident even when they were very inaccurate, and many of them were, in fact, inaccurate. Similarly, memories of the September 11 attacks also tend to be inaccurate (Conway, Skitka, Hemmerich, & Kershaw, 2009; Greenberg, 2004; Lee & Brown, 2003, Pezdek, 2003; Talarico & Rubin, 2003; Tekcan, Ece, Gulgoz, & Er, 2003).

Of course, flashbulb memories involve stress at the time of encoding, which may enhance children's memories – at least for certain aspects of the event (e.g., Buchanan & Lovallo, 2001; see Christianson, 1992; McGaugh, 2003). Some theorize that stress may narrow children's focus to central aspects of distressing events so that they remember these central aspects well (e.g., the identity of the assailant) while remembering peripheral aspects in less detail (e.g., the colour of the assailant's shirt; see Christianson, 1992). As indicated above, however, this hypothesis has not been well established.

Of course, stress at encoding and its potential effect on later recall is not under the interviewers' control, but interviewers *can* affect stress at the time of memory retrieval. In general, children typically have more difficulty than adults retrieving information from memory (Bjorklund, 2005), and young children often need more cueing and prompting than adults to recount information retained in memory (e.g., Fivush, 1993;

Lamb *et al.*, 2003; Price & Goodman, 1990). Children may also fail to access the appropriate memories (i.e., of the alleged crime) because they do not understand the 'rules' of forensic and courtroom contexts or know what information the interviewer is seeking (e.g., Cordon, Saetermoe, & Goodman, 2005). In addition, the stressfulness of the interview context may interfere with retrieval by consuming some of their cognitive resources. Children may need to devote some of their cognitive/attentional resources to coping with their emotions instead of to memory retrieval (e.g., Quas *et al.*, 2004).

Children, like adults, often find encounters with the legal system stressful. Testifying in open court (or while facing the defendant) and being cross-examined are among the most distressing aspects (for a detailed review see Chapter 16), and these same factors are associated with poorer memory performance (e.g., Nathanson & Saywitz, 2003). In one well-known field study, Goodman *et al.* (1992) found that children who were more fearful about testifying in front of the defendant were less able to answer prosecutors' questions than those who were less fearful. In experimental studies, where it is possible to verify the accuracy of children's memory, children's free recall is less complete and their responses to direct questions are less accurate when they are questioned in a courtroom than in a more familiar location (e.g., a classroom) or less intimidating environment (e.g., Hill & Hill, 1987). Similarly, Saywitz, and Nathanson (1993) found that children who rated the 'legal process' as stressful provided less information about staged events than children who rated it as less stressful.

The accuracy of children's responses during cross-examination, one of the most feared parts of legal involvement, has also been examined experimentally. Zajac and Hayne (2003) interviewed 5- and 6-year-olds about a visit to a police station using both direct and cross-examination. During the cross-examination, interviewers used several techniques often observed in actual court cases (e.g., complex, leading, irrelevant questions; challenges to children's certainty; expressions of disbelief), and most (over 85%) of the children changed some answers that they had provided during direct testimony. The changes occurred regardless of whether children's original responses were accurate or inaccurate. Some changes were considered small alterations in specific details, whereas others represented total retractions of children's original reports. In fact, nearly one-third of the children changed all of their original responses. Although the researchers did not measure children's stress during the cross-examination, it is possible that the cross-examinations increased children's anxiety and nervousness, leading them to change answers and provide inconsistent and often inaccurate responses.

CONCLUSIONS

Memory research has had an important role in the development of investigative interview guidelines, and an understanding of how memory works is useful for the investigative interviewer. The aspects of memory described in this chapter have received much attention from researchers and are well established and agreed upon. Of course, researchers will continue to advance knowledge and scientific understanding about human memory. However, our knowledge of the basic concepts discussed in this chapter is unlikely to change given the clear areas of consensus about the basic memory issues discussed above.

It is vital for investigative interviewers and other legal professionals to recognize that memory abilities develop dramatically throughout childhood. Interviewers must be careful not to interview in a way that exceeds children's cognitive abilities or places unreasonable expectations on them regarding the amount or specificity of information recalled. Although there are major improvements in memory across childhood, it is important to note that even among adults and even for stressful, traumatic or 'highly memorable' experiences, memory does not work like a video recorder capturing detailed experiences and playing them back exactly as they happened. Memory has its own 'laws' which frequently do not fit neatly within legal systems that specify the need for specific and detailed evidence. How legal systems can better accommodate the workings and limitations of human memory remains a challenge.

REFERENCES

Ackil, J., Van Abbema, D., & Bauer, P. (2003). After the storm: Enduring differences in mother–child recollections of traumatic and nontraumatic events. *Journal of Experimental Child Psychology*, *84*, 286–309.

Atkinson, R.C., & Shiffrin, R.M. (1968). A proposed system and its control processes. In K.W. Spence, & J.T. Spence (Eds), *The Psychology of Learning and Motivation: Advances in Research and Theory* (Vol. 2, pp. 89–195). New York: Academic Press.

Atkinson, R.C., & Shiffrin, R.M. (1971). The control of short term memory. *Scientific American*, 80–92.

Ballard, P.B. (1913). Oblivescence and reminiscence. *British Journal of Psychology*, *1*, 1–82.

Bartlett, F.C. (1932). *Remembering: A Study in Experimental and Social Psychology*. Cambridge: Cambridge University Press.

Bauer, P.J. (2006a). Constructing a past in infancy: A neuro-developmental account. *Trends in Cognitive Sciences*, *10*, 175–181.

Bauer, P.J. (2006b). Event memory. In W. Damon, & R.M. Lerner (Editors-in-Chief). *Handbook of Child Psychology* (6th edn.), D. Kuhn, & R. Siegler (Volume Eds) *Volume 2: Cognition, Perception, and Language* (pp. 373–425). Hoboken, NJ: John Wiley & Sons.

Bjorklund, D. (2005). *Children's Thinking*. Belmont, CA: Wadsworth.

Brainerd, C.J., Reyna, V.F., Howe, M.L., & Kingma, J. (1990). The development of forgetting and reminiscence. *Monographs of the Society for Research in Child Development*, *55* (Serial No. 222).

Brown, R., & Kulik, J. (1977). Flashbulb memories. *Cognition*, *5*, 73–99.

Bruck, M., Ceci, S.J., Francouer, E., & Renick, A. (1995). Anatomically detailed dolls do not facilitate preschoolers' reports of a pediatric examination involving genital touching. *Journal of Experimental Psychology*, *1*, 95–109.

Bruck, M., Ceci, S.J., & Hembrooke, H. (2002). The nature of children's true and false narratives. *Developmental Review*, *22*, 520–554.

Buchanan, T.W., & Lovallo, W.R. (2001). Enhanced memory for emotional material following stress-level cortisol treatment in humans. *Psychoneuroendocrinology*, *26*, 307–317.

Ceci, S.J., Ross, D.F., & Toglia, M.P. (1987). Suggestibility of children's memory: Psycholegal implications. *Journal of Experimental Psychology: General*, *116*, 38–49.

Christianson, S. (1992). Emotional stress and eyewitness memory: A critical review. *Psychological Bulletin*, *112*, 284–309.

Conway, A.R.A., Skitka, L.J., Hemmerich, J.A., & Kershaw, T.C. (2009). Flashbulb memory for 11 September 2001. *Applied Cognitive Psychology*, *23*, 605–623.

Cordon, I.M., Saetermoe, C.L., & Goodman, G.S. (2005). Facilitating children's accurate responses: Conversational rules and interview style. *Applied Cognitive Psychology*, *19*, 249–266.

Dent, H.R., & Stephenson, G.M. (1979). An experimental study of the effectiveness of different techniques of questioning child witnesses. *British Journal of Social and Clinical Psychology*, *18*, 41–51.

Ebbinghaus, H. (1964/1885). *Memory: A Contribution to Experimental Psychology*. New York: Dover. (Trans. 1964).

Erdelyi, M.H. (1996). *The Recovery of Unconscious Memories: Hypermnesia and Reminiscence*: Chicago, IL: University of Chicago Press.

Erdelyi, M.H. (2010). The ups and downs of memory. *American Psychologist*, *65*, 623–633.

Fivush, R. (1993). Developmental perspectives on autobiographical recall. In G.S. Goodman, & B.L. Bottoms (Eds), *Child Victims, Child Witnesses: Understanding and Improving Children's Testimony* (pp. 1–24). NY: Guilford.

Fivush, R., Gray, J.T., & Fromhoff, F.A. (1987). Two-year-olds talk about the past. *Cognitive Development*, *2*, 393–409.

Fivush, R., Hamond, N.R., Harsch, N., Singer, N., & Wolf, A. (1991). Content and consistency in young children's autobiographical recall. *Discourse Processes*, *14*, 373–388.

Fivush, R., McDermott Sales, J., Goldberg, A., Bahrick, L., & Parker, J. (2004). Weathering the storm: Children's long-term recall of Hurricane Andrew. *Memory*, *12*, 104–118.

Fivush, R., & Schwarzmueller, A. (1995). Say it once again: Effects of repeated questions on children's event recall. *Journal of Traumatic Stress*, *8*, 555–580.

Fivush, R., & Shukat, J. (1995). What young children recall: issues of content, consistency and coherence of early autobiographical recall. In M.S. Zaragoza, J.R. Graham, G.C.N. Hall, R. Hirchman, & Y.S. Ben-Porath (Eds), *Memory and Testimony in the Child Witness* (pp. 5–23). Thousand Oaks, CA: Sage.

Gilbert, J.A.E., & Fisher, R.P. (2006). The effects of varied retrieval cues on reminiscence in eyewitness memory. *Applied Cognitive Psychology*, *20*, 723–739.

Goodman, G.S., Hirschman, J.E., Hepps, D., & Rudy, L. (1991). Children's memory for stressful events. *Merrill-Palmer Quarterly*, *37*, 109–158.

Goodman, G.S., Taub, E.P., Jones, D.P., England, P., Port, L.K., Rudy, L., & Prado, L. (1992). Testifying in criminal court: Emotional effects on child sexual assault victims. *Monographs of the Society for Research in Child Development*, *57*, v–142.

Greenberg, D.L. (2004). President Bush's false 'flashbulb' memory of 9/11/01. *Applied Cognitive Psychology*, *18*, 363–370.

Greenstock, J., & Pipe M.E. (1997). Are two heads better that one? Peer support and children's eyewitness reports. *Applied Cognitive Psychology*, *11*, 461–483.

Hamond, N.R., & Fivush, R. (1991). Memories of Mickey Mouse: Young children recount their trip to Disneyworld. *Cognitive Development*, *6*, 433–448.

Hartshorn, K., Rovee-Collier, C., Gerhardstein, P.C., Bhatt, R.S., Wondoloski, T.L., Klein, P., Gilch, J., Wurtzel, N., & Campos-de-Carvalho, M. (1998). Ontogeny of long-term memory over the first year-and-a-half of life. *Developmental Psychobiology*, *32*, 69–89.

Hayne, H. (2004). Infant memory development: Implications for childhood amnesia. *Developmental Review*, *24*, 33–73.

Hershkowitz, I., Orbach, Y., Lamb, M.E., Sternberg, K.J., Horowitz, D., & Hovav, M. (1998). Visiting the scene of the crime: Effects on children's recall of alleged abuse. *Legal and Criminological Psychology*, *3*, 195–207.

Hill, P.E., & Hill, S.M. (1987). Videotaping children's testimony: An empirical view. *Michigan Law Review*, *85*, 809–833.

Howe, M.L., Toth, S., & Cicchetti, D. (2006). Memory and developmental psychopathology. In Cicchetti, D. & Cohen, D. (Eds), *Developmental Psychopathology* (2nd edn). *Volume 2: Developmental Neuroscience* (pp. 629–655). New York: Wiley.

Howie, P., Sheehan, M., Mojarrad, T., & Wrzesinska, M. (2004). 'Undesirable' and 'desirable' shifts in children's responses to repeated questions: Age differences in the effect of providing a rationale for repetition. *Applied Cognitive Psychology*, *18*, 1161–1180.

Jones, C.H., & Pipe, ME. (2002). How quickly do children forget events? A systematic study of children's event reports as a function of delay. *Applied Cognitive Psychology*, *16*, 755–768.

La Rooy, D., Lamb, M.E., & Pipe, ME. (2009). Repeated interviewing: A critical evaluation of the risks and potential benefits. In K. Kuehnle, & M. Connell (Eds), *The Evaluation of Child Sexual Abuse Allegations: A Comprehensive Guide to Assessment and Testimony* (pp. 327–361). Wiley.

La Rooy, D., Pipe, M.E., & Murray, J.E. (2005). Reminiscence and hypermnesia in children's eyewitness memory. *Journal of Experimental Child Psychology*, *90*, 235–254.

La Rooy, D., Pipe, M.E., & Murray, J.E. (2007). Enhancing children's event recall after long delays. *Applied Cognitive Psychology*, *21*, 1–17.

Lamb, M.E., Sternberg, K.J., Orbach, Y., Esplin, P.W., Stewhart, H., & Mitchell, S. (2003). Age differences in young children's responses to open-ended invitations in the course of forensic interviews. *Journal of Consulting and Clinical Psychology*, *71*, 926–934.

Lee, P.J., & Brown, N.R. (2003). Delay related changes in personal memories for September 11, 2001. *Applied Cognitive Psychology*, *17*, 1007–1015.

Leichtman, M.D., & Ceci, S.J. (1995). The effects of stereotypes and suggestions on preschoolers' reports. *Developmental Psychology*, *31*, 568–578.

Leippe, M.R., Manion, A.P., & Romanczyk, A. (1992). Eyewitness persuasion: How and how well do fact finders judge the accuracy of adults' and children's memory reports? *Journal of Personality and Social Psychology*, *63*, 181–197.

Loftus, E.F. (2005). Planting misinformation in the human mind: A 30-year investigation of the malleability of memory. *Learning and Memory*, *12*, 361–366.

Lyon, T. (2002). Applying suggestibility research to the real world: The case of repeated questions. *Law and Contemporary Problems*, *65*, 97–126.

McGaugh, J.L. (2003). *Memory and Emotion: The Making of Lasting Memories*. New York: Columbia University Press.

Melnyk, L., & Bruck, M. (2004). Timing moderates the effects of repeated suggestive interviewing on children's eyewitness memory. *Applied Cognitive Psychology*, *18*, 613–631.

Melton, A.W. (1963). Implications of short-term memory for a general theory of memory. *Journal of Verbal Learning and Verbal Behaviour*, *2*, 1–21.

Murachver, T., Pipe, M.E., Gordon, R., Owens, J.L., & Fivush, R. (1996). Do, show, and tell: Children's event memories acquired through direct experience, observation, and stories. *Child Development*, *67*, 3029–3044.

Nathanson, R., & Saywitz, K.J. (2003). The effects of the courtroom context on children's memory and anxiety. *Journal of Psychiatry and Law*, *31*, 67–98.

Neisser, U., & Harsch, N. (1992). Phantom flashbulbs: False recollections of hearing the news about Challenger. In E. Winograd, & U. Neisser (Eds), *Affect and Accuracy in Recall: Studies of 'Flashbulb' Memories* (pp. 9–31). Emory Symposia in Cognition 4. Cambridge: Cambridge University Press.

Orbach, Y., Hershkowitz, I., Lamb, M.E., Sternberg, K.J., & Horowitz, D. (2000). Interviewing at the scene of the crime: Effects on children's recall of alleged abuse. *Legal and Criminological Psychology*, *5*, 135–147.

Orbach, Y., & Lamb, M.E. (2001). The relationship between within-interview contradictions and eliciting interviewer utterances. *Child Abuse and Neglect*, *25*, 323–333.

Ornstein, P.A., Gordon, B., & Larus, D.M. (1992). Children's memory for a personally experienced event: Implications for testimony. *Applied Cognitive Psychology*, *6*, 49–60.

Ornstein, P.A., Shapiro, L.R., Clubb, P.A., Follmer, A., & Baker-Ward, L. (1997). The influence of prior knowledge on children's memory for salient medical experiences. In N.L. Stein, P.A. Ornstein, C.J. Brainerd, & B. Tversky (Eds), *Memory for Everyday and Emotional Events* (pp. 83–111). Hillsdale, NJ: Erlbaum.

Peterson, C. (1999). Children's memory for medical emergencies: 2 years later. *Developmental Psychology*, *35*, 1493–1506.

Peterson, C., Moores, L., & White, G. (2001). Recounting the same events again and again: Children's consistency across multiple interviews. *Applied Cognitive Psychology*, *15*, 353–371.

Peterson, C., & Parsons, B. (2005) Interviewing former 1- and 2-year olds about medical emergencies 5 years later. *Law and Human Behavior, 29*, 743–754.

Pezdek, K. (2003). Event memory and autobiographical memory for the events of September 11, 2001. *Applied Cognitive Psychology, 17*, 1033–1045.

Pezdek, K., & Lam, S. (2007). What research paradigms have cognitive psychologists used to study 'False memory,' and what are the implications of these choices? *Consciousness and Cognition, 16*, 2–17.

Pillemer, D.B., & White, S.H. (1989). Childhood events recalled by children and adults. In H.W. Reese (Ed.), *Advances in Child Development and Behavior* (Vol. 21, pp. 297–340). Orlando, FL: Academic Press.

Pipe, M.E., Sutherland, R., Webster, N., Jones, C.H., & La Rooy, D. (2004). Do early interviews affect children's long-term recall? *Applied Cognitive Psychology, 18*, 1–17.

Pipe, M.E., & Wilson, J.C. (1994). Cues and secrets: Influences on children's event reports. *Developmental Psychology, 30*, 515–525.

Poole, D.A., & White, L.T. (1991). Effects of question repetition on the eyewitness testimony of children and adults. *Developmental Psychology, 27*, 975–986.

Poole, D.A., & White, L.T. (1993). Two years later: Effects of question repetition and retention interval on the eyewitness testimony of children and adults. *Developmental Psychology, 29*, 844–853.

Price, D.W.W., & Goodman, G.S. (1990). Visiting the wizard: Children's memory for a recurring event. *Child Development, 61*, 664–680.

Priestley, G., Roberts, S., & Pipe, M.E. (1999). Returning to the scene: Reminders and context reinstatement enhance children's recall. *Developmental Psychology, 35*, 1006–1019.

Quas, J.A., Bauer, A., & Boyce, W.T.B. (2004). Physiological reactivity, social support, and memory in early childhood. *Child Development, 75*, 1–18.

Quas, J.A., Goodman, G.S., Bidrose, S., Pipe, M.E., Craw, S., & Ablin, D.S. (1999). Emotion and memory: Children's long-term remembering, forgetting, and suggestibility. *Journal of Experimental Child Psychology, 72*, 235–270.

Quas, J.A., & Schaaf, J.M. (2002). Children's memories of experienced and non-experienced events following repeated interviews. *Journal of Experimental Child Psychology, 83*, 304–338.

Quas, J.A., Thompson, W.C., & Clarke-Stewart, K.A. (2005). Do jurors 'know' what isn't so about child witnesses? *Law and Human Behavior, 29*, 425–456.

Saywitz, K.J., & Nathanson, R. (1993). Children's testimony and their perceptions of stress in and out of the courtroom. *Child Abuse and Neglect, 17*, 613–622.

Sheingold, K., & Tenney, Y.J. (1982). Memory for a salient childhood event. In U. Neisser (Ed.), *Memory Observed* (pp. 201–212). San Francisco, CA: Freeman.

Talarico, J.M., & Rubin, D.C. (2003). Confidence, not consistency, characterizes flashbulb memories. *Psychological Science, 14*, 455–461.

Tekcan, A.I., Ece, B., Gulgoz, S., & Er, N. (2003). Autobiographical and event memory for 9/11: Changes across one year. *Applied Cognitive Psychology, 17*, 1057–1066.

Tulving, E. (1974). Cue-dependant forgetting. *American Scientist, 62*, 74–82.

Tulving, E. (1983). *Elements of Episodic Memory*. New York: Oxford University Press.

Usher, J.A., & Neisser, U. (1993). Childhood amnesia and the beginnings of memory for four early life events. *Journal of Experimental Psychology: General*, *122*, 155–165.

Weaver, C.A. III (1993). Do you need a 'flash' to form a flashbulb memory? *Journal of Experimental Psychology: General*, *122*, 39–46.

Wilkinson, J. (1988). Context effects in children's event memory. In M.M. Gruneberg, P.E. Morris, & R.N. Sykes (Eds), *Practical Aspects of Memory: Current Research Issues* (Vol. 1, pp. 107–111). New York: Wiley.

Zajac, R., & Hayne, H. (2003). I don't think that's what really happened: The effect of cross-examination on the accuracy of children's reports. *Journal of Experimental Psychology: Applied*, *9*, 187–195.

4

Assessing the Competency of Child Witnesses: Best Practice Informed by Psychology and Law

Thomas D. Lyon

Key Points

- The law recognizes two types of child witness competency: basic competency and truth–lie competency. Jurisdictions vary in the extent to which they require that children demonstrate these competencies before being allowed to testify.
- Basic competency, which concerns the child's ability to perceive, remember and communicate, can be demonstrated by eliciting a child's report of a recent event.
- Truth–lie competency, which concerns the child's understanding of the difference between truth and lies and the importance of telling the truth, can be demonstrated by asking the child whether simple statements are the truth, and by asking the child to promise to tell the truth.
- Tests of children's truth–lie competency *do not* predict honesty, but eliciting a child's promise to tell the truth *does* increase honesty.

Children's Testimony: A Handbook of Psychological Research and Forensic Practice, Second Edition.
Edited by Michael E. Lamb, David J. La Rooy, Lindsay C. Malloy, and Carmit Katz.

In the courts, questions about the competency of child witnesses may arise in two respects. A child's competency *at trial* affects whether she will be allowed to testify. Because of the rules regarding the admissibility of hearsay, a child's competency *during a pre-trial interview* may affect the admissibility of her interview statements at trial. For these reasons, both attorneys and forensic interviewers are interested in how competency can best be assessed.

Witness competency is often said to include the capacity to observe, remember, communicate and to tell the truth (Hoyano & Keenan, 2007). The first three capacities can be thought of as *basic* competency. Many jurisdictions have eliminated specific requirements of basic competency. Nevertheless, rules requiring that evidence be relevant essentially establish a minimum level of basic competency, and therefore children are sometimes questioned about their ability to observe, remember, and communicate. The ability to tell the truth can be called *truth–lie* competency. Truth–lie competency is still popular in many courts, because witnesses are expected to testify under oath, and questions about truth–lie competency test whether a child understands the meaning of the oath. Therefore, children are often asked about their understanding of the truth and lies.

This chapter surveys both psychology and law. Based on what psychology teaches and what the law requires, it recommends approaches for both attorneys questioning child witnesses in court and interviewers questioning children before trial. Necessarily, compromises must be made, and what seems most sensible to psychologists must often be trumped by the requirements of the law. Nevertheless, understanding both psychology and law enables practitioners to avoid needless mistakes; many common practices are ill-informed by assumptions that psychologists make about the law and vice versa.

This chapter recommends practices for both eliciting testimony at trial and questioning before trial. At trial, a good rapport-building device – asking the child to narrate a recent event – doubles as a test of basic competency, and is therefore highly recommended. It is also extremely useful in pre-trial interviews. With respect to truth–lie competency, questions about truth and lies have little intrinsic value; they do not predict honesty, and they are not a foolproof means of determining what the child actually knows about the truth and lies. Truth–lie questions are not recommended unless they are legally required. The same recommendation applies to pre-trial interviews. On the other hand, there are good reasons for asking children to promise to tell the truth. Research has found that eliciting a promise to tell the truth from children increases honesty.

BASIC COMPETENCY: PERCEPTION, MEMORY, AND NARRATION

There are several reasons why one might reject any inquiry into a child's basic competency. First, an appreciation of a child's ability to perceive, remember, and communicate is arguably best obtained by letting the child testify. The proof is in the pudding. Recommending this approach, the renowned American evidence scholar, John Henry Wigmore, argued, 'the effort to measure *a priori* the degrees of trustworthiness in children's statements, and to distinguish the point at which they cease to be totally incredible and acquire suddenly some degree of credibility, is futile and unprofitable' (Wigmore, 1904, p. 640). New Zealand and Scotland have explicitly rejected any preliminary inquiry into a child witness's competency by the court (Hoyano & Keenan, 2007).

On the other hand, there are reasons why some preliminary assessment of basic competency is likely. Even without competency requirements, there are legal restrictions on witness testimony. The rule of relevance requires that evidence has some tendency to prove what it is intended to prove. The rule of prejudice states that relevant evidence may nevertheless be excluded if its evidentiary value is outweighed by the likelihood that the evidence will be misused or unfairly weighed by the fact finder. (The fact finder is either the judge or the jury, depending on the type of trial.) For example, in the United States, the Federal Rules of Evidence state that '[e]very person is competent to be a witness except as otherwise provided in these rules', and the advisory committee who drafted the rules emphasize that '[a] witness wholly without capacity is difficult to imagine' (Federal Rules of Evidence, 2010). Forty-two of the 50 states in the United States have adopted evidence codes very similar to the federal rules (Mueller & Kirkpatrick, 2009) and the 'every person is competent' language is quite common (National Center for the Prosecution of Child Abuse, 2009). Nevertheless, one often still encounters *some* preliminary inquiries of child witnesses, and the justification for those inquiries is that if a child is unintelligible, or otherwise incapable of answering questions, his or her testimony is of little or no relevance, and may simply have prejudicial effect (Lyon, 2000). Some believe that any testimony from a child, no matter how incoherent or inconsistent, will help the party who presents the child's testimony. Jurors' sympathies with a child (and, possibly, their anger at any attempts to cross-examine the child) might create prejudice. And even if this were not so, attorneys are quite adept at communicating their theory of the case through questions, regardless of the answers. The best argument against allowing the child's testimony to 'speak for itself' is that any declaration of irrelevance after a child's testimony comes too late. If the case is tried before a jury, and the judge concludes that the child's testimony was irrelevant and prejudicial, the judge must provide the awkward instruction that the jury should disregard what they just heard. This type of instruction has been analogized to throwing a skunk into the jury box and telling the jury to ignore the smell (*Dunn v. United States,* 1962).

Because of concerns regarding relevance and prejudice, many countries allow for limited inquiry into child witnesses' competency. The child must be capable of understanding and answering questions (Hoyano & Keenan, 2007, discussing the United Kingdom, Canada, and both the federal system and the provinces/states in Australia).

Can psychologists provide any guidance into the questions that should be asked? Developmental psychologists specialize in mapping children's growing abilities to observe, remember and communicate, and one might expect researchers to have developed standardized tests to measure these abilities. However, there are good reasons for doubting the validity of any preliminary assessments of children's testimonial competency. Tests are inherently limited by the fact that a child's capacities in response to a test is at best an imperfect measure of her capacities with respect to the subject of her testimony.

Some researchers have developed tests for children's suggestibility (Candel, Merckelbach, & Muris, 2000; Endres, Poggenpohl, & Erben, 1999; Finnilä, Mahlberga, Santtilaa, & Niemib, 2003; Scullin & Ceci, 2001), and one might turn to these for assistance in assessing a child's competency. However, suggestibility assessments present their own difficulties. A child's suggestibility determines how well (or how poorly) the child responds to suggestive questioning, and not whether the child is capable of providing relevant testimony. If a child has not been subjected to highly suggestive questioning before testifying, and is not subjected to suggestive questioning in the case-in-chief, the child's suggestibility is of little relevance to basic competency. Even if suggestive influences are proven, the tests are designed to identify children along a continuum of suggestibility, rather than to distinguish between competent and incompetent. Any performance above chance would constitute relevant evidence (Lyon & Koehler, 1996). Finally, the scales are of limited validity; for example, the age range within which they predict performance is often quite narrow (Melinder, Scullin, Gravvold, & Iverson, 2007; Scullin, Kanaya, & Ceci, 2002).

A good solution is to look to research on interviewing, and to borrow a technique originally designed to build rapport and increase the productivity of children's reports: narrative practice. The interviewer begins by asking the child questions about her interests ('Tell us about things you like to do'), and then asks the child witness to narrate a recent innocuous event (e.g., 'Tell us about your last birthday. Tell us everything that happened, from the beginning to the end'). The child's responses can establish basic competency, and will provide additional benefits as well. Preliminary questions about innocuous topics in court would allow the child witness to acclimate herself to the courtroom and to relax before the topic of interest is introduced. Through a series of open-ended questions asking the child to elaborate on her narrative (e.g., 'You said you hit a piñata. Tell us what happened next' or 'You said you played in a bouncy. Tell us about playing in the bouncy'), the attorney could accustom the child to provide a chronological narrative without the need for leading or closed-ended questions. Research has established that narrative practice in interviews increases the productivity of children's abuse disclosures (Hershkowitz, 2009; Sternberg *et al.*, 1997), with no evidence of impaired accuracy (Roberts, Lamb, & Sternberg, 2004).

TRUTH–LIE COMPETENCY: SINCERITY

Psychologists are likely to be surprised at the emphasis that the law places on the dangers of insincerity, particularly in the case of young children. Surely the dangers of the youngest witnesses have to do with errors in memory or the influence of adults rather than deliberate falsehoods. Nevertheless, in many jurisdictions witnesses are expected to affirm in some manner that they will tell the truth, typically by taking the oath, and a common concern is that child witnesses may be too young to meaningfully understand what they are asked to do. Because of these concerns, child witnesses are more often asked about their understanding of the meaning and morality of lying than about their understanding and ability to answer questions more generally.

The seriousness with which the law treats children's truth–lie competency can be placed on a continuum. At its most strict, the law mandates that all witnesses take a formal oath, and requires that child witnesses understand the 'danger and impiety of falsehoods' in order to qualify as testimonially competent (*R. v. Brasier*, 1779). 'Danger and impiety' suggests an understanding of both earthly punishment for perjury and additional punishment in the hereafter. At its most liberal, the law abandons both the oath and any tests for truth–lie competency for child witnesses. Examination of the courts in the United States, the United Kingdom, Australia, New Zealand, Scotland, and Canada reveals a wide diversity of approaches.

The United States probably ranks first with respect to the rigors of truth–lie competency: some form of oath or affirmation is near-universally required, and truth–lie competency inquiries are still very common. This may come as a surprise. Psychology commentators have asserted that courts in the United States have eliminated all competency inquiries (Bruck, Ceci, & Hembrooke, 1998; Goodman & Reed, 1986). Commentators sometime make reference to a federal law that allows for 'competency examinations' only upon written motion and a demonstration of 'compelling reasons' (18 U.S.C. 3509(c)(2)(4) (1999)). However, a federal court interpreting the law held that preliminary questioning of child witnesses regarding their understanding of the oath does not constitute a 'competency examination' (*United States v. Allen J.*, 1997).

The reason for the confusion is that commentators fail to distinguish between basic competency and truth–lie competency. The reader will recall that Federal Rule of Evidence 601 states that all witnesses are competent. At the same time, Federal Rule of Evidence 603 requires that '[b]efore testifying, every witness shall be required to declare that the witness will testify truthfully, by oath or affirmation administered in a form calculated to awaken the witness' conscience and impress the witness' mind with the duty to do so' (Federal Rules of Evidence, 2010). The language of Rule 603 does not *necessitate* a preliminary inquiry into the witness's understanding of the meaning of the truth and his/her duty to tell it, but it is routinely used as a justification for such an inquiry. The reader will also recall that most states in the United States have modelled their evidence codes after the Federal Rules, and states that have done so also have a Rule 603. Furthermore, 15 states have explicit provisions in their competency statutes that statutorily require understanding of duty to tell the truth (or at least the capacity to testify truthfully; National Center for the Prosecution of Child Abuse, 2009).

Provisions for unsworn testimony are quite rare. Because of the allowance in Rule 603 for an 'affirmation', witnesses need not take a formal oath, but they must at least signal their intention to tell the truth. I am aware of only two states in which unsworn testimony is allowed, by statute in Florida (1999) and New York (1999). In Florida, child witnesses are nevertheless expected to 'understand. . .the duty to tell the truth or the duty not to lie.' One US Federal Court of Appeals has even concluded that some form of the oath, and in turn some demonstration of competency to take the oath, is required by the Constitution (*Haliym v. Mitchell*, 2007; but see *Walters v. McCormick*, 1997, for the opposite view from a different Court of Appeal).

The US Supreme Court has not decided whether some form of the oath is required of all witnesses. However, it has increased the significance of children's truth–lie competency through a series of cases involving defendant's confrontation rights against the admissibility of certain types of hearsay. The Court has held that 'testimonial' hearsay is inadmissible against a criminal defendant unless that defendant is given the opportunity to cross-examine the hearsay declarant (the person who made the hearsay statement) (*Crawford v. Washington*, 2004). 'Testimonial' hearsay includes most statements to the police. In a number of cases, criminal convictions have been overturned because a child witness failed to qualify as competent, and his/her testimonial hearsay was admitted against the defendant (e.g., *State v. Hooper*, 2007; *State v. Henderson*, 2007). The legal justification for reversing the convictions was not that the child's hearsay was inaccurate, but that the defendant's constitutional right to cross-examine the child was denied when the child failed to qualify.

Jurisdictions in Australia vary somewhat in their requirements (Evidence Act, 1906 (Western Australia); Evidence Act, 1929 (South Australia); Evidence Act, 1977 (Queensland); Evidence Act, 1995 (Commonwealth of Australia); Evidence Act, 2001 (Tasmania); Evidence Act, 2008 (Victoria); Evidence Act, 1995 (New South Wales)). All jurisdictions require that any witness taking the oath must understand his/her obligations to tell the truth, which entails an understanding of the meaning and special importance of telling the truth in court (e.g., *R. v. Climas*, 1999 (South Australia)). All jurisdictions allow for unsworn testimony if a witness is incompetent to take the oath. However, in two jurisdictions (South Australia and) children testifying unsworn must nevertheless understand the difference between the truth and lies, and must affirm that they 'will not tell lies.'

The United Kingdom has gradually liberalized the rules with respect to child witnesses, and has virtually abolished truth–lie competency requirements in the criminal courts. By 1991, the law required that testimony by children under 14 years of age be unsworn, and by 1999, the only requirement for unsworn testimony was that the witness understand questions and be capable of giving understandable answers (Hoyano & Keenan, 2007). Curiously, the law with respect to civil cases (including family law and child protection proceedings) is more strict, retaining the requirement that even children testifying unsworn must demonstrate that they understand the importance of telling the truth (Hoyano & Keenan, 2007).

Perhaps the most liberal approaches toward allowing children to testify without a demonstration of truth–lie competency have been adopted by Scotland and Canada. Scotland barred any inquiry into children's understanding of truth and lies in 2004 (Bala, Lee,

Lindsay, & Talwar, 2010). In 2005, Canada adopted a similar ban, and all children under 14 are asked to promise to tell the truth rather than administered a formal oath (Bala, Evans, & Bala, 2010).

The justification for the change in law in Canada was that there is little or no relation between children's understanding of truth and lies and their honesty (Bala *et al.*, 2010). There is substantial empirical evidence supporting this claim. Several studies have found that children's eyewitness performance is not related to their understanding of truth and lies (Feben, 1985; Goodman, Aman, & Hirshman, 1987; London & Nunez, 2002; Pipe & Wilson, 1994; Talwar, Lee, Bala, & Lindsay, 2002). When research does find a relation between performance and children's understanding, it is in contexts in which children may be motivated to make deliberately false reports and are then urged to tell the truth or asked to promise to do so (Lyon & Dorado, 2008; Lyon, Malloy, Quas, & Talwar, 2008; Talwar, Lee, Bala, & Lindsay, 2004). This suggests that the efficacy of 'I promise to tell the truth' depends to some extent on the child's comprehension of 'truth'; it does not mean that there is a general relation between understanding of truth and lies and honesty. And even in this context, one should not assume that an apparent failure to comprehend the meaning and morality of truth and lies justifies an assumption that a promise to tell the truth is ineffective. Lyon *et al.* (2008) found that children who failed to perform well on a truth–lie understanding task were nevertheless more honest after promising to tell the truth. The probable reason for this finding is that comprehension tasks likely underestimate what children understand.

The difficulty of accurately assessing children's understanding of the truth and lies provides another argument against competency inquiries. Competency questions are likely to confound children for reasons unrelated to their actual understanding of the meaning and importance of truth-telling. Children are much better at identifying statements as truth or lie than they are at providing even the simplest definitions of 'truth' and 'lie' (such as 'a lie is not the truth') or explaining the difference between the words (Lyon & Saywitz, 1999). Children who are quite adept at assessing whether statements are the truth or not may fail to identify false statements as lies (Lyon, Carrick, & Quas, 2010). They appear reluctant to label false statements lies, because of their awareness of the badness of lying. Children are better able to explain the negative consequences of lying when presented with a hypothetical child than when asked what would happen to themselves if they lied (Lyon, Saywitz, Kaplan, & Dorado, 2001). Young children appear to treat hypothetical questions ('What would happen to you if you lied?') as suggestions, and, again because of their acute awareness of the badness of lying, reject the premises rather than entertain the hypothetical outcomes. Even 2-year-olds adhere to a principle that one ought to say true things – they reliably reject statements that are clearly false (Hummer, Wimmer, & Antes, 1993; Pea, 1982) – well before they are able to articulate an understanding of the concept 'true statement' and 'false statement' (T.D. Lyon, N. Carrick, & J.A. Quas, manuscript in preparation).

It is fair to conclude that an interviewer's assessment of a child's understanding of truth or lie has virtually no value in assessing the child's honesty, and is likely to make matters worse. Indeed, recent research suggests that children with an incipient understanding of truth and lies are *better* able to make false statements (B. Ahern, T.D. Lyon, & J.A. Quas, manuscript in preparation). In other words, it is more difficult for the child who *does not* know the difference between 'truth' and 'lie' to tell a lie. This finding should not be surprising, because both the understanding of truth and lies and the ability to lie are related to children's cognitive development. Indeed, adults are probably the best liars, and they are of course quite capable of defining truth and lie.

If inquiries into a child's comprehension of truth and lies are not justified at the time the child testifies at trial, there is even less justification for such inquiries in investigative or other pre-trial interviews. Forensic interviewers primarily ask children truth–lie competency questions for two reasons:

1. To determine if the child will qualify as competent at trial, and
2. To increase the likelihood that the interview with the child will be admissible at trial under exceptions to the rule against hearsay.

Neither of these reasons is compelling.

The first justification is obviously undermined in jurisdictions that have abolished inquiries into truth–lie understanding at trial. A child who fails truth–lie questions but who is capable of understanding and intelligibly responding to questions of relevance to the case will qualify as competent in many courts. Truth–lie inquiries are of questionable value even in jurisdictions that retain competency requirements at trial. Given the long delays between investigation and trial and young children's rapid development, young children are quite likely to acquire truth–lie understanding between the time they are first interviewed and the time they testify.

The second justification – that truth–lie competency is a prerequisite for the admissibility of hearsay – is overstated. I am aware of no jurisdictions in which truth–lie competency is a necessary precondition for hearsay to be admitted (Hoyano & Keenan, 2007; Myers, 2005). Courts will sometimes cite truth–lie competency as a factor to be considered in assessing the reliability of children's statements (Myers, 2005), but as the research clearly documents, this is unwarranted. The use of truth–lie questions in interviews will unjustifiably undermine the credibility of children who fail the questions, and unjustifiably bolster the credibility of children who succeed. It also creates the impression that the interviewer (and, if the interviewer is working for law enforcement or social services, the state) believes that the inquiry has some value in assessing the child's story.

Truth–lie questions are quite common in forensic interviews. Studies of forensic interviewing have found large percentages asking about truth–lies in the United States (Huffman, Warren, & Larson, 1999; Sternberg, Lamb, Orbach, Esplin, & Mitchell, 2001; Walker & Hunt, 1998); the United Kingdom (Westcott & Kynan, 2006); New Zealand (Davies & Seymour, 1998); and Scotland (La Rooy, Lamb, & Memon, in press).

One would expect that with the liberalization of truth–lie competency requirements, the use of truth–lie questions in forensic interviews would diminish. However, there is little evidence that this is occurring. To a large extent, psychologists who recommend such questions assume some sort of legal need, and legal experts who recommend such questions assume psychological validity. As we shall see, both types of professional are somewhat misinformed. It is rather like the couple who go to a less preferred show, each attempting to please the other.

First, practitioners are likely influenced by practice guides that incorporated truth–lie discussions into their recommendations. For example, Poole and Lamb (1998) recommend a truth–lie discussion, and inquiry into children's understanding is part of the National Institute of Child Health and Human Development (NICHD) structured interview (Lamb, Hershkowitz, Orbach, & Esplin, 2008). What may be overlooked is that the recommendations were based on legal and not psychological considerations. Poole and Lamb (1998) emphasized that there is no empirical support for the use of the discussions as a key to accuracy, and recommended the questions only because 'such conversations are currently considered satisfactory demonstrations in jurisdictions that require explicit discussions of the truth' (p. 125). Similarly, the NICHD protocol incorporated truth–lie questions at the behest of law enforcement, and modification of those questions 'would not do violence to the Protocol' (Lyon, Lamb, & Myers, 2009, p. 73).

Second, in some jurisdictions, governmental guidelines continue to prescribe truth–lie discussions despite liberalization of the rules for child witnesses. Both the Home Office (2001) in the United Kingdom and the Scottish Executive (Richards, Morris, & Richards, 2008) recommend that investigative interviewers continue to inquire into children's understanding of the meaning and importance of truth and lies. The purported justification is that the truth–lie discussion remains relevant for assessing the likelihood that the child was telling the truth. The reader will recall that questions regarding children's basic competency are justified by the courts as much by rules of relevance and prejudice as on competency requirements. The reasoning underlying retention of truth–lie questions is analogous. Hence, the Home Office (2001) suggests retaining the truth–lie inquiry on the grounds that 'admissibility of the statements may be of very little weight, and their admissibility prejudicial to the defendant' (p. 13). Similarly, the Scottish Executive warns that 'the court will still have to make a judgement of the witness's truthfulness and reliability, therefore any interview should still clarify, in age appropriate ways, the witness's level of understanding. This exploration will assist the court in determining issues of credibility and reliability' (Richards *et al.*, 2008, quoting Scottish Executive, p. 21).

These recommendations are puzzling, in so far as the justification for abolishing inquiries into children's truth–lie understanding is that their answers fail to correlate with their honesty. If a child's failure to answer truth–lie questions is not a basis for deeming her incompetent, it is no better basis for deeming her statements irrelevant or prejudicial. Even in those cases where there is some relation exists between accuracy and understanding (when the child has promised to tell the truth but does not know the meaning of the word 'truth'), the relation is imperfect and likely to be overstated. That is, truth–lie questions are themselves objectionable as of little relevance and likely prejudicial.

Third, interviewers might argue that although the prosecution may avoid truth–lie questions, the defence may insist on their right to do so, and the defence naturally has little inclination (and perhaps limited ability) to ask age-appropriate questions. Although Canadian law now prohibits questions about children's truth–lie understanding, a Canadian appellate court has held that these issues may still be inquired into on cross-examination (Bala *et al.*, 2010). Review of criminal court transcripts in the United States suggests that defence attorneys do indeed capitalize on children's difficulty with certain types of truth–lie questions (such as children's tendency to respond 'no' when asked 'Have you ever told a lie?') (A. Evans & T.D. Lyon, manuscript in preparation). However, prosecutors can object to defence attorneys' truth–lie questions as irrelevant and prejudicial, because they have little or no relation to honesty and they are likely to mislead the jury (Dufraimont, 2007).

Finally, there exists the concern that children's understanding should be demonstrated, because otherwise juries will be skeptical of unsworn child witnesses. Hoyano and Keenan (2007) warn that:

> Jurors will not have to be particularly astute to notice that they have not been sworn to tell the truth, and may infer that their testimony is devalued by the criminal justice system. It is natural for jurors to want to be satisfied that the child can distinguish between truth and falsehood, and does understand the importance of telling the truth, given the implications for the accused (p. 604).

However, it would be preferable to ask the child witness to promise to tell the truth than to inquire into the child's apparent understanding of the truth and lies. Research has demonstrated that eliciting an age-appropriate oath from children (such as 'Do you promise that you will tell the truth?') increases children's honesty (Lyon & Dorado, 2008; Lyon, Malloy, Quas, & Talwar, 2008; Talwar, Lee, Bala, & Lindsay, 2002, 2004), even among children who fail truth–lie competency tasks (Lyon *et al.*, 2008). The fact that the court no longer elicits an oath does not prevent the attorney presenting the child witness from eliciting a promise.

When it is legally necessary to inquire into children's understanding, the most sensitive means of assessing young children's understanding is by asking the child to identify whether accurate and inaccurate statements uttered by a story child are the truth or not the truth (see Figure 4.1, stimuli from Lyon, Carrick, & Quas, 2010). In the depicted example, the interviewer shows the child the picture, and first points at the truck, asking 'What is this?' When the child responds 'truck', the interviewer says 'OK, that's a truck. This girl (pointing to the girl) looks at the truck and says "that's a plane".' The interviewer then asks the child 'Did the girl tell the truth?'

For the very young child who has not clearly acquired an articulable concept of 'truth', interviewers can ask the child to accept or reject a false label. In the previous example, the interviewer could omit the question 'Did the girl tell the truth?' Instead, the interviewer would point at the truck and ask 'Is that a plane?' As noted above, children evince a tendency to reject false statements by 2 years of age (Hummer *et al.*, 1993; Pea, 1982), and most children acquire a basic understanding of 'truth' before their fourth birthday (Lyon, Carrick, & Quas, manuscript in preparation); of course, children with language delays are likely to lag somewhat (Lyon, Carrick, & Quas, 2010).

A task this simple has a number of advantages. Children's potential reluctance to call statements lies is avoided by only asking about truth.

Figure 4.1 Task for asking children about the meaning of 'truth' (Lyon, Carrick, & Quas, 2010, manuscript in preparation).

The statements are uttered by a story child rather than the adult questioner or the child herself, which reduces reluctance to challenge an adult or to acknowledge making false statements. Issues of intent and wrongdoing are also avoided. For reasons that are not fully explained, commentators have sometimes urged that the truth–lie questions focus on lies about wrongdoing that are intended to deceive (Home Office, 2001; Hoyano & Keenan, 2007; McCarron, Ridgway, & Williams, 2004). The problem is that adding information about either wrongdoing or speaker intent complicates the scenarios and potentially misleads children (Aldridge & Wood, 1998; Lyon, Carrick, & Quas, 2010). Hoyano and Keenan (2007) argue that if the false statements are obviously false, children will not take the interview seriously, but this conflates the purpose of the truth–lie questions with the purpose of a promise to tell the truth; the former simply tests the child's understanding of the word 'truth', and the latter is what communicates the seriousness of the interview.

CONCLUSIONS

In summary, this review of competency requirements suggests that interviewers and attorneys can elicit a narrative of an innocuous event during rapport-building as a means of establishing children's basic competency: their ability to perceive, remember, and communicate. Interviewers need not ask children truth–lie competency questions, but can profitably elicit a promise to tell the truth. When a legal requirement forces examination of young children's truth–lie understanding, the most sensitive approach entails asking the child whether statements are the truth, and eliciting a promise from the child that she will tell the truth. Competency requirements should not serve as a bar to the admissibility of relevant evidence from children.

ACKNOWLEDGEMENT

Preparation of this article was supported in part by National Institute of Child Health and Human Development Grant HD047290.

REFERENCES

Aldridge, M., & Wood, J. (1998). *Interviewing Children: A Guide for Child Care and Forensic Practitioners*. Chichester, UK: Wiley.
Bala, N., Evans, A., & Bala, E. (2010). *Child and Family Law Quarterly*, *22*, 21–45.
Bala, N., Lee, K., Lindsay, R.C.L., & Talwar, V. (2010). The competency of children to testify: Psychological research informing Canadian law reform. *International Journal of Children's Rights*, *18*, 53–77.
Bruck, M., Ceci, S.J., & Hembrooke, H. (1998). Reliability and credibility of young children's reports. *American Psychologist*, *53*, 136–151.
Candel, I., Merckelbach, H., & Muris, P. (2000). Measuring interrogative suggestibility in children: Reliability and validity of the Bonn Test of Statement Suggestibility. *Psychology, Crime and Law*, *6*, 61–70.
Crawford v. Washington, 541 U.S. 36 (2004).
Davies, E., & Seymour, F.W. (1998). Questioning child complainants of sexual abuse: Analysis of criminal court transcripts in New Zealand. *Psychiatry, Psychology, and Law*, *5*, 47–61.
Dufraimont, L. (2007). Care in cross-examining child witnesses. *Criminal Reports*, *48*, 357.
Dunn v. United States, 307 F.2d 883, 886 (5th Cir. 1962).
Endres, J., Poggenpohl, C., & Erben, C. (1999). Repetitions, warnings, and video: Cognitive and motivational components in preschool children's suggestibility. *Legal and Criminological Psychology*, *4*, 129–146.
Evidence Act, 1906 (Western Australia).

Evidence Act, 1929 (South Australia).
Evidence Act, 1977 (Queensland).
Evidence Act, 1995 (Commonwealth of Australia).
Evidence Act, 1995 (New South Wales).
Evidence Act, 2001 (Tasmania).
Evidence Act, 2008 (Victoria).
Feben, D.J. (1985). Age of witness competency: Cognitive correlates. Unpublished honours thesis, Monash University, Clayton, Australia.
Federal Rules of Evidence (2010) (United States).
Finnilä, K., Mahlberga, N., Santtilaa, P., & Niemib, P. (2003). Validity of a test of children's suggestibility for predicting responses to two interview situations differing in degree of suggestiveness. *Journal of Experimental Child Psychology*, *85*, 32–49.
Goodman, G.S., Aman, C.J., & Hirschman, J. (1987). Child sexual and physical abuse: Children's testimony. In S.J. Ceci, M.P. Toglia, & D.F. Ross (Eds), *Children's Eyewitness Memory* (pp. 1–23). New York: Springer-Verlag.
Goodman, G.S., & Reed, R.S. (1986). Age differences in eyewitness testimony. *Law and Human Behavior*, *10*, 317–332.
Haliym v. Mitchell, 492 F.3d 680 (6th Cir. 2007).
Hershkowitz, I. (2009). Socioemotional factors in child sexual abuse investigations. *Child Maltreatment*, *14*, 172–181.
Home Office (2001). *Achieving Best Evidence in Criminal Proceedings: Guidance for Vulnerable or Intimidated Witnesses, Including Children*. London: Home Office.
Hoyano, L., & Keenan, C. (2007). *Child Abuse: Law and Policy Across Boundaries*. Oxford, UK: Oxford University Press.
Huffman, M.L., Warren, A.R., & Larson, S.M. (1999). Discussing truth and lies in interviews with children: Whether, why, and how? *Applied Developmental Science*, *1*, 6–15.
Hummer, P., Wimmer, H., & Antes, G. (1993). On the origins of denial negation. *Journal of Child Language*, *20*, 607–618.
Lamb, M.E., Hershkowitz, I., Orbach, Y., & Esplin, P.W. (2008). *Tell Me What Happened: Structured Investigative Interviews of Child Victims and Witnesses*. West Sussex, UK: Wiley.
La Rooy, D., Lamb, M.E., & Memon, A. (in press). Forensic interviews with children in Scotland: A survey of interview practices among police. *Journal of Police and Criminal Psychology*.
London, K., & Nunez, N. (2002). Examining the efficacy of truth/lie discussions in predicting and increasing the veracity of children's reports. *Journal of Experimental Child Psychology*, *83*, 131–147.
Lyon, T.D. (2000). Child witnesses and the oath: empirical evidence. *Southern California Law Review*, *73*, 1017–1074.
Lyon, T.D., Carrick, N., & Quas, J.A. (2010). Young children's competency to take the oath: Effects of task, maltreatment, and age. *Law and Human Behavior*, *34*, 141–149.
Lyon, T.D., & Dorado, J. (2008). Truth induction in young maltreated children: The effects of oath-taking and reassurance on true and false disclosures. *Child Abuse and Neglect*, *32*, 738–748.
Lyon, T.D., & Koehler, J.J. (1996). The relevance ratio: Evaluating the probative value of expert testimony in child sexual abuse cases. *Cornell Law Review*, *82*, 43–78.

Lyon, T.D., Lamb, M.E., & Myers, J. (2009). Authors' response to Vieth (2008): Legal and psychological support for the NICHD Interviewing Protocol. *Child Abuse and Neglect*, *33*, 71–74.
Lyon, T.D., Malloy, L.C., Quas, J.A., & Talwar, V. (2008). Coaching, truth induction, and young maltreated children's false allegations and false denials. *Child Development*, *79*, 914–929.
Lyon, T.D., & Saywitz, K.J. (1999). Young maltreated children's competence to take the oath. *Applied Developmental Science*, *3*, 16–27.
Lyon, T.D., Saywitz, K.J., Kaplan, D.L., & Dorado, J.S. (2001). Reducing maltreated children's reluctance to answer hypothetical oath-taking competency questions. *Law and Human Behavior*, *25*, 81–92.
McCarron, A.L., Ridgway, S., & Williams, A. (2004). The truth and lie story: Developing a tool for assessing child witnesses' ability to differentiate between truth and lies. *Child Abuse Review*, *13*, 42–50.
Melinder, A., Scullin, M.H., Gravvold, T., & Iversen, M.K. (2007). The stability and generalizability of young children's suggestibility over a 44-month interval. *Psychology, Crime, and Law*, *13*, 459–468.
Mueller, C.B., & Kirkpatrick, L.C. (2009). *Evidence* (4th edn.). Austin, TX: Wolters Kluwer.
Myers, J.E.B. (2005). *Myers on Evidence in Child, Domestic, and Elder Abuse Cases*. New York: Aspen.
National Center for the Prosecution of Child Abuse (2009). Legislation and case law regarding the competency of child witnesses to testify in criminal proceedings. Available at http://www.ndaa.org/pdf/Competency_of_Child_Witnesses_%282009%29.pdf. Last accessed July 2009.
N.Y. Crim. Proc. Law 60.20(2) (McKinney 1999).
Pea, R.D. (1982). Origins of verbal logic: Spontaneous denials by two- and three-year-olds. *Journal of Child Language*, *9*, 597–626.
Pipe, M.E., & Wilson, J.C. (1994). Cues and secrets: Influences on children's event reports. *Developmental Psychology*, *30*, 515–525.
Poole, D.A., & Lamb, M.E. (1998). *Investigative Interviews of Children: A Guide for Helping Professionals*. Washington, DC: American Psychological Association.
R v. Brasier, 1 Leach 199, 168 Eng. Rep. 202 (K.B.) (1779).
R v. Climas, 74 S.A.S.R. 411 (1999).
Richards, P., Morris, S., & Richards, E. (2008). *Turning up the Volume: The Vulnerable Witnesses (Scotland) Act 2004*. Edinburgh: Scottish Government Social Research.
Roberts, K.P., Lamb, M.E., & Sternberg, K.J. (2004). The effects of rapport-building style on children's reports of a staged event. *Applied Cognitive Psychology*, *18*, 189–202.
Scullin, M.H., & Ceci, S.J. (2001). A suggestibility scale for children. *Personality and Individual Differences*, *30*, 843–856.
Scullin, M.H., Kanaya, T., & Ceci, S.J. (2002). Measurement of individual differences in children's suggestibility across situations. *Journal of Experimental Psychology: Applied*, *8*, 233–246.
State v. Henderson, 160 P.3d 776 (Kan. 2007).
State v. Hooper, 176 P.3d 911 (Idaho 2007).
Sternberg, K.J., Lamb, M.E., Hershkowitz, I., Yudilevitch, L., Orbach, Y., Esplin, P.W., & Hovav, M. (1997). Effects of introductory style on children's

abilities to describe experiences of sexual abuse. *Child Abuse and Neglect, 21*, 1133–1146.
Sternberg, K., Lamb, M., Orbach, Y., Esplin, P., & Mitchell, S. (2001). Use of a structured investigative protocol enhances young children's responses to free-recall prompts in the course of forensic interviews. *Journal of Applied Psychology, 86*, 997–1005.
Talwar, V., Lee, K., Bala, N., & Lindsay, R.C.L. (2002). Children's conceptual knowledge of lying and its relation to their actual behaviors: Implications for court competence examinations. *Law and Human Behavior, 26*, 395–415.
Talwar, V., Lee, K., Bala, N., & Lindsay, R.C.L. (2004). Children's lie-telling to conceal a parent's transgression: Legal implications. *Law and Human Behavior, 28*, 411–435.
United States v. Allen J., 127 F.3d 1292 (10th Cir. 1997).
Walker, N.E., & Hunt, J.S. (1998). Interviewing child victim-witnesses: How you ask is what you get. In C.P. Thompson, D.J. Herrmann, J.D. Read, D. Bruce, D.G. Payne, & M.P. Toglia (Eds), *Eyewitness Memory: Theoretical and Applied Perspectives* (pp. 55–87). Mahwah, NJ: Lawrence Erlbaum.
Westcott, H.L., & Kynan, S. (2006). Interviewer practice in investigative interviews for suspected child sexual abuse. *Psychology, Crime and Law, 12*, 367–382.
Walters v. McCormick, 122 F.3d. 1172 (9th Cir. 1997).
Wigmore, J.H. (1904). *A Treatise on the System of Evidence in Trials at Common Law (Vol. 1)*. Boston: Little Brown.

5

Planning the Interview

Kevin Smith and Rebecca Milne

Key Points

- Planning investigative interviews is an essential aspect of the interview process.
- Planning involves collating and assessing available information about the child and the suspected offence.
- Planning makes it possible to decide how the interview will proceed and what objectives it should pursue.
- Interview plans should be reviewed and modified in the light of new information.

This chapter is about the planning that an interviewer should complete before conducting an interview. Planning an interview is important in any country; however, England and Wales will be used as an example throughout this chapter. Planning is not a luxury that can be dispensed with when the interviewer is busy; it is integral to the interview process. In the absence of planning, interviewers are unlikely to have a clear idea about what they are setting out to achieve and how they might best achieve it in the interview. This is likely to have an adverse consequence on the structure of the interview, notably on the sequence in which the

Children's Testimony: A Handbook of Psychological Research and Forensic Practice, Second Edition.
Edited by Michael E. Lamb, David J. La Rooy, Lindsay C. Malloy, and Carmit Katz.

various investigative topic areas are introduced, and on the efficacy of the techniques used.

On some occasions such planning will take place in the context of an interview strategy (Smith & Tilney, 2007). In England and Wales, interview strategies are the responsibility of investigating officers; they are usually developed by an interview adviser who has the responsibility for the overall management of the interview or a number of interviews within the investigation (for an outline of the tiered approach to investigative interviewing in England and Wales see Griffiths & Milne, 2005). Interview strategies set the conditions in which the interview takes place, including the topics and the sequence in which they should be covered. While interview strategies are usually the responsibility of an interview adviser, interview plans are very much the responsibility of the interviewer. An interview plan should always take account of the interview strategy. Unlike an interview strategy, an interview plan tends to focus on the detail of the interview, for example the techniques to be used to initiate and probe an account. A strategy determines *what* needs to be covered; an interview plan sets out *how* it is to be dealt with.

This chapter covers the following key concepts:

- Planning information:
  - witness assessment;
  - minimal offence information;
  - information important to the investigation.
- Using planning information:
  - objective setting;
  - decision making; and
- Interview preparation.

PLANNING INFORMATION

In a nutshell, planning consists of using information about the child and the investigation to develop an interview plan. Information about the child is established by means of a witness assessment. Finding information out about the investigation means acquiring a limited knowledge of the alleged offence and establishing what general and, so far as is possible, specific background material may be relevant to the inquiry. What is known about the witness and the investigation is then used to identify the most appropriate approach to be taken in the interview.

Witness Assessment

Witness assessment consists of:

1. Collating information about the child's circumstances;
2. Issues of consent; and
3. The welfare of the child.

The child's circumstances The information about the child that should be established for the purposes of planning the interview includes the following:

- Age of the child;
- Gender;
- Culture, ethnicity, religion and first language;
- Preferred name;
- Domestic circumstances (including whether the child is currently in a 'safe' environment);
- The implications of any physical or learning disability or mental disorder for the interview process;
- The implications of any medication taken for the interview process;
- Current emotional state, including
  - trauma
  - distress
  - fears of intimidation
  - recrimination
  - any other recent significant stressful events experienced (e.g., bereavement);
- Likely impact of recalling traumatic events on the behaviour of the witness;
- Current or previous contact with public services (including previous contact with police, the children's services department of the local authority or health professionals); and
- Relationship to the alleged offender.

Some of these factors may merit specialist advice (e.g., from a paediatrician or a psychologist). This is particularly true of culture, ethnicity and religion, and in relation to physical or learning disability or mental disorder, including the implications of any medication taken for the interview process. Specialist advice can be very useful in these circumstances but, unless the specialist knows the child well, it should always be tempered with information about the child who is to be interviewed because the broad parameters of culture and diagnostic features of many disabilities and disorders often manifest themselves in families and individuals in different ways (Office for Criminal Justice Reform, 2007a). For this reason, it may be useful to talk to the specialist about these issues before talking to those who know the child well about them; broad cultural issues and the diagnostic features of disability can then help to guide the interviewer as to what to ask those who know the child well. For example, an understanding that children with autism are likely to have a rather inflexible approach to routine (e.g., see Attwood, 1998) may lead an interviewer to ask the child's carers how they manage a change in routine, something that could be very useful when preparing the child for the interview.

Consent Witness interviews should take place with the informed consent of the interviewee. Such consent should be obtained as soon as sufficient information has been obtained as to whether the witness can understand what they are being asked to consent to. Where a witness is under 17 years in England and Wales interviewers need to consider the guidelines specified by Lord Fraser in the case involving Victoria Gillick (*Gillick v. West Norfolk and Wisbech AHA,* 1985). The effect of the Fraser guidelines is that a child can consent in their own right if they are capable of understanding the implications of what they are being asked to consent to. If a child can understand the implications of being interviewed as a witness and, where the interview is to be video recorded, the use to which the recording is to be put they can consent in their own right. If a child cannot understand these implications the consent of a parent or a guardian is required, or the consent of the local authority where the child is the subject of a care order or interim care order unless a court has already given their permission via an Emergency Protection Order.[1] It is important to note that *Achieving Best Evidence* (Office for Criminal Justice Reform, 2007a) deals with the issue of informing a child's parents/guardians separately to consent: other than in wholly exceptional circumstances parents/guardians should be informed even where the child has the capacity to consent.

'Informed consent' in this context refers to the understanding about the purpose of the interview (e.g., to be played as evidence-in-chief or, in the case of a written statement, to help the lawyer for the prosecution guide the witness through live evidence-in-chief). Informed consent is not only a moral imperative in England and Wales, it is also a procedural requirement that arises from the *Code of Practice for Victims of Crime* (Office for Criminal Justice Reform, 2005) and the *Witness Charter* (Office for Criminal Justice Reform, 2007b). Both the *Code of*

[1]Section 44 Children Act 1989.

Practice for Victims of Crime and the *Witness Charter* oblige the police to *explain* special measures to vulnerable and intimidated victims and witnesses. Such an explanation should include the following points in England and Wales:[2]

- That the witness may have access to special measures if the court agrees but that no guarantees can be given that the recording will be played;
- That video recorded evidence-in-chief is an *option*;
- That video recorded evidence-in-chief means playing the video in open court, although an application could also be made for the evidence to be heard in private[3] by clearing the public gallery;
- That the witness still needs to be available for cross-examination, usually via a live television link;[4]
- That the reason for video recording the interview for the purposes of evidence-in-chief is to reduce the potential stress on the witness by limiting the extent to which they might otherwise need to repeat their account;
- That the video recording will be served on the defence with the rest of the prosecution case papers (as would be the case with a written statement).

As can be seen in England and Wales, the video recorded interview forms a dual function: (i) it has an investigative purpose, to establish what has occurred (if anything) and who has committed the offence; and (ii) an evidential one as a child's evidence-in-chief. This thus has to be acknowledged in the planning.

Welfare The practice issues associated with child protection and the multi-agency context in which it is investigated is covered elsewhere in this book. In situations in which the police are involved and child protection is not an obvious issue, the children's services department should still be consulted prior to the interview. The child or their family may already be known to the local authority or may warrant assessment to establish whether they are in need.

Where a child is injured or traumatized, or is already undergoing a course of medical or psychological treatment, it will be necessary to

[2]In other jurisdictions an explanation of the purpose of conducting an interview with a child on video should take account of the legal provisions in the country where the interview is to take place.
[3]Section 25 Youth Justice and Criminal Evidence Act 1999.
[4]Section 24 Youth Justice and Criminal Evidence Act 1999.

establish whether they are fit to be interviewed by asking the person in charge of their treatment. If they are not fit to be interviewed an attempt should be made to find out what their prognosis is likely to be following treatment, particularly in respect of when, if ever, they are likely to be fit to be interviewed. If they are fit to be interviewed the 'terms and conditions' of the interview (e.g., maximum duration of the interview sessions, minimum period of time between interview sessions) should be established. Where a child is in hospital it may also be useful to find out whether they have said anything about the matter that is to form the basis of the interview and what, if anything, they have been told about it by visitors and those involved in their treatment because this may be of relevance when subsequently evaluating the interview for reliability. For example, a child who has been rendered unconscious as a result of an assault may wake up in hospital enquiring how they got there. In these circumstances, distinguishing between a simple repetition of what the child was told in response to such a query and a memory of the event during which the assault took place is likely to be a crucial consideration when the interview is evaluated for reliability.

Minimal Alleged Offence Information

Ideally, interviewers should only have minimal alleged offence information because of the potential of such knowledge to contaminate the interview. Such minimal information includes:

- The nature of the alleged offence;
- The time, frequency and location of the alleged offence;
- How the alleged offence came to the notice of the police;
- The nature of any threats or intimidation alleged to have been used by the suspect or their family or associates.

Limiting an interviewer's knowledge of the offence to this minimal information is desirable because it reduces the scope for confirmation bias. 'Confirmation bias' is a process in which interviewers and investigators wittingly or unwittingly guide their decision making and the questioning itself to confirm pre-existing views they may have (for more on this concept see Ask & Granhag, 2005; Savage & Milne, 2007).

While such a limited knowledge of the offence on the part of interviewers is certainly desirable, it is rarely achievable. Indeed, it can only be achieved in high profile investigations of the most serious kind (e.g., a child witness to a murder) where resources in terms of the number of potential interviewers are readily available and where an interview adviser can drip-feed information to the interviewer at the appropriate time in the interview as and where necessary and in accordance with the interview strategy. In most cases, however, a minimal knowledge of the offence on the part of the interviewer is usually unachievable because of the extent of their involvement in the investigation. For example, in England and Wales, police officers involved in investigating allegations of child abuse within a family will usually have attended a planning meeting with social services prior to conducting an interview; in these circumstances the alleged offences are necessarily discussed in order to determine the most appropriate course of action. In such cases it can only be hoped that an awareness of the possibility of confirmation bias on the part of the interviewer will minimize its effects, although, in the absence of any research on the subject, it must be accepted that this not entirely clear how effective simply having such an awareness is likely to be.

Information Important to the Investigation

Information important to the investigation can be thought of as falling into two categories:

1. Matters of general investigative practice; and
2. Case-specific material.

Matters of general investigative practice include:

- Points to prove the offence;
- Case law (e.g., in the *R v. Turnbull* (1977) case in respect of eyewitnesses in England and Wales); and
- Good investigative practice (e.g., 'Have you told anyone else about this?').

As is suggested in the name, case-specific material very much depends on the particular circumstances of the case. It could include:

- The antecedence of the victim;
- The background to a relationship;
- A history of the alleged abuse experienced by a victim;
- The victim's usual routine;
- The ownership, control or use of property such as vehicles, mobile telephones, and computers;
- Access to weapons;
- Access to a crime scene;

- Access to material that could be used to conceal or cleanse a crime scene; and
- Significant omissions or inconsistencies between the witness's account and other material.

Matters of general investigative practice are invariably of evidential value, whereas case-specific material often has little or no evidential value (highlighting the dual role of the interview noted earlier). The principal function of case-specific material is to aid the investigative process by contributing to the investigator's understanding of the alleged offence and by generating lines of inquiry.

Interviewers should know as much as possible about matters of general investigative practice when they prepare for interview. The amount of case-specific material that interviewers can have access to prior to the interview is, however, dependent upon on how much they know about the alleged offence. The interview plan will need to take account of situations in which interviewers have only limited knowledge of the offence and thus no knowledge of some or all of the case-specific material (to help stop interviewer bias as noted earlier). In these circumstances the case-specific material might be handled either by being 'drip-fed' to the interviewers at a suitable point in the interview by someone monitoring the process (e.g., an interview adviser) or, where the case is complex, by the interview taking place in two parts separated by a break during which the interviewers can be briefed about the case-specific material.

USING THE PLANNING INFORMATION

The use of the planning information to plan the interview is a decision-making process. Such decisions should be made by the interviewers as a team effort. Where an interview plan is developed in the broader context of an interview strategy, the decisions made by the interviewers are open to amendment by their managers, or by the interview adviser appointed to develop the strategy on behalf of their managers.

Objective Setting

After all the planning information has been obtained it should be used to plan the interview. As a first step it should be used to set the objectives for the interview. These objectives should be clear, precise, and topic-based and clearly identify the incident-related topics (e.g., the child's movements at the time of the alleged offence) and the case-specific information important to the investigation (e.g., the history of any relationship between the child and the alleged perpetrator) that the interview is to focus on. General objectives such as 'to find out what the witness knows about the offence' are of little use in determining the ground to be covered during the interview.

Setting out the objectives in a way that clearly distinguishes the incident-related topics from the case-specific information important to the investigation reflects the dual purpose of the interview; to play the recording as evidence-in-chief and to advance the investigation. These purposes are seldom entirely consistent with each other; the kind of background material that is regarded as case-specific information important to the investigation can prove absolutely crucial in solving a crime, corroborating an account or in locating an offender but it relies on semantic rather than episodic memory (see planning 'interview structure and techniques' below) and it is not usually the stuff of evidence. For these reasons it is essential that the differences between the different kinds of objectives are taken into account during the planning phase when the structure of the interview is considered for two reasons:

1. Memory recall may become unnecessarily difficult for a witness if they are frequently asked to switch between different kinds of memory; and
2. The courts may be reluctant to permit the playing of a lengthy recording when they consider that much of the material in it is irrelevant to the proceedings (i.e., not evidence) if it cannot be edited as a result of the interview being poorly structured and the topics being muddled up.

Decision Making

The planning information should then be used to determine the following:

- The most appropriate structure and techniques for the interview;
- The method of recording the interview;
- The location of the interview;
- The equipment to be used to record the interview;
- Any props and exhibits that should be available to the interviewers;
- The people to be present during the interview:
  - interviewers;
  - camera operator;
  - interview monitor;
  - witness supporter;

  - ○ interpreter;
  - ○ intermediary;[5]
- The timing, likely duration and pace, and number of interview sessions.

Interview structures and interview techniques An interview structure describes the component parts of an interview in terms of its phases and the topic areas to be dealt with and the order in which they should be covered. Interview techniques refer to the methods to be used within each phase or while covering each topic area. Interview techniques and structures are covered elsewhere in this book.

Method of recording Video recording of interviews with children has the advantage of providing a more complete record of what was communicated, verbally and non-verbally, in the interview than is ever likely to be possible with handwritten notes alone (e.g., see Wolchover & Heaton-Armstrong, 2007). In addition to this, such a recording could also serve to reduce the stress on the child by limiting the number of times that they have to repeat their account (Home Office, 1989) because it can be played back in a variety of settings in England and Wales including the criminal courts by way of evidence-in-chief, civil court cases involved in resolving child care issues, and disciplinary proceedings concerning inappropriate behaviour by adult employees towards children (Office for Criminal Justice Reform, 2007a). Decisions about the method of recording should take account of what is known about the child, including the child's wishes and those of their carers, and what is known about the offence. For example, it is likely to be appropriate to audio record an interview with a child who consents to be interviewed but who is reluctant to appear on camera as a result of an offence involving witness intimidation in circumstances where their identity is not already known to the alleged offender and an application for witness anonymity is a realistic possibility according to the legislation in England and Wales. It is important that the witness assessment and the circumstances of the offence are considered carefully when making a decision as to the most appropriate method of recording. However, it is difficult to provide general advice on this issue because it is important that every child is treated as an individual but matters such as the chronological and developmental age of the child as well as the emotional impact the alleged offence is likely to have on them, including

[5]See definition later in this chapter and O'Mahony, Smith and Milne (in press) for more on the role of the intermediary.

the potential for recrimination and intimidation, are likely to feature in decisions as to the most appropriate method of recording.

Location Video recorded interviews should ideally take place in purpose-built interview suites because they are designed to keep background noise and visual distractions down to a minimum. Memory retrieval requires intense concentration and thus to obtain detailed accounts from interviewees appropriate distraction-free environments and a place where the victim feels at ease and safe is essential.

Portable video recording equipment should only be used where it is not practical to access a purpose-built interview suite. Where portable equipment is used all possible steps should be taken to minimize auditory distractions such a mobile telephones ringing and the sounds from radios or televisions elsewhere in the premises. In some instances it may also be worth considering the use of screens to reduce visual distractions in the background where this is practical.

Where the interview is to take place in an institution such as a hospital, finding out about the cleaning and meal-time routines may also serve to minimize auditory distractions, particularly where cleaning equipment such as vacuum cleaners and floor buffers are used.

Equipment Most interview suites in England and Wales are equipped with one Pan Tilt Zoom (PTZ) camera that is used to focus on the witness and a wide-angle lens camera that records the events in the whole room during the interview. Most portable equipment consists either of a single PTZ camera or a PTZ camera and a wide-angle lens camera. This equipment may be either analogue VHS tapes or digital DVD disks, although it is likely that digital recording will progress to storage on a secure central server in due course, when funding permits (Griffiths, 2008). This equipment is likely to be perfectly adequate for most witness interviews with children.

However, additional cameras may be necessary where a child uses an augmentative or alternative form of communication that involves the use of signs or symbols. Where a child and the interpreter or intermediary are signing a single PTZ camera may not be able to record what both are doing, given that the camera should focus on the witness (Office for Criminal Justice Reform, 2007a, Appendix H, paragraph 9) and a wide-angle lens camera is unlikely to have the resolution needed to discriminate between some of the more subtle signs. In these circumstances it may be worth considering the use of an additional PTZ camera to record what the signer is doing in order to preserve the integrity of the interview. A similar issue may arise where the child is using symbols to communicate; an additional PTZ camera placed behind the child should be able to record more accurately which symbols are being pointed at.

Props and exhibits Props are dealt with in Chapter 17. If it is necessary to ask the child to identify an item of property as something that is of relevance to their account the interviewers will need to have it on hand. In these circumstances it will usually be appropriate to keep the property out of the sight of the child until the point in the interview when it is mentioned and then to produce it and ask the child if they can identify it. The property may be kept either in the control room or in a locked cabinet in the interview room.

People present Other than the child, the people present in the interview might include:

- Interviewers;
- Camera operator;
- Interview monitor;
- Interview supporter;
- Interpreter; and
- Intermediary.

Interviewers The training of interviewers is dealt with elsewhere in this book. In addition to training it is important to take account of the skills and experience of the interviewer and the likelihood of them being able to build a rapport with the child. The gender of the interviewer may also be important for some children in some circumstances (e.g., as a result of culture, sexuality or the nature of the offence), although no assumptions should be made about this and the child and their carers should always be consulted. Other personal qualities such as the age or cultural background of the interviewer might also be a consideration; in instances where the child or their carers express a preference it should be accommodated as far as possible in the circumstances (Office for Criminal Justice Reform, 2007a).

Interviewer welfare issues should also be considered. Such welfare issues may relate to apparently minor issues that are likely to distract or put unnecessary pressure on the interview, such as the time that they have available to conduct the interview or they might include a major event such as a bereavement that could make them less able to manage an emotionally charged disclosure. Where the interview or the potential interviewer is likely to be adversely affected by welfare concerns managers should be open to considering the use of another interviewer. In these circumstances managers will clearly need to ensure that they act in a tactful and supportive way to potential interviewers who are not to be used as a result of the welfare issues surrounding them.

A decision should also be made during the planning of the interview as to whether a second interviewer should be present. Such a decision should take account of the complexity of the case, the age and emotional condition of the child and the resources available to the interview team. The possibility that the child might feel intimidated by the presence of too many people in the interview room must also be considered in determining whether a second interviewer should be present in the interview room, particularly where several other people also need to be there (e.g., interpreters, intermediaries and interview supporters). If a decision is made that a second interviewer is to be present it is important that there is a clear understanding about who will lead the interview and that it is agreed when and how the second interviewer will be given the opportunity to contribute towards the interview (e.g., by being explicitly invited to do so after the lead interviewer has finished probing each topic).

Camera operator A camera operator should always be present when the interview is video recorded. The practice of a lone interviewer setting up the recording equipment before the interview begins raises two difficulties:

1. The PTZ camera needs to be set up in such a way that it focuses on the child from a few inches above their head down to their waist. This is so because a clear picture of them might help the court determine what they have said and to assess their emotional state. If the camera is set up in this way and the child moves position posture, even to a small imperceptible degree, there is every chance that they will be completely or partially lost from the picture;
2. If the recording equipment fails during the interview the interviewer will not discover it until the interview has been completed, this could potentially give rise to the loss of important material.

Interview monitor There may be occasions on which it is thought helpful to have someone in addition to the camera operator to observe the interview in order to identify any confusion that arises in the communication between the child and the interviewer, to identify any gaps or inconsistencies that emerge in the child's account, to make sure that the child's needs are taken into consideration (e.g. for a break) and to ensure that everything that needs to be covered in the interview is adequately dealt with. Such an interview monitor is likely to be particularly useful in cases where the alleged incident is a complex one or where the information important to the investigation contains much case-specific material. Where an interview monitor is used the plan should clearly identify how and when they will be given the opportunity to contribute towards the interview. This might be by the interviewer telling the child that they need to check that they have not missed anything with the monitor at the end of each major topic or just prior to the closure phase of the interview. Alternatively, wireless earpieces might be used so that the interview monitor can make suggestions to the interviewer as the interview progresses; however, such earpieces should only be used after careful consideration because they can distract both the interviewer and the interviewee. In addition, they could also be perceived suspiciously by the interviewee and be unnerving for the child.

Witness supporters A supporter may be present with the agreement of the witness to provide them with emotional support during the interview. The possibility of a witness supporter being present during the interview should certainly be a consideration where the witness assessment and the circumstances of the case suggest that the presence of a supporter might be useful. For example, where the child is young or has a learning disability and finds it more difficult than others to adjust to new people in unfamiliar environments or where the witness is particularly traumatized. Witness supporters cannot be other witnesses in the case. *Achieving Best Evidence* generally discourages the use parents or carers as supporters because they can be an additional source of stress for the witness (Office for Criminal Justice Reform, 2007a, paragraph 2.104). Witness supporters should not be confused with appropriate adults in England and Wales; appropriate adults should only to be used in interviews with suspected offenders (O'Mahony, Smith, & Milne, in press). It is important to note that the role of the interview supporter is a rather passive one in England and Wales in that they 'must be clearly instructed not to participate in the interview itself, whether by instructing or correcting the child, answering the interviewer's questions, head nodding or facial expressions' (Office for Criminal Justice Reform, 2007a).

Interpreters Children should usually be interviewed in their first language unless there is a good operational reason for not doing so. For example, an immediate concern for the safety of the child who speaks an unusual language or uses an unusual dialect in addition to being able to communicate in English where the only people available to translate for them in their first language are suspected of being involved in committing an offence against them. Where the child or their family express a preference for an interpreter of a particular gender, religious background or ethnicity and it is not possible to accommodate them the reasons should be carefully explained to them. Where the society from which the family's values originate is stratified into social groups it might be useful to obtain cultural advice to establish whether there is likely to be an issue if the interpreter comes from a different social group to the child.

Non-English language interpreters should be accredited with an appropriate body in England and Wales. Where an interpreter is not so accredited it is important that they meet the same standards as those on the national register.

A sign language interpreter who is registered with an appropriate body in England and Wales will also be required where the child is deaf. Before engaging such an interpreter, however, it is important to find out which form of sign language the child is using. The most common form of sign language used in the United Kingdom is British Sign Language (BSL), but BSL is by no means the only form of sign language. Even where the child uses BSL it should be noted that there are a number of different regional dialects in use across the United Kingdom and that it cannot be assumed that a signer proficient in one will necessarily be able to communicate with a child using another. Younger children who are deaf may not be fully proficient in BSL; in these circumstances consideration should be given to commissioning a registered intermediary[6] (see next section) rather than an interpreter. Children who have a learning disability may use sign language as either an augmentative or alternative form of communication; in these circumstances the sign language used is unlikely to be BSL and an intermediary who is competent in the use of other signing systems such as Makaton[7] should be called.

Whenever an interpreter is used it is important to understand that translation from one language to another is seldom literal; translation tends to take place on the basis of meaning. In view of this it is essential that interpreters are involved at some point in the planning process, perhaps after the objectives have been set and when the interviewer has a good idea of what they want to achieve but before firm decisions have been made about the use of any specific techniques.

[6]The register of intermediaries includes a number deaf people who are capable of facilitating communication in non-standard sign language.
[7]See www.makaton.org for further information.

Intermediaries Intermediaries are one of the special measures in England and Wales that are provided for in Part 2 Youth Justice and Criminal Evidence Act 1999 (YJCEA). In particular, Section 29 points out that the function of an intermediary is to communicate: (i) questions put to the witness; and (ii) answers given by the witness, and to explain such questions and answers so far as is necessary to enable them to be understood by the person asking the questions of the witness.

Intermediaries are available during the investigative interview and during any court proceedings that follow it. Where an intermediary is used during an interview it is necessary to make an application retrospectively for their use when the case comes to court (for more on the role of the intermediary see O'Mahony, Smith, & Milne, in press).

Intermediaries are professional people from a variety of backgrounds which include speech and language therapy, clinical and forensic psychology, special needs education and mental health. They are selected and trained by the Ministry of Justice in England and Wales then put on a register. The process of accessing the register is one of matching the communication needs of the child with the skills of the intermediary. The matching service is managed by the Specialist Operations Centre for the National Policing Improvement Agency.

All vulnerable witnesses are eligible for an intermediary. Section 16 of the YJCEA defines vulnerable witnesses as children, and people of any age with a mental disorder, learning disability or physical disorder or disability that has an adverse impact on their ability to communicate. Eligibility is one thing; however, actually getting access to an intermediary is another. To gain access to an intermediary it will be necessary to demonstrate to the court that the child's evidence is likely to be maximized by their use. There are no precise guidelines about how to make a judgement as to whether an intermediary is required; in practice it is likely to be a matter of witness assessment, focusing on the child's age where communication is age-appropriate and the nature of their disability where it is not.

Intermediaries need to assess the witness before the interview to ensure that they have the skills needed to facilitate the dialogue with the witness and establish the most appropriate methods of communication during the interview. A police officer should usually be present during the assessment to corroborate and act upon any unsolicited comments that might be of significance to the investigation. The details of the assessment vary according to needs of the witness but they can include:

- Extent of vocabulary (verbal/sign/symbol);
- Use of auditory memory;
- Attention span (including concentration);

- Turn-taking;
- Use of abstract concepts and concrete words;
- Understanding of questions beginning with where, what, when, why, and how;
- Likely response to open questions;
- Maximum words likely to be understood in a question;
- Use of non-verbal communication;
- Acquiescence and suggestibility;
- Causality;
- Concept of time;
- Use of narrative conventions when providing an account, including the sequencing of events; and
- Taking the perspective of others (theory of mind[8]).

This list is by no means exhaustive and is only presented to give the reader an insight into what is involved in the assessment.

Having assessed the child's communication skills it is essential that intermediaries are involved in planning the interview after the objectives have been set and when the interviewer has a good idea of what they want to achieve. Given the range of communication skills involved, children can sometimes be tired after the assessment. For this reason and because the intermediary needs to be involved in planning, the assessment often takes place on a different day to the interview.

In most cases, having conducted the assessment and been involved in planning, the role of the intermediary during an interview is quite different to the role of an interpreter. An interpreter serves as a translation point through which both the interviewer and the witness have to go whereas intermediaries often only speak during an interview when a question is asked or an answer is given that is not likely to be understood. In instances involving the use of alternative systems of communication such as the use of signs or symbols, however, it may be that the intermediary will adopt a role more akin to that of an interpreter during the interview.

Timing, duration and pace, number of interview sessions The interview should take place as soon as possible, certainly where the matter under investigation relates to a recent event (for a discussion about the retention interval in memory see Murdock, 1974). Questions may be raised about the accuracy of the child's memory if there is an unreasonable delay in conducting the interview, particularly where the child is young.[9]

[8]For example, Baron-Cohen, Leslie and Frith (1986).
[9]As was the case in *R v. Powell* (2006).

However, the need to act quickly should never be used as an excuse for failing to plan the interview properly. Given that the consequences of a failure to plan may be a poor interview and that a poor interview may have adverse consequences for the investigation and on any legal proceedings that follow it, it is incumbent on those responsible for managing interviewers to ensure that interviewers are given enough time for planning.

The timing of the interview should take account of factors such as the child's routine and the effects of any medication they are using (e.g., if they have been prescribed a slow-release drug that makes them drowsy in the afternoon the best time for the interview is likely to be the morning).

Similarly, the duration and pace of the interview must be influenced by what is known about the child, including their age, medical, mental and emotional condition. In complex cases or cases in which the witness cannot be interviewed for more than a short period of time, it may be appropriate for the interview to take place over a number of sessions. These sessions can take place over more than one day if necessary.

PREPARING THE WITNESS FOR THE INTERVIEW

It is important that the interview plan sets out the arrangements for preparing the child for the interview. In some cases preparation may take place just before the interview but in cases where the age, developmental level or emotional condition of the child is such that time will be needed to give them an opportunity to familiarize themselves with the interviewer and build some trust in their relationship preparation is likely to take place a day or two before the interview. In some cases preparation might even extend to a number of sessions several days before the interview.

Overall, interview preparation should:

1. Begin the process of rapport building between the child and the interviewer;
2. Help the child to gain an understanding of the particular conversational rules that apply in an investigative interview;
3. Give the child an understanding of the overall structure of the interview;
4. Provide the interviewer with an opportunity to supplement their knowledge of the child's developmental level and emotional condition.

Interview preparation should, therefore, include:

- An explanation of the role of the interviewer(s);
- An explanation of the purpose of the interview without discussing the details of the offence being investigated;
- The ground rules for the interview (e.g., not making any assumptions about the interviewer's knowledge of what was witnessed);
- An outline of structure of the interview without discussing the details of the offence being investigated.

In England and Wales it is rarely practical to make an electronic recording of interview preparation. Written records have routinely been made of interview preparation since video recorded interviews for use as evidence-in-chief were introduced for children in October 1992 and very few challenges suggesting that the witness was coached have been made in the English and Welsh courts. Such allegations could equally apply to other interactions with the child that are also not practical to electronically record such as initial contact with the police, the journey to the interview suite and any time taken to show the child around the facility prior to the recording equipment being switched on. Interviewers should ensure that the written record of the interview preparation and any other pre-interview contact with the child is as comprehensive as possible so that they are in a position to rebut any subsequent suggestion of coaching.

Interview preparation is not intended to include a discussion about the matter under investigation; this should be left until the investigative interview. Sometimes, however, despite the best intentions of the interviewer, children can make unsolicited comments that might be relevant to the investigation, including a reference to the allegation under investigation. In these circumstances the rules governing initial contact with the witness[10] should be applied to interview. These rules may be summarized as follows:

- Listen to the child, do not interrupt them;
- If it is not necessary to ask any questions, acknowledge what the child has said and tell them that the matter will be explored further during the investigative interview;
- Only ask questions if it is necessary to take some form of immediate action (e.g., to protect another child, to ensure the recovery of forensic material);

[10]As set out in *Achieving Best Evidence*, Office for Criminal Justice Reform (2007a) paragraph 2.29.

- Where it is necessary to ask questions try to limit them to the type of questions commonly used in investigative interviews (e.g., open-ended and specific closed); and
- Make a comprehensive written record of what was said and the circumstances in which it was said as soon as possible.

It should always be remembered that a child witness could refer to previous conversations with the interviewer during the video recorded interview itself and that the lawyers acting for the accused person may therefore ask what was said. For this reason, in England and Wales, written records of interview preparation and any other pre-interview interaction with the child are disclosed to the Crown Prosecution Service (CPS) in the event of the matter subsequently being referred to them. The CPS will then forward a copy of these records, along with the other prosecution papers, to the lawyers acting for the accused person, thus ensuring that the whole process is as transparent as possible.

The interview plan should be reviewed and revised as necessary following interview preparation.

CONCLUSIONS

This chapter has described the process of planning an interview with a child victim or witness. In essence, planning consists of the following:

- Collating information about the child and conducting an assessment of that information (witness assessment);
- Establishing minimal information about the offence;
- Identifying what information that the child may have access to that is important to the investigation.

This information is then used to set the objectives for the interview and to make decisions about the interview process relating to:

- Structure and techniques;
- Recording method;
- Location;
- Recording equipment;
- Props and exhibits;
- People to be present; and
- Timing, duration, pace and number of sessions.

The child should then be prepared for the interview and the plan reviewed and revised if necessary.

Planning should be an integral part of the interview process; it is not a luxury that can be dispensed with when the interviewer is busy. Without effective planning there can be no effective interview. If interviewers do not know who they are talking to or what they are talking about we should not be surprised if the interview has a less than satisfactory outcome.

REFERENCES

Ask, K., & Granhag, P.A. (2005). Motivational sources of confirmation bias in criminal investigations: the need for cognitive closure. *Journal of Investigative Psychology and Offender Profiling*, *2*, 43–63.

Attwood T. (1998). *Asperger's Syndrome: A Guide for Parents and Professionals*. London: Jessica Kingsley.

Baron-Cohen S., Leslie, A.M., & Frith, U. (1985). Does the autistic child have a 'theory of mind'? *Cognition*, *21*, 37–46.

Gillick v. West Norfolk and Wisbech AHA [1985] 3 All ER 402.

Griffiths, A. (2008). Setting digital standards. *Investigative Practice Journal* (20 March 2008), pp. 28–29.

Griffiths, A., & Milne, R. (2005). Will it all end in tiers? Police interviews with suspects in Britain. In T. Williamson (Ed.), *Investigative Interviewing: Rights, Research, Regulation*. Cullompton, UK: Willan.

Home Office. (1989). *Report of the Advisory Group on Video Evidence*. London: Home Office.

Murdock, B. (1974). *Human Memory: Theory and Data*. Potomac: Lawrence Erlbaum.

Office for Criminal Justice Reform. (2005). *Code of Practice for Victims of Crime*. London: Office for Criminal Justice Reform.

Office for Criminal Justice Reform. (2007a). *Achieving Best Evidence in Criminal Proceedings: Guidance on Interviewing Victims and Witnesses, and Using Special Measures*. London: Office for Criminal Justice Reform.

Office for Criminal Justice Reform. (2007b). *Witness Charter*. London: Office for Criminal Justice Reform.

O'Mahony, B., Smith, K., & Milne, R. (in press). The early identification of the vulnerable witness prior to the investigative interview. *British Journal of Forensic Practice*.

R v. Powell (2006) EWCA Crim 3.

R v. Turnbull (1977) QB224.

Savage, S., & Milne, R. (2007). Miscarriages of justice: the role of the investigative process. In T. Newburn, T. Williamson, & A. Wright (Eds), *Handbook of Criminal Investigation* (pp. 610–627). Cullompton, UK: Willan.

Smith K., & Tilney S. (2007). *Vulnerable Adult and Child Witnesses*. Oxford: Oxford University Press.

Wolchover D., & Heaton-Armstrong A. (2007). Woeful neglect. *New Law Journal*, 624–625.

6

Rapport Building in Investigative Interviews of Children

IRIT HERSHKOWITZ

Key Points

- Establishing rapport with children is an essential step in investigative interviews and should precede any discussion of suspected child abuse.
- Rapport building should be based on open-ended invitations prompting children to tell about personally meaningful experiences and should involve a supportive approach.
- During rapport building, interviewers should assess children's verbal and non-verbal responses to ensure that they are involved and cooperative.
- Reluctant children may need longer and more supportive rapport building before they are ready to discuss their abuse. Those who remain reluctant may benefit from another opportunity to establish rapport in a second interview.
- During the substantive part of the interview, investigators should maintain rapport with children by providing non-suggestive support.

Field professionals and researchers are largely in agreement about the necessity for effective rapport building in forensic interviews of

Children's Testimony: A Handbook of Psychological Research and Forensic Practice, Second Edition.
Edited by Michael E. Lamb, David J. La Rooy, Lindsay C. Malloy, and Carmit Katz.

children who are alleged victims of sexual abuse (Collins, Lincoln, & Frank, 2002; Goodman, Bottoms, Schwartz-Kenney, & Rudy, 1991; Lamb, Orbach, Warren, Esplin, & Hershkowitz, 2007; Sternberg *et al.*, 1997). When approached by unfamiliar adults or authority figures, some children may be reluctant to describe personally meaningful experiences that are intimate or embarrassing (e.g., Saywitz, Goodman, Nicholas, & Moan, 1991). Research shows that a substantial proportion of children are reluctant to disclose their abuse when interviewed (London, Bruck, Ceci, & Shuman, 2005, 2007). Therefore, professionals who are unknown to children must first establish rapport before bringing up the topic of suspected abuse. Establishing rapport has been shown to help facilitate communication with children and to encourage them to affirm and describe traumatic experiences in clinical (Boggs & Eyberg, 1990; Morgan & Friedemann, 1988), evaluative (Kanfer, Eyberg, & Krahn, 1992; Powell & Lancaster, 2003) or investigative interviews (Aldridge & Wood, 1998; Goodman & Bottoms, 1993; Hynan, 1999; McBride, 1996; Powell & Thomson,1994). Thus, rapport building can be crucial in motivating children, particularly reluctant disclosers, to talk about abuse by decreasing their anxiety and discomfort (e.g., Siegman & Reynolds, 1983). When interviewers familiarize themselves with children and show warm and supportive behavior, it can also reduce children's suggestibility and increase the accuracy of their statements (e.g., Goodman *et al.*, 1991, Hershkowitz, Orbach, Lamb, Sternberg, & Horowitz, 2006).

In field contexts, research has demonstrated the beneficial effects of rapport on children's production. Wood, McClure and Birch (1996) found that children who seemed reticent and were uncommunicative at the beginning of an interview were more likely to reveal their experiences to the interviewer later when rapport building was conducted well. Ruddock's findings also highlight the importance of the quality of rapport for the amount of information provided by children. Ruddock (2006) examined 98 transcripts of child sexual abuse investigative interviews conducted by trained social workers in a children's hospital and reported that better rapport was associated with longer responses from the children, and emotional rapport positively predicted the number of details that children provided. Effective rapport building appears to make children more comfortable, reduces their anxiety, enhances their trust in the interviewers, and motivates them to be cooperative interlocutors. Rapport building may exert these effects via social support. As discussed next, research concerning the effects of social support on children's memory performance provides compelling evidence for the value of rapport building with children during investigative interviews.

EFFECTS OF SOCIAL SUPPORT

Although findings have been mixed, research evidence generally shows positive effects of supportive interviewing on children's memory performance. Most studies of social support in interviews with children are laboratory analogue studies; only a few involve direct observations of the effects of social support in interviews concerning child abuse. Analogue studies show that supportive environments can improve the accuracy of the information that children report (Greenstock & Pipe, 1997, exp. 2; Moston, 1992) and reduce their suggestibility (Cornah & Memon, 1996; Greenstock & Pipe, 1997, exp. 1; but see also Greenstock & Pipe, 1996). Familiar interviewers such as parents (Goodman, Sharma, Thomas, & Considine, 1995; Ricci, Beal, & Dekle, 1996) and other non-official interviewers (Tobey & Goodman, 1992) also seem to have a positive effect on children's accuracy, at least in some parts of the interview.

In a few analogue studies, the interviewers' interpersonal style, including their supportiveness, was directly manipulated. Although supportiveness was not always associated with increased accuracy of the children's reports, there was evidence of the beneficial effects of support and no evidence of harmful effects. For example, Goodman *et al.* (1991) found that 3- to 7-year-olds were more accurate in their free-recall descriptions of inoculation experiences when the interviewers were supportive than when they were neutral. After a 4-week delay and under supportive conditions, younger children were as resistant as older children to misleading questions regarding possible abuse, although their reports regarding peripheral aspects of the events were less complete than those of older children. Similarly, Carter, Bottoms, and Levine (1996) reported that 5- to 7-year-old children were more resistant to misleading questions under supportive than under intimidating conditions, but support did not specifically affect their free-recall descriptions of a play session. Finally, consistent with the two previous studies, Davis and Bottoms (2002) found that 6- to 7-year-old children who were interviewed with no delay by a supportive interviewer about a play session were more resistant to misleading suggestions than were children who were interviewed by an intimidating interviewer. This study, unlike Goodman *et al.*'s, failed to show the effect of support on children's free-recall accuracy, but a re-examination of the children's memory after a delay revealed such an effect. In a later study (reported in Bottoms, Quas, & Davis, 2007), Davis and Bottoms re-interviewed the children who participated in the original study 1 year later. Children interviewed by supportive interviewers reported more accurate and less inaccurate information in free recall and made fewer errors of commission in response to specific and misleading questions. The researchers also proposed and tested a potential mechanism underlying the effects of interview support. Their findings suggest that support fosters a sense of self-efficacy, which improves children's resistance to misleading information.

By contrast, Imhoff and Baker-Ward (1999) failed to show similar effects of support on children's performance in interviews. They examined young (3- to-4 year-old) children's descriptions of a classroom demonstration after a 2-week delay. No effects of supportive versus neutral interviewing on children's accuracy in yes–no or direct questions emerged, and the children's resistance to misleading questions was similarly unaffected by interview supportiveness. After a 4-week delay, no effect of support was evident in their responses to all type of questions, including free-recall questions (Imhoff, 1999).

In an attempt to explain inconsistencies across studies, researchers (Davis & Bottoms, 2002; Imhoff & Baker-Ward, 1999) have suggested that the manipulation of the interviewers' support might be responsible for differences in the findings because the effects seem more consistent when supportive interviewers are contrasted with intimidating interviewers than when they are compared with neutral interviewers. This observation suggests that the findings may reflect the harmful effects of intimidating conditions rather than the beneficial effects of supportive conditions. Researchers have also suggested that the effects of support might be mediated by individual differences in children such as social support reserves, attachment style, or working memory capacity (Davies & Bottoms, 2002). However, these researchers clarified that while some children may benefit from interviewers' support more than other children, there is no evidence that interviewer's support is harmful to children.

Overall, research findings illustrate that social support helps decrease children's suggestibility and enhances their memory performance while showing no evidence of harmful effects. However, because empirical evidence is scarce and relevant studies vary in their methodology, it is difficult to specify the conditions under which interviewers' support enhances children's reporting competency. In addition, the effects of interviewers' support have been studied primarily in laboratory analogue studies. In such studies, it is not possible to manipulate the levels of stress associated with events such as sexual abuse or the stress associated with difficult retrieval conditions such as forensic investigations. Children undergoing sexual abuse investigations may need more emotional support to report painful experiences and to cope with the stressful nature of forensic investigations. Only a few studies have examined the effects of supportive behaviour by interviewers on children's performance in real life investigations using the National Institute of Child Health and Human Development (NICHD) Protocol, which is described more fully later in the chapter.

In her study, Hershkowitz (2009) examined the level of support interviewers provided to alleged child sexual abuse victims who were interviewed using the NICHD Protocol. Support was identified when the interviewers personally addressed the child by his/her name (e.g., 'Now, Daniel, tell me everything that happened from the beginning to the end' or 'Tell me more about this person, Sharon') and when neutral reinforcements, unrelated to the content of the child's response, were included (e.g., 'You are doing just fine', 'You are really helping me to understand what happened'). Interviewers provided, on average, seven prompts containing support across the entire interview, and there were no differences based on age or talkativeness in the amount of support directed to children. Interviewers' support significantly predicted the children's production of free-recall details following open-ended prompts. That is, the more supportive comments addressed to children by interviewers, the more details that were obtained from children. To investigate this finding in greater detail, Hershkowitz examined more and less talkative children as well as older and younger children separately. While interviewers' support led to the production of more details among the group of children who were less talkative, interviewers' support failed to produce more details among the more talkative children. Similarly, interviewers' support predicted the number of details following open-ended prompts for the older (7–9 years), but not for the younger children (4–6 years). Although this study shed some light on the dynamics of support in investigative interviews, it focused on cooperative or non-reluctant children and thus did not reveal how rapport building might affect the reports of reluctant children.

Using the same operationalization of interviewers' support, Hershkowitz *et al.* (2006) compared only the pre-substantive parts of NICHD Protocol interviews with cooperative and reluctant children. They reported that responsiveness by the children during the pre-substantive portion of the interview and actual disclosures of abuse in the substantive portion of the interview were associated with a more supportive interviewer style. Paradoxically, interviewers were less supportive of reluctant children than of cooperative children, even though reluctant children probably needed more rather than less support.

This limited evidence indirectly shows that an effective rapport-building session at the beginning of the interview and a supportive approach from interviewers throughout the interview can help children disclose abuse and describe it in more detail. However, despite the professional recommendations to develop rapport in investigative interviews with children, and despite empirical evidence supporting those recommendations, it seems that investigators often fail to adequately establish rapport with children. Field studies of investigative interviews with alleged child abuse victims clearly indicate that investigators typically do not make the necessary efforts to develop rapport with their interviewees before shifting the focus to the topic of abuse and that the presence and quality of rapport building are often unsatisfying (Warren, Woodall, Hunt, & Perry, 1996; Westcott & Kynan, 2006).

Acknowledging the value of rapport building in investigative interviews of alleged child abuse victims and observing that child investigators rarely establish appropriate rapport with children, experts have formulated various guidelines for interviewing children, which include specific instructions for establishing rapport.

PRACTICAL GUIDELINES FOR ESTABLISHING RAPPORT

Recommendations that forensic interviewers establish rapport before prompting children to talk about suspected abuse are formulated in different ways in the existing suggested guidelines (e.g., Fisher & Geiselman, 1992; Home Office, 2002; Lamb, Sternberg, & Esplin, 1998; Poole & Lamb, 1998; Yuille, Hunter, Joffe, & Zaparniuk, 1993). One of the best-studied guidelines for conducting forensic interviews with children is the NICHD Investigative Interview Protocol (Lamb, Hershkowitz, Orbach, & Esplin, 2008; Orbach *et al.*, 2000). This Protocol, which covers all phases of the investigative interview (e.g., pre-substantive phase including rapport building and narrative practice, substantive phase, disclosure phase, closure) was designed to translate professional recommendations into operational guidelines and guide interviewers to use prompts and techniques that maximize the amount of information elicited from free-recall memory. The Protocol's effectiveness in improving the quality of interviewer questions and testimony from children has been demonstrated in numerous field and laboratory studies (Lamb *et al.*, 2008) and will be described in greater detail later in this volume (see Chapters 9 and 10).

The NICHD Protocol includes a structured rapport-building session in the pre-substantive part of the interview, during which open-ended invitations are used to explore the child's everyday life and a particular past event. In this Protocol, rapport building comprises two sections: the first is a structured open-ended section designed to encourage children to provide personally meaningful information about both positive and negative experiences. In the second section, children are prompted to share with the interviewer one recently experienced event of personal significance to them, such as their last birthday party, and to describe it in detail. Note that the NICHD Protocol includes in the rapport-building session two 'training' functions: general free-narrative training and specific episodic-memory retrieval training. Although rapport building and 'training' are not separate in the interview, they are discussed separately in this book because they involve different mechanisms and purposes. The training functions of this session are further elaborated in the next chapter, while the current chapter focuses on the emotional function of rapport building.

In the NICHD Protocol, rapport building starts after an introductory phase, in which the interviewer introduces him/herself, clarifies the child's task (the need to describe events in detail and to tell the truth), and explains the ground rules and expectations (i.e., that the child can and should, if appropriate, say 'I don't remember', 'I don't know', 'I don't understand', or correct the interviewer). Then, the Protocol suggests a sequence of open-ended structured prompts aimed at evoking a narrative about positive and negative experiences, as follows:

1. Now, [*child's name*], I want to get to know you better. Tell me about things you like to do.
2. I really want to know you better. Tell me more about what you like to do.
3. Tell me more about [*one activity the child mentioned*].
4. Tell me about something fun that has happened to you.
5. Tell me more about [*one activity the child mentioned*].
6. Tell me about something unpleasant that has happened to you.
7. Tell me more about [*one activity the child mentioned*].
8. See, [*child's name*], you can talk to me about both good things and bad things that have happened to you.

Then, the second section of rapport building begins, and children are encouraged to focus on one meaningful recently experienced event and are prompted to describe it in detail.

1. [*child's name*], I want to know more about you and the things you do. A few [*days/weeks*] ago was [*a holiday/birthday party/the first day of school/another event*]. Tell me everything that happened on [*the event*].
2. [Repeat the first activity the child has mentioned and ask] And then what happened? (Use this question as many times as needed until you have a full account of the event.)

3. Now I want you to tell me everything that happened from the moment [*an activity the child mentioned*] to the moment [*a subsequent activity*]. (Use this question to cover various time segments of the event.)
4. Earlier you mentioned [*an activity / figure / object*]. Tell me everything about [*this activity / figure / object*]. (Repeat this question using various cues drawn from the child's narrative.)
5. In our conversation, it is very important that you tell me every detail about things that have really happened to you. (Important. If the child's narrative remains brief, make additional efforts to elicit an account of a different event. You may prompt for a description of the same day or the previous day with the next invitation followed by prompts 2–5.)
6. I really want to know about things that happened to you. Tell me everything that happened today [*yesterday*], from the time you woke up until you arrived here.

A standardized rapport-building section like that included in the NICHD Protocol has made it possible for researchers to explore a variety of important issues. Researchers have recently started exploring practical questions related to rapport building. What is the preferred style of prompts to be used when attempting to build rapport with children? How long should interviewers engage in rapport building with children? How do the age and personal characteristics of the children affect their behavior during and after rapport building? How do reluctant children respond to rapport-building attempts, and what strategies should be used when interviewing them?

STYLE OF RAPPORT BUILDING

A few studies have empirically assessed different styles of rapport building in investigative interviews with children (Hershkowitz, 2009; Roberts, Lamb, & Sternberg, 2004; Sternberg *et al.*, 1997) and have systematically revealed the advantage of using open-ended prompts when attempting to establish rapport with children (e.g., 'Tell me about something fun that happened to you'). In her recent field study, Hershkowitz (2009) demonstrated that, in interviews following the NICHD Protocol, an open-ended rapport-building style was associated with greater amounts of free-recall information about the alleged abuse: the proportion of invitations posed during rapport building significantly predicted the average number of details children provided following open-ended prompts in the substantive part of the interview.

The demonstrable value of open-ended rapport building may be attributable to the empowering function of this style which conveys to children that they have a central role in the interaction, that their personal experiences are a valued source of information and that they are being listened to carefully. In addition, researchers have underscored the modelling function of an open-ended pre-substantive rapport-building session. The next chapter of this book makes clear that this session can simulate both the investigative strategies used in the substantive phase and the related pattern of interaction between interviewers and children, while demonstrating to children the specific level of detail expected of them.

LENGTH OF RAPPORT BUILDING

The effect of the length of rapport building in investigative interviews was the focus of several studies. Davies, Westcott, and Horan (2000) compared interviews including short (less than 8 minutes) with long (over 8 minutes) rapport building on the amount of abuse-relevant information obtained. They found that short rapport building was associated with longer answers containing more Criterion Based Content Analysis (CBCA) criteria. They speculated that longer rapport building may have reduced children's attention and/or interviewers' efforts during the substantive questioning. An alternative explanation that they raised was that longer rapport building was provided to children who were less comfortable and more hesitant to provide information; it might be helpful to control for this individual difference in future research.

Teoh and Lamb (2010) have similarly found a negative association between the length of rapport building and children's production, although they specified that the longer the interviewers spoke, the less information young children gave in the substantive phase. Neither Davies *et al.* nor Teoh and Lamb studied Protocol interviews.

In her study of NICHD Protocol interviews, Hershkowitz (2009) supported the conclusion that very lengthy rapport building can be counterproductive. This study also showed that longer rapport building was characterized by a lower proportion of open-ended prompts than shorter rapport building, suggesting that the questioning style perhaps interacted with the length of rapport building to decrease production. In this study, the length of rapport building was a significant predictor of the amount of free-recall information provided in the substantive part of the interview.

These studies led researchers to recommend that interviewers should take the necessary time to establish rapport with children but avoid too lengthy rapport building which may be counter-productive. This recommendation is based on the recognition that cognitive resources and attention span are limited in children and that effective interviewing should aim to maintain children's attention throughout the interview. An excessive use of cognitive resources in the rapport-building phase may leave the children unable to process the many cognitive requests during the substantive part of the interview.

It should be noted, however, that these studies are correlational in nature, meaning that, while they demonstrate a *connection* between shorter rapport building and increased production, they do not demonstrate causal links. It is possible, for example, that shorter rapport building is associated with other factors that enhance production. Indeed, in the samples studied, a short rapport-building session was associated with a high proportion of invitations and with low number of words spoken by the interviewer, which are both associated with increased production. The limitations of the studies underscore the need for more research and specifically for better controlled field experiments before we can clearly identify how much rapport building is typically needed. Also, it is important to note that the amount of rapport building with an individual child needs to be determined based on his/her level of engagement and cooperation rather than by a particular time prescription. As it is made clear later, rapport-building efforts should preferably continue until the interviewer feels confident that the child is ready to discuss any unpleasant experiences with the interviewer if they have indeed occurred.

AGE AND INDIVIDUAL DIFFERENCES

While researchers have demonstrated the advantage of rapport building for children and adolescents (4–15 years) and there is consensus that both younger and older children benefit from rapport building, two studies used planned age comparisons to explore developmental differences in children's responses to the style and the length of rapport building. Hershkowitz (2009) observed that the length of rapport building was negatively associated with substantive production in both 4- to 6-year-olds and 7- to 9-year-olds. However, Teoh and Lamb (2010) also studied even older children and found that the negative correlation between the length of rapport building and substantive production was evident only among younger children (5–7 years), but not among older children (8–12 and 13–15 years). Paradoxically, the youngest children in this sample were addressed with proportionally more rapport-building prompts, with more words spoken by interviewers, than the older children, a pattern that was apparently counter-productive.

The effects of the rapport-building style on children's production also differed for younger and older children. In the sample studied by Hershkowitz (2009), a greater proportion of invitations during rapport building was predictive of increased free-recall production in the substantive portion. However, when the two age groups (4–6 and 7–9 years) were examined separately, the proportion of invitations showed a significant effect only for the older children, perhaps because young children were not given the chance to cope with open-ended prompts in the rapport building as were the older children. It seems therefore that interviewers act counter-productively when attempting to establish rapport with preschoolers by posing too many focused questions.

Because some children are shyer and less talkative than others, Hershkowitz (2009) also attempted to test whether two defined groups of more and less talkative children differed in terms of the extent to which they benefitted from short and open-style rapport building. The children were divided into more and less talkative groups by median split. The proportion of invitations and the length of rapport building predicted the amount of substantive information provided by the less talkative children but not the amount provided by more talkative children. Again, paradoxically, interviewers treated less talkative children with longer rapport building and fewer invitations, which again appeared to be counter-productive.

In summary, the limited research on the effects of age and individual differences on children's responses to rapport building suggests that the length of rapport building is associated with substantive informativeness for younger (but not for older) and for less talkative children while the open style rapport building is more beneficial for older children although it is also beneficial for younger children.

ESTABLISHING RAPPORT WITH RELUCTANT CHILDREN

A few studies shed light on the effects of rapport on reluctant children's willingness to disclose abuse experiences. The literature indicates that a substantial proportion of alleged victims are reluctant to disclose abuse when formally interviewed, with estimates varying depending on the context in which the interviews were conducted (London, Bruck, Ceci, & Shuman, 2005, 2007). In the context of forensic or assessment interviews, disclosure rates range from 45% to 74%. It is especially concerning that the lowest rates of disclosure were reported in the most serious cases of abuse such as when the suspects were parental figures or when the abuse involved repeated incidents and severe forms of abuse (Hershkowitz, Horowitz, & Lamb, 2005, 2007). Reluctance may not only affect willingness to disclose but also the amount of abuse-related information children provide once they have disclosed (Orbach, Shiloach, & Lamb, 2007). Therefore, it is crucial to help reluctant children talk about their abuse by building trusting relationships with interviewers.

There is evidence that children who seemed reticent or were uncommunicative in non-protocol interviews were more likely to talk or open up to the interviewer later when rapport building was conducted well (Wood *et al.*, 1996), and the effects of rapport building with reluctant children have been further explored in recent systematic field studies involving NICHD Protocol interviews. Hershkowitz *et al.* (2006) studied the dynamics of interviews with 50 children who failed to disclose validated instances of abuse and compared them with interviews conducted with cooperative children who did disclose abuse. The researchers reported that disclosers received fewer questions during rapport building than non-disclosers. The questioning style used in the rapport-building sessions also differed among the groups. Rapport building in interviews with children who later disclosed abuse was characterized by higher proportions of free-recall prompts than interviews of children who failed to disclose abuse. Interestingly, children's responsiveness during rapport building was predictive of disclosure, with children showing disengagement in one or more responses being most likely not to disclose abuse that was known to have occurred. This study makes clear that interviewers acted counter-productively in interviews with reluctant children, providing them with less rather than more supportive and open-ended prompts.

Interestingly, reluctance can be manifested by children during rapport building both verbally and non-verbally. In a recent field study, C. Katz, I. Hershkowitz, L.C. Malloy, M.E. Lamb, M. Atabaki, and S. Spindler (manuscript in preparation) observed the non-verbal cues that disclosers and non-disclosers of documented abuse displayed during the pre-substantive phase of investigative interviews conducted using the NICHD Protocol. This study revealed that non-disclosers were more likely to use gestures indicating disengagement than disclosers, and that these differences appeared early in the interview, even before rapport building started, intensifying during rapport building.

The studies by Hershkowitz *et al.* and by Katz *et al.* (manuscript in preparation) emphasize that rapport building is not just about using structured prompts but about evoking trust, cooperation and engagement from the children. These studies underscore both the possibility and the importance of evaluating children's responsiveness during rapport building while providing useful measures for identifying reluctance early in the interview and for anticipating the risk of non-disclosure. The authors suggested that steps for enhancing rapport with children should be taken as soon as reluctance is identified. They recommended that interviewers spend more time and efforts overcoming reluctance and building rapport while refraining from exploring the possibility that abuse took place if children remain reluctant. They also suggested that when necessary, interviewers should attempt to engage in an additional rapport-building session in a second interview.

DIFFICULTIES INVESTIGATORS FACE ESTABLISHING RAPPORT WITH CHILDREN USING EXISTING GUIDELINES

Although the NICHD Protocol offers structured guidelines for establishing rapport with children in a pre-substantive part of the interview, both researchers and field supervisors point to apparent difficulties interviewers face establishing rapport effectively. One major obstacle identified in research is the engagement of child investigators in negative dynamics when children seem uncooperative; interviewers sometimes react with frustration and counter-productive strategies such as withdrawing their support. Informing interviewers about the multi-source emotional distress that these children may experience and their need for support may evoke more empathy rather than frustration among interviewers. In addition, making interviewers conscious of how their own reactions may affect children and providing interviewers with alternative or complementary guidelines for establishing rapport more effectively may help them break this cycle.

Another difficulty interviewers may experience in creating meaningful rapport with children during investigative interviews stems from their concerns that showing empathy and providing support to the children may be criticized in court as a suggestive practice that may increase children's eagerness to please interviewers by providing information that they think interviewers want to hear. In order to avoid such criticism, many interviewers refrain from providing emotional support in investigative interviews and rather adapt a neutral style. However, as discussed later in this chapter, it is possible to design a non-suggestive yet supportive rapport-building session which better meets the emotional needs of allegedly abused children.

NEW GUIDELINES FOR ENHANCING RAPPORT BUILDING

Recognizing the need to enhance rapport with allegedly abused children, and especially with reluctant children, I. Hershkowitz, M.E. Lamb, and C. Katz (manuscript in preparation) have begun revising the NICHD Protocol. Insights from previous studies indicated that supportive comments and prompts should be built into this revision of the NICHD Protocol.

In order to enhance children's trust and cooperation, accordingly, rapport building precedes (rather than follows) the explanation of the ground rules and expectations, and additional guidance is provided to interviewers with respect to building and maintaining rapport. In addition to inviting a narrative about recent experiences during the rapport-building phase, interviewers are encouraged to express interest in the children's experiences, both verbally and non-verbally, specifying that body posture (leaning toward the children), smiling and eye contact may signal their interest. Because the NICHD Protocol did not include instructions to address feelings expressed by the children, the revised Protocol specifies the need to address children's feelings by one or more of the following means: acknowledging the feelings, echoing them, or exploring them with open-ended invitations. Expressions of empathy with the children's expressed feelings regarding the interview experience, but not regarding past experiences, were also encouraged. Similarly, positive reinforcement of the children's efforts, but not the specific content of their statements, was also recommended.

In a recent study conducted in Israel, 1424 4- to 13-year-old suspected victims of intra-familial abuse, who are more likely to be reluctant than suspected victims of extra-familial abuse (Hershkowitz, Lamb, & Horowitz, 2007), were interviewed using either the conventional NICHD Investigative Interview Protocol (n = 613) or the revised version (n = 811). Although a more systematic exploration of the data is still needed, preliminary analyses point to the beneficial effects of the revised Protocol on both children's willingness to disclose abuse and on reduced reluctance during the interview once they have disclosed. In addition, a second interview in which interviewers had another opportunity to establish and further strengthen rapport with the children further enhanced disclosure even among the most reluctant children.

In addition to the revised NICHD Protocol, a new version of the NICHD Protocol has been designed for children and adults with learning difficulties. Because evidence shows that people with learning difficulties are more likely to experience abuse but at the same time less likely to disclose the abuse (see Chapter 13; Hershkowitz *et al.*, 2007), the special guidelines included instructions for enhancing rapport and support. This Protocol is currently being applied and tested in Israel.

THE CHALLENGE FOR CHILD INVESTIGATORS: PROVIDING NON-SUGGESTIVE SUPPORT

The employment of supportive techniques may reduce anxiety among children and help them cope with feelings of shame and guilt during the interview, thereby allowing them to discuss the abuse. However, interviewer's support is a double-edged sword and may be highly suggestive if interviewers use support to selectively reinforce certain kinds of statements or to approve feelings associated with the abuse. Thus, it is crucial that only non-suggestive support be used and that this support involves positive reinforcement of the children's efforts, but not of the specific content of their statements. Similarly, expressions of empathy with the children's expressed feelings regarding the interview experience, but not regarding past experiences, are recommended. The following suggested techniques can be used to encourage truthful disclosures and to enhance narrative production once children have disclosed abuse.

Non-specific Support

1. *Welcoming the child:* I am glad to meet you today/glad we get to talk.
2. *Expression of personal interest in the child:* I really want to get to know you/ about things that have happened to you.
3. *Expression of care:* I care about you/your well-being is important to me.
4. *Checking on the child's feelings:* How are you doing?/How do you feel now?
5. *Reinforcement:* You are really helping me to understand/You are working very hard, and that is important.
6. *Small gestures of good will:* Are you cold?/Let me show you where the toilet is/Here is a glass of water for you.
7. *Thanks and appreciation:* I want to thank you for your help/I really appreciate your efforts.

When the child has *expressed* specific difficulties disclosing/elaborating:

8. *Empathy:* I know it is difficult for you to talk/I know it's been a long interview.

9. *Legitimating expressions:* You can talk about bad things and good things/In this office, you can talk about everything/It is OK to tell this kind of thing/to say these words/bad words.
10. *Generalization of the child's difficulties:* Many children find it difficult to tell/feel ashamed initially.
11. *Expression of confidence / optimism:* You can make it/Of course you can tell.
12. *Reassurance:* Don't worry, I won't tell other children/you won't be late for the bus/nobody is going to arrest you/we will finish shortly.
13. *Offering help:* What can help you tell?/You can write that/You start talking, and I will help you.

When the child shows reluctance to disclose/elaborate. Note: The following techniques should be used *only* if there is strong evidence for the abuse. If evidence is weak, these prompts can be formalized in a generalized way as follows:

14. *Expression of worry:* I am worried about you/that something happened to you. [*Generalized way:* My job is to check that children are well, and I am worried when things happen to them.]
15. *Containment:* I am here to listen to you if something happened I am the person to tell/you can trust me if... [*Generalized way:* I listen to children when something has happened to them/Children can trust me when something has happened to them.]
16. *Encouragement:* Please tell me if something has happened to you/It is really important that you tell if... [*Generalized way:* Children need to tell if.../It is important that children tell if . . .]
17. *Removing responsibility from the child:* If something has happened, it is not your fault/You are not responsible for that. [*Generalized way:* When something happens to children, it's not their fault/Children are not responsible when things happen to them.]

When the child *expresses* distressing emotions. Note: In this input-free format, the following prompts can be used also to address emotions experienced during the substantive event and reported by the child:

18. *Exploring emotions:* Tell me more about your fear/What are you ashamed about?
19. *Acceptance:* You say. . . . I understand what you say/I see what you are saying.
20. *Echoing the child's words:* You say you were frightened.

Inappropriate responses:

21. *Ignoring the child's emotion/difficulties/worries/wishes:* Child: Mom hit me and I was sad; Interviewer: What happened after your Mom hit you?
22. *Negative response to expressed difficulties:* Come on, you are not a little child/We are wasting time.
23. *Suggestive support:* Any of the above techniques used to reinforce the contents of the statements or the use of 14–17 when there is no evidence of abuse.

CONCLUSIONS

There is growing evidence that attempts should be made by interviewers to establish rapport with all children, and particularly with less talkative or reluctant children, when conducting investigative interviews. Rapport building should preferably involve open-ended invitations that encourage children to describe personally meaningful experiences. The preferred duration of rapport building should be a function of the children's attention span and based on the optimization of their cognitive resources; too lengthy rapport building can be counterproductive, at least for preschoolers. The NICHD Investigative Protocol includes a useful sequence of prompts designed to help build rapport with children in the pre-substantive part of the interview. However, effective rapport building is not just about addressing those prompts to the children, but also about evaluating their verbal and non-verbal responses to these prompts and ensuring that children are engaged and cooperative before any discussion of the possibility of abuse begins. A promising supportive approach to rapport building is currently being tested in the field. Child investigators are urged to continue employing a supportive approach when first exploring the possibility that abuse occurred and throughout the entire interview in order to maintain the motivation and competency of the children. It is crucial that supportive comments in the substantive phase of the interview be carefully worded in a non-suggestive manner to avoid the risks of contamination. A list of suggested supportive techniques to be used and those to be avoided is provided above, together with examples illustrating the contexts in which they can be used safely.

REFERENCES

Aldridge, M., & Wood, J. (1998). *Interviewing Children: A Guide for Child Care and Forensic Practitioners*. New York, USA: John Wiley & Sons Ltd.

Boggs, S.R., & Eyberg, S. (1990). Through the eyes of the child: Obtaining self-reports from children and adolescents. In A.M. La Greca (Ed.), *Interview Techniques and Establishing Rapport* (pp. 85–108). Needham Heights, MA: Allyn & Bacon.

Bottoms, B.L., Quas, J.A., & Davis, S.L. (2007). The influence of the interviewer-provided social support on children's suggestibility, memory and disclosures. In M.E. Pipe, M.E. Lamb, Y. Orbach, & A.C. Cederborg (Eds), *Child Sexual Abuse: Disclosure, Delay, and Denial* (pp. 135–157). Mahwah, NJ: Erlbaum.

Carter, C.A., Bottoms, B.L., & Levine, M. (1996). Linguistic and socioemotional influences on the accuracy of children's reports. *Law and Human Behavior*, *20*, 335–358.

Collins, R., Lincoln, R., & Frank, M.G. (2002). The effect of rapport in forensic interviewing. *Psychiatry, Psychology and Law*, *9*, 69–78.

Cornah, C.E., & Memon, A. (1996). Improving children's testimony: The effects of social support. Presented at the biennial meeting of the American Psychology–Law Society, Hilton Head, TX.

Davies, G.M., Westcott, H.L., & Horan, N. (2000). The impact of questioning style on the content of investigative interviews with suspected child sexual abuse victims. *Psychology, Crime and Law*, *6*, 81–97.

Davis, S.L., & Bottoms, B.L. (2002). Effects of social support on children's eyewitness reports: A test of the underlying mechanism. *Law & Human Behavior*, *26*, 185–215.

Fisher, R.P., & Geiselman, R.E. (1992). *Memory-Enhancing Techniques for Investigative Interviewing: The Cognitive Interview*. Springfield, IL: Charles C. Thomas.

Goodman, G.S., & Bottoms, B.L. (1993). *Child Victims, Child Witnesses: Understanding and Improving Testimony*. New York, NY: Guilford Press.

Goodman, G.S., Bottoms, B.L., Schwartz-Kenney, B., & Rudy, L. (1991). Children's memory for a stressful event: Improving children's reports. *Journal of Narrative and Life History*, *1*, 69–99.

Goodman, G.S., Sharma, A., Thomas, S.F., & Considine, M.G. (1995). Mother knows best: Effects of relationship status and interviewer bias on children's memory. *Journal of Experimental Child Psychology*, *60*, 195–228.

Greenstock, J., & Pipe, M.E. (1996). Interviewing children about past events: The influence of peer support and misleading questions. *Child Abuse and Neglect*, *20*, 69–80.

Greenstock, J., & Pipe, M.E. (1997). Are two heads better than one? Peer support and children's eyewitness reports. *Applied Cognitive Psychology*, *11*, 461–483.

Hershkowitz, I. (2009). Socioemotional factors in child abuse investigations. *Child Maltreatment*, *14* (2), 172–181.

Hershkowitz, I., Horowitz, D., & Lamb, M.E. (2005). Trends in children's disclosure of abuse in Israel: A national study. *Child Abuse and Neglect*, *29*, 1203–1214.

Hershkowitz, I., Horowitz, D., & Lamb, M.E. Individual and family variables in non-allegations of abuse. (2007). In M.E. Pipe, M.E. Lamb, Y. Orbach, & A.C. Cederborg (Eds), *Child Sexual Abuse: Disclosure, Delay, and Denial*. Mahwah, NJ: Erlbaum.

Hershkowitz, I., Lamb, M.E., & Horowitz, D. (2007). Victimization of children with disabilities. *American Journal of Orthopsychiatry*, 77(4), 629–635.

Hershkowitz, I., Orbach, Y., Lamb, M.E., Sternberg, K.J., & Horowitz, D. (2006). Dynamics of forensic interviews with suspected abuse victims who do not disclose abuse. *Child Abuse and Neglect*, *30*, 753–769.
Home Office. (2002). *Achieving Best Evidence in Criminal Proceedings: Guidance for Vulnerable and Intimidated Witnesses, Including Children*. London: Home Office.
Hynan, D.J. (1999). Interviewing: Forensic psychological interviews with children. *Forensic Examiner*, *8*, 25–28.
Imhoff, M.C., & Baker-Ward, L. (1999). Preschoolers' suggestibility: Effects of developmentally appropriate language and interviewer supportiveness. *Journal of Applied Developmental Psychology*, *20*, 407–429.
Kanfer, R., Eyberg, S.M., & Krahn, G.L. (1992). Handbook of clinical child psychology. In C.E. Walker, & M.C. Roberts (Eds), *Interviewing Strategies in Child Assessment* (pp. 49–62). Oxford, UK: John Wiley & Sons.
Lamb, M.E., Hershkowitz, I., Orbach, Y., & Esplin, P.W. (2008). *Tell Me What Happened: Structured Investigative Interviews of Child Victims and Witnesses*. New York and Chichester, England: Wiley.
Lamb, M.E., Orbach, Y., Warren, A.R., Esplin, P.W., & Hershkowitz. I. (2007). Enhancing performance: Factors affecting the informativeness of young witnesses. In M.P. Toglia, J.D. Read, D.F. Ross, & R.C.L. Lindsay (Eds), *Handbook of Eyewitness Psychology*, Volume 1: *Memory for Events* (pp. 429–451). Mahwah, NJ: Erlbaum.
Lamb, M.E., Sternberg, K.J., & Esplin, P.W. (1998). Conducting investigative interviews of alleged sexual abuse victims. *Child Abuse and Neglect*, *22*, 813–823.
London, K., Bruck, M., Ceci, S.J., & Shuman, D.W. (2005). Disclosure of child sexual abuse: What does the research tell us about the ways that children tell? *Psychology, Public Policy, and the Law*, *11*, 194–226.
London, K., Bruck, M., Ceci, S.J., & Shuman, D.W. (2007). Disclosure of child sexual abuse: A review of the contemporary empirical literature. In M.E. Pipe, M.E. Lamb, Y. Orbach, & A.C. Cederborg (Eds.), *Child Sexual Abuse: Disclosure, Delay and Denial* (pp. 11–40). Mahwah, NJ: Erlbaum.
McBride, K.L (1996). Child sexual abuse investigations: A joint investigative approach combining the expertise of mental health and law enforcement professionals. *Dissertation Abstracts International: Section B: The Sciences and Engineering*, 56, 51–52.
Morgan, M.K., & Friedemann,V.M. (1988). Abuse and religion: When praying isn't enough. In A.L. Horton, & J.A. Williamson (Eds), *Interviewing Children about Sensitive Topics* (pp. 145–155). Lexington, MA: Lexington Books/D.C. Heath and Co.
Moston, S. (1992). Social support and children's eyewitness testimony. In H. Dent, & R. Flin (Eds), *Children as Witnesses* (pp. 33–46). Oxford, UK: John Wiley & Sons.
Orbach, Y., Hershkowitz, I., Lamb, M.E., Sternberg, K.J., Esplin, P.W., & Horowitz, D. (2000). Assessing the value of structured protocols for forensic interviews of alleged child abuse victims. *Child Abuse and Neglect*, *24*, 733–752.
Orbach,Y., Shiloach, H., & Lamb, M.E. (2007). Reluctant disclosers of child sexual abuse. In M.E. Pipe, M.E. Lamb, Y. Orbach, & A.C. Cederborg (Eds), *Child Sexual Abuse: Disclosure, Delay and Denial* (pp. 115–134). Mahwah, NJ: Erlbaum.

Poole, D.A., & Lamb, M.E. (1998). *Investigative Interviews of Children: A Guide for Helping Professionals*. Washington, DC: American Psychological Association.

Powell, M.B., & Lancaster, S. (2003). Guidelines for interviewing children during child custody evaluations. *Australian Psychologist, 38*, 46–54.

Powell, M.B., & Thomson, D.M. (1994). Children's eyewitness-memory research: Implications for practice. *Families in Society, 75*, 204–216.

Ricci, C.M., Beal, C.R., & Dekle, D.J. (1996). The effect of parent versus unfamiliar interviewers on children's eyewitness memory and identification accuracy. *Law and Human Behavior, 20*, 483–500.

Roberts, K.P., Lamb, M.E., & Sternberg, K.J. (2004). The effects of rapport-building style on children's reports of a staged event. *Applied Cognitive Psychology, 18*, 189–202.

Ruddock, A.C. (2006). The relationship of interviewer rapport behaviors to the amount and type of disclosure from children during child abuse investigations. Dissertation Abstracts International: Section B: The Sciences and Engineering, *67*(4-B), 2241.

Saywitz, K.J., Goodman, G.S., Nicholas, E., & Moan, S.F. (1991). Children's memories of a physical examination involving genital touch: Implications for reports of child sexual abuse. *Journal of Consulting and Clinical Psychology, 59*, 682–691.

Siegman, A.W., & Reynolds, M.A. (1983). Effects of mutual invisibility and topical intimacy on verbal fluency in dyadic communication. *Journal of Psycholinguistic Research, 12*, 443–455.

Sternberg, K.J., Lamb, M.E., Hershkowitz, I., Yudilevitch, L., Orbach, Y., Esplin, P.W., & Hovav, M. (1997). Effects of introductory style on children's abilities to describe experiences of sexual abuse. *Child Abuse and Neglect, 21*, 1133–1146.

Tobey, A.E., & Goodman, G.S. (1992). Children's eyewitness memory: Effects of participation and forensic context. *Child Abuse and Neglect, 16*, 779–796.

Teo, Y.S., & Lamb, M.E. (2010). Preparing children for investigative interviews: Rapport-building, instruction, and evaluation. *Applied Developmental Science, 14*, 154–163.

Warren, A.R., Woodall, C.E., Hunt, J.S., & Perry, N.W. (1996). 'It sounds good in theory, but . . .': Do investigative interviewers follow guidelines based on memory research? *Child Maltreatment, 1*, 231–245.

Westcott, H.L., & Kynan, S. (2006). Interviewer practice in investigative interviews for suspected child sexual abuse. *Psychology, Crime and Law, 12*, 367–382.

Wood, J.M., McClure, K.A., & Birch, R.A. (1996). Suggestions for improving interviews in child protection agencies. *Child Maltreatment, 1*, 223–230.

Yuille, J.C., Hunter, R., Joffe, R., & Zaparniuk, J. (1993). Interviewing children in sex abuse cases. In G. Goodman, & B. Bottoms (Eds), *Child Victims, Child Witnesses: Understanding and Improving Children's Testimony: Clinical, Developmental and Legal Implications* (pp. 95–115). New York: Guilford Press.

7

Practice Narratives

Kim P. Roberts, Sonja P. Brubacher, Martine B. Powell, and Heather L. Price

Key Points

- *Memory practice:* children need to practise remembering information. This reduces the mental effort needed when the allegations are later discussed.
- *Practice narrative/practice interview:* asking children questions about a recent event before the allegations are raised.
- *Substantive phase:* the part of the interview where the allegations are discussed. This occurs immediately after the practice interview.
- *Rapport building:* time spent early on in the interview helping children to feel comfortable and that the interviewer is interested in them and what they have to say.
- *Episodic memory:* memory for an event (an 'episode') that takes place at a specific time and place.
- *Repeated-event memory:* memory for events that have happened more than once.
- *Open-ended questions:* questions that invite children to choose what information to report and to report it in their own words (e.g., 'Tell me what happened.' 'You said that he played a game with you. Tell me everything that happened when he played the game.')

Children's Testimony: A Handbook of Psychological Research and Forensic Practice, Second Edition.
Edited by Michael E. Lamb, David J. La Rooy, Lindsay C. Malloy, and Carmit Katz.

- Giving the child practice in remembering and reporting information from memory subsequently leads to longer and more accurate reports about the allegations.
- Giving the interviewer practice in asking open-ended questions reduces the chances that less desirable questions are asked in the substantive phase.
- Good practice interviews follow the same recommendations as all investigative interviewing (i.e., reliance on open-ended questions).
- Practice interviews lead to a decrease in the number of questions interviewers have to ask.
- Interviews containing practice interviews do not take longer than interviews without practice interviews.

An investigative interview is a complex social situation which can place great demands on both the interviewee and the interviewer. Simple and easy-to-use techniques that enhance the accuracy and completeness of witness and victim statements are highly valued. One such technique is known as the practice interview or practice narrative phase. A practice narrative phase comprises a few minutes in the interview when child witnesses and interviewers have the opportunity, respectively, to practise responding to and asking questions similar to those recommended by experts when asking about alleged abuse. Importantly, this narrative practice takes place *within* the same investigative interview and not at a different time; the practice is ideally done immediately before children are interviewed about any allegations. An extract from a practice narrative is shown in Box 7.1.

Box 7.1: Excerpt from practice interview

Interviewer: Was there something fun or special that has happened in your life recently?
Child: Um, well, getting an A plus plus on my presentation today.
I: Yep.
C: Really um, makes me happy. Because usually my mum helps me a lot with uh, my pres uh my presentations and I always get really good marks. And I've never thought that I'd be able to get a good mark on my own, and so I tried it and I did get a really good mark.
I: Good for you.
(pause)
I: Well you know what, I'd really like to know more about that. So I would like you to tell me everything that you can remember about your presentation, from the very beginning to the very end.

C: Well, um, um, we're doing autobiographies and biographies and we get to pretend that we're a person that we read about.
I: Yep.
C: And I pretended to be J.K. Rowling, the author of uh, Harry Potter.
I: Mmm-hmm (positive)
C: And so I brought in all my Harry Potter books and I bought a little doll, pretending it's my baby. And then, I gathered a whole bunch of information and put it into a presentation.
I: Mmm-hmm (positive)
C: But first it started out like um, my real name is Joanne Kathleen instead of J.K. Rowling.
I: Mmm-hmm (positive)
C: And uh, I told them about uh, stuff that uh, stuff that happened to J.K. Rowling in her life and um, like what her books are called.
I: (interrupts) Yeah.
C: Stuff that happened in her books and uh how her her first book was ch- uh it's title was changed.
I: Mmm-hmm (positive)
C: And um, . . .uh I talked about all her other books and I brought in a little safe with a Terry Fox coin cause I um, another boy did Terry Fox and I thought I'd say 'Oh well when I was getting a tour of the school I saw Terry Fox so I thought I'd bring in a coin.' And um, then I started talking about J.K. Rowling's life, like her husband, and her daughter.

The results of this practice interview are obvious. The 10-year-old witness is responding fully and informatively to the questions and requests from the interviewer. Further, the child is describing a personal event, much like they will be asked to do when the interviewer moves on to talk about the allegations. It is highly likely that the child will continue responding in this informative way throughout the remainder of the interview.

In this chapter, we provide clear evidence of the benefits of incorporating practice into investigative interviews. The evidence is based on carefully conducted research on investigative interviews of children as well as research conducted with a high degree of experimental control in research laboratories. Collectively, these studies and their authors support the use of the practice interview. We begin the chapter by demonstrating the logged benefits of a practice interview, followed by a breakdown of the specific advantages that can be achieved. Although the benefits are clear, there are several concerns that need to be addressed when considering the use of a practice interview. Such concerns include the time it takes to conduct a practice interview and the fear that the child becomes fatigued before full disclosure is achieved. We address each concern in turn and hope to demonstrate that these concerns are either unjustified, minimal or are greatly outweighed by the benefits. We conclude by addressing practical ways to conduct a good-quality practice interview.

RATIONALE: WHY A PRACTICE NARRATIVE IS IMPORTANT AND USEFUL

Several researchers have documented clear evidence that what occurs immediately before discussing the allegations is closely related to the quality of reports about those allegations (Roberts, Lamb, & Sternberg, 2004; Sternberg *et al.*, 1997). For example, Sternberg *et al.* (1997) asked investigative interviewers to establish rapport with alleged victims using either open-ended questions (e.g., 'Tell me about yourself') or direct focused questions (e.g., 'How old are you?'). When subsequently asked about the alleged incidents, children in the open-ended condition reported 2.5 times more relevant details in their first response than did children in the direct condition. Sternberg *et al.* argued that children in the open-ended condition had learned how to answer open-ended questions informatively.

More recently, Price, Collins, and Roberts (2009) have found that the quality of interactions prior to asking about the allegations is followed by predictable behaviour. Price *et al.* found that when investigative interviewers conduct practice interviews using a high proportion of open-ended questions (i.e., a quality practice interview), children go on to report proportionally more information about alleged abuse in response to open-ended prompts than children who received a practice interview characterized by fewer open-ended questions.

As the research by Sternberg *et al.* and Price *et al.* was conducted in the field with the participation of investigative interviewers and alleged child victims of abuse, these studies provide clear evidence that using a practice interview is related to the quality of children's testimony in investigations of abuse. As none of the alleged incidents of abuse were recorded, however, we do not know whether the practice affected the accuracy of children's reports. A critic might wonder whether children are merely feeling pressured to talk, and consequently describe events regardless of whether they happened or not.

The issue of accuracy was explored in the study by Roberts *et al.* (2004), which attempted to replicate Sternberg *et al.*'s (1997) findings under controlled conditions. Children aged 3–9 years participated in a staged event comprising forensically relevant details such as dressing, undressing and taking photographs. The children were interviewed 1 week or 1 month later. Immediately before asking about the staged event, interviewers attempted to establish rapport using open-ended or direct styles, as in Sternberg *et al.*'s study. Interviewers followed a script when asking about the staged event to control for differences between interviewers. Children in the open-ended condition provided more accurate reports than children in the direct condition after both short and long delays. These effects were observed even for very young children. With the exception of responses to the first question, 3- to 4-year-olds provided more accurate reports after practice responding to open-ended questions than counterparts in the direct condition.

As well as rapport building, practice interviews can help children practise retrieving information from memory. The National Institite of Child Health and Human Development (NICHD) Interview Protocol (see Chapter 6) includes a recommendation to use the practice phase to ask children about a recent event (e.g., first day of school). Price *et al.* (2009) examined child abuse allegations made after a practice narrative phase. After participating in a practice interview, children provided a greater average number of details in response to each question than allegations made in interviews without a practice phase. That is, practised children were willing to talk longer each time a question was posed. Importantly, interviewers who conducted a practice phase also asked fewer questions in the allegations phase, yet their witnesses provided the most detailed reports.

Collectively, these studies conducted in the field and in controlled laboratory settings show that asking children open-ended questions to establish rapport or encourage reports about a recent event are often followed by longer and more accurate reports about events relevant to the investigation. We can therefore conclude that practice interviews serve a very important purpose and we recommend their use in investigative interviews.

WHAT SHOULD YOU EXPECT FROM A PRACTICE NARRATIVE? COGNITIVE AND MOTIVATIONAL ADVANTAGES OF PRACTICING NARRATIVES

The importance of language and memory in investigative interviews is obvious. Comprehending questions, retrieving memories, and describing memories are cognitive skills that children develop gradually. Using these cognitive skills can also greatly tax children's attention and lead to mental fatigue. Using a practice interview can lessen the cognitive demands of an interview and the evidence for this assertion is presented below. Even if children are able to complete an investigative interview without much mental effort, it does not guarantee that they will cooperate. As well as being able to retrieve relevant information, children must be willing to disclose information. Thus, we also outline below the ways in which practice interviews can be used to increase children's willingness to talk. The advantages of practice interviews are summarized in Box 7.2.

Box 7.2: Summary of benefits of narrative practice

- Enables child to practise remembering events
- Enables child to retrieve specific details about individual events rather than just the gist
- Enables child to practise responding to open-ended questions
- Helps build and maintain rapport between child and interviewer
- Motivates child to provide full descriptions of what happened
- Gives interviewer practice in asking the recommended type of questions

Memory Practice

Psychologists sometimes test children's mental flexibility using a sorting task. For example, imagine 20 cards lain out on a table top; some cards have pictures of rabbits on them and some have trucks; 10 rabbit and 10 truck cards are yellow, the rest are red. Children are first asked to sort objects as fast as they can by, for example, colour ('Give me the red pictures'). When children have shown successful mastery on this criterion, they are asked to sort by a different criterion, for example, objects ('Give me the rabbit pictures'). Children typically make predictable errors on the first few trials of a new criterion; they continue to use the old criterion, for example, sorting by colour even though the colour is no longer relevant. This is known as *perseverance* because children persevere with an old strategy that is no longer appropriate for the new task. Although these errors decrease with age, their presence continues into adulthood (Zelazo, Frye, & Rapus, 1996).

However, it is possible to harness children's perseverance 'errors' to enhance their testimony. In a quality practice interview using open-ended questions, children practise retrieving information without external cues from interviewers, and practise reporting the information in narrative form (e.g., as a description of an event including details about actions, conversations, the order in which things happened). Persevering in using the memory and language skills that children have been using in the practice phase, then, ensures that the same skills are used when they are asked about the allegations. As there is sometimes suspicion that young children, especially, cannot answer open-ended questions (Lamb, Sternberg, & Esplin, 2000), such memory practice is critical to a narrative account of the alleged events.

Episodic Recall

Many jurisdictions require that alleged child victims of abuse provide descriptions of events that specify a particular episode (*R. v. B.(G.)*, 1990; *S. v. R.*, 1989). A description of a specific episode influences the charge that can be laid against the alleged perpetrator, gives him/her an opportunity to fully defend the allegations and influences sentencing if found guilty (Powell, Roberts, & Guadagno, 2007).

The way children talk about an event, or series of events, is strongly influenced through their interactions with adults with whom they converse, and is shaped by their expectations of what the adult is asking (Fivush & Shukat, 1995). As such, practising recalling and reporting episodic information should translate into a substantive phase that is characterized by a high proportion of episodic details, language and interviewer prompts. Episodic language use is often indicated by past tense verbs (e.g., 'we went'), and reference to temporal markers (e.g., 'it was Tuesday'), and is contrasted with generic language which is characterized by the use of the impersonal pronoun 'you' and the present tense ('the timeless present'; Nelson & Gruendel, 1986).

The excerpt in Box 7.1 shows how the interviewer is encouraging the child to describe a specific event bounded by time and place. Notice how this child is using 'episodic language' when reporting what she remembers, for example, saying *I bought* and *I gathered* (thus referring to distinct actions) rather than the more generic 'I buy' and 'I gather' (which refer to these actions in general, as in 'I buy toys at holiday time').

Thus, the goal of engaging in episodic recall practice (i.e., describing an autobiographical event from the past) is to assist children in enhancing the amount of event-specific or episodic information they can provide, and to minimize use of generic statements.

Practice in recalling episodes is especially important when children make allegations of a repeated nature. Roughly 50% of child complainants in published studies of investigative interviews of child abuse allege that the abuse was repeated. Children find it easier to describe what usually happens when an event has been repeated than to describe a specific episode such as what happened the 'last time' they engaged in the activity (Fivush, Hudson, & Nelson, 1984). Even children as young as 3 years can describe highly familiar events, such as going to a restaurant, in general terms, although their narratives include relatively few details (Hudson, Fivush, & Kuebli, 1992). However, research has also shown that children can be encouraged to describe individual events episodically when asked directly about specific episodes (e.g., Fivush *et al.*, 1984). The issue, then, is that children naturally tend to describe repeated events in generic terms (describing what usually happens) but legal systems require descriptions of one or more specific episodes.

Thus, it is especially important to give children an opportunity to practise recalling specific episodes to offset the natural tendency to describe events in general if the child has been the victim of multiple and chronic abuse.

Responding to Open-ended Questions

During the practice phase, interviewers have the opportunity to 'train' children in the types of questions/prompts that will be used when the allegations are later discussed, and to give children realistic expectations about how much detail is needed in response to these prompts (Lamb, Hershkowitz, Orbach, & Esplin, 2008). There is clear consensus on the most desirable types of questions in investigative interviews of children, and the recommendation is to use 'open-ended' questions (Lamb *et al.*, 2008). Open-ended questions are those that give witnesses freedom to report what information they choose, they do not include information not yet mentioned by children and they encourage narrative responses (i.e., descriptions in sentences or pseudo-sentences). Take a look at the excerpt in Box 7.1 and see if you can find an interviewer utterance that meets the criteria of an open-ended question.

One example in the excerpt is the invitation to describe the presentation that the child just mentioned: 'I would like you to tell me everything that you can remember about your presentation, from the very beginning to the very end.' Notice how the interviewer has not specified what kind of information he/she wants the child to describe as would be the case with more focused prompts like 'What was your presentation about?', 'Tell me who went first' and 'Do you like giving presentations?' What is important about open-ended questions is that they encourage children to provide spontaneous descriptions and elaborative details (Saywitz & Snyder, 1996; Sternberg *et al.*, 1997; Sternberg, Lamb, Orbach, Esplin, & Mitchell, 2001).

Saywitz and Snyder (1996) have demonstrated training effects in children who learned to provide more elaborative responses prior to recall of a target (staged) event. These children were given instructions to talk about everything that happened, including the small details, but without making anything up. Visual cues were provided, the strategies were modelled for the children and feedback was given. These children reported a greater number of correct details about the event than children who were not as well trained in providing detailed descriptions. Importantly, the trained children did not report any more errors than untrained children.

Although using visual cues is usually not feasible in investigative interviews, Saywitz and Snyder's study shows that children clearly have the capacity to benefit from training in a practice phase.

Building Rapport

Children's abilities to communicate are influenced by social context and the general feeling of the interview environment (Lamb, Sternberg, & Esplin, 1995; Saywitz, Nathanson, & Snyder, 1993). From a child's perspective, an interview is an unusual, and possibly confusing, context; the child has to interact with an unfamiliar adult (Fisher & McCauley, 1995) and likely has to provide details that may be embarrassing, or that are not usually discussed outside of the family, or anywhere, for that matter. Additionally, children are quite used to being questioned by adults about things that they know the adult knows the answer to, which is usually not the case in an investigative interview (Fisher & McCauley, 1995). Thus, the practice phase allows the child to feel more familiar with the interviewer and the physical context.

The practice phase can be conducted as an extension to a rapport-building phase or in combination with a rapport-building phase. As the aim of a practice phase is to encourage children to describe a recent event that has some personal significance, the attentive listening of interviewers can signal interviewers' interest and sincerity towards child interviewees.

Thus, the practice phase can be used to build rapport between child and interviewer and, if rapport has already been established, the interactions in a practice phase can solidify and maintain rapport.

Increases in Motivation to Disclose

Practice in providing a narrative offers an opportunity for the child to feel successful. A good practice interview engages the child in active conversation, transfers control of the interview to the child and allows the child to feel as though he/she has something of value to contribute to the interaction. This enhanced feeling of control and usefulness, together with the rapport building described above, can give a child the motivation to continue to work to provide details through what can often be an arduous task. When a child feels motivated, it is likely that he/she will then also be willing to share more information with relatively less prompting. Indeed, Price *et al.* (2009) found that after participating in a practice interview, children in investigative interviews provided a greater amount of information in response to each question than children who were not practised. Fewer questions were posed by interviewers following practice phases and so it appears that practised children were willing to talk longer even though they were prompted less than the unpractised children. As the practised children were more likely to spontaneously describe events, there is a greater chance that their reports were more accurate than reports gleaned with much focused prompting by the interviewer.

Practice for the Interviewer

Finally, the advantages of practice interviews extend not just to the child, but also to the interviewer. Asking open-ended questions in real time during interviews takes considerable skill. The practice phase is an opportunity for interviewers to also 'get settled', get to know the children they are interviewing and to identify any cognitive or social issues that may be helpful to bear in mind such as regular mispronunciations or lack of eye contact. The practice phase is also a time to give interviewers practice in crafting questions that are open-ended in style and practice inhibiting the tendency to rush in with questions that limit children's responses.

Thus, the practice phase is important for interviewers to reach their own interviewing standards.

COMMON REASONS FOR NOT CONDUCTING A PRACTICE NARRATIVE

The benefits of using practice interviews are clear. But might there be some disadvantages that outweigh the benefits? Next, we document the most common concerns we have heard from investigative interviewers in our training courses, and consider the rationale and evidence behind the concerns. The concerns are summarized in Box 7.3.

Box 7.3: Most common concerns about the use of practice narratives

Fatigue/time issues

- Time constraints – engaging in a practice narrative might unduly lengthen the interview
- Fatigue – children may become too tired to subsequently talk fully about the alleged events
- Wanting to get to the point – interviewers must secure an account of abuse in order for a charge to be laid, and so may not want to 'waste time' talking about irrelevant information

Motivational issues

- The child has already disclosed – it may seem foolish or insensitive to stop the child talking about the alleged abuse
- Worries about losing/not establishing rapport – children may be suspicious as to why the interviewer is asking about recent events
- It might be difficult to find a suitable event to discuss
- Hard to see the purpose to a practice interview

Concerns About the Length of the Interview and Child Fatigue

On the surface, it seems logical that any time spent building rapport and practising episodic recall will add minutes to the interview. Supposing that were true, the research on the benefits of practice interviews detailed in this chapter show that those minutes have great payoffs. In a study by Brubacher, Roberts, and Powell (in press), the benefits of practising narratives were observed when interviewers were limited to 5–7 minutes of practice. In their analysis of practice interviews in child abuse investigations, Price *et al.* (2009) found that interviews with practice phases were *no longer* than interviews without practice. This may have been because interviewers had to ask more questions when children had not been given practice in providing narrative descriptions of events, thus lengthening the interview. Thus, practice interviews need not take a lengthy period of time.

Rather than making children tired, the practice phase prepares children to talk by focusing on events of interest to the children. We have described several studies to demonstrate that children provide *more* information if practised (Brubacher *et al.*, in press; Price *et al.*, 2009;

Sternberg *et al.*, 1997, 2001). As children who are practised willingly provide more information than children who are not given practice, it is hard to argue logically that practice interviews lead to fatigue. In all of the studies published thus far, children were alert, willing and able, after practice, to provide extensive amounts of information.

Sometimes, children might appear to 'want to get to the point', especially if they are uncomfortable in an interview context. A major component of a good interview is the child's willingness to talk (Lamb *et al.*, 2008) and so it may seem like a good idea to harness children's eagerness to talk and begin discussing allegations immediately. There are two potential downsides to getting the allegation before a practice phase has been conducted. First, children who do not provide much information in the practice phase are also reluctant to talk in the allegation phase, while the reverse is true for children who respond informatively and extensively in the practice phase (Hershkowitz *et al.*, 2006). It is possible that children who do not make descriptive allegations were never abused, but in Hershkowitz's study, there was 'compelling evidence' that all children had been abused. Secondly, it is highly unlikely that children will know just how much detail investigators need. Children may report the gist of what happened and be unaware that investigators need episodic detail about particular events. The bottom line: if children have not been adequately prepared, the interviewer risks never actually 'getting to the point'.

Motivational Issues

Because attentively listening to children describe a recent significant event conveys interest, concern and respect for children's knowledge and willingness to describe such knowledge, the practice interview is more likely to foster and maintain rapport than lead to a breakdown in rapport. In Hershkowitz *et al.*'s (2006) study, interviewers used fewer open-ended prompts, relied on risky focused questions and offered less support to the children who provided little information. The children who were the least likely to disclose, then, were the ones most in need of extended practice. According to Hershkowitz *et al.* (2006), 'using this simple, easy to apply, predictive indicator of informativeness, many reluctant disclosers can apparently be identified and given additional rapport-building and support before substantive issues are broached' (p. 767). Thus, practice interviews are ideal for establishing and maintaining rapport with witnesses.

Care must be taken to determine a suitable event to use for practice. Although often good candidate events, a holiday or birthday may not always be suitable for discussion (e.g., not recent enough, child does not celebrate occasion). In their field study, Price *et al.* (2009) report anecdotal information from interviewers suggesting difficulty in choosing a topic, and noted that more guidelines are needed in this area. Some suggestions for events are provided in the next section.

Finally, the purpose of a practice interview is not just to train child witnesses but to give interviewers important information that can be put to good use throughout the interview and investigation. Interviewers can learn about children's developmental levels, potential sources of misunderstanding, language capabilities and so on (Saywitz *et al.*, 1993). Spending 5 minutes talking about a neutral or positive event, then, can increase the chances that the investigator gets the full and reliable report that is desired and needed.

PRACTICAL GUIDELINES FOR PRACTICE NARRATIVE

In this final section we offer some practical suggestions for conducting practice interviews. These suggestions come from the scientific evidence reviewed above and our experience with investigators in a number of different jurisdictions. The primary aim of the practice interview is to model the upcoming interaction about the substantive issue(s). That is, the practice interview should establish the pattern of communication the interviewer expects will elicit the most, and most accurate, recall when the allegations are discussed. Thus, many of the features of a quality practice interview will overlap with those recommended for effective investigative interviewing, and are summarized in Box 7.4.

Box 7.4: Features of a 'good' practice interview

- Identification of an episodic event of interest to the child (e.g., first trip to Disney World, a national holiday, recent birthday, winning a swimming competition – event must be a specific episode)
- Consistent use of open-ended prompts (e.g., 'Tell me everything that happened at your Grandma's 90th birthday party.' 'What else happened?')
- Consistent use of episodic language (e.g., 'Tell me about the last time she hit you' (vs. 'Tell me about the hitting'), 'I'd really like to hear what happened' (vs. 'I'd really like to hear what happens')
- Selective use of motivational phrases (e.g., 'I'm really interested in hearing more about X')
- One- to two-second pauses between prompts so the child can collect her/his thoughts

- Appropriate closure of the practice interview (e.g., 'You did a great job telling me all about Halloween')
- Clear transition to substantive issue (e.g., 'Now that I know you better, I'd like to talk about why I'm here today')

Identification of an Episodic Event

Price *et al.* (2009) found that many of the interviewers in their study reported difficulty choosing a topic for discussion, and suggested that perhaps a 'cheat sheet' could be created with a list of possible topics. Some possible events are in the public domain, such as the first day of school and national holidays such as Independence Days. Other possible events are tied to a particular culture or religion such as Christmas Day, the first day of Hannukah, or Ramadan. These latter events are suitable when interviewers have knowledge about children's cultural background and children can identify a specific episode. It is also possible to ask parents, teachers, siblings, and so on about what recent significant events have happened in the child witness' life. Another possibility is to ask children about their hobbies, interests, and lessons during rapport building, and then use one of these as a topic for discussion in the practice phase. Brubacher *et al.* (in press) found that recreational activities (e.g., swimming, hockey, soccer) or other weekly activities/meetings (e.g., church, scouts, girl guides) were popular events. Some children in their study did not engage in any type of organized activity, and so interviewers asked them to describe specific classes in a subject that was only held once or twice a week (e.g., music, art).

It is essential that the chosen event refers to an event that has only happened once or a specific episode of a repeated event. Brubacher *et al.* (in press) had children aged 5–8 years participate in a similar event on four different days. When children were later asked to practise recalling an episode of a repeated event (parents nominated events, e.g., the child's last dance lesson), clear benefits were observed for the younger children (5- to 6-year-olds). These children reported more details specific to one of the four events than children who practised recalling general features (e.g., what dance lessons are like). They were also much more likely to tell the interviewer early on in the interview that they had done the event multiple times, and they spontaneously mentioned more differences across the four events (e.g., by saying the badge they wore each day was different). The children who practised general features of events provided less distinctive information, that is, the kind of information that helps particularize a single episode, including temporal and other contextual information that would assist in laying a charge (Powell *et al.*, 2007).

Consistent Use of Open-ended Prompts and Episodic Language

Open-ended prompts are, without doubt, the most successful type of interview question in producing spontaneous descriptions from children. Many studies have demonstrated that open-ended questions elicit more information from children about the allegations (e.g., Lamb *et al.*, 1996; Sternberg *et al.*, 1996), and this information also tends to be more often confirmed, and thus more likely to be accurate (Lamb, Orbach, Hershkowitz, Esplin, & Horowitz, 2007). Interviewers may find themselves, however, slipping into more focused questioning, and so the practice phase allows interviewers to practise crafting open-ended questions and thus prevent the use of risky techniques in the allegation phase.

Children should be encouraged to use episodic language in their practice narratives. If children use the present tense when describing the past, it can signal that they are actually describing 'what usually happens' during a series of repeated events (e.g., 'we go', 'you have fun'). It is important for interviewers to be aware of such language so that they can ensure that children are talking about just one experience. When describing the child's *last* birthday, statements such as 'we *get* cake' and 'my mum *puts* the presents on the front table and I *can't* open them until after everyone *comes*', are indicative that the child is not accessing a specific episode. It then becomes important for interviewers to guide children back to episodic recall.

The easiest way of encouraging children to report an episode/single event is for the interviewer to use episodic language. In a recent laboratory study by Brubacher *et al.* (in press), interviewers were trained to conduct a practice phase using episodic language ('Tell me what happened') or generic language ('Tell me what happens'). The children in this study responded in kind; when interviewers used episodic language, 93% of the children's utterances were episodic, whereas only 19% were episodic when interviewers used generic language. Further, the children who gave episodic narratives continued to use episodic language when asked about the target event suggesting that they were accessing memories of one-time episodes.

CONCLUSIONS

The scientific evidence is clear: providing practice for children to recall and report events from memory enhances the quality of children's testimony. Spending just a few minutes encouraging children to talk freely about a recent event that is meaningful to them can subsequently lead to the reporting of critical, forensically relevant information that might otherwise not be obtained. As rapport is enhanced in a practice phase, child witnesses also benefit from a greater level of comfort in interview contexts. Thus, for social and cognitive reasons, we fully recommend the incorporation of a practice narrative phase in investigative interviews of alleged child abuse victims.

REFERENCES

Brubacher, S.P., Roberts, K.P., & Powell, M.B. (in press). Interviewing children about a repeated event: Does prior practice in describing a specific instance of an unrelated repeated event improve the amount and quality of elicited information? *Psychology, Public Policy, & Law*.

Fisher, R.P., & McCauley, M.R. (1995). Improving eyewitness testimony with the cognitive interview. In M.S. Zaragosa, J.R. Graham, G.C.N. Hall, R. Hirschman, & Y.S. Ben-Porath (Eds), *Memory and Testimony in the Child Witness* (Vol. 1, pp. 141–159). Thousand Oaks, CA: Sage.

Fivush, R., Hudson, J.A., & Nelson, K. (1984). Children's long-term memory for a novel event: An exploratory study. *Merrill-Palmer Quarterly*, *30*, 303–316.

Fivush, R., & Shukat, J.R. (1995). Content, consistency, and coherence of early autobiographical recall. In M.S. Zaragoza, J.R. Graham, G.C.N. Hall, R. Hirschman, & Y.S. Ben-Porath (Eds), *Memory and Testimony in the Child Witness* (Vol. 1, pp. 5–23). Thousand Oaks, CA: Sage.

Hershkowitz, I., Orbach, Y., Lamb, M.E., Sternberg, K.J., Pipe, M.E., & Horowitz, D. (2006). Dynamics of forensic interviews with suspected abuse victims who do not disclose abuse. *Child Abuse and Neglect*, *30*, 753–769.

Hudson, J.A., Fivush, R., & Kuebli, J. (1992). Scripts and episodes: The development of event memory. *Applied Cognitive Psychology*, *6*, 483–505.

Lamb, M.E., Hershkowitz, I., Orbach, Y., & Esplin, P.W. (2008). *Tell Me What Happened: Structured Investigative Interviews of Child Victims and Witnesses*. Chichester: John Wiley & Sons.

Lamb, M.E., Hershkowitz, I., Sternberg, K.J., Esplin, P., Hovav, M., Manor, T., & Yudilevitch, L. (1996). Effects of investigative utterance types on Israeli children's responses. *International Journal of Behavioural Development*, *19*, 627–637.

Lamb, M.E., Orbach, Y., Hershkowitz, I., Esplin, P., & Horowitz, D. (2007). Structured forensic interview protocols improve the quality and informativeness of investigative interviews with children. *Child Abuse and Neglect*, *31*, 1201–1231.

Lamb, M.E., Sternberg, K.J., & Esplin, P.W. (1995). Making children into competent witnesses: Reactions to the amicus brief in re Michaels. *Psychology, Public Policy, & Law*, *1*, 438–449.

Lamb, M.E., Sternberg, K.J., & Esplin, P.W. (2000). Effects of age and delay on the amount of information provided by alleged sexual abuse victims in investigative interviews. *Child Development*, *71*, 1586–1596.

Nelson, K., & Gruendel, J. (1986). Children's scripts. In J. Gruendel (Ed.), *Event knowledge: Structure and Function in Development*. Erlbaum: Hillsdale, NJ.

Powell, M.B., Roberts, K.P., & Guadagno, B. (2007). Particularisation of child abuse offences: Common problems when interviewing child witnesses. *Current Issues in Criminal Justice*, *19*, 64–74.

Price, H.L., Collins, A., & Roberts, K.P. (2009). The effects of a practice interview on interviewer behaviour and the informativeness of children's reports. Paper presented at the meeting of the American Psychology–Law Society, San Antonio, Texas, USA, March 2009.

R. v. B.(G.), [1990] 2 S.C.R. 3.

Roberts, K.P., Lamb, M.E., & Sternberg, K.J. (2004). The effects of rapport-building style on children's reports of a staged event. *Applied Cognitive Psychology*, *18*, 189–202.

S. v. R. (1989). 89 A.L.R., 321.

Saywitz, K.J., Nathanson, R., & Snyder, L.S. (1993). Credibility of child witnesses: The role of communicative competence. *Topics in Language Disorders*, *13*, 59–78.

Saywitz, K.J., & Snyder, L.S. (1996). Narrative elaboration: Test of a new procedure for interviewing children. *Journal of Consulting and Clinical Psychology*, *64*, 1347–1357.

Sternberg, K.J., Lamb, M.E., Hershkowitz, I., Esplin, P., Redlich, A., & Sunshine, N. (1996). The relation between investigative utterance types and the informativeness of child witnesses. *Journal of Applied Developmental Psychology*, *17*, 439–451.

Sternberg, K.J., Lamb, M.E., Hershkowitz, I., Yudilevitch, L., Orbach, Y., Esplin, P.W., & Hovav, M. (1997). Effects of introductory style on children's abilities to describe experiences of sexual abuse. *Child Abuse and Neglect*, *21*, 1133–1146.

Sternberg, K.J., Lamb, M.E., Orbach, Y., Esplin, P.W., & Mitchell, S. (2001). Use of a structured investigative interview protocol enhances young children's responses to free recall prompts in the course of forensic interviews. *Journal of Applied Psychology*, *86*, 997–1005.

Zelazo, P.D., Frye, D., & Rapus, T. (1996). An age-related dissociation between knowing rules and using them. *Cognitive Development*, *11*, 37–63.

8

Investigating Substantive Issues

Yael Orbach and Margaret-Ellen Pipe

Key Points

- *Substantive phase*: the substantive phase is the part of the forensic interview during which the interviewer obtains information about a suspected/alleged event.
- *Objective*: the goal of the substantive phase is to obtain as much uncontaminated allegation-specific information about the event as possible.
- *Interviewing strategy*: the interviewing strategy involves an evidence-based plan dictating the optimal procedures for fulfilling the objective.
- *Recommended practices*:
  - Giving priority to open-ended 'input-free' prompts and techniques to elicit testimony from free-recall memory in the child's own words.
  - Minimizing potential contamination by delaying the use of focused prompts until open-ended prompts and techniques have been exhausted and by eliminating suggestive practices.
  - Adapting interviewing practices to children's strengths and limitations, as well as to their motivational level.
  - Enhancing support for child witnesses, especially those who are reluctant to disclose their suspected experiences of abuse.
  - Providing extended feedback monitored training to investigators.

Children's Testimony: A Handbook of Psychological Research and Forensic Practice, Second Edition.
Edited by Michael E. Lamb, David J. La Rooy, Lindsay C. Malloy, and Carmit Katz.

- *Rationale*:
  - Input-free prompts and techniques tap children's *'free-recall'* processes, which are more likely than *'recognition memory'* processes to involve the retrieval of highly accurate information.
  - Focused prompts like *'yes / no'* and *'choice questions'* tap 'recognition memory' processes, which are more likely than *'input-free'* prompts to elicit erroneous information.
- *Structure*: a funnel-shaped hierarchical structure is recommended, with open-ended prompts used early in the interview, and progressively more focused questions used only later in the interview.
- *Conclusion*: enhancing the informativeness of forensic interviews would help child protective services, clinicians, police detectives, and law professionals to make informed decisions, thus protecting vulnerable children from further abuse and avoiding the wrongful incrimination of innocent persons.

THE SUBSTANTIVE PHASE OF INVESTIGATIVE INTERVIEWS

The substantive phase of an investigative interview is the portion of the interview during which the interviewer obtains information from a witness on the suspected/alleged incident(s) under investigation. Although the forensic interview is only a part of the investigative process and has to be viewed in the context of the complete investigation, it is a highly significant source of forensic evidence, often from a sole witness to the investigated event. Evidence gained in forensic interviews with child witnesses is particularly important in legal systems that recognize the 'hearsay exception', allowing children's videotaped out of court statements and forensic interviews with no corroborative evidence to be presented in court in lieu of testimony (e.g., *Ohio v. Roberts,* US Supreme Court, 1980; see Chapter 15). Although in the United States the Supreme Court ruling in *Crawford v. Washington* in 2004 (US Supreme Court, 2004) limited the hearsay exception to 'non-testimonial' statements (in addition to those admitted under 'excited utterances' and 'statements provided during medical diagnosis and treatment'), which could have had important implications for cases of child sexual abuse, it is argued that the court decision of 2004 "may not impact most child abuse cases" (Vieth, 2004, p. 2; for discussion see also Goodman, 2006; Myers, 2006). In many countries, moreover, there is no legal obstacle to the introduction of investigative interviews as evidence in court.

Both the structure and interviewing practices recommended for the substantive phase of forensic interviews draw heavily on empirical evidence generated in laboratory and field research. This research has led to broad consensus about children's limitations and competencies as witnesses and suggests that children can remember and report accurate information about incidents they have experienced, provided they are positively motivated and appropriately interviewed. In other words, much of the burden of responsibility is on the investigative interviewers. Their main challenge during the substantive phase is to motivate child witnesses to be cooperative and to provide effective retrieval conditions that prompt children to provide reliable, informative, and rich accounts of their suspected/alleged experiences. In line with these objectives, the substantive interview draws on the pre-substantive preparation of child witnesses for their task as information providers, both motivationally, through supportive rapport building and the empowerment of children as unique sources of information (see Chapter 6), and cognitively, through clarification of the interview ground rules and practice opportunities with the substantive questioning procedures, the expected response type and the level of detail (see Chapter 8). Indeed, it is important to recognize that although our focus in this chapter is on the substantive phase of the investigative interview, effective elicitation of substantive information during this phase is highly likely to depend on the 'groundwork' of the pre-substantive phase on which it builds. Readers are encouraged to review these earlier chapters to place the recommendations outlined here in the appropriate context.

In order to minimize the degrading effects of delay on the quality, completeness, and richness of children's testimony and on their susceptibility to suggestion, it is recommended that children be interviewed as soon as possible after the occurrence, disclosure, or suspicions of the suspected/alleged offence(s). Further, interviewers should elicit forensically relevant information using primarily open-ended 'input-free' prompts to obtain children's testimony from free-recall memory in the child's own words, to both minimize potential contamination and maximize the quality and accuracy of the provided information. The 'quality' of the substantive information obtained from suspected/alleged victims of abuse, both how central it is to the investigated allegation(s) and how it is elicited, is likely to have a significant effect on the witness's perceived credibility and reliability, the admissibility of the child's statement under the exceptions to the rule against hearsay, as well as the nature of the charges on which the suspect is convicted/acquitted. Ultimately, it is also likely to affect legal decision making in the criminal justice system (Pipe, Orbach, Lamb, Abbott, & Stewart, 2009). Adherence to recommended interviewing practices during the substantive phase therefore not only contributes to the protection of victimized children, but also minimizes the risks of eliciting false reports of abuse when abuse did not occur, thus avoiding false incriminations of innocent persons.

INTERVIEWING STRATEGIES AND PRACTICES AND RATIONALE FOR THEIR USE

Research conducted in controlled laboratory settings where the accuracy of information can be determined, together with that conducted in the field based on actual investigative interviews in which an objective record of the investigated incident was available, has demonstrated that the most important determinant of the accuracy and richness of detail of the information elicited from young children is the way the information is elicited. Appropriately, much attention has focused on investigative prompts and techniques most likely to yield reliable detailed disclosures and accounts from children suspected of having been abused.

Many research studies, in particular controlled laboratory-based studies, have been concerned with how the formulation of a question affects the accuracy and detail in children's responses, comparing, for example, 'WH'-questions ('who', 'when', 'where', 'what'); 'yes/no' questions ('Did he have a bird?'); 'choice' questions ('Were your pants on or off at that time?'); or 'tag' questions ('He was drunk, wasn't he?'). In forensic contexts, however, an analysis of the effect of prompt type on the quality or likely accuracy of the elicited information cannot solely rely on how a question has been formulated or posed. The following, for example, is an interviewer prompt taken from a field forensic interview and illustrates the problem: 'Tell me about everything that happened when you were in the bathtub.' This prompt may seem like an open-ended 'invitation' to tell everything that happened. However, because prior to the introduction of this prompt, the child had only mentioned that the perpetrator *asked him/her* to get into the bathtub, and not that he/she actually *did* that, this open-ended prompt is in fact highly 'suggestive'; it assumes the occurrence of an unreported action and asks the child to elaborate on that assumed (and potentially forensically significant) action (see Chapter 2).

Researchers at the National Institute of Child Health and Human Development (NICHD) therefore introduced a categorization system that takes account not only of the way in which a question or prompt is posed, but also whether the interviewer introduces, either implicitly or explicitly, information that the child has not already reported ('interviewer input'; Orbach *et al.*, 2000; Sternberg, Lamb, Orbach,

Esplin, & Mitchell, 2001). In this analysis, prompts range from the most open-ended input-free, to the most closed option-posing or even suggestive questions where the interviewer provides the response alternatives and/or suggests the appropriate response. The inclusion of interviewer input in the analysis means that identically formulated prompts that have been introduced at different temporal points within the substantive interview may be very different with respect to their suggestiveness (and potentially contaminating content), depending on the information disclosed by the child prior to their introduction. It is therefore important that the interviewer is aware of the need not only to avoid 'suggestive questions' and particular types of questions, but also to avoid introducing previously undisclosed details and implying that they may have been part of the investigated event, until the end of the interview when other means of eliciting critical details have been exhausted. The way questions are formulated is, of course, still important, especially when, for example, questions are repeated and there is pressure to respond. For instance, a third repetition of a 'yes/no' question that, by implication, casts doubt on the truthfulness of child's response (e.g., 'Are you sure?' or 'Is that true?'), or repeatedly asking about the same (interviewer-introduced) issue, might exert pressure on the interviewee to doubt or change his/her earlier response and would be highly suggestive. We discuss styles of prompting that are suggestive and are to be avoided in further detail below.

The effectiveness of retrieval prompts and techniques in eliciting accurate information from children is highly correlated with the type of memory processes they tap. Input-free prompts and techniques tap children's 'free-recall' processes, which are more likely than recognition memory processes to involve the retrieval of highly accurate information. Most focused prompts – 'yes/no' and 'choice questions' – that tap 'recognition memory' processes involve the confirmation, negation or selection of interviewer-given rather than child-generated options and are more likely than input-free prompts to elicit erroneous information (see Chapter 3).

Experimental studies in both analogue and forensic contexts have shown that freely recalled information, elicited in response to open-ended input-free prompts (e.g., 'Tell me everything you remember…') in the child's own words, is three to five times longer, more detailed and more accurate than information elicited in response to focused-recognition questions, involving the selection of interviewer-given options (e.g., 'Did that happen before or after he locked the door?'). Such focused-recognition prompts typically increase the probability of erroneous responses, regardless of the child's age (e.g., Bruck & Ceci, 1999). Therefore, reliance on open-ended prompts and techniques during the early stages of the substantive investigative interview, before the interviewer introduces any information, can be expected to yield greater amounts of uncontaminated information as well as to reduce acquiescence to misleading information introduced later in the interview. In addition, longer narrative accounts that are elicited by appropriate open-ended input-free prompting are more amenable to credibility assessment, using the Criterion Based Content Analysis (CBCA). A broad-based international consensus has been reached regarding the superiority of open-ended input-free interviewing strategies.

HIERARCHICAL STRUCTURE OF THE SUBSTANTIVE INTERVIEW

The structure of the substantive phase of the forensic interview is designed to enhance its unique function to elicit reliable, accurate, and rich forensically informative accounts. A funnel-shaped hierarchical structure (modelled after Yuille & Cutshall, 1986, 1989), is recommended with open-ended input-free prompts and techniques, the most desirable means of eliciting information, represented by the top wider end of the funnel, and focused-recognition prompts, the least desirable eliciting means, represented by the bottom narrower end of the funnel. Thus, the funnel represents the desired distribution of prompts, prioritizing open-ended input-free prompts and techniques as the most desirable eliciting means in terms of both how often and when they are used. Note that the funnel approach applies to the structure of the substantive phase of the interview *as a whole* in the first instance, and not to questioning about specific incidents or topics within the interview. Interviewers adhering to the best-practice recommendations would not only use more input-free practices throughout the interview, they would also postpone the introduction of any focused question until after the exhaustion of open-ended techniques and then only use them if essential information is still missing, avoiding the use of direct questioning for topics that have already been described in response to open-ended prompts. Postponing the introduction of more focused prompts and questions until after the disclosure of most of the allegation information minimizes the potential for contamination of children's accounts by interviewer input. Moreover, focused questions would only be introduced toward the end of the interview if open-ended techniques have failed to elicit information critical to the investigation: it is not mandatory that the funnel be pursued from top to bottom; if children provide the necessary detail in response to the most open-ended prompting, this approach should be pursued.

The use of the 'verbal contextual cueing' techniques and the 'pairing' principle, described in more detail below, facilitate the maintenance of this optimal structure even when it has been necessary to be more focused in eliciting specific information of interest. Field studies of investigative interviews have demonstrated that contextual cueing techniques (Tulving, 1983), based on the interviewee's verbal reports, and the 'pairing' principle (i.e., following each of the child's responses to focused prompts with input-free questioning) offer effective alternatives to focused-recognition prompts and enable interviewers to extend input-free questioning without reverting to less desirable recognition prompts. By extending input-free practices, both techniques create additional 'mini funnels' in the final stages of the substantive interview.

SEQUENTIAL ORGANIZATION OF THE SUBSTANTIVE INTERVIEW

Transition to Substantive Issues

The transition to the substantive phase of the interview starts when the interviewer attempts to shift attention from the pre-substantive rapport building and preparation to substantive issues, using a series of prompts intended to non-suggestively probe the identification of the target event(s) under investigation. The series of 'getting the allegation' (GTA) prompts ranges from open-ended to option-posing (options presented by the interviewer), each anchored by a rationale for its specific wording and order in the sequence. It opens with a sequence of input-free open-ended prompts designed to probe the child to raise a source of concern or make an allegation, while avoiding any interviewer input about a possible incident, beginning with 'Now that I know you a little better, I want to talk about why [you are here] today.' If the child does not make any reference to an issue that would be a cause for concern, the interviewer continues with a more direct statement: 'I understand that something may have happened to you. Tell me everything that happened from the beginning to the end.' If the child still does not identify the target event(s) and does not make any reference to an issue that would be a cause for concern, the interviewer continues with gradually more focused prompts and may use some external information (when applicable), for example, 'I've heard that you talked to [a doctor/a teacher/a social worker/any other professional] at [time/location]. Tell me what you talked about' or 'Did someone do something to you that you don't think was right?' At any moment during the transition phase, if the child makes reference to an issue that might be a cause for concern or makes an allegation, the interviewer would start the substantive open-ended phase by prompting free-recall: 'Tell me everything that happened from the beginning to the end' (expected to trigger the child's first narrative response about the investigated incident). If the child does not make an allegation in response to the last prompt in the series of the transition prompts, the interviewer shifts to the closing section of the interview, while communicating to the child that if he/she wishes to talk at a later time the interviewer will always be available (while providing the child with contact information).

Open-ended Free-recall Phase

Once the child makes an allegation, the interviewer begins the free-recall investigative phase with the first scripted substantive invitation: 'Tell me everything that happened from the beginning to the end as best you can.' As soon as the first narrative is completed, the interviewer prompts the child to indicate whether the incident occurred 'one time or more than one time', before proceeding to secure incident-specific information using open-ended prompts and techniques. If the incident occurred more than one time, the interviewer should communicate to the child the need to report event-specific memories and should direct the child to start reporting about the event he/she remembers the best, while labelling each event with the order of its occurrence (i.e., first, last or the one you remember the best), or with the label used by the child (e.g., indicating 'location' or a witness). For example: 'Tell me everything about the last time [the first time/the time in [some location]/the time [some specified activity/another time you remember well] something happened', or 'Tell me about the time at your grandma's house' [when a time at grandma's house has been mentioned by the child]. Focusing on event-specific information will help to differentiate among multiple occurrences of abuse and will minimize the retrieval of generic statements and script descriptions based on features common to the multiple events, typical of reports of multiple similar occurrences, rather than on the distinctive features of each specific event.

Open-ended Input-free Elaboration

After securing event-specific information, interviewers make use of input-free invitational prompts for eliciting additional uncontaminated free-recall elaboration, including, *general invitations*, making reference to the disclosed allegation (e.g., 'Tell me everything about...'), *follow-up invitations*, making reference to the latest content mentioned (e.g., 'Then what happened?' or 'Tell me more about that'), *cued-invitations*, making references to specific details mentioned by the child, for requesting free-recall elaboration (e.g., 'Earlier you mentioned a [person/object/action]. Tell me everything about that'), or *temporal invitational cues*, making reference to disclosed actions for requesting free-recall elaboration on what happened during a segment of time immediately prior, following, or between the disclosed actions (e.g., 'Tell me everything that happened before/after [a disclosed action]', or 'Tell me everything that happened from the time of [a disclosed action] to the time of [another disclosed action]'. Following the retrieval of the first narrative in the substantive phase, the interviewers are given only general guidance regarding desirable practices to employ (i.e., prioritizing free-recall and recall prompts and techniques) and undesirable practices to avoid (i.e., prompts introducing information that the child has not reported, options suggested by the interviewer), while adapting their investigative practices to children's responses, without having to follow an inflexible script. The interviewers may continue, using a variety of follow-up input-free open-ended prompts (e.g., 'Tell me more about that'; 'Then what happened?') and cueing techniques, focusing on contents disclosed by the child (e.g., 'Tell me more about [person/object/activity mentioned by the child]'; 'Think back to that [day/night] and tell me everything that happened from [some preceding action mentioned by the child] until [the most recent action described by the child])' to investigate the allegation. Interviewers are encouraged to maximize the opportunities provided to children of all ages to recall information in response to input-free prompts and techniques, to give children the opportunity to elaborate on all allegation-specific (central) details of each specific incident before shifting attention to another alleged incident in cases of multiple incidents, and to check that they have indeed covered all the allegation aspects, using open-ended practices, before moving on to the use of directive prompts.

Using Focused Directive Prompts

After exhausting the use of free-recall prompts and techniques for exploring the alleged incident(s), if details critical to the investigation have not yet been provided by the child, interviewers may proceed to directive questions that refer to previously disclosed details and provide a category (mostly 'WH') for requesting undisclosed central allegation-related information (e.g., 'Where was it?'; 'When did it happen?'), necessary to fully investigate the disclosed allegation. It is recommended that interviewers first refocus the child's attention on the detail he/she mentioned, and then ask the direct question, for example, 'You mentioned [person/object/activity], when/what/where [completion of the direct question]?'. Whenever possible, following directive prompts with open-ended invitations (a practice labelled as 'pairing') is recommended.

A Break

It is recommended that once interviewers feel that they have exhausted all open-ended practices for investigating the allegations and have reached the stage at which open-ended prompts are no longer effective in producing new information and the contextual cues (cued invitations) that can be generated from the child's narrative have been exhausted, they would pause for a short break to consult with colleagues, who have been monitoring the process of the interview from remote, on any missing issue in their investigation that they could follow up on still using open-ended practices, prior to using recognition prompts. Only then interviewers would continue to carefully plan their use of recognition prompts to investigate critical allegation-related issues that were not disclosed by the child in the open-ended phase of the interview. Using a scripted prompt: 'Now I want to make sure I understood everything and see if there is anything else I need to ask. I will just [think about what you told me/go over my notes/go and check with X],' the interviewer conveys that to the child. While planning the rest of the interview, interviewers should plan to pair focused questioning with open-ended prompts (e.g., 'Tell me all about that') whenever possible. If the child has not made an allegation by this point, however, the interviewer may review possible barriers and additional strategies to explore, or may decide to end the interview and continue it at another time. During interviewers' consultation, the child remains in the interview room. There are, at present, no scripted instructions for the child during this break although a common activity used is counting to 100. This is an area in which further research is necessary. Clearly, the child should not be engaged in any activity that is likely to lead to confusion when the interviewer returns as to the purpose of the interview and the focus on the alleged events.

Using Recognition Prompts

Optimally, it is not until all open-ended retrieval means have been exhausted that a limited number of focused-recognition prompts (i.e., 'yes/no' and 'choice' questions) may be introduced during the substantive phase of the forensic interviews, and that is only recommended for obtaining missing forensically crucial information at the end of the interview, so as to minimize the potential for contamination of the information reported following it. It is recommended that even when interviewers uses focused (directive or recognition) prompts to obtain undisclosed forensically important information, the information request is contextualize (e.g., 'When you told me about [specific incident identified by time or location] you mentioned [person/object/activity]. Did/was [focused questions]?'), and upon receiving a response to each of the focused prompt, interviewers revert back to open-ended practices (i.e., 'pairing').

Obtaining Information About the Disclosure

Although children's reports on how information about the investigated event(s) became known to persons other than the victim, suspect and witnesses, if there were any, does not constitute substantive information, some field practitioners found that posing disclosure questions following the substantive phase of the interview may elicit investigative leads that will contribute to obtaining substantive evidence and to better understanding of substantive issues. As a result, questions concerning disclosure history have been developed as a follow-up to the substantive phase of the interview, prior to shifting to neutral non-substantive conversation. If the child has mentioned telling someone about the incident(s), the interviewer asks: 'Tell me everything you can about how [the first person mentioned by the child] found out,' and continues with a series of scripted questions (e.g., 'Now I want to understand how other people found out about [the last incident]'; or 'Who was the first person besides you and [the perpetrator] to find out about [alleged abuse as described by the child]?'), repeating the entire section with respect to each of the incidents described by the child.

Closing

Upon the completion of the substantive questioning phase, interviewers give children an opportunity to ask questions, if they have any, and then thank children for their cooperation and assistance in providing valuable information, shifting to neutral topics for closing.

IMPLEMENTING INTERVIEWING STRATEGIES: PROMPT TYPES AND RATIONALE FOR THEIR USE

The whole structure of the investigative interview follows from the interviewing strategies and is, therefore, in turn based on the rationale and evidence base for these strategies. The following is the sequence of interviewing prompt types and techniques, based on the extent of interviewer input, from the most to the least open, and their recommended use.

Input-free Open-ended Free-Recall Prompts and Techniques

Input-free open-ended prompts and techniques include questions, statements or imperatives, as well as contextual cues, built on disclosed information, prompting free-recall responses in the child's own words. They may be formulated as '*invitations*' – including '*general invitations*', which do not delimit the child's focus except in a general way (e.g., 'Tell me everything that happened from the beginning to the end, as best as you can remember'); '*follow-up invitations*', which limit the child's response to what happened following the last disclosed action or invite elaboration on the last disclosed content (e.g., 'Then what happened?'; 'Tell me more about that'); '*cued invitations*', referencing a disclosed content and prompting for additional free-recall elaboration (e.g., 'Earlier you mentioned a [person/object/action]. Tell me everything about that'); or '*time segmenting cues*', using a disclosed action as a temporal reference point for prompting additional information about segments of time prior to, following or during two such actions (e.g., 'Tell me everything that happened before/after you went into the bathroom' ['we went into the bathroom' was mentioned by the child]; 'Tell me everything that happened from the time you went into the bathroom to the time you came out of the bathroom' [both actions were mentioned by the child]); or '*summaries*' – accurate input-free restatements of what the child has just said, without any explicit request for information or further questioning built on the rephrased statement (e.g., 'You said that you locked the door because he asked you to do that').

Note that '*facilitators*' – non-suggestive encouragement to continue with an ongoing response (e.g. 'OK', 'Uhuh' or repetition of the last few words spoken by the child) are not considered independent utterances, because they have been shown to encourage children to continue their ongoing responses to the preceding prompt (Hershkowitz, 2002). Thus, information provided by children following facilitators is attributed to the preceding utterance.

Maximizing Input-free Open-ended Prompts and Techniques

It is recommended that interviewers prioritize input-free open-ended prompts and delay the introduction of directive prompts until they have exhausted input-free prompts and techniques. Reliance on input-free open-ended prompts and techniques during the early stages of the substantive investigative interview, prior to the introduction of any input, including the 'WH' category input intrinsic to the open-ended directive prompts, is expected to contribute to maximizing the amounts of free recall information provided by child witnesses in the initial phase of the substantive interview. It is expected that 'WH' information about the investigated event would be provided by children either spontaneously, in response to invitations or in response to input-free contextual cues, used by the interviewers to enhance memory elaboration (Lamb *et al.*, 2003).

Directive Prompts

Directive prompts refocus children's attention on details of the alleged incident they had already given, and request additional information, mostly using 'WH' categories. These are formulated as either open-ended prompts – who, what, where, when, how (e.g., 'When did that happen?'; 'Where were you when that happened?'; 'What did he say?' [when 'he talked to me' was mentioned by the child]) or focused (narrow) prompts – 'WH' question plus a content category (e.g., 'What colour was his car?' [when 'his car' was mentioned]; 'Who locked the door?' [when 'the door was locked' was mentioned]).

Focused Recognition Prompts (Option-posing)

Option-posing prompts reference new issues that the child has not addressed earlier in the interview and present interviewer-given options for confirming, negating or selecting, mostly using 'yes/no' or 'choice' questions, *without implying the expected response*; or casting doubt over children's statements.

Option-posing prompts may be formulated as 'yes/no' questions (e.g., 'Did he say anything when he did that?'; '*choice*' questions (e.g., 'Did he touch you over or under your clothes?'), or '*casting doubt*' (e.g., 'Is what you're telling me true?'; 'Are you sure?') questions.

Minimizing the Use of Focused Recognition Prompts

Minimizing the use of focused 'yes/no' and 'choice' questions, limiting their use only for obtaining undisclosed forensically essential information, delaying their introduction to the end of the interview and 'pairing' them with a series of open-ended questioning, would reduce the risk of contaminating and compromising children's testimony, especially when the interviewees are very young (Lamb, Hershkowitz, Orbach, & Esplin, 2008; Poole & Lamb, 1998).

Suggestive Prompts

One of interviewers' challenges in conducting forensic interviews is to avoid the use of suggestive prompts and practices. *Suggestive* prompts introduce undisclosed input – contents unmentioned by children earlier in the interview, *mostly communicating the expected response*, and potentially contaminating any further information provided by the child. Suggestive prompts may mislead children into responding affirmatively, confirming non-experienced events or event components, or acquiescing to interviewers' explicit or implicit assumptions. Such potentially contaminating prompts may be drawn on the interviewers' own hypotheses, interpretations, or knowledge from external sources. Suggestive prompts may be formulated as either statements (e.g., "I understand that he told you to keep it a secret" ['secret' was not mentioned]), or questions (including 'open-ended', e.g., 'What did he say to you?' [when 'saying/talking' was not mentioned]; 'focused recognition', e.g., 'Was your mother there when he touched you?' [when the child did not mention that he/she was touched], or "Did it hurt when he touched you?' [when 'touch' was not mentioned]; 'tag', e.g., 'He must have touched you, didn't he?' [when 'touch' was not mentioned]; or repeated 'casting doubt' on the truthfulness of the witness' account, e.g., 'Is what you are telling me true?'; 'Did that really happen?'; 'Are you sure?').

Eliminating All Suggestive Practices

Although most guidelines and interviewing protocols recommend that suggestive utterances and practices are totally eliminated, failure of the child to mention crucial information (e.g., the suspect's name, the location of the incident, details of the allegation), assumed by the interviewer, or known to him/her from an external source (e.g., other witnesses, suspect, social worker, or parents), often triggers its introduction by the interviewer during the interview.

USING RESEARCH-BASED MEMORY ENHANCING TECHNIQUES

The broad consensus among experts and professional groups on children's abilities and limitations as witnesses, as well as on what constitutes best interviewing practices, led to many attempts to develop non-suggestive memory-enhancing techniques that will maximize the elicitation of free-recall information from child witnesses. Examples of memory-enhancing techniques demonstrated to be highly effective in field forensic interviewing.

Verbal Contextual Cueing

'*Verbal contextual cueing*' techniques, include '*cued-invitations*' and '*time segmenting cues*', use contents disclosed by the child earlier in the interview as contextual cues for eliciting further input-free elaboration on their initial disclosure, as an alternative to the risky recognition prompts (Lamb *et al.*, 2008; Orbach & Lamb, 2000); '*mental context reinstatement*' (MCR), a technique involving a free-recall guided mental reconstruction of the investigated event – a component of the cognitive interview (Geiselman *et al.*, 1984), adapted for use with child witnesses by Geiselman and Padilla (1988); and '*report every detail*', an input-free encouragement to report every detail of the investigated event, regardless of the perceived importance of the information – a component of the cognitive interview, adapted for use with child witnesses by Geiselman & Padilla (1988).

Representational Interviewing Aids

'*Representational Interviewing aids*', include the '*narrative elaboration technique*' (NET) – a cueing technique, using pictorial cards presenting four elaboration categories (participants, setting/location, actions and conversations) as reminders of what to talk about when reporting memories about experienced events (Dorado & Saywitz, 2001; Saywitz & Snyder, 1996), as well as '*drawings*', '*body diagrams*' and '*anatomically detailed dolls*', which provide children with alternative response modes to verbal communication for reporting bodily contact during alleged experiences of abuse (for review see Chapter 18).

ADAPTING INTERVIEWING PRACTICES TO CHILDREN'S DEVELOPMENTAL LEVEL

The reporting of episodic event memories involves different aspects of location and time. The development of different spatial (where an event occurred) and temporal (when an event occurred) concepts and the mastery of the related linguistic vocabulary are acquired by children at different developmental levels, however. The findings of a recent study on children's ability to report temporal information about experienced events demonstrate that although children as young as 4 years of age can reconstruct the temporal sequences of events they had experienced, the amount and types of information they provide about the timing of events (e.g., dating, temporal sequence, order, duration and frequency; Orbach & Lamb, 2007) steadily increase with age. Children's ability to temporally date events (i.e., indicate the month of a year, or a day of a month), for example, develops only after the age 10 years. Being aware of developmental trends, including children's age-related strengths and limitations, will enhance investigative interviewers' ability to obtain essential forensic information from children using age-appropriate techniques and discourage decision makers during the judicial process from discrediting children, or doubting their competence as witnesses, when they 'fail' to provide age-inappropriate conceptual information.

CONCLUSIONS

Maximizing non-suggestive input-free interviewing strategies, while adapting interviewing prompts and techniques to children's motivation level and to their developmentally related strengths and limitations, would enhance the elicitation of reliable information from child witnesses during the substantive phase of forensic interviews. Recommended interviewing strategies, 'translated' into easy to follow operational guidelines, along with extended feedback monitored training (see Chapter 11) should provide practitioners in the field with effective tools to maximize the elicitation of free-recall information from child witnesses of all ages. Moreover, memory-enhancing techniques would facilitate the elicitation of further free-recall elaboration from children, including preschoolers, once general invitations cease to be effective. In addition, enhancing support to child witnesses, including those who are reluctant to disclose their suspected experiences of abuse, would build up children's trust, motivation and cooperation, resulting in a retrieval of more complete forensically informative accounts.

In summary, ongoing effort to adapt optimal interviewing practices to children of all ages and to extend them to very young children and special witnesses' groups would further enhance the effectiveness of forensic interviewers in achieving their objective – obtaining allegation-specific information of superior quality and centrality, likely to be accurate, reliable and rich in detail, which would help child protective services, clinicians and law professionals make informed decisions both during treatment and throughout the legal procedures in the criminal justice system, thus protect vulnerable children from further abuse and avoid the wrongful incrimination of innocent persons.

REFERENCES

Bruck, M., & Ceci, S.J. (1999). The suggestibility of children's memory. *Annual Reviews of Psychology*, *50*, 419–439.

Crawford v. Washington, US Supreme Court (2004) (Lexis 1838).

Dorado, J.S., & Saywitz, K.J. (2001). Interviewing preschoolers from low- and middle-SES communities: A test of the Narrative Elaboration Recall Improvement technique. *Journal of Clinical Child Psychology*, *30*, 568–580.

Geiselman, R.E., Fisher, R.P., Firstenberg, I., Hutton, L.A., Sullivan, S.J., Avetissian, I.V., & Prosk, A.L. (1984). Enhancement of eyewitness memory: An empirical evaluation of the Cognitive Interview. *Journal of Police Science and Administration*, *12*, 74–80.

Geiselman, R.E., & Padilla, J. (1988). Cognitive interviewing with child witnesses. *Journal of Police Science and Administration*, *16*, 236–242.

Goodman, G.S. (2006). Children's eyewitness memory: a modern history and contemporary commentary. *Journal of Social Issues*, *62*, 811–832.

Hershkowitz, I. (2002). The role of facilitative prompts in investigative interviews with children. *Legal and Criminological Psychology*, *7*, 63–71.

Lamb, M.E., Hershkowitz, I., Orbach, Y., & Esplin, P.W. (2008). *Tell Me What Happened: Structured Investigative Interviews of Child Victims and Witnesses.* Oxford: Wiley-Blackwell.

Lamb, M.E., Sternberg, K.J., Orbach, Y., Esplin, P.W., Stewart, H., & Mitchell, S. (2003). Age differences in young children's responses to open-ended invitations in the course of forensic interviews. *Journal of Consulting and Clinical Psychology*, *71*, 926–934.

Myers, J.E.B. (2006). *Myers on Evidence in Child, Domestic and Elder Abuse Cases*. New York, NY: Aspen.

Ohio v. Roberts, US Supreme Court (1980) (No. 02-9410).

Orbach, Y., Hershkowitz, I., Lamb, M.E., Sternberg, K.J., Esplin, P.W., & Horowitz, D. (2000). Assessing the value of structured protocols for forensic interviews of alleged child abuse victims. *Child Abuse and Neglect*, *24*, 733–752.

Orbach, Y., & Lamb, M.E. (2000). Enhancing children's narratives in investigative interviews. *Child Abuse and Neglect*, *24*, 1631–1648.

Orbach, Y., & Lamb, M.E. (2007). Young children's references to temporal attributes of allegedly experienced events in the course of forensic interviews. *Child Development*, *78*, 1100–1120.

Pipe, ME., Orbach, Y., Lamb, M.E., Abbott, C., & Stewart, H. (2009). *Do Best Practice Interviews with Child Abuse Victims Influence Case Outcomes?* A paper summarizing a research project on the impact of the use of the NICHD Investigative Interview Protocol on case prosecution outcomes; funded under the NIJ FY06 Crime and Justice Research, National Institute of Justice Office of Justice Programs for Research Foundation of the City University of New York.

Poole, D.A., & Lamb, M.E. (1998). *Investigative Interviews of Children: A Guide for Helping Professionals*. Washington, DC: American Psychological Association.

Saywitz, K.J., & Snyder, L. (1996). Narrative elaboration: Test of a new procedure for interviewing children. *Journal of Consulting and Clinical Psychology*, *64*, 1347–1357.

Sternberg, K.J., Lamb, M.E., Orbach, Y., Esplin, P.W., & Mitchell, S. (2001). Use of a structured investigative protocol enhances young children's responses to free recall prompts in the course of forensic interviews. *Journal of Applied Psychology*, *86*, 997–1005.

Tulving, E. (1983). *Elements of Episodic Memory*. Oxford: Clarendon Press.

Vieth, V.I. (2004) Keeping the balance true: Admitting child hearsay in the wake of *Crawford v. Washington. American Prosecutors Research Institute (APRI), National Center for Prosecution of Child Abuse, Update 16*, Alexandria, VA.

Yuille, J.C., & Cutshall, J.L. (1986). A case study of eyewitness memory of a crime. *Journal of Applied Psychology*, *71*, 291–301.

Yuille, J.C., & Cutshall, J. (1989). Analysis of the statements of victims, witnesses and suspects. In J.C. Yuille (Ed.), *Credibility Assessment* (pp. 175–191). Norwell, MA: Kluwer Academic.

9

Reviewing the Case (Post-interview)

Trond Myklebust and Gavin E. Oxburgh

Key Points

In the investigation of an alleged offence, the investigative interview is one of the most, if not the single most, important component in the investigative process. In this chapter we outline the investigators' review of the case (post-interview) through the following key concepts:

- *The review process:* the importance of following up leads and of viewing the interview as simply a part of the entire investigation. Both the amount (quantity) and relevance (quality) of the information obtained in the interview are important issues. Evaluation methods such as Statement Validity Analysis (SVA) could be used in the analysis and review of the relevant investigative information.
- *The progression of cases:* despite international differences in judicial systems, the objective of the interview and the investigation is always the same – to gather reliable information. The main reason for lack of case progress is typically a shortage of valid and reliable information.
- *Decision-making processes:* to avoid investigative decisions based only on the investigators' individual heuristics, knowledge-based approaches at individual, group, and strategic levels are important.

Children's Testimony: A Handbook of Psychological Research and Forensic Practice, Second Edition.
Edited by Michael E. Lamb, David J. La Rooy, Lindsay C. Malloy, and Carmit Katz.

Implementation of modern and dynamic investigative procedures poses challenges for the management and leadership of the investigative process.

- *If the case is not ready to move forward, what happens next?*: stagnation in any case should call for thorough analysis of all relevant aspects using strategic approaches such as SWOT (Strengths, Weaknesses, Opportunities, and Threats) or content analysis such as SVA. In addition to ensuring that the mandatory legal processes and extant practice guidelines are followed, investigators and decision makers need to work out a concrete action plan about what should be done next to progress the case and to obtain further information of appropriate quality.

Following any interview, investigative teams must analyse the child's reports and make a decision about when (or if) the case is ready to move forward. The basic investigative questions to be raised by the investigators in their decision-making process include the following:

1. Is the information obtained from the child relevant to the investigation?
2. Are there other witnesses who need to be interviewed?
3. Is there any forensic evidence (e.g., medical, biological or electronic) that should be retrieved and analysed?
4. Is the child's account coherent and testable given any available or possible future evidence?
5. Does the child need to be re-interviewed?
6. Has any suspect/s been identified?
7. Do any other children require protection?

Whatever decision is made regarding the case moving forward, the reasons for this must be clear, agreed and documented by the investigation team. We now consider various issues that affect case progression and subsequent decision-making processes.

IS THE INFORMATION OBTAINED FROM THE CHILD RELEVANT TO THE INVESTIGATION?

To our knowledge, there exists no general and widely accepted classification system within police organizations to guide the effective analysis of the information gained from the child's interview. However, we would argue that, both nationally and internationally, investigators' decisions about the progress of the investigative process are based upon ad hoc considerations without reference to scientific studies. The information obtained from interviews has two main components: (i) the *quantity*, and (ii) the *quality*. If we consider the *quantity*, or amount of information, we could say that the more information available, the easier it is to make decisions about the likely outcomes. But it is also vitally important that all interviews should elicit good *quality* relevant information that establishes: (i) what happened; (ii) how the crime was committed; (iii) the persons involved; (iv) when and where the crime took place; and (v) any items that were used (if any) to assist in the commission of the offence(s) (Yuille & Cutshall, 1986).

One way to help determine whether the information obtained from a witness is truthful has been to use Statement Validity Analysis (SVA; Köhnken, 2004). The rationale behind SVA is the belief that a statement derived from the victim's memory of an actual experience differs in content and quality from a statement based on invention or fantasy. This is because truth tellers and fabricators have to meet different cognitive and motivational demands to appear credible (Steller, 1989; Undeutsch, 1967, 1982; Vrij, 2008). SVA consists of four stages: (i) a case-file analysis to gain insight into the case; (ii) a semi-structured interview to obtain a statement from the interviewee; (iii) a Criteria Based Content Analysis (CBCA) that systematically assesses the quality of statements; and (iv) an evaluation of the CBCA outcome via a set of questions (Validity Checklist). SVA is seen as an objective approach for joint police–social work investigative teams in England and Wales, employed to evaluate witness statements (Bradford, 1994), and is widely accepted in Europe. Others have urged caution and query the reliability and validity of the test (Davies, 1994). Like any other diagnostic procedure, it has its strengths, weaknesses and limitations (for an overview see Köhnken, 2004; Vrij, 2008).

There are various other aspects involved in the investigative process following the child's interview, including *objective* and *subjective* factors. The former includes details of the offence (e.g., physical abuse, sexual assaults), the number and duration of the offences (the account) and indeed whether the child was a victim or witness to the crime. The subjective factors are related to the child's perception of the event, and may include previous experiences and vulnerability in the situation. Regarding the child's account, there are three aspects that are often referred to by the investigators: the amount of relevant information in the child's statement; the child's emotions during the alleged offence; and the linguistic ability of the child. Unfortunately, it is demanding in the investigation process to separate between the child's linguistic ability, their respective emotions and details from the event. Not all countries have separate evaluation of the child's linguistic competence; hence, in some countries (e.g., Norway), the investigators, in most cases, have no prior knowledge about the child's linguistic or cognitive ability before the interview takes place. Considering all of the above information will help interviewers decide whether the child should be re-interviewed, especially when evidential inconsistencies arise during the investigation, and the investigator needs to decide whether other persons should be interviewed.

FORENSIC EVIDENCE TO BE RETRIEVED AND ANALYSED

Investigations must also be focused on additional forensic evidence. Such evidence includes medical and/or biological evidence (DNA, blood, hair, semen, and other human secretions) and electronic evidence (data stored in mobile devices, cameras, personal computers, and computer network servers). When obtaining additional forensic evidence, there is great potential, but challenges also arise. For example, in the case of electronic evidence, the law relating to enforcement agencies obtaining information stored on network servers differs greatly between countries. Forensic examination of impounded electronic equipment can also take several weeks or even months to analyse because of the amount of information involved. Information gathered through the child's interview will attempt to establish the allegation(s) and will have to be verified by statements from possible witnesses in addition to other forensic evidence as detailed above. Furthermore, in most cases, the child's description of the crime scene will have to be investigated in detail via a visit/inspection of the actual scene by members of the investigation team. Deciding how likely it is that an alleged offence took place does not follow nationally or internationally agreed clear guidelines; rather, an individual investigator makes decisions based upon his/her implicit assumptions about the evidence obtained (which includes the information provided in the child's interview).

CASE PROGRESSION

Regarding whether a case progresses, there are some differences in the decision-making procedures that are related to the individuals responsible, the legal jurisdiction and how the child will cope (emotionally and cognitively) in potential subsequent court procedures. For example, in England and Wales, the police are in charge of the entire investigation and forward each case to the Crown Prosecution Service (CPS) for legal advice on whether the case is ready for court purposes. In other judicial systems (e.g., Norway), the police conduct the initial investigation and work together with representatives from the prosecutors' office throughout the entire investigation. In Sweden, a preliminary pre-investigation is undertaken by the police, and this pre-investigation is then evaluated by the prosecution office who decide if a full investigation is required. The full investigation is then led by the police and transferred to the prosecution office for a decision whether the case evidence is sufficient to forward to the court for prosecution.

In the Nordic countries (Norway, Sweden, Finland, Denmark, and Iceland), the video of the child's interview is accepted in court as the evidence-in-chief, thus negating the requirement for the child to attend court, provide evidence or be cross-examined. In other words, the child's involvement in the judicial process, in almost all circumstances, comes to an end after the interview, even if the case is appealed (see Chapter 14). In Norway, the interview process is conducted by highly trained police officers in specially designed video interview suites, while a judge and counsel (prosecution, defence lawyer, and a legal representative* for the child) observe the interview in an adjoining monitor room via video link. The process of the interview and the presence of observers in the monitor room are normally explained to the child in a such a way that the child will understand. Towards the end of the interview, the interviewer is able to consult the judge, away from the child, for legal advice pertaining to the interview, and also to ask if the judge and/or counsel have further questions that they would like the interviewer to ask the child. Following this consultation process, the interview is concluded (Justisdepartementet, 1998; Myklebust, 2005, 2009). Next, the interview is transcribed, and this transcript will accompany the video and other case documents to the prosecutor who will decide on the progress of the case.

REASONS FOR LACK OF CASE PROGRESS

The lack of case progress is generally related to a shortage of valid and reliable information meeting the requirement to proceed. A challenge in many investigations is that almost all available information gathered through interviews of the victim, witnesses, and suspected offenders are verbal accounts of what happened with varying levels of detail and accuracy. Other factors that may affect case progress include the complexity of the case, the type of offence, number of investigating officers, the relationship between the victim and the offender, the delay since the alleged events occurred, and the effects of the case on the child's emotional needs (see Chapter 10) and intellectual ability (see Chapter 13). It is also important to gauge whether caregivers or other

*Appointed by the court pursuant of the Criminal Procedure Act.

individuals known to the child have suggestively influenced the child. Of critical importance is the degree to which the interviewer adhered to best-practice guidelines and whether they can justify any departures (see Chapter 17).

These aspects characterize the complexity and distinctiveness found in many cases and it is a challenge to decide where to focus resources in an effort to progress the case. If cases are forwarded to the court before enough evidence/information is available, the court may rule that there is insufficient evidence to proceed.

INVESTIGATIVE DECISION-MAKING PROCESSES

Generally, a large amount of research on decision making has been conducted in the field of cognitive psychology (Eysenck & Keane, 2010). Broadly speaking, many scientific papers show that people make restricted decisions when they are obliged to consider a large amount of information. Usually, we follow 'rules of thumb', also known as heuristics, when we make decisions. There are various factors that can affect the quality of decision making including novelty of the situation, individual habits, expectations, previous experiences, timing and seriousness of events, emotional reactions, and forgetting. In 1944, the German psychologist Fritz Heider published important articles that pioneered the concept of social perception and causal attribution. Heider argued that we explain the behaviour of others and ourselves either by attributing it to personal dispositions (e.g., personality traits, motives, attitudes), or to situational factors (e.g., external pressure, social norms, peer pressure, accidents of the environment, random chance). Heider stated that people tend to overstate internal dispositional causes compared to external situational causes when they observe others' behaviour (Heider, 1944; Heider & Simmel, 1944), and this principle has been described as the *fundamental attribution error* or *correspondence bias* (Fiske & Taylor, 1991; Jones, 1979, 1990; Ross 1977).

The decision about the case progress could also be affected by any sympathy/empathy the investigators have toward the alleged victims/witnesses and suspected offenders. Maass, Salvi, Arcuri, and Semin (1989) and Maass and Arcuri (1992) found that people will use different terms to describe others and that their decisions vary depending upon their degree of sympathy/empathy. For instance, when we observe positive actions performed by friends, we may describe their actions as typical examples of their 'goodness'. When the same friend behaves negatively, such as by being unhelpful, our descriptions will be concrete and only related to the one specific event or situation.

Conversely, when we observe positive actions performed by people for whom we do not feel sympathy/empathy, we will consider these as unique positive events. Our negative impressions of people who lack our sympathy/empathy will be of general character and serve as general descriptions of those persons (Heider, 1944; Heider & Simmel, 1944).

In most countries, police officers learn decsion making following the 'master–apprentice' principle, with older officers transferring their experiences to younger officers. Since the 1990s, the education of police officers has gradually become more knowledge-based with a strong emphasis on the international literature relating to different aspects of police work. This development from an ad hoc trial and error decision-making process to knowledge-based decisions continues to evolve. Many factors have contributed to the enhanced quality of the decision-making processes. Internationally, it appears that more attention is paid to police work and education of officers, both on a general and specialized level. The increased number of scientific papers and doctorial degrees compiled by serving and ex-police officers indicate that police services across the world are able to generate competence which serves as a basic foundation for their investigative procedures and decisions, resulting in more critical thinking and open-mindedness when making decisions about case progress.

Previously, any decision relating to specific case progress was based upon single-minded determinations by individual investigators and prosecutors, based upon political, humanitarian, financial, and administrative arguments. Today, an understanding of the benefits of a team-based approach also affects how investigative efforts should be conducted. In addition, the complexity of several forensic cases demands a broader approach generating more hypotheses than can be covered by a single investigator. The importance of leadership in decision making by police investigators is also very important.

IF THE CASE IS NOT READY TO MOVE FORWARD, WHAT HAPPENS NEXT?

Basically, an analysis of the reasons for lack of case progress constitutes the foundations of decisions about what should be done next. One strategic approach is known as a SWOT analysis (Hoff, 2009; Hoff *et al.*, 2009), which is a mnemonic for strengths, weaknesses, opportunities, and threats in any given situation (such as an investigation or specific investigative interview). At a strategic level, continuous evaluation of strengths (S) and weaknesses (W) in the case generates information necessary to develop and assess specific actions plans for additional investigative procedures. The action plans should include opportunities (O) for further efforts and realistic evaluations of the threats (T) that might obstruct effective progress in the case. Depending on the nature of the investigation, the complexity of such a SWOT analysis will demand cooperation between all agencies and individuals involved in the investigation. The responsibility for such an analysis lies with the management and leadership of the respective case. An action plan that arises might include consideration of any other children who may require protection, the re-interviewing of victims, witnesses and suspects, consultation with specialists to evaluate the evidence, re-examination of the crime scene, increasing the number of investigators, and/or replacing the current members of the team with new ones.

Although all of the above points are equally important, we will now explore some aspects in more detail.

Examination of the Crime Scene

Despite the fact that Crime Scene Investigators (CSI) might well have already visited the scene(s) of an alleged offence, it is of paramount importance that, following the initial interview of any child witness, especially those alleging physical or sexual assault, a member (or members) of the investigation team visit (or revisit) the alleged crime scene. Some of the main aims of attending a crime scene are to:

1. Preserve and recover any evidence and possible intelligence;
2. Minimize possible contamination of evidence, and;
3. Maximize the potential to detect crime, apprehend offenders and exonerate the innocent.

The latter point will ensure that any allegations can be appropriately verified (where possible). For example, during an investigation of an alleged sexual assault against a young girl by the second author, investigators decided to visit the crime scene to establish the veracity of the information that the girl provided during the initial interview. She had alleged that her stepfather, on various occasions, had entered her bedroom and climbed on top of the bunk-bed (where she slept on the top bunk), knelt upright and removed items of his clothing before sexually assaulting her. At the time of the interview, everything in her version of events appeared feasible; however, on visiting the alleged crime scene, it soon became apparent that the gap between the top bunk and the ceiling would have made it impossible for the stepfather to do what she had alleged. Although the child witness maintained her version of events in a subsequent interview, given the findings of the crime scene visit, the case was not progressed by the legal services. Thus, the importance of visiting (or revisiting) the crime scene, for verification purposes, cannot be over-emphasized.

Repeated Interviews of Children

Investigation teams should always consider whether having another interview is in the child's best interest. Traditionally, repeated interviews of children have been considered to be distressing because they generate painful memories, and also increase the likelihood of inaccurate information being suggestively introduced by the interviewers (Lamb, Hershkowitz, Orbach, & Esplin, 2008; La Rooy, Katz, Malloy, & Lamb, 2010; La Rooy, Lamb & Pipe, 2009; Malloy & Quas, 2009). However, despite holding an initial interview, which should have been thoroughly planned beforehand, a further interview is often necessary to ask the child about significant new information that has become relevant to the investigation team (e.g., information from the suspected offender and/or other witnesses), or to discuss new information that the child witness has subsequently remembered.

The likelihood of divergent information between several interviews of the same child has been studied primarily in experimental laboratory-based situations and not in 'real life' interviews. There is also a need for further investigation of the potential impact of the personal characteristics of the interviewers and training procedures, the time delay before and between any interviews, the age of the child and the suggestiveness of the interviews. Interestingly, repeated interviews are not inherently suggestive, but can maximize the effects of suggestive interviewing (Lamb *et al.*, 2008; La Rooy *et al.*, 2009; Malloy & Quas, 2009).

Interviews with Suspects

Following any allegation by a child witness that an offence may have been committed against them, the suspect, if known, must be interviewed to establish the veracity of the allegations. The Senior Investigating Officer (SIO) is required to make decisions on the basis of the information available, which may be limited, flawed, and/or unclear. Such decisions include: (i) the interview strategy, and (ii) which officers will conduct the interview. When choosing interviewers, the SIO should ensure that only those trained in appropriate non-leading and non-coercive specialist interview techniques (specific to the type of offence) are utilized and are fully briefed on the progress of the case to date.

Following the initial interview with the suspect, the investigation team (through the SIO) should ensure that the nominated interviewing officers are the most effective. If not, or if there is any doubt, consideration should always be given to replacing the interviewer(s). Because child abuse cases are often more complex than other investigations, it is vitally important that, if the inquiry becomes protracted, all appropriate steps are taken by the investigation team to minimize, wherever possible, any significant adverse disruption of or psychological impact on the suspect's personal and/or professional life.

Are There Any Other Children that Require Protection?

During the course of any investigation, a key consideration, especially following an initial interview of a child witness, is whether any other children require protection. If it becomes apparent that other children may be at risk, the investigation team should take the appropriate steps (in accordance with local guidelines and protocols) to safeguard the children identified.

Consultation with Specialists

There are numerous and varied specialists who can be utilized during an investigation such as interview advisors, intermediaries, and psychologists. Following an interview of a child, there may be instances where the investigation team (through the SIO) may wish to seek specialist assistance to aid the investigation, before or after the interview, or to evaluate the veracity of the child's account. For example, in the United Kingdom, police forces have a formalized system where they have access to National Interview Advisors. These advisors are able to provide advice and guidance in relation to the interviewing of victims, witnesses, and suspects. In particular, they can offer support and advice regarding interview strategies, the analysis of interviews and written statements, and the evaluation of the interview process.

Although investigation teams should always consider the use of intermediaries before the initial interview, there may be occasions where it is decided that one is required in subsequent interviews. Intermediaries can communicate directly with children of all ages, or assist the investigation team per se, especially where a child has a speech or communication impediment.

Many investigations utilize the specialist knowledge of psychologists, specifically forensic psychologists, who are devoted to psychological aspects of legal processes in courts. They can also assist in the application of psychological theory to assist in the investigation, providing expert assistance to the investigation team and providing expert witness testimony in court.

Regardless of any specialist used in the investigation, the SIO must ensure that he/she is appropriately qualified and uses scientifically accepted methods.

CONCLUSIONS

In this chapter, we have highlighted the key issues regarding child interviews that investigation teams need to consider in order to progress the case forward, following the initial interview, in addition to the key factors related to how decisions concerning case progress are made in different countries. We have outlined various methods in which full analyses of interviews can be undertaken by investigation teams to ensure that all interviews maximize (i) the *quantity* of information, and (ii) *quality* of information. Most importantly, investigators should ensure that all interviews adhere to local regulations and using well-documented and empirical-based guidelines. Both practitioners and academics have a fundamental role in translating knowledge into practice.

REFERENCES

Bradford, D. (1994). Developing an objective approach to assessing allegations of sexual abuse. *Child Abuse Review*, *3*, 93–101.

Davies, G.M. (1994). Statement validity analysis: An art or a science? Commentary on Bradford. *Child Abuse Review*, *3*(2), 104–106.

Eysenck, M.W., & Keane, M.T. (2010). *Cognitive Psychology: A Student's Handbook* (6th edn). Hove: Psychology Press.

Fiske, S.T., & Taylor, S.E. (1991). *Social Cognition* (2nd edn). New York: McGraw-Hill.

Heider, F. (1944). Social perception and phenomenal causality. *Psychological Review*, *51*, 358–374.

Heider, F., & Simmel, M. (1944). An experimental study of apparent behavior. *American Journal of Psychology*, *57*, 243–259.

Hoff, T. (2009). Mapping the organizational climate for innovation: Introducing SWOT as a Process Based Tool. In Østreng, W. (Ed.), *Confluence: Interdisiplinary Communications 2007/2008, Centre for Advanced Study – Norwegian Academy of Science and Letters* (pp. 76–80).

Hoff, T., Flakke, E., Larsen, A.K., Lone, J.A., Bjørkli, C.A., & Bjørklund, R.A. *(2009)*. On the validity of M-SWOT for innovation climate development. *Scandinavian Journal of Organizational Psychology*, *1*(1), 3–11.

Jones, E.E. (1979). The rocky road from acts to dispositions. *American Psychologist, 34*, 107–117.
Jones, E.E. (1990). *Interpersonal Perception*. New York: Freeman.
Justisdepartementet (1998). *Rundskriv G-70/98 om forskrift 2 oktober 1998 nr 925 om dommeravhør og observasjon og om endringer i straffeprosessloven, straffeloven og påtaleinstruksen [Regulations concerning out of court judicial examination and observation]*. Oslo: Det Kongelige Justis-og politidepartement.
Köhnken, G. (2004). Statement Validity Analysis and the 'detection of the truth'. In P.A. Granhag, & L.A. Strömwall (Eds), *The Detection of Deception in Forensic Contexts* (pp. 41–63). Cambridge: Cambridge University Press.
Lamb, M.E., Hershkowitz, I., Orbach, Y., & Esplin, P.W. (2008). *Tell Me What Happened: Structured Investigative Interviews of Child Victims and Witnesses*. Chichester: John Wiley & Sons.
La Rooy, D., Katz, C., Malloy, L.C., & Lamb, M.E. (2010). Do we need to rethink guidance on repeated interviews? *Psychology, Public Policy and Law, 16*, 373–392.
La Rooy, D., Lamb, M.E., & Pipe, M.E. (2009). Repeated interviewing: A critical evaluation of the risks and potential benefits. In: K. Kuehnle, & M. Connell (Eds), *The Evaluation of Child Sexual Abuse Allegations: A Comprehensive Guide to Assessment and Testimony* (pp 327–361). New Jersey: Wiley.
Maass, A., & Arcuri, L. (1992). The role of language in the persistence of stereotypes. In G.R. Semin, & K. Fiedler (Eds), *Language, Interaction and Social Cognition* (pp. 131–143). Thousand Oaks: Sage.
Maass, A., Salvi, D., Arcuri, L., & Semin, G.R. (1989). Language use in intergroup contexts: The linguistic intergroup bias. *Journal of Personality and Social Psychology, 57*, 981–993.
Malloy, L.C., & Quas, J.A. (2009). Children's areas of consensus and controversy. In: K. Kuehnle, & M. Connell (Eds), *The Evaluation of Child Sexual Abuse Allegations: A Comprehensive Guide to Assessment and Testimony* (pp. 267–297). New Jersey: Wiley.
Myklebust, T. (2005). Dommeravhør av barn i Norge: intensjon og fakta [Investigative interviews of children in Norway: intention and facts]. In M. Egge, & J. Strype (Eds), *Politirollen gjennom 100 år: Tradisjon og endring [The role of the police in 100 years: Tradition and changes]* (pp. 142–172). Oslo: PHS Forskning.
Myklebust, T. (2009). *Analysis of Field Investigative Interviews of Children Conducted by Specially Trained Police Investigators*. Oslo: UniPub.
Ross, L. (1977). The intuitive psychologist and his shortcomings: Distortions in the attribution process. In L. Berkowitz (Ed.), *Advances in Experimental Social Psychology* (Vol. 10, pp. 173–220). Orlando, FL: Academic Press.
Steller, M. (1989). Recent develpments in statement analysis. In J.C. Yuille (Ed.), *Credibility Assessment* (pp. 135–154). Deventer, The Netherlands: Kluwer.
Undeutsch, U. (1967). Beurteilung der Glaubhaftigkeit von Aussagen. In U. Undeutsch (Ed.), *Handbuch der Psychologie*, Vol. 11: *Forensiche Psychologie* (pp. 26–181). Göttingen: Hogefe.
Undeutsch, U. (1982). Statement reality analysis. In A. Trankell (Ed.), *Reconstructing the Past: The Role of Psychologists in Criminal Trials* (pp. 27–56). Stockholm, Sweden: P.A. Norstedt & Söners.

Vrij, A. (2008). *Detecting Lies and Deceit. Pitfalls and Opportunities* (2nd edn). Chichester, UK: John Wiley & Sons.

Yuille, J.C., & Cutshall, J.L. (1986). A case study of eyewitness memory of a crime. *Journal of Applied Psychology*, *71*, 291–301.

10

Managing Children's Emotional and Clinical Needs

Kathryn Kuehnle and Mary Connell

Key Points

- The time period between a report of child maltreatment to state authorities and the legal determination of the child's abuse status allows for the child to experience further stress and potentially traumatic experiences.
- Children's unique vulnerabilities and resiliency should be determined prior to providing interventions.
- When alleged victims of abuse and neglect exhibit behavioural and emotional problems but their maltreatment status is undetermined by the legal system, efficacious interventions may provide these children the opportunity to develop pro-social interpersonal relationships, may reinforce coping strategies and may foster instrumentality.
- Alleged victims of abuse should not be provided abuse specific therapy until abuse status has been legally determined.
- Because some cases are not resolved in a timely manner, alleged victims of abuse should be provided comprehensive forensic evaluations with videotaped interviews and, if treatment needs are urgent,

Children's Testimony: A Handbook of Psychological Research and Forensic Practice, Second Edition.
Edited by Michael E. Lamb, David J. La Rooy, Lindsay C. Malloy, and Carmit Katz.

provided abuse-specific therapy even though such intervention could compromise the judicial process.

A focus on the child's well-being is paramount, after an allegation of child maltreatment has been reported to Child Protective Services (CPS)[1] and/or law enforcement. Following identification to authorities that a child may be abused or neglected, the child and family are swept into a potentially distressing legal process. During the investigative phase, the child may endure multiple contacts with legal authorities and repeated interviews that may create further feelings of instability and apprehension. Numerous interviewers may attempt to determine the veracity of the allegation and the safety of the child in the home, as well as assist in gathering information for the prosecution of the alleged perpetrator. Troxel, Ogle, Cordon, Lawler, and Goodman (2009) identify the potential chronology of interviews an alleged child victim may experience:

1. A call to police or child protective services is made. A police officer or social worker then interviews the child.
2. A detective is assigned to the case. The detective will likely also interview the child.
3. If the case is accepted for prosecution, the prosecutor will interview the child several months after the case was reported to authorities.
4. A victim advocate (e.g., a social worker who works with the courts) may be assigned to help explain the legal system to the child and family, and to guide them through the criminal court process.
5. The child may testify in depositions and/or preliminary hearings.
6. A trial date is set, although the trial date may be postponed one or more times, each time possibly requiring the child to emotionally prepare to testify and wait at the courthouse for hours.
7. The child may be called as a witness in the trial; if so, he/she would generally be treated like an adult witness (e.g., face the defendant, submit to cross-examination).
8. If the defendant is found guilty, the child might be encouraged to testify at the sentencing hearing.
9. Especially in child abuse prosecutions, at the same time as the criminal case is winding its way through to trial, the child may also be

[1]Child protection agencies operate under a variety of names across jurisdictions but generally have similar roles – to investigate allegations of abuse or neglect and provide intervention. For convenience we will refer to the agency fulfilling this role as Child Protective Services (CPS) even though in a specific jurisdiction it may be referred to by a different name.

involved in a juvenile court dependency case to determine if the child should be removed from home (Troxel *et al.*, 2009, pp. 151–152).

As noted by Troxel *et al.* (2009), the case may change courses at any point as a consequence of plea bargain or dismissal of charges, in which case the child's involvement in the prosecution would end without the child having to testify. Conversely, if a conviction is appealed, the legal case could start all over again. Throughout this process there are a number of professionals with whom the child may interact, including a CPS caseworker, a police officer, a forensic interviewer, perhaps a sexual assault nurse examiner or other medical professionals, a victim's advocate, a prosecutor, a forensic psychologist or psychiatrist who conducts a comprehensive assessment, and a therapist. Although a purpose for the multi-agency collaboration called Child Advocacy Centers was to reduce the number of interviews the child must undergo, children continue to experience numerous interviews regarding the alleged maltreatment (see National Children's Alliance web site). It is not difficult to see how this process of investigation and prosecution of maltreatment might create distress for the child – but as yet it is not empirically known whether therapy reduces the distress. Our focus in this article will be on therapeutic interventions during the period of time when the abuse status of the child has not been legally determined.

It has been our observation that there is an assumption by many professionals that if a child is an *alleged* victim of maltreatment the child should be provided abuse-specific therapy prior to the legal determination of the child's abuse status. We believe this to be a mistaken assumption.

FORENSIC AND CLINICAL ROLES

Before addressing the basis for our challenge of the assumption that abuse-specific therapy is generally an appropriate intervention for children whose abuse status is undetermined, it is useful to define the unique roles of diverse professionals in child maltreatment cases. Professionals, whether acting in the role of forensic interviewer, mental health forensic evaluator, or clinical evaluator/therapist, may greatly influence both the course of the child's experience and the outcome of the legal process, depending upon how well they understand and maintain the boundaries of their roles.

Forensic Interviewer

The purpose of the 'forensic interview' conducted by law enforcement, CPS or a Child Advocacy Center interviewer is to determine whether the child needs protection and if legal action may be warranted (Saywitz, Esplin, & Romanoff, 2007). Forensic interviewers are fact gatherers who provide children an opportunity to tell as much as possible about the suspected interpersonal violence incident(s) in their own words. The aim is to gather accurate information, and, although interviewer is sensitive to the child's emotional and clinical needs, the forensic interviewer does not engage in treatment or work to reduce the child's symptoms. The forensic interviewer has limited contact with the child and does not enter into an ongoing advocacy relationship with the child.

In communicating with other professionals, it is important for the forensic interviewer to retain professional independence rather than to convey an advocacy position. Although CPS is required to determine whether the abuse allegation has merit (Substantiated or Unsubstantiated), research indicates that based on the child's statement alone, false negatives (an abused child is inaccurately determined to not be a victim of abuse) and false positives (a non-abused child is inaccurately determined to be a victim of abuse) may be a significant risk (Herman, 2009).

Secondly, it is imperative that the interviewer retain objectivity so as to be receptive to new information, to be available to testify, if necessary, about the events surrounding the interview and the interview itself, and to avoid contaminating the child's or the caretaker's knowledge about the case. Communication with other professionals should be directed toward the logistics of the case, rather than the contents of the interview, and should be documented.

Forensic Mental Health Evaluator

Children who are suspected victims or witnesses to interpersonal violence may also be referred for a mental health forensic evaluation. The forensic evaluation, similarly to the forensic interview, involves gathering facts and information and both roles require a stance of neutrality. The mental health forensic evaluator, in contrast to the forensic interviewer, has access to multiple sources of information. This information may include interviews with and testing of children and parents; review of school, medical, and legal records; and interviews with potentially important collateral sources. The obtained information is typically integrated into a report for the trier of fact who may rely, in part, on the forensic evaluation in determining the truth of the matter. Forensic evaluators may offer conclusions about children's behavioural, emotional, or cognitive functioning and offer hypotheses regarding a child's capacity to accurately report events or the likelihood of the accuracy of the allegation. Although there are differing opinions by experts on whether forensic evaluators should answer the ultimate issue regarding whether a child is a witness or victim of interpersonal violence, the authors of this chapter do not support mental health professions addressing the ultimate issue. If the forensic evaluator is successful in assisting the court, children may be better protected as victims of interpersonal violence or protected from false allegations. The forensic evaluator has a unique role, then, that is distinct from the forensic interviewer or from the therapist.

Forensic evaluators, like forensic interviewers, do not engage in treatment of the child, but may make treatment recommendations. Their reports may form the basis for the court's rulings regarding a number of issues including, in Family and Dependency Courts, the child's placement and contact with parents or other family members. The recommendations of the forensic evaluator may directly or obliquely address the child's clinical and emotional needs. However, it is not the role of the forensic evaluator to taken on a treatment role or 'helping' role in the traditional clinical sense.

Clinical Mental Health Evaluator

Children who are suspected to have witnessed or been victim to interpersonal violence may also be referred for clinical evaluation. Unlike the forensic evaluation, the purpose of clinical evaluation is to determine if the child manifests psychological disorders or symptoms and, if so, formulate a plan for treatment. Mental health therapists have the very specific role to determine the need for and then carry out psychological treatment, in contrast to the forensic evaluator's role to assist the trier of fact. The clinical mental health evaluator's role is to assist in designing a treatment plan to effect change in the child's behaviour, emotions, or cognitions.

Mental health treatment providers may be called upon to provide psychotherapy during the investigative phase of allegations of children's exposure to interpersonal violence in order to either support children, or, problematically, to assist in cultivating evidence or to treat symptoms assumed to be associated with the exposure to violence. These different goals of treatment will be further discussed below; for the present it is sufficient to note that there are a number of roles the therapist may have, including those roles supported by empirical research, professional ethics, and the legal context or those that lack such support.

DETERMINING THE INDIVIDUAL NEEDS OF THE ALLEGED CHILD VICTIM

In order to meet each child's needs, we must understand the particular impact, on the child, of the exposure to maltreatment or the mistaken belief the child has been exposed to maltreatment, including:

1. The circumstances surrounding the abuse allegation;
2. Other traumatic external events;
3. Life changes following the report to authorities such as loss of a parent or parents; lost contact with extended family members and friends; change of schools;
4. The current placement of the child.

The period of time between a report of child maltreatment to authorities and the legal determination regarding the abuse allegation can be a stressful time for the child. During this time, well-intentioned interventions may moderate or exacerbate stress. We propose that stress will be moderated when children are provided interventions based on their unique individual needs rather than based on the premature and potentially inaccurate assumption that these allegedly maltreated children are members of a homogeneous group who require similar interventions.

Maltreated Children and their Families

The incidence of child maltreatment is significantly higher in families with low income and chronic economic hardship than in families with greater economic resources (Sedlak & Broadhurst, 1996). Therefore, many maltreated children may have been subjected to other potentially damaging experiences to their development in addition to abuse or neglect. There is considerable research to suggest that economic hardship is associated with problems in family functioning, including increased psychological distress, decreased capacity for sensitive and consistent child rearing (Conger *et al.*, 1992), and parents' serious psychiatric disorders – for example, substance abuse and depressive disorders (Chaffin, Kelleher, & Hollenberg, 1996; Luthar, 1999; Mayes & Truman, 2002). In some child maltreatment research samples, the percentage of maltreated children living in families suffering economic hardship reaches approximately 90% (Bolger & Patterson, 2003).

Diverse Effects of Traumatic Experiences

Each child is a unique individual whose totality of experiences forms the child's personality. The impact of traumatic experiences of maltreatment on a particular child is not predictable, although estimates on increased risk for poor life time adjustment can be made. The specific impact of a potentially traumatic event depends on a number of factors and trauma may affect children in diverse ways. Internal risk and resiliency factors such as personality characteristics and the personal interpretation of the abuse event are related to differences on the psychological impact of maltreatment experiences. External factors, such as family chaos vs. family stability or the parents' responses following disclosure, also are associated with children's risk and resiliency (Kendall-Tackett, Williams, & Finkelhor, 1993). Furthermore, characteristics of the abuse experience, such as timing, duration, frequency, severity, degree of threat, and relationship to the perpetrator are all associated with better or worse outcomes (Keiley, Howe, Dodge, Bates, & Pettit, 2001; Manly, Kim, Rogosch, & Cicchetti, 2001).

Children abused and neglected by their parents or caretakers show greater vulnerability to long-term psychological problems. There is a growing body of research that indicates chronic maltreatment commencing in early childhood and continuing into adolescence has the most deleterious effects on the foundation of children's psychological development (Aguilar, Sroufe, Egeland, & Carlson, 2000). A substantial number of maltreated children also experience more than one form of maltreatment (American Psychological Association Presidential Task Force on Posttraumatic Stress Disorder and Trauma in Children and Adolescents, 2008). Risk rather than resiliency defines the majority of these children. There is evidence that children experiencing the combinations of abuse and neglect, multiple forms of abuse or abuse with exposure to intimate partner violence have decreased odds of stable psychological functioning compared with children experiencing a single maltreatment form (Bolger & Patterson, 2003; Holden, Geffner, & Jouriles, 1998). Bolger and Patterson found that experiencing the combination of neglect and child sexual abuse put children at greater risk than children experiencing either form of these specific maltreatments independently. Silvern *et al.* (1995) found that after accounting for the effects of being abused, adult reports of their witnessing interparental violence during childhood still accounted for a significant degree of their problems as children.

Identifying the Individual Needs of Each Child

If the needs of a child are to be met after an allegation of child maltreatment has been reported to CPS and/or law enforcement, we must look at the child as an individual rather than as one amorphous figure in a homogeneous group. Following the allegation of child maltreatment it is unknown if:

1. The child is a victim of maltreatment;
2. Whether the investigative process itself will be traumatic for the child regardless of abuse status; and
3. What specific needs, if any, the child may have.

CPS, law enforcement, or the forensic interviewer, as first responders, may make referrals to mental health providers for therapeutic interventions without understanding that some types of therapy may taint children's memories and thwart successful prosecution of a criminal case or produce iatrogenic effects. Rather than receiving abuse-specific therapy, many alleged child victims may be better served through interventions that assist children with needs not related to the alleged maltreatment. Such interventions may include cognitive behaviour therapy to reduce symptomatic behaviour, academic tutors, resilient pro-social play partners, and, where indicated, parent training or other interventions for the child's parent. Cognitive behaviour therapy, an evidence-based intervention, has been found to be effective in reducing aggressive and acting out behaviours that may be related to any number of potentially traumatic childhood events (Cohen, Berliner, & Mannarino, 2010). Abuse-specific support services at this early point, before the child's abuse status is legally determined, may include court educator/advocate, comprehensive forensic assessment, or therapy addressing the child's symptomatic behaviours without providing therapy for the alleged abuse that may or may not have occurred.

TREATMENT CHALLENGES

When a concern about possible child maltreatment arises, there must be a report to CPS. CPS may find that there is some basis for concern about maltreatment, a strong basis to believe the child has been maltreated or no evidence to support the concern that maltreatment has occurred. CPS agencies use various terms to describe the level of concern and for purposes of discussion we will refer to these as 'Unsubstantiated', 'Some Indicators' and 'Substantiated'. These terms, when used by CPS, are not legal findings and do not confirm an allegedly maltreating person's guilt or innocence or whether the child has been maltreated, which is a determination that can only be made judicially.

After CPS has reached a determination, CPS investigators or forensic interviewers, as first responders, may have the most significant impact on whether the alleged child victim receives therapy and potentially what kind of therapy the child receives. We will explore a number of treatment pathways that may be chosen when a child is alleged to be maltreated. For clarity see Figure 10.1 summarizing recommended interventions depending on CPS findings and the child's presentation as asymptomatic or symptomatic.

Treatment Recommendations by First Responders

Forensic interviewers or CPS workers make the initial assessment about whether to refer for treatment. In some cases it may be obvious that the child is experiencing serious emotional distress as the allegation first becomes articulated. The child may break down and become so distressed that he/she cries during the forensic interview or may appear painfully withdrawn or anxious. In order to maintain an objective fact-finding posture,[2] interviewers refrain from shifting to the role of therapist (e.g., 'That must have been terrible'; 'He should not have done that to you. It's not your fault'). Instead, interviewers inquire about children's feelings and then, exhibiting sensitive concern but remaining task-focused, ask if the child can continue the interview. The interviewer does not move into the therapeutic mode of verbalizing judgements about the child's alleged experiences or making negative comments about the alleged perpetrator in order to validate the child's feelings. At the conclusion of the interview a further brief inquiry of the caretaker about referral for therapy is appropriate to gauge receptivity or to learn whether the child is already in therapy. Depending on the child's age, it may be appropriate for the interviewer to ask the child if it would help to have someone to talk to, not necessarily about the (alleged) incidents but about how the child is doing, what worries the child may face, and so on. This distinction between therapy to explore the alleged abuse and therapy to support the child or address peripheral issues is an important one and will be further discussed.

Allegation Facilitating Therapy: A Misnomer

The term 'therapy' is a misnomer for the intervention called allegation facilitating therapy, because the focus is on the possibility of obtaining a disclosure or a more detailed disclosure from the child. This extended

[2] An objective fact-finding posture is not synonymous with a cold and indifferent posture.

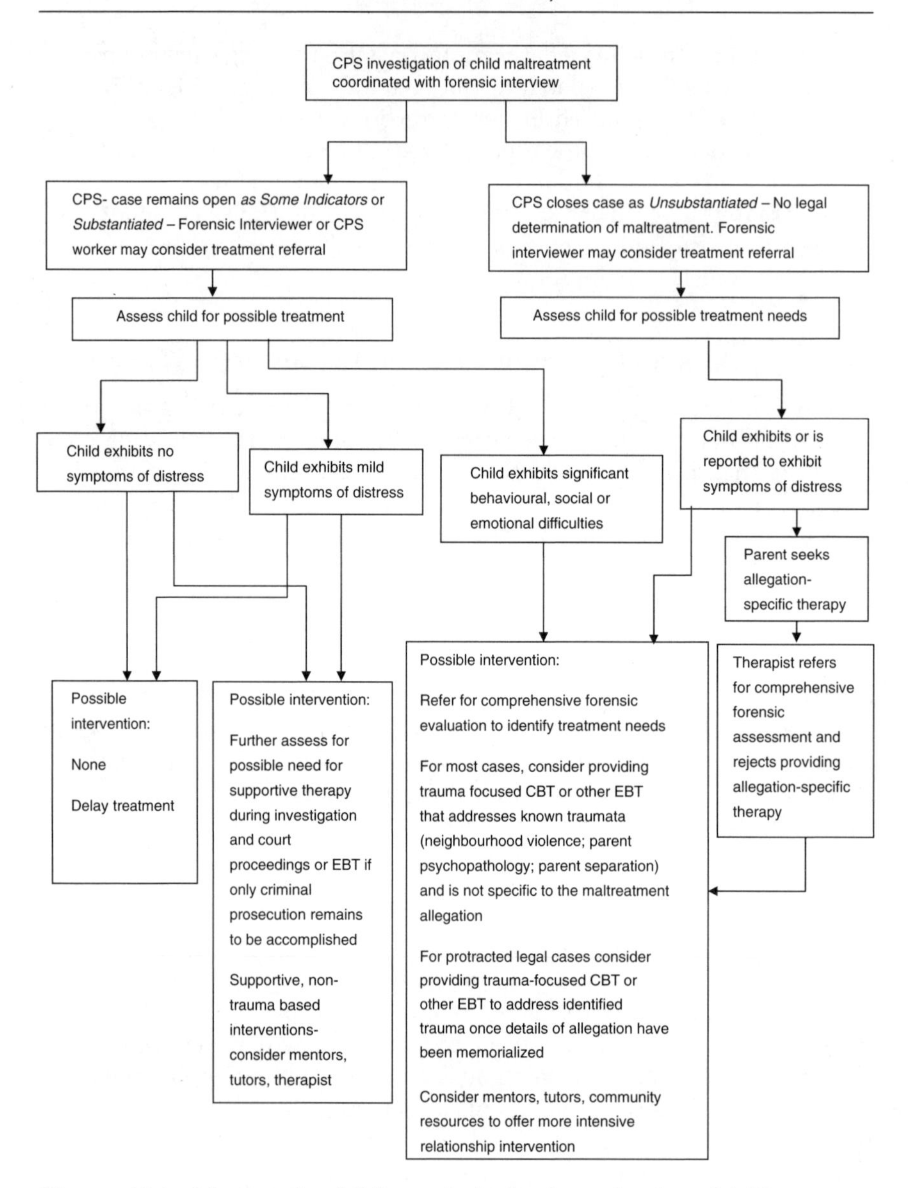

Figure 10.1 Meeting the child's needs during investigation of child maltreatment.

interviewing was developed for use in Child Advocacy Centers and titled the Extended Forensic Evaluation (Carnes, Nelson-Gardell, Wilson, & Orgassa, 2001; Carnes, Wilson, & Nelson-Gardell, 1999; but for a critical review see Connell, 2009). The title Extended Forensic Evaluation is also a misnomer because this allegation facilitating process is not a forensic evaluation, which involves the analysis of multiple data sets, but instead is extended interviewing.

A parent or a prosecutor may request allegation facilitating therapy when it is believed the child may have been maltreated but the child has not made a clear statement. The forensic interviewer may be in a unique position to manage this request and ensure that the child is not subjected to intervention that might include suggestive questioning. Interviewers are trained to understand the problems with leading or suggestive questioning and can explain to parents or prosecutors, and to therapists to whom the child may be referred, the importance of letting the child initiate any discussion about the suspected maltreatment.

They may also caution about repeatedly questioning the child and vilifying the suspected abuser. All of these problems can potentially contaminate the child's perceptions and/or eventual statements. Whereas the forensic interviewer may generally assume therapists to be the experts at deciding treatment issues, in these cases, we argue, the forensic interviewer has greater knowledge about the dangers of an atmosphere of bias and should screen therapists for their ability to maintain an appropriate posture of neutrality on the question of maltreatment.

Allegation facilitating therapy may commence with a neutral posture or begin with the assumption that the suspected maltreatment did in fact occur, that the child has not been able to disclose it or describe it fully, and that the child needs to be in a treatment relationship in order to fully narrate the abuse. Concerns are raised that repeated questioning, especially by biased therapists who believe they know what has happened, may alter children's memories (Bruck, Ceci, & Hembrooke, 2002; La Rooy, Lamb, & Pipe, 2009). Further, there is a risk that allegation facilitating therapy may continue until an allegation is elicited, which may make it difficult to determine if the allegation is true or false. With the goal of facilitating more salient disclosures from children, allegation facilitating therapists may inadvertently use techniques of data gathering that result in the creation or reinforcement of false allegations. This could cause harm to both children who were not victims and to children who were victims but whose memories may be contaminated and subsequently be viewed as unreliable.

Empirical review of extending the information gathering phase in therapy sessions has not been provided with well-designed research studies. These extended information gathering therapy sessions are generally not conducted in a way that preserves the information gathering process for later examination, such as videotaping sessions. Malloy and Quas (2009) wrote that discrepant research findings have made it difficult to draw definitive conclusions about the effects of repeated interviews, and they opined that researchers have yet to adequately disentangle the factors of repetition, delays of questioning, and interviewer bias. For these reasons, when the allegation facilitating therapy process is utilized as an information gathering structure to provide non-reporting or ambiguously reporting children the opportunity to tell about suspected maltreatment, the authors of this article strongly advocate for video recording each extended session.

Through video recording the extended interviewer can provide, when necessary, concrete information regarding the techniques utilized to acquire the child's statement. This may be helpful to refute allegations of extended interviewer bias affecting the child's statements. The initial forensic interviewer may explicitly request such recording when making referral for further exploration of the suspected child maltreatment – exploration that may be risky if the therapist departs from the careful questioning that is familiar to forensic interviewers but may be altogether foreign to the extended interviewer. Extreme caution is warranted in considering such referral and in ensuring that, if the referral is made, it is to a follow-up interviewer therapist who understands the importance of neutrality, non-leading and non-suggestive discourse and questioning, and recording in extensive detail both the data that support the possibility of abuse and the data that argue against it having occurred.

We believe it is empirically justified to avoid allegation facilitating therapy and instead to call for a court appointed comprehensive forensic evaluation for allegedly maltreated children with or without ambiguous allegations. These forensic evaluations are conducted in a transparent way, have a beginning and end point, and do not rely solely on the child's statements. Unlike allegation facilitating therapy, the comprehensive forensic evaluation provides the opportunity to put the pieces of the puzzle together through the thorough exploration of data such as: triggers or motives for the timing of the allegation, prior suspicions of the child's victimization, family dynamics, relationship between the alleged offender and alleged victim, and previous questioning of the alleged child victim.

Maltreated children who have not made credible disclosures may be unable to do so. Therefore, the determination of maltreatment, especially sexual abuse that leaves no physical evidence, must be made using multiple data sets, in addition to or other than a child's statements. Professionals must accept that in some cases the accurate abuse status of the child may never be known. The focus of professionals then must be on protection of the alleged child victim, and if the alleged perpetrator is a parent, protection of the parent–child relationship with safety of the child made paramount.

Therapeutic Interventions

There are two issues with the historical treatment of alleged and known maltreated children. The first issue is the problem of individual abuse-focused therapy as the major and usually sole intervention for these children. The second issue is the problem of providing abuse-focused therapy to children whose abuse status and resiliency has yet to be determined. As noted by Cohen *et al.*, 'If the child has not experienced a trauma or does not have significant trauma-related symptoms (e.g., PTSD including avoidance; depressive symptoms; self-blame; maladaptive coping strategies; attachment or relationship problems, etc.), trauma-focused treatment is not appropriate. An Evidence Based Treatment (EBT)[3] for the child's other problems is likely indicated' (Cohen, Berliner, & Mannarino, 2010, p. 217). There is robust research to show that abuse specific cognitive therapy has a significantly positive effect on sexually abused children (Substance Abuse Mental Health Services Administration, 2002). However, this intervention should be prudently recommended until the abuse status of the alleged maltreated child is legally determined, or determined by medical evidence, a credible eyewitness report or some other indisputable evidence and treatment needs can be determined. We further argue that there are a number of interventions based on the resiliency literature that can be considered prior to placing the child in individual or group psychotherapy.

Our premise is that any designated intervention for alleged victims of abuse and neglect must distinguish between the suspected maltreatment and other known potential traumas (e.g., exposure to family or neighbourhood violence; children as pawns in parents' high conflict separation and divorce). We propose when alleged victims of

[3]The term Evidence-Based Treatment (EBT) or Empirically Supported Treatment (EST) refers to preferential use of mental and behavioral health interventions for which systematic empirical research has provided evidence of statistically significant effectiveness as treatments for specific problems. In recent years, EBT has been stressed by professional organizations such as the American Psychological Association so that patients with differing problems will receive appropriate and successful therapy.

abuse and neglect exhibit behavioural and emotional problems but their maltreatment status is undetermined by the legal system, efficacious EBT may be provided to many of these children to promote pro-social interpersonal relationships, reinforce coping strategies and foster instrumentality. A comprehensive forensic evaluation of the child should be conducted, in a timely manner, and should include videotaped interviews of the child's allegation. Based on the evaluation findings, the appropriate therapy can be recommended for alleged victims, including placement in evidence-based sexual abuse specific therapy or other evidenced-based therapies. As emphasized by Saywitz, Mannarino, Berliner, and Cohen (2000), if intervention is delayed for too long for maltreated children, symptoms may become worse or may become chronic and resistant to treatment. Although there is risk that abuse-specific therapy may alter some of the child's recollections and interfere in the prosecution phase, in many cases the benefit of abuse specific therapy will outweigh this risk. As noted by Myers (see Chapter 15), judicial decision making may take into account the fact that therapeutic interventions may taint children's memories and render them incompetent (unreliable) witnesses – yet, children alleged to be victims of abuse may nevertheless need therapy.

Therapeutic Intervention: Building Resiliency

Therapy focusing on providing support, pro-social relationship building, strengthening coping mechanisms, and decreasing symptomatic behaviour may be helpful to many alleged victims of maltreatment whether the maltreatment allegation is eventually legally determined to be accurate or inaccurate. In contrast, therapies such as allegation facilitating therapy and abuse-specific trauma therapy, which focus on alleged experiences of maltreatment must be used judiciously prior to a legal determination of a child's abuse status.

INTERVENTIONS FOR CHILDREN: CLASSIFIED UNSUBSTANTIATED, SOME INDICATORS, OR SUBSTANTIATED

The forensic interviewer may appraise the child's needs as the initial investigation unfolds. The data collected in initial interviews, the child's apparent or reported level of distress, and the findings of the CPS and police investigations of corroborative evidence may determine whether to refer the child for further services. In some settings this may not be considered to be part of the role of the forensic interviewer but may instead be the purview of the CPS investigator.

Cases Classified 'Unsubstantiated' – Concern Remains the Child is a Victim

There are children alleged to have been maltreated by a parent or extended family member and who have consequently been evaluated, in some cases repeatedly, by child protection or law enforcement with resulting 'Unsubstantiated' findings. Unsubstantiated is not synonymous with non-abused, it simply indicates that CPS did not find any factors that would support an abuse finding. In such cases, we are in support of parents or other authorities seeking a comprehensive forensic evaluation when they continue to have suspicions that the child is a victim of maltreatment, despite the CPS finding.

The parent or an agency representative may, however, sidestep forensic evaluation and directly seek therapeutic intervention to either facilitate a narrative of abuse from the child or to treat the child for the alleged maltreatment, despite CPS case disposition. In some of these cases the therapist gathers information from only one parent and provides abuse-specific therapy to a child who may or may not be a victim of sexual abuse. Such children may become symptomatic due to the anxiety of the alleging parent, repeated interviewing and/or iatrogenic therapy effects.

Cases Classified 'Some Indicators' or 'Substantiated' – Child is Assumed to be a Victim

When CPS designates a finding of 'Some Indicators' or 'Substantiated' the alleged child victim may be referred for treatment. The therapist must make an assessment of the child that is abuse-informed, rather than abuse-specific (Saunders, Berliner, & Hanson, 2004). The therapist should evaluate not only those potential problems that may be attributable to the alleged abuse, but also any other difficulties the child may have and other environmental factors that may contribute to the child's symptoms. Importantly, when a legal case is pending in Criminal Court, the child may be in a state of limbo for months or, not uncommonly, a year or even longer while the machinations of the legal system move the case forward (Troxel *et al.*, 2009). During this time the status of the allegation is not legally determined and yet the child may be experiencing distress caused by any of several contributors: conflicts or instability in the home or neighbourhood; the abuse if it did occur; and the necessary interviews and examinations necessitated by the legal process.

For children who are functioning well in social, emotional, and academic domains, psychotherapy interventions may not be beneficial until the child's maltreatment status has been legally determined and treatment goals, if any, can be accurately identified. In place of therapy, a forensic evaluation may be of greater relevance at this stage to assist the court in its effort to determine the veracity of the abuse allegation. The forensic evaluation can also assist the child by providing a further opportunity for the child to impart relevant details.

Some alleged victims of maltreatment may exhibit mild to severe social, emotional, and/or academic problems that interfere in their daily functioning. Forensic or clinical assessment may address the potential utility of more novel interventions such as provision of a mentor or academic tutor, or development of a pro-social peer relationship. The evaluator may also craft a treatment plan that addresses known traumata (neighbourhood violence, parent psychopathology, parent separation, repeated and distressing interviews). The child may be referred for more traditional therapy, such as cognitive therapy, to decrease symptoms and develop self-enhancing coping skills during the period between the maltreatment report to authorities and judicial determination. These interventions are justified whether or not the child was abused and do not risk contaminating the child's testimony or, worse, harming the child by providing a child not actually abused with abuse focused therapy. Such interventions do not negate a therapist listening to a child's disclosure of abuse and responding in a supportive manner.

Children who are involved with CPS may live in multi-problem family environments including parents with mental health problems or chemical dependency, underemployment or impoverishment, neighbourhood violence, and significant difficulties in a number of other areas. It may be that weekly therapy sessions will simply be inadequate to assist the child who faces such challenges on a daily basis in the home, school, and neighbourhood. In addition to psychotherapy, CPS workers and therapists must creatively explore adjunctive interventions. Mentors, academic tutors and other community resources might be utilized to offer wrap around interventions.

CONCLUSIONS

During the time period between a report of child maltreatment to the state authorities and the legal determination of the child's abuse status, the child is at risk to experience further stress and potentially traumatic experiences such as loss of family and community and repeated questioning by attorneys and other authorities. A child's vulnerability and resiliency must be considered in order to develop the most efficacious interventions during this time.

Maltreated children may live in impoverished households or face other challenges in addition to experiencing abuse and/or neglect. Individual therapy alone may not be the most effective intervention for these alleged victims who may live with significantly impaired parents and in violent families and neighbourhoods. Alternative treatments include supportive socialization experiences, enhancement of family and community strengths, and fostering the child's capacity to activate existent coping skills. When abuse status has not been legally determined, the majority of alleged victims of abuse and neglect should not be provided abuse-specific therapy until their maltreatment status has been legally determined and the psychological impact of the abuse is also determined. For those children whose cases are protracted, and who may wait years for a legal determination of abuse, a forensic evaluation with detailed documentation and video recorded interviews should be utilized to secure evidence of the child's initial statements and to provide for assessment of treatment needs, including the appropriateness of abuse-specific therapy or other evidence-based therapies, to be provided prior to a legal determination of abuse status.

Forensic interviewers occupy a unique position to assist in ensuring that children are referred for appropriate services. As first responders, they have the opportunity to make at least a cursory assessment of the chronic and situational stressors the child may be experiencing. Many forensic interviewers can apply their own sophisticated appreciation for the preservation of the child's independent account of alleged maltreatment in considering intervention options:

- It cannot be assumed that child maltreatment affects most or all children similarly.
- The determination about whether allegations of maltreatment are true is made by the court; pending that, all opinions must be considered tentative.
- Abuse facilitation therapy, which is used to assist alleged maltreatment victims to make disclosures or facilitate more detailed disclosures, should only be implemented if each facilitation session is videotaped in order to document how the allegation was elicited and to provide opportunities to review the methods used by the interviewer to facilitate the child's statements.

- The use of a child's statement as the sole criteria to determine abuse, in contrast to a comprehensive forensic evaluation that relies on multiple data sets may increase the risk of false negative and false positive conclusions.
- Children who are alleged to have witnessed or experienced traumatic interpersonal events may have behavioral, cognitive and emotional difficulties related to the events, the legal process, and/or fractured family life.
- During the investigation of child maltreatment many alleged victims may benefit from EBT that focuses on alleviation of the child's symptoms, such as anxiety, depression, and other emotional distress.
- Abuse-specific therapy should be avoided until a legal determination can be rendered on the child's abuse status and appropriate interventions can be determined.
- Alleged child victims whose legal cases are protracted for years may benefit from the immediate commencement of abuse-specific therapy prior to legal determination of the child's abuse status. This should be initiated only upon recommendations following a comprehensive forensic evaluation and in consideration of the relative risks and benefits of such treatment, which may significantly impede the judicial process.

REFERENCES

American Psychological Association Presidential Task Force on Posttraumatic Stress Disorder and Trauma in Children and Adolescents. (2008). Children and trauma: Update for mental health professionals. Washington, DC: APA. Retrieved 30 May 2010 from http://www.apa.org/pi/families/resources/update.pdf

Aguilar, B., Sroufe, L.A., Egeland, B., & Carlson, E. (2000). Distinguishing the early-onset/persistent and adolescent-onset antisocial behavior type: From birth to 16 years. *Development and Psychopathology*, *12*, 109–132.

Bolger, K.E., & Patterson, C.J. (2003). Sequelae of child maltreatment: Vulnerability and Resilience. In S.S. Luthar (Ed.), *Resiliency and Vulnerability* (pp. 156–181). New York, NY: Cambridge University Press.

Bruck, M., Ceci, S.J., & Hembrooke, H. (2002). The nature of children's true and false narratives. *Developmental Review*, *22*, 520–554.

Carnes, C.N., Nelson-Gardell, D., Wilson, C., & Orgassa, U.C. (2001). Extended forensic evaluation when sexual abuse is suspected: A multisite field study. *Child Maltreatment*, *6*, 230–242.

Carnes, C.N., Wilson, C., & Nelson-Gardell, D. (1999). Extended forensic evaluations when sexual abuse is suspected: A model and preliminary data. *Child Maltreatment*, *4*, 242–254.

Chaffin, M., Kelleher, K., & Hollenberg, J. (1996). Onset of physical abuse and neglect: Psychiatric, substance abuse, and social risk factors from prospective community data. *Child Abuse and Neglect, 20*, 191–203.

Cohen, J., Berliner, L., & Mannarino, A. (2010). Trauma focused CBT for children with co-occurring trauma and behavior problems. *Abuse and Neglect, 34*, 215–224.

Conger, R.D., Conger, K.J., Elder, G.H., Lorenz, F.O., Simons, R.L., & Whitbeck, L.B. (1992). A family process model of economic hardship and adjustment of early adolescent boys. *Child Development, 63*, 526–541.

Connell, M. (2009). Extended forensic evaluation. In K. Kuehnle, & M. Connell (Eds), *The Evaluation of Child Sexual Abuse Allegations: A Comprehensive Guide to Assessment and Testimony* (pp. 451–487). Hoboken, NJ: John Wiley & Sons.

Herman. S. (2009) Forensic child sexual abuse evaluations: Accuracy, ethics, and admissibility. In K. Kuehnle, & M. Connell (Eds), *The Evaluation of Child Sexual Abuse Allegations: A Comprehensive Guide to Assessment and Testimony* (pp. 247–266). Hoboken, NJ: John Wiley & Sons.

Holden, G.W., Geffner, R., & Jouriles, E.N. (1998). *Children Exposed to Marital Violence*. Washington DC: American Psychological Association.

Keiley, M.K., Howe, T.R., Dodge, K.A., Bates, J.E., & Pettit, G.S. (2001). The timing of child physical maltreatment. A crossdomain growth analysis of impact on adolescent externalising and internalising problems. *Development and Psychopathology, 13*, 891–912.

Kendall-Tackett, K.A, Williams, L.M., & Finkelhor, D. (1993). Impact of sexual abuse on children: A review and synthesis of recent empirical studies. *Psychological Bulletin, 113*, 164–180.

La Rooy, D., Lamb, M.E., & Pipe, M.E. (2009). Repeated interviewing: A critical evaluation of the risks and potential benefits. In K. Kuehnle, & M. Connell (Eds), *The Evaluation of Child Sexual Abuse Allegations: A Comprehensive Guide to Assessment and Testimony* (pp. 327–361). Hoboken, NJ: John Wiley & Sons.

Luthar, S.S. (1999). *Poverty and Children's Adjustment*. Thousand Oaks, CA: Sage.

Malloy, L.C., & Quas, J.A. (2009). Children's suggestibility: Areas of consensus and controversy. In K. Kuehnle, & M. Connell (Eds), *The Evaluation of Child Sexual Abuse Allegations: A Comprehensive Guide to Assessment and Testimony* (pp. 327–361). Hoboken, NJ: John Wiley & Sons.

Manly, J.T., Kim, J.E., Rogosch, F.A., & Cicchetti, D. (2001). Dimensions of child maltreatment and children's adjustment: Contributions of developmental timing and subtype. *Development and Psychopathology, 13*, 759–782.

Mayes, I.C., & Truman, S.D. (2002). Substance abuse and parenting. In M. Bornstein (Ed.), *Handbook of Parenting* (3rd edn, Vol. 4, pp. 329–359). Mahwah, NJ: Erlbaum.

National Children's Alliance. Mission. Retrieved 14 June 2010 from the National Children's Alliance web site, http://www.nationalchildrensalliance.org/index.php?s=24

Saunders, B.E., Berliner, L., & Hanson, R.F. (Eds). (2004). *Child Physical and Sexual Abuse: Guidelines for Treatment* (Revised Report: 26 April 2004). Charleston, SC: National Crime Victims Research and Treatment Center. Document can be downloaded at: http://www.musc.edu/cvc/

Saywitz, K.J., Esplin, P., & Romanoff, S.L. (2007). A holistic aproah to interviewing and treating children in the legal system. In M.E. Pipe, M.E. Lamb, Y. Orbach, & A.C. Cederborg (Eds), *Child Sexual Abuse: Disclosure, Delay, and Denial* (pp. 219–249). Mahwah, NJ: Lawrence Erlbaum.

Saywitz, K.J., Mannarino, A.P., Berliner, L., & Cohen, J.A. (2000). Treatment for sexually abused children and adolescents. *American Psychologist, 55*, 1040–1049.

Sedak, A.J., & Broadhurst, D.D. (1996). *Third National Incidence Study of Child Abuse and Neglect, final report*. Washington, DC: US Department of Health and Human Services.

Silvern, L., Karyl, J., Waelde, L., Hodges, W.F., Starek, J., Heidt, E., & Min, K. (1995). Retrospective reports of parental partner abuse: Relationships to depression, trauma symptoms and self-esteem among college students. *Journal of Family Violence, 10*, 177–202.

Substance Abuse Mental Health Services Administration (SAMHSA). (2002). Mental health: A report of the Surgeon General. Rockville, MD: US Department of Health and Human Services, Substance Abuse and Mental Health Services Administration, Center for Mental Health Services. Retrieved 14 June 2010 from http://mentalhealth.samhsa.gov/cre/toc.asp

Troxel, N., Ogle, C., Cordon, I. Lawler, M., & Goodman, G.S. (2009). Child witnesses in criminal court. In B.L. Bottoms, G.S. Goodman, & C.J. Najdowski (Eds), *Children as Victims, Witnesses, and Offenders: Psychological Science and the Law* (pp. 150–166). New York, NY: Guilford Press.

11

Training Forensic Interviewers

HEATHER STEWART, CARMIT KATZ, AND DAVID J. LA ROOY

Key Points

- The training forensic interviewers receive should be based on methods that have been the subject of scientific study and proven to work.
- The initial training should begin with the introduction of the NICHD structured interview protocol along with information about the research base supporting the approach.
- Training programmes should be continuous and ongoing (i.e., monthly) so that the quality of interviewing is maintained at the highest standards possible.

GOAL OF INVESTIGATIVE INTERVIEWER TRAINING

The outcome of investigative interviewer training is to enable interviewers to conduct investigative interviews that adhere to recommended guidelines. Interviewers must learn to reflect critically on the skills and techniques required to conduct effective interviews through a variety of methods which include seminar presentations, practice interviews with experienced police officers and actors, as well as detailed individual and group feedback sessions. Interviewers need to become competent in building rapport and communicating with children using

Children's Testimony: A Handbook of Psychological Research and Forensic Practice, Second Edition.
Edited by Michael E. Lamb, David J. La Rooy, Lindsay C. Malloy, and Carmit Katz.

appropriate prompts and questions. Interviewers must also be aware of the evidence requirements that apply in their jurisdictions as well as possessing the skills to give evidence in court proceedings and defend their practice.

The training of interviewers is therefore of fundamental importance because without appropriate training and support it is not possible to translate the best practice discussed in this book into practice. It is all too easy to criticize interviewers when they depart from guidelines but responsibility for interviewer shortcomings must also be borne by interviewer trainers, management teams, and others involved in the delivery of training programmes to investigative interviewers. Fortunately, there is a growing research base that has evaluated training methods and their effectiveness which we can learn from. Research shows that successful training of interviewers must involve two important ingredients. First, interviewers must begin their training using a structured interview such as the National Institute for Child Health and Human Development (NICHD) Protocol which has proven to be successful in helping interviewers adhere to recommended best practice, as evidenced in many field studies. Secondly, successful training programmes must be ongoing and continuously deliver feedback to interviewers about the quality of their work and provide opportunities for interviewers to develop their skills.

In this chapter we describe training methods used in different jurisdictions. These methods have been developed based on the results of scientific research examining the most effective training methods for promoting interviews of a high standard. We pay particular attention to the specific content of the training as well as the manner of training delivery. Of course, there is no 'one size fits all' solution to training interviewers so new developments should also be accompanied by research to measure their success whenever possible.

IMPORTANCE OF A STRUCTURED APPROACH TO INTERVIEWING

Forensic interviewers have a duty to be familiar with current interview methods and the supporting literature. It is expected that interviewers be trained, knowledgeable, and skilled so that they can conduct interviews effectively and to accepted high standards. This has never been more important because over the years prosecutors and defense attorneys have become more knowledgeable about what constitutes a 'good' interview, and standards for filing charges and moving cases forward through the judicial process have become increasingly higher.

Therefore, adhering to a research-based training method maximizes the defensibility of the procedures that are used by forensic interviewers and increases interviewer confidence.

The most well-known and widely studied interviewer training system is the freely available NICHD Protocol (see Chapter 10 and Appendix). It was developed with reference to child development issues, including linguistic capabilities, memory and suggestibility, forensic needs, interviewer behaviour, and the effects of stress and trauma by a team of researchers, interviewers, police officers, and legal professionals. Research over the last decade has shown that effective interviewer training can begin with the proper use of the NICHD Protocol because it allows interviewers to maximize the amount of information obtained from free-recall memory (which is deemed most accurate) by using open-ended questions thereby requiring fewer, more risky, focused questions be used (Lamb *et al.*, 2008, 2009; Orbach *et al.*, 2000; Sternberg *et al.*, 2001b). The overarching goal for effective training is to operationalize these professional recommendations and maximize the interviewers' adherence to these procedures (Sternberg *et al.*, 2001b).

While there can be some initial resistance by interviewers to the idea that that a structured approach to interviewing is the most desirable, the benefits are obvious in terms of how much more easily interviewers are able to learn how an interview should be conducted, and the way children should be prompted for information. Moreover, using the same standardized approach with all children has other advantages: it levels the playing field, giving every child who is interviewed an equal opportunity to disclose or not disclose alleged abuse. Personal biases such as underestimating children's capabilities, or those resulting from certain case characteristics, are minimized. Forensic interviewers may sometime also lack self-awareness or self-monitoring regarding interviewing practices and thus a standardized format aids in efforts to maintain desirable interview standards.

IMPORTANCE OF ONGOING FEEDBACK AND TRAINING FOR INTERVIEWERS

It is absolutely crucial, however, to understand that the publication and teaching of professional guidelines must be accompanied with ongoing feedback. It has emerged from research conducted in many countries over the last decade that although there is a consensus as to what best-practice interviewing should involve, investigative interviewers, even after intensive training about 'best practice', often fail to modify and improve their own interviewing behaviour accordingly (e.g.,

Cederborg, Orbach, Sternberg, & Lamb, 2000; Craig, Scheibe, Kircher, Raskin, & Dodd, 1999; Lamb *et al.*, 1996; Sternberg *et al.*, 2001a). The disappointing results of these studies showed that although the interviewers understood how they should interview children, no measurable improvement in the quality of their interviews was observed. Studies with British police officers (Sternberg *et al.*, 2001a), US police officers (Sternberg *et al.*, 1996), and Israeli youth investigators (Lamb *et al.*, 1996) have all shown that although it seems that the investigative interviewers learn and appreciate the rationale of best practice during the training, they nonetheless later fail to use the desirable interventions and instead use techniques that they were told to avoid when they conducted real interviews. Thus, there is awareness that initial training programmes that do not dovetail with ongoing training feedback for interviewers are not sufficient in improving investigative interviewing in the long term.

Other research has shown that ongoing training that provides continuous feedback beyond initial training sessions is effective at maintaining high standards (Lamb, Sternberg, Orbach, Esplin, & Mitchell, 2002a; Lamb *et al.*, 2002b). These studies showed that interviewers who were provided with initial training on how to use the NICHD Protocol, followed by ongoing group and individual training and feedback, conducted interviews containing higher proportions of open-ended prompts and lower proportions of option-posing and suggestive utterances. However, when the training and ongoing supervision stopped, there was a decline in the proportion of open-ended prompts used and an increase in the proportion of more risky option-posing questions.

In a recent field study conducted in Israel by Katz and Hershkowitz (2010), a group of nine investigative interviewers were trained on two different sets of protocols: the NICHD Protocol integrating the use of drawing and the NICHD Protocol integrating repeated open questioning. The interviewers were provided with individual and group training once a month. The initial training took place over 2 days and during these training sessions the interviewers were exposed to the interview protocols and to their rationale. The interviewers themselves were fully involved in shaping these guidelines based on their previous experiences with children, which was found to be very important not only for their engagement with and commitment to the use of the protocols, but also their involvement considerably improved the protocols in the first place. The initial training also included presentation of the main concepts supporting the use of these protocols, including discussion of the main findings from laboratory and field studies concerning drawings and repeated interviews. While communicating research findings to interviewers, it is important to be aware of their time constraints and recognize that it is difficult for interviewers to find the time to search for the pertinent literature, read the relevant studies, and remember the most critical information. That is why trainers selected relevant studies beforehand and prepared briefings specifically suited for their training needs.

Following the initial training, the structure of both the individual and the group training involved analysing transcripts, together identifying strengths that need to be maintained and weaknesses that need to be improved while documenting and following the improvement from one meeting to the next. This training achieved exceptional results with interviewers using, on average, 87% open-ended questions and no suggestive interventions.

In summary, effective training begins with introducing interviewers to the structured NICHD Protocol followed by intensive and systematic training which provides ongoing individual and group supervision and feedback. The successful implementation of strategies used by interview trainers that have been developed on the basis of this research are detailed in the following sections.

INITIAL TRAINING

Initial training is a critical tool while working on the improvement of the investigative interviews and it is a great opportunity for interviewers, who often come from different backgrounds, have different experiences, and who may have different attitudes and beliefs about forensic interviewing, to meet each other. The initial training is also a great opportunity to make clear what will be expected from interviewers, how they can meet these expectations, and to convey the message that 'we are all in this together'.

The initial training should be intensive and last for 5–10 days, with the same group of interviewers trained by the same people. A positive group environment is very important and makes the training easier to deliver and helps the ultimate success of the training session. Although it has yet to be documented empirically, based on our experiences, it is sometimes difficult enough for interviewers to grapple with 'best practice' and address their own interviewing behaviour. Thus, tension in the training sessions is especially counter-productive. Of course, some tension will always exist, but if it is focused on the professional aspects of interviewing then it can be used effectively. However, if the group dynamic is destructive and if there is a negative or overly anxious atmosphere between the interviewers and the trainers, there is an increased chance that the training will be a failure, regardless of everyone's best intentions. That is why the first step of the trainer should be to establish rapport with the group. The best way to do this is to start the initial training by giving each one of the interviewers the opportunity to share their expectations of the sessions and their beliefs and feelings. Creating intimacy and respect within the group is highly beneficial and can also emphasize the critical impact of the rapport building in the interviews that they will conduct with children. After rapport building is achieved within the group, the 'substantive' training phase can start.

What are the aims of the initial training 'substantive' phase? The first aim should be a continuation of the intimacy and respect among the group; no change can happen unless the interviewers feel safe in the group. Initial training programmes should include a combination of instruction, recorded interview examples, and role play practice sessions. There should be an exhaustive explanation of the structured interview tool. Participants should not just be instructed to adopt a new method; they must begin to understand why they are using the guidelines recommended to them. Recorded interviews help solidify the instructional pieces by demonstrating the components being discussed. Extensive role play allows participants to demonstrate what they have learned, acclimatize to the challenges of adopting new techniques in a supportive learning environment, and receive feedback, before conducting real interviews. This decreases anxiety and builds confidence. Critically, it sets the tone and expectations for future feedback to be solicited, welcomed, and incorporated. The initial training should also cover the following content:

1. Discussion of the importance of forensic interviews with children, the fact that children can be reliable witnesses, and the role of the investigative interviewer in promoting the well-being of children in the forensic context. This discussion should include historic aspects and developments in children's testimony and also should be the time when the interviewers share their thoughts, attitudes, and beliefs about forensic interviewing with children.
2. The importance of learning about child development in order to conduct appropriate interviews (basic concepts in memory, language, time and touch concepts, attention, social and cognitive abilities, authority). On the one hand, the information relating to these concepts should be up-to-date and detailed enough to create an understanding but, on the other hand, it should not be too detailed. It is important to integrate into this section both experimental and applied studies of forensic interviewing.
3. Detailed discussion of the different components of a best-practice interview: ground rules, rapport building, the practice interview, and

questioning children about substantive issues using different kinds of techniques, focusing on appropriate interviewer prompts. This is the core of the initial training and should include the following techniques by the trainer: discussion of each one of these parts should include a detailed rationale of its importance using up-to-date studies (e.g., open-ended questions, lab and field studies relating to it). After this introduction, the trainer should expose the interviewers (preferably a videotape but a transcript can be useful as well) to real interviews that present questions, dilemmas, and difficulties concerning the discussed issues. Finally, exercises in role play for all the participants should take place; the exercises should be followed by detailed feedback from the group members and at the end by the trainer.

4. During the initial training it is highly important to involve in the discussions experienced forensic interviewers who can share their experiences concerning the importance of using the guidelines and the challenges of presenting their work in the legal context. This also should be taken as an opportunity for the interviewers to have informal discussions with the experienced interviewers about the work that is expected of them.
5. The importance of corroboration in child abuse investigations should be discussed and how following up investigative leads provided during the interview is essential. Because legal jurisdictions vary in their requirements, it is worth considering having a local prosecutor and defense attorney review their perspectives relative to child forensic interviews and how they may strengthen or weaken a case.
6. The final component of the initial training programme should involve a short summary of the main contents that were covered during the training and an opportunity for the interviewers to share their experience from the training – the group environment, the trainer, questions, dilemmas, and anxieties that remain unresolved. The ideal situation is that in the final stage of this initial training it is clear for each interviewer when, how often, by whom, and with whom the ongoing training (individual and group) will take place.

INITIAL FEEDBACK OPPORTUNITIES

Feedback can begin the moment that the interviewer is conducting an interview. It can be beneficial for interviewers to take at least one 'break' during the interview so that they can confer with another team member or partner in the investigation. Feedback can be provided at this time and can also be continued during the debriefing process immediately following each interview. Both positive and negative interviewer behaviour can be addressed immediately. Feedback at the time can be very meaningful and effective. Without the passage of time, the interviewer is more likely to recall the case specifics and they can avoid the same mistakes in subsequent interviews. It can also have a direct impact on the case at hand rather than delaying feedback, allowing interviewers to continue with poor interview practices longer than necessary. Another effective mechanism for monitoring and feedback is to involve immediate supervisors of those conducting forensic interviews. Supervisors and police sergeants should attend the same training as the interviewers so that they are in a position to recognize and provide feedback on interview practices. To this end, they should be encouraged to watch their staff's interviews in progress or afterwards and provide evaluation. In general, people tend to perform better given the expectation that their work will be shared and evaluated.

FEEDBACK IN TEAM MEETINGS

Feedback in team meetings is an effective method when applied to a team situation and can be accomplished by scheduling regular team meetings to review interviews and provide feedback. It is critical that team members (caseworkers, detectives, prosecutors) also be trained in best practices in forensic interviews so they can provide constructive and accurate comments to the interviewer and they should be invited to attend feedback sessions. This provides a time for self-reflection and to view their own behaviour outside the confines of the interview itself. This provides an opportunity to observe behaviours that may not be readily apparent or ones we are not initially conscious of. The interviewer should then share what they learnt from this self-reflection process with trainers and their peers.

Building a network of trainees is also useful to help keep professionals updated on changes and emerging research as the field evolves; internal newsletters, blogs, and list-serves are worth considering. These groups can also come together for advanced forensic interview training or to discuss special topics and issues that arise.

ONGOING INDIVIDUAL AND GROUP TRAINING AND FEEDBACK

It is important to maintain the knowledge of best practice that was acquired during the initial training and promote the quality of interventions from the investigative interviewers. Although the main aims of individual and group feedback are similar, there is a basic difference between these two formats – while in individual training there is follow-up on the work of one specific interviewer, in group training the focus is on the interviews without focus on a specific person. So why is there a need for both formats? Ideally, the individual training and the group training together will accomplish the main aim of maintaining and promoting the quality of the forensic interviews, with the individual training paying attention to the specific characteristics of the interviewer, and with the group training taking into consideration the development of the group and their team.

Individual Training

In individual training the trainer will usually be someone more experienced than the interviewer. The ideal frequency of individual training is once every 3 weeks or a month. The structure of each meeting should be as follows: each month there will be a focus on one element that reflects difficulty or dilemma in the interviewer's work, with the interviewer selecting one transcript or recorded interview that emphasizes this issue (many places do not have the luxury of transcribing interviews plus viewing the actual DVD of the interview helps focus attention and provides the opportunity to view/discuss non-verbal things that happen). It is highly important that before each meeting both the trainer and the interviewer read the transcript closely and evaluate it according to the matter to be discussed. For example, if the matter chosen is working on elaboration of open-ended prompts, both the trainer and the interviewer need to analyse the case according to this aspect and identify relevant aspects of the interview. During the individual meeting it is important, within an environment of trust and respect, to cover all the 'should be maintained' items in the interview and the 'should be changed' items. At the end of the meeting there should be a summary of the most important points that were covered and a decision of what will be the main issue for the next meeting and how there will be evaluation of the progress of the current matter (e.g., choosing some random transcripts for the next meeting and evaluating the use of open-ended questions). Ideally, the interviewer will give a written summary of the meeting to the trainer so both of them will know what they discussed and agreed on. All the summaries, coded transcripts, and evaluations should be kept in one place and be available both to the trainer and the interviewer. These meetings should form the basis of an individual development plan so that over time interviewers can see how they are improving.

Group Training

In group training there are two formats: a *peer review*, which is a facilitated review and discussion of interviews among the interviewers themselves, and the other is when the trainer is a permanent person, usually much more experienced than the trainees. Currently, peer review is perhaps the method with the most notoriety intended to maintain desirable practices in forensic interviews. Effective from January 2010, all child advocacy centres (CACs) must demonstrate 'continuous quality improvement activities' by instituting a formalized peer review process. The specific details of this process can be determined by individual communities or agencies. Peer review programmes per se for forensic interviewers are relatively new and have not been empirically tested. The suggested outline may provide a framework for the peer review process:

1. Peer review should be conducted in a professional, respectful, and supportive manner. Refer to Appendix A for a sample letter that can be given to peer review participants ahead of time and sets the tone for a positive non-threatening interaction.
2. A feedback sheet, or a report card of sorts, should be developed. It may include desired practices, prompts, and elements of the interview. Overall impressions of the interview, interviewer strengths, and areas for improvement should also be included (Appendix B).
3. An interview expert, trainer, forensic interviewer supervisor, or peer review leader should view the interview to be critiqued. This can be done prior to meeting as a group or in the meeting if time is short. Ideally, a recorded interview is best but a transcript will suffice if that is the only format available. The interviews reviewed should be closed cases and if referred to the criminal justice system should be adjudicated. This is so the interview is not unduly subject to attack before or during a court proceeding.
4. Each interview can be evaluated as a whole or special attention can be given to key elements. The results of the evaluation of the interview can be shared one-to-one with the interviewer before presenting it to the group if that is needed to increase the interviewer's comfort. Then either the entire interview or demonstrative excerpts previously identified by the peer review leader are viewed by the group. Good examples can be shown to demonstrate elements of the interview (i.e., effective use of ground rules, narrative elaboration by the child, open-ended prompts by the interviewer, and proper timing and formulation of option posing questions). In this way, ideas are shared about how to handle issues in future interviews. When

undesirable interview practices have been used, suggestions for improvement can be solicited from the peer review group. They can help one another find solutions. This promotes a 'we're all in this together' mentality that it is hoped will continue to flourish in subsequent training.

5. It is beneficial to discuss existing trends for this group of interviewers. They learn from observing one another. They may have adopted good and bad habits by modelling each other. It is important to point this out. Inform them that this information is specific to those sitting in the room. Otherwise, they will think it applies to everyone except them. If one-to-one feedback has already been conducted with their interviews, this information will sound familiar and will be reinforced.

Examples include the following:

- Allow the child to provide a narrative response. Do not interrupt them to fulfill the interviewer's need to ask a direct question.
- Separate multiple incidences as soon as possible. Have the child describe specific details about a specific incident. Avoid allowing the child to continue to disclose scripted memories, encourage them to describe episodic memories.

CONTENT OF THE TRAINING PROGRAMMES

The quality of the interview is the main issue of concern both for researchers and practitioners; its effects on the interview outcomes have been proven systematically to be critical. However, beyond maintaining a high quality of interview, it is also very important to dedicate part of the initial and the ongoing training to other issues. These could include the way interviewers communicate their work to other practitioners in the legal system and how interviewers handle motivational factors during the interviews are also highly important for the interview outcomes. For example, anecdotally, interviewers often talk about cases in which the quality of the interview was good but presenting it in court and defending it required much more than just conducting a good interview. As discussed above, the interviewer needs to show he/she is no less knowledgeable in the relevant updated information than other practitioners in the field. So, when working with interviewers on this matter, whether it is in individual or group training, it is important to work on the skills of identifying main themes in the interview that are relevant in each specific case for court. For example, if the interview was conducted with a young child, aged 4, and multiple incidents of abuse were alleged, it is very important for the interviewer to address the difficulties that young children's greater reliance on script memory and potential difficulties in retrieving information from specific episodes. After identifying these themes, it is important for the interviewer to reflect when and how during the interview the child handles these issues. If all the group members are aware of useful techniques to assist in preparing a case for court, then presenting it in front of their peers can be very effective.

As for the issue of reluctant children, it is highly important to work with the interviewers on how they feel and consequently how they react to a reluctant child. A study by Hershkowitz *et al.* (2006) demonstrated that while interviewing reluctant children, interviewers tend to decrease their supportiveness, contrary to what those interviewers expected from their own behaviour. In a recent study by Katz, Hershkowitz, and Lamb (2010), an individual training session was conducted on the topic of interviewing reluctant children. The main focus of the training was not on studies and empirically based findings but rather on re-engaging the interviewers and helping them to be aware of their own emotions and thoughts as a source of something that can affect their interventions during the interview. This first step helped those interviewers to later on employ new recommended techniques in handling reluctant children (a 'Revised' NICHD Protocol) and brought a significant increase in the rates of disclosure (55% in interviews that followed the new instructions vs. 49% in interviews with the standard protocol). Over 30% of the allegations that were elicited using the 'Revised' Protocol were initiated spontaneously by the children or in response to open-ended questions, while over 50% of the allegations using the standard NICHD Protocol were elicited using coercive interventions (e.g., 'I heard that you talked with your teacher, I wanted to check with you whether...'). One of the main needs that was emphasized by the interviewers was their need for emotional support given the unique characteristic of their job; however, barriers such as time constraints make it very hard for training to take place in a systematic way, and when that happens in most organizations the main aim will be to improve the quality of the interviews so less attention and resources will be spent on the interviewers' personal difficulties.

BARRIERS TO TRAINING

Change can be a tough proposition for many, especially if new methods compete with natural instincts, previous training, and other habits that have formed. Empirical evidence of efficacy is not always the most significant criteria for selecting interview methods. Traditionally, in the field of forensic interviewing, awareness and incorporation of science has not been part of the culture. In the past, forensic interviewing has been viewed as an 'art form'. There has been an over-reliance on personal experience and anecdotal information rather than research. Interviewers have viewed themselves as eclectic, talented at picking and choosing different techniques based upon each case and the characteristics of each child. This approach is not supported by research.

Even with the understanding that in order to achieve best practice interviewers should follow closely a structured interview protocol and in order to maintain high quality of interviews they should be part of an ongoing training, several barriers exist that make implementing a desirable model quite a daunting task. In some communities, budget constraints, lack of specialized resources, demands of overwhelming caseloads, and lack of accessibility to quality training prevail. Often there are competing interests with other professional duties of the forensic interviewer; for example, safety planning, suspect interrogations, and court testimony to name a few. This lack of time and money can thwart the ability to obtain proper training. Creative solutions need to be sought in each community to make ongoing training a priority. Collaboration between agencies and CACs is critical as ongoing training and peer review programmes are emerging so that effective methods can be shared. If quality interviewing is expected, then proper training should be required and made available. Interviewers need to be supported in the tough work they do.

Training is crucial to the work of forensic interviewers and should be mandatory. In addition, because of the barriers that exist, it is highly important to make the time not only for the initial training, but also for ongoing training. This understanding should be presented to policy makers in different countries and the training should become a basic part of the forensic interviewer's work.

CONCLUSIONS

The forensic interview has a crucial role in the context of child abuse investigations and it often determines how the rest of the investigation progresses. Consequently, proper training of forensic interviewers is paramount. Forensic interviewers should receive training in methods that have scientific backing and proven efficacy. Initial training, however intensive, is simply not enough to maintain best practices and should always be accompanied by a continuous ongoing training throughout an interviewer's career. In order for this approach to be successful, it must be supported by everyone on the team including administrators and managers. If forensic interviewers are expected to carry out such important work, they need to be properly equipped with the support and tools necessary to be successful.

REFERENCES

Cederborg, A.C., Orbach, Y., Sternberg, K.J., & Lamb, M.E. (2000). Investigative interviews of child witnesses in Sweden. *Child Abuse and Neglect*, *24*, 1355–1361.

Craig, R.A., Scheibe, R., Kircher, J., Raskin, D.C., & Dodd, D. (1999). Interviewer questions and content analysis of children's statements of sexual abuse. *Applied Developmental Science*, *3*, 77–85.

Hershkowitz, I., Orbach, Y., Lamb, M.E., Sternberg, K.J., Pipe, M.E., & Horowitz, D. (2006). Dynamics of forensic interviews with suspected abuse victims who do not disclose abuse. *Child Abuse and Neglect*, *30*, 753–769.

Katz, C. & Hershkowitz, I. (2010). The effect of drawing on the richness of accounts provided by alleged victims of child sexual abuse. *Child Maltreatment*, *15*, 171–179.

Katz, C., Hershkowitz, I., & Lamb, M.E. (2010). Enhancing abuse disclosure by reluctant children: A test of the revised NICHD protocol. Paper presented at the annual meeting of the American Psychology Law Society, Vancouver, Canada, March 2010.

Lamb, M.E., Hershkowitz, I., Orbach, Y., Esplin, P.W. (2008). *Tell Me What Happened: Structured Investigative Interviews of Child Victims and Witnesses.* West Sussex, England: John Wiley & Sons Ltd.

Lamb, M.E., Hershkowitz, I., Sternberg, K.J., Esplin, P.W., Hovav, M., Manor, T., & Yudilevitch, L. (1996). Effects of investigative utterance types on Israeli children's responses. *International Journal of Behavioural Development*, *19*, 627–637.

Lamb, M.E., Orbach, Y., Sternberg, K.J., Aldridge, J., Pearson, S., Stewart, H., Esplin, P.W., & Bowler, L. (2009). Use of a structured investigative protocol enhances the quality of investigative interviews with alleged victims of child sexual abuse in Britain. *Applied Cognitive Psychology*, *23*, 449–467.

Lamb, M.E., Sternberg, K.J., Orbach, Y., Esplin, P.W., & Mitchell, S. (2002a). Is ongoing feedback necessary to maintain the quality of investigative interviews with allegedly abused children? *Applied Developmental Science*, *6*, 35–41.

Lamb, M.E., Sternberg, K.J., Orbach, Y., Hershkowitz, I., Horowitz, D., & Esplin, P.W. (2002b). The effects of intensive training and ongoing supervision on the quality of investigative interviews with alleged sex abuse victims. *Applied Developmental Science*, *6*, 114–125.

Orbach, Y., Hershkowitz, I., Lamb, M.E., Sternberg, K.J., Esplin, P.W., & Horowitz, D. (2000). Assessing the value of structured protocols for forensic interviews of alleged child abuse victims. *Child Abuse and Neglect*, *24*, 733–752.

Sternberg, K.J., Lamb, M.E., Davies, G.A., & Westcott, H.L. (2001a). The memorandum of good practice: theory versus application. *Child Abuse and Neglect*, *25*, 669–681.

Sternberg, K.J., Lamb, M.E., Orbach, Y., Esplin, P.W., & Mitchell, S. (2001b). Use of a structured investigative protocol enhance young children's responses to free recall prompts in the course of forensic interviews. *Journal of Applied Psychology*, *86*, 997–1005.

Sternberg, K.J., Lamb, M.E., Hershkowitz, I., Esplin, P.W., Redlich, A., & Sunshine, N. (1996). The relation between investigative utterance types and the informativeness of child witnesses. *Journal of Applied Developmental Psychology*, *17*, 439–451.

APPENDIX A

Thank you for participating in the new Peer Review process which was created with input and support from local child protective service workers, law enforcement and prosecutors, as well as trainers from the forensic interview training program.

The training experience is designed to provide supportive feedback to investigators to promote best practice methods in the child abuse forensic interview process. All investigators in our county will be asked to participate in this process annually. It is a requirement from the National Children's Alliance to comply with accreditation requirements.

We want to assure you that your peer review session is confidential and those conducting the session shall only discuss the feedback with your team at the time of the peer review training. You will receive written comments that will be provided to you and your supervisor indicating areas of strengths and areas for improvement.

To get the most positive experience from this peer review session, please consider the following:

1. Know that there is no such thing as the perfect interview and you are not being held to an unrealistic standard.
2. Have an open mind to listen and hear the guidance you will receive, it will not compromise your cases.
3. You do not have to defend why you did things in the past, the reasons are very likely good ones, but the guidance will expand your options and skill sets that will work well for you and for the child.
4. Interviewing victims is one of the most challenging parts of an investigation and you are respected and appreciated for your efforts.

The objective of the session is to ensure that forensic interviews are being conducted at the best practice level on a consistent basis to ensure the highest likelihood for protection and justice for child victims.

Providing supportive feedback and guidance to help investigators accomplish these techniques is the best method to achieve the objective. Supervisors play a key role in providing ongoing support and guidance after the peer review session is completed to sustain the gains accomplished in the session.

Thank you for your hard work which is never appreciated enough for the burdens placed on you every day. We hope you will feel that this was a valuable experience.

APPENDIX B: FEEDBACK/GUIDANCE

Interview Review

Child: Female
Age: 12

☑ Introduce self
☑ Tell the truth
☑ If you don't understand me
☑ If I don't understand you
☑ Don't guess – say I don't know
☑ Correct me
☑ Demonstrates ground rules
☑ Things you like to do
☑ Happy
☑ Unhappy
☑ Episodic memory training
☑ Narrative elaboration
☑ Time segmentation
☑ Cued recall
☑ Engaged child and established rapport
☑ Proper progression of getting the allegation questions
☑ Tell me everything/more about _______ (after initial disclosure)
☑ Attempt to elicit narrative from the child
☑ Time segmentation
☑ Cued recall
☑ And then what happened?
☑ Did it happen one time or more than one time?
☑ If more than one time:
☑ Tell me about the last time
☑ Tell me about the first time
☑ Tell me about another time you remember well/or that was different

BREAK

☑ Appropriate questions asked after the break
☑ Anything like that happened to you before?
☑ Anyone talk with you about what to tell me today
☑ Who else knows about this/How did others find out?
☑ Anything else you think I should know/you want to tell me/any questions for me?
☑ Interrupts the child
☑ Interprets child's words instead of asking child to explain
☑ Not enough use of open-ended questions
☑ Asks 'can you' questions
☑ Listen, eye contact, limit note taking
☑ Probed for more detail with non-leading questions
☑ Asks child to clarify when necessary
☑ Asks about other possible victims/perpetrators when necessary
☑ Separation and ample detail when there are multiple incidents
☑ NEUTRAL FACT FINDER

Overall Impression of Interview

The interviewer's flow is very natural. The child is very cooperative and provides narrative responses. Interviewer's use of open-ended questions is excellent. Interviewer's follow up questions are effective and well timed. Interviewer's patience, kindness, and honesty to the child's questions at the end of the interview is impressive.

Interviewer Strengths

Excellent use of time segmentation and 'and then what happened' prompts throughout the interview. Interviewer counteracted child's reluctance by being appropriately persistent, asking open-ended questions during the disclosure, and by effectively using pauses.

Interviewer effectively uses the prompt 'and then what happened' throughout the interview which yielded crucial information. Interviewer asks for clarification throughout the interview when it is necessary. In an effort to help the child organize her narrative, the interviewer asks things like 'As soon as you woke up, tell me the very next thing that happened?' – superb technique.

It was important that the interviewer followed up on how others found out and who else knows about the sexual abuse for corroborative value and to assess mother's potential for being supportive of this child.

It was a good idea to ask this child if her stepfather ever had her do anything to him or touch him. This question was appropriate in this case, was formulated well, and was perfectly timed (after the break).

Areas for Improvement/Recommendations

Do not take your cell phone into the interview room or make sure it is turned off.

Interviewer asks more than once 'how many times/how often?' This question has no value. If the child would have provided a number it likely would have been a guess. This child was very clear throughout the interview that the sexual abuse occurred many times, in many locations, and in several different ways since third grade. Focus on specific details about specific incidents.

12

The Use of Supplementary Techniques in Forensic Interviews with Children

DEIRDRE A. BROWN

Key Points

- Interviewers may use supplementary techniques (e.g., introducing props, toys, photographs, dolls, context reinstatement or drawing exercises, truth induction strategies) to assist children in providing more detailed accounts of their experiences.
- These communication aids may serve a variety of purposes (e.g., facilitate rapport between the interviewer and child, reduce the social and emotional demands of the interview, provide retrieval cues to assist in recalling further information, overcome linguistic deficits, or provide a non-verbal response option).
- Research indicates that the various aids that have been employed differ in their effectiveness at supporting children's recall and reporting. Consideration must be given to what aids are used, the timing and manner in which they are introduced into the interview, and the developmental capacities of the children.
- Although supplementary techniques introduced in the substantive portion of the interview may lead to new details being reported

Children's Testimony: A Handbook of Psychological Research and Forensic Practice, Second Edition.
Edited by Michael E. Lamb, David J. La Rooy, Lindsay C. Malloy, and Carmit Katz.

the accuracy or reliability of this information tends to be lower than for information spontaneously reported, especially with younger children.
- Techniques that allow children to provide their own retrieval cues (rather than being provided by the interviewer) tend to have better support from research studies.
- Caution must be used to ensure children's direct interactions with aids (e.g., the content of their drawings, play or exploration with props or toys) is not interpreted as communication of their experiences.

It is now generally accepted that the amount and reliability of information reported by children in forensic interviews will reflect the interaction of a number of variables pertaining to the child (e.g., developmental level, communicative ability), the event in question (e.g., how many times it occurred, how long ago it was), and, importantly, how the children are interviewed (for reviews see Brown, Lamb, Pipe, & Orbach, 2008; Pipe, Lamb, Orbach, & Esplin, 2004). While factors relating to the child and the event are typically unable to be modified when pursuing an allegation, how children are interviewed is able to be controlled and has been the focus of extensive research attention over the past three decades (for reviews see Brown & Lamb, 2009; Lamb, Hershkowitz, Orbach, & Esplin, 2008). This research has consistently demonstrated that the amount of information *spontaneously* reported by children (especially those under 5 years), although typically very accurate, is often insufficiently detailed to be of use to investigators seeking to determine whether there is a case to answer. As such an important question has been how best to support children in providing as much detail as possible about the event to assist with establishing the specific details of an incident required for successful prosecution, without inadvertently compromising the truthfulness of their accounts (e.g., via provision of misleading information or use of suggestive techniques). The impact of introducing prop items (e.g., real items, toys, models, photographs, drawings, dolls) on children's testimony has been thought to provide a means of addressing some of the developmental limitations children bring to the interview context. Early research indicated that such techniques were common in interviews conducted by professionals from a range of backgrounds (e.g, social work, mental health, law, policing), with a survey of American interviewers indicating 92% included anatomically detailed dolls in interviews, 66% used anatomically detailed drawings, 87% used free drawings, and 47% used puppets or other toys (Conte, Sorenson, Fogarty, & Rosa, 1991). A more recent survey of professionals conducting investigations of child sexual abuse in the context of child custody cases indicated 67.5% included projective drawing tests in their evaluations, 54% used timelines, 44% used anatomical drawings, 21% used anatomical dolls, and 34% used puppets or other toys (e.g., dolls' houses) (Bow, Quinnell, Zaroff, & Assemany, 2002). It is difficult to establish the extent to which supplementary techniques are included in contemporary practice; however, recent professional protocols and consultation documents suggest that dolls and body diagrams remain part of an interviewer's repertoire of techniques, and may even be utilized in the courtroom (e.g., APRI, 2003; APSAC, 2002; Home Office, 2002; Plotnikoff & Woolfson, 2009a,b).

RATIONALE FOR USING SUPPLEMENTARY TECHNIQUES IN INTERVIEWS WITH CHILDREN

The interview context itself is a novel and unfamiliar one for children, with a variety of implicit expectations and assumptions that differ from children's typical interactions with adults (for a review see Lamb & Brown, 2006), which may lead to minimal responding from children. For example, investigative interviews require that children engage with unfamiliar adults, often on their own, in an unfamiliar place. Children are unlikely to perform at their best unless they are comfortable with the adults conducting the assessment and understand what is expected from them. The forensic interview context is also novel in that children typically interact with adults in contexts where the adult knows more than them. In an interview, however, the alleged victims of abuse are often the 'experts' – the sole sources of information about the suspected events. As such, developing rapport with the children, establishing their communicative level and relevant idiosyncratic vocabulary, and providing information about the purpose and ground rules of the interview is an important part of the forensic interview process. Providing toys for the children to play with or asking the children to engage in a drawing task prior to introducing the interview proper may help to put children at their ease, meaning they are more productive during the substantive part of the interview.

Normal conversational expectations mean that responses to questions such as 'What did you do today?' will be brief *summaries* of the key activities that occurred during the day (Sternberg *et al.*, 2002). Young children, in particular, typically respond to such questions with even greater brevity (e.g., 'I played'). Although in all likelihood very accurate, such responses are not particularly useful in forensic interviews where typical conversational conventions do not apply – victim/witnesses need to provide *elaborative* responses that provide as much detail as possible about their experiences (Wattam, 1992). Forensic interviewers must, therefore, help children elaborate on their spontaneous disclosures without compromising the accuracy of the information elicited. Providing props in an interview has been proposed as one way of encouraging children to be more responsive – possibly as a result of the props helping children to recall more information about their experience, or by encouraging them to report details they may not otherwise have included.

The forensic interview also differs from typical adult–child communication via the goal of the interaction. The purpose is to establish the credibility of allegations, assess the safeness of children's living arrangements, and evaluate the viability of criminal charges. As a result, the outcomes of the conversations between children and forensic interviewers are more significant than those of everyday conversations and may have far-reaching consequences (e.g., disruption of the family). The extent to which children are aware of the purpose of the interview and its possible outcomes may affect their willingness to disclose and discuss their experiences. In contrast to everyday conversations, forensic interviews also require children to talk about subjects that may be embarrassing and/or traumatic, which may adversely affect their willingness to converse with interviewers. It is important to note, however, that children are not necessarily unduly emotional when recounting experiences of maltreatment. Indeed, a recent study of children's emotional expression when talking about experiences of abuse demonstrated the majority (75%) did not display any negative emotional expression when disclosing abuse (Sayfan, Mitchell, Goodman, Eisen, & Qin, 2008). Further, children (especially very young children) may lack the knowledge and vocabulary to communicate adequately what happened to them, or may use idiosyncratic language to describe, for example, body parts or actions that took place. The task of forensic interviewers is thus to create an atmosphere in which children are willing to discuss topics that are not normally sanctioned, and may not be well understood, and provision of non-verbal methods of communication (e.g., by pointing, showing or re-enacting) may assist with this. Table 12.1 summarizes the research evaluating various supplementary techniques, which are described in detail below.

ANATOMICALLY DETAILED DOLLS

The use of anatomically detailed (AD) dolls was initially thought to provide children with a means of communicating their experiences when developmental, cognitive, or motivational challenges might provide a barrier, by allowing them to show rather than tell what had occurred.

Table 12.1 Summary of research evaluating supplementary techniques to facilitate children's recall and reporting of their experiences

Technique	Empirical support	Age groups studied	Positive benefits	Risks	Use
Anatomically detailed dolls	Laboratory and field studies	Preschool and school age	May increase information reported	May invite play/exploration	Eliciting child's vocabulary for body parts
	Contradictory evidence – results range from positive, negative, and no effects			May increase errors and decrease overall accuracy	Clarify verbal accounts
					Elicit new information
					Limit direct interaction; play should *not* be interpreted
Body diagrams	Laboratory and field studies	School age	May increase information reported	May increase errors especially regarding genital touch	Elicit child's vocabulary for body parts
	Field study showed increased detail			Decreases accuracy	Clarify verbal accounts
	Laboratory studies show increase errors			Omission of details common	Use open-ended questions to elicit elaborative details of any touch indicated
					Avoid yes/no questions
					Best support is for clarifying location of touch rather than actions associated with it

(*Continued*)

Table 12.1 (*Continued*)

Technique	Empirical support	Age groups studied	Positive benefits	Risks	Use
Real items	Laboratory studies	3–10 years	Increase in detail without affecting overall accuracy	Increase in plausible errors	Have items visible but limit direct interaction
				Accuracy decreases if distracter items included and over repeated interviews	
Toys and scale models	Laboratory studies	2.5–6 years	Increase in correct information reported	Increase in errors, with overall decrease in accuracy	Better outcome if uniquely associated with event and not a strong identity as a toy Unlikely to achieve this, presence may be suggestive Children need to interact with items for benefit to emerge
Photographs	Laboratory studies	3–11 years	Increase in information reported	May trigger false reports across repeated interviews	Over long delays require activity-based content to be useful

Picture cue cards	Laboratory studies	Preschool and school age	Increase in information reported	None identified	Effect apparent when cards introduced (no effect on free recall) Verbal prompting for categories just as effective Cards without preparation/ training not effective
Physical context reinstatement	Laboratory and field studies Mixed results – no effects and positive effects	School age	May elicit increase in information reported	May elicit errors if context not uniquely associated with event	Can only use once child has disclosed location – may interrupt recall process to travel to location
Mental context reinstatement	Laboratory and field studies	Preschool and school age	Increase in information reported	None identified	Instructions to recreate context given prior to interview
Drawing and talk	Laboratory and field studies	Preschool and school age	Increase in information reported Longer interviews	Increase in false reports if suggestive questions used Accuracy may decrease over long delays	Introduce alongside verbal interview Content of drawings not analysed Less useful with preschool children

(Continued)

Table 12.1 *(Continued)*

Technique	Empirical support	Age groups studied	Positive benefits	Risks	Use
Projective drawings	No methodologically sound empirical studies	School age	May indicate psychological distress	No reliable signs identified as accurate indicators of maltreatment	Not supported
				No normative data Rater bias in interpretation May reflect psychopathology arising from other causes than maltreatment	
				May reflect play/imagination Coding manuals contradictory	
Truth induction					
Reassurance	Laboratory studies with maltreated children	Preschool and school age	Increase in truth telling with oath competent children	May elicit false reports if children do not have understanding of truth/lies	Prior to interview, following a competency assessment (understanding and consequences of truth/lies)
Oath/promises to tell truth	Laboratory studies	School age	Increase in truth telling (even with oath incompetent children)	Increase false reports if highly suggestive questioning used (i.e., does not protect from effects)	Avoid highly suggestive questions
Discussions of truth/lies			Increase in truth telling	None	

AD dolls have attracted significant controversy, however, because of a number of concerns identified in research and raised by the courts (Ceci & Bruck, 1995; Dickinson, Poole, & Bruck, 2005). One issue relates to the possibility that the dolls themselves are inherently suggestive, implicitly indicating that the children are expected to use them in some way, or inviting exploratory play because of the novelty of the anatomical detail, which may be interpreted as actual experience. Given that there are no supported 'signs' of children's play or behaviour with AD dolls that reliably diagnose abuse (i.e., children's play cannot distinguish children who have experienced abuse from those who have not; see Murrie, Martindale, & Epstein, 2009) critics of including AD dolls in forensic interviews have proposed that the risk of inaccurate conclusions being drawn from observations of children's interactions with AD dolls is too high to support their use.

A second concern relates to children's developing cognitive capacities. The use of AD dolls as a means for children to demonstrate their experience requires that they appreciate that the doll has a dual identity – on the one hand its typical identity as a doll and plaything and on the other hand its identity as a symbol for the child (DeLoache, 2000, 2004; DeLoache & Marzolf, 1995). While young children may be able to appreciate that a doll can represent a person, being able to use them in that way while simultaneously recalling and reporting their experiences (i.e., under a high cognitive load) seems to exceed their abilities. Despite these concerns, AD dolls are still recommended in some professional guidelines, albeit in the context of specific uses and protocols (Everson & Boat, 2002). These uses include eliciting children's names for body parts, assessing sexual knowledge and knowledge of bodily functions, providing a means for the child to demonstrate where touch occurred, providing a visual retrieval cue for prompting recall of specific details relating to the allegation, and screening of possible abuse (i.e., the child is allowed to interact freely with the doll and then the interviewer poses questions based on what they have observed).

Research investigating the effectiveness of AD dolls has demonstrated that benefits in terms of eliciting increased information are typically accompanied by decreased accuracy (Pipe & Salmon, 2009; Salmon, 2001). The majority of research has explored recall in children under 5 years, presumably because they are the children most likely to require additional support because of their cognitive and communicative immaturity. While some studies have shown that children's free recall of events involving touch are more complete when they are interviewed with AD dolls (e.g., Goodman, Quas, Batterman-Faunce, Riddlesberger, & Kuhn, 1997), others have demonstrated reduced reporting (e.g., Goodman & Aman, 1990). When accompanied by verbal questions, especially those that are suggestive (leading or misleading) then the presence of AD dolls does not help children to be more accurate, and in some studies has increased error rates or inflated their susceptibility to suggestion (e.g., Bruck, Ceci, Francouer, & Renick, 1995). When introduced to elicit new information (i.e., previously unreported details), accuracy is compromised, although the design of the studies has meant it is difficult to separate out the influence of the dolls from the questions asked. The pattern is much the same in the few studies conducted with older children (e.g., Saywitz, Goodman, Nicholas, & Moan, 1991). That is, including AD dolls may lead to increased reporting of information, including that about genital touch; however, when accompanied by leading questions error rates increase as do false reports of touch from children who did not experience any. Field studies examining the effects of inclusion of AD dolls in actual investigative interviews have shown either no or a negative effect of the dolls (e.g., Lamb, Hershkowitz, Sternberg, Boat, & Everson, 1996; Thierry, Lamb, Orbach, & Pipe, 2005). In these studies, however, the interviewers did not follow the relevant professional guidelines (APSAC, 2002), presenting the dolls alongside other toys, allowing the children to interact directly with the dolls and introducing them with some children before any abuse-related information had been disclosed. As such it is difficult to isolate the effect of the dolls themselves from these other factors.

In summary, then, AD dolls may be useful for eliciting children's own vocabulary for various body parts, to aid the interviewer in clarifying and understanding what they report, and for clarifying the location of touch that the children have spontaneously reported. However, there is limited evidence that they provide any benefits over and above careful verbal interviewing techniques, in terms of eliciting new details or additional information. The risk of eliciting inaccurate statements increases if the dolls are presented in the context of suggestive questioning techniques, if children are allowed to play with or interact with the dolls directly, and if they are presented alongside other toys or props. There is no evidence that the content of children's interactions or play with dolls provides a reliable diagnostic indicator of abuse. AD dolls should not be used with very young (pre-school) children.

BODY DIAGRAMS

Body diagrams are also referred to as anatomically detailed (AD) drawings, human figure diagrams or drawings, and body maps. They vary across practitioners and research studies in terms of how they are presented – some are gender-specific and anatomically detailed, some are gender-neutral (no genital detail included), some clothed, some unclothed, some are realistic line drawings, others still are presented as cartoon or 'gingerbread' figures. The various pros and cons and relative efficacy associated with each have not been systematically examined. Body diagrams are thought to offer a safer alternative to AD dolls for a variety of reasons. Given their two-dimensional nature, body diagrams offer less opportunity for children to explore and interact with them directly and are therefore less inherently suggestive. However, as with AD dolls, the criticism still remains that the presence of diagrams in an interview may communicate to the child that they ought to use them. Body diagrams provide a more concrete symbolic representation of a person than dolls by virtue of avoiding the problem of dual identity, meaning they may pose less of a cognitive load for children. They also do not have the same strong association with play that dolls do. As with AD dolls, body diagrams are recommended for assisting to establish children's own labels for various body parts and for demonstrating the location of any touch the child has spontaneously reported.

There is limited research evaluating the usefulness of body diagrams for helping children to talk about touch they have experienced. Eight studies (Aldridge *et al.*, 2004; Brown, Pipe, Lewis, Lamb, & Orbach, 2007, unpublished manuscript; Bruck, 2009; Steward *et al.*, 1996; Teoh, Yang, Lamb, & Larsson, 2010; Wilcock, Morgan, & Hayne, 2006; P.J. Yang, Y.S. Teoh, & M.E. Lamb, unpublished manuscript) have explored different types of body diagrams in the context of staged or naturally occurring events, and one field study. Irrespective of the delay used in the studies the researchers found that although body diagrams were associated with reporting of new information, they also elicited false information about touch, particularly when paired with direct (yes/no) questions about touch to different parts of the body. All of the studies showed that children's reporting of touch was typically incomplete, and this did not improve when children were provided with brief training in how to use a body diagram to report touch immediately prior to the interview. That is, they were more likely to leave out incidences of touch than to include touch that did not occur. Body diagrams did elicit false reports of genital touch in all of the studies, although this was typically clarified as innocuous with further questioning (Brown *et al.*, 2007, unpublished manuscript). It is important to note that all of the laboratory studies presented the body diagrams following a verbal interview with the aim of *eliciting new information* about touch, rather than clarifying previously reported information. Although given the opportunity to report touch in the free-recall sections of the interviews, children typically did not do so. One field study has examined whether presenting gender neutral body diagrams to children to elicit elaboration about touch reported in the verbal part of the interview was effective (Aldridge *et al.*, 2004). Children (4–13 years) presented with the diagrams after an exhaustive verbal interview consistent with best-practice guidelines to clarify previously reported touch reported many new forensically relevant details, and this was particularly the case for the youngest children. The diagrams were also associated with an increased use of direct and yes/no questions, however, which are typically associated with decreased accuracy, and so the usefulness of the diagrams could not be separated from the type of question that accompanied them, nor could the accuracy of the details elicited be established. Follow-up studies using this data set examined the type and clarity of detail reported about touch (Teoh *et al.,* 2010), and the clarity of details reported about the identity of the body parts identified or actions associated with touch (Yang *et al.*, unpublished manuscript). Teoh *et al.* demonstrated that while children of all ages reported new information about touch in response to the diagrams, they elicited more elaboration about body parts and the nature of the touch experienced than new information. The youngest children were less likely to provide clear accounts of touch than the older children, especially about the nature of the touch experienced. Yang *et al.* demonstrated an increase in the clarity of details reported about body parts (i.e., the location of the touch) but not actions associated with it for all children, irrespective of age. As in the original Aldridge study, in both of these studies the accuracy of the children's statements could not be assessed. Taken together these studies suggest the most likely benefit of introducing body diagrams into interviews is to clarify the location of touch that has been spontaneously reported during the verbal part of an interview rather than eliciting elaborative detail or new accounts of touch.

The research examining the usefulness and safety of including body diagrams in forensic interviews with young children has yet to address several key questions, such as whether they support children to clarify information they have already reported, what form the diagrams should take, and when in the interview they should be introduced. The existing research suggests that children may not understand the concept of touch well, at least when it occurs as part of a wider event (i.e., the touch itself does not define the event). Introducing body diagrams may lead to small increases in the level of details reported, but they are also likely to elicit ambiguous, inaccurate, and possibly forensically relevant (and misleading) information. As such their use is not strongly supported by empirical evidence, and they have certainly not been established as more effective than verbal questioning techniques on their own. Any information reported in response to the presentation of a body diagram should be explored using open-ended questioning to elicit further detail and context to clarify the child's communication.

PROPS: REAL ITEMS, TOYS, AND PHOTOGRAPHS

Introducing props into an interview is, like dolls, thought to provide a means by which children may overcome communication difficulties (e.g., limited vocabulary, poor comprehension of the event) by enabling re-enactment or demonstration using the items provided. In addition the provision of props is based on the premise that they will increase the similarity between the context of the event in question and the interview, thereby encouraging additional retrieval and reporting of information. Concerns relate to the extent to which children may become distracted by the items from the task of reporting an actual experience and engage in play or exploration with them. Additionally, children may interpret the presence of the props in the interview as an expectation that they are relevant and should be referred to in some way. Various types of props have been explored in laboratory- or analogue-based studies (for reviews see Pipe & Salmon, 2009; Salmon, 2001); however, there has been limited examination of their inclusion in actual forensic interviews. The evidence relating to the various types of props is summarized below.

Real Props

Real props include actual items from the event the children experienced (e.g., pieces of a costume the child wore). Laboratory studies examining their effectiveness have generally demonstrated increased reporting of correct information, even across long delays, for children aged 3–10 years. Although an increase in errors is also often observed, the overall accuracy (proportion of correct to total information reported) remains stable. Any errors reported are of concern, of course, and it appears that the errors children tend to report are consistent with the general theme of the event, and therefore may seem highly plausible. Errors are particularly likely to occur (and accuracy decrease) when children are allowed to interact with the props, if distracter items are included, and if they are exposed to multiple interviews over a delay. Merely having the props visible can also increase the amount of correct information children report (although to a lesser extent than when children are able to interact with them), and is much less likely to degrade accuracy even if distracter items are included. The effectiveness of providing real items in interviews with older children has not been established, nor have any field studies been conducted to explore the effect of introducing real props (which may serve as corroborating evidence) on children's responses. Of course, simply having these items present may also serve a suggestive purpose, implying that the children ought to reference them in their accounts, meaning their evidence may face challenge in court. Issues also arise when considering what items can/should be present in an interview (e.g., some items may have a generic familiarity to children, whereas others may be uniquely associated with an instance of abuse) and who decides what to include.

Toys and Scale Models

The use of toys and models have been examined in younger (2.5–6 years) children. Similar effects as real items have been observed in increasing correct information; however, they also elicit a disproportionate amount of incorrect information, leading to a decrease in overall accuracy. Accuracy is higher when the items are more similar to those from the event – that is, scale models or objects are superior to toys. Simply having the toys present or visible achieves little in the way of enhancing reporting; increases in information have been demonstrated in studies that allow children to use them for re-enactment. In an extensive review of the use of props in interviews with children, Salmon (2001) concludes 'optimal performance is obtained with scale models that convey highly specific information about the event, that do not have a strong identity as toys, and that are not easily manipulated as objects of play' (p. 287). However, in a field setting, it may be highly suggestive to do this, implying that children ought to respond to these items in their accounts. Given that it is unlikely that forensic interviewers will be able to meet these conditions, when identification of items from the event and exclusion of distracter items is likely to be difficult, the inclusion of toys and scales models is likely to compromise rather than enhance the reliability of children's reports.

Photographs

Photographs may reduce some of the challenges associated with other props. Unlike toys and dolls, photographs are defined by being representations of other things (i.e., there is no dual representation) and thus may facilitate recall of information by reminding children of details they may not otherwise spontaneously report. There is limited research, however, on the efficacy of photographs as aids for supporting children's reporting of their experiences. Two published studies (Ascherman, Danneberg, & Schultz, 1998; Hudson & Fivush, 1991) have examined the effect of presenting children (3–7 years) with photographs from an event on their verbal reports. Both showed an increase in the amount of information children reported; however, over very long delays the children required presentation of highly specific activity-based photographs to provide additional details, which are unlikely to be available to forensic interviewers. Further research is needed to establish the conditions under which photographs (especially generic or scene-based as opposed to activity-based) pictures assist children in recounting their experiences. With the advent of the digital age, photographs no longer hold the same level of infallibility as representations of true events as in earlier times. Photographs can be easily manipulated to demonstrate or imply false details of an event, and research has demonstrated that they can serve as powerful triggers for the formation of entirely false memories (e.g., Lindsay, Hagen, Read, Wade, & Garry, 2004; Wade, Garry, Read, & Lindsay, 2002). A study with children not only replicated this effect but demonstrated that, following repeated interviewing, children would confidently narrate 'memories' of both plausible (e.g., a hot-air balloon ride) and implausible (having a cup of tea with Prince Charles) events (Strange, Sutherland, & Garry, 2006). A recent study also demonstrated the powerful effect of presenting a photograph as a memory cue. Strange, Hayne, and Garry (2008) asked children to talk about three events across three interviews, within 1 week. One of the events was false. Some of the children saw a doctored photograph of them participating in the false event, others simply saw a photo of the false event (without them present). The remaining events were true, and children were also shown photos of these (in one they were present, in the other they were not). Irrespective of the child's presence in the false event photo, some children reported details suggestive of an episodic memory by the final interview, although this was more likely if the child featured in the photo (overall rates were 47% for child present, and 18% for child absent). Adult raters were unable to distinguish reliably between true accounts and false ones. It is worth noting, however, that even in the strongly suggestive condition (child present in photo) less than 30% of children reported false memories in the final interview. Nevertheless, these findings highlight the risks of using photographs as cues to prompt recall – they may in fact elicit false recall that appears valid.

Cue Cards for Forensically Relevant Categories of Information

Saywitz and her colleagues developed an innovative interviewing technique, Narrative Elaboration Training (NET), to explore the effectiveness of pre-interview training and practice in talking about the past, and providing generic pictorial cues for prompting children to talk about forensically relevant categories of information (people, setting, actions, conversation, and affect; Saywitz & Snyder, 1993, 1996). Research has demonstrated that the NET helps children, including preschoolers, to report events more completely, without compromising accuracy (e.g., Brown & Pipe, 2003b; Dorado & Saywitz, 2001; Saywitz & Snyder, 1996) and does not prompt false event reports (Camparo, Wagner, & Saywitz, 2001). The benefits are particularly apparent on introduction of the cue cards (i.e., the children do not provide more complete free-recall accounts). Verbal prompting for categories of information, without training, can be just as effective as the NET (e.g., Brown & Pipe, 2003a; Elischberger & Roebers, 2001). The effect of training alone (without pictorial or verbal prompts for categories of information) has not been examined, and the NET has yet to be evaluated in the context of more ecologically valid events, in field studies, and across repeated interviews.

Summary

In summary, although having props (real items, toys, models, and photographs) present in an interview may elicit additional information, there is also the risk of eliciting inaccurate information, thus compromising the reliability of the children's accounts. This is particularly likely if children are allowed to interact with the props and if nonrelevant props are included. Given that it is unlikely that forensic interviewers will be able to establish just what is relevant to the event, their use is hazardous. Furthermore, errors that are reported tend to be those relating to general knowledge of events or the items presented – this may be a concern in forensic interviews given that the information may seem plausible in the context of the allegation and thus indistinguishable from accurate information. This may be particularly the case if children have experienced or witnessed multiple instances of abuse and thus developed a 'script' of what generally happens, and therefore have a detrimental effect on interviewer's ability to ascertain what happened during a specific incident. Providing generic pictorial or verbal prompts for general categories of information (e.g., people, place, actions, conversations) may assist children in giving more detailed accounts, even in the absence of prior training with the prompts, without compromising accuracy.

REINSTATEMENT OF CONTEXT

Drawing from theories of memory and information processing, researchers have also explored the impact of reinstating the context of the event on children's ability to report what occurred. Reinstatement of context increases the similarity of the conditions between the event and those at recall, which should make information more accessible for reporting (Tulving & Thomson, 1973). Context reinstatement also allows for re-enactment of events, addressing communication difficulties that may arise as a result of children's developmental stage or motivation. Researchers have speculated that is more likely to be effective with older children who may have integrated contextual details into their experience (meaning they are more likely to serve as retrieval cues). To the extent that the event context is unique or defines the event and the activities therein, however, context reinstatement may also benefit younger children. There have been a limited number of studies exploring the utility of reinstating the physical context of the event that children experienced, and the findings have been mixed. One study showed no effect of context reinstatement alone relative to a verbal interview (Pipe & Wilson, 1994) (although context reinstatement in conjunction with the presence of real items from the event was associated with increased recall), whereas another showed children who returned to the place where the event occurred reported more information (Wilkinson, 1988). A field study examined the effectiveness of re-interviewing children at the alleged scene of abuse, following an exhaustive verbal interview. Children reported additional details at the scene, although whether this was due to a further (repeated) opportunity for recall or being in context was unable to be determined (Hershkowitz *et al.*, 1998). A follow-up study separated out the possible confounding effects of a repeated interview by interviewing children either in the interviewer's office or at the scene once a location was disclosed. This study did not demonstrate any advantage of being in context, although the authors speculated this may have been because children's initial recall and reporting was interrupted to travel to the scene (Orbach, Hershkowitz, Lamb, Sternberg, & Horowitz, 2000). Further research is needed to establish the conditions under which context reinstatement is effective and can be utilized in a way that is relevant for the forensic context. It is possible that the effects will vary to the extent that the context is familiar vs. uniquely associated with the child's experience.

Studies of mentally (as opposed to physically) reinstating the context of a child's experience indicate that this can be a useful technique for helping children to retrieve as much information as possible (Brown, Lamb, Pipe, & Orbach, 2008). Children are instructed to think about different sensory features of the event (e.g., what they could hear, see, smell) and different aspects of the event (e.g., what the place looked like) to reconstruct the scene before beginning to recount verbally what they remember. Consistent with the expectation that mental reinstatement of context will help witnesses to travel back mentally in time and 'relive' the experience, mental context reinstatement (MCR) increases the similarity between the conditions at recall and those at the time of the experience, thereby making the information associated with the event more accessible. One advantage of MCR is that it does not require that the interviewer have knowledge of the event in question, and the child, rather than the interviewer, generates the retrieval cues.

MCR is one of the main components of the Cognitive Interview (Fisher, Geiselman, Raymond, Jurkevich, & Warhaftig, 1987), which is used widely by police officers interviewing adult witnesses. The Cognitive Interview has also been used successfully with children (e.g., Köhnken, Milne, Memon, & Bull, 1999) although some of the component techniques (e.g., changing perspectives, changing the temporal ordering) may make demands that exceed the cognitive abilities of children under 8 years of age. Significant gains have been demonstrated with young children when using only the MCR and instructions-to-tell-everything components of the Cognitive Interview (Hayes & Delamothe, 1997). In addition, a field study (Hershkowitz, Orbach, Lamb, Sternberg, & Horowitz, 2001) demonstrated that, while not increasing the overall amount of information reported, MCR assisted 4- to 13-year-old children (especially the youngest children) in providing more detailed accounts earlier in the interviews (i.e., in response to open-ended or free-recall questions). Finally, a field study comparing the relative effectiveness of physical context reinstatement with MCR and with a control interview also demonstrated increased details reported in response to the main invitation, in the children's first narrative and in response to subsequent open ended (free-recall) prompts by children given MCR instructions relative to those interviewed in context or with a control interview (who did not differ; Hershkowitz, Orbach, Lamb, Sternberg, & Horowitz, 2002). A substantial body of evidence has demonstrated the superiority of the quality of information reported to these kinds of prompts (see Chapter 8) and more detailed responses earlier in the interview reduces the need for further interviewer-led questioning and possible introduction of leading questions.

The evidence for the utility of physically reinstating the context of an event is equivocal. Furthermore, abuse frequently occurs in well-known situations or contexts that are familiar or associated with other events or experiences. As such, establishing the actual psychological context (over and above the physical context) may be hard to capture, thereby reducing the effectiveness of the location as a retrieval cue. In contrast, MCR appears to benefit children in providing more detailed reports without increasing errors or affecting overall accuracy. MCR has the advantage of being child-led and does not require any information from the interviewer, thus avoiding the possibility of contaminating children's evidence or leading the child by introducing information they have not already reported.

DRAWINGS

Drawings have been used in two distinct ways in assessing children's experiences. One approach, the draw-and-talk method, provides children with the opportunity to draw while recounting their experiences, with only their verbal responses being of interest (i.e., the content of the drawing is not evaluated). The facilitative effects of allowing children to draw while talking are thought to be derived from a number of possible mechanisms. Drawing allows children to generate their own retrieval cues, much in the same way as MCR, by reminding them of additional event-related details as they construct their drawings. Drawing may also serve to make the interview context more comfortable by giving the children a focus other than the interviewer. Finally, interviews that include drawings tend to be longer than verbal interviews alone, which may extend the opportunity for recall and reporting.

Studies examining the use of drawings to enhance children's reports of personally experienced events have shown that, under ideal circumstances (i.e., when asking children about true events using nonsuggestive questioning), drawing while talking yields an increase in the amount of information recalled, without compromising accuracy (e.g., Gross & Hayne, 1998; Salmon, Roncolato, & Gleitzman, 2003; Wesson & Salmon, 2001). A recent field study demonstrated increases in information reported about alleged abuse when children were given the opportunity to draw a picture of their experience after an exhaustive verbal interview (Katz & Hershkowitz, 2010). When children were asked to recount their experience again, with the drawing present, they reported more information than those who had not drawn, although the accuracy of this information could not be established. However, increases in information reported have not been demonstrated with very young (3- to 4-year old) children (Butler, Gross, & Hayne, 1995). Only two studies have examined the effectiveness of including drawing in an interview after a long delay, with one showing drawing decreasing the accuracy of children's accounts (Salmon & Pipe, 2000), while the other showed increased reporting relative to a verbal condition with no effect on accuracy (Gross & Hayne, 1999). Several studies have also demonstrated that in addition to encouraging more complete recall of true events, drawing may also encourage children to report information about events that never occurred (e.g., Bruck, Melnyk, &

Ceci, 2000; Gross, Hayne, & Poole, 2006; Strange, Garry, & Sutherland, 2003). Taken together, these studies suggest that drawing and talking may generally increase children's responsiveness – about both true and false events. Thus, as with other supplementary techniques, the context in which children are asked to draw is a paramount consideration – when used with school-aged children and in conjunction with appropriate verbal questioning (i.e., open-ended prompting) drawing appears to aid children in recalling and reporting their experiences. When accompanied by misleading information or suggestive questioning, however, the additional information elicited is likely to be highly unreliable.

A second way in which drawing may be utilized in assessments with children is in the use of projective drawing tests, which are based on the premise that global impressions formed about the drawings or the presence of specific features in a drawing can be used to evaluate the likelihood of abuse experiences, assess emotional functioning, or identify psychopathology associated with abuse. Such techniques include Draw-A-Person, House–Tree–Person, and Kinetic Family Drawings (for reviews see Lally, 2001; Murrie *et al.*, 2009). A number of criticisms have been levelled at the use of projective drawing techniques for screening or identifying maltreatment in children. The most widely reported challenge to the validity of these techniques is the lack of scientific evidence for a set of behaviours, symptoms, or indicators (signs) in drawings that accurately identify children who have been abused and reliably discriminate them from children who are not suspected of having experienced maltreatment (Gurley, Kuehnle, & Kirkpatrick, 2009; Murrie *et al.*, 2009; Poole & Wolfe, 2009). Thus, although some symptoms may be frequently observed in children who are maltreated, they also occur in non-maltreated children (e.g., those with psychopathology arising from other factors). Projective drawing techniques have also been criticized due to poor test–retest reliability. That is, across a series of drawings the presence or absence of critical signs and the quality of drawings may vary so much as to produce significantly different conclusions. It has been suggested that, rather than necessarily reflecting children's direct experiences, the content of the drawings could just as easily be interpreted as representing other processes (e.g., perception of self, what the child would like to be, perceptions of impairment, or compensation). Given the strong association that drawing has with play activity, the content of the drawings may also simply reflect the child's creative process, including imaginative or fantastic elements, rather than reality.

The reliability of conclusions derived from projective drawings has also been challenged on the basis of how they have been scored or interpreted. Some evaluators form a global impression, based on clinical experience, and some use the presence or absence of signs or features in the drawing. Neither approach has good support in the literature in terms of reliability across different raters, and associations with other measures. Identification of signs also often requires subjective judgements of the relative size, placement, and style of items in the drawing, and the manuals often include contradictory indicators as being equally representative of concern (e.g., lack of details but also excessive details included in the drawing). Given the subjective nature of many of the items scored, concern has also been expressed that evaluators may fall prey to rater bias (i.e., identifying features because of a pre-conceived notion about the child's status) or project their own issues when scoring. Finally, no normative data exists from which to identify extreme or unusual scores which may be indicative of maltreatment.

By far the most major criticism of projective drawing techniques, however, is that they lack adequate empirical support from well-conducted scientific studies. The quality of studies conducted to examine differences in children's responses to projective drawing techniques according to suspected maltreatment status have varied considerably. Many lack a suitable control group, are based on single case studies, small samples, or do not control for comorbid psychopathology, which in itself may account for the children's responses. The general consensus in the scientific literature is that there is no empirical validation for the use of projective drawing techniques, and those studies purporting to show their ability to discriminate abused children from those who have not been abused are plagued by methodological issues that affect the conclusions reached (Gurley *et al.*, 2009; Murrie *et al.*, 2009; Poole & Wolfe, 2009).

In summary, drawing techniques have been used in different ways in investigative interviews with children. The draw-and-talk technique seems to support children in talking about their experiences when interviewed a short time after the event without compromising accuracy, if presented in the context of appropriate verbal questioning. When presented after a delay, or when used with very young children, the evidence for their effectiveness is less clear. When associated with misleading or suggestive questioning children are prone to making more errors or recounting entirely false events at a higher rate than children interviewed without drawing. Projective drawing techniques should not be used in forensic interviews with children, because of a lack of scientific evidence supporting their reliability.

TRUTH INDUCTION

Truth induction refers to strategies employed to overcome children's tendency to deny or minimize their own or other's transgressions. These include emphasizing the necessity of telling the truth (e.g., child-friendly versions of the oath, promises to tell the truth), and minimizing the negative consequences of disclosure (or highlighting the negative consequences of *non*-disclosure; e.g., via discussion or provision of examples or vignettes). Children's knowledge about truth and lies (both the meaning of these concepts and their consequences) may not parallel or predict their behaviour during an interview. Studies have shown truth telling may be increased by eliciting promises to tell the truth or including a discussion of the morality of truth and lies prior to interviewing them (e.g., Talwar, Lee, Bala, & Lindsay, 2002). Studies of the effectiveness of highlighting the negative consequences of non-disclosure have focused on emphasizing the need to tell the truth. Indeed, many interview protocol and professional guidelines recommend the inclusion of a 'truth–lie ceremony' (e.g., NICHD protocol, see Lamb *et al.*, 2008 for summary of research with the protocol; *Achieving Best Evidence*, Home Office, 2002), which includes emphasizing the importance of telling the truth and practising the difference between the truth and a lie. Some version of oath taking or promising to tell the truth is a feature of the judicial process in many countries (e.g., UK, USA, Canada, New Zealand, Australia). Lyon and Dorado (2008) recently examined the effects of reassurance or minimizing negative consequences compared with a child-friendly version of the oath and with no special instructions or preparation on 6- to 7-year-old children's truth telling or disclosure of their own and an adult confederate's minor transgression (play that the confederate warned 'might get [them] in trouble'). The children had all experienced substantiated maltreatment and had passed a basic competency assessment required by US law for children to be able to give evidence (assessing meaning and consequences of truth and lies). Both reassurance and oath taking increased truthfulness. A second study examined these strategies with children (5–7 years) who had not passed the initial competency test and also assessed whether children who had not actually transgressed would be induced to falsely assent to direct (yes/no) and suggestive (tag) questions. Results showed no evidence that the oath had any negative effects, even in conjunction with suggestive questions and when children had not achieved a basic understanding of the meaning and consequences of truth and lies. Reassurance, although effective with children who had passed the competency test, was associated with acquiescence to both yes/no and more suggestive questions in children who did not pass the competency test. Lyon, Malloy, Quas, and Talwar (2008) examined the effects of the two truth induction strategies on the accuracy of maltreated 4- to 7-year-old children's reports when they had been coached to provide a false report (either denying play that had occurred or affirming play that had not occurred), and examined whether reassurance was effective when it was general (rather than about a specific behaviour as in the previous studies). The oath had positive effects in overcoming the coaching to provide false accounts for all children, especially for those coached to deny play that had occurred. Reassurance was less effective than in the previous studies, neither eliciting false reports or increasing the children's accuracy. Neither strategy was effective in ameliorating the effects of highly suggestive questioning.

In summary, then, providing reassurance to children to encourage truth telling may be effective with children who have a basic understanding of the meaning and consequences of telling the truth or lies but it is less effective with children who lack this understanding and when it is generic rather than specific to the event in question. Administering a child-friendly oath to children exerts a positive effect on accuracy and truth telling, irrespective of children's understanding of truth and lies, even when they have been extensively coached to provide a false account. Future research is needed to explore the effectiveness of these strategies with non-maltreated children, those with developmental disabilities, and with older children and adolescents. It will also be important to explore their effectiveness when there is a strong relationship between the child and the adult confederate (thus more closely mimicking situations where the alleged perpetrator of abuse is familiar to the child).

LEGAL ISSUES

There are a number of issues that arise when applying the research on supplementary interview techniques to the consideration of a particular case before the courts. The first relates to the ecological validity of the studies conducted. That is, how well do the studies match real life contexts in which their findings are to be applied to? Studies of children's eyewitness testimony have used a variety of stimulus or target events, ranging from naturally occurring events (e.g., medical procedures, natural disasters), staged events (e.g., a trip to the pirate), and witnessed events (e.g., interactions occurring at the front of the class, short video clips). Studies have further varied as to the level of the participation required from the child – some events are individually experienced, some experienced as a class, and in some the child observes an interaction – and how many times the child experiences an event. Events tend to be very unique or novel, so as naturally occurring events in the child's life do not contaminate memory for the event in the interim between staging it and the child being interviewed. Ethical considerations preclude reconstructing analogues to maltreatment, and so the question is often asked how well can findings from analogue studies using unique occurrences of pleasant, novel events be generalized to the real world context to which they are meant to apply? Early analogue studies produced inconsistent findings with respect to the influence of stress on memory, with some studies showing a positive effect and others showing a negative effect or no effect at all (for reviews see Cordón, Pipe, Sayfan, Melinder, & Goodman, 2004; Howe, 1997; Ogle *et al.*, 2008). The inconsistencies may arise, in part, from the degree of stress (or distress) experienced, methodological differences in the definition and measurement of stress across studies, differing delay intervals, and differences in the assessment of memory (e.g., central vs. peripheral information, reliability vs. suggestibility). In general, studies indicate stress may be associated with increased memory and decreased forgetting over time, particularly with respect to central or core information. Nonetheless, studies involving less stressful experiences still make a valid contribution to forensic psychology, because abuse victims may not always perceive their experiences as painful or traumatic, and children's ignorance or misunderstanding of events may decrease their salience (Pipe *et al.*, 2007). Moreover, analogue studies provide a basis for the development of safe and effective forensic interview techniques. Field studies, by contrast, examine interviewer and child contributions to investigative interviews in the actual context. Very few studies are able to compare children's reports with an objective record of what has occurred, however, and as such accuracy can only be inferred from examining the types of prompts used to elicit the information (which in turn is informed by analogue studies), or assessed indirectly by examining the consistency of repeated responses during an interview. It is the convergence of evidence resulting from the two approaches to the study of how best to support children's recall and reporting in investigative interviews that provides the best guidance for forensic interviewers.

The next issue is to what extent findings from group-based studies can be applied to a particular case under investigation. While studies may consistently demonstrate an effect between two different groups (e.g., those interviewed with props and without), *within* each group there will be children who do not fit the general trend. That is, while the majority of children in a group may benefit from the provision of additional support in an interview, some children may not. Or put another way, while some children may report more errors, others may report additional information without including any errors. As such, it is important that when consulting the research, interviewers consider the size or meaningfulness of the difference between groups (often indicated by the inclusion of effect size calculations) and conduct a risk–benefit analysis of their own in considering whether the risks of eliciting highly unreliable information are outweighed by gaining further detail. Investigators must also consider the context in which the research has been conducted to determine how much they can draw from it (e.g., does the delay match the case under investigation, what style of verbal questioning will be used, etc.). Research provides an important evidence base from which to make this analysis, and where findings are highly contradictory or limited research has been conducted, investigators must be prepared for their decision making around the use of supplementary techniques to be susceptible to challenge in the courts.

Another issue that arises is the limited amount of research examining the effectiveness of supplementary techniques across delays that are similar to those encountered in the legal process. Most case evaluations in forensic contexts are delayed for at least weeks or months (Hershkowitz, Horowitz, & Lamb, 2005) and several additional months may pass before investigations reach court. A survey of young witnesses in the United Kingdom showed delays averaging 11.6 months (Plotnikoff & Woolfson, 1995), for example, and similarly long delays have been found in the United States (Pipe, Orbach, Lamb, Abbott, & Stewart, 2008). While it can be assumed that any negative effects of techniques demonstrated at short delays might only be exacerbated after longer delays when children's memory is even more fragile as a result of natural forgetting processes, research has not generally documented what happens to any positive effects (i.e., do techniques retain their usefulness or become more hazardous?).

FUTURE RESEARCH

Despite substantial research conducted exploring supportive techniques for use in forensic interviews with children, several important questions still warrant further attention. As highlighted throughout the chapter, many of these techniques have not been examined when substantial delays akin to those observed in the forensic process are incorporated into the study design. The usefulness of these techniques have also typically not been examined with older children and adolescents, who may well derive benefit from them because of their more advanced cognitive development, and yet at the same time may be more susceptible to the implicit social demands that they may present (e.g., that there is more tell).

Another important area for research is the extent to which children with various developmental, behavioural, communicative, or intellectual disabilities may benefit from (or be compromised by) the use of supplementary techniques in interviews (see Chapter 13). Children with disabilities are a particularly vulnerable group of witnesses. They are both more likely to experience or witness abuse (e.g., Sullivan & Knutson, 1998, 2000) and yet less likely to have their complaints heard and investigated. Furthermore, field studies of interviews that do occur with this group suggest that the children are unlikely to be interviewed in a developmentally appropriate manner (Cederborg & Lamb, 2008), and have their capacities and limitations recognized and provided for in court (Cederborg & Lamb, 2006; Westcott & Jones, 1999). While there may be intuitive appeal to the introduction of aids such as props, drawings, dolls, or toys into interviews to overcome cognitive and language deficits (e.g., with children with intellectual disabilities or receptive or expressive language disorders), the nature of their disabilities may, in fact, render such techniques dangerous. For example, children with intellectual disabilities or autism spectrum disorders (ASD) may have difficulty with the symbolic skills needed to interact with toys, dolls, or props intended to represent aspects of their experience. Children with attention deficit hyperactivity disorder (ADHD) may have difficulty with impulse control and distractibility which may make them more vulnerable to suggestive techniques or play-based interaction with props which is interpreted as representing their experiences. More research is required to document the strengths and vulnerabilities of children with various disabilities and diagnoses, to understand how best to support them in interviews without compromising the reliability of their reports.

Another area of research that has received limited attention is how best to support children to recall temporal information (e.g., sequencing of events (both within and across events), dating events) and indicate numerosity (e.g., frequency of repeated events) (Lyon & Saywitz, 2006). Inclusion (or omission) of such information can affect juror assessments of the credibility of the child's account and this information is also important for the 'particularization', or establishment of salient details of the event which may affect judgements about the worthiness of progressing a case from investigative interview to laying of formal charges, and whether a child will appear in court. Limited research has been conducted in the forensic context regarding children's understanding of and emerging ability to respond to questions relating to these concepts and ways in which they might be supported to do so (e.g., via timelines, personal time intervals (e.g., age, significant events) or landmark events to date their experiences). Recent evidence suggests children have difficulty using such strategies (e.g., Friedman & Lyon, 2005); however, more research is required that approximates the time intervals or delays likely to be relevant in forensic contexts and that uses personally salient, experienced (rather than observed) events.

CONCLUSIONS

The usefulness of introducing supplementary techniques into forensic interviews with children varies according to the type of technique, the age of the child, how the technique is presented, when in the interview it is introduced, the level of interaction the child is allowed (e.g., with props), and, most importantly, the verbal instructions that accompany them. There is limited or equivocal support for their effectiveness with very young (e.g., preschool) children, who are most in need of support to recall and recount what they know. Introducing props and AD dolls into interviews is most likely to result in challenges to the reliability of the child's evidence, especially if children are allowed to interact directly with them. There are no reliable 'signs' of maltreatment in doll play or children's drawings that identify and differentiate children from those who have not experienced abuse or neglect. Body diagrams do not appear to be particularly useful in assisting children to report new information about touch they have experienced; however, their use for clarifying or elaborating on children's spontaneous accounts has not yet been examined. The strongest evidence for supporting children's recall is associated with asking children to draw while talking and for mental reinstatement of context prior to beginning their accounts (although drawing may increase children's general responsiveness and thus elicit inaccurate information if presented in conjunction with misleading information). Both of these techniques have the advantage of being child-led (i.e., the child provides their own retrieval cues), and thus require less input from the interviewer. Providing reassurance to children about the importance of disclosing and minimizing negative consequences associated with it may encourage children who understand the concepts of truth and lies to disclose, but may elicit false accounts from children who do not understand these concepts. Administering a child-friendly version of the oath has been demonstrated to be effective at enhancing disclosures of both the child's and other's actions, without increasing false reports. The usefulness of these techniques across substantial delays, with older children and adolescents, and with those who have developmental disabilities has yet to be well established. As with verbal interviewing techniques, the use of supplementary techniques in interviews with children needs to be carefully considered, taking into account the child's developmental stage, the context of the interview and the nature of the event under investigation. The benefits of eliciting additional detail need to be weighed against the risk of the quality of the information elicited being poor, which may result in the child's testimony being vigorously challenged in court.

In summary, then, research shows:

- Researchers and practitioners have been interested in finding ways of supporting children to provide detailed accounts of their experiences.
- Introducing aids into interviews (e.g., dolls, diagrams, toys, scale models, photographs, cue cards, drawing exercise or exercises to reinstate the context of the event) may assist with helping children to remember additional information, or report it non-verbally.
- Research has demonstrated that most techniques can assist children in reporting additional information, but the accuracy of this information may be poor.
- Should aids be introduced into the interview children should not be allowed to interact with them directly, nor should the content of their interactions or drawings be taken as indicative of their experiences.
- Clarifying any information reported using appropriate verbal interviewing strategies is important.
- The nature of the verbal instructions or questions accompanying the aids is likely to influence how effective they are.
- Administering a developmentally appropriate (child-friendly) oath to children prior to interview may increase accurate disclosure of details.
- Further research is needed to establish the effectiveness of the various techniques when long delays have occurred since the child's experience, to explore their use with older children and adolescents, and with children who have developmental, communicative, behavioural, or intellectual disabilities.

REFERENCES

Aldridge, J., Lamb, M.E., Sternberg, K.J., Orbach, Y., Esplin, P.W., & Bowler, L. (2004). Using a human figure drawing to elicit information from alleged victims of child sexual abuse. *Journal of Consulting and Clinical Psychology*, *72*, 304–316.

American Professional Society on the Abuse of Children (APSAC). (2002). *Investigating Cases of Alleged Child Abuse.* Practice Guidelines.

American Prosecutors Research Insitutue (APRI). (2003). *Finding Words: Half a Nation by 2010. Interviewing Children and Preparing for Court.* Virginia, USA: APRI.

Aschermann, E., Dannenberg, U., & Schultz, A.P. (1998). Photographs as retrieval cues for children. *Applied Cognitive Psychology*, *12*, 55–66.

Bow, J.N., Quinnell, F.A., Zaroff, M., & Assemany, A. (2002). Assessment of sexual abuse allegations in child custody cases. *Professional Psychology: Research and Practice*, *33*, 566–575.

Brown, D.A., & Lamb, M.E. (2009). A two-way street: Supporting interviewers in adhering to best practice recommendations and enhancing children's capabilities in forensic interviews. In K. Kuehnle, & M. Connell (Eds), *The*

Evaluation of Child Sexual Abuse Allegations: A Comprehensive Guide to Assessment and Testimony (pp. 299–326). New Jersey: Wiley.

Brown, D.A., Lamb, M.E., Pipe, M.E., & Orbach, Y. (2008). Pursuing 'the truth, the whole truth, and nothing but the truth': forensic interviews with child victims or witnesses of abuse. In M.L Howe, G.S. Goodman, & D. Cicchetti (Eds), *Stress, Trauma, and Children's Memory Development: Neurobiological, Cognitive, Clinical, and Legal Perspectives*. (pp. 267–301). New York: Oxford University Press.

Brown, D.A., & Pipe, M.E. (2003a). Individual differences in children's event memory reports and the narrative elaboration technique. *Journal of Applied Psychology, 88*, 195–206.

Brown, D.A., & Pipe, M.E. (2003b). Variations on a technique: Enhancing children's recall using narrative elaboration training. *Applied Cognitive Psychology, 17*, 377–399.

Brown, D.A., Pipe, M.E., Lewis, C., Lamb, M.E., & Orbach, Y. (2007). Supportive or suggestive: Do human figure drawings help 5–7 year old children to report touch? *Journal of Consulting and Clinical Psychology, 75*, 33–42.

Bruck, M. (2009). Human figure drawings and children's recall of touching. *Journal of Experimental Psychology: Applied, 15*, 361–374.

Bruck, M., Ceci, S.J., Francoeur, E., & Renick, A. (1995). Anatomically detailed dolls do not facilitate preschoolers' reports of a pediatric examination involving genital touching. *Journal of Experimental Psychology: Applied, 1*, 95–109.

Bruck, M., Melnyk, L., & Ceci, S.J. (2000). Draw it again Sam: The effect of drawing on children's suggestibility and source monitoring ability. *Journal of Experimental Child Psychology, 77*, 169–196.

Butler, S., Gross, J., & Hayne, H. (1995). The effect of drawing on memory performance in young children. *Developmental Psychology, 31*, 597–608.

Camparo, L.B., Wagner, J.T., & Saywitz, K.J. (2001). Interviewing children about real and fictitious events: Revisiting the narrative elaboration procedure. *Law and Human Behavior, 25*, 63–80.

Ceci, S.J., & Bruck, M. (1995). *Jeopardy in the Courtroom: A Scientific Analysis of Children's Testimony.* Washington, DC: American Psychological Association.

Cederborg, A.C., & Lamb, M.E. (2006). How does the legal system respond when disabled children are victimized? *Child Abuse and Neglect, 30*, 537–547.

Cederborg, A.C., & Lamb, M.E. (2008). Interviewing alleged victims with intellectual disabilities. *Journal of Intellectual Disability Research, 52*, 49–58.

Conte, J.R., Sorenson, E., Fogarty, L., & Rosa, J.D. (1991). Evaluating children's reports of sexual abuse: Results from a survey of professionals. *American Journal of Orthopsychiatry, 61*, 428–437.

Cordón, I.M., Pipe, M.E., Sayfan, L., Melinder, A., & Goodman, G.S. (2004). Memory for traumatic experiences in early childhood. *Developmental Review, 24*, 101–132.

DeLoache, J.S. (2000). Dual representation and young children's use of scale models. *Child Development, 71*, 329–338.

DeLoache, J.S. (2004). Becoming symbol minded. *Trends in Cognitive Sciences, 8*, 66–70.

DeLoache, J., & Marzolf, D.P. (1995). The use of dolls to interview young children: Issues of symbolic representation. *Journal of Experimental Child Psychology, 60*, 155–173.

Dickinson, J.J., Poole, D.A., & Bruck, M. (2005). Back to the future: A comment on the use of anatomical dolls in forensic interviews. *Journal of Forensic Psychology Practice*, *5*, 63–74.

Dorado, J.S., & Saywitz, K.J. (2001). Interviewing preschoolers from low- and middle-SES communities: A test of the Narrative Elaboration recall improvement technique. *Journal of Clinical Child Psychology*, *30*, 566–578.

Elischberger, H.B., & Roebers, C.M. (2001). Improving young children's free narratives about an observed event: The effects of nonspecific verbal prompts. *International Journal of Behavioral Development*, *25*, 160–166.

Everson, M.D., & Boat, B.W. (2002). The utility of anatomical dolls and drawings in child forensic interviews. In M.L. Eisen, J.A. Quas, & G.S. Goodman (Eds), *Memory and Suggestibility in the Forensic Interview* (pp. 383–408). Mahwah, NJ: Erlbaum.

Fisher, R.P., Geiselman, R.E., Raymond, D.S., Jurkevich, L.M., & Warhaftig, M.L. (1987). Enhancing enhanced eyewitness memory: Refining the cognitive interview. *Journal of Police Science and Administration*, *15*, 291–297.

Friedman, W.J., & Lyon, T.D. (2005). Development of temporal-reconstructive abilities. *Child Development*, *76*, 1202–1216.

Goodman, G.S., & Aman, C. (1990). Children's use of anatomically detailed dolls to recount an event. *Child Development*, *61*, 1859–1871.

Goodman, G.S., Quas, J.A., Batterman-Faunce, J.M., Riddlesberger, M.M., & Kuhn, J. (1997). Children's reactions to and memory for a stressful event: Influences of age, anatomical dolls, knowledge, and parental attachment. *Applied Developmental Sciences*, *1*, 54–75.

Gross, J., & Hayne, H. (1998). Drawing facilitates children's verbal reports of emotionally laden events. *Journal of Experimental Psychology: Applied*, *14*, 163–179.

Gross, J., & Hayne, H. (1999). Drawing facilitates children's verbal reports after long delays. *Journal of Experimental Psychology: Applied*, *5*, 265–283.

Gross, J., Hayne, H., & Poole, A. (2006). The use of drawing in interviews with children: A potential pitfall. In J.R. Marrow (Ed.), *Focus on Child Psychology Research* (pp. 119–144). New York: Nova Publishers.

Gurley, J., Kuehnle, K., & Kirkpatrick, H.D. (2009). The continuum of children's sexual behavior: Discriminative categories and the need for public policy change. In K. Kuehnle, & M. Connell (Eds), *The Evaluation of Child Sexual Abuse Allegations: A Comprehensive Guide to Assessment and Testimony* (pp. 129–150). New Jersey: Wiley.

Hayes, B.K., & Delamothe, K. (1997). Cognitive interviewing procedures and suggestibility in children's recall. *Journal of Applied Psychology*, *82*, 562–577.

Hershkowitz, I., Orbach, Y., Lamb, M.E., Sternberg, K.J., Horowitz, D., & Hovav, M. (1998). Visiting the scene of the crime: Effects on children's recall of alleged abuse. *Legal and Criminological Psychology*, *3*, 195–207.

Hershokowitz, I., Horowitz, D., & Lamb, M.E. (2005). Trends in children's disclosure of abuse in Israel: A national study. *Child Abuse and Neglect*, *29*, 1203–1214.

Hershkowitz, I., Orbach, Y., Lamb, M.E., Sternberg, K.J., & Horowitz, D. (2001). The effects of mental context reinstatement on children's accounts of sexual abuse. *Applied Cognitive Psychology*, *15*, 235–248.

Hershkowitz, I., Orbach, Y., Lamb, M.E., Sternberg, K.J., & Horowitz, D. (2002). A comparison of mental and physical context reinstatement in forensic

interviews with alleged victims of sexual abuse. *Applied Cognitive Psychology*, *16*, 429–441.
Home Office. (2002). *Achieving the Best Evidence in Criminal Proceedings: Guidance for Vulnerable and Intimidated Witnesses, Including Children.* London: Home Office.
Howe, M.L. (1997). Children's memory for traumatic experiences. *Learning and Individual Differences*, *9*, 153–174.
Hudson, J.A., & Fivush, R. (1991). As times go by: Sixth grade children recall a kindergarten experience. *Applied Cognitive Psychology*, *5*, 347–360.
Katz, C., & Hershkowitz, I. (2010). The effects of drawing on children's accounts of sexual abuse. *Child Maltreatment*, *15*, 171–179.
Köhnken, G., Milne, R., Memon, A., & Bull, R. (1999). The cognitive interview: A meta-analysis. *Psychology, Crime, and Law*, *5*, 3–27.
Lally, S.J. (2001). Should human figure drawings be admitted into court? *Journal of Personality Assessment*, *76*, 135–149.
Lamb, M.E., & Brown, D.A. (2006). Conversational apprentices: Helping children become competent informants about their own experiences. *British Journal of Developmental Psychology*, *24*, 215–234.
Lamb, M.E., Hershkowitz, I., Orbach, Y., & Esplin, P.W. (2008). *Tell Me What Happened: Structured Investigative Interviews of Child Victims and Witnesses.* Chichester, UK: Wiley.
Lamb, M.E., Hershkowitz, I., Sternberg, K.J., Boat, B., & Everson, M.D. (1996). Investigative interviews of alleged sexual abuse victims with and without anatomical dolls. *Child Abuse and Neglect*, *20*, 1239–1247.
Lindsay, D.S., Hagen, L., Read, J.D., Wade, K.A., & Garry, M. (2004). True photographs and false memories. *Psychological Science*, *15*, 149–154.
Lyon, T.D., & Dorado, J.S. (2008). Truth induction in young maltreated children: The effects of oath-taking and reassurance on true and false disclosures. *Child Abuse & Neglect*, *32*, 738–748.
Lyon, T.D., Malloy, L.C., Quas, J.A., & Talwar, V.A. (2008). Coaching, truth induction, and young maltreated children's false allegations and false denials. *Child Development*, *79*, 914–929.
Lyon, T.D., & Saywitz, K.J. (2006). From post-mortem to preventive medicine: Next steps for research on child witnesses. *Journal of Social Issues*, *62*, 833–861.
Murrie, D., Martindale, D.A., & Epstein, M. (2009). Unsupported assessment techniques in child sexual abuse evaluations. In K. Kuehnle, & M. Connell (Eds), *The Evaluation of Child Sexual Abuse Allegations: A Comprehensive Guide to Assessment and Testimony* (pp. 397–420). New Jersey: Wiley.
Ogle, C.M., Block, S.D., Harris, L.S., Culver, M., Augusti, E.M., Timmer, S., Urquiza, A., & Goodman, G.S. (2008). Accuracy and specificity of autobiographical memory in childhood trauma victims: Developmental considerations. In M.L. Howe, G.S. Goodman & D. Cicchetti (Eds), *Stress, Trauma, and Children's Memory Development: Neurobiological, Cognitive, Clinical, and Legal Perspectives* (pp. 171–203). New York, NY: Oxford University Press.
Orbach, Y., Hershkowitz, I., Lamb, M.E., Sternberg, K.J., & Horowitz, D. (2000). Interviewing at the scene of the crime: Effects on children's recall of alleged abuse. *Legal and Criminological Psychology*, *5*, 135–147.
Pipe, M.E., Lamb, M.E., Orbach, Y., & Esplin, P.W. (2004). Recent research on children's testimony about experienced and witnessed events. *Developmental Review*, *24*, 440–468.

Pipe, M.E., Lamb, M.E., Orbach, Y., Sternberg, K.J., Stewart, H.L., & Esplin, P.W. (2007). Factors associated with nondisclosure of suspected abuse during forensic interviews. In M.E. Pipe, M.E. Lamb, Y. Orbach, & A.C. Cederborg (Eds), *Child Sexual Abuse: Disclosure, Delay, and Denial* (pp. 77–96). Mahwah, NJ: Lawrence Erlbaum.

Pipe, M.E., Orbach, Y., Lamb, M., Abbott, C., & Stewart, H. (2008). *Do best practice interviews with child sexual abuse victims influence case outcomes?* Final Technical Report to the National Institute of Justice, Grant Number 2006-IJ-CX-0019.

Pipe, M.E., & Salmon, K. (2009). Dolls, drawing, body diagrams, and other props: Role of props in investigative interviews. In K. Kuehnle, & M. Connell (Eds), *The Evaluation of Child Sexual Abuse Allegations: A Comprehensive Guide to Assessment and Testimony* (pp. 365–398). New Jersey: Wiley.

Pipe, M.E., & Wilson, J.C. (1994). Cues and secrets: Influences on children's event reports. *Developmental Psychology*, *30*, 515–525.

Plotnikoff, J., & Woolfson, R. (1995). *Prosecuting Child Abuse: An Evaluation of the Government's Speedy Progress Policy*. London: Blackstone Press.

Plotnikoff, J., & Woolfson, R. (2009a). *Measuring up? Evaluating Implementation of Government Commitments to Young Witnesses in Criminal Proceedings*. London: NSPCC.

Plotnikoff, J., & Woolfson, R. (2009b). *Measuring up? Evaluating implementation of Government Commitments to Young Witnesses in Criminal Proceedings. Good Practice Guidance in Managing Young Witness Cases and Questioning Children*. London: NSPCC.

Poole, D.A., & Wolfe, M.A. (2009). Child development: Normative sexual and nonsexual behaviors that may be confused with symptoms of sexual abuse. In K. Kuehnle & M. Connell (Eds), *The Evaluation of Child Sexual Abuse Allegations: A Comprehensive Guide to Assessment and Testimony* (pp. 101–128). New Jersey: Wiley.

Salmon, K. (2001). Remembering and reporting by children: The influence of cues and props. *Clinical Psychology Review*, *21*, 267–300.

Salmon, K., & Pipe, M.E. (2000). Recalling an event one year later: The impact of props, drawing and a prior interview. *Applied Cognitive Psychology*, *14*, 261–292.

Salmon, K., Roncolato, W., & Gleitzman, M. (2003). Children's report of emotionally laden events: Adapting the interview to the child. *Applied Cognitive Psychology*, *17*, 65–80.

Sayfan, L., Mitchell, E.B., Goodman, G.S., Eisen, M.L., & Qin, J. (2008). Children's expressed emotions when disclosing maltreatment. *Child Abuse and Neglect*, *32*, 1026–1036.

Saywitz, K.J., Goodman, G.S., Nicholas, E., & Moan, S.F. (1991). Children's memories of a physical examination involving genital touch: Implications for reports of child sexual abuse. *Journal of Consulting and Clinical Psychology*, *59*, 682–691.

Saywitz, K.J., & Snyder, L. (1993). Improving children's testimony with preparation. In G.S. Goodman & B.L. Bottoms (Eds), *Child Victims, Child Witnesses: Understanding and Improving Testimony* (pp. 117–146). New York: Guilford.

Saywitz, K.J., & Snyder, L. (1996). Narrative elaboration: Test of a new procedure for interviewing children. *Journal of Consulting and Clinical Psychology*, *64*, 1347–1357.

Sternberg, K.J., Lamb, M.E., Esplin, P.W., Orbach, Y., & Hershkowitz, I. (2002). Using a structured protocol to improve the quality of investigative interviews. In M. Eisen, G. Goodman, & J. Quas (Eds), *Memory and Suggestibility in the Forensic Interview* (pp. 409–436). Mahwah, NJ: Erlbaum.

Steward, M.S., Steward, D.S., Farquar, L., Myers, J.E.B., Reinhart, M., Welker, J., Joye, N., Driskill, J., & Morgan, J. (1996). Interviewing young children about body touch and handling. *Monographs of the Society for Research in Child Development, 61*(4–5, Serial No. 248).

Strange, D., Garry, M., & Sutherland, R. (2003). Drawing out children's false memories. *Applied Cognitive Psychology, 17*, 607–619.

Strange, D., Sutherland, R., & Garry, M. (2006). Event plausibility does not determine children's false memories. *Memory, 14*, 937–951.

Sullivan, P.M., & Knutson, J.F. (1998). The association between child maltreatment and disabilities in a hospital-based epidemiological study. *Child Abuse and Neglect, 22*, 271–288.

Sullivan, P.M., & Knutson, J.F. (2000). Maltreatment and disabilities: A population-based epidemiological study. *Child Abuse and Neglect, 24*, 1257–1273.

Talwar, V., Lee, K., Bala, N., & Lindsay, R.C.L. (2002). Children's conceptual knowledge of lying and its relation to their actual behaviors: Implications for court competence examinations. *Law and Human Behavior, 26*, 395–415.

Teoh, Y.S., Yang, P.J., Lamb, M.E., & Larsson, A. (2010). Do human figure diagrams help alleged victims of sexual abuse provide elaborate and clear accounts of physical contact with alleged perpetrators? *Applied Cognitive Psychology, 24*, 287–300.

Thierry, K.L., Lamb, M.E., Orbach, Y., & Pipe, M.E. (2005). Developmental differences in the function and use of anatomical dolls during interviews with alleged sexual abuse victims. *Journal of Consulting and Clinical Psychology, 73*, 1135–1134.

Tulving, E., & Thomson, D.M. (1973). Encoding specificity and retrieval processes in episodic memory. *Psychological Review, 80*, 359–380.

Wade, K.A., Garry, M., Lindsay, D.S., & Read, J.D. (2002). A picture is worth a thousand lies: Using false photographs to create false childhood memories. *Psychonomic Bulletin and Review, 9*, 597–603.

Wattam, C. (1992). *Making a Case in Child Protection.* Harlow: Longman.

Wesson, M., & Salmon, K. (2001). Drawing and showing: Helping children to report emotionally laden events. *Applied Cognitive Psychology, 15*, 301–320.

Westcott, H.L., & Jones, D.P.H. (1999). Annotation: The abuse of disabled children. *Journal of Child Psychology and Psychiatry, 40*, 497–506.

Wilkinson, J. (1988). Context effects in children's event memory. In M.M. Gruneberg, P.E. Morris, & R.N. Sykes (Eds), *Practical Aspects of Memory: Vol. 1. Current Research Issues* (pp. 107–111). New York: Wiley.

Willcock, E., Morgan, K., & Hayne, H. (2006). Body maps do not facilitate children's reports of touch. *Applied Cognitive Psychology, 20*, 607–615.

13

Children with Intellectual Disabilities and Developmental Disorders

LUCY A. HENRY, CAROLINE BETTENAY, AND DANIEL P.J. CARNEY

Key Points

- Children with disabilities are more vulnerable to abuse and maltreatment than their typically developing peers, yet their participation in the criminal justice system is rare.
- Children with mild to moderate intellectual disabilities can recall forensically useful information. Experimental research indicates that mental age level is a reasonably good guide to performance.
- Children with Down syndrome are likely to have language problems, verbal short-term memory difficulties, and may also be difficult to understand because of expressive language difficulties; however, recall of visual and spatial details may be a relative strength.
- Children with autism spectrum disorders may have difficulties with remembering personal and/or social dimensions of an event and expressing themselves, because of language problems and reduced social awareness; but they may also find it difficult to mislead an interviewer.

Children's Testimony: A Handbook of Psychological Research and Forensic Practice, Second Edition.
Edited by Michael E. Lamb, David J. La Rooy, Lindsay C. Malloy, and Carmit Katz.

- Children with Williams syndrome may have apparently advanced language skills, but their ability to recall and understand visual and spatial details or concepts is likely to be weak.
- Best practice for interviewing children with intellectual and developmental disabilities is to adopt relevant guidelines for typical children and, in addition: (i) gather information on the child's profile of strengths and weaknesses before planning interviews; (ii) structure interview questions so that they are simple, short, and carefully paced; (iii) begin with/emphasize free recall, which is likely to be accurate; (iv) avoid the repetition of questions; and (v) provide relevant support (e.g., an intermediary) and adaptations (e.g., more frequent breaks/reassurance).

SOME KEY CONCEPTS

- *Intellectual disabilities*: reduced cognitive capacity as measured by a standardized IQ test, plus difficulties with daily living.
- *Developmental disorder*: maturation in a manner not in line with the typical developmental path.
- *Chronological versus mental age*: children's mental age (MA) is determined by their IQ score in comparison with their peers of the same chronological age (CA); it is important in establishing where developmentally a child's performance on a given task may be, in comparison with typically developing children of the same age.

Children with disabilities are more likely to be maltreated and abused than their typically developing peers (Hershkowitz, Lamb, & Horowitz, 2007; Sullivan & Knutson, 2000), and those with intellectual disabilities are particularly vulnerable to sexual violence (Lin, Yen, Kuo, Wu, & Lin, 2009). Yet, despite being more likely to experience abuse in many forms (Mencap, 1999), individuals with intellectual disabilities are less likely to participate fully in the legal system (Kebbell & Hatton, 1999). Previous chapters have examined typically developing children's potential strengths and weaknesses as witnesses. This chapter examines the types of additional factors that may need to be taken into account for children with intellectual disabilities, and whether these may influence the quality of their testimony. We focus first on child witnesses with general learning difficulties (which we refer to as non-specific intellectual disabilities (ID)). Following this, we go on to examine the possible impact of having an ID *and* a specific developmental disorder, in relation to Down syndrome, autism spectrum disorder, and Williams syndrome.

A BRIEF INTRODUCTION TO INTELLECTUAL DISABILITIES

This section outlines some key issues that are important in understanding intellectual disability. As such, it is relevant for all four of the groups of children that are discussed subsequently. Although the term 'learning difficulties' is widely used in the United Kingdom, particularly in educational settings, this term has a different meaning in the United States, where it refers to specific difficulties with particular skills such as reading or mathematics. Therefore, we use the term 'intellectual disabilities' (ID) as it is less open to misinterpretation.

ID is 'the most common developmental disorder and the most handicapping of the disorders beginning in childhood' (Harris, 2006). Individuals with ID have significant deficits in cognitive abilities, compared with typically developing individuals of the same age (*DSM-IV*, American Psychiatric Association, 2000). For a formal diagnosis, the ID has to have been evident from early childhood (Emerson, Hatton, Felce, & Murphy, 2001), as measured by an IQ of lower than 70. Equally importantly, the person diagnosed with ID must also present with difficulties in adaptive functioning (areas such as self-care, communication, social development, and interpersonal skills). Both *DSM-IV-TR* and *ICD-10* (World Health Organization, 2007) classify those who achieve IQ scores of less than 70 further as follows: a person with an IQ score of 50–69 would be classified as having mild ID; those with scores in the range of 35–49 as having moderate ID; those scoring 25–35 as having severe ID; and anyone with a score less than 20–25 as having profound ID. However, it is difficult to derive accurate and valid scores on many IQ tests below a level of around 40. Most diagnoses of ID (80%) fall within the mild range and have a favourable prognosis in terms of living independently. There is a 1.5 : 1 ratio of males to females with ID.

According to Volkmar and Dykens (2002), if we look only at those with an IQ of less than 70, rates of ID are between 2% and 3% of the population. If we also require a degree of social impairment (e.g., sufficient to require services), rates of ID are somewhat lower at around 1% of the population. Many with milder forms of ID in the pre-school years will not yet have come to the attention of services; equally, many will acquire better adaptive skills as they grow up and achieve independence by adulthood. In other words, rates of ID may be lower in pre-schoolers and adults than in school-age children.

Children and adults with ID are a vulnerable population (Westcott & Jones, 1999). They are at increased risk of abuse (e.g., Brown & Stein, 1998; Westcott, 1991), with studies reporting risk factors 2–4 times higher in those with ID than typically developing peers (Lin *et al.*, 2009; Sullivan & Kuntson, 2000). Vulnerability is increased by the lack of power and influence within society of those with ID, their increased dependence on caregivers and intervention services, and a lack of education regarding sexual abuse (Lin *et al.*, 2009). Those with ID can also be the only witnesses to others' victimization in care settings (Milne, 2000). Increased severity of ID appears to correlate with increased severity of abuse (Hershkowitz *et al.*, 2007; Williams, 1995; Wilson & Brewer, 1992). The majority of cases of physical, sexual, and verbal abuse are rarely reported despite being often repeated and chronic (Sobsey & Doe, 1991); but when they are, do not often lead to prosecution or other punishment such as disciplinary action at work (Mencap, 1999; Sharp, 2001). However, despite being more at risk, children with ID are an under-researched group in the eyewitness testimony literature. As children with ID represent a substantial part of the community likely to be victims of crime, it is important to understand their relative strengths and weaknesses in court settings. This is especially important given the importance of witness testimony to the success of a case (Leippe, 1980; Visher, 1987).

As well as discussing potential witnesses for the defence who may have ID, it is important to point out that many defendants also have ID (Barron, Hassiotis, & Banes, 2004). Gudjonsson, Clare, Rutter, and Pearse (1993) observed that the mean IQ for 162 suspects at two police stations was 82 (range 61–131), with 9% recording an IQ below 70, and one-third a score of 75 or less.

Earlier authors have noted that the skills required in encoding, storing, and retrieving memories for events may be less well developed in younger children, with consequent reductions in their ability to process and respond appropriately to questions (e.g., Saywitz, 2002). These issues need careful consideration in children who have ID are likely to be cognitively less mature than typically developing children of the same age (Brown & Geislman, 1990).

It is important to note that not all witnesses with a disability, intellectual or otherwise, would define themselves as vulnerable. Research with a range of child witnesses (Plotnikoff & Woolfson, 2004) has shown that the most important point is that children's wishes as individuals should be taken into account. Children with ID deserve this treatment too, in conjunction with clinical and diagnostic advice. Neither should it be assumed that all people with a given disability should be treated the same. One cannot make assumptions regarding the severity of abilities and deficits in children with a given disorder, as there is a high degree of variability, both within and between disorders.

IDENTIFYING CHILDREN WITH INTELLECTUAL DISABILITIES

Children may be identified as having ID through a requirement to be in a special school or being placed into special programmes in mainstream schools. This may be as a result of low IQ or other associated learning problems, or it may be because of the child having a diagnosed developmental disorder that is often or usually associated with ID, such as Down syndrome, Williams syndrome, or autism spectrum disorder (note that although the majority of individuals with Down and Williams syndrome also have ID, the proportion of individuals with autism spectrum disorders and ID is lower, at around 50–80%). It is important to bear in mind that overall IQ scores on their own tell us nothing about the cognitive and behavioural profile of children with ID, and, as with typically developing individuals, those with ID may share a raw IQ score but differ in the pattern of abilities and disabilities they present across the range of cognitive functions. This may be particularly true for children with ID and a specific developmental disorder, as discussed later in the chapter. Therefore, additional diagnostic evidence pertaining to an individual's relative strengths and weaknesses is very valuable.

Describing the performance of children with ID can be in terms of their abilities in each area compared with norms of others of the same chronological age. Alternatively a child's mental age can be determined by comparing their scores with the norms derived from samples of other age groups. Mental age is often used as a general descriptor for the broad level of intellectual functioning of a child with ID, and can be helpful to put the child's abilities in developmental context.

Two theories of the cognitive development of those with ID are also helpful. The 'developmental model' (Zigler, 1969) assumes that stepwise progression towards cognitive competence happens over time in children with non-specific ID. It further assumes that development occurs in the same manner as in typically developing children, but at a slower rate. The 'difference model' assumes that development in children with ID produces cognitive abilities that are qualitatively different to those shown by typically developing children (Ellis, 1969), and that early differences have a detrimental knock-on effect on subsequent development. The two positions may be complementary, and it is probable that some disorders produce specific profiles of cognitive functioning, which affect both developmental rate and the nature of cognitive performance achieved.

FORENSIC ISSUES RELEVANT TO ALL VULNERABLE WITNESSES

The *Achieving Best Evidence* (ABE) guidelines are now in their second edition (Home Office, 2007) and a brief outline is provided here.

ABE provides guidance for the treatment of a number of witness groups such as intimidated, vulnerable, and significant witnesses. Vulnerable witnesses are able to gain assistance in testifying in criminal cases where they are deemed eligible for 'special measures', such as the removal of gowns/wigs and giving evidence behind a screen. These guidelines stipulate that all witnesses aged 17 or under at the time of the hearing are deemed vulnerable and entitled to have their evidence-in-chief submitted as a video recording, and to be examined and cross-examined via video link. Three other categories of vulnerable witnesses are defined within the guidelines: any witness classified as having a mental disorder; any witness with a learning disability; and anyone with a physical disability. In addition, a complainant in a sexual offence case is deemed to be an intimidated witness and eligible for special measures. It can be seen that any child with ID on its own, or an ID plus a specific developmental disorder, will clearly fall into the vulnerable category, and may also be classed within the intimidated category.

During police interviews and any subsequent court processes, can we determine the likely performance of a child with ID? In answering this question, one might assess whether the child is able to recall and verbalize memories of events, people, and places to the level of their chronological age peers, their peers of the same mental age, or neither of these groups.

As already noted, development in typically developing children and children with ID/developmental disorders may follow the same trajectory; or those with ID/developmental disorders may follow a different path altogether. Additionally, some children with ID/developmental disorders may have a degree of difficulty with language and communication over and above what we might expect based on their mental age. One example of this is Down syndrome, where difficulties with articulating ideas, comprehending questions, and producing easily understandable speech may cause practical problems to interviewers.

A limited amount of research with adults who have ID has given us some insight into their capabilities. Adults with ID are less likely to understand complex instructions such as having their rights read or explaining the meaning of the oath; they tend to be more acquiescent; and they may not understand the consequences of making a given statement (Clare & Gudjonsson, 1995; Gudjonsson, Murphy, & Clare, 2000). However, if questioned correctly, adults with ID are capable of giving evidence on matters they clearly remember (Gudjonnsson & Gunn, 1982) and making correct suspect identifications (Ericson & Isaacs, 2003). Similarly, research has shown that with the correct questioning, adult witnesses with ID are capable of providing accurate testimony (Perlman, Ericson, Esses, & Isaacs, 1994).

We will now move on to considering how well children with non-specific ID, and three different developmental disorders (Down syndrome, autism spectrum disorder, Williams syndrome), deal with questioning procedures. Some developmental disorders are almost always associated with ID (Down and Williams syndromes), and others are often, but not always, associated with ID (autism spectrum disorder). Children with autism spectrum disorder may display other symptoms such as social dysfunction along a continuum of severity, which may affect the way they react to and respond to questions. In addition, 'comorbidity' (i.e., where a child has more than one disorder) is common, and symptoms may interact and possibly exacerbate the child's difficulties. Assessment is therefore crucial to ascertain the strengths and weakness of the individual witness, regardless of the diagnostic symptomatology with which they present.

The following sections give brief overviews of relevant forensic research on children with: (i) non-specific ID; (ii) Down syndrome; (iii) autism spectrum disorder; and (iv) Williams syndrome.

CHILDREN WITH NON-SPECIFIC INTELLECTUAL DISABILITIES

A small body of experimental evidence has developed over the past 20 years, addressing the issue of how well children with non-specific ID are likely to perform as witnesses. In general, the studies involve children watching or participating in a live event, and then taking part in a subsequent evidence-gathering interview, designed to assess their accuracy of recall and often also their suggestibility. Most studies have included three broad types of questions:

1. 'Free recall', whereby the child is asked to remember as much as possible about the witnessed event (e.g. 'Tell me everything you can remember about what happened...');

2. 'General questions', which are open-ended prompts designed to follow up free recall and elicit further narrative answers ('Tell me more about the lady that spoke to you...'); and
3. 'Specific questions', which probe particular details and are designed to have short, or one word answers ('What did the lady take out of her bag?').

Note that some experimental studies also include *leading* questions (indicating or suggesting to the interviewee an answer (e.g., 'The lady was wearing a hat, wasn't she?'). In fact, leading questions can be *correctly* leading, whereby the correct answer is suggested; or *misleading* whereby a mistaken answer is suggested (e.g., 'The man took a picture of you with his mobile phone', when he did not). Clearly, absolute truth regarding whether a question is correctly leading or misleading is known in experimental studies using staged events. Leading questions, however, are not recommended in ABE guidelines.

Turning now to the literature, Dent (1986) tested 33 children (aged 8–11 years) with IQs ranging from 49 to 70, using different questioning techniques. She found that they recalled less information in response to free-recall and specific questions, but more in response to general questions. This finding ties in well with subsequent research showing that children with ID may produce sparse amounts of detail in response to free-recall instructions, but that this information is nevertheless very accurate, with around 94% accuracy or higher being a common finding (Henry & Gudjonsson, 1999, 2004; Michel, Gordon, Ornstein, & Simpson, 2000). However, Dent did not compare the performance of children with ID to that of comparison groups, so it was not possible to evaluate whether their performance might reach chronological age levels, or more closely resemble typically developing peers of a similar mental age.

A later experimental study by Henry and Gudjonsson (1999) looked at just this issue. They evaluated the eyewitness skills of 11- to 12-year-old children with ID (IQ 60, range 40–78, MA 7 years), comparing them with typically developing children who were either of the same mental age (younger children) or the same chronological age. Henry and Gudjonsson (1999) found that children with ID recalled slightly fewer details in response to free-recall instructions than typically developing children of the same age, but that this difference was not significant. This rather good level of performance was also found for general questions and a range of other specific questions. Where the children with ID had difficulties was in responding to misleading questions phrased in a 'yes/no' style (e.g., 'The man said hello to you, didn't he?', when he did not). Here, the children with ID were more suggestible than typically developing comparisons of the same chronological age. Nevertheless, they were not more suggestible than the comparison group matched for mental age. These results implied that children with ID could provide a good range of detail about an event in response to a range of question types, even in comparison to chronological age peers but that they were slightly more vulnerable to misleading 'yes/no' questions.

This research was followed up by Henry and Gudjonsson (2003) to examine whether those with more marked ID might have greater difficulties with witnessing skills than those with milder ID. This was, indeed, the case. Children aged 11–12 years with mild ID (IQ 66, range 55–79, MA 8 years) recalled just as much information in response to free-recall instructions as typically developing children of the same chronological age; and were no more suggestible. Overall therefore, the performance on those with mild ID was very good, although they did show slightly weaker performance on general questions and some types of specific questions. By contrast, 11-to 12-year-old children with moderate ID (IQ 46, range 40–54, MA 6 years) showed weaknesses on all question types compared with chronological age comparisons.

However, one important finding from this study was that even the children with moderate ID did not perform below their mental age level. Therefore, we might expect that the witnessing skills of children with moderate ID should be in line with their mental age. Somewhat higher expectations may even be appropriate for those with milder forms of ID.

Henry and Gudjonsson (2003) did, nevertheless, find one marked weakness that was characteristic of children with both mild and moderate ID. When evidence gathering interviews were re-administered 2 weeks later, children with ID changed their responses to specific questions more often than either comparison group. These results imply that interviewers must take particular care with repeated questions/interviews, as children with ID may be prone to interpreting a repeated question as a signal that their original answer was incorrect. Similarly, Cederborg, Danielsson, La Rooy, and Lamb (2009) examined real life transcripts of evidence-gathering interviews with children and young people with ID (some also had autism spectrum disorder, so this was a very mixed sample), relating to sexual abuse allegations. Cederborg *et al.* (2009) found that 9% of 'focused' (specific) questions were repeated in these interviews, and that the children and young people with ID changed their answers to these repeated questions on 40% of occasions. Although these authors did not include a control group, the rates of changed responses to repeated questions were very high.

Other experimental work has broadly supported the view that the witnessing skills of those with non-specific ID are in line with mental age. For example, Michel *et al.* (2000) found that 9- to 14-year-old children with ID (IQ 58, standard deviation 15, MA 6.5 years, CA 11.5 years) recalled as much information about a simulated health check (and obtained the same levels of suggestibility) as children of the same mental age; although they did not reach the performance levels of chronological age comparisons. Jens, Gordon, and Shaddock (1990) also found that 10-year-old children with ID (IQ 63, range 47–77, MA 6.5 years) obtained levels of recall and suggestibility in line with their mental age; a result that was largely replicated in a new sample of 10-year-old children with ID (IQ 57, range not reported, MA 6.5 years) by Gordon, Jens, Hollings, and Watson (1994).

It is tempting to summarize the implications of these findings by saying that children with ID show at least 'mental age-appropriate' witness skills. However, there is one study to suggest that such a conclusion should be made cautiously. Agnew and Powell (2004) found that 9- to 12-year-old children with ID recalled fewer items of information about a magic show they participated in than children of the same mental age. This was true for free recall as well as a range of specific questions including those phrased as a 'forced choice' between alternatives. Less comprehensive and accurate answers were provided, and the participants in both mild (IQ 63, range 56–75) and moderate ID (IQ less than 55, but not exactly determined as the test used did not measure IQs below 55) groups required more questioning to elicit information. The authors attributed this to possible language deficits and to less efficient explicit memory processing. However, the children with ID were not more suggestible than typically developing children of the same mental or chronological age. Agnew and Powell (2004) also noted that all of the children were able to provide forensically useful and accurate information about more than half of the target items when the interview as a whole was looked at.

However, it is important to note that the experimental studies reviewed here did not concern traumatic events, and there were no consequences following the evidence-gathering interviews. Instances of abuse allegations in relation to children with disabilities are more likely to concern parents or parent figures, and the psychological and physical dependence of these children on their abusers may account for their reduced likelihood of disclosure (Hershkowitz *et al.*, 2007). In addition, court settings may be particularly problematic for those with ID. Research shows their comprehension of legal terms as adults does not match typically developing peers (Ericson & Perlman, 2001). During complex questioning, particularly under cross-examination, professionals do not appear to make allowances for those with ID (Kebbell, Hatton, & Johnson, 2004). Neither do judges intervene on their behalf as they are allowed to do by law (O'Kelly, Kebbell, Hatton, & Johnson, 2003). Thus, further research is required to assess whether the promising performance of children with ID on experimental witnessing tasks can be reproduced in real forensic settings.

Forensic Implications

Despite these caveats, the main point to emerge is that children with ID can provide forensically useful and relatively accurate information about an event. If forensic interviews are conducted in line with best-practice models such as that published by the Home Office (2007), this should optimize their responses. In fact, Agnew, Powell, and Snow (2006) have recently investigated this, utilizing real police interviewers in an experimental study of event recall in 9- to 13-year-old children with ID (IQ in the range 75 and below, but the IQ test did not measure IQs under 55). Agnew *et al.* (2006) found that police officers did broadly adopt best-practice guidelines, but made frequent interruptions and did not use many 'minimal encouragers' to increase the amount of recall.

The most important points to bear in mind about the structure and planning of evidence-gathering interviews with children have been covered already in other chapters, and remain highly relevant for children with ID. However, it is worth re-emphasizing the importance of question order when interviewing children with ID. Interviews should begin with open-ended requests for 'free recall', because this has been found to be very accurate, if sometimes rather sparse. General prompts should come next, to try to elicit more free narrative, again because this is likely to be accurate. Specific questions should be left until last, because children with ID may answer such questions to please an interviewer, or try to provide the answer they think is wanted. In addition, specific questions should not be repeated, given evidence that children with ID are prone to changing answers when specific questions are repeated (Cederborg *et al.*, 2009; Henry & Gudjonsson, 2003).

It is always important to tailor interviews with children to their developmental level, and this is particularly important for children with ID. We have suggested that mental age might be an approximate guide to a child's developmental level, if no other information is available. Questions should be worded in a simple manner, free from jargon and abstract ideas or words. Each question should be short and restricted to just one point (children with ID often have poor verbal short-term memory; e.g., Henry & Winfield, 2010), not too directive or suggestive, and without double negatives ('She was not unhappy'). Thorough and timely preparation for an evidence gathering-interview with children who have ID (or suspected ID) is strongly recommended.

Additional factors to bear in mind when interviewing children and young people with non-specific ID include:

1. Does the child need more frequent breaks and a familiar environment with very few distractions.
2. Would the child benefit from having a familiar person or 'supporter' present, or at the very least regular reassurance from the interviewer.
3. Are there any language weaknesses or idiosyncratic uses of language that need to be taken into account.
4. Should the questions proceed at a slower pace, as individuals with ID can have slower speeds of information processing (Anderson, 2001).
5. Does the child know that the interviewer does not know what happened – children with ID may assume that the interviewer knows already.
6. Does the child know that the interviewer needs full details – children with ID may not appreciate this.
7. Is there adequate time to establish rapport and allow the interviewer to judge the child's level of social, emotional, and cognitive maturity.
8. Would the child benefit from an 'intermediary' (all child witnesses, particularly those with communication difficulties, are entitled to an intermediary to assess their communicative skills and assist interviewers, barristers, and judges in communicating with the child throughout the investigative process prior to and during evidence-gathering interviews, as well as in court).

Cross-Examination

Our adversarial system recognizes a defendant's right to challenge and test the evidence against them. Thus, conflict is inherent in attempting to balance the rights of the defendant with those of the witness. 'While it is important to cater for a child's needs and comfort, judicial efforts to that end should never be such as to amount to a suggestion that the child's evidence is likely to be more credible than that of any another witness. Consistently with that, steps to limit the distress experienced by a child must not overcome the necessity of ensuring that a party has been given a proper opportunity to challenge the evidence of the child' (Judicial Studies Board, 2008).

In court settings, typically developing children can experience anxiety and stress as a result of questioning from verbose and aggressive defence lawyers, such that they are likely to change their answers, regardless of initial accuracy, under cross-examination (Zajac & Hayne, 2003). This is unrelated to telling lies. Lyon and Saywitz (1999) asked

96 abused and neglected children to distinguish between truth and lies in three tasks, showing that at age 5, children were able to identify these differences successfully. Nevertheless, children may be overawed by the authority figure posing questions, may remember details and events differently from adults, and are known to be more suggestible than adults. They seldom request clarification of questions, despite the complexity of the language used in court, and are highly inconsistent when cross-examined, with 75% of 5- to 7-year-olds changing at least one piece of their evidence in a study of real court transcripts (Zajac, Gross, & Hayne, 2003). If typically developing children experience this stress to a point where their performance suffers, what can we expect from children with ID?

As we have seen earlier, even when matched for mental age and therefore cognitive ability, children with ID appear more likely than other children to change their answers when evidence-gathering interviews are repeated (Henry & Gudjonsson, 2003). While this may be a result of social factors (e.g., eagerness to please, increased sensitivity to desired cued responses), which are also present in typically developing children, it is possible that such phenomena may be exacerbated in children with ID.

However, recent research (Bettenay, 2010) undertaken with children who had non-specific ID indicated that they were broadly no more susceptible to changing their answers under cross-examination (by real trainee barristers) than children of the same mental age, either for gist questions (general questions relating to the event and its meaning) or verbatim questions (specific details of the event). In fact, very large numbers of primary school age children, whether they had ID or not, changed their responses in a 'mock' cross-examination.

Summary: Children with Non-specific Intellectual Disabilities

- Children with ID have broad difficulties with thinking and learning, usually expressed as low IQ, and difficulties with daily living skills.
- Research evidence indicates that children and young people with non-specific ID (there is no diagnosed cause for the ID) can recall forensically relevant and valuable information about witnessed events.
- Forensic interviews both prior to and during court appearances may be most effective if carried out with the expectation that the performance of children with ID will compare with children of a similar mental age (i.e., their equivalent in a measure of cognitive ability rather than their equivalent in actual years). However, all children with ID are individuals, and there is substantial variation in witness

performance within both typically developing and intellectually disabled populations.
- Performance may vary depending on a number of factors; some relating to the child's profile of cognitive skills and whether the ID is mild or moderate, and others concerning the particular social and emotional circumstances of the interview.
- Children and young people with ID may benefit from intermediaries to facilitate their communication, but there is as yet no research evidence on this issue.
- Following ABE Guidelines for vulnerable witnesses will help interviewers to obtain the most accurate accounts from children with non-specific ID, but a number of additional considerations have been outlined. Repeated questions, in particular, are best avoided with this population of children, as their tendency to change responses may adversely affect the credibility of their evidence.

CHILDREN WITH DOWN SYNDROME

Down syndrome (DS) is the most frequently observed genetic disorder (Pennington, Moon, Edgin, Stedron, & Nadel, 2003) and the most common genetic cause of ID (Caselli, Monaco, Trasciani, & Vicari, 2008). The condition occurs in approximately 1 in every 700–1000 live births (Kittler, Krinsky-McHale, & Devenny, 2007), and is almost uniformly caused by trisomy 21, an extra copy of genetic material on chromosome 21 (Pennington *et al.*, 2003), with around 95% of individuals with DS displaying this anomaly (Seung & Chapman, 2004). Physical features associated with DS include distinctive 'flattened' facial features and poor muscle tone (Nadal *et al.*, 1996). In addition, there are increased risks of congenital heart disease, leukaemia (Korenberg, Bradley, & Disteche, 1992), hearing difficulties (Dahle & McCollister, 1986), immunological deficiencies (Goldacre, Wotton, Seagroatt, & Yeates, 2004) and speech–motor problems (Fowler, 1995).

Psychologically, the condition is primarily characterized by ID, with IQ usually in the moderate to severe range (i.e., 25–55; Pennington *et al.*, 2003). However, despite severe ID being typical, Epstein (1989) points out that the IQs of some individuals with DS are in the normal range. Furthermore, recent advances in educational provision, coupled with higher expectations, have meant that many children with DS are now educated in mainstream settings.

DS also carries a significantly increased risk of age-related cognitive decline and early onset of Alzheimer's-type dementia (Numminen, Service, Ahonen, & Ruoppila, 2001; Rowe, Lavender, & Turk, 2006), with Johanson *et al.* (1991) reporting clinical dementia to be observable in 25–30% of those with DS aged 40 years and under, rising to 75% prevalence by the age of 60. Co-occurrence of DS and autistic spectrum disorder is also relatively common, with 5–10% of individuals with DS estimated to display sufficient autistic traits for diagnosis (Kent, Evans, Paul, & Sharp, 1999; Rasmussen, Börjesson, Wentz, & Gilberg, 2001).

Behaviourally, those with DS have often been characterized as friendly, cooperative, and mild-mannered, and likely to show fewer adaptive behaviour problems than individuals with other types of developmental disorder (e.g., Chapman & Hesketh, 2000). However, some authors have reported a significantly higher level of problem behaviours, such as non-compliance, aggression, and social withdrawal, in comparison with typically developing individuals (Coe *et al.*, 1999; Cuskelly & Dadds, 1992).

A principal feature of the DS ability profile is a marked impairment in expressive language (i.e., language that is produced rather than simply heard) (Fowler, Gelman, & Gleitman, 1994). Within this domain, individuals with DS show deficits in a number of areas, including vocabulary, utterance length, sentence construction (or syntax), and intelligibility, in comparison with typically developing comparisons matched for non-verbal mental age (e.g., Chapman, Seung, Schwartz, & Kay-Raining Bird, 1998). Verbal short-term memory deficits, in the absence of specific hearing impairments (which may compromise performance upon verbal memory tasks) have also been observed (e.g., Jarrold & Baddeley, 1997; Jarrold, Baddeley, & Hewes, 2000). Some researchers suggest that the expressive language impairments in DS may be directly related to these verbal STM problems (Chapman, 1995; Fowler, 1998).

In contrast, receptive language (i.e., understanding and processing of language) and non-verbal skills, while still generally impaired in comparison with the performance of typically developing individuals, has often been observed to be superior to expressive language (e.g., Chapman, Schwartz, & Kay-Raining Bird, 1991). Although the cognitive profile associated with DS has been reasonably well defined, Reeves, Baxter, and Richtmeier (2001) point out that people with the condition vary in terms of the severity of the characteristics with which they present.

Forensic Implications

The points raised in the previous section on interviewing children with ID will be equally relevant when interviewing children who have DS. However, there are a number of additional points to keep in mind for this population of children. Although we are not aware of any specific research that has examined the performance of children with DS in investigative interview situations, existing knowledge of the verbal/nonverbal ability profile associated with the condition enables the identification of factors that may potentially be of influence, and of which practitioners should be aware.

In particular, the poorer verbal than non-verbal abilities shown by individuals with DS, especially when considered in combination with their documented expressive language deficit, may mean that children with DS will be better equipped to recall visual and spatial information than verbal material. However, because of language production difficulties, it may be advisable – and less stressful for the child – to enable them to communicate this information non-verbally wherever possible (e.g., tracing a route manually on a floor plan drawing).

In terms of questioning, although the verbal understanding of children with DS is likely to outstrip their ability to communicate information, receptive language abilities in DS are still usually below those of chronological age-matched typically developing children. Interviewers should, therefore, employ clear, simple language wherever possible, and avoid using lengthy phrases and questions. The latter is particularly important because of the known difficulties with verbal short-term memory. Interviewers should also ascertain whether a child with DS has any hearing difficulties, as these are relatively common.

Where children with DS are required to give verbal responses, difficulties with articulation and/or intelligibility may make it hard for them to be fully understood. It is advisable that, where possible, children are interviewed in the presence of an individual who knows them well enough to be able to clarify anything they say that may be difficult to decipher or understand. The use of intermediaries to facilitate communication and understanding, and avoid important misinterpretations throughout the investigative process is strongly recommended for children with DS. Children with DS are also routinely reported to use significantly shorter sentences when communicating than typically developing children (e.g., Chapman *et al.*, 1998). While this may be a result of expressive language difficulties, it is highly plausible that, for some children, a lack of communicative confidence may be implicated. It is thus advisable not only to allocate more time than usual to the interview process, and rephrase key questions if necessary, but also to offer encouragement and approval at every opportunity, in order to facilitate freer communication.

Lastly, because of the wide ability range that has been observed in the DS population, it is possible that some children may have difficulty grasping certain key contextual aspects of the interview situation. For instance, a witness with DS may find it hard to understand that he/she is not directly in trouble. Simply being interviewed in a police station may prompt greater anxiety, fear, and reluctance to communicate than the 'being a witness' situation might usually provoke in typically developing individuals. It is therefore important to establish early on in the investigative process that the child understands exactly why he/she is there, that he/she is not trouble, and to periodically reinforce this information.

Summary: Children with Down Syndrome

- DS is a developmental disorder associated with ID, in the moderate to severe range (IQ 20–55).
- Interviewers should be aware that hearing difficulties and speech motor problems (leading to reduced intelligibility) are relatively common among children with DS. Taken together with the fact that children with DS have difficulties with expressive language, the use of an intermediary is strongly recommended.
- Immediate verbal short-term memory difficulties are also characteristic of DS; this means that questions must be kept very short and simple.
- Relative strengths in those with DS include good non-verbal skills and better receptive than expressive language. This means that children may understand more than they can express verbally; interviewers might also consider using non-verbal methods to elicit information.
- Like any vulnerable witness, a child with DS may require regular reassurance in an interview situation.

CHILDREN WITH AUTISM SPECTRUM DISORDER

Autism spectrum disorder (ASD) is a lifelong developmental disorder included in the *DSM-IV-TR* broader category of Pervasive Developmental Disorder (PDD). ASD encompasses a wide range of symptoms, but three main characteristics/impairments are particularly marked: difficulties in reciprocal social interaction; difficulties in communication; and restricted/repetitive behaviours and interests. It affects around four times more boys than girls (Volkmar, Szatmari, & Sparrow, 1993), and the overall prevalence of the broader category of PDD may be as high as 1 in 1000 (Fombonne, 2002). Although ASD is understood to present with early onset (before 36 months), distinct patterns of non-typical behaviours can routinely be clinically observed around 3 years of age (Howlin & Moore, 1997; Matson, Nebel-Schwalm, & Matson, 2007).

Individuals with ASD vary in the severity of their symptoms from high functioning individuals, possibly with a diagnosis of Asperger syndrome and relatively intact language and intelligence (Joliffee & Baron-Cohen, 1999), to those with more severe symptoms. However, they all share poor social relationships and rigid behaviour patterns. There appears to be a lack of ability in children with ASD to mentally represent the thoughts and feelings of themselves and others; for example, they cannot predict others' behaviour, understand jokes, sarcasm, or metaphors and do not interpret lying behaviour (Martin & McDonald, 2003). Conscious and deliberate effort is required to deduce logically what others may be thinking or feeling (Grandin & Scariano, 1986). Researchers (e.g., Hobson, 1993) note that those on the autism spectrum may experience problems with personal pronouns (I, you) and struggle to interpret terms for space and time (here, there, come, go).

Obsessional interests are often evident, as children and adults with ASD attend to small details within a larger subject such as train timetables, cardboard boxes, and straight lines (Watts & Swinbourne, 2001). Anxiety is prevalent, and may be exacerbated by the cognitive and social deficits described above in children and adolescents with ASD (MacNeil, Lopes, & Minnes, 2009). Situational anxiety, particularly when routines are disrupted, strangers are present, or other events occur that the individual feels deviate from their normal experience, will be high in most individuals on the autism spectrum regardless of cognitive ability.

ASD can co-occur with other disorders, most often with ID; around 50–80% of individuals with ASD have ID (Matson & Shoemaker, 2009). Matson and Shoemaker (2009) also note that because of increased effectiveness of available testing techniques and an increase in knowledge about the research area, comorbidity is now understood to occur often with mood and anxiety disorders, schizophrenia, obsessive–compulsive disorder, and attention deficit hyperactivity disorder (ADHD).

Depending upon where the individual's symptoms lie on the autism spectrum, behaviour can be rigid and inflexible (e.g., routines must be followed exactly); and perseveration can be common, perhaps repeating one set of behaviours over and over again. One of the authors notes that this adherence to rules can sometimes manifest itself as a preoccupation with the law, the police, and legal aspects of life generally. Even in the absence of such a preoccupation, any interview situation may induce high levels of anxiety, as well as necessitating the breaking of routines, which may be stressful in itself. Individuals with ASD may also experience difficulties in planning for the future or even thinking about the future – they do not anticipate the long-term consequences of their behaviour.

Forensic Implications

As many individuals with ASD also have ID, the general comments made earlier regarding interviewing children with ID will be relevant. There is also some specifically relevant research evidence on examining witnessing skills more directly in children with ASD, as well as some general research on memory development in those with ASD which has forensic implications. We will now touch on both of these areas.

Research on general memory functioning in those with ASD has identified difficulties with the recall of 'gist', or abstracted meaning, information. For example, although some individuals with ASD show remarkable and richly developed memory for 'facts' (some individuals have 'savant' skills in this area), these remembering skills tend to be narrow and rigid, and are not suited to recalling the gist of an event (Jordan, 2008). Recounting events with a 'personal' dimension or point of view may also be problematic for those with ASD, because of their difficulties with social relationships and the understanding of self (Jordan, 2008). Finally, memory for faces and voices, whether the newly encountered or familiar, seems to be impaired in those with ASD (Webb, 2008).

Some relevant research has recently been carried out on autobiographical memory and witnessing skills in children with ASD. For example, McCrory, Henry, and Happé (2007) looked at memory and suggestibility in young people (11–14 years) with Asperger syndrome. Although these individuals generally do not have language difficulties or ID, they do demonstrate the social difficulties and rigid behaviour patterns characteristic of ASD. McCrory *et al.* (2007) found that young people with Asperger syndrome did not differ from chronological age-matched (and IQ-matched) comparisons on their overall accuracy or suggestibility in recalling a recently witnessed, staged, live event. However, there were subtle differences in performance. Those with Asperger syndrome recalled less information in response to free-recall instructions, particularly for social details about the event. They were also less able to recall the five key ('gist') aspects of the event.

Similarly, Bruck, London, Landa, and Goodman (2007) evaluated autobiographical memory for recent and past life events, as well as including an assessment of how well a recently experienced magic show could be recalled. These authors focused on children with ASD that were 'high functioning', with IQs in the average range. Bruck *et al.*

(2007) found that children with ASD provided fewer accurate details than typically developing comparisons on virtually every measure they included. Children with ASD did not make more errors (of confabulation or distortion), they simply produced much sparser reports. These findings tie in well with reports that children and young people with ASD have difficulty with recalling gist information about events, particularly in relation to social details or events of personal relevance. However, it is important to note that the experimental studies we have quoted concern only high functioning children with ASD, and this work should be extended to children who have ASD plus ID.

Despite these documented difficulties with recalling gist information, children and young people with ASD may have enhanced abilities to recall specific detailed information that others miss, provided that the information is of interest to them. Therefore, it is possible that a child with ASD could provide better evidence about some types of details than a child with no disability. As noted by Baron-Cohen (2002), 'In the social world there is no great benefit to such a precise eye for detail, but in the world of maths, computing, cataloguing, music, linguistics, craft, engineering or science, such an eye for detail can lead to success rather than disability.'

Another potentially positive feature about those with ASD is that they should have difficulty deliberately misleading an interviewer, or lying, because their understanding of these concepts is often limited. However, the other side of this is that the relative inability of children with ASD to show empathy toward others may mean details of how other players in an event were acting may be lost. When interviewing, it should also be borne in mind that individuals with ASD are not able to process metaphors or allusions given their literal interpretation of language. 'It's raining cats and dogs' may mean exactly that to an individual on the autistic spectrum. Therefore, use of these phrases could induce confusion and heighten anxiety.

Care must be taken not to over-generalize with respect to individuals with ASD, given the wide range of symptoms children with this disorder present with. Children at the mild end of the spectrum may simply have problems with social skills, while those at the far end may have little or no language or ability to interact socially, and repetitive behaviours which further impede communication. While language skills may be preserved in those with Asperger syndrome, their restricted interests and social difficulties may mean that details in the surrounding environment and socially salient information remain of little interest to them.

In children with more severe symptoms, language skills may be severely depleted or non-existent. For example, echolalia is a sign of delayed language development in those with autism (Durand, 2005). However, young children also repeat speech from others as an intermediate step to full language acquisition. Some children with ASD may be 'stuck' at that stage of development, but it must not be assumed that the child does not comprehend what is being said. The intervention of an intermediary (many intermediaries are qualified speech and language therapists) would be essential in such cases where language development is severely delayed or unusual.

Summary: Children with Autism Spectrum Disorder

- Children and young people with ASD have difficulties with reciprocal social interaction, communication difficulties, narrow and obsessional interests, and rigid or inflexible behaviour. Intellectual disability is also present in 50–80% of those with ASD.
- The large range and variation in severity of symptoms in ASD means that generalizing about individual performance can be difficult. For example, those with Asperger syndrome do not tend to show difficulties with language, nor do they have ID, but they will still show social and behavioural difficulties.
- Lack of expressive language, unusual or severely delayed language skills, and/or unusual social skills in a proportion of individuals with ASD may impede interviews. Intermediaries, therefore, are highly recommended for children who have limited language skills.
- Research evidence suggests that individuals with ASD show poor memory for the gist of an event, especially in relation to social aspects of the situation. However, it is possible that they may remember large amounts of specific detail if this coincides with their area(s) of interest.
- Children and young people with ASD are unlikely to perform well on face or voice recognition, given research evidence that these skills are impaired.
- Children with ASD are, however, expected to find lying or misleading an interviewer difficult, as their understanding of such concepts is limited.

CHILDREN WITH WILLIAMS SYNDROME

Williams syndrome (WS) is a rare developmental disorder resulting from a deletion of genetic material on chromosome 7 (Peoples *et al.*, 2000), with a prevalence of approximately 1 in 20 000 (Brown *et al.*, 2003). Physical features of the condition include 'elfin' facial features

(Morris & Mervis, 1999), growth deficiency (Udwin, Davies, & Howlin, 1996), poor muscle tone, excessive blood calcium levels (Morris, Demsey, Leonard, Dilts, & Blackburn, 1988), cardiac/kidney problems, and hypersensitivity to certain sounds (Laskari, Smith, & Graham, 1999).

The psychological profiles of individuals with WS are generally characterized by mild to moderate ID, and an uneven pattern of abilities; namely a relative strength in verbal skills alongside marked non-verbal difficulties in problem solving (e.g., Bellugi, Bihrle, Neville, Jernigan, & Doherty, 1992), numerical (e.g., Udwin *et al.*, 1996) and spatial processing (e.g., Bellugi, Wang, & Jernigan, 1994). However, an area of strength within the spatial domain has been observed, with individuals with WS sometimes reported to show face recognition or face processing skills at a level similar to that of mental age-matched comparisons (e.g., Deruelle, Mancini, Livet, Casse-Perrot, & de Schonen, 1999; Gagliardi *et al.*, 2003). This is in direct contrast to other aspects of spatial performance, which have been consistently observed to be weak (e.g., Bihrle, Bellugi, Delis, & Marks, 1989).

Behaviourally, individuals with WS generally present as sociable, talkative, empathic, and uninhibited (e.g., Jones *et al.*, 2000; Porter, Coltheart, & Langdon, 2007). While some studies have indicated that social interaction skills in those with WS may be impaired or at least atypical (e.g., Stojanovik, 2006), such observably 'hypersociable' behaviour is a striking aspect of the condition. Restlessness, hyperactivity, and anxiety – both generalized and specific – have also been reported (e.g., Davies, Udwin, & Howlin, 1998; Dykens, 2003).

Despite the relatively defined psychological, social, and behavioural profile which has come to be associated with WS, it is undoubtedly important for practitioners to remember that individuals with the condition can vary considerably in terms of the extent to which they manifest each of the traits discussed (Porter & Coltheart, 2005). Nevertheless, Bellugi, Lichtenberger, Jones, Lai, and St George (1994) note that the long-term circumstances of individuals with WS are generally characterized by special educational placement with heavily supported living in adulthood, with adults with WS usually residing in the parental home or in a supervised care setting.

Forensic Implications

As with DS, we are not aware of any specific research that has examined the performance of children with WS in investigative interview situations, but earlier comments regarding interviewing those with non-specific ID will be relevant. In addition, we have used existing knowledge of the verbal/non-verbal ability profile associated with the condition to identify some potentially relevant factors specific to those with WS.

The cognitive abilities of those with WS are – generally speaking – the reverse of DS, with verbal skills being relatively preserved compared with those with DS. In addition, processing of faces seems to be an area of strength. It may be reasonable to expect that such a profile may determine how well – or how poorly – different types of material are recalled or reported. For instance, research suggests that verbal memory in children with WS is superior to memory for spatial material (e.g., Jarrold, Baddeley, & Hewes, 1999; Wang & Bellugi, 1994). Therefore, it might be that individuals with WS, when being interviewed or cross-examined, may find it easier to remember specific verbal material than material of a visual or spatial nature. In other words, they may be more likely to remember 'what was said' than they would a particular route taken or the spatial location of a person or object at a scene. Furthermore, with regard to spatial language, research has indicated that children with WS may often misuse spatial prepositions (Rubba & Klima, 1991) or overgeneralize when using such devices (e.g. 'by' rather than 'in front of/behind'; Bellugi *et al*., 2000). However, they may show relative superiority when recalling aspects of, or identifying, unfamiliar faces.

Although children with WS often appear to be fluent speakers and able conversationalists, assumptions should not be made about what children may mean when speaking, and what they may have understood when listening. A number of parents of children with WS have informally expressed to one of the authors that they feel their children are routinely 'over-rated' in terms of overall ability, and that this may be because of a combination of verbal strengths and a tendency to present well in social and conversational situations.

Despite most children with WS qualifying under current jurisdiction for vulnerable witness status (at least) as a result of associated ID, it is highly plausible that the formalized nature of interview room/court situations, whether evidence is being given remotely or not, will cause high levels of anxiety. Although this is a pertinent concern with regard to any child, practitioners should remain conscious of the heightened anxiety which has frequently been associated with WS.

In addition to anxiety which may arise from the interview situation, other aspects of the WS profile may also affect the nature of the responses given. Specific, narrow interests (a phenomenon common to individuals with WS) may cause children to fixate on one particular aspect of a recalled scenario, at the expense of other factors that are equally, if not more, meaningful. Alternatively, possible difficulties with inhibition/self-regulation with regard to verbal material (e.g., Porter *et al.*, 2007) – or simply a desire to interact – may lead to responses that are unnecessarily long or garrulous and, as a function of this, characterized by a high level of irrelevant information. Practitioners may find it useful to ensure that the child is not only aware of what type of information is required from them, but also that they are periodically reminded of this. Such contextual reinforcement will help children to not only stay 'on track' but also plan and structure their responses appropriately.

Some children with WS may also, as a function of heightened sociability, try to 'turn the tables' and ask the interviewer questions that are irrelevant. While this may prove useful in establishing a rapport and reducing anxiety, efforts should again be made to remind children why they are there and what is required from them. Social motivation may also lead them to be keen to give the perceived desired response to interviewers, at the possible expense of factual accuracy. Any such tendency is especially relevant when the usage of deliberately misleading questions in cross-examination is considered. Intermediaries are recommended to ensure that communication misunderstandings are avoided and the relevance and focus of interviews is maintained.

Summary: Children with Williams Syndrome

- WS is characterized by mild to moderate ID, and an uneven pattern of abilities, namely a relative strength in verbal skills alongside marked non-verbal difficulties.
- Therefore, individuals with WS, when being interviewed or cross-examined, may find it easier to remember verbal material than material of a visual or spatial nature.
- Face recollection may also be a strength for those with WS.
- Those with WS are often described as sociable, talkative, empathic, and uninhibited. Although these characteristics may facilitate interviews, professionals should be aware of the heightened anxiety that has frequently been associated with WS and which might become a factor in very formal situations. Children and young people with WS can also suffer from hyperactivity which may make interviews challenging.
- Despite the documented verbal strengths of those with WS and a tendency to present well in social and conversational situations, the factual accuracy of their recollections has not been systematically assessed and may be over-rated.
- Children and young people with WS may give responses that are unnecessarily long, garrulous, and/or irrelevant.

- Intermediaries may be a very useful aid to communication for children and young people with WS, by helping to keep interviews focused on relevant information and alerting interviewers/practitioners to occasions when superficially good language skills may hide a lack of understanding.

CONCLUSIONS

Research shows that indivduals with ID and developmental disorders associated with ID do not often get their day in court (Kebbell & Hatton, 1999). Although we do not have extensive research evidence in relation to the witnessing skills of individuals with specific developmental disorders associated with ID, research among populations of children with non-specific ID suggests that they are able to provide accurate detail at least in line with typically developing children of the same mental age (Henry & Gudjonsson, 1999, 2003). They also appear to be broadly as able as their peers to resist cross-examination (Bettenay, 2010). Using other available literature, we have made some inferences concerning useful measures that could be taken with children who have specific developmental disorders in addition to ID. The key general points to emerge were as follows:

- Wherever possible, interviewers should establish the nature and extent of the person's ID beforehand, as well as determining whether a specific developmental disorder has been diagnosed. This will guide the style, speed, and nature of the interview and perhaps highlight the need for extra precautions to be taken.
- Most children with ID, if not all, would benefit from the presence of a support person, ideally an intermediary, as many children and young people with ID have communication difficulties.
- Interviewers should not make negative assumptions about the abilities of a child or young person based solely on their having ID. The research reviewed here suggests that children and young people with ID can recall forensically relevant information. When interviewing any child or young person with ID, adherence to the ABE (2007) guidelines is essential. Beginning with free narrative, gradually increasing the specificity of the questions and avoiding repeated questions helps to produce the most accurate accounts.
- Children and young people with ID and specific developmental disorders present with different profiles of cognitive abilities and disabilities even where they share the same IQ score. These cognitive

(and also relevant social and behavioural) factors should be taken into account in planning interviews.
- Employing additional straightforward measures will increase the effectiveness of the interview, such as:
  - using simple sentences;
  - avoiding leading questions;
  - allowing extra time for responses;
  - avoiding the introduction of abstract ideas; and
  - resisting the temptation to interrupt.
- Interviewers should prepare the environment wherever possible to avoid distractions, and allow for shorter interview sessions.

Great strides have been made in the last 15 years with regard to gathering evidence from children, and some progress has been made with children who have ID. However, further research, particularly in assessing the performance of children with specific developmental disorders, would consolidate our knowledge and provide practitioners with an empirical basis on which to structure their interviews with children depending upon their particular profile of abilities and disabilities.

REFERENCES

Agnew, S., & Powell, M. (2004). The effect of intellectual disability on children's recall of an event across different question types. *Law and Human Behavior*, *28*, 273–294.

Agnew, S.E., Powell, M.B., & Snow, P.C. (2006). An examination of the questioning styles of police officers and caregivers when interviewing children with intellectual disabilities. *Legal and Criminological Psychology*, *11*, 35–53.

American Psychiatric Association. (2000). *Diagnostic and Statistical Manual of Mental Disorders* (4th edn, text revised). Washington, DC: APA.

Anderson, M. (2001). Annotation: Conceptions of intelligence. *Journal of Child Psychology and Psychiatry*, *42*, 287–298.

Baron-Cohen, S. (2002). Is Asperger syndrome necessarily viewed as a disability? *Focus on Autism and Other Developmental Disabilities*, *17*, 186–191.

Barron, P., Hassiotis, A., & Banes, J. (2004). Offenders with intellectual disability: A prospective comparative study. *Journal of Intellectual Disability Research, 48*, 69–76.

Bellugi, U., Bihrle, A., Neville, H., Jernigan, T., & Doherty, S. (1992). Language, cognition, and brain organization in a neurodevelopmental disorder. In M. Gunnar & C. Nelson (Eds), *Developmental Behavioral Neuroscience* (pp. 201–232). Hillsdale, NJ: Lawrence Erlbaum.

Bellugi, U., Lichtenberger, L., Jones, W., Lai, Z., & St George, M. (2000). The neurocognitive profile of Williams syndrome: A complex pattern of strengths and weaknesses. *Journal of Cognitive Neuroscience*, *12*(1), 7–29.

Bellugi, U., Wang, P.P., & Jernigan, T. (1994). Williams syndrome: An unusual neuropsychological profile. In S.H. Broman & J. Grafman (Eds), *Atypical Cognitive Deficit in Developmental Disorders: Implications for Brain Function* (pp. 23–56). Hillsdale, NJ: Lawrence Erlbaum.

Bettenay, C. (2010). Memory of children under cross-examination with and without intellectual disabilities. Unpublished doctoral dissertation. London South Bank University, UK.

Bihrle A.M., Bellugi, U., Delis, D., & Marks, S. (1989). Seeing either the forest or the trees: Dissociation in visuospatial processing. *Brain and Cognition, 11*(1), 37–49.

Brown C.L., & Geiselman R.E. (1990). Eyewitness testimony of mentally retarded: Effect of the cognitive interview. *Journal of Police and Criminal Psychology*, *6*, 14–21.

Brown, H., & Stein, J. (1998) Implementing Adult Protection Policies in Kent and East Sussex. *Journal of Social Policy*, *27*, 371–396.

Brown, J.H., Johnson, M.H, Paterson, S.J., Gilmore, R., Longhi, E., & Karmiloff-Smith, A. (2003). Spatial representation and attention in toddlers with Williams syndrome and Down syndrome. *Neuropsychologia*, *41*, 1037–1046.

Bruck, M., London, K., Landa, R., & Goodman, J. (2007). Autobiographical memory and suggestibility in children with autism spectrum disorder. *Development and Psychopathology*, *19*, 73–95.

Caselli, M.C., Monaco, L., Trasciani, M., & Vicari, S. (2008). Language in Italian children with Down syndrome and with Specific Language Impairment. *Neuropsychology*, *22*, 27–35.

Cederborg, A.C., Danielsson, H., La Rooy, D., & Lamb, M.E. (2009). Repetition of contaminating question types when children and youth with intellectual disabilities are interviewed. *Journal of Intellectual Disability Research*, *53*(5), 440–449.

Chapman, R.S. (1995). Language development in children and adolescents with Down syndrome. In P. Fletcher & B. MacWhinney (Eds), *Handbook of Child Language* (pp. 641–663). Oxford: Blackwell Publishers.

Chapman, R.S., & Hesketh, L. (2000). The behavioural phenotype of Down syndrome. *Mental Retardation and Developmental Disabilities Research Review*, *6*, 84–95.

Chapman, R.S., Schwartz, S.E., & Kay-Raining Bird, E. (1991). Language skills of children and adolescents with Down syndrome: I: Comprehension. *Journal of Speech and Hearing Research*, *34*, 1106–1120.

Chapman, R.S., Seung, H., Schwartz, S.E., & Kay-Raining Bird, E. (1998). Language skills of children and adolescents with Down syndrome: II: Production. *Journal of Speech, Language, and Hearing Research*, *41*, 861–873.

Clare, I.C.H., & Gudjonsson, G.H. (1995). The vulnerability of suspects with intellectual disabilities during police interviews: A review and experimental study of decision making. *Mental Handicap Research*, *8*, 110–128.

Coe, D.A., Matson, J.L., Russell, D.W., Slifer, K.J., Capone, G.T., Baglio, C., & Stallings, S. (1999). Behavior problems of children with Down syndrome and life events. *Journal of Autism and Developmental Disorders*, *39*, 149–156.

Cuskelly, M., & Dadds, M. (1992). Behavioural problems in children with Down's syndrome and their siblings. *Journal of Child Psychology and Psychiatry*, *33*(4), 749–761.

Dahle, A., & McCollister, F. (1986). Hearing and otologic disorders in children with Down syndrome. *American Journal of Mental Deficiency*, *90*, 636–642.

Davies, M., Udwin, O., & Howlin, O. (1998). Adults with Williams syndrome. Preliminary study of social, emotional and behavioural difficulties. *British Journal of Psychiatry*, *172*, 273–276.

Dent, H. (1986). An experimental study of the effectiveness of different techniques of questioning mentally handicapped child witnesses. *British Journal of Clinical Psychology*, *25*, 13–17.

Deruelle, C., Mancini, J., Livet, M.O., Casse-Perrot, C., & de Schonen, S. (1999). Configural and local processing of faces in children with Williams syndrome. *Brain and Cognition*, *41*(3), 276–298.

Durand, V. (2005). Past present and emerging directions in education. In D. Zager (Ed.), *Autism Spectrum Disorder: Identification, Education, and Treatment* (3rd edn, pp. 89–109). Hillsdale, NJ: Erlbaum.

Dykens, E.M. (2003). The Williams syndrome behavioral phenotype: The 'whole person' is missing. *Current Opinion in Psychiatry*, *16*(5), 523–528.

Ellis, N.R. (1969). A behavioural research strategy in mental retardation: Defence and critique. *American Journal of Mental Deficiency*, *73*, 557–567.

Emerson, E., Hatton, C., Felce, D., & Murphy, G. (2001). *Learning Disabilities: The Fundamental Facts*. London: Foundation for People with Learning Disabilities.

Epstein, C.J. (1989). Down syndrome. In C.R. Scriver, A.L. Beaudet, W.S. Sly, & P. Valle (Eds), *The Metabolic Basis of Inherited Disease* (pp. 291–396). New York: McGraw-Hill.

Ericson, K., & Isaacs, B. (2003). Eyewitness identification accuracy: A comparison of adults with and those without intellectual disabilities. *Mental Retardation*, *41*(3), 161–173.

Ericson, K., & Perlman, N. (2001). Knowledge of legal terminology and court proceedings in adults with developmental disabilities. *Law and Human Behavior*, *25*, 529–545.

Fombonne, E. (2002). Epidemiological trends in rates of autism. *Molecular Psychiatry*, *7*, 4–6.

Fowler, A.E. (1995). Linguistic variability in persons with Down syndrome. In L. Nadel and D. Rosenthal (Eds), *Down Syndrome: Living and Learning in the Community*. New York: Wiley.

Fowler, A.E. (1998). Language in mental retardation: Associations with and dissociations from general cognition. In J.A. Burack, R.M. Hodapp, & E. Zigler (Eds), *Handbook of Mental Retardation and Development* (pp. 290–333). Cambridge: Cambridge University Press.

Fowler, A.E., Gelman, R., & Gleitman, L., (1994). The course of language learning in children with Down syndrome. In H. Tager-Flusberg (Ed.), *Constraints on Language Acquisition: Studies of Atypical Children*. Hillsdale, NJ: Lawrence Erlbaum.

Gagliardi, C., Frigerio, E., Burt, D.M., Ilaria Cazzaniga, I., Perrett, D.I., & Borgatti, R. (2003). Facial expression recognition in Williams syndrome. *Neuropsychologia*, *41*, 733–738.

Goldacre, M.J., Wotton, C.J., Seagroatt, V., & Yeates, D. (2004). Cancers and immune related diseases associated with Down's syndrome: A record linkage study. *Archives of Disease in Childhood*, *89*(11), 1014–1017.

Gordon, B.N., Jens, K.G., Hollings, R., & Watson, T.E. (1994). Remembering activities performed versus those imagined: Implications for testimony of children with mental retardation. *Journal of Clinical Child Psychology*, *23*, 239–248.

Grandin, T., & Scariano, M. (1986). *Emergence; Labelled Autistic*. New York: Warner Books.

Gudjonsson, G.H., Clare, I., Rutter, S., & Pearse, J. (1993). *Persons At Risk During Interviews in Police Custody: The Identification of Vulnerabilities*. London: Royal Commission Criminal Justice, HMSO.

Gudjonsson, G.H., & Gunn J. (1982). The competence and reliability of a witness in a criminal court. *British Journal of Psychiatry, 141*, 624–627.

Gudjonsson, G.H., Murphy, G.H., & Clare, I.C.H. (2000). Assessing the capacity of people with intellectual disabilities to be witnesses in court. *Psychological Medicine, 30*, 307–314.

Harris, J.C. (2006). *Intellectual Disability: Understanding its Development, Causes, Classification, Evaluation and Treatment*. Oxford: Oxford University Press.

Henry, L.A., & Gudjonsson, G.H. (1999). Eyewitness memory and suggestibility in children with mental retardation. *American Journal on Mental Retardation, 104*, 491–508.

Henry, L.A., & Gudjonsson, G.H. (2003). Eyewitness memory, suggestibility and repeated recall sessions in children with mild and moderate intellectual disabilities. *Law and Human Behavior, 27*, 481–505.

Henry, L.A., & Gudjonsson, G.H. (2004). The effects of memory trace strength on eyewitness recall in children with and without intellectual disabilities. *Journal of Experimental Child Psychology, 89*, 53–71.

Henry, L.A., & Winfield, J. (2010). Working memory and educational achievement in children with intellectual disabilities. *Journal of Intellectual Disability Research, 54*, 354–365.

Hershkowitz, I., Lamb, M.E., & Horowitz, D. (2007). Victimisation of children with disabilities. *American Journal of Orthopsychiatry, 77*(4), 629–635.

Hobson, R.P. (1993). The emotional origins of social understanding. *Philosophical Psychology, 6*(3), 227–249.

Home Office. (2007). *Achieving Best Evidence in Criminal Proceedings: Guidance on Interviewing Victims and Witnesses, and Using Special Measures*. London: Home Office.

Howlin, P., & Moore, A. (1997). Diagnosis in Autism: A survey of over 1200 patients in the UK, *Autism, 1*, 135–162.

Jarrold C., & Baddeley A.D. (1997). Short-term memory for verbal and visuospatial information in Down's syndrome. *Cognitive Neuropsychiatry, 1*, 101–122.

Jarrold, C., Baddeley, A.D., & Hewes, A.K. (1999). Genetically dissociated components of working memory: Evidence from Down's and Williams' syndrome. *Neuropsychologia, 37*, 637–651.

Jarrold, C., Baddeley, A.D., & Hewes, A.K. (2000). Verbal short-term memory deficits in Down syndrome: a consequence of problems in rehearsal? *Journal of Child Psychology and Psychiatry, 41*, 233–244.

Jens, K.G., Gordon, B.N., & Shaddock, A.J. (1990). Remembering activities performed versus imagined: A comparison of children with mental retardation and children with normal intelligence. *International Journal of Disability, Development and Education, 37*, 201–213.

Johanson, A., Gustafson, L., Brun, A., Risberg, J., Rosen, I., & Tideman, E. (1991). A longitudinal study of dementia of Alzheimer type in Down's syndrome. *Dementia, 2*, 159–168.

Jolliffe, T., & Baron-Cohen, S. (1999). A test of central coherence theory: Linguistic processing in high-functioning adults with autism or Asperger's syndrome – is local coherence impaired? *Cognition*, *71*, 149–185.

Jones, W., Bellugi, U., Lai, Z., Chiles, M., Reilly, J., Lincoln, A., & Adophs, R. (2000). Hypersociability in Williams syndrome. *Journal of Cognitive Neuroscience*, *12*, 30–46.

Jordan, R.R. (2008). Practical implications of memory characteristics in autistic spectrum disorders. In J. Boucher & D. Bowler (Eds), *Memory in Autism: Theory and Evidence* (pp. 293–310). Cambridge: Cambridge University Press.

Judicial Studies Board. (2008). *Equal Treatment Bench Book*. London: Judicial Studies Board.

Kebbell, M.R., & Hatton, C. (1999). People with mental retardation as witnesses in court: A review. *Mental Retardation*, *37*(3), 179–187.

Kebbell, M.R., Hatton, C., & Johnson, S.D. (2004). Witnesses with intellectual disabilities in court: What questions are asked and what influence do they have? *Legal and Criminological Psychology*, *9*, 1–13.

Kent, L., Evans, J., Paul, M., & Sharp, M. (1999). Comorbidity of autistic spectrum disorders in children with Down syndrome. *Developmental Medicine and Child Neurology*, *41*, 153–158.

Kittler, P.M., Krinsky-McHale, S.J., & Devenny, D.A. (2007). Dual-task processing as a measure of executive function: a comparison between adults with Williams and Down syndromes. *American Journal on Mental Retardation*, *113*, 117–132.

Korenberg, J.R., Bradley, C., & Disteche, C.M. (1992). Down syndrome: Molecular mapping of the congenital heart disease and duodenal stenosis. *American Journal of Human Genetics*, *50*, 294–302.

Laskari, A., Smith, A., & Graham, J. (1999). Williams–Beuren syndrome: an update and review for the primary physician. *Clinical Pediatrics*, *38*, 189–208.

Leippe, M.R. (1980). Effects of integrative and memorial processes on thecorrespondence of eyewitness accuracy and confidence. *Law and Human Behaviour*, *4*, 261–274.

Lin, L.P., Yen, C.F., Kuo, FY., Wu, J.L., & Lin, J.D. (2009). Sexual assault of people with disabilities: Results of a 2002–2007 national report in Taiwan. *Research in Developmental Disabilities*, *30*, 969–975.

Lyon, T.D., & Saywitz, K.J. (1999). Young maltreated children's competence to take the oath. *Applied Developmental Science: Special issue: New research on child witnesses: I*, *3*(1), 16–27.

MacNeil, B.M., Lopes, V.A., & Minnes, P.M. (2009). Anxiety in children and adolescents with Autism Spectrum Disorders. *Research in Autism Spectrum Disorders*, *3*, 1–21.

Martin, I., & McDonald, S. (2003). Weak coherence, no theory of mind, or executive dysfunction? Solving the puzzle of pragmatic language disorders. *Brain and Language*, *85*(3), 451–466.

Matson, J.L., Nebel-Schwalm M., & Matson, M.L (2007). A review of methodological issues in the differential diagnosis of autism spectrum disorders in children. *Research in Autism Spectrum Disorders*, *1*, 38–54.

Matson, J.L, & Shoemaker, M. (2009). Intellectual disability and its relationship to autism spectrum disorders. *Research in Developmental Disabilities*, *30*, 1107–1114.

McCrory, E., Henry, L.A., & Happe, F. (2007). Eyewitness memory and suggestibility in children with Asperger syndrome. *Journal of Child Psychology and Psychiatry*, *48*, 482–489.
Mencap. (1999). *Living in Fear*. London: Mencap.
Michel, M.K., Gordon, B.N., Ornstein, P.A., & Simpson, M.A. (2000). The abilities of children with mental retardation to remember personal experiences: Implications for testimony. *Journal of Clinical Child Psychology*, *29*, 453–463.
Milne, R. (2000). Interviewing children with learning disabilities. In A. Memon & R. Bull (Eds), *Handbook of the Psychology of Interviewing* (pp. 165–180). West Sussex, UK: Wiley and Sons.
Morris, C.A., Demsey, S., Leonard, C., Dilts, C., & Blackburn, B. (1988). Natural history of Williams syndrome: Physical characteristics. *Journal of Pediatrics*, *113*, 318–326.
Morris, C.A., & Mervis, C.B. (1999). Williams syndrome. In S. Goldstein, & C.R. Reynolds (Eds), *Handbook of Neurodevelopmental and Genetic Disorders in Children* (pp. 555–590). New York: Guilford Press.
Nadal, M., Milà, M., Pritchard, M., Mur, A., Pujals, J., Blouin, J., Antonarakis, S.E., Ballesta, F., & Estivill, X. (1996). YAC and cosmid FISH mapping of an unbalanced chromosomal translocation causing partial trisomy 21 and Down syndrome. *Human Genetics*, *4*, 460–466.
Numminen, H., Service, E., Ahonen, T., & Ruoppila, I. (2001). Working memory and everyday cognition in adults with Down's syndrome. *Journal of Intellectual Disability Research*, *45*, 157.
O'Kelly, C.M.E., Kebbell, M.R., Hatton, C., & Johnson, S.D. (2003). When do judges intervene in cases involving people with learning disabilities? *Legal and Criminological Psychology*, *8*, 229–240.
Peoples, R., Franke, Y., Wang, Y., Perez-Jurado, L., Paperna, T., Cisco, M., & Francke, U. (2000). A physical map, including a BAC/PAC clone contig, of the Williams–Beuren syndrome deletion region at 7q11.23. *American Journal of Human Genetics*, *66*, 47–68.
Pennington, B.F., Moon, J., Edgin, J., Stedron, J., & Nadel, L. (2003). The neuropsychology of Down syndrome: Evidence for hippocampal dysfunction. *Child Development*, *74*, 75–93.
Perlman N.B., Ericson K.I., Esses V.M., & Isaacs B.J. (1994) The developmentally handicapped witness: Competency as a function of question format. *Law and Human Behavior*, *18*, 171–187.
Plotnikoff, J., & Woolfson, R. (2004). *In Their Own Words: The Experiences of 50 Young Witnesses in Criminal Proceedings*. London: NSPCC.
Porter, M.A., & Coltheart, M. (2005). Cognitive heterogeneity in Williams syndrome. *Developmental Neuropsychology*, *27*(2), 275–306.
Porter, M.A., Coltheart, M., & Langdon, R. (2007). The neuropsychological basis of hypersociability in Williams and Down syndromes. *Neuropsychologia*, *45*, 2839–2849.
Rasmussen, P., Börjesson, O., Wentz, E., & Gilberg, C. (2001). Autistic disorders in Down syndrome: background factors and clinical correlates. *Developmental Medicine and Child Neurology*, *43*, 750–754.
Reeves, R.H., Baxter, L.L., & Richtsmeier, J.T. (2001). Too much of a good thing: Mechanisms of gene action in Down syndrome. *Trends in Genetics*, *17*, 83–88.

Rowe, J., Lavender, A., & Turk, V. (2006). Cognitive executive function in Down's syndrome. *British Journal of Clinical Psychology*, *45*, 5–17.

Rubba, J., & Klima, E.S. (1991). Preposition use in a speaker with Williams syndrome: Some cognitive grammar proposals. *Center for Research on Language Newsletter, University of California at San Diego*, *5*(3), 3–12.

Saywitz, K. (2002). Developmental Underpinnings of Children's Testimony In H.L. Seung, H.K., & Chapman, R.S. (2004). Sentence memory of individuals with Down's syndrome and typically developing children. *Journal of Intellectual Disability Research, 48*, 160–171.

Sharp, H. (2001). Challenging crime and harassment against people with learning difficulties. *Mental Health Care and Learning Disabilities*, *4*, 398–400.

Sobsey, D., & Doe, T. (1991). Patterns of sexual abuse and assault. *Sexuality and Disability*, *9*, 243–259.

Stojanovik, V. (2006). Social interaction and conversational inadequacy in Williams syndrome. *Journal of Neurolinguistics*, *19*, 157–173.

Sullivan, P.M., & Knutson, J.F. (2000). Maltreatment and disabilities: A population-based epidemiological study. *Child Abuse and Neglect*, *24*(10), 1257–1273.

Udwin, O., Davies, M., & Howlin, P. (1996). A longitudinal study of cognitive abilities and educational attainment in Williams syndrome. *Developmental Medicine and Child Neurology*, *38*, 1020–1029.

Visher, C.A. (1987). Juror decision making: The importance of evidence. *Law and Human Behavior*, *11*, 1–17.

Volkmar, F., & Dykens, E.M. (2002). Mental retardation. In M. Rutter, & E. Taylor (Eds), *Child and Adolescent Psychiatry: Modern Approaches* (4th edn, pp. 697–710). Oxford, UK: Blackwell Science.

Volkmar, F., Szatmari, P., & Sparrow, S.S. (1993). Sex differences in pervasive developmental disorders. *Journal of Autism and Developmental Disorders*, *23*, 579–591.

Wang, P.P., & Bellugi, U. (1994). Evidence from two genetic syndromes for a dissociation between verbal and visual-spatial short-term memory. *Journal of Clinical and Experimental Neuropsychology*, *16*, 317–322.

Watts, J., & Swinbourne, H. (2001). *Smiling at Shadows*. Sydney: Harper Collins.

Webb, S.J. (2008). Impairments in social memory in autism? Evidence from behaviour and neuroimaging. In J. Boucher, & D. Bowler (Eds), *Memory in Autism: Theory and Evidence* (pp. 188–209). Cambridge: Cambridge University Press.

Westcott, H. (1991). The abuse of disabled children: A review of the literature. *Child Care Health and Development*, *174*, 243–258.

Westcott, H., & Jones, D. (1999). Annotation: The abuse of disabled children. *Journal of Child Psychology and Psychiatry*, *40*(4), 497–506.

Williams, C. (1995). *Invisible Victims: Crime and Abuse against People with Learning Difficulties*. London: Jessica Kingsley.

Wilson, C., & Brewer, N. (1992). The incidence of criminal victimisation of individuals with an intellectual disability. *Australian Psychologist*, *27*, 114–117.

World Health Organization (WHO). (2007). *International Statistical Classification of Diseases and Related Health Problems, 10th Revision (ICD-10)*. Geneva, Switzerland: WHO.

Zajac, R., Gross, J., & Hayne, H. (2003). Asked and answered: Questioning children in the courtroom. *Psychiatry, Psychology and Law*, *10*, 199–210.

Zajac, R., & Hayne, H. (2003). I don't think that's what really happened: The effect of cross examination on the accuracy of children's reports. *Journal of Experimental Psychology: Applied*, *9*, 187–195.
Zigler, E. (1969) Developmental versus difference theories of mental retardation and the problem of motivation. *American Journal of Mental Deficiency*, *73*, 536–556.

14

Evidence and Cross-Examination

John R. Spencer

Key Points

- Cross-examination is widely believed to have an important role in facilitating the pursuit of justice and safeguarding defendants' rights.
- The right to cross-examine is an integral part of adversarial legal systems in the United States and it is constitutionally protected.
- Cross-examination that is delayed until the eventual trial creates obvious problems for witnesses who are vulnerable, including children and adolescents.
- The recommendations of the Pigot Report, which involve the defence questioning children in a second pre-trial interview, could mitigate these problems and should be implemented fully.

As readers will discover, this chapter is in two parts. The first, which is general, discusses in broad terms the different notions present in different legal traditions as to the most effective way for the courts to collect reliable evidence from witnesses, and the place of cross-examination in the lawyer's theoretical scheme of things. The second part, which is specific, explains the current law and practice governing the cross-examination of child witnesses in England and Wales. Although this second part is self-confessedly Anglocentric, some references will be made to the law in other parts of the United Kingdom, and the rest of the English-speaking world.

Children's Testimony: A Handbook of Psychological Research and Forensic Practice, Second Edition.
Edited by Michael E. Lamb, David J. La Rooy, Lindsay C. Malloy, and Carmit Katz.

CROSS-EXAMINATION AS A LEGAL INSTITUTION

Broadly speaking, the legal traditions of the world enshrine two different and competing notions as to the most effective means by which accurate information can be obtained from witnesses as the basis for decision making by the courts. The first assumes that best way is to have them examined, quietly and in private, and ahead of trial, by a neutral person who writes down their statement, and transmits the resulting deposition to the court of trial. By analogy with the institution of 'confession' in the Catholic church, in what follows I have called this concept the 'confessional model'. The second and contrasting concept assumes that the best way is to make the witness communicate his evidence to the court of trial orally and in person, at a hearing in which questions are put to him by the interested parties. In what follows, I have called this second concept the 'adversarial model'. Again broadly speaking, it is the first method that is traditionally favoured by the inquisitorial tradition of justice that developed in continental Europe, and the second by the adversarial tradition that was an integral part of the common law that grew up in England, and which is dominant today not only in the United Kingdom but also in the rest of the 'common law world', alias the 'Anglo-Saxon legal world': that is to say, the United States and most of the other parts of world that at one time were under British rule or influence.

The merits of the 'adversarial model' over the 'confessional model' were proclaimed in the seventeenth century by one of the 'fathers' of the common law, Sir Matthew Hale, when describing what he saw as the strong points of the English jury trial:

> 2ndly, That it is *ore tenus* personally, and not in writing, wherein oftentimes, yea too often, a crafty clerk, commissioner or examiner, will make a witness speak what he truly never meant, by his dressing of it up in his own terms, phrases, and expressions; whereas on the other hand, many times the very manner of a witness's delivering his testimony will give a probable indication whether he speaks truly or falsely; and by this means also he has opportunity to correct, amend or explain his testimony upon further questioning with him, which he can never have after a deposition is set down in writing.
>
> 3dly, That by this course of personal and open examination, there is opportunity for all persons concerned, viz. the judge, or any of the jury, or parties, or their council or attornies, to propound occasional questions, which beats and boults out the truth much better than when the witness only delivers a formal series of his knowledge without being interrogated; and on the other side, preparatory,

> limited and formal interrogatories in writing, preclude this way of occasional interrogations, and the best method of searching and sifting out the truth is choked and suppressed.
>
> 4thly, Also by this personal appearance and testimony of witnesses, there is opportunity of confronting the adverse witnesses, of observing the contradiction of witnesses sometimes of the same side, and by this means great opportunities are gained for the true and clear discovery of the truth. (Hale, c.1670, pp. 290–291)

Some 250 years later, the opposite view was eloquently put by a French judge and legal writer, François Gorphe:

> The Anglo-American system has grave faults which cry out for it to be abolished. In the first place, it over-uses the right of questioning, to which it attributes an exaggerated efficiency in the case of suspect witnesses, whilst paying insufficient respect to witnesses who are sincere. Even more deplorably, it takes absolutely no precautions against the witness being influenced, or even badgered, and it takes no account of the distorting effect of suggestive questions, which get worse as the case is more bitterly contested. This, as Schneikert [a German public prosecutor] says, is 'the best means of working upon witnesses and leading them astray'. Wouldn't the wretched witness need to be made of marble to stay calm and unruffled under the crossfire of interrogation and counter-interrogation, examination, cross-examination and re-examination which he must endure at the hands of the two adversarial opponents? Just think of a frightened witness, a weak one, or a child having to give evidence under such conditions! In reality, truth and justice cannot see the light of day except in an atmosphere of calmness and serenity. (Gorphe 1927, p. 90)

A moment's reflection will show that there is truth in both these statements, sharply opposed as they appear to be. Both the 'confessional method' and the 'adversarial method' have their merits and their faults, and which is more effective in a given case will depend upon the circumstances (Spencer & Flin, 1993, Chapter 10). If the trial follows quickly after the disputed incident, and the witness is self-confident, the 'adversarial method' has obvious advantages – particularly if the witness has strong motives for being less than wholly truthful. But where the trial will take place after a significant delay, and the witness is timid, and has no reason to be untruthful, the 'confessional method' is likely to produce evidence that is both fuller and more reliable.

Furthermore, the two methods are not completely incompatible. Legal procedures can be devised in which both are used; as in French criminal procedure, for example, where the trial court will sometimes have, as the evidence of a given witness, both the written deposition taken by *juge d'instruction* at a private hearing, and the oral testimony that he later gives at the trial; or as in English criminal procedure, where nowadays the evidence of a child in a sex case is likely to consist of two elements: evidence-in-chief in the form of a videotape of an early examination conducted privately, and evidence in cross-examination, given orally under an adversarial examination carried out at trial.

Although the 'Anglo-Saxon' legal world traditionally favours the adversarial method, England – the cradle of the common law and the original 'Anglo-Saxon' legal jurisdiction – has abandoned the adversarial method in favour of the confessional method of obtaining evidence from children when this is necessary to determine civil proceedings involving them. In public law proceedings where the state intervenes to take children away from parents who are believed to be abusing or neglecting them, and in private law proceedings where separated parents fight one another over questions of residence and access, hearsay evidence is freely admissible. And in civil proceedings of these types, the evidence of a child as to what has been happening or not happening in his life will in practice almost always take the form of a report, or oral evidence, from an adult who has interviewed the child, plus or minus a videotape of the interview. In theory it is possible for children in such cases to be called as witnesses and examined orally before the court, but in practice this is almost never done, and the judges who handle such cases are strongly opposed to it, and usually resist attempts to call them. In a recent case (*Re W (Children) (Concurrent Criminal and Care Proceedings)* (2009) in which a local authority had removed a child from a family on the ground that her stepfather was sexually abusing her, the stepfather appealed against the ruling on a variety of grounds, one of which was that the child should have been produced to give oral evidence. Upholding the decision of the court below, Wall LJ in the Court of Appeal said this:

> [55] Like Wilson LJ in *LM v. Medway Council* (2007)... in my 11 years as a judge in the Family Division, I never had an application to compel the attendance of a child for cross-examination on allegations of abuse made by the that child, or allegedly committed on that child, and no child was ever called to give such evidence in my court. At the same time, and during the same period, I attended numerous conferences at which every child and adolescent psychiatrist to whom I spoke, or whom I heard speak, condemned as abusive the process in criminal law whereby a child was required to attend court to be cross-examined, often many months and sometimes years after the event in order to have his or credibility impugned over abuse allegations...

> [59] ... I respectfully agree with Butler-Sloss LJ ... in *B County Council ex p. P* (1991) that it will be rare in family cases in which a child will be compelled to attend and give oral evidence to the judge.
>
> At one time it was even thought that, in civil cases involving children, there was a presumption that they should never be called to give live evidence. However, in another case also called *Re W*, which reached the Supreme Court in 2010, the justices rejected this. The child should be called as a witness, they said, whenever this was necessary to achieve a fair trial: but this, they said, meant a trial that was fair to the child as well as to the other participants, and hence judges are entitled to proceed without it.

In criminal proceedings in the 'Anglo-Saxon' legal world, however, the 'adversarial method' is firmly entrenched, even in proceedings where the key witnesses are children. This is not merely because most 'Anglo-Saxon' lawyers believe that it is the soundest method of extracting and testing evidence – though many do. It is also because it is felt, rightly, that defendants must be given an opportunity to put questions to prosecution witnesses, in order to reduce the risk of wrongful convictions based on evidence that is false. Aside from utilitarian considerations of this sort, there is a widespread and deep-seated feeling that, in criminal proceedings, it is an essential ingredient of a fair trial that the defendant should be given the opportunity to confront and challenge his accusers. In the United States this feeling was so strong that it was incorporated into the Constitution. The Sixth Amendment to the US Constitution provides that 'In all criminal prosecutions, the accused shall enjoy the right ... to be confronted with the witnesses against him.'

What exactly is the scope of this constitutional guarantee? Does it merely guarantee the defendant the right to cross-examine those persons whom the prosecution calls to give evidence against him as live witnesses at trial? Or does it go further, and also inhibit them from using against him what common lawyers call 'hearsay evidence': statements about material facts, delivered to the court not as oral first-hand testimony from someone who personally experienced them, but delivered to the court by some means – for example, a police officer who had interviewed the witness and taken a written statement from him? For many years, US case-law interpreted this constitutional requirement in a limited sense: it meant that the defendant had a right to be confronted with those who were called to testify against him at trial, but if the out-of-court statement of an absent witness was admitted in evidence against him under an exception to the hearsay rule he was unable to complain of an infringement of his Sixth Amendment rights. In

2004, however, the US Supreme Court changed direction, and took the position that the defendant's right to confrontation could in principle be infringed by the admission of hearsay evidence (*Crawford v. State of Washington* 2004).

A guarantee that is similar, but expressed in rather more muted terms, was included in the European Convention on Human Rights in 1951 – an international instrument drawn up after the Second World War, with a large amount of input from common lawyers (Marston, 1993; Straw, 2008). So far as relevant, Article 6 is as follows:

1. In the determination of his civil rights and obligations or of any criminal charge against him, everyone is entitled to *a fair and public hearing* within a reasonable time by an independent and impartial tribunal established by law...
2. Everyone charged with a criminal offence shall be presumed innocent until proved guilty according to law.
3. *Everyone charged with a criminal offence has the following minimum rights: ...*
   to examine or have examined witnesses against him and to obtain the attendance and examination of witnesses on his behalf under the same conditions as witnesses against him...

This guarantee, together with the rest of the Convention, is officially recognized by all 47 of the states that have joined the Council of Europe: a group which, besides all 27 of the EU Member States (one of which of course is the United Kingdom) includes, among other countries, Albania, Turkey, the Russian Federation, and – at the opposite end of the physical scale – the Republic of San Marino. A failure by a signatory state to respect Article 6, or any of the other guarantees set out in the Convention, can result in the condemnation of the state concerned by the European Court of Human Rights at Strasbourg.

One of the functions of the Strasbourg Court is to interpret the Convention and, like the US Supreme Court with the Sixth Amendment, it has been called upon to determine the limits of the 'confrontation' guarantee contained in Article 6(3)(d). In a series of cases starting with *Unterpertinger v. Austria* (1986) it has adopted a broadly similar approach to the one now taken by the US Supreme Court: Article 6(3)(d) guarantees the defendant's right not only to put questions or have questions put to those whom the prosecution call to give evidence at trial, but also other people who are 'witnesses' in the wider sense of being persons who have fed information, consciously and voluntarily, into a criminal justice system, the ears of which have been officially open to it (Spencer, 2008, Chapter 2).

This interpretation has caused some embarrassment to countries in continental Europe which traditionally favoured what I have called the 'confessional approach' to child witnesses, to the extent of allowing criminal courts to convict defendants on the basis of statements from child complainants to whom the defendant had been unable to put any questions. In *P.S. v. Germany* (2001) a child's account of what had happened was relayed to the court via her mother and a police officer, and the court convicted the defendant on this evidence, supplemented by a report from a child psychologist who had examined the child and expressed the view that her statements were credible. At no stage did the defence have any input into her questioning. The convicted defendant made an application to Strasbourg, which upheld his complaint, and condemned Germany for breach of Article 6(3)(d).

However, although the Strasbourg case-law makes it clear that the defendant in a criminal case has a right to have his side of the story put to a child complainant, it does not go so far as to guarantee him the right to force the child to undergo a live cross-examination, conducted by his barrister at trial, which is a characteristic feature of Anglo-American criminal procedure. In a series of cases it has been made clear that the defendant's right under Article 6(3)(d) of the Convention is also satisfied if the defence had the opportunity to have their questions put to the child witness at an interview conducted out of court ahead of trial. In *S.N. v. Sweden* (2002) a defendant was convicted of a sexual offence against a child on the basis of tape-recorded police interviews with the child complainant, before one of which the suspect's lawyer had agreed with the police officer which aspects of the case he wished to be explored. In dismissing the defendant's application the Strasbourg Court said:

> Having regard to the special features of criminal proceedings concerning sexual offences. . ., [Article 6(3)(d)] cannot be interpreted as requiring in all cases that the questions be put directly by the accused or his or her defence counsel, through cross-examination or other means.

So a scheme recommended for England and Wales in 1989 by the Pigot Committee – discussed below – would clearly satisfy the requirements of the European Convention.

Does the guarantee contained in Article 6(3)(d) mean that it would be a breach of the defendant's Convention rights to convict him on the basis of a convincing statement from a child (or indeed an adult) witness where circumstances conspired to make it simply impossible for the defence to put their questions to the witness at any stage? For example, if at trial a child witness simply refused to submit to cross-examination, or if a witness, having given a statement to the police, then dies before the trial? On this important issue there is an ongoing conflict between the Strasbourg Court and the Supreme Court of the United Kingdom (which replaced the House of Lords as the final court of appeal in the UK with effect from October 2009). In *Al-Khawaja and Tahery v. UK* (2009) a Division of the Strasbourg Court said that a conviction in such circumstances infringes the defendant's rights under the Convention if the statement is the 'sole or decisive' evidence against him, and on that basis condemned the UK in respect of two convictions, in one of which the crucial piece of evidence was a statement from a witness who had died before the trial, and in other a statement from a witness who had been excused attendance because he feared reprisals. (In each case the statement, though constituting hearsay, was admissible in England under statutory exceptions to the general ban on hearsay evidence in criminal proceedings.) In *R v. Horncastle and others* (2009) the UK Supreme Court refused to accept this, holding that if the statement is properly admitted under the provisions of the Criminal Justice Act 2003 that set out a scheme of exceptions to the hearsay rule, the defendant's trial is 'fair' even if the 'sole or decisive' piece of evidence is the statement from an absent witness whom the defence have been unable to examine (Spencer, 2010a). At the request of the UK government the Al-Khawaja case was referred to the Grand Chamber, where it was reheard, with greater formality, before an enlarged court consisting of 20 judges. At the time of writing, the outcome is awaited.

THE CURRENT LAW IN RELATION TO THE CROSS-EXAMINATION OF CHILD WITNESSES IN CRIMINAL PROCEEDINGS IN ENGLAND AND WALES

In 1989 a Home Office committee chaired by Judge Pigot QC condemned the existing system for taking evidence from child witnesses in cases where adults were accused of committing offences against them and recommended a new scheme, making use of video technology, under which the evidence of children would be taken in two stages. When the complaint first came the light, the child would be interviewed by a trained examiner according to a code of practice; if in this interview the child described the commission of an offence, the video recording of this interview would replace the child's live evidence-in-chief at the eventual trial, if there should be one. As soon as possible after this initial interview the defence should be given the opportunity to put their questions to the child at a similar informal hearing; and at the eventual trial, should there be one, a video recording of this second interview should replace the child's live cross-examination (Pigot, 1989). This would enable the child to drop out of the legal picture at an early stage, and – at least in some cases – it would lead to a more meaningful interaction with the child during cross-examination than is likely to occur in the formal setting of a trial, particularly one that takes place a long time afterwards.

Although this proposal attracted widespread support there were also fears that the second part of Pigot scheme would be unfair to the defendant. The defence would not be able to cross-examine the child effectively until it had received full disclosure of all the evidence the police and prosecution had collected, and at the point in time when the child would be cross-examined under the Pigot scheme this material might not yet have reached the hands of the defence. The government was impressed by this argument, and instead of introducing legislation to enact the whole of the Pigot scheme it produced proposals, later enacted in the Criminal Justice Act 1991, to provide for the first stage of the Pigot scheme without the second. Under the government's 'half-Pigot' scheme, a video of the child's initial interview normally replaces the child's live evidence-in-chief, but the child is obliged to come to court to undergo a live cross-examination: albeit one normally conducted through a live video link with the child in an adjoining room, rather than present in the body of the courtroom.

In 1999, the Youth Justice and Criminal Evidence Act (YJCEA) repealed the child witness provisions of the 1991 Act and replaced them with wider provisions about 'special measures' that apply not only to children but to other categories of vulnerable witness too. As a step towards implementing the 'full Pigot', section 28 of the YJCEA created the possibility of holding the cross-examination of a vulnerable witness ahead of trial. This change, however, has never been implemented, and it now most unlikely that it ever will be (Spencer, 2008). One of the reasons that section 28 has been (in effect) abandoned is that it falls far short of what the Pigot Committee actually intended. The out-of-court cross-examination that section 28 presupposes is one that would take place late, not early: shortly before the eventual trial, in other words, and not, as Pigot wanted, shortly after the initial video interview. As such it would, in essence, carry most if not all of the disadvantages of cross-examination at trial, and also fail to provide the main advantages of the sort of early cross-examination that Pigot had in mind. So it is hardly surprising that the government concluded, on reflection, that it would add a complication to criminal proceedings in which child witnesses were involved without yielding any genuine benefits in return. And so it is that, at least for now, it is still the 'half-Pigot' scheme originally enacted in 1991 that governs the examination and cross-examination of child witnesses in criminal trials in England and Wales today.

If the scheme currently in force meets the objections expressed by some defence lawyers to the 'full Pigot', for child witnesses it has disadvantages that are grave and obvious. Whereas the 'full Pigot' would have enabled the child to drop out of the picture from the point at which the second video-recorded interview had taken place, under the 'half-Pigot' scheme children who are to give evidence in criminal cases cannot do this, and must keep the incident alive in their minds until the trial, at which point they have to relive it once again as they first watch the video of the original interview, and then undergo a cross-examination. For a child who has really been the victim of some grave act or course of abuse, it goes without saying that this can be extremely stressful.

The 'half-Pigot' scheme can also fail the purposes of justice, particularly where the child is very young. A scenario that all too frequently occurs is that, when it comes to the eventual trial, a young child who gave a fairly coherent account the initial video interview is completely tongue-tied and no intelligible communication with him is possible. One example – sadly, out of many – is the case of *R v. Powell* (2006), where at a video interview held 9 weeks after the alleged incident a child of 3.5 years described how the defendant had licked her private parts, and at the eventual trial, which took place 7 months after that, she could not be persuaded to answer questions about it. (For other cases see Spencer, 2010b).

In English law, section 53 of the YJCEA 1999 currently provides that witnesses 'whatever their age' are competent to give evidence provided they can 'understand questions put to him' and 'give answers to them which can be understood'. As interpreted by the Court of Appeal in *Powell* and later cases, a child witness who is giving evidence under the 'half-Pigot' procedure must satisfy this test not only at the time of the initial video interview, but also when he or she is cross-examined at the trial. It follows that, where the situation arises that occurred in *Powell*, the evidence in-chief that was provided by the video interview must be retrospectively excluded. Unless there is other cogent evidence, this will inevitably mean that the judge or magistrates must stop the case.

The courts, naturally, feel uncomfortable about stopping cases in these circumstances where the child's video evidence-in-chief seems credible. In the light of that, they are prepared to accept a rudimentary degree of communication with the defence lawyers during cross-examination as showing that the child satisfies the competency test, and as satisfying the requirement that the witness be cross-examined. This message emerges clearly from the recent, and much publicized case of *R v. Barker* (2010). The complainant, a little girl, was born in November 2004. After she was taken into care in August 2007 she made a series of unsolicited disclosures indicating that Barker, with whom she had lived before she was taken into care, had anally penetrated her on a number of occasions. In the light of this she was video interviewed by a police officer, with a view to Barker's possible prosecution for rape, in April 2008, when she was 3.5 years. In this interview she described how he had 'put his willy' in her, indicating where by pointing to her bottom, and then demonstrating the positions of their bodies when he did this by lying on her stomach on the floor. When Barker's trial eventually took place in May 2009 – a year later, following his trial and conviction for involvement in the death of the complainant's brother – she was subjected to cross-examination. By this stage, she was now 4.5 years. After the video interview was played to the jury, Barker's counsel, an eminent QC at the criminal bar, did his best to question her, but made little headway: many of her responses were monosyllables, or non-verbal answers, in the form of nods or shakes of the head. On her evidence the jury convicted. The Court of Appeal upheld the conviction, holding that the limited interchange that had taken place justified the judge in deciding that she satisfied the competency requirement, and rejecting the defendant's argument that the attempt to cross-examine the child had proved 'futile', so making the resulting conviction in consequence unfair. (The Court also upheld the trial judge's sentence: life imprisonment, with a specified minimum period of 20 years.)

If there seems little reason to doubt the justice of the verdict in this case, like the decision in *Powell* it leaves us with the feeling that the 'half-Pigot' procedure is inherently unsatisfactory. In *Barker* the cross-examination of the child took place over a year after the video interview that constituted her evidence-in-chief. It is impossible not to feel some degree of sympathy with defence counsel, who argued that to cross-examine a child as young as this so long after the video interview did not really give him an opportunity to engage in meaningful dialogue with the complainant. If the defence is to have a genuine chance to put its questions to a child as young as this, surely this must be done very soon after the initial interview: as the Pigot Committee proposed. (Though that said, even an interview at this early stage would produce a meaningful exchange only if the person asking the questions used language that was appropriate to the age of the child; and depressingly, a series of studies suggests that, even today, lawyers who question child witnesses frequently use language that is beyond the child's ability to understand: see Plotnikoff & Woolfson, 2009, section 9.2.)

Given that the 'half Pigot' scheme currently in force in England and Wales in principle requires child witnesses in contested cases to attend the trial in order to undergo a live cross-examination, does the law provide any means by which a vulnerable child may be spared the worse rigours that this process normally entails? In fact there are a number, and the next section of this chapter briefly examines each in turn.

(i) Admitting the Child's Statement as Hearsay

First, in certain cases it may be possible to circumvent the need for cross-examination by putting the child's initial interview before the court, not as the first instalment of the child's giving evidence as a witness, but as a piece of 'hearsay evidence' admissible under the exceptions to the hearsay rule set out in Part 11 of the Criminal Justice Act 2003. Under section 116 of this Act, an out-of-court statement from an absent witness is in principle admissible where the witness is 'unavailable' for any of five reasons: death, illness, absence abroad, disappearance without trace, and – provided the court grants leave – where the witness does not give evidence 'through fear'. Of this list of possibilities, the second (unfitness to give evidence 'because of his bodily or mental condition'), and the last (failure to give oral evidence 'through fear') are both potentially applicable to a number of child witnesses.

However, section 116 provides that hearsay evidence may only be given in the last of these situations only where the court grants leave; and, more generally, under section 78 of the Police and Criminal Evidence Act (PACE) 1978 the court has a power to prohibit the prosecution from adducing any piece of evidence if it believes that it would have the effect of making the proceedings 'unfair'. If the statement of the 'unavailable' witness is of central importance to the case, and the judge believes that a cross-examination, had it been possible, might have seriously dented it, section 78 of PACE may well be used to suppress it. In practice, the statement of a child who is a prosecution witness is unlikely to be admitted as hearsay evidence except where the defence do not wish to dispute its contents; as, for example, in the notorious case of Michael Stone. Stone, it will be remembered, was accused (and eventually convicted) of a murderous attack on a young family with a hammer. The 9-year-old daughter who had survived the attack was able to describe what happened, but not in such a way as to implicate the defendant; her evidence was put before the court as hearsay, by agreement between prosecution and defence (*R v. Stone* 2001).

The hearsay provisions of the Criminal Justice Act 2003 also contain a further provision, section 114(1)(d), which gives the court an 'inclusionary discretion' to admit any piece of otherwise inadmissible hearsay if it 'is satisfied that it is in the interests of justice for it to be admissible'. This provision has been used in at least one case to admit evidence of out of court statements made by a very young child whom it would have been impracticable to use as a formal witness. In *R v. J* (2009), someone penetrated the vagina of a little girl aged 30 months, in such a way as to cause extensive cuts and bruises. This happened at a time when the defendant (who had been drinking heavily) was the only person who had ready access to the bedroom in which the incident occurred, though it was theoretically possible for a stranger to have entered unobserved, assaulted her, and having done so quietly departed. After the incident the child told her mother that the person who had hurt her was the defendant. At trial, the judge admitted the mother's account of what the child had said by virtue of the 'inclusionary discretion'. The Court of Appeal endorsed the judge's ruling, and the defendant's conviction was affirmed.

(ii) Examining the Child Witness via an Intermediary

Secondly, as one of the 'special measures' provided to help vulnerable witnesses, section 29 of the YJCEA 1999 makes it possible for the court to order 'any examination of the witness (however and wherever conducted) to be conducted through an interpreter or other person approved by the court for the purposes of this section ("an intermediary")'. Section 29 provides that this procedure may be used in respect of any witness who is under 17 – to be raised to 18, when a recent amendment made by the Coroners and Justice Act 2009 comes into force. This provision can be used, obviously, to facilitate communication with a child who is very young, or an older one with speech problems.

Its use is not limited to these cases, and intermediaries are increasingly being appointed for 'ordinary' children of all ages if they have a communication need in the court context. By section 19 of the YJCEA, the key question for the court to consider is whether the measure would 'be likely to improve the quality of the evidence given by the witness'. This would potentially include the case where a child needs help who would otherwise be unable to detect and cope with some misunderstanding.

However, as interpreted by the government in the official manuals it has produced (Office of Criminal Justice Reform, 2005), the role of an 'intermediary' is a fairly limited one. The intermediary is not someone to whom the would-be cross-examiner communicates a series of issues that the defence wants to have explored, leaving the intermediary to do it in the way that he thinks most appropriate. In principle, his role is more like that of an interpreter dealing with a witness who has little or no English (Ellison, 2002). In practice, the role is often even more limited than this: the intermediary assesses the witnesses, advises the court and advocates how best the witness can be questioned, and intervenes only if a miscommunication is likely. In consequence, a study carried out by Plotnikoff and Woolfson found that intermediaries have 'the potential to improve professionals' interaction with vulnerable witnesses, but only where the practitioners themselves were sufficiently skilled to adapt their approach to the witness's communication needs'. In other words, the appointment of an intermediary only helps where the advocate is sufficiently skilled to take on board the intermediary's advice in making the questions developmentally appropriate (Plotnikoff & Woolfson, 2008).

Thirdly, a child witness who has to undergo a cross-examination may benefit from one or more of a range of statutory provisions enacted in recent years to shield witnesses of all ages from some of the worst abuses of adversarial cross-examination.

(iii)(a) Statutory Ban on Cross-examination Conducted in Person by Defendants who are Unrepresented

In past years a particular abuse was the defendant accused of a sex offence who sacked his lawyer and conducted his own defence, in the process cross-examining the complainant himself. This was particularly distressing for the witness, and, conversely, for certain defendants – as in the case of *R v. Brown* (1998) – a source of sadistic pleasure. Sections 34–39 of the YJCEA 1999 now ban unrepresented defendants in sex cases from cross-examining the complainant (of whatever age) and also ban unrepresented defendants accused of any of a range of offences against children from cross-examining witnesses who are children. In these situations, the court appoints a lawyer to conduct the cross-examination for him.

(iii)(b) Statutory Restriction on Cross-examination of Complainants in Sex Cases

Another abuse was the practice of asking complainants in a sex cases embarrassing questions about aspects of their sex lives that had no obvious connection with facts of the case before the court. Section 41 of the YJCEA attempts to stamp this practice out by banning such questions except in certain very limited circumstances, which are spelt out in detail in the section. A difficult issue arises when the complainant in a sex case has made sexual allegations about other people in the past, and the defence wish to cross-examine the complainant about these, in order to suggest that she is a habitual maker of false allegations. The case-law allows this to be done, but only where the defence have an 'evidential basis' to suggest that the previous complaint was false – as against merely disbelieved (*R v. V* 2006; Spencer, 2009, section 3.35).

In practice, this 'rape shield' provision has proved to be something of a disappointment. It is extremely complicated and in consequence has given rise to an extensive body of case-law (Munday, 2009, sections 4.67–4.82). Research published by the Home Office suggests that it fails to provide the protection that its promoters hoped for, inter alia, because prosecutors tend to not to object when defence advocates ask questions that the provision in principle forbids (Kelly, Temkin, & Griffiths, 2006).

(iii)(c) Statutory Restriction on Cross-examining Witnesses to Show 'Bad Character'

A related and more general problem was the practice of cross-examiners to question witnesses about minor pieces of discreditable conduct of which they had been guilty in the past, in order to suggest that they were therefore rogues whose word was unworthy of belief. If taken to excess this could be oppressive and embarrassing, and in order to curtail it section 100 of the Criminal Justice Act 2003 forbids the asking of such questions unless the leave of the court is first obtained; leave which is to be given only where (to paraphrase the wording of the statute) it really does serve to shed light upon the credibility of the witness, or some other matter of genuine importance (Spencer, 2009, Chapter 3).

(iv) Judicial Control of Cross-Examination

Fourthly, the law both permits and encourages judges (and magistrates) to exercise a measure of control over the conduct of cross-examinations as part of the statutory duty, imposed on them by Rule 1 of the Criminal Procedure Rules (2010), to further the 'overriding objective' of dealing with cases 'justly': a concept that is elaborated in Rule 1.2, which provides that dealing with cases justly includes a list of stated factors, at the head of which is 'acquitting the innocent and convicting the guilty'. (Readers will find Rule 1 set out in full as an appendix to this chapter.) This means, in essence, that judges and magistrates are both bound and entitled to intervene to check a cross-examination that appears to be hindering the court from reaching a truthful outcome, rather than helping it to do so.

In this spirit, the judge is entitled to put a time-limit on cross-examination that is needlessly prolix. In *R v. B* (2005) a defendant appealed against his conviction for rape on the ground that the judge, having gently encouraged defence counsel several times to bring her cross-examination to a close, gave her a time-limit of 10 more minutes, and when she overran it, cut her off. In upholding the conviction, the Court of Appeal said that where 'counsel indulges in prolix and repetitious questioning, judges are fully entitled, and indeed we would say obliged, to impose reasonable time limits'. The Court of Appeal has also held that a judge is entitled to curb a cross-examination if the witness becomes ill (*R v. Stretton* 1988) or seriously distressed (*R v. Wyatt* 1990). More radically, it has also made it clear that a judge is entitled to take over the cross-examination of a vulnerable witness himself if defence counsel's attempts are generating more heat than light. It so held in *R v. Cameron* (2001), a case where the witness, a complainant in a rape case, was a 14-year-old girl.

Similarly, a judge or magistrate is entitled to intervene to stop a line of cross-examination that appears to be confusing the witness in such a way as to produce answers that are untrue or misleading. English books on the law of evidence are replete with comments such as 'The court may disallow cross-examination used simply to oppress and not for the purposes of justice' (Phipson, 2009, section 12.30). Fleshing the matter out in greater detail, section 85 of the New Zealand Evidence Act 2006 provides as follows:

> Unacceptable questions
>
> (1) In any proceeding, the Judge may disallow, or direct that a witness is not obliged to answer, any question that the Judge considers improper, unfair, misleading, needlessly repetitive, or expressed in language that is too complicated for the witness to understand.
>
> (2) Without limiting the matters that the Judge may take into account for the purposes of subsection (1), the Judge may have regard to—
>
> (a) the age or maturity of the witness; and
>
> (b) any physical, intellectual, psychological, or psychiatric impairment of the witness; and
>
> (c) the linguistic or cultural background or religious beliefs of the witness; and
>
> (d) the nature of the proceeding; and
>
> (e) in the case of a hypothetical question, whether the hypothesis has been or will be proved by other evidence in the proceeding.

This provision, I believe, accurately reflects the legal position as it is understood by English judges, even if there is no British statute to similar effect.

In theory, judges and magistrates are also bound and entitled to stop two other practices by cross-examiners which the law officially regards as abusive. These are making adverse comments on the witness's answers (*R v. Hardy* 1794), and 'argumentative questions': questions that are rhetorical, and designed to provoke argument rather than to extract further information, such as 'Do you seriously expect the court to believe this nonsense?' (*R v. Baldwin* 1925). However, in reality both practices do occur, and judges do not always intervene to check them. The truth of the matter is that there is something of a gap between the role the law officially prescribes for cross-examination, and the way that advocates commonly perceive it. The law conceives cross-examination as a tool for testing the truth of what the witness has already said and extracting further information from him, but many advocates see it as a further opportunity for oratory. As a New Zealand barrister once candidly explained to a researcher: 'In a trial I have three speeches: my opening, my cross-examination, and my closing' (Henderson, 2001, p. 282).

A feature of cross-examination that many children find particularly distressing is that they are accused of telling lies. In principle, judges and magistrates have no power to prevent this, because it is a convention of the law of evidence that, where the defence that an advocate is putting forward involves as a necessary step in the reasoning that a prosecution witness has not told the truth, he must confront the witness with the suggestion and give him the chance to answer it. However, this does not mean that an advocate who is cross-examining a child is entitled to ask him, as sometimes happens, 'Do you ever tell lies?' Another principle of the law of evidence is that suggestions that witnesses are guilty of misbehaviour are not to be made in cross-examination unless the suggestion appears to the advocate 'to be supported by reasonable grounds' (Code of Conduct for the Bar, 2004, section 708(j)). So it would be improper for a cross-examiner to ask a child this question unless he had some reason for believing not merely that the evidence the child has given is untrue, but that he is an habitual liar.

CONCLUSIONS

Time to Implement the Pigot Proposals

For truthful children, having their accuracy and sincerity impugned is bound to be an uncomfortable experience. But, regrettably or otherwise, justice clearly requires the defence in criminal cases to have a proper chance to put their questions to prosecution witnesses, including those who are children. Issues of ideology and tradition aside, this is a necessary safeguard against the risk of false convictions. Though many of those who are accused of harming or abusing children are unquestionably guilty, some are innocent; and the chance to question the accusing witnesses may be crucial to avoid their being convicted wrongly. A disquieting object lesson on this point is a cause célèbre: the abortive trial, in 2002, of the first group of youths accused of murdering the 10-year-old Nigerian boy, Damilola Taylor. A key figure in the proceedings was a girl of 12, whom the police and prosecution had put forward as a truthful witness, but whose unreliability was amply demonstrated in the course of a lengthy cross-examination. Following the acquittal of these defendants, and an official inquiry (Sentamu, Blakely, & Nove, 2002), police investigations were renewed, and eventually a different group of youths were put on trial, and in due course convicted of the crime (*R v. Preddy and others* 2006).

The key question is how, where witnesses are children, this can best be done. In principle, the law should identify the way that tests their evidence most thoroughly, while causing them the least amount of distress. This, it is suggested, is not necessarily the traditional type of in-court cross-examination.

The leading American writer on the law of evidence once famously described cross-examination as 'the greatest engine ever invented for the discovery of truth' (Wigmore, 1974, V, section 1367). The consensus of informed opinion is that for child witnesses the traditional in-court adversarial cross-examination is a tool that is frequently inept. Far from extracting information that is truthful it often confuses them, gets them to produce information that is misleading or inaccurate, and in the process causes them severe distress (Brennan & Brennan, 1988). This is often so, even if the process is 'tamed' in the ways that have been described in previous pages. With young child witnesses, this is obvious. Less obviously, this is often so with older children too. Research conducted for the National Society for the Prevention of Cruelty to Children in 2009 suggests that the questioning of older children is also often developmentally inappropriate. Older children reported as many problems with questions as the younger ones and found it equally difficult to communicate with the court (Plotnikoff & Woolfson, 2009). Indeed, it has been suggested that teenagers may actually be at greater risk of miscommunication because of adults' higher expectations of their ability to understand court language (Walker, 1999).

A much better means of testing the evidence of child witnesses – or at any rate, the younger ones – would surely be to have them questioned about the matters the defence want to explore at a second informal interview, held shortly after the first one, as proposed by the Pigot Committee in 1989. This is, of course, how the evidence of young children is managed in many other countries. The case of *S.N. v. Sweden*, mentioned earlier in this chapter, shows how it operates there; and incidentally also shows that a system constructed on those lines is viewed by Strasbourg as adequately protecting the defendant's right to confront his accusers as guaranteed by Article 6(3)(d) of the European Court of Human Rights.

So far, the implementation of the 'full Pigot' scheme has been resisted in England and Wales on the ground that, in order to carry out an effective cross-examination, the defence would first need to consider all the evidence, including any 'unused material' extracted (under the usual tortuous processes) from the prosecution; and because of this, any cross-examination earlier than the eventual trial would serve no useful purpose.

In certain types of case, this may be true. But in many child abuse cases the issues are very simple, the questions the defence need to put to the child are obvious from the outset, and the sort of early questioning Pigot had in mind would give the defence everything they need. Indeed, the case of *R v. Powell*, where the prosecution eventually failed because no effective cross-examination of the child was possible at trial – was just such a case as this: as indeed were a number of other cases in the law reports where prosecutions failed for the same reason (Spencer, 2010b). Even if it would not solve the problem in every case, the 'full Pigot' would clearly solve it in many of them. So it would be an improvement, even if it would not be a panacea. The fact that a reform would not solve every problem is no reason for rejecting a reform that would solve many of them. As Wall LJ said in *Re W (Children) (Concurrent Criminal and Care Proceedings)* – the case quoted earlier in which he explained that in civil proceedings child witnesses are not subjected to cross-examination – the reasons for not implementing the Pigot proposals in full are less than convincing.

The obvious reason for implementing the full proposals of the Pigot Committee is that what they provide would be a more efficient and less painful method of equipping courts with the information necessary to reach factually correct outcomes than the 'half Pigot' scheme currently in force. There is a further reason, which is that it appears to be required by European Union law. Under the constitution arrangements created by the Maastrict Treaty, the Council of the EU acquired the power to adopt instruments called 'Framework Decisions', requiring Member States to amend their rules of criminal law or criminal procedure. In 2001, it adopted a Framework Decision on the Rights of

Victims, which required all EU Member States to put in place various protections for victims of crime, including, for victims who are vulnerable, mechanisms enabling their evidence to be given without them having to appear in open court. On this account, in 2005 the Court of Justice of the European Communities held Italy to have failed to implement its obligation under EU law, because as Italian law then stood, it did not provide a mechanism for the evidence of young children in a case of physical abuse to be taken ahead of trial (*Criminal Proceedings Against Pupino* 2005; see Spencer, 2005). The same criticism can be made, surely, of arrangements that currently operate in England and Wales.

Behind all this there is a basic point that must be stressed. This is the need for young witnesses to be questioned in a manner and a language that is developmentally appropriate. If a child does not understand the question, the answer that he gives will not further the overriding objective of criminal procedure: which, as the Criminal Procedure Rules remind us, is first and foremost the acquittal of the innocent and the conviction of the guilty. This is so, whether the question is asked by a police officer, a social worker, a barrister, or a judge; in a 'rape suite' at a police station or in a courtroom; adversarially or inquisitorially; in examination or in cross-examination; privately in the early stages of the proceedings, or publicly at the eventual trial. Furthermore, an initial interview in which the child misunderstood the questions will have an adverse impact on the cross-examination. If in cross-examination the child gives different answers, this will discredit his testimony by suggesting that the witness has given two conflicting accounts, when what he really meant to say at the initial interview was in fact consistent.

ACKNOWLEDGEMENTS

I am grateful to Joyce Plotnikoff and to Emily Henderson for their helpful comments on an earlier draft of this chapter. Any remaining errors are entirely mine.

REFERENCES

Brennan, M., & Brennan, R. (1988). *Strange Language* (2nd edn). Wagga Wagga: Riverina Institute of Higher Education.
Code of Conduct for the Bar of England and Wales (2004).
Council Framework Decision of 15 March 2001 on the Standing of Victims in Criminal Proceedings, 2001/220/JHA, [2001] OJ L82/1.

Criminal Procedure Rules 2010, S.I. 2010/60, (L.2)
Ellison, L.E. [2002] Cross-examination and the intermediary: bridging the language divide? *Criminal Law Review*, 114–127.
Gorphe, F. (1927). *La Critique du Témoignage*, 2nd edn. Paris: Dalloz.
Hale, M. (c. 1670). *The History of the Common Law of England* (4th edn). Runnington (Ed.), 1779.
Henderson, E. (2002) Persuading and controlling: The theory of cross-examination in relation to children. In Westcott, H., Davies, G., & Bull, R. (Eds), *Children's Testimony: A Handbook of Psychological Research and Forensic Practice* (pp. 279–294). Chichester: Wiley.
Kelly, L., Temkin, J., & Griffiths, S. (2006). *Section 41: An Evaluation of New Legislation Limiting Sexual History Evidence in Rape Trials*. Home Office Online Report 20/26. Available at http://www.homeoffice.gov.uk/rds/pdfs06/rdsolr2006.pdf
Marston, G. (1993). The United Kingdom's part in the preparation of the European Convention on Human Rights, 1950. *International and Comparative Law Quarterly*, *42*, 796–826.
Munday, R. (2009). *Evidence* (5th edn). Oxford: Oxford University Press.
Office of Criminal Justice Reform (OJCR). (2005). *Intermediary Procedural Guidance Manual*. Available at http://www.homeoffice.gov.uk/documents/intermediary-procedural-guidance/manual_front_page_Oct_05.pdf?view=Binary
Phipson. (2009) *Phipson on Evidence* (17th edn). Malek H.M. and others (Ed.): London: Sweet & Maxwell.
Pigot, T. (1989). *Report of the Advisory Group on Video-recorded Evidence*. London: Home Office.
Plotnikoff, J., & Woolfson, R. (2008). Making the best use of the intermediary special measure at trial. *Criminal Law Review*, 91–104.
Plotnikoff, J., & Woolfson, R. (2009). *Measuring Up? Evaluating Implementation of Government Commitments to Young Witnesses in Criminal Proceedings*. Nuffield Foundation/NSPCC. Available at http://www.nspcc.org.uk/inform/research/findings/measuring_up_summary_wdf66580.pdf.
Sentamu, J., Blakely, J., & Nove, P. (2002). *The Damilola Taylor Murder Investigation Review*. *The Report of the Oversight Panel.*
Spencer, J.R. (2005). Child witnesses and the European Union. *Cambridge Law Journal*, *64*, 569–572.
Spencer, J.R. (2008). *Hearsay Evidence in Criminal Proceedings*. Oxford: Hart Publishing.
Spencer, J.R. (2009). *Evidence of Bad Character* (2nd edn). Oxford: Hart Publishing.
Spencer, J.R. (2010a). Squaring up to Strasbourg: *Horncastle* in the Supreme Court. *Archbold Review*, *1*, 6–9.
Spencer, J.R. (2010b). Children's evidence: the *Barker* case and the case for Pigot. *Archbold Review*, *3*, 5–8.
Spencer, J.R., & Flin, R. (1993). *The Evidence of Children, the Law and the Psychology* (2nd edn). Blackstone Press.
Straw, J. (2008). Human rights in the twenty-first century. In Barnard, C. (Ed.), *Cambridge Yearbook of European Legal Studies 2007–2008* (Vol. 10, Chapter 16). Oxford: Hart Publishing.
Walker, A.G. (1999). *Handbook on Questioning Children: A Linguistic Perspective*. American Bar Association.

Wigmore, J.H. (1974). *Evidence at Trials at Common Law* (revised by J.H. Chadbourn). Boston: Little, Brown and Co.

Cases

Al-Khwaja and Tahery v. UK (2009) 49 European Human Rights Reports 1
B County Council, ex pte P [1991] 1 WLR 221
Crawford v. State of Washington 124 S Ct 1354 (2004)
Criminal Proceedings Against Pupino [2005] 3 WLR 1102; Case C-105/03; noted [2005] CLJ 569
LM v. Medway Council [2007] EWCA Civ 9
P.S. v. Germany (2001) 36 European Human Rights Reports 61
R v. B [2005] EWCA Crim 805
R v. Baldwin (1925) 18 Criminal Appeal Reports 175
R v. Barker [2010] EWCA Crim 4
R v. Brown [1998] 2 Criminal Appeal Reports 364
R v. Cameron [2001] EWCA Crim 562
R v. Hardy (1794) 24 State Trials 199
R v. Horncastle and others [2009] EWCA Crim 964, [2009] UKSC 14, [2010] 2 AC 373
R v. J (S) [2009] EWCA Crim 1869
R v. Powell [2006] EWCA Crim 3, [2006] 1 Criminal Appeal Reports 31
R v. Preddy and others, Central Criminal Court, September 2006; BBC News, 20 September 2006.
R v. Stone [2001] EWCA Crim 297; [2005] EWCA Crim 105
R v. Stretton (1988) 86 Criminal Appeal Reports 7
R v. V [2006] EWCA Crim 1901
R v. Wyatt [1990] Criminal Law Review 343
Re W (Children) (Concurrent Criminal and Care Proceedings) [2009] EWCA Civ 644; [2009] 2 Criminal Appeal Reports 23
Re W (Children) (Family Proceedings: Evidence) [2010] UKSC 12, [2010] 1 WLR 701
S.N. v. Sweden (2002), 39 European Hhuman Rights Reports 13
Unterpertinger v. Austria (1986) 13 European Human Rights Reports 175

APPENDIX: CRIMINAL PROCEDURE RULES (2010) RULE 1

The Overriding Objective

1. The overriding objective of this new code is that criminal cases be dealt with justly.
2. Dealing with a criminal case justly includes—
   (a) acquitting the innocent and convicting the guilty;
   (b) dealing with the prosecution and the defence fairly;
   (c) recognising the rights of a defendant, particularly those under Article 6 of the European Convention on Human Rights;
   (d) respecting the interests of witnesses, victims and jurors and keeping them informed of the progress of the case;

(e) dealing with the case efficiently and expeditiously;
(f) ensuring that appropriate information is available to the court when bail and sentence are considered; and
(g) dealing with the case in ways that take into account—
  i. the gravity of the offence alleged,
  ii. the complexity of what is in issue,
  iii. the severity of the consequences for the defendant and others affected, and
  iv. the needs of other cases.

The Duty of the Participants in a Criminal Case

1. Each participant, in the conduct of each case, must—
   (a) prepare and conduct the case in accordance with the overriding objective;
   (b) comply with these Rules, practice directions and directions made by the court; and
   (c) at once inform the court and all parties of any significant failure (whether or not that participant is responsible for that failure) to take any procedural step required by these Rules, any practice direction or any direction of the court. A failure is significant if it might hinder the court in furthering the overriding objective.
2. Anyone involved in any way with a criminal case is a participant in its conduct for the purposes of this rule.

The Application by the Court of the Overriding Objective

The court must further the overriding objective in particular when—

(a) exercising any power given to it by legislation (including these Rules);
(b) applying any practice direction; or
(c) interpreting any rule or practice direction.

15

Children's Disclosure Statements as Evidence in the United States Legal System

JOHN E.B. MYERS

Key Points

- Children's disclosure statements are powerful evidence that can be used to protect children and that need to be documents and recorded correctly by all those involved in child abuse investigations.
- A child's disclosure can provide evidence needed to arrest a suspect.
- Children's disclosure statements are typically hearsay, and all US states have a rule against hearsay.
- What is hearsay?
- There are exceptions to the rule against hearsay, and this chapter describes the three exceptions that are most important in child abuse litigation: (i) excited utterances; (ii) statements for purposes of medical diagnosis or treatment; and (iii) residual or catch-all exceptions.

Children experience crime as direct victims and as eyewitnesses to the victimization of others. In a case from the US state of Illinois, for example, a mother drove her 4- and 5-year-old sons to a shopping centre. While parked outside the centre, a man with a gun approached

Children's Testimony: A Handbook of Psychological Research and Forensic Practice, Second Edition.
Edited by Michael E. Lamb, David J. La Rooy, Lindsay C. Malloy, and Carmit Katz.

the car and demanded the mother get out. When she refused to leave her children, the man dragged her out of the car and shot her. The man then drove away with the children in the back seat. When the killer realized the children were in the car he ordered them out. Six years later the killer was brought to trial and the older boy, then 11, testified to the murder of his mother (*People v. Banks* 2010).

In the aftermath of crime, a child may discuss what happened with parents, friends, teachers, and others. If the case comes to official attention, the child may be interviewed by police officers, social workers, doctors, forensic interviewers, mental health professionals, and attorneys. What children reveal often provides critical evidence, and this chapter discusses the forensic uses in US law of children's disclosures.

INVESTIGATIVE DECISIONS BASED ON CHILDREN'S DISCLOSURE STATEMENTS

Long before proceedings are commenced in court, children's disclosure statements have important roles. Police officers often begin investigations based on children's disclosures. If investigation points to a particular suspect, a police officer wishing to make an arrest must have probable cause to believe the suspect committed a crime. Probable cause exists when a police officer possesses reasonably trustworthy information that would lead a cautious officer to believe there is a fair probability of criminal activity (*Illinois v. Gates* 1983). A child's reliable disclosure can constitute probable cause for arrest. In *Burke v. County of Alameda* (2009), the court wrote, 'A victim's report of abuse ... is compelling evidence' (p. 731). However, not all disclosures are sufficiently reliable for probable cause. In *Stoot v. City of Everett* (2009), the court ruled that a police officer acted improperly in relying solely on the uncorroborated inconsistent statements of a 4-year-old in deciding to arrest the teenager suspected of molesting the child. The court wrote, 'Law enforcement officers may obviously rely on statements made by the victims of a crime to identify potential suspects. But such information does not, on its own, support a finding of probable cause if the information is not reasonably trustworthy or reliable' (p. 919). The court was troubled by the victim's youth, her inconsistency, and the fact that at one point she confused the suspect with another boy. The court wrote, 'These three circumstances, considered together, point to the need for further investigation and corroboration to establish probable cause' (p. 920).

Although a child's reliable disclosure can suffice for probable cause to arrest, in most cases police look for evidence to corroborate the child's words. In *Brodnicki v. City of Omaha* (1996), for example, a 9-year-old provided police a detailed description of the man who tried to kidnap her. The child's description was corroborated by other evidence and was sufficient for probable cause to arrest the suspect.

In addition to supplying probable cause for arrest, a child's reliable disclosure can support probable cause for a search warrant of a suspect's home.

Changing the focus from police to child protection social workers, a child's disclosure is sufficient to launch an investigation into possible maltreatment. A recurring theme in child protection work is the amount of evidence social workers need to remove an endangered child from the home over parental objection. US law requires a social worker to obtain a court order *before* removing a child. In emergencies, however, when there is no time for a court order, a social worker (typically working with police) may remove a child in imminent danger.

Emergency removal is justified when a social worker has sufficient evidence that maltreatment occurred or is very likely to occur. A 'mere possibility' of maltreatment will not suffice (*Gomes v. Wood* 2006). Some US courts require that the evidence of danger must rise to the level of 'probable cause' (*Doe v. Kearney* 2003). Other courts require 'reasonable cause' to suspect maltreatment (*Greene v. Camreta* 2009). It is unclear the difference (if there is one) between 'probable cause' and 'reasonable cause'. Still other courts hold that evidence less than probable cause will suffice for emergency removal. In *Gomes v. Wood* (2006), the court specified that 'reasonable suspicion' is required for emergency removal. The filaments separating probable cause, reasonable cause, and reasonable suspicion are elusive. Moreover, the fact that different courts in different parts of the country impose slightly different standards for emergency removal causes uncertainty among professionals. Hopefully, the US Supreme Court will some day clarify the law in this area. Obviously, the stronger the evidence of risk, the more confidence a social worker can take in the decision to remove. Children's disclosure statements are often the most cogent evidence of danger, particularly in cases of suspected sexual abuse.

Clearly, children's disclosure statements have a central role at the investigative stage of child protection, and every reasonable effort must be make to enhance the reliability of children's disclosures.

CHILDREN'S DISCLOSURE STATEMENTS IN COURT – HEARSAY

When children's disclosure statements are repeated in court to prove maltreatment, the statements are hearsay (Lyon & LaMagna, 2007).

Hearsay has a critical role in child abuse litigation. The Delaware Supreme Court observed, 'Admission of hearsay evidence is sometimes essential in these cases' (*McGriff v. State* 1996, p. 1028), and a federal court noted that in child sexual abuse cases, 'the need for the victim's out-of-court statements about the crime is likely to be great' (*Guam v. Ignacio* 1993, p. 612).

The law governing hearsay developed in England, and was applied in England's colonies. Thus, the rule against hearsay evidence was thoroughly established in North America by the time the United States gained independence. Since then, hearsay law evolved along parallel but not identical lines in England, Australia, Canada, New Zealand, and the United States (for analysis of hearsay outside the United States see Hoyano & Keenan, 2007).

Hearsay is a statement that is made *prior* to court proceedings, and that is repeated in court. Hearsay has three components:

1. A person made a statement describing an event (e.g., 'The car went through the red light.' 'He touched my privates');
2. The person made the statement prior to court proceedings where the statement is repeated (the statement was *out*-of-court and is repeated *in* court); and
3. The statement is repeated in court to prove that what the person said actually happened (the car went through the red light; the defendant touched the victim's private parts).

In every US state, hearsay is inadmissible unless it meets the requirements of an exception to the rule against hearsay.

It should be noted that in the United States, as in other nations, the rule against hearsay is enforced most assiduously in criminal cases. In non-criminal cases, including juvenile and family court proceedings to protect children from maltreatment, many US states relax the rule against hearsay.

To come to grips with the definition of hearsay, consider an example. Sally is being examined by a physician for possible sexual abuse. The doctor asks, 'What happened?' and Sally says, 'Uncle Fred took off his clothes and my clothes. His pee-pee was big and hard, but soft too, and he made me touch it, and white glue popped out and got all over me.' Fred is charged with child sexual abuse. At Fred's trial the prosecutor asks the doctor to testify and repeat Sally's graphic description of abuse. Before the doctor can repeat Sally's words, however, Fred's defence attorney objects that Sally's words are hearsay and thus inadmissible in court. Is the defence attorney correct? Is Sally's disclosure hearsay? First, Sally described something that happened.

Secondly, Sally's disclosure was out-of-court, that is, prior to the court proceeding where the doctor is asked to repeat Sally's words. Thirdly, the prosecutor wants to use Sally's words to prove that Fred sexually abused Sally. Thus, Sally's disclosure is hearsay, and will not be allowed in court unless the prosecutor can convince the judge that the disclosure meets the requirements of an exception to the rule against hearsay.

Most people understand that there are limits on the use of hearsay in court. Few people outside the legal community, however, fully understand *why* these limits exist. Why is there a rule against hearsay? The answer is that the rule against hearsay is intended to keep unreliable evidence out of court. To understand the rule against hearsay, it is necessary to understand the adversary system of litigation employed in the United States and other countries modelled on English law.

In the adversary system, each side of a lawsuit prepares for trial by marshalling the evidence that is most favourable to its position. Evidence consists of anything that is presented to the senses of the jury or judge (the trier of fact) and that has a tendency in logic to prove something that is relevant to the case. Thus, evidence includes the testimony of witnesses, documents, things (e.g., drugs in a drug trafficking case; money in a bank robbery), *and hearsay*.

In a trial, the parties take turns presenting the evidence they hope will convince the trier of fact. Each party has the right to challenge the evidence presented by the opponent. Lawyers use a set of tools to challenge the opponent's evidence. When it comes to challenging witnesses, the chief tool is cross-examination. The cross-examiner can ask questions to determine whether the witness: (i) accurately perceived the event in question; (ii) correctly remembers what happened; (iii) is narrating a coherent story; and (iv) is lying or telling the truth. Cross-examination is the principal mechanism for challenging testimony. If a witness cannot be cross-examined, it is not possible to test the witness's perception, memory, narration, and sincerity.

A person who makes a hearsay statement is, in a very real sense, a witness even if the person never sets foot in court. Consider Sally who disclosed abuse to the doctor. Sally's words – repeated in court by the doctor – are powerful evidence of abuse. Yet, if Sally does not testify, Fred's defence attorney cannot cross-examine Sally to test her perception, memory, narration, and sincerity. It is true that the defence attorney can cross-examine the doctor, but the evidence comes from *Sally*, not the doctor. The doctor is a mere conduit for Sally's hearsay.

The hearsay rule exists because it is not possible to cross-examine the person who made the hearsay statement. Cross-examining the person who testifies and repeats the hearsay statement is not a satisfactory substitute for cross-examining the person who made the statement. In the final analysis, the goal of the rule against hearsay is to exclude evidence that has not been examined under the microscope of cross-examination.

In some cases, the person who made a hearsay statement *does* testify in court and repeats their own out-of-court statement. Suppose, for example, that Sally testifies and repeats what she told the doctor: 'I told the doctor, "Uncle Fred took off his clothes and my clothes. His pee-pee was big and hard, but soft too, and he made me touch it, and white glue popped out and got all over me."' Because Sally testifies, she *can* be cross-examined about her statement. Is Sally's statement nevertheless hearsay? The traditional answer is yes. Sally's disclosure meets the three-part definition of hearsay: an out-of-court statement repeated in court to prove the truth of the statement. There is a gradual movement in the United States to remove out-of-court statements from the definition of hearsay when the person who made the statement testifies and is subject to cross-examination.

Before leaving the definition of hearsay, it is important to avoid confusion by clarifying what *is* and *is not* hearsay. The rule against hearsay does not prohibit Sally from testifying in court and describing the abuse. Sally may testify, 'Uncle Fred took off his clothes and my clothes. His pee-pee was big and hard, but soft too, and he made me touch it, and white glue popped out and got all over me.' What Sally may not do without offending the rule against hearsay is testify, 'I told the doctor, "Uncle Fred took off his clothes and my clothes. His pee-pee was big and hard, but soft too, and he made me touch it, and white glue popped out and got all over me."' It is the repetition of an earlier out-of-statement that runs afoul of the hearsay rule.

In summary, the rule against hearsay is intended to exclude unreliable evidence from court. Judges and lawyers have long understood, however, that not all hearsay is unreliable. Indeed, hearsay is sometimes *more* reliable than testimony in court. Over the centuries, judges carved out exceptions to the rule against hearsay. Today there are more than 30 exceptions to the rule against hearsay. Exceptions are based on the belief that certain types of hearsay are sufficiently reliable that they should be allowed in court despite lack of cross-examination.

In child sexual abuse litigation in the United States, the three most important hearsay exceptions are: (i) the excited utterance exception, (ii) the medical diagnosis or treatment exception, and (iii) the residual hearsay exception. These three exceptions to the rule against hearsay are described below. (For in-depth analysis of these and other hearsay exceptions in US litigation see Myers, 2011.)

THE EXCITED UTTERANCE EXCEPTION

An excited utterance is a hearsay statement that describes a startling event. The statement must be made while the child is under the emotional stress caused by the startling event. The theory behind the excited utterance exception is that statements made under significant stress shortly following a traumatic event are likely to be true. All US states have a version of the excited utterance exception. Other countries with legal systems founded on English law refer to this exception as *res geste* (Hoyano & Keenan, 2007).

When a judge is considering whether a hearsay statement is an excited utterance, the judge evaluates the following factors:

Nature of the event Some events are more startling than others, and the judge considers the likely impact a particular event would have on a child of similar age and experience. In many cases sexual abuse is sufficiently startling to satisfy the excited utterance exception.

Amount of time elapsed between the startling event and the child's statement relating to the event The more time that passes between a startling event and a child's hearsay statement describing the event, the less likely a judge is to conclude that the statement is an excited utterance. Although passage of time is important, elapsed time is not the only factor judges consider. Judges have approved delays ranging from a few minutes to many hours.

Indications the child was emotionally upset when the child spoke The judge considers whether the child was crying, frightened, or otherwise upset when the statement was made. If the child was injured or in pain, the judge is more likely to find an excited utterance.

Child's speech pattern In some cases the way a child speaks (e.g., pressured or hurried speech) indicates excitement.

Extent to which child's statement was spontaneous Spontaneity is a key factor in the excited utterance exception. The more spontaneous the statement, the more likely it meets the requirements of the exception.

Questions used to elicit child's statement Asking questions does not necessarily destroy the spontaneity required for the excited utterance exception. As questions become suggestive, however, spontaneity may dissipate, undermining the exception.

First safe opportunity In many abuse cases, children remain under the control of the abuser for hours after an abusive incident. When the child is finally released to a trusted adult, the child has the first safe opportunity to disclose what happened. A child's statement at the first safe opportunity may qualify as an excited utterance even though considerable time has elapsed since the abuse occurred.

Rekindled excitement A startling event such as abuse may be followed by a period of calm during which excitement abates. If the child is later exposed to a stimulus that reminds the child of the startling event, the child's excitement may be rekindled. Rekindled excitement sometimes satisfies the excited utterance exception to the rule against hearsay.

The excited utterance exception and other hearsay exceptions were created by judges based on their knowledge of law and their lay understanding of psychology. The psychological premise of the excited utterance exception is that statements made under stress are (as a group) more reliable than statements in the absence of stress. But is that true? Very little psychological research has been carried out to evaluate the assumptions undergirding hearsay exceptions. Myers, Cordon, Ghetti, and Goodman (2002) are among the few to examine hearsay exceptions in light of psychological science. After reviewing the available research, Myers *et al.* wrote, 'The heart of the excited utterance exception is the belief that traumatic stress inhibits lying. On this key point, psychology has little direct evidence, although there is indirect evidence indicating that individuals may lie with more difficulty under stressful circumstances' (p. 8). Although the excited utterance exception may stand on shaky psychological ground, the thousands of excited utterance cases attest to how firmly ensconced this exception is in US law.

MEDICAL DIAGNOSIS OR TREATMENT EXCEPTION

All US states have a 'diagnosis or treatment' exception to the rule against hearsay. This exception to the rule against hearsay allows use in court of certain out-of-court statements made to professionals providing diagnostic or treatment services. The professional to whom the child spoke may be a physician, psychiatrist, psychologist, nurse, clinical social worker, paramedic, or medical technician.

The diagnosis or treatment exception includes a child's statements describing medical history as well as statements describing present symptoms, pain, and other sensations. The exception includes the child's description of the cause of illness or injury. Unlike the excited utterance exception, the child does not have to be upset for the medical diagnosis or treatment exception to apply.

In many cases the child is the one who makes the hearsay statement that is admissible under the diagnosis or treatment exception. However, sometimes an adult describes the child's history and symptoms to the professional. So long as the adult's motive is to obtain diagnosis or treatment for the child, the adult's statements are admissible under the exception.

The rationale for the diagnosis or treatment exception is that hearsay statements to professionals providing diagnostic or treatment services are reliable because the patient has an incentive to be truthful with the professional. This rationale is applicable for older children and adolescents. Some young children, however, may not understand the need for accuracy with healthcare providers. When a child does not understand that the child's personal well-being may be affected by the accuracy of what is said, the rationale for the diagnosis or treatment exception evaporates.

Psychology sheds light on whether young children understand the clinical significance of providing accurate information to medical professionals. Psychologists have studied children's developing understanding of illness, medical care, and the role of medical professionals (e.g., Bibace & Walsh, 1981; Steward & Regalbuto, 1975; Steward & Steward, 1981). Herbst, Steward, Myers, & Hansen (1999) studied the medical knowledge of 3- to 6-year-olds. Herbst *et al.* wrote, 'Our data indicate that young children are more likely to report painful than benign touch and that they understand the necessity to provide an accurate narrative to persons in authority' (p. 247). Herbst *et al.* asked children about lying to a doctor. Three- and 4-year-old children thought the doctor would be angry. One child said, 'You're in big trouble now.' About half the older children (5- and 6-year-olds) understood that the doctor needed accurate information to help them. Kato, Lyon, and Rasco (1998) examined the understanding of healthy and chronically ill 3- and 4-year-olds regarding illness and treatment. Kato *et al.* wrote, 'When children as young as 4 years of age are asked to recognize the causes of illness rather than to generate causal explanations, they show an impressive understanding.... As in many other contexts, children can recognize what they cannot articulate" (p. 69).

Psychological research provides a measure of insight into whether the rationale supporting the diagnosis or treatment exception – the patient has a personal incentive to tell the truth – applies to young children. Medical professionals can increase the likelihood children will understand the importance of telling the truth by informing children of their professional role, 'I'm a doctor, and I'm going to give you a check up today.' The child can be informed of the importance of telling the truth, 'I'll ask you some questions. When you answer my questions, it is important for you to tell me the truth. Tell me only things that really happened, OK?'

RESIDUAL HEARSAY EXCEPTIONS

Most US states have a hearsay exception known as a residual or catch-all exception. This exception allows use in court of reliable hearsay that does not meet the requirements of one of the traditional hearsay exceptions (e.g., excited utterance, medical diagnosis or treatment). In addition to the residual exception, which applies in all types of litigation, a majority of states have a specialized residual exception that allows use of children's reliable hearsay in child abuse cases.

When a child's hearsay statement is offered under a residual exception, the most important question for the judge is whether the statement is reliable. Judges consider the factors listed below to assess reliability. Myers *et al.* (2002) reviewed the psychological research on these factors.

Children's disclosure statements often have a ring of veracity. Indeed, Sir William Blackstone, the most famous expositor of English common law, observed centuries ago that children 'often give the clearest and truest testimony' (Blackstone, 1769, p. 214). With very young children, disclosures indicating developmentally inappropriate sexual knowledge often provide disturbing and powerful evidence of abuse. A young child said, for example, 'white bubbly stuff' came out of his penis (*Bockting v. Bayer* 2007). Another child said, 'His too-too spit on me' (*Bishop v. State* 2008). A third youngster said, 'Penises grow and then melt' (*Re L.N.* 2004). Statements like these can be utilized to prove abuse and protect children.

Spontaneity The more spontaneous a child's statement, the more likely a judge is to find it reliable.

Statements elicited by questioning The reliability of a child's statement may be influenced by the type of questions asked. When questions are suggestive or leading, the possibility increases that the questioner influenced the child's statement. The smaller the number of suggestive and leading questions, the more likely a judge is to conclude that a child's statement is sufficiently reliable to be admitted in evidence.

Consistent statements Reliability may be enhanced if the child's description of abuse is consistent over time.

Play or gestures that corroborate child's hearsay statement The play or gestures of a young child may strengthen confidence in the child's statement.

Developmentally unusual sexual knowledge As mentioned above, a young child's developmentally unusual knowledge of sexual acts or anatomy can support the reliability of the child's statement.

Idiosyncratic detail Presence in a child's statement of idiosyncratic details of sexual acts points to reliability. Jones (1992) wrote, 'The interview can be examined for signs of unique or distinguishing detail. This may be found both within the account of the sexual encounter and/or in unrelated recollections. Examples include children who describe smells and tastes associated with rectal, vaginal, or oral sex' (p. 53).

Child's or adult's motive to fabricate Evidence that the child or an adult had or lacked a motive to fabricate affects reliability.

Medical evidence of abuse The child's statement may be corroborated by medical evidence.

Taped interviews When a child's disclosure of abuse is audiotaped or videotaped, the judge can evaluate first-hand whether improper questions were asked. In *United States v. Cabral* (1996), the 4-year-old victim of sexual abuse was interviewed by an agent of the Air Force Office of Special Investigations. The agent videotaped the substantive portion of the interview, but did not tape the rapport-building phase. Although the Air Force Court of Criminal Appeals found the taped interview reliable, the court wrote, 'We do not encourage investigators to selectively videotape their contact with child witnesses – all of the interview should be taped, including "rapport building" sessions. In a closer case, an investigator's failure to tape an initial "rapport" session could be the scale-tipper' (p. 811). In *State v. Branch* (2005), the New Jersey Supreme Court considered whether a child's statement to the police detective was admissible. The detective destroyed his initial notes of his interview with the child. The Supreme Court wrote, 'We register our displeasure that police officers engage in the seemingly routine practice of destroying their contemporaneous notes of witness interviews after the preparation of formal reports' (p. 690).

Mental health counselling before statement Following abuse, the victim may receive mental health services. During counselling sessions, the child may be asked about abuse. In *State v. Carlson* (1991), the Washington State Court of Appeals considered whether a child's participation in counselling undermined the reliability of statements the child made following counselling. The court wrote:

> We recognize that a lapse of time and intervening counseling could affect the reliability of a child's statements regarding abuse. However, these factors will not affect reliability in all cases. Such a rule would be unworkable in any event. Were the courts to hold as a matter of law that counseling affects a child's reliability, an abused child would be prevented from receiving much needed help until after trial. We hold, therefore, that a trial judge may find child hearsay statements unreliable on the ground that there has been a lapse of time and intervening counseling between the abuse and the statements at issue only when the evidence demonstrates that the lapse or counseling somehow affected the child's statements. (*State v. Carlson* 1991, p. 540)

There are thousands of US cases where children's hearsay statements describing abuse have been allowed in court under a residual exception (Myers, 2011). The residual exception has a vital role in child protection in the United States.

CONCLUSIONS

Given the forensic importance of children's disclosure statements regarding abuse, what steps should professionals take to increase the likelihood children's statements can be used in court to protect them?

First, professionals who interact with children – teachers, police, mental health and medical professionals, child care providers – should be trained on the importance of documenting precisely what children say when they disclose abuse.

Secondly, it is not enough to preserve children's exact words. In addition, professionals should watch for and document the factors – outlined above – that judges consider in deciding whether children's statements meet the requirements of hearsay exceptions. Although it is a lawyer's responsibility to suggest a hearsay exception to a judge, and a judge's responsibility to decide whether a child's hearsay statement fits an exception, it is non-legal professionals in the field and the clinic who are in the best position to document the factors that are essential to deciding whether a child's hearsay statement is admissible in court. Even the most skillful attorney may fail to convince a judge to admit a child's hearsay statement if the professional in the field who heard the statement failed to document the factors that are essential for admission of hearsay in court. Unfortunately, there is little training for front line professionals on what hearsay factors to look for and document.

Thirdly, the most important factor in admitting hearsay is reliability. Judicial findings of reliability are tied closely to the suggestiveness of questions used to elicit children's statements. The more suggestive the questions, the less likely a child's hearsay will be allowed in court. Thus, it is vital to train all professionals – not just forensic interviewers – about the legal dangers of suggestive questions when talking to children about maltreatment.

REFERENCES

Bibace, R., & Walsh, M. (1981). Children's conceptions of illness. In R. Bibace & M. Walsh (Eds), *New Directions for Child Development: Children's Conceptions of Health, Illness, and Bodily Functions* (pp. 31–48). San Francisco, CA: Jossey-Bass.

Bishop v. State (2008) 982 So.2d 371 (Miss.)

Blackstone, W. (1769) *Commentaries on the Law of England* (Vol. 4). Oxford.

Bockting v. Bayer (2007) 505 F.3d 973 (9th Cir.)

Brodnicki v. City of Omaha (1996) 75 F.3d 1261 (8th Cir.)

Burke v. County of Alameda (2009) 586 F.3d 725 (9th Cir.)

Doe v. Kearney (2003) 329 F.3d 1295 (11th Cir.)

Gomes v. Wood (2006) 451 F.3d 1122 (10th Cir.)

Greene v. Camreta (2009) 588 F.3d 1011 (9th Cir.)

Guam v. Ignacio (1993) 10 F.3d 608 (9th Cir.)

Herbst, M.R., Steward, M.S., Myers, J.E.B., & Hansen, R.L. (1999) Young children's understanding of the physician's role and the medical hearsay exception. In M. Siegal & C.C. Peterson (Eds), *Children's Understanding of Biology and Health*, (pp. 235–256). Cambridge University Press.

Hoyano, L., & Keenan, C. (2007). *Child Abuse: Law and Policy Across Boundaries*. Oxford, UK: Oxford University Press.

Illinois v. Gates (1983) 462 US 213.

Jones, D.P.H. (1992). *Interviewing the Sexually Abused Child: Investigation of Suspected Abuse*. London: Gaskell. Royal College of Psychiatrists.

Kato, P.M., Lyon, T.D., Rasco, C. (1998). Reasoning about moral aspects of illness and treatment by preschoolers who are healthy or who have chronic illness. *Journal of Developmental and Behavioral Pediatrics, 19*, 68–76.

Lyon, T.D., & LaMagna, R. (2007). The history of children's hearsay: From Old Bailey to post-Davis. *Indiana Law Journal, 82*, 1029–1058.

McGriff v. State (1996) 672 A.2d 1027 (Del.)

Myers, J.E.B. (2011). *Myers on Evidence in Child, Domestic, Rape, Stalking, and Elder Abuse Cases*. New York: Aspen.

Myers, J.E.B., Cordon, I., Ghetti, S., & Goodman, G.S. (2002). Hearsay exceptions: Adjusting the ratio of intuition to psychological science. *Law and Contemporary Problems*, *65*, 3–46.
People v. Banks (2010) West Law 572105 (Ill.)
Re L.N. (2004) 91 P.3d 836 (Utah Ct. App.)
State v. Branch (2005) 865 A.2d 673 (N.J.)
State v. Carlson (1991) 812 P.2d 536 (Wash. Ct. App.)
Steward M.S., & Regalbuto, G. (1975). Do doctors know what children know? *American Journal of Orthopsychiatry*, *45*, 146–149.
Steward M.S., & Steward, D.S. (1981). Children's conceptions of medical procedures. In R. Bibace & M. Walsh (Eds), *New Directions for Child Development: Children's Conceptions of Health, Illness, and Bodily Functions* (pp. 67–83). San Francisco, CA: Jossey-Bass.
Stoot v. City of Everett (2009) 582 F.3d 910 (9th Cir.)
United States v. Cabral (1996) 43 M.J. 808 (A.F. Ct. Crim. App.)

16

Consequences of Legal Involvement on Child Victims of Maltreatment

Jodi A. Quas and Mariya Sumaroka

Key Points

- Child victims involved in a legal case are likely at risk even before involvement begins because they already experienced some form of maltreatment or violence.
- Children may participate as witnesses in a criminal court, dependency court, or both.
- Characteristics of children most likely to become involved in the two systems often vary:
  - Children involved in criminal cases are most often victims of sexual abuse, are more likely to be female, and are more likely to be older children or adolescents rather than younger children; their case length varies, but lasts, on average, about 1 year); and children may be required to testify, either live or via some alternative means.
  - Children involved in dependency cases are most often victims of non-sexual forms of maltreatment that occurred at the hands of a caregiver, are more likely to be younger rather than older children, and are likely from lower income and ethnic minority backgrounds;

Children's Testimony: A Handbook of Psychological Research and Forensic Practice, Second Edition.
Edited by Michael E. Lamb, David J. La Rooy, Lindsay C. Malloy, and Carmit Katz.

legal involvement often includes removal from home, cases regularly last several years, and children rarely testify, although in a few jurisdictions they may attend hearings in which their case is discussed.

- Aspects of legal involvement that increase children's risk for negative consequences include:
  - testifying repeatedly in court, and possibly the anticipation of testifying,
  - lack of understanding of the legal process and children's own legal situation,
  - exposure to repeated interviews,
  - multiple delays and continuances,
  - lack of support from a non-offending caregiver, and
  - adverse case outcomes.

> The little girl's halting account of what happened to her, given when she was only three, was recorded on video and played to the Old Bailey... Her obvious distress – and tough questioning at the hands of two defence lawyers – raises disturbing questions about how the criminal justice system deals with very young witnesses. (Allen, *Daily Mail*, 2 May 2009; see also Chapter 14)

During the past two decades, a large body of scientific research has emerged concerning the conditions under which children can – and cannot – remember events well enough to be reliable witnesses in legal contexts. This work, much of which is reviewed in other chapters in this volume, has been incredibly important in shaping forensic interview training to facilitate children's eyewitness capabilities, in cross-national legal decisions that rely on children's statements as evidence, and in national and international doctrine regarding the acceptance of testimony from children (Ceci & Bruck, 1993; *Commonwealth v. Baran* 2009; Flin, Bull, Boon, & Knox, 1992; Goodman, Quas, & Ogle, 2010; *Lillie & Reed v. Newcastle City Council & Ors* 2002; Scotland Criminal Procedure Act of 1995; *Stronger v. Brook* 2003; United Kingdom Youth Justice and Criminal Evidence Act of 1999). Yet, as is evident even from a simple quote taken from a newspaper, children's experiences in a legal case go well beyond providing eyewitness testimony. Children are subjected to multiple interviews, each of which may be conducted by a different, unfamiliar, and potentially intimidating adult. They may undergo physical and psychological evaluations. They may go to court expecting to testify, but then not actually take the stand, for instance because of continuances, appeals, or plea bargains. Eventually, some children testify, and, in doing so, must recount, in an intimidating context, experiences that were likely frightening and painful, and answer questions posed by potentially hostile attorneys. In other cases, children do not testify but may nonetheless attend court hearings and listen while the judge, attorneys, and other professionals discuss the children's experiences, their family, and their needs. Finally, children may receive periodic notifications (e.g., via mail) about the status of the case or their responsibilities. These notices are written in formal legal language that many adults, not to mention children, fail to understand. And yet, children are supposed to respond to and possibly even, act on the information that they are given.

Given the range of experiences children may have as a result of participating in a legal case, combined with the austere, formal, and intimidating context surrounding the case, it is imperative that research concerning child witnesses addresses not only questions about their eyewitness capabilities, but also questions how well children can participate in a legal case and the effects of that participation on their well-being. Fortunately, such questions have been addressed, albeit not in as extensive a manner as questions concerning children's eyewitness testimony. Answers are already highlighting aspects of children's legal experiences that are particularly likely to lead to adverse outcomes.

The purpose of this chapter is to review key findings from this emerging body of research. We begin with a brief description of characteristics and experiences of children most likely to come into contact with the legal system as victims of or witnesses to crime. We then discuss findings concerning children's reactions to legal involvement, both initially and over time. Throughout our review we describe procedural modifications and interventions that have been developed to reduce potential adverse effects of legal involvement on children. We also offer suggestions for future research needs.

Of note, our review is somewhat slanted toward the United States, in large part because a majority of research to date on this topic has been conducted there. However, some research has been conducted in other countries, and we describe this research when possible. Also, some findings generalize across countries, regardless of procedural and legal variations; however, other findings do not. Cross-national differences in policy, legislative structure, and laws themselves need to be considered when evaluating the research and its implications for child witnesses.

CHARACTERISTICS OF CHILD VICTIMS INVOLVED IN LEGAL CASES

A useful starting point when trying to understand the consequences of legal involvement on children is to consider what 'legal involvement' may entail and the types of children most likely to experience that involvement. Unfortunately, children – like adults – may be exposed to any number of crimes, ranging from witnessing theft, a car accident, or violence between others, to personally experiencing assault or rape. Following this exposure, children may be questioned by the authorities, and, if the evidence is strong enough, a legal case may ensue.

Despite children possibly enduring any number of types of crimes, the most common crimes that lead to legal involvement by children are exposure to maltreatment or witnessing family violence (Goodman, Quas, Bulkley, & Shapiro, 1999; Plotnikoff & Woolfson, 2009). Allegations of serious maltreatment may lead to criminal charges being filed against the perpetrator, for example, in the Crown Court in England. The allegations may also lead to a family or juvenile dependency case (at times referred to as 'care proceedings') being filed to protect a child from further harm, or lead to both types of cases being filed. The two systems (hence referred to as criminal and dependency, respectively) as well as the maltreatment that led to the case's being filed vary in important ways (Cross, DeVos, & Whitcomb, 1994; Jones, Walsh, & Cross, 2007) that have implications for children's legal experiences and possibly well-being.

Turning first to criminal court, the basic purpose of a case is to determine the innocence or guilt of the defendant, and, if guilty, how the defendant should be punished. The child, in such cases, is thus simply a witness who has been asked to provide evidence, for instance via forensic interviews and possibly testifying in court, on behalf of either the defence or prosecution. Some efforts may be made to facilitate children's involvement, but, because the child's needs are not the central reason for the case, those needs are secondary to the main purpose. The vast majority of child witnesses involved in criminal cases, especially in the United States where one of the only large-scale surveys of reasons for criminal court involvement has been conducted, experienced sexual abuse. The next most frequent types of crimes are domestic violence and assault (Goodman *et al.*, 1999; Plotnikoff & Woolfson, 2009). The defendant is most often male, and, at least among cases that end up in criminal court, is slightly more likely to be a stranger than a parent figure (Cross *et al.*, 1994; Menard & Ruback, 2003; Stroud, Martens, & Barker, 2000). Although girls are more likely to be victims of sexual abuse and hence are more likely to come into contact with the criminal system as a witness, it is not clear whether proportionally there are differences in how often cases against girls versus boys result in criminal case filings (Cross, Jones, Walsh, Simone, & Kolko, 2007). Age differences, however, have emerged. Older witnesses are more likely take part in a criminal case than younger witnesses (e.g., preschool-age;

Cross *et al.*, 1994; Goodman *et al.*, 1992; Stroud *et al.*, 2000; Whitcomb *et al.*, 1991), a pattern that may be a result of greater reluctance to file cases involving young children, perhaps because of perceptions of their reduced credibility or ability to provide evidence. Finally, the length of criminal cases varies considerably, from a few months to several years. In the United States, cases last, on average, between 1 and 2 years from the initial filing to the final disposition (Walsh, Lipeert, Cross, Maurice, & Davison, 2008). In Great Britain, Plotnikoff and Woolfson (2004) reported that almost a year delay for the Crown Court between the start of the case and when child witnesses took the stand, and about a 10-month delay in a magistrates court. Thus, the length to disposition would be slightly longer.

Many maltreatment allegations are filed not in criminal court, but instead in dependency court. This is most common with allegations of neglect or physical abuse. The primary purpose of a dependency court is to protect children from harm that either occurred at the hands of a parent or for which a parent is not able or willing to protect them. Thus, unlike in criminal court for which the defendant's guilt is of primary concern, in a dependency court, children's well-being is of primary concern. In theory, then, considerable efforts are made to accommodate children's needs. Also, because in dependency cases the maltreatment likely occurred at the hands of one or both parents, significant concerns are often raised about whether there are supportive adults available to facilitate children's adjustment.

The demographic characteristics and legal experiences of children in the dependency system are often quite different from the characteristics of children in the criminal system. Children in the dependency system tend to be from ethnic minorities, economically disadvantaged backgrounds, and are also younger (e.g., preschool-age) rather than older (e.g., school-age; US Department of Health and Human Services, 2009). When a dependency case is filed, children may be interviewed by a child protection worker, and, if they are believed to be in imminent danger of harm, they may be removed from home and placed in an emergency shelter. Children may be subjected to additional interviews (e.g., by social workers) about the maltreatment, their needs, and placement preferences. Hearings are held to evaluate the allegations, determine children's best interests, and identify appropriate caregivers. Children rarely (i.e., only in a small number of jurisdictions, states, and countries) attend these hearings, and, with a few select exceptions, do not take the stand (Khoury, 2006; Quas, Cooper, & Wandrey, 2009). It is not known how often children are actually informed of decisions that are made, despite the significance of these decisions for their lives. Finally, although some dependency cases may be resolved quickly, many last several years, much longer than criminal cases typically do, and there is often no clear, simple identifiable outcome (Bishop *et al.*, 2000; Malloy, Lyon, & Quas, 2007). Instead, numerous decisions may be made during each hearing, with separate decisions that affect the children, their relationship with their parents, their living arrangements, or their treatment.

Two other issues need to be considered when evaluating children's legal involvement. First, regardless of whether a case is filed in criminal or dependency court, most children have already experienced some form of maltreatment or witnessed a potentially violent crime. As such, the children are already at risk for mental and physical health problems, even before participating in the legal case (Crooks, Scott, Wolfe, Chiodo, & Killip, 2007; Ellis & Wolfe, 2009; Friedrich, 1993; Hébert, Tremblay, Parent, Daignault, & Piché, 2006; Hunter, Goodwin, & Wilson, 1992; Mannarino, Cohen, & Berman, 1994). At the same time, maltreated children whose allegations are reported and who subsequently end up in legal cases likely differ from maltreated children who do not end up in the legal system, the latter of whom, for example, may not have disclosed the abuse or may have recanted their claim (Gray, 1993; Malloy *et al.*, 2007). Children involved in legal cases may be more forthcoming, less closely related to the perpetrator, and have higher levels of maternal or caregiver support, all of which can affect their willingness to disclose and maintain allegations of abuse and may reduce at least some of their risks for harm as a result of maltreatment relative to children not involved in legal cases (Goodman-Brown, Edelstein, Goodman, Jones, & Gordon, 2003; Malloy *et al.*, 2007). Stated another way, maltreated children entering the legal system are not representative of children more generally or of children whose maltreatment is never reported, and legal samples of maltreated children have unique characteristics and needs that must be considered when evaluating the consequences of legal involvement on their well-being.

Second, we heuristically described child witnesses as participating in *either* the criminal or dependency system. However, some child witnesses are involved in both systems, possibly concurrently. A parent may be prosecuted criminally for sexual abuse of a child, while the child has been removed from home and placed in foster care to be protected from further harm. These types of situations often involve the most serious acts of maltreatment, which come with their own risks. In so far as varying of participation in the criminal and dependency systems emerge, it is critical to consider how children involved in both systems fare.

In summary, children who endure maltreatment, and as such are already quite vulnerable, may become involved in a criminal case against the perpetrator, a dependency case focused on their safety and well-being, or both types of cases. Child witnesses in the criminal system tend to be older rather than younger and most likely endured some form of child sexual abuse. Their relationship to the perpetrator varies considerably, from parent to stranger. The nature of the relationship between the perpetrator and child has implications for parental supportiveness of children following discovery of maltreatment and during legal case, and for children's subsequent adjustment. Criminal court involvement by children most often involves providing evidence, for example, in interviews or in court, and cases typically end with a clear, single decision about the guilt or innocence of the defendant. Child witnesses in the dependency system are in many ways likely even more vulnerable than child witnesses in the criminal system. Children in the dependency system tend to be younger and be from ethnic minority and economically disadvantaged backgrounds. They were likely maltreated at the hands of a caregiver and thus are likely to lack parental support. Finally, dependency cases often last much longer than criminal cases and the outcomes are much more nebulous, making it difficult for children to understand, react to, and recover following dependency case decisions.

CONSEQUENCES OF LEGAL INVOLVEMENT

Given the many vulnerabilities inherent in child witnesses, it should come as no surprise that considerable concerns have been raised about whether participating in a legal case serves as a form of secondary victimization, further traumatizing children who have already endured violence and maltreatment. These concerns are evident in legal debates, legislation, and international doctrine (e.g., Canada's Child and Family Services Act of 1990; New Zealand's Children, Young Persons and their Families Act of 1989; United Kingdom's Children Act of 1989), all of which tout the need to protect children from harm that may occur as a result of their involvement in a legal case. For example, the United Nations Guidelines on Justice in Matters Involving Child Victims and Witnesses of Crime (2009) is designed to assist in the creation and implication of legal practices and procedures that protect children's rights and well-being, while concurrently considering the rights of the defendant. Similarly, the United Nations Convention on the Rights of the Child (1990) and the Council of Europe's Convention on the Protection of Children against Sexual Exploitation and Sexual Abuse (2007) both acknowledge specific limitations in children's mental and cognitive development and mandate that special care is provided to child witnesses during the legal process.

Empirical research has also taken up the question of whether children are harmed as a result of participation in a legal case, most often in the criminal system (Goodman *et al.*, 1992; Oates & Tong, 1987; Quas *et al.*, 2005; Sas, Austin, Wolfe, & Hurley, 1991). Findings reveal several aspects of children's legal experiences that appear to be especially distressing, both initially and over time. These aspects are not likely the only negative parts of children's participation, but these are now fairly well documented across several empirical studies. We now review this research, which concerns consequences linked to: (i) testifying repeatedly in court, (ii) not understanding legal procedures and language, (iii) exposure to repeated interviews, and (iv) other case characteristics (e.g., caregiver support, continuances, delays, case verdict). When possible, we also describe procedural innovations and courtroom alterations that have been proposed or used to reduce at least some negative outcomes associated with these aspects of children's participation.

Testifying

Perhaps the most well-studied component of children's participation in a legal case is that of taking the stand, that is, testifying in court. On the one hand, legal doctrines (e.g., Section 1, Article 6[3] in the European Convention on Human Rights, the US Constitution's 6th amendment) afford defendants the right to face their accused in court, which often requires that children provide evidence formally, most often by testifying. This 'face-to-face confrontation' is often considered necessary for justice. In theory, facing one's accuser compels the witness to speak the truth. However, facing a defendant, especially one who threatened or harmed a victim, or to whom loyalty is felt, can be traumatic. Adults can at least reason about justice and weigh, somewhat rationally, the need for their testimony against experiences of distress while doing so. However, developmental differences in reasoning about the legal system (Grisso, 1997) and coping (Compas, Connor-Smith, Saltzman, Thomsen, & Wadsworth, 2001) may limit children's understanding of why they must testify, increase their distress, and cause longer-term harm (for legal arguments concerning the latter position, see, e.g., the United Kingdom's Children Act of 1989; United Kingdom's Youth Justice and Criminal Evidence Act, 1999; United Nations Convention on the Rights of the Child, 1990; US Child Abuse and Treatment Act of 1974).

Numerous studies have examined children's reactions to and consequences of testifying, at least in criminal cases involving alleged sexual abuse (Goodman *et al.*, 1992; Henry, 1997; Whitcomb, 1991). Findings reveal first that, before actually taking the stand, preparing to testify is distressing to children. Secondly, testifying is at times associated with increased distress and adverse outcomes, but this is primarily the case when testifying is combined with several additional risk factors.

With regard to the anticipation of testifying, research suggests that children are often distressed well before they take the stand. In a large survey of several hundred children who participated in criminal cases in England, Wales, and Northern Ireland, for example, Plotnikoff and Woolfson (2009) found that 70% of children had been worried about going to court, and over half experienced stress symptoms before the trial date. Other studies, conducted in the United States and Canada, have similarly reported increased distress, loss of sleep and appetite, poor health, and increases in behavioural and emotional problems in children awaiting testimony (Goodman *et al.*, 1992; Sas, Hurley, Hatch, Malla, & Dick, 1993). At least a part of this distress may be caused by the uncertainty associated with when children will actually testify. Pre-trial delays and continuances (requests by either party to postpone a requested legal action) are common and may lead to perceived helplessness because children must continually prepare to testify only to have the trial date changed, requiring that they prepare again with no clear sense of when they will take the stand (Berliner & Conte, 1995; Edelstein *et al.*, 2002; Runyan, Everson, Edelsohn, Hunter, & Coulter 1988).

This anticipatory distress is not short-lived. Pre-testimony distress has been linked to adverse outcomes months and years after the trial has ended. Berliner and Conte (1995), for example, reported that distress while waiting to testify predicted poorer adjustment later. Quas *et al.* (2005) interviewed former child victims of sexual abuse who testified in criminal court over a decade earlier and found a positive association between pre-testifying anticipatory stress (obtained at the time of the original case) and subsequent behaviour problems, even with other potentially important child and case characteristics statistically controlled (e.g., child age, mental health problems at the start of case, number of times children had testified).

With regard to actually testifying, consider for a moment what it must be like to take the stand: children answer questions, at times posed by hostile attorneys, about frightening, violent, and perhaps intimate details, often while facing the individual they are accusing of the crime. This individual may be a trusted caregiver to whom the children feel love and loyalty or a violent stranger who has killed in the past. Some children are incredibly distressed while testifying, even to the point of being incapable of communicating (*Maryland v. Craig* 1990). Others, however, appear quite calm (Goodman *et al.*, 1992; Whitcomb *et al.*, 1991), which is often unexpected to jurors (McAuliff, Maurice, Neal, & Diaz, 2008). Perhaps somewhat surprising, older children are more negative while testifying, both according to observer and self-report, than younger children (Goodman *et al.*, 1992). However, older children often testify for longer, are treated more harshly, and are more likely to have their honesty questioned (Bottoms & Goodman, 1994; Goodman *et al.*, 1992; Whitcomb *et al.*, 1991), all of which likely contribute to their increased distress.

Children who are closely related to the defendant are more variable and inconsistent in their emotional reactions than children who are not closely related to the defendant. Goodman *et al.* (1992), for example, observed child sex abuse victims while testifying. Those who were closely related to the alleged perpetrator displayed less anger and more sympathy toward the defendant but were also less cooperative when answering the defence attorneys' questions (Goodman *et al.*, 1992). Children involved in cases against a parental figure may well experience a range of conflicting emotions while testifying, which certainly could be expressed via inconsistent emotions and behaviours.

What is perhaps more important than whether children are distressed while testifying, which may simply be an inevitable reaction for all witnesses – adults and children alike (e.g., see Scalia's dissent in *Maryland v. Craig* 1990) – is whether this distress is related to adverse outcomes, initially and over time. Increased distress while recounting prior experiences has been associated with poorer memory, increased suggestibility, and reduced ability to communicate, both in laboratory analogue studies and in actual legal settings (e.g., Goodman *et al.*, 1992; Quas & Lench, 2007; Saywitz & Nathanson, 1993). Moreover, for important subsets of children, the distress does not end when children step off the stand. Instead, for some children, negative outcomes remain after their testimony is complete. These subsets of children include those whose cases lack corroborative evidence, who do not have maternal support during the case, who endured particularly severe sexual abuse, or who testify repeatedly. Lack of corroborative evidence (regardless of allegation veracity) can mean the case rests largely on a child's report, which could increase stress associated with taking the stand. Caregiver support of child victims is crucial for their well-being, regardless of legal or testifying experiences (Liang, Williams, & Siegel, 2006; Malloy & Lyon, 2006; Sas *et al.*,1993). Without caregiver support, the stress of testifying may simply overwhelm children's coping resources. (In fact, Goodman *et al.*, 1992, found that caregivers were less likely to be present when a child testified in cases involving a closely related perpetrator than cases involving an acquaintance or stranger perpetrator; not being present may well be indicative of lack of support.) Finally, recounting on multiple occasions, in open court, details of severe abuse, which involved repeated abuse, penetration, and/or a closely related perpetrator, may constitute a repeated stressor, which may well underlie longer term adverse outcomes (Quas *et al.*, 2005).

One caveat worth mentioning with regard to research to date is that virtually all studies have only included child victims participating in sexual abuse cases. Whether testifying in cases involving other types of crime also relates to adverse outcomes is not clear (for descriptive information suggesting similar outcomes, see Plotnikoff & Woolfson, 2009). Nor have the effects of testifying in dependency cases, which occurs very rarely, been systematically examined. One exception is a study conducted by Runyan *et al.* (1988) of 79 victims of sexual abuse, aged 6–17 years, who were interviewed shortly after abuse was reported to the authorities and again 5 months later. At the 5-month follow-up, 45% of the allegations had resulted in dependency filings, and 12 children had testified. Those who had testified evinced larger improvements in well-being compared with those who had not testified. However, the two groups (testifiers and non-testifiers) also differed even before they testified, and their cases' lengths varied (testifiers cases had ended more quickly), making it difficult to interpret precisely why the testifiers had improved while the non-testifiers had not. Overall, the research highlights the need for further studies concerning the relations between testifying in a variety of types of cases, especially dependency cases, and children's functioning.

Of importance, a few studies indicate that, under certain conditions, not testifying may predict poorer outcomes. For instance, when a case involves less severe abuse, children may need to have some clear acknowledgment that, not only did the abuse occur, but the abuse was sufficiently wrong as to warrant public intervention. Testifying may provide such acknowledgment, at least in part (Henry, 1997). Quas *et al.* (2005), in a long-term follow-up of child sexual abuse victims who participated in criminal proceedings in the United States, found that not testifying in cases involving less severe abuse (e.g., the abuse lasted only a short duration, the perpetrator was unknown to children) predicted poorer functioning. Also, Goodman *et al.* (1992) and Quas *et al.* (2005) found that non-testifiers reported more negative feelings about their case than did testifiers. Specifically, non-testifiers reported feeling worse about not having testified when the case outcome was not guilty (either through a plea bargain or court decision) rather than guilty (testifiers' feelings did not vary depending on case outcome). Additionally, years later, the former victims who had not testified in their case reported that the legal system was less fair than did the former victims who had testified.

Testifying in open court while facing a defendant occurs in many countries; however, it is most common in the United States partly as a result of the 6th amendment, often referred to as the confrontation clause, which affords the defendant the right to look his/her accusers in the eye. Many European countries, unhampered by such an amendment, have laws that protect children somewhat from the stress of facing the defendant. For instance, closed-circuit television testimony, commonly referred to as live link (where a child answers questions live, but from a location separate from the actual courtroom), is regularly used in England, Wales, Belgium, Germany, and Australia (see the International Association of Prosecutor's Annotated Model Guidelines for the Effective Prosecution of Children, 2001). Live link is the default for children in some countries, whereas in others (e.g., Scotland) the court reviews case features (e.g., child's age, relationship to the perpetrator) and makes a decision about whether live link is appropriate (Scotland Criminal Procedure Act of 1995). Overall, studies consistently find decreases in children's self- and observer-rated distress as a result of testifying via live link rather than in open court (Cashmore, 1992; Davies & Noon, 1991; Goodman *et al.*, 1998). In a few countries, such as Sweden, children rarely if ever testify, including via live link, but instead provide videotaped narrative statements before a trial which are then presented in lieu of live testimony (for a discussion of different practices see International Children's Bureau, 2005). Whether children then need to be available for cross-examination, which may take place in open-court or via live link, again varies across countries.

Having children testify via live link predicts reduced levels of distress relative to testifying in open court. Showing videotaped statements in lieu of having children testify at all eliminates this distress completely. However, the longer term effects of removing children entirely from the process are not clear. That is, perhaps even though in the short-term children may be distressed by testifying, it may be better in the long-run for them to have had their day in court, so long as that day was not a repeated occurrence and additional safeguards are in place, in a manner similar to that observed in adults who often report more positive feelings about the legal system when they feel that they were able to participate and the process was fair (Tyler, 1990; Tyler & Lind, 2001). What exactly 'testifying' would need to entail though, needs to be determined. That is, it is unknown as to whether testifying via live link or with shields to preclude a child from seeing a defendant, jury, or others in the court adequately serves the dual purpose of making children feel as though they have a voice and protecting them from enduring high levels of distress as a result of testifying against a defendant. Further empirical investigations in this area will be critical (Hall & Sales, 2008).

Legal Knowledge

A potentially critical source of distress for children involved in legal cases is children's knowledge, or rather lack thereof, about the legal system broadly and about their case and situation specifically. This lack of knowledge can induce a sense of uncertainty in children about their responsibility or self-blame for the case. It may also underlie fears associated with providing testimony, may lead children to be unwilling to testify or contribute to inaccuracies while they are testifying, or may create feelings of resentment or fear of punishment (Perry *et al.*, 1995; Sas *et al.*, 1993; Saywitz, Goodman, & Lyon, 2002; Saywitz, Nathanson, Snyder, & Lamphear, 1993; Zajac, Gross, & Hayne, 2003).

What is particularly striking is the magnitude of children's lack of understanding, which is evident in a myriad of ways. First, children often fail to understand the language used in legal contexts (Flin, Stevenson, & Davies, 1989; Perry *et al.*, 1995; Peterson-Badali, Abramovitch, & Duda, 1997; Saywitz *et al.*, 1993; Zajac *et al.*, 2003). Indeed, even adults are often unclear as to the meaning of commonly used jargon in legal cases (Perry *et al.*, 1995). Sentence structures are complex and sentences regularly contain multiple embedded clauses, both of which can lead to inaccurate responses and increase children's confusion and anxiety (Saywitz, Jaenicke, & Camparo, 1990; Walker, 1993; Zajac *et al.*, 2003). In Plotnikoff and Woolfson's (2009) survey, for example, nearly half of the child witnesses who gave evidence in magistrates' court and well over half of those who gave evidence in Crown Court reported not understanding some questions and expressed negative feelings about the complexity of questions.

Answering questions during cross-examination appears to be especially challenging for children, who have described it as 'confusing, complex, rushed, repetitive, bullying and frightening' (Plotnikoff & Woolfson, 2004). The purpose of cross-examination is to discredit witnesses' claims. It is thus not surprising that defence attorneys frequently ask disconnected, hard-to-follow questions, and embed complex phrases and legal jargon into questions (Brennan & Brennan, 1988; Ghetti, Alexander, & Goodman, 2002; Hall & Sales, 2008). Yet, even prosecutors often use developmentally inappropriate, overly complex language (Goodman *et al.*, 1992), and legal professionals regularly overestimate children's legal understanding (Eltringham & Aldridge, 2000), leading to developmentally inappropriate questions and statements. Given that children rarely ask for clarification when they do not understand a question or information, their inability to comprehend legal language often goes undetected.

Children are often unaware of the precise roles and responsibilities of legal professionals and fail to understand the purpose of many legal procedures. This is evident even among older children and children who have had extensive contact with the legal system as a victim or defendant (Cauffman & Steinberg, 2000; Cooper, Wallin, Quas, & Lyon, 2010; Flin *et al.*, 1989; Putnam, 2003; Saywitz *et al.*, 1990). For instance, Quas, Wallin, Horwitz, Davis, and Lyon (2009) interviewed maltreated 4- to 15-year-olds awaiting dependency hearing in the United States about their understanding of legal terms and the function of various legal professionals (e.g., attorney, judge). Although children's accuracy, both in defining terms and describing legal professionals' roles, improved dramatically with age, none of the oldest children was at ceiling (i.e., answered all questions accurately), and many had difficulty providing accurate answers to some questions. Also, even children who attend hearings, whether they testify (e.g., in a criminal case) or not (e.g., in a dependency case), fail to fully grasp what is happening and the decisions being made. Again, the language is complex, the pace is fast, and the adults often talk at a level far above the developmental level of the child participants.

Studies of children's understanding of decisions made in dependency hearings that they attended provide clear evidence of children's difficulties. When asked immediately afterward what decision was made, many fail to answer correctly. Block, Oran, Oran, Baumrind, & Goodman (2010), for example, interviewed 7- to 10-year-old maltreated children at the courthouse after they had attended a dependency hearing (for approximately 50% of the children, the hearing corresponded to the initial hearing held subsequent to their emergency removal, whereas for the remaining children the hearings focused on evaluating ongoing cases). When asked why they had to go to court, 65% of the children responded that they did not know or because they had 'been bad'. Only a minority correctly responded that it was to keep them safe or to talk to the judge. Similarly, Quas *et al.* (2009) asked 63 4- to 15-year-olds who had just attended their hearings (e.g., trials, placement review proceedings) what the judge had decided. Older children were more accurate than younger children, but even the oldest children erred at times: 33% of the 12- to 15-year-olds correctly describing the judge's decision, 50% provided an incomplete, but correct response, and 17% provided no correct information. Across age, one-third of the total sample provided no correct information about the judge's decision, and half of these children were actually incorrect in their responses. Thus, lack of understanding, even of their own situation, is quite prevalent.

Of course, what is most relevant to the current chapter is that lack of legal knowledge is predictive of increases in children's distress (Hall &

Sales, 2008; Quas *et al.*, 2009). This pattern has emerged in dependency cases when children attend their hearings, as well as in criminal cases when children are called upon to testify. Less complete legal understanding is predictive of increased anxiety about taking the stand (Goodman *et al.*, 1998), and to higher levels of reported and expressed fear while in the courtroom (Quas *et al.*, 2009; Sas *et al.*, 1991). Whether this increased distress persists over long periods of time has not been examined empirically, but remains a critically important next step in research concerning children's reactions to the legal environment.

Several countries and jurisdictions have recognized how little children understand about the legal process, and, as a result, have employed various strategies to facilitate children's understanding. The formality of these strategies varies, ranging from an informal conversations with a staff member to intensive multi-session training sessions to familiarize children with the nuances of their participation in a legal case.

Informal programmes typically include brief court tours or summaries of generic information about court, legal personnel, or the process of a legal case. In the United States, investigators, attorneys, or victim advocates may give child witnesses a tour of the courtroom or a cursory overview of the facts of a case to help acclimatize children to the process (Goodman *et al.*, 1999; Saywitz & Snyder, 1993). In England, most child witnesses are given the opportunity to tour the courtroom prior to testifying in what is called a familiarization visit (Plotnikoff & Woolfson, 2009). In Los Angeles County, California, where children over the age of 4 years attend many of their dependency proceedings, an orientation video is shown to the children on the day of their visit describing the general function of key personnel with whom the children interact at court.

Other interventions target children's ability to interpret and respond to trial questions. In Australia, for instance, a communicator, such as a school teacher, can be present while a child testifies (including when the child testifies via live link). This individual will help the child understand and respond to complicated legal questions (see the International Association of Prosecutors' Annotated Model Guidelines for the Effective Prosecution of Children, 2001). A similar approach is taken in Ireland and New Zealand. Children under age 17 can have an intermediary appointed who will assist during the live link phase by rewording questions in age-appropriate language (see, e.g., New Zealand Evidence Act of 1998).

Formal programmes have specific trained individuals or materials that assist child victims during the legal process. The individual or material provides children with general knowledge about the process as well as case-specific information. In Ontario, Canada, for example, the Ministry of the Attorney General oversees the Child Victim/Witness Program, which provides children's families with case information (e.g., court dates, bail conditions), gives the children court orientation sessions and tours, and assigns a support person to children who testify. The Program also gives children aged 6–12 years an activity book, 'What's my job in court', to help them understand the court process and key personnel. The Safe Passage Program in Colorado Springs, Colorado collaborates with police departments, social service agencies, and district attorney offices to prepare children to testify in criminal cases by individually working with children to get them ready for court, by providing a support person to children during the trial, and by holding orientation and communication sessions for caregivers. In Huntsville, Alabama (Keeney, Amacher, & Kastanakis, 1992), child witnesses are offered a series of structured sessions to address their uncertainties (e.g., about who the judge is) and fears (e.g., about facing the defendant and answering prosecutors' and defence attorneys' questions) concerning testifying in court.

The goals of informal and formal programmes are to enhance children's legal understanding, reduce their anxiety and distress, and facilitate the progression of the case. Although children regularly cite lack of knowledge as an important source of distress, and children regularly ask to be more informed about their case, very few scientific investigations have evaluated, using an experimental design, the precise effects of enhancing knowledge on children's well-being or on the case itself. Research from medical settings, which indicates that children are less distressed about impending medical procedures when they know what will happen, and anecdotal accounts of children in legal contexts certainly suggest that greater knowledge should help them during the process, but additional empirical research with legal samples is needed. This research, importantly, has to focus not only on the effects of knowledge, but also on how that knowledge should be provided so that it is developmentally appropriate and can be linked by children to their own experiences and concerns.

Repeated Interviews

During the course of a legal case, children are routinely subjected to multiple interviews. At least some of this repetition may be necessary: Both sides must gather evidence to support their claims, additional information may become available, the evidence provided by children needs to be clarified, or children's placement or needs change. According to studies in the United States, children involved in child sexual abuse legal cases, including those filed in criminal or dependency court, undergo between two and six formal interviews about the allegations (Cross *et al.*, 2007; Goodman *et al.*, 1992; Malloy *et al.*, 2007). Whether children endure a similar numbers of interviews in other countries is not known. However, policies that promote videotaped or collaborative interviews with child witnesses (e.g., by police and attorneys) should reduce the total number of interviews children complete. As an example, in Denmark – through the use of earpieces – legal professionals can direct a single interviewer to ask particular questions or clarify information as the interview is ongoing, which in theory reduces the need for at least some follow-up interviews (see the Danish Association of Parents for the Protection of Children's Report to the UN Committee on the Rights of the Child, 2001).

Regardless of the total number of interviews, any repetition can be quite controversial. On the one hand, in so far as repeated interviews highlight concerns for children's well-being and foster a positive relationship between a child and an interviewer (Tedesco & Schnell, 1987), positive effects may ensue. For instance, children become more familiar with the interviewer, which could increase their comfort and trust in the individual, who then becomes a potentially important (and beneficial) source of support (Faller, 2007; Thompson, 1994). Interviewer familiarity is also associated with increased accuracy in mock forensic interview settings and may help children communicate information by increasing their comfort, for example in refuting false suggestions (Goodman, Sharma, Thomas, & Considine, 1995; Quas & Schaaf, 2002).

However, numerous negative effects are believed to occur as a result of repeated interviews. The Council of Europe's (2007) Convention on the Protection of Children against Sexual Exploitation and Sexual Abuse report, for example, contains explicit language directing its members to restrict the number of interviews child victims must endure to reduce the harm these interviews cause. Similar language can be found in Article 13 in the United Nations Guidelines on Justice Matters involving Child Victims and Witnesses of Crime (2009). Consistent with these admonitions, there is evidence that repeated interviewing may lead some children to re-experience the trauma or negative emotions associated with the event (Brennan & Brennan, 1988; Ghetti *et al.*, 2002; Malloy *et al.*, 2007; Quas & McAuliff, 2009; United Nations Annual Convention on the Rights of the Child, 1990) and may lead children to have negative attitudes toward the legal system (Goodman *et al.*, 1992; Tedesco & Schnell, 1987), which could affect their willingness to report details of a crime or participate fully in interviews or trials.

In addition to concerns about the emotional effects of repeated interviewing, there has been concern that such practices can affect the quality of children's testimony. For example, the US Supreme Court, in a decision banning the death penalty for non-capital offenses (*Kennedy v. Louisiana* 2008), specifically mentioned that repeatedly interviewing a child could lead to unreliable testimony. Even if repetition per se did not affect children's accuracy (see, e.g., Goodman & Quas, 2008; Lyon, 2002), perceptions that repetition reduces the accuracy of children's reports could still lead to harsher, more skeptical, and less supportive questioning, all of which would increase children's distress.

Several national and international polices have directed attention toward reducing the number of interviews in which children take part. In Scotland, for example, the prosecution must make interview reports available to the defence in order to avoid repeated interviewing of the child by the defence (International Association of Prosecutors, 2001). Videotaping of interviews is also quite widely supported. Interviews may be conducted jointly by a social worker and a prosecutor (e.g., in Finland) and may be shown in court as evidence in lieu of children's live testimony (e.g., in Sweden). Many US jurisdictions have created multidisciplinary interview or child advocacy centres (CACs) that centralize forensic interviewing, evaluation, and service delivery for victims of maltreatment. Because children are questioned at a single location, often by highly trained interviewers, the quality of the information may be better. Also, a larger number of individuals may be involved in setting up the interview, leading to higher quality and potentially fewer overall interviews conducted.

As a final note regarding repeated interviews, there remain considerable controversies regarding their use irrespective of the potential effect of interview repetition on children's functioning. As briefly discussed, repeated interviews are often claimed to be an important factor that can lead to false allegations. This belief is not only promoted by some academic researchers (Brainerd & Reyna, 2005), but is also believed by laypersons (Quas, Thompson, & Clarke-Stewart, 2005) and has even been mentioned in actual legal decisions as a reason not to trust children's allegations (e.g., the US Supreme Court's decision in *Kennedy v. Louisiana* 2008, mentioned previously). However, actual empirical evidence demonstrating causal links between repeated interviews per se and children's errors is much more scant, with many studies failing to report significant increases in inaccuracies simply as a function of interview repetition (Ceci, Huffman, Smith, & Loftus, 1994; Quas *et al.*, 2007). Indeed, LaRooy *et al.* (2009) observed that it is suggestive interviewing, especially when repeated, rather than repeated interviewing per se, that needs to be avoided. Thus, repeated interviews may not adversely affect the quality of children's reports (Goodman & Quas, 2008; La Rooy, Lamb, & Pipe, 2009), but may need to be avoided as much as possible because they may be psychologically stressful for children.

Other Case Characteristics.

Certainly, testifying multiple times, lack of understanding, and repeated interviews are not only characteristics that may contribute to adverse outcomes in children following legal involvement, other characteristics exist as well. Those that have been identified in empirical research include case length (e.g., continuances and delays), lack of caregiver support, and case outcome.

First, the length of legal cases involving child witnesses varies tremendously, and longer lasting cases have been associated with poorer outcomes. In the United States, for instance, criminal cases last on average between 1 to 2 years from the time a case is referred for prosecution to the initial verdict (Smith & Elstein, 1993; Walsh *et al.*, 2008), and dependency cases commonly last 2 years or more (Johnson & Wagner, 2005; White, Albers, & Biotini, 1996). In England, Plotnikoff and Woolfson (2004) reported that, for cases involving child witnesses, the average time between the referral of a case and the trial in the Crown Court was 11.6 months, with this time decreasing only slightly to 9.9 months for cases in a magistrate's court. Furthermore, only 44% of the children who testified in court did do so on the first scheduled date, and about 25% of the children had to return two or three times because of rescheduling before taking the stand. In a follow-up survey, Plotnikoff and Woolfson (2009) found a slight decrease in the overall case length, but delays and continuances remained common: 30% of trials were rescheduled one or more times; only half of the children in England and Wales began providing testimony on the first day of their court attendance, and a mere 8% of the children in Northern Ireland did so. Such delays and continuances, which are largely out of children's control, are believed to create feelings of helplessness (Batterman-Faunce & Goodman, 1993). Moreover, when children do not know when they will take the stand, and when children prepare to testify only to have a date changed, their anxiety is kept at high levels for long periods of time, increasing their risk of adverse consequences (Goodman *et al.*, 1992; Runyan *et al.*, 1988).

Second, the absence of a supportive adult has been linked to numerous negative outcomes in children participating in a legal case. Besides not having critically necessary emotional support, children who lack a support person may be less likely to receive information and updates about their case, and may feel more uncertain, helpless, and distressed. Indeed, numerous studies of the consequences of legal involvement for child victims of sexual abuse have uncovered significant differences in children's well-being depending on whether a supportive adult is available (Goodman *et al.*, 1992; Malloy *et al.*, 2007; Quas *et al.*, 2005; Runyan *et al.*, 1988). For instance, Sas *et al.* (1993) found that, even among children taking part in an intervention programme to facilitate their ability to participate in a sexual abuse criminal case, those who did not receive maternal support at the time of disclosure were more depressed both initially and several years after the case ended than those who had received maternal support. Goodman *et al.* (1992) and Whitcomb *et al.* (1991) similarly found that maternal support was positively related to children's improved functioning during the course of a legal case. Children who lacked maternal support failed to show such improvement. These associations were still evident years later: lack of caregiver support predicted greater internalizing problems over a decade after the cases ended (Quas *et al.*, 2005).

Third, case outcome has numerous implications for the consequences of legal involvement, especially for children's attitudes about the legal system, testifying, and the process in their case. In an early evaluation of the Child Witness Project in Ontario, Canada, Sas *et al.* (1991, 1993) found that children whose cases ended in not guilty rather than guilty verdicts reported more negative feelings about their legal experiences. Goodman *et al.* (1992) and Quas *et al.* (2005) similarly found that case outcome was strongly related to former child sexual abuse victims' legal attitudes. Immediately after the case ended, children reported feeling more negative about the case, their legal experiences, testifying, and the legal system generally when the case was dropped, the defendant was acquitted, or the defendant received a lenient than when a guilty or more severe sentence was delivered (Goodman *et al.*, 1992). These negative feelings did not dissipate. Years later, the former victims whose cases resulted in less severe outcomes for the defendants continued to feel more negative about the case, even with initial mental health, age, abuse characteristics, and testifying controlled statistically (Quas *et al.*, 2005). Of course, unlike testifying or legal knowledge, it is not possible to intervene by 'changing' the outcome. However, it should be possible to help children better understand, in a developmentally manner, the outcome of a trial or at least better understand their role (or perhaps their lack of role) in contributing to that outcome. Such knowledge may well reduce some of children's negative feelings and help them adjust, over time, to an outcome they view as unfavourable.

How to intervene and promote maternal (or perhaps non-offending caregiver) support, though, is a difficult endeavour. One method is to increase parents' involvement in and knowledge of the legal process and their children's cases, a strategy attempted by many CACs in the United States. By increasing parents' involvement, the various challenges children may encounter during the course of a trial may be more evident, leading parents to be more attentive to their children's needs (Cross *et al.*, 2007, 2008). One study found that parents with children being seen at CACs were less negative about the process than parents with children seen at non-CACs (e.g., police stations). Whether parents' negativity affects children's distress has not been examined directly, and our idea that by reducing negative feelings in parents, children will receive greater support, is only speculative without direct empirical investigations.

Another strategy is to provide children with an adult who can act as a support person. This latter approach is most common in criminal cases when children testify. Legal provisions in several countries allow for such an individual (United Kingdom's Children Act of 1989; US Child Abuse and Treatment Act of 1974), who may be responsible for providing the child with information about the upcoming trial, preparing the child to testify, and then being present while the child testifies. At times, the support person is a parent, but the individual is more often a court-appointed advocate. In so far as a positive relationship is created between the support person and child, improved adjustment may occur (Tedesco & Schnell, 1987).

A few studies have examined, albeit somewhat indirectly, how of the presence of a support person may relate to children's functioning and ability to participate in a legal case. In Goodman *et al.*'s (1992) investigation of children who testified in sexual abuse cases, those who testified with a non-offending parent or loved one present were rated as less frightened while testifying, were less likely to provide inconsistent testimony about details of the abuse, and were better able to answer prosecutors' questions than children without such an individual present. Santilla, Korkman, and Sandnabba (2004) analysed investigative interviews of suspected child abuse victims in Finland and found that support person use was associated with interviewers' behaviours and children's responses, although in a direction opposite of what one might expect. The presence of a support person was associated with longer, more suggestive interviewer utterances and shorter, less detailed responses from children. The contradictory findings across studies, in concert with limitations inherent in correlational research (i.e., inability to make causal inferences or control for confounding variables), highlight the need for additional research to clarify the precise nature of the associations between support person use and children's experiences in court as well as outcomes after children's legal involvement has ended.

CONCLUSIONS

Every year, substantial numbers of children are exposed to crime and, as a result, end up involved in a legal case. Their ability to participate fully in the case is imperative in order to protect them and others from further harm and to ensure that justice prevails (National Society for the Prevention of Cruelty to Children, 2009). A growing body of literature concerning the effects of legal involvement on children reveals first that they are able to take part in legal proceedings, which includes getting on the stand and testifying. Second, however, the literature highlights when harmful outcomes are likely to emerge and provides important hints at ways that at least some of these outcomes may be reduced.

The most well-studied characteristics of legal proceedings that are associated with increased risk for harm, including both in the domains of mental health outcomes and negative attitudes in children include:

1. Testifying repeatedly in court, especially in cases that lack corroborative evidence, that contain multiple continuances and delays, and for which the child victims lack caregiver support.
2. Anticipation of testifying, even when children do not actually take the stand.
3. Lack of legal knowledge, both about the legal system generally and about children's own legal situation specifically; lack of legal knowledge's associations with adverse outcomes are evident even among older children, whose legal understanding is often overestimated.
4. Delays and continuances, which often keep children's anxiety high and preclude them from recovering.
5. Unfavourable case outcomes which children may not fully understand and/or for which they may feel responsible.

Certainly it is not feasible to eliminate children's participation in or distress during legal cases entirely, and children often want – and may even need – to have some voice after they endure a crime. At the same time, it is imperative to recognize the inherent vulnerabilities of child witnesses and continue, as many countries are already doing, to identify the best ways to accommodate these children as they face the challenges associated with their participation in a legal case.

REFERENCES

Allen, V. (2009). She called it the 'evil room' – the video suite where a little girl was grilled for 45 minutes by lawyers. *Mail Online*, 2 May 2009. Available at www.dailymail.co.uk.

Batterman-Faunce, J.M., & Goodman, G.S. (1993). Effects of context on the accuracy and suggestibility of children witnesses. In G.S. Goodman, & B.L. Bottoms (Eds), *Child Victims, Child Witnesses* (pp. 301–330). New York: Guilford Press.

Berliner, L., & Conte, J. (1995). The effects of disclosure and intervention on sexually abused children. *Child Abuse and Neglect, 19*, 371–384.

Bishop, S.J., Murphy, J.M., Hicks, R., Quinn, D., Lewis, P.J., Grace, M., & Jellinek, M. (2000). What progress has been made in meeting the needs of seriously maltreated children? The course of 200 cases through the Boston Juvenile Court. *Child Abuse and Neglect, 24*, 599–610.

Block, S., Oran, D., Oran, H., Baumrind, N., & Goodman, G.S. (2010). Abused and neglected children in court: Knowledge and attitudes. *Child Abuse and Neglect, 34*, 659–670.

Bottoms, B.L., & Goodman, G. (1994). Perceptions of children's credibility in sexual assault cases. *Journal of Applied Social Psychology, 24*, 702–732.

Brainerd, C.J., & Reyna, V.F. (2005). *The Science of False Memory*. Oxford, UK: Oxford University Press.

Brennan, M., & Brennan, R.E. (1988). *Strange Language: Child Victims Under Cross Examination* (3rd edn). Wagga Wagga, NSW, Australia: Riverina Murray Institute of Higher Education.

Canada, Child and Family Services Act (1990).

Cashmore, J. (1992). *The use of closed-circuit television for child witnesses in the ACT*. Sydney, Australia: Australian Law Reform Committee.

Cauffman, E., & Steinberg, L. (2000). (Im)maturity of judgment in adolescence: Why adolescents may be less culpable than adults. *Behavioral Sciences and the Law, 18*, 741–760.

Ceci, S.J., & Bruck, M. (1993). Suggestibility of the child witness: A historical review and synthesis. *Psychological Bulletin, 113*, 403–439.

Ceci, S.J., Huffman, M.L.C., Smith, E., & Loftus, E.F. (1994). Repeatedly thinking about a non-event: Source misattributions among preschoolers. *Consciousness and Cognition, 3*, 388–407.

Commonwealth v. Baran, 74 Mass. App. Ct. 256, 274 n. 25 (2009).

Compas, B.E., Connor-Smith, J.K., Saltzman, H., Thomsen, A.H., & Wadsworth, M.E. (2001). Coping with stress during childhood and adolescence: Problems, progress, and potential in theory and research. *Psychological Bulletin, 127*, 87–127.

Cooper, A., Wallin, A.R., Quas, J.A., & Lyon, T.D. (2010). Maltreated and non-maltreated children's knowledge of the dependency court system. *Child Maltreatment, 15*, 255–260.

Council of Europe. (2007). *Convention on the Protection of Children against Sexual Exploitation and Sexual Abuse Report*. Council of Europe Treaty Series No 201.

Crooks, C., Scott, K., Wolfe, D.A., Chiodo, D., & Killip, S. (2007). Understanding the link between childhood maltreatment and violent delinquency: What do schools have to add? *Child Maltreatment, 12*, 269–280.

Cross, T.P., DeVos, E., & Whitcomb, D. (1994). Prosecution of child sexual abuse: Which cases are accepted? *Child Abuse and Neglect, 18*, 663–677.

Cross T.P., Jones L.M., Walsh W.A., Simone M., & Kolko D. (2007). Child forensic interviewing in Children's Advocacy Centers: empirical data on a practice model. *Child Abuse and Neglect, 10*, 1031–1052.

Cross, T.P., Jones, L.J., Walsh, W., Simone, M., Kolko, D.J., Szczepanski, J., Lippert, T., Davison, K., Cryns, A., Sosnowski, P., Shadoin, A., & Magnuson,

S. (2008). *The multi-site evaluation of children's advocacy centers: Overview of the results and implications for practice*. OJJDP Crimes Against Children Series Bulletin. Washington, DC: Office of Juvenile Justice and Delinquency Prevention.

Danish Association of Parents for the Protection of Children. (2001). Report to the UN Committee on the Rights of the Child. Retrieved on 20 December 2010 from http://www.crin.org/docs/resources/treaties/crc.27/Denmark-FBB.pdf.

Davies, G., & Noon, E. (1991) *An Evaluation of the Live Link for Child Witnesses*. Home Office report.

Edelstein, R.S., Goodman, G.S., Ghetti, S, Alexander, K.W., Quas, J.A., Redlich, A.D., Schaaf, J.M., & Cordon, I.M. (2002). Child witnesses' experiences post-court: The effects of legal involvement. In H.L Westcott, G.M. Davies, & R.H.C. Bull (Eds), *Children's Testimony in Context* (pp. 261–278). NY: John Wiley & Sons.

Ellis, W.E., & Wolfe, D.A. (2009). Understanding the association between maltreatment history and adolescent risk behavior by examining popularity motivations and peer group control. *Journal of Youth and Adolescence, 38*, 1253–1263.

Eltringham, S., & Aldridge, J. (2000). The extent of children's knowledge of court as estimated by guardians ad litem. *Child Abuse Review*, *9*, 275–286.

European Convention on Human Rights, Section 1, Article 6[3] (1953).

Faller, K.C. (2007). *Interviewing Children About Sexual Abuse: Controversies and Best Practice.* New York: Oxford University Press.

Flin, R., Boon, J., Knox, A., & Bull, R. (1992). The effects of a five month delay on children's and adults' eyewitness memory. *British Journal of Psychology*, *83*, 323–336.

Flin, R.H., Stevenson, Y., & Davies, G.M. (1989). Children's knowledge of court proceedings. *British Journal of Psychology*, *80*, 285–297.

Friedrich, W.N. (1993). Sexual victimization and sexual behavior in children: A review of recent literature. *Child Abuse and Neglect*, *17*, 59–66.

Ghetti, S., Alexander, K.W., Goodman, G.S. (2002). Legal involvement in child sexual abuse cases: Consequences and interventions. *International Journal of Law and Psychiatry. Special Issue: Children in the Forensic System*, *25*, 235–251.

Goodman, G.S., & Quas, J.A. (2008). Repeated interviews and children's memory: It's more than just how many. *Current Directions in Psychological Science*, *17*, 386–390.

Goodman, G.S., Quas, J.A., Bulkley, J., & Shapiro, C. (1999). Innovations for child witnesses: A national survey. *Psychology, Public Policy, and the Law*, *5*, 255–281.

Goodman,G.S., Quas, J.A., & Ogle, C.M. (2010). Child maltreatment and memory. *Annual Review of Psychology*, *61*, 325–351.

Goodman, G.S., Sharma, A., Thomas, S.F, & Considine, M.G. (1995). Mother knows best: Effects of relationship status and interviewer bias on children's memory. *Journal of Experimental Child Psychology*, *60*, 195–228.

Goodman, G.S., Taub, E.P., Jones, P.P., England, P., Port, L.K. & Prado, L. (1992). Testifying in criminal court: Emotional effects on child sexual assault victims. *Monographs of the Society for Research in Child Development*, *57*(5), Serial No. 229.

Goodman, G.S., Toby, A.E., Batterman-Faunce, J.M., Orcutt, H., Thomas, S., Shapiro, C., & Sashsenmaier, T. (1998). Face to face confrontation: Effects of closed circuit technology on children's eyewitness testimony and juror's decision. *Law and Human Behavior, 22*, 165–203.

Goodman-Brown, T.B., Edelstein, R.S., Goodman, G.S., Jones, D.P.H., & Gordon, D.S. (2003). Why children tell: A model of children's disclosure of sexual abuse. *Child Abuse and Neglect, 27*, 525–540.

Gray, E. (1993). *Unequal Justice: The Prosecution of Child Sexual Abuse*. New York, NY: Free Press.

Grisso, T. (1997). The competence of adolescents as trial defendants. *Psychology, Public Policy, and Law, 3*, 3–32.

Hall, S., & Sales, B. (2008). *Courtroom Modifications for Child Witnesses*. Washington, DC: APA.

Hébert, M., Tremblay, C., Parent, N., Daignault, I. V., & Piché, C. (2006). Correlates of behavioral outcomes in sexually abused children. *Journal of Family Violence, 21*, 287–299.

Henry, J. (1997). System intervention trauma to child sexual abuse victims following disclosure. *Journal of Interpersonal Violence, 12*(4), 499–513.

Hunter, J.A., Goodwin, D.W., & Wilson, R.J. (1992). Attributions of blame in child sexual abuse victims: An analysis of age and gender influences. *Journal of Child Sexual Abuse, 1*, 75–89.

International Children's Bureau. (2005). *The Rights of Child Victims and Witnesses of Crime: A Compilation of Selected Provisions Drawn from International and Regional Instruments* (2nd edn). Montréal, Canada: International Children's Bureau.

International Association of Prosecutors. (2001). *Annotated Model Guidelines for the Effective Prosecution of Children, 2001*. Retrieved 20 December 2010 from http://www.icclr.law.ubc.ca/Site%20Map/Programs/Model_Guidelines.htm.

Jones, L.M., Walsh, W.A., & Cross, T.P. (2007). Do Children's Advocacy Centers improve families' experiences of child sexual abuse investigations? *Child Abuse and Neglect, 31*, 1069–1085.

Johnson, K., & Wagner, D. (2005). Evaluation of Michigan's foster care case management system. *Research on Social Work Practice, 15*, 372–380.

Kennedy v. Louisiana, 128 S. Ct. 2641 (2008).

Keeney, K.S., Amacher, E., & Kastanakis, J.A. (1992). The court prep group: A vital part of the court process. In H. Dent, & R. Flin (Eds), *Children as Witnesses* (pp. 201–209). Chichester, UK: Wiley.

Khoury, A. (2006). Seen and heard: Involving children in dependency court. *Child Law Practice, 25*, 145–155.

La Rooy, D., Lamb, M.E., & Pipe, M.E. (2009). Repeated interviewing: A critical evaluation of the risks and potential benefits. In K. Kuehnle, & M. Connell (Eds), *The Evaluation of Child Sexual Abuse Allegations: A Comprehensive Guide to Assessment and Testimony* (pp. 327–362). Chichester, UK: Wiley.

Liang, B., Williams, L., & Siegel, J. (2006). Relational outcomes of childhood sexual trauma in female survivors: A longitudinal study. *Journal of Interpersonal Violence, 21*, 1–16.

Lillie & Reed v. Newcastle City Council & Ors. (1994). EWHC 252 (QB).

Lyon, T.D. (2002). Applying suggestibility research to the real world: The case of repeated questions. *Law and Contemporary Problems, 65*, 97–126.

Malloy, L.C., & Lyon, T.D. (2006). Caregiver support and child sexual abuse: Why does it matter? *Journal of Child Sexual Abuse, 15*, 97–103.

Malloy, L.C., Lyon, T.D., & Quas, J.A. (2007). Filial dependency and recantations of child sexual abuse allegations. *Journal of the American Academy of Child and Adolescent Psychiatry*, *46*, 162–170.

Mannarino, A.P., Cohen, J.A., & Berman, S.R. (1994). Children's Attribution and Perception Scale: A new measure of sexual abuse-related factors. *Journal of Clinical Psychology*, *23*, 204–211.

Maryland v. Craig (1990). 497 US 836, 110 S. Ct. 3157.

McAuliff, B. D., Maurice, K. A., Neal, E. S., & Diaz, A. (2008). 'She should have been more upset. . .': Expectancy violation theory and jurors' perceptions of child victims. Paper presented at the annual meeting of the American Psychology–Law Society, Jacksonville, FL.

Menard, K.S., & Ruback, R.B. (2003). Prevalence and processing of child sexual abuse: A multi-data-set analysis of urban and rural counties. *Law and Human Behavior*, *27*, 385–402.

National Society for the Prevention of Cruelty to Children. (2009). Policy summary: Young witness support. Retrieved 20 December 2010 from http://www.nspcc.org.uk/Inform/policyandpublicaffairs/policysummaries/YoungWitnessSupport_wdf61908.pdf.

New Zealand, Children, Young Persons and Their Families Act (1989).

Oates, R.K., & Tong, L. (1987). Sexual abuse of children: An area with room for professional reforms. *Medical Journal of Australia*, *147*, 544–548.

Perry, N., McAuliffe, B.D., Tam, P., Claycomb, L., Dostal, C., & Flanagan, C. (1995). When lawyers question children. Is justice served? *Law and Human Behavior*, *19*, 609–629.

Peterson-Badali, M., Abramovitch, R., & Duda, J. (1997). Young children's legal knowledge and reasoning ability. *Canadian Journal of Criminology*, *39*, 145–170.

Plotnikoff, J., & Woolfson, R. (2004). *In Their Own Words: The Experiences of 50 Young Witnesses in Criminal Proceedings*. London: NSPCC.

Plotnikoff, J., & Woolfson, R. (2009). *Measuring Up? Evaluating Implementation of Government Commitments to Young Witnesses in Criminal Proceedings*. NSPCC: London.

Putnam, F.W. (2003). Ten-year research update review: Child sexual abuse. *Journal of the American Academy of Child and Adolescent Psychiatry*, *42*(3), 269–278.

Quas, J.A., Cooper, A., & Wandrey, L. (2009). Child victims in dependency court. In B. L. Bottoms, C.J. Najdowski, & G.S. Goodman (Eds), *Children as Victims, Witnesses, and Offenders: Psychological Science and the Law* (pp. 128–149), New York: Guilford Press.

Quas, J.A., Goodman, G.S., Ghetti, S., Alexander, K.W., Edelstein, R., Redlich, A.D., Cordon, I.M., & Jones, D.P.H. (2005). Childhood sexual assault victims: Long-term outcomes after testifying in criminal court. *Monographs of the Society for Research in Child Development*, *70*, 1–145.

Quas, J.A., & Lench, H. (2007). Arousal at encoding, arousal at retrieval, interviewer support, and children's memory for a mild stressor. *Applied Cognitive Psychology*, *21*, 289–305.

Quas, J.A., Malloy, L., Melinder, A.M., D'Mello, M., Goodman, G.S., & Schaaf, J. (2007). Developmental differences in the effects of repeated interviews and interviewer bias on young children's event memory and false reports. *Developmental Psychology*, *43*, 823–837.

Quas, J.A., & McAuliff, B.D. (2009). Accommodating child witnesses in the criminal justice system: implications for death penalty cases. In R.F. Schopp,

R.L. Wiener, B.H. Bornstein, & S.L. Willborn (Eds), *Mental Disorder and Criminal Law: Responsibility, Punishment and Competence* (pp. 79–102). New York: Springer.

Quas, J.A., & Schaaf, J.M. (2002). Children's memories of personal experiences following repeated questioning. *Journal of Experimental Child Psychology*, *83*, 304–338.

Quas, J.A., Thompson, W.C., & Clarke-Stewart, A. (2005). Do jurors know what isn't so about child witnesses? *Law and Human Behavior*, *29*, 425–456.

Quas, J.A., Wallin, A.R., Horwitz, B., Davis, E., & Lyon, T.D. (2009). Maltreated children's understanding of and emotional reactions to dependency court involvement. *Behavioral Sciences and the Law*, *27*, 97–117.

Runyan, D., Everson, M., Edelson, G., Hunter, W., & Coulter, M. (1988). Impact of legal intervention on sexually abused children. *Journal of Pediatrics*, *113*, 647–653.

Santilla, P., Korkman, J., & Sandnabba, N. (2004). Effects of interview phase, repeated interviewing, presence of a support person, and anatomically detailed dolls on child sexual abuse interviews. *Psychology, Crime, and Law*, *10*, 21–35.

Sas, L., Austin, G., Wolfe, D., & Hurley, P. (1991). *Reducing the system induced trauma for child sexual abuse victims through court preparation, assessment, and follow-up*. Ottawa: NationalWelfare Grant Division, Health and Welfare Canada.

Sas, L.D., Hurley, P., Hatch, A., Malla, S., & Dick, T. (1993). *Three years after the verdict: a longitudinal study of the social and psychological adjustment of child witnesses referred to the child witness project*. Ottawa, Canada: Health and Welfare Canada.

Saywitz, K.J., Goodman, G.S., & Lyon, T.D. (2002). Interviewing children in and out of court: Current research and practice implications. In J.E.B. Myers, & L. Berliner (Eds), *The APSAC Handbook on Child Maltreatment* (2nd edn, pp. 349–377). Thousand Oaks, CA: Sage.

Saywitz, K., Jaenicke, C., & Camparo, L. (1990). Children's knowledge of legal terminology. *Law and Human Behavior*, *14*, 523–535.

Saywitz, K., & Nathanson, R. (1993). Children's testimony and perceived stress in and out of the courtroom. *Child Abuse and Neglect*, *17*(5), 613–622.

Saywitz, K.J., Nathanson, R., Snyder, L., & Lamphear, V. (1993). *Preparing Children for the Investigative and Judicial Process: Improving Communication, Memory and Emotional Resiliency* (Report No. 90CA1179). Washington DC: National Center on Child Abuse and Neglect.

Saywitz, K.J., & Snyder, L. (1993). Improving children's testimony with preparation. In G. Goodman, & B. Bottoms (Eds), *Child Victims, Child Witnesses: Understanding and Improving Children's Testimony* (pp. 117–146). New York: Guilford Press.

Scotland Criminal Procedure Act (1995).

Smith, S.E., & Elstein, G.S. (1993). *The Prosecution of Child Sexual and Physical Abuse Cases*. Washington, DC: American Bar Association Fund for Justice and Education.

Stroud, D.D., Martens, S.L., & Barker, J. (2000). Criminal investigation of child sexual abuse: A comparison of cases referred to the prosecutor to those not referred. *Child Abuse and Neglect*, *24*, 689–700.

Stronger v. Brook, 539 US 607, 649 (2003).

Tedesco, J.F., & Schnell, S.V. (1987). Children's reactions to sex abuse investigation and litigation. *Child Abuse and Neglect*, *11*, 267–272.

Thompson, R.A. (1994). Social support and the prevention of child maltreatment. In G.B. Melton, & F. Barry (Eds), *Protecting Children from Abuse and Neglect* (pp. 40–130). New York: Guilford.

Tyler, T.R. (1990). *Why People Obey the Law.* New Haven, CT: Yale University Press.

Tyler, T.R., & Lind, E.A. (2001). Procedural justice. In J. Sanders, & V.L. Hamilton (Eds), *Handbook of Justice Research in Law* (pp. 65–92). Dordrecht, Netherlands: Kluwer.

United Kingdom, Children Act (1989).

United Kingdom, Youth Justice and Criminal Evidence Act (1999).

United Nations Convention on the Rights of the Child (1990).

United Nations Guidelines on Justice in Matters Involving Child Victims and Witnesses of Crime (2009).

US Child Abuse and Treatment Act (1974).

US Department of Health and Human Services, Children's Bureau. (2009). *Child Maltreatment 2008*. Retrieved 10 May 2010 from www.acf.hhs.gov/programs/cb/pubs/cm07/index.htm.

Walker, A.G. (1993). Questioning young children in court: A linguistic case study. *Law and Human Behavior*, *17*, 59–81.

Walsh, W.A., Lippert, T., Cross, T.P., Maurice, D.M., & Davison, K. (2008). How long to prosecute child sexual abuse for a community using a children's advocacy center and two comparison communities? *Child Maltreatment*, *13*, 3–13.

Whitcomb, D. (1991). Improving the investigation and prosecution of child sexual-abuse cases: Research findings, questions, and implications for public policy. In D.D. Knudsen, & J.L. Miller (Eds), *Abused and Battered: Social and Legal Responses to Family Violence* (pp. 181–190). New York: A. de Gruyter.

Whitcomb, D., Runyan, D., De Vos, E., Hunter, W., Cross, T., Everson, M., Peeler, N., Porter, C., Toth, P., & Cropper, C. (1991). *The Child Victim as a Witness*. Washington, DC: Office of Juvenile Justice and Delinquency Prevention.

White, M., Albers, E., & Bitonti, C. (1996). Factors in length of foster care: Worker activities and parent–child visitation. *Journal of Sociology and Social Welfare*, *23*, 75–84.

Zajac, R., Gross, J., & Hayne, H. (2003). Asked and answered: Questioning children in the courtroom. *Psychiatry, Psychology and Law*, *10*, 199–209.

17

Expert Testimony

Bryan Tully

WHAT IS EXPECTED FROM EXPERT TESTIMONY?

This chapter arises from my two decades of experience as an expert witness providing testimony throughout the United Kingdom as a registered clinical and forensic psychologist, and chartered neuropsychologist. The courts are increasingly turning to psychologists for assistance in an increasingly broad range of matters. In my experience, these have included disputed confessions made to police by vulnerable people, juvenile and vulnerable witnesses and complainants, personal injury outcomes, parental capacity, and post-traumatic stress disorder. To be considered an expert, capacity in three main areas is needed. First, the expert must have a detailed understanding of the research in the field and be sensitive to (and willing to report) alternative points of view about the data gathered. Secondly, the expert must be able to apply those findings professionally to the facts of the case and inquire after further facts if that turns out to be necessary. Thirdly, the expert sometimes has to undertake assessments of memory, cognitive functioning, language ability, psychological disorders, and the emotional and developmental status of children and adults.

Children's Testimony: A Handbook of Psychological Research and Forensic Practice, Second Edition.
Edited by Michael E. Lamb, David J. La Rooy, Lindsay C. Malloy, and Carmit Katz.

The field of children's testimony demands on occasion all the above capacities. The expert witness psychologist is therefore called to offer an opinion in those legal cases where any or all parties consider there may be factors in the gathering or presentation of children's testimony which may support confidence in that testimony or question the confidence that can be placed in it and so add caution to such consideration. The ultimate question as to whether that testimony directly or indirectly supports the issue before the court is, of course, a matter for the court alone. The expert must understand this difference clearly, else he/she may add to the problems of evidential evaluation rather than assisting. The expert is expected to interpret the evidence-based research that is available and to apply that research to the case in hand. Each requires its own skill and competence.

Much of the research into children's testimony concerns the investigative interview (Lamb, Hershkowitz, Orbach, & Esplin, 2008). That is of core and critical importance of course but it is only one part of the wider investigation. The psychologist must have a good grasp of other issues that will bear on credibility and indeed those issues should have been of concern to investigators. One such issue is the developmental status of the child. Much research on children's testimony is age-related (Westcott, Davies, & Bull, 2002). More often than not this issue is glossed over by investigators who assume normal development. This is a key area which a critical expert will address if the investigator has ignored the issue. The answer, from the investigator's point of view, is not to ignore it. Expert witnesses in children's testimony cases are seldom asked to assess a child themselves (e.g., to take a psychological history and administer assessment instruments and protocols). This may have been undertaken by someone else and the original data may or may not have been provided and need interpretation in the context of the interview and how the child has been managed before the investigative interview has taken place. Assessment issues which may affect the conduct of the interview and the credibility of the resulting evidence, include developmental and intellectual levels or emotional and communication disabilities. In many cases the expert may only have to hand an impression gained from the performance of the child in one or more interviews.

Sometimes investigators detect that a child has a 'communication difficulty' which may or may not be related to general developmental delay or may be very specific arising out of a distinctive and diagnosable developmental disorder. Where it is assumed that the communication difficulty is due to such a developmental disorder (and not just lack of motivation or emotional conflict), some jurisdictions allow for an intermediary to facilitate the children's capacity to provide intelligible answers or narrative or to appreciate what the interviewer is asking. Such intermediaries are often developmental therapists (such as speech and language therapists). They have their own protocols which are supposedly good fits with the protocols that comprise the guidance to the investigative interviewer. For example, in the United Kingdom, the interviewing guidance is *Achieving Best Evidence in Criminal Proceedings* (ABE; Home Office, 2007). The guidance is designed to optimize the collection of children's testimony at a standard that will be good enough for criminal proceedings, although the same video-recorded interviews are actually used even more frequently in family proceedings where the welfare of the child is paramount. The intermediaries are supposed to follow their own *Intermediary Procedure Guidance Manual* (Criminal Justice System, 2005). General principles are similar to those found in the ABE protocols but there are enough differences to make the task of expert evidence more complex where an intermediary has been used. There is ground for conflict of evidence because intermediaries are likely to think of themselves as something of an expert in the field of the communication disability that they are addressing. In spite of their guidance, they are usually unaware of the large area of research that indicates how children's testimony can be jeopardized. This means there is a danger they come to the aid of an interviewer who is getting little response, offering techniques such as pictures and stick figures. Their own protocol requires that their preliminary assessment demonstrates that the techniques work in the way they are supposed to *with that child*. The savvy expert will ask for that evidence. The least controversial aspect of intermediaries' work is where they help the interviewer plan carefully how to ask questions and how to check the child has properly understood, before the interview starts. That can help avoid pitfalls. As Mahoney has pointed out: 'When an Intermediary is used as part of the interviewing process it adds a new dynamic to the interview room' (Mahoney, 2009). This is a key area for the investigative interviewer because if he/she employs an intermediary and causes significant delay as a result or lets the intermediary take the initiative in 'facilitating' testimony from a child, then the investigator may find him/herself criticized for losing control of the interviewing protocol laid down in the guidelines. The answer is to learn from the intermediary but maintain control of the interview.

The provenance of the accounts or utterances which come to be considered evidence of abuse or wrongdoing is very important. It may be that a single comment made by a child has led to a detailed formal structured and recorded interview within 24 hours. That is ideal. Far from ideal and far more frequent are cases where a child may have made a number of utterances and been questioned on those by parents or other caretakers who are neither trained interviewers nor aware of the risks of suggestive questions and of providing misleading information. Such adults seldom make much of a record of what has been said and very rarely keep a verbatim contemporaneous record. The expert has to form some overall view of how far this has happened and what impact it is likely to have and whether any sign of what has happened at this stage appears in the structured and recorded interviews with the child protection investigator. This is a key area for the investigator to consider, partly because most guidelines imply that the interviewer should be aware of all these provenances when planning the interview. Failing to do so when this other evidence will be addressed by any competent expert, is to invite an attack on the probative value of whatever has come out of the interview. The answer is not to fail to take this into account when planning and to have developed a reasonable view of the earlier exchanges with the child, before being asked about this for the first time in the witness box.

A particular form of provenance affecting the child's account of an event is therapy. Where the court, properly informed, appreciates a child's need for psychological therapy, then such therapy may be authorized for the benefit of the child even if that may compromise evidence for legal proceedings. The informed therapist will have liaised with the prosecutor or civil court to ensure that all is done properly and that inadvertent occasions of contaminating or 'tainting' testimony are avoided as far as is practical. The therapist will take a careful history and evaluate the intensity or seriousness of the presenting difficulties. As time passes, comparative evaluations should give an idea of improvement in the child's functioning or not. This, as part of continuing history, may cast light on the assumed abuse and may show that some abuse actually started earlier or some other life history event is far more closely associated with the psychological difficulty than the index suspected abuse. All of this will be evident from good records kept throughout and thus available to the expert and the court. It can do nothing but assist the investigative interviewer to be aware of how this other narrative has been unfolding and how far that fits with what is emerging in the investigative interview. This too is a key area for the investigative interviewer. Failing to appreciate the harm or the help such therapeutic interviews may cause to the perceived veracity of the child's testimony will only make the evidence collector look less competent and hence, by implication, diminish the value of the child's evidence itself. Discovering from therapeutic notes that the child has tried to cope with the alleged offences, or tried successfully or unsuccessfully to avoid the circumstances or persons associated with abuse, will provide the interviewer with additional points to cue the child's narrative, which he/she might not otherwise have chosen, especially if trying to employ open questions.

Many abusive experiences leave a child victimized which may affect their patterns of attachmen-related behaviours, their sexualized behaviours, and their poor emotional regulation, which may be attributable to disordered/disorganized attachment, conduct difficulties, attention deficit hyperactivity disorder (ADHD), and so on. These are all 'look alike' presentations up to a point. At interview, investigators usually do their best to overcome these behaviours because what they seek are specific narratives of particular abusive acts committed at one time or another, or repeated in one place or another. However, the display of these behaviours, when linked in the narrative to the history of the allegations, can help the interviewer refer to and consolidate one kind of evidence (e.g., coping reactions) with another (e.g., assertions of what happened). That comes across as more telling and persuasive. Criminal proceedings require specific indictments and the child's evidence has to be specific and credible enough to support each indictment. This usually leads to the investigators missing or deliberately avoiding exploring issues of the full presentation of distress and difficulty the child may have in one or more settings. There are some adult behaviours that are offence-related although not necessarily *so* related so as to be useable in criminal proceedings. The presence of those behaviours and patterns of relationship, however, may help a Family Court to conclude that a child has been abused or neglected and that no-one has intervened when it would have been reasonable to do so. That may be enough to help a Family Court decide a child has been harmed and is at risk of further harm without some kind of court order. Since the investigative interviews may only pick up fragments and suggestions of these issues for the reasons given above, the expert may further assist by spelling out what needs to be looked for in other settings (e.g., observed contact sessions with a suspected parent). The collection of evidence is not always a one-off interview, especially in complex cases. Where an interviewer detects unresolved comments or styles of behaviour, this can assist an expert to advise on further settings and approaches to collect further evidence. Although the proceedings may be legally adversarial, all professionals involved with the court need to understand that their job is to cooperate to assist the court in its fact-finding mission. Interviewers and experts are not opponents save where they are genuinely offering conflicting evidence.

In England and Wales, the ABE guidance is in its second edition, and the first, issued in 2001, was an update on the original *Memorandum of Good Practice* (Home Office, 1992). The original and its successors represent a most careful attempt to incorporate a large range of findings from developmental and investigative psychology, including, of course, issues of memory and its reconstructive malleability, with the rules of evidence needed for court proceedings. The verbatim records allow any party or court to see exactly what was said and how, and in response to exactly what series of questions. It is an enormous benefit that the child can see and hear what he/she said before a trial which may be many months afterwards. The video record can be played in court as evidence-in-chief. Guidelines concerning interviewing practice are becoming increasingly detailed and specific. The more items of instructed perfection listed, the more a diligent expert or lawyer can pick out those as having been 'in breach'. The most common breaches are using leading and alternative (option posing) questions and failing to establish the ground rules of the interview with the child adequately. Do breaches matter? Presumably they do, or there would be no point in going to all the trouble to try to get things right. The expert's task is to take these breaches and relate them to the implications that arise from the research and apply those to the particular case. This is not always easy. A similar issue faces those who evaluate disputed or query false or compromised confessions to police (Gudjonsson, 2003). From the interviewer's point of view, it is essential to be aware of what breaches or departures from protocol have been committed. It is better to steal thunder, as they say, by advancing these self-criticisms and weighing those against more persuasive reasons which would support resilience of the evidence. For example, even a series of leading and suggestive questions can be mitigated by pointing out how often the interviewee corrected or failed to follow a suggested lead. Leading and suggestive questions do most damage in the context of uncertain memory. A similar or coherent answer found in a completely different part of the interview record may well support credibility even when one of those utterances was obtained in a less than satisfactory way. However, interviewers must be their own critics first and have such mastery over their material that they can perform this rebuttal function in the witness box.

WEAKNESSES IN, AND ATTACKS ON THE VERACITY OF CHILDREN'S TESTIMONY

The diligent expert is likely to be instructed at different times by all kinds of parties in legal proceedings. It is a duty whoever instructs to look searchingly for any factor that may have jeopardized a child's testimony and to state that clearly. If instructed by a prosecutor, the prosecutor may withdraw the case or a judge dismiss at an early stage. Those decisions are not the responsibility of the expert. As already intimated, investigators insofar as trained with an awareness of research-based good practice, should apply their own critical minds to what has been produced in the course of their investigations to see if any weaknesses may be redressed or that other evidence could be brought forward to weigh in the overall balance. Neither investigator nor expert will have heard all the evidence. Trials have a funny habit of taking their own course and fresh evidence suddenly produced half-way through or later may have an unexpected consequence.

Some aspects of weakness in children's testimony arise more frequently than others. If there are any aspects of a child's development that have implications for memory then for the interviewer not to know this and to plough on during the interview using normal adult grammar and vocabulary is asking for trouble, even if that trouble is only detected on one or two occasions. Doubts may generalize to other issues. Children with certain developmental disabilities (including autistic spectrum disorders) may be more prone to incorporate what an interviewer seems to be looking for and echoing the interviewer's words. On one occasion when an interviewer late in the day began to wonder about this and asked again how a child actually knew something, he received a series of repeated comments 'lucky guess'. That pretty well ruined the interview. It can be difficult to interview a child who is not keen to be interviewed, is distracted, or genuinely not interested. If at all possible, it is worth the interviewer *understanding* exactly why this is and trying to deal with this then or on other occasions, before going into the evidential issues. Further inquiry as to the child's usual behaviour and demeanour and how that varies, and ensuring that the interview does not run onto the evidential issues before the child seems happy being interviewed on non-evidential issues (and giving longer answers) are practical ways for the investigative interviewer to forestall this kind of criticism in court. This criticism will be forthcoming from lawyers and experts where the child's answers are extracted as if pulling teeth, are given with a casual throwaway tone, or as one of several topics switched between rapidly. Where a child hops from one topic to another without giving the suspected events the seriousness that might be expected, this may come across unconvincingly.

It is worth bearing in mind that in many jurisdictions, no expert can bolster the evidence of a complainant in criminal proceedings. The complainant witness must be convincing in and of themselves. An exception is made where the defence, for example, calls an expert who proceeds to identify various weaknesses or breaches which are argued to erode confidence so much the material cannot be accepted. If that opinion is controversial, then the prosecution can call its own expert who may rebut what has been said by the other. The interviewer may or may not get a chance to say much. Courts do not like experts disagreeing or 'battles of experts' and there is often an inclination (in the United Kingdom at least) for the experts to be directed to meet, discuss, and then draw up lists of common opinions about which there is agreement. In real life practice, experts (called only when court proceedings are imminent) and investigative interviewers rarely talk to each other, the highway of communication being led throughout by lawyers. Whether formally or informally, interviewers can decide to do otherwise and it would likely enhance their practice in the long run. Workshops and conferences are the obvious opportunity for such exchanges.

INTERVIEWERS AVOIDING PITFALLS

The guidances to interviewers are based on research-based evidence and therefore it behoves interviewers to follow those guidelines as far as possible and depart only when there is a careful, well thought out reason to do so. Interviewing the older, intellectually capable child, about recent events, is easier and can be conducted without taking so much time dealing with ground rules and rapport. Some children clearly get frustrated as the interviewer ploughs his/her way through a lot of preliminaries, clearly unnecessary to that particular case. Most guidances emphasize how important it is for interviewers to prepare for their interviews (see Chapter 5). That is certainly worthwhile. Failure to even realize a child has been doing poorly at school, has been referred for speech therapy, has been interviewed before and said certain things to a different interviewer, is asking for trouble and the throwing of doubt by other parties and their experts. If asked whether having now appreciated what was not understood before makes any difference to the way the interviewer *would have* conducted part of the interviewer, that invites the interviewer to weaken the confidence that can be placed on that part of the interview, almost whatever answer they give, especially a simple 'yes' or 'no'. Experts also find these sorts of questions difficult to field if they have not anticipated them.

It is worth thinking twice about explaining that the purpose of the interview is just to let the nice police lady interviewer 'sort things out' when the clear purpose is to get enough evidence to arrest dad. The pitfall here, especially with the older child who may have his/her own agenda about prosecutions and break up of the family, is that a retraction is made further down the line once the child realizes what is happening. That child's view may be open to many influences. Usually, a retraction by the main or only complainant is fatal to a prosecution case in criminal proceedings. Often the retraction is brief or with a note. However, occasionally investigators have conducted a structured video-recorded interview concerning this new and contrary evidence. The outcome, as we shall see below under the topic of the child's credibility, can be surprisingly helpful to the investigative interviewer. The interviewer needs to think in advance of an age-appropriate way of telling the child what is going on without misleading them. Picking up whether the child has a view about what should happen to the accused person can be informative and alert the interviewer to problems that might arise later. Some older children especially, can come to a point where they agree that a wise judge should decide what happens eventually, rather than the child being responsible for outcomes.

Even, or especially if obtaining an account is difficult, exploring how the child feels about the suspected person is worthwhile (i.e., can be productive and aid understanding). Children often go on to say something once their natural talk begins to flow. Dad may be nice *except* when he starts to do certain things. It would be good if that stopped. Perhaps the child does recall first time, second time, and last time clearly and differentiates them. If not, the attempt to solicit such recall in those terms may lead to an account that will vary in future cross-examination. Very often a child recalls a script memory of repeated abuse acts. It is worth allowing the child to report fully in gist fashion, without interruption, if that seems the most natural way for them to report in the first instance. They can subsequently be asked if certain events have happened one time or more than one time. Sometimes the cognitive process of generating the gist memory narrative by the child will prompt a retrieved recall of an instance or episode where things went differently, perhaps not as much or as bad as before, or because of a complication or interruption. Such exceptionality is recalled because that exceptionality was important to the child. It may be a fragment of episodic memory but it will count all the more if it arises spontaneously. There is no rule to say that fragments of episodic memory need be in any sense complete. It is good if the child spontaneously provides accounts of efforts to avoid abuse but the child may say nothing because there was no *effective* effort. Bringing this up at the appropriate time and without any hint of reproach, may prompt the child to tell the interviewer of *mental* efforts to avoid by distraction and so on. If that is new material spontaneously given from that point on that is good evidence. Once speaking of subjective mental states the child may speak of other such states or find excusing states for the suspected perpetrator. That can be convincing and telling evidence. A similar effect may be found when combining invitational open questions with having the child make a drawing. The act itself seems to help the child to comment on what was happening (Katz, Yang Lamb, & La Rooy, 2009).

Perhaps the most common pitfall is the desire on the part of interviewers to extract every tiny detail a child might provide in answer to numerous questions. If a child spontaneously offers blocks of free narrative then of course collecting as much as possible is a good idea. However, a long drawn out process where virtually all the child's answers are very short, or answers to alternative/option posing questions, creates a hostage to fortune. A child will try and answer where a reasonable guess can be figured out, and that is *not* an episodic memory per se. Asking which hand or which finger was used is a frequent example of a question that does not need to be asked, and where later the same question may elicit an equally reasonable answer but a different one. A child may recall her knickers being taken down but asking whether it was a straight pull or if the waistband was folded over is not smart. Neither is asking a child what he/she was wearing on an occasion weeks or months before. Contextualized cued open questions can be very useful if the interviewer feels this is something they really need to know: 'Are you able to remember anything else about *that*?'

The original *Memorandum of Good Practice* (Home Office, 1992) in the United Kingdom was partially developed with a view that spontaneous free narrative would allow certain features of that narrative to emerge which could be used for credibility assessment. Those features will be discussed below more fully, but the point to be made here is that if the interviewer and monitor of the interview are not detecting any such features then the earlier they ask *why*, the better. There can be authentic reasons why the real memory of an abusive event is rendered with few of the recognizable features that are associated with credibility, but it is easiest to establish those early on. On the other hand, where these sorts of features are forthcoming in relation to a particular event or relationship, it is a mistake to change the subject too quickly before all such commentary (sometimes called the emotional commentary) is expressed. Once a child (or indeed adult) realizes that his/her reactions and subjective feelings are just as important as which room he/she was in and which pyjamas he/she was wearing, the more likely he/she will provide that sort of narrative in relation to the course of events (Griffiths, 1985).

Another pitfall is to make it all too obvious that the interview is simply a collection device for quantities of evidence which, once the basket is full, will be used for prosecution. That may happen if there has been a preliminary interview in which the interviewer has asked questions, not recorded them verbatim, and decided in their mind the child has been abused. Following that, the subsequently videotaped

ABE/structured interview may come across as a rehearsed performance on both sides. There is little truly 'investigative' in such interviews. Failing to ask about other unhappy victimizing events may result in other genuine acts of abuse being overlooked, or to an alert that this is one of those rare children who are persistent complainers with usual psychopathology associated. A frequent defence by accused estranged partners/parents is that the child was coached by a malicious resident parent opposing contact. All hypotheses should be given due consideration and the child should be gently questioned about what he/she has said to others and what mother thinks, or auntie thinks, keeping the investigator's views (whatever they may be) neutral and non-judgemental. A child cannot *guess* what an adult is thinking, but asked that question they often spontaneously give an episode of speech or action that supports their view. If significant material of this kind is only brought out by others later, then the investigative interviewer begins to looked naïve and biased.

DEFENDING ATTACKS ON INTERVIEWS WITH CHILDREN

Adherence to Guidelines

The guidances are for guidance. Most aspects do not have a force of law. Nevertheless, the fact that the guidance is researched-based makes any inadvertent departure seem incompetent and careless of the quality of evidence. If significant departures are to be made, have good information or argument ready to support what was a thoughtful decision. The best way an interviewer can protect their interview and the evidence so gathered is to try and scrupulously keep to the guidances that have been developed. If the interviewer can anticipate what a fair advocate would ask when acting for the accused person, it will help to ask that in the present and in a neutral way. If a child is asked about various other adults, for example, and the child makes accusations against each of those adults, there is reason to question why.

Repetition of Questions

Asking questions twice within a short time period just because the first time did not elicit much or what was expected, has disadvantages. Research shows that when questions are repeated in interviews with children they sometimes produce answers that are different to their previous ones. This is so, even when in experiments the first answer is known to be right (Krahenbuhl, Blades, & Eiser, 2009). However, it is also true that retrieval maybe less than 100% on any given occasion, and motivational variables may be more favourable on another occasion. A second interview some time later may be the best way of eliciting important new memories which are not just elaborations or efforts to please or alternatives which a child produces because their first answer is thought by them to be wrong because the interviewer is asking twice within the same interview. Where an investigative interviewer can see at an early stage that a child is difficult to interview or needs to make clear to the child the need for details – without at the same time coaxing and suggesting – then allowing the first interview to be a practice interview where the child recalls detail of a neutral episodic memory of a significant life event, can be useful. Preliminary research supports the idea that the child *learns* to be a better interviewee in the substantive interview without the interviewer *then* resorting to closed or leading questions (see Chapter 7). This reduces potential criticism which an expert witness may make on the validity of the investigative interview.

Summaries

Another way that investigative interviewers try to protect the solidity of their evidence is to recapitulate what the child has (apparently) said. Guidances such as ABE do allow for such a summary to be made towards the end of the interview, and should there be a major misunderstanding, then this is one more opportunity for the child to say so and qualify. If the summary is clearly wrong or in conflict with what has been said in the body of the interview, then anyone can see that and raise the issue. Some British police interviewers, however, have taken to recapitulating after every few minutes of question and answer. This doubles the length of the interview, which is not an inconsiderable matter for the child and all who come afterwards to view the video record. However, it is almost impossible to repeat exactly what a child has said and the adult's summary or gist may include small but significant upgrades to the child's utterances which then become incorporated into the next stage of the interview. The savvy expert witness will spot and document all these. The effect may be to undermine the child's testimony because it is now so mixed with the adult's summarization. The lesson for the investigative interviewer is to keep such 'Am I correctly understanding you?' checks to a minimum and when such are really called for.

Confidence in Memory

It is a general principle in human cognitive psychology that the subjective confidence of any memory may not be a good guide to the likely accuracy. That is all the more so with immature individuals including children. The confidence with which a child tells a story can be detected and judged, but if the interviewer attempts to shore this up with a question, 'Are you sure?' then the child may regard this as a challenge and either back down or insist that of course they are sure. This doubles the issue of uncertainty there may be. The expert will point this out.

Aftermath Information

Many of the systems of credibility assessment of especially sexual victimization such as Statement Validity Assessment (SVA) have been developed on the basis of what a child or older person states about the alleged abusive event itself, rather than the aftermath experience following the abusive event or after the ending of a series of events. Because it is true that interviewers want to elicit narratives that come across as credible (whether using a particular system of evaluation or none at all), then it is not surprising that the interviewing protocols are related to those credibility features. The (US) National Institute of Child Health and Human Development (NICHD) Protocol is the best known and most extensively tested and promulgated (Lamb *et al.*, 2008). Those who use such a protocol or the ABE in the United Kingdom often stop their investigative interview at the time the abusive events are said to have ended. It is rare for the interview to continue into the aftermath. SVA does not have criterionized codes for aftermath experience. However, the importance of the aftermath experience should not be underestimated. The credit for documenting the importance of this lies not with research psychologists, but with the US military police (Griffiths, 1985). This original research and documentation was based on adult rape victims. However, the principle that the offence is not over when the perpetrator finishes his/her action, generalizes to all. There are a host of adaptive and maladaptive emotional and behavioural aftermath reactions, some overt and some subjective and covert. The aftermath life and relationships for an abused child or older person goes through stages, and recovery, relapse, and reminders all play a part. Of course, the ability to identify aftermath states and actions will be better with older, more mature children. Often, however, the effort by a child to speak of a generally good relationship with a parent which has been spoiled because sometimes he wants her to do things to him, itself opens up new or confirms previous narrative. This subjective interview evidence is far more telling than an expert simply noting that a child has difficulty sleeping or eating, and so on, any of which could be a clinical sign of post abuse maladjustment, but none are good enough to comprise a post abuse forensic signature. If the interviewer gathers aftermath information that can be related to more objective behavioural difficulties then that is likely to be far more telling. The good expert will say so.

EVALUATING THE CREDIBILITY OF THE CHILD'S EVIDENCE

Although investigative interviewers are supposed to be investigating, it is often the case that they give the impression that they believe everything a child states from the beginning and their only issue is how to get the child to say a sufficient quantity that by itself will convince. This is another key area for interviewers because a lack of perceived impartiality on their part may compromise perceived credibility of the child's evidence. Some kind of credibility monitoring is as essential at the investigative stage as at trial. If the interviewer realizes that there are serious inconsistencies or a lack of features associated with credibility (e.g., subjective mental states) where they might be expected, then it makes sense for the interviewer to explore this gently. These questions are likely to be asked during cross-examination when the child's memory may not be so good or the child so trusting of his/her questioner. In an alleged satanic ritual abuse case in Scotland, children claimed various reptiles had been put into their orifices. There was a complete lack of subjective reaction and, further, once those children had been initially taken into care, there was delight described in the case notes when they visited the reptile house at the local zoo. Had the interviewer explored this unlikely post abuse lack of subjective aftermath, she may have kept a more open mind about what had really happened and saved a local panic reaction from becoming overblown.

It is axiomatic that bad interviews can sometimes produce really good evidence. Sadly, the opposite is also true. Therefore, the expert witness in children's testimony is often asked after reviewing the evidence collection process whether there are features in the child's evidence or behaviour that indicate support for the allegations as made or are grounds for suspecting veracity has been compromised. The interviewer needs to understand that others will judge the credibility of their interview output whether it carries 'the ring of truth' – whatever that is, or is based on a more systematic approach. The best known and researched-based methodology is SVA, originally developed by Undeutsch (1982) and then further revised by Stellar and Kohnken (1989). It was developed for investigators but it tends these days to be used by post investigation trial experts. The investigative interviewer with a sound interest in credibility and its discernment will take an interest in the approaches that are used, and have some appreciation and comment to make about either the presence or absence of features that tend to be more likely associated with real as opposed to fabricated accounts.

The SVA procedure requires a background analysis of facts and history or provenance of the allegations. This is followed by an interview which is best semi-structured along the lines of the NICHD Protocol. It is no surprise that better interviews give rise to more material that exhibit credibility features (Lamb *et al.*, 2008). The narrative of the interview is then subjected to a search for features or criteria that are known to be more likely found in accounts arising from authentic real experience (usually of sexual abuse) than in deliberate fabrication. After Stellar and Kohnken's (1989) revisions there are some 19 criteria of different kinds and each defined more or less tightly or loosely. The procedure of searching for and classifying slices of narrative as exhibiting one or another criteria is called Criteria Based Content Analysis (CBCA). Following that there is a review of the total exercise by way of a Validity Checklist. Researchers have focused primarily on CBCA (sometimes writing as if that was the validation procedure all by itself). CBCA is most easily operationalized and researchers can even assign numbers to absence or presence of criteria so that comparisons can be made between narratives believed to come from true stories as opposed to false.

To be succinct, researchers have generally found that more CBCA criteria are identified in accounts that arise from authentic experience than from those that are false (Tully, 1999; Vrij, 2008). However, sometimes the narratives cannot be so easily distinguished, and sometimes the number of criteria in certain true narratives are not much different from the false. Taking many and varied accounts, the statistical differentiation based on CBCA alone is limited and not always so good as to provide a confident conclusion. Some researchers think that is a basis for not using SVA in court, although what is often meant by that sort of statement is that the results should not be used as a 'decision-making' basis to accept a disputed account of what a child complainant states in criminal proceedings. As we have seen, there is a legal bar to that particular exercise in any case. SVA is often misunderstood by researchers who may not have read what expert witnesses actually say to courts in their reports and live evidence. In a sense SVA is based on scientific knowledge and research but is not a standardized scientific technique as, say, DNA analysis. The critical issue is whether the examiner/expert can see whether the evidence is there strongly or not. The stronger the evidence is, the more transparent that becomes to the finder of fact and the less likely the outcome will be disputed.

It may be worthwhile to give an example from an actual case of a fragment comprising a reply to a bad leading question. The child is aged 4 years, nearly 5.

Q Did you see anything coming out of Jack's willy?

A (pause)...No....I didn't see anything...because it was only when he put his willy in my mouth and then he wee'd and it was all salty and horrible. I had to go and get a glass of water afterwards to get rid if it.

First we can see that the bad question does not *in this case* just lead the child on to a guessed answer. She struggles because she cannot answer *that* question. Her *own* memory is eventually retrieved and that explains why she must correct the interviewer. Of course, a child correcting a presumptive interviewer cannot be relied upon. The girl does not fully understand what has happened inside her mouth. That is one of the classic criteria from CBCA (accurate detail misunderstood). There is a fairly strong sensory detail given regarding taste. Some researchers, being very strict, would have difficulty in assigning that to one specific of the 19 CBCA criteria and those trained to rate might say it could belong to either of one or two. That brings down the 'inter-rater reliability' and hence the 'reliability' of the whole procedure if it is insisted it must be standardized in a manner required in a research study which has the purpose to test a hypothesis. Finally, we get an immediate aftermath coping reaction from the child of having to go and get a glass of water when (presumably) the willy has been removed. This then is *supportive* of credibility and that must be considered alongside all the other relevant evidence. This is as strong a statement that a sensible well-grounded expert will come to. The expert witness using SVA is like the forensic pathologist, not just an expert in a technique per se, but rather in how that particular technique does or does not *in a particular case* give rise to data that are open to interpretation. That interpretation is made in the context of expert knowledge of either sexual victimology, for example, or the causes of death in bodies in the case of the pathologist. To put this another way, SVA adds incremental validity to the judgement of overall authenticity in the absence of any better evidence. It enables the finder of fact to see and appreciate the evidence of the child (not the psychologist) with greater acuity and understanding. The investigative interviewer may feel somewhat left out of arguments over credibility (depending on jurisdiction, type of proceeding, and stage to trial) but it is in his/her interests to have an appreciation of the credibility qualities of the testimony being elicited from a child witness. Such awareness can better inform the direction and checking that further interviewing may take.

It was mentioned earlier that one pitfall of an interviewer pressing on regardless of the motivational agenda of the older child, risks a retraction. Younger children retract also, but it is not always easy to find out the reason why they have done so. In some few cases where structured interviews have been carried out on retractions it is also possible to carry out a modified SVA on the retraction statement. The retraction of a false statement requires some account of why and how the idea of producing a false statement first arose and how much time and effort went into composing what seemed like (say) a moderately credible statement by SVA standards. The outcome was obviously not the one expected. How and when did that realization dawn? Then there is the tricky position the fabricator is in now. How to provide a retraction with sufficient excuse for the false allegation so that others will believe the retraction and not consider it false. Generally, retractions which are suspected of being false retractions made after true allegations emerge as woefully thin compared to the allegation. Where there is a combination of moderately credible allegation and woefully thin retraction, both being subjected to examination, in these circumstances, then it can be argued that this actually *adds* probative value to the initial allegation rather than simply detract on the grounds of contradiction (Tully, 2001). Care must be exercised that the simple fact of a retraction should not be for seen as a forensic sign of abuse per se, as came to be held by some who took Summit's (1983) 'child sexual abuse accommodation syndrome' rather too literally.

UNUSUAL AND RARE PRESENTATIONS

Any expert or investigator should be aware of unusual and rare circumstances where the history and narrative of a case have been more carefully and intentionally fabricated than is usual. That has a considerable tendency to mislead. Cases of factitious disorder or factitious victimization often look like terrible real cases of victimization until a particularly incontrovertible piece of evidence throws doubt on the whole narrative. Apart from such obvious incontrovertible issues of fact pointing to at least one matter of falsehood, a suspicious cluster of more than one of the following should alert the investigator or expert to seek advice from someone in this speciality:

- Evidence of teen precursor behaviour of Emotionally Unstable Personality Disorder aka Borderline Personality Disorder.
- Evidence of intense sibling rivalry and/or poor peer relationships.
- Lacking of contextual and psychological details as would be normally expected of a child of that age and experience of serious and repeated abuse.

- The keeping of a diary where fantastic elements are generated before disclosure.
- Demanding of unusual amounts time and 'trust' from serially trusted adults, each given only certain elements of the abusive history or history of abductions with rules of secrecy imposed.
- Lack of subjective aftermath experiences or thoughts save very general dysfunctional behaviour (e.g., self-harming).
- Resistance to investigators or therapists going further than the victim wishes and controls to an unusual degree of efficacy.
- Alleged offender behaviour highly atypical.
- Reports of 'sleep paralysis' phenomena, albeit presented as 'post traumatic'.
- Repeated escalation of story of abuse often going back further than any sign of psychological dysfunction or the early life period of normal infantile amnesia.
- Unwillingness to speak in fluent detail but to make use of nodding or confirmatory writing to anxious investigators who are encouraged to lead by guessing what has happened.
- Withdrawal of limited cooperation when threatened with circumstances that might demonstrate falsity of narrative.

There has been very little research material published on young and teenage presenters of such rare but striking dysfunctions (see Feldman & Eisendrath, 1996; Howells, 1995).

Unlike investigative interviewers or other professional witnesses, expert witnesses are expected to give opinions on matters and data that lie outside their personal purview and examination. Where an opinion arises from a hypothesis that is in any way controversial and there is a significant divergence of opinion, the expert must state this in their report and give reasons why they prefer one opinion over another. The expert can be challenged by a lawyer or indirectly by another expert but any investigative interviewer will be better placed to make rebuttal of an unfair expert opinion (as it applies to them) if they are aware of sources of theoretical support which are less than a library of psychology textbooks. A challenged expert must always be ready to offer the court the scholarly research on which their opinion is based. Two very handy sources (useful for lawyers, investigators, and experts alike) are provided by Heaton-Armstrong, Shepherd, and Wolchover (1999) and Heaton-Armstrong, Shepherd, Gudjonsson, and Wolchover (2006). These volumes are edited by authors from both law and psychology and are written more akin to a legal text. Indeed, they are designed for legal practitioners particularly. Within it is quite easy to find the key research (e.g., why confidence in a memory is not a sure sign of its accuracy). The later volume is an updated edition of the first, but certain topics are dealt very fully in the first and not at all in the second. Therefore, both volumes are extremely useful to refer to.

The work of investigative interviewers and the expert witness psychologists who come along afterwards to see if any holes may be found is one of the most challenging, absorbing, and satisfying realms of professional endeavour. Because of the amount of high quality research on which this work is now based, experts in this field are in high demand. The best fighting armour the investigative interviewer can find for their work to be properly appreciated, is much of the same learning.

REFERENCES

Criminal Justice System. (2005). *Intermediary Procedure Guidance Manual*. London, UK: Ministry of Justice.

Feldman, M., & Eisendrath, S. (1996). *The Spectrum of Factitious Disorders*. Washington DC: American Psychiatric Press.

Griffiths, G. (1985). The overlooked evidence in rape investigations. *FBI Law Enforcement Bulletin* (April 1985, pp. 8–16).

Gudjonsson, G. (2003). *The Psychology of Interrogations and Confessions*. Chichester, UK: Wiley.

Heaton-Armstrong, A., Shepherd, E., & Wolchover, D. (Eds) (1999). *Analysing Witness Testimony; A Guide for Legal Practitioners & Other Professionals*. London: Blackstone.

Heaton-Armstrong, A., Shepherd, E., Gudjonsson, G., & Wolchover, D. (Eds) (2006). *Witness Testimony*. Oxford, UK: Oxford University Press.

Home Office. (1992). *Memorandum of Good Practice*. London UK: Home Office and Department of Health, HMSO.

Home Office. (2001/2007). *Achieving Best Evidence in Criminal Proceedings*. Home Office, Lord Chancellor's Department, Crown Prosecution Service, Department of Health, National Assembly for Wales.

Katz, C., Yang, P.J., Lamb, M., & La Rooy, D. (2009). Finding out 'more' about what happening: The use of drawing, diagrams, and repeated investigative interviews with children. Paper presented to the 2nd International Investigative Interviewing Conference, University of Teesside, UK.

Krahenbuhl, S., Blades, M., & Eiser, C. (2009). The effect of repeated questioning on children's accuracy and consistency in eyewitness testimony. *Legal and Criminological Psychology*, *14* (2), 263–278.

Lamb, M., Hershkowitz, I., Orbach, Y., & Esplin, P. (2008). *Tell Me What Happened: Structured Investigative Interviews of Child Interviews and Witnesses*. Chichester, UK: Wiley.

Mahoney, B. (2009). Achieving best evidence: The role of the registered Intermediary in assisting vulnerable witnesses, police suspects, and defendants to communicate their account to the police and the court. *iIIRG Bulletin*, *2*(1), 226–229.

Stellar, M., & Kohnken, G. (1989). Criteria-based content analysis. In D. Raskin (Ed.), *Psychological Methods for Criminal Investigation and Evidence* (pp. 000–000). New York: Springer.

Summit, R. (1983). The 'child sexual abuse accommodation syndrome'. *Child Abuse and Neglect*, 7, 177–193.
Tully, B. (1999). Statement validation. In D. Canter & L. Allison (Eds), *Interviewing and Deception* (pp. 000–000). Dartmouth, UK: Ashgate.
Tully, B. (2001). The evaluations of retractions in sexual abuse cases. *Child Abuse Review*, *11*, 94–102.
Undeutsch, U. (1982). Statement reality analysis. In A. Trankell (Ed.), *Reconstructing the Past: The Role of Psychologists in Criminal Trials* (pp. 000–000). Stockholm: Norstedt.
Vrij, A. (2008). *Detecting Lies and Deceit* (2nd edn). Chichester, UK: Wiley.
Westcott, H., Davies, G., & Bull, R. (2002). *Children's Testimony: A Handbook of Psychological Research and Forensic Practice*. Chichester, UK: Wiley.

18

Relationship between Research and Practice

Graham M. Davies and Lindsay C. Malloy

Key Points

- In the field of children's eyewitness testimony, there is much to be learned from examining the successes and challenges of the past – from debates about the reliability of children's memory, through conducting investigative interviews with children, to special measures designed for the presentation of children's evidence in court.
- Both basic research and applied research have contributed to advancements in children's testimony.
- Practitioners should pay particular attention to the ecological validity of studies when evaluating research. Researchers have developed creative ways to increase the ecological validity of child witness studies.
- It is important to recognize that simply publishing best-practice guidelines may not be enough to lead to lasting and effective change – training and evaluation are invaluable.
- It is critical for science to inform practice and vice versa. Both researchers and practitioners must be cooperative, respectful, and open to achieve successful outcomes.

Children's Testimony: A Handbook of Psychological Research and Forensic Practice, Second Edition.
Edited by Michael E. Lamb, David J. La Rooy, Lindsay C. Malloy, and Carmit Katz.

- In order to develop good practice, it is imperative that up-to-date research findings reach those who practice in the field. Researchers should consider modes of dissemination that will reach end-users, rather than simply publishing in specialized academic journals.

RELATIONSHIP BETWEEN RESEARCH AND PRACTICE

In the 1990s, the psychological world was convulsed by a debate over the status of 'recovered memories': memories of long-forgotten traumatic events from childhood that surfaced in adulthood, often in the context of therapy. The status of such memories launched what came to be known as the 'memory wars', with practitioners and researchers facing up to each other in conference halls and across courtrooms in cases where the prosecution relied upon a victim's recovered memories (Johnston, 1997; Loftus, 1993, Maclean, 1993). The researchers, drawing on findings demonstrating the malleability of memory, argued that these 'memories' were no more than fictitious constructs encouraged by the suggestions of therapists. The practitioners, based on their clinical experience, argued that partial or complete recovery of stressful childhood occurrences was a regular experience for patients in therapy.

In an effort to dispel this increasingly polarized debate, professional societies, such as the British Psychological Society and the American Psychological Association (APA), formed working parties of researchers and practitioners in an attempt to produce a consensus view. When the APA report eventually appeared (APA Working Group, 1996), after 2 years of wrangling, no consensus had emerged between the practitioners and researchers and they settled for a summary of their rival positions, headed by a short list of points of agreement and those where dissension continued. It is important that the polarized debate illustrated by the recovered memories controversy in adults is not repeated in the current concerns over the qualities of children's memory and event reports. We need to ensure both that research findings translate into effective practice and that guidance acknowledges the realities and complexities that invest 'real life' as opposed to the neat and sterile world of the laboratory.

Getting decisions right in the forensic context is essential, not merely for psychological science, but also for the lives of the vulnerable, particularly children. Lawyers, judges, jurors, social workers, and parents make life-altering decisions affecting children every day and it is important that, whenever possible, such decisions are guided by practice grounded in reliable and applicable research. In this chapter, we begin by considering the sometimes differing goals of basic and applied research and the strengths and drawbacks of these different traditions. We then illustrate the interactions between these two traditions in relation to, first, the ongoing debate on the reliability of children's testimony; secondly, the conduct of investigative interviews with young witnesses; and, thirdly, the presentation of their evidence at court. For each area, we illustrate how basic and applied research has been translated into practical guidance for professionals and the lessons this holds for researchers and practitioners. Finally, we consider the reciprocal benefits for both researchers and practitioners of working more closely together and avoiding the damaging schisms so vividly illustrated by the 'memory wars'.

Basic Research

Instruction in basic research methods forms the bedrock of most first degrees in psychology. Students learn the rudiments of experimental design, the importance of isolating and controlling variables, and generating clear hypotheses from existing psychological theory. Most basic research, whether a student lab report or a submission to an experimental journal, will be judged by these criteria. Following these rules will enable students to contribute to knowledge.

These same rules apply to basic research with children, which will usually be 'motivated by the desire to expand knowledge' (Zigler & Finn-Stevenson, 1999, p. 555). Where attempts are made to seek directly applicable findings, for instance to the memory competencies of young witnesses, it will normally use a sample of conventional school pupils and be conducted in a well-controlled environment such as a mobile laboratory or silent schoolroom. The aim of such research is to develop and test theories regarding memory and suggestibility within a context of rigorous control and sound experimental design. Ethical concerns inevitably limit the range of materials and experiences to which child participants can be exposed. Methodological rigour may dictate the use of questioning procedures or time lags between study and test that bear little resemblance to real-life investigations. As a consequence, there will be an inevitable gap, sometimes amounting to a chasm, between children's experiences under laboratory conditions and those typically relayed by child witnesses at court (Lyon, 1999). For those offering guidance to practitioners, the generalizability and representativeness of even the best-controlled basic research studies will be a perennial concern.

Applied Research

As a consequence, recent years have seen a growth in applied research on memory. The attractions of what is sometimes termed 'real world' or 'everyday memory' research are obvious for both research and practice. A successful demonstration of an effect in the 'real world' of a phenomenon first shown in the laboratory will bolster the robustness and applicability of a theory developed in the laboratory. Conversely, a failure to replicate may suggest factors operating in the wider environment which had not been captured in basic research. Applied memory research has not been without controversy and concerns have been expressed that some studies, in their rush to embrace reality, may flout some of the cannons of good experimental design (Banaji & Crowder, 1989), but researchers and practitioners alike now regard applied studies as a necessary and complementary adjunct to basic research (Gathercole & Collins, 1992).

While some applied research may be aimed at developing and testing a theory in the real world, other research is driven by the more immediate goal of solving a practical problem. For child witnesses and the law, such problems revolve around how law enforcement and the courts may best gather and then accommodate the evidence of children and the weight that can be attached to their statements. The endpoint of such research is usually the production of guidance for practitioners or information for legislators; any contribution to theory is typically a secondary consideration. Such research is frequently undertaken at the request of government departments or other state agencies, such as the police or law commissions. It is sometimes termed 'policy-driven research' or 'action scholarship' (Groark & McCall, 2005) because its aim is to provide knowledge relevant to a particular set of circumstances or in reaction to a specific issue. Furthermore, it is normally conducted in a real-world setting such as a courtroom or interview suite using information provided by actual witnesses. The results of such research are more likely to be published in journals devoted to social policy than experimental research or enjoy even more limited circulation as reports for the practitioners or government departments who commissioned the work.

Basic vs. Applied Research

Both the basic and applied research traditions have contributed to the memory literature and knowledge concerning children's eyewitness testimony, and researchers and practitioners alike need to be aware of the strengths and weaknesses of these two approaches. As we have noted, basic research prizes objectivity and control but may miss out on critical features of realism (sometimes termed 'ecological validity') either in terms of the setting or materials employed or the participants involved. Applied research majors on realism but often the operational requirements of the police or the courts can lead to less than optimal experimental designs (McCall & Green, 2004). No one paradigm has a monopoly of virtue, and good research in both genres is necessary in order to provide a comprehensive guide to theory and practice with regard to child witnesses.

In an ideal world, basic and applied research would enjoy a reciprocal relationship and arrive at the same conclusions, thus achieving 'convergent validity' or 'triangulation'. However, as we shall note in relation to research on children's eyewitness memory, while some areas show this virtuous convergence, others demonstrate that different forms of research do not always lead unequivocally to the same answer. Where convergence fails to occur, this can be caused by several factors including the laboratory research being insufficiently realistic; the applied research lacking some essential control; or its rationale being insufficiently developed or just plain wrong. With these possibilities in mind, we now turn to the first and the most central of the three key areas of debate in the field of children's eyewitness testimony: the reliability of children's memory.

RESEARCH ON THE RELIABILITY OF CHILDREN'S MEMORY

The research literature on child witnesses shows a curious U-shaped curve: it either dates from before the First World War or has been undertaken in the last 40 years. The reasons for this tell us much about the development of psychology as a discipline. When researchers began to explore the mysteries of memory, they were drawn to witnessing as one of the early areas of application, but the advent of behaviourism, with its focus on basic learning processes and rejection of 'memory' as too mentalistic a concept, stunted progress (Miller, 2003). It was only with the growth of cognitive psychology in the 1980s, coupled with increasing social concerns surrounding the reliability and credibility of witnesses, which brought the topic once more to the forefront.

Early Research on Children's Testimony

The first wave of experimental research emphasized the vulnerability of children to suggestion and leading questions, and reached pessimistic conclusions regarding their reliability as witnesses (Binet, 1900; Stern, 1910; Varendonck, 1911). Judged by the standards of today, some of these studies inevitably suffer from methodological weaknesses and limitations, but many of their insights had to await rediscovery by a later generation of researchers. Varendonck (1911), for instance, was one of the first to demonstrate high levels of suggestibility in response to leading questions in his studies involving groups of 7- and 8-year-old Belgian schoolchildren. Many of the children did not merely accede to a suggestion concerning a non-existent stranger on school premises, but went on to describe the individual and the circumstances in which they had observed him (confabulation). Varendonck used these findings as part of his testimony for the defence in a murder trial, where the principal evidence against the accused came from two witnesses of a similar age who had been asked questions similar to those used by Varendonck in his research. On the basis of this one study, he concluded that children could not be relied upon to give accurate testimony and that their suggestibility was inexhaustible.

Binet (1900) had reported similar effects some years previously, but his analysis of the process by which children report false information was altogether more subtle. Binet noted that some children went along with a misleading statement, only to confide the correct answer to him outside of the experimental situation. These findings led Binet to conclude that suggestibility was as much a product of social conformity and compliance to authority as to actual changes in memory representations. It seems likely that all three factors contributed to the very high levels of suggestibility observed in Varendonck's research (Davies, 2003).

Alongside theoretical insights, there were also important methodological distinctions in the early research concerning children's suggestibility. Stern (1910) conducted a developmental study involving young people from 7 to 18 years observing and recalling the content of a picture. He observed that accuracy of free recall was least effected by age, but that younger children were much more influenced in their reports by leading questions than older children or young adults. Stern also introduced the important distinction between 'picture tests' of the kind used in his own and Binet's studies and 'event tests' involving an unexpected incident staged in front of unprepared participants (though Stern himself appears never to have used this technique with children; Ceci & Bruck, 1995). The skepticism as to children's witness competency reflected in these early studies also paralleled the thrust of the law in the United Kingdom and the United States, which had established formidable legal obstacles to prevent the courts from hearing the evidence of children or expert testimony from psychologists or psychiatrists regarding their prowess (Spencer & Flin, 1993).

Revival of Research Interest in Children's Testimony

In the late 1970s, increasing concerns over the prevalence of child sexual and physical abuse and the need for a proper evidence-base on which to assess the reliability of children's allegations led to a revival of research interest, led by the US researcher, Gail Goodman. Goodman's new research emphasized the importance of gauging the likely qualities of children's event memories by simulating the intimate one-on-one nature of abusive behaviour. Goodman's choice of 'event tests' involved eliciting accounts of medical procedures such as inoculations or intimate examinations, events that involved physical contact between a powerful adult and a child and some degree of novelty and immediate distress. She argued that such incidents in which the child was an active participant offered a better analogue for sexual or physical abuse than the passive observation epitomized by the 'picture tests' of Stern and Binet (Goodman, 1984).

The results that emerged from these more realistic studies painted a far more positive picture of the mnemonic capacities of children than the tenor of the earlier generation of research. As Stern had reported 70 years earlier, Goodman conveyed that the free accounts of children across the age range showed high levels of accuracy. Contrary to Stern, however, on these more involving events, children showed high levels of resistance to leading and repeated questions and, on occasion, any age differences in performance were eliminated for all but the very youngest (3-year-old) children (Goodman, Bottoms, Schwartz-Kennedy, & Rudy, 1991; Goodman, Hirschman, Hepps, & Rudy, 1991). Where children did go along with the implication of a leading question, these were much more likely to concern what Goodman described as 'peripheral' features of an event (the colour of the consulting room curtains) than what she termed 'central' features (who did what to whom). Goodman and Schwartz-Kenney (1992) emphasized that developmental age as such was not the only or even the most significant factor in determining children's memory capacity; the nature, familiarity, and frequency of events, the social and emotional maturity of the child, and the style of interviewing adopted by the questioner, all influenced what the child said or did not say.

Goodman's more positive view of children's competencies undoubtedly influenced legislation and the training of child protection professionals in Britain (Spencer & Flin, 1993) and North America (Ceci & Bruck, 1995). It also strengthened the hand of those calling for changes in legal procedure to make the gathering of children's evidence and testifying at court a less stressful process, reflected in such innovations as pre-recorded videotaped interviews and remote testimony delivered via closed-circuit television. However, amid this new optimism, there was an inevitable backlash.

The Backlash

As more children had their testimony heard at court, cases emerged on both sides of the Atlantic of actual or potential miscarriages of justice caused by their testimony (Hechler, 1988). The McMartin case in 1987 (Butler, Fukurai, Dimitrius, & Krooth, 2001) was but the first in a series of high-profile cases alleging sexual abuse by adults which rested exclusively on the testimony of preschool children secured through investigative interviews conducted by experienced child professionals (for a detailed discussion of this case see Chapter 2). In the United Kingdom, also in 1987, over 200 children in Cleveland were removed from their parents on the basis of a new and unproven technique for medically diagnosing abuse. Many of the children were then interviewed by professionals to try to gather information to back up these diagnoses. Following an outcry, all the children were returned to their parents and the resulting official inquiry contained serious criticisms of the interviewing practices employed, highlighting the use of leading or suggestive questioning (Butler-Sloss, 1988). These and similar cases reawakened serious concerns regarding the suggestibility of young children and their vulnerability to leading or coercive interviewing techniques which in turn produced misleading, inconsistent, and sometimes bizarre allegations (Ceci & Bruck, 1993, 1995).

Academic research and debate also reflected concerns that children's vulnerabilities as witnesses were being overlooked by existing research. At a series of international conferences, Ceci and Loftus both argued that the issue of children's suggestibility had been underplayed in Goodman's research (e.g., Doris, 1991; Ornstein & Davies, 1997). A subsequent review by Ceci and Bruck (1993) of nearly a century of research on the issue concluded that there was overwhelming evidence that suggestibility was age-related and challenged the view of Goodman, Rudy, Bottoms, and Aman (1990) that its influence was attenuated when 'central' as opposed to the 'peripheral' features of an event were being probed or when the child was an actor rather than an observer.

To support their position, Ceci and colleagues had also embarked on a series of important studies examining the memory and suggestibility of children from the age group represented in the McMartin and other preschool cases (for review see Bruck, Ceci, & Hembrooke, 1998; Bruck, Ceci, & Principe, 2006). Leichtman and Ceci (1995) had a stranger, 'Sam Stone', pay a brief and innocuous visit to a daycare centre. When the children were asked 10 weeks later whether Sam had damaged a book or a teddy bear during his visit, fewer than 10% of the children responded positively, a result entirely consistent with Goodman's work. However, if the children were exposed to a combination of negative stereotyping before Sam's visit regarding his alleged clumsiness and misleading suggestions at a subsequent interview, then the proportion of children making an allegation of damage among 3- to 4-year-olds rose to 70%, of whom 20% continued to maintain that they had seen him do it under gentle questioning. Ceci argued that this latter condition was closer to the realities of abuse investigations, where children might be exposed to relentlessly negative stories about the alleged offender and leading questions at interview.

Ceci, Huffman, Smith, and Loftus (1994a) demonstrated that repeatedly questioning children of the same age group about fictitious events in the context of remembering real incidents from their childhood led over half to confirm that at least one of the fictitious events had actually occurred. As Stern had noted many years earlier, Ceci *et al.* found that many of the youngsters involved did not merely accede to the false information, but actively elaborated it through fictitious and sometimes plausible detail. In informal tests, Leichtman and Ceci (1995) found that legal and child care professionals were unable to distinguish between true and false accounts on the basis of the children's interviews alone.

In 1995, Ceci and Bruck published *Jeopardy in the Courtroom: A Scientific Analysis of Children's Testimony*, which presented findings from their own research and their concerns over current professional practice in the context of controversial trials involving the evidence of children. The authors highlighted what they saw as poor interviewing practices and misleading advocacy at court by expert practitioners, which were not grounded in rigorous research. The authors emphasized that they did not wish to deny the reality of child abuse or to claim that children could not, under a range of unspecified circumstances, provide accurate testimony, but argued for a more evidence-based approach rather than potentially misleading advocacy.

Ceci and Bruck's book undoubtedly had a profound and lasting impact on both professional training and practice and the attitude of the courts toward children's testimony. However, their pleas for a purely evidence-based approach were criticized as unrealistic by many child protection specialists, and their presentation of the McMartin and Michaels' cases as typical of those coming before the courts was questioned (Lyon, 1999; Westcott, 1998). Goodman and Schaaf (1997) queried whether the academic and judicial pendulum had now swung too far toward scepticism and that an interview doctrine based purely on asking open-ended questions (generally regarded as the most reliable form of questioning with witnesses of all ages) would be unlikely to elicit information from frightened or intimidated children sufficient to secure a conviction. They called for greater interactions and integration between researchers and practitioners if an appropriate balance was to be struck.

How Representative is Research of Practice?

Ceci and colleagues' own research has not escaped criticism. Some expressed ethical concerns: for example, was it ever appropriate for researchers to inculcate memories of non-existent events in a child in the interests of science (Goodman, Quas, & Redlich, 1998; Hermann & Yoder, 1998)? Lyon (1999) has provided an extensive critique of the representativeness of Ceci *et al.*'s research as typical of the child abuse cases that reach the courts. The children involved in their studies were generally very young; but even within this limited age range, there were strong developmental effects. For instance, in the Leichtman and Ceci (1995) study, the proportion of children asserting that they had positively seen Sam Stone misbehaving fell from over 40% at 3–4 years to around 10% by age 5–6. Lyon argued that such dramatic effects would not be anticipated for children closer to the typical age of those involved in sexual abuse trials: 13 years in the United States and 10–14 years in the United Kingdom (Davies & Noon, 1991).

Lyon went on to point out that the typical defendant in a child sexual abuse case would be a member of the child's immediate family or another familiar adult, rather than a complete stranger, and such close relationships imposed a potentially different dynamic which could increase or decrease the likely impact of suggestive responding. There were also differences in the nature of the alleged offence. In the Leichtman and Ceci study, children were repeatedly told stories illustrating Sam's clumsiness, behaviour with which most children could empathize and provide plausible elaborations upon if they responded positively to the suggestion that he had been responsible for damage to the book or teddy bear. For most children (though sadly not all) knowledge of sexual matters, particularly the mechanics of the most frequent forms of abuse, will be poorly understood, so that attempts at fictitious elaboration may fall well short in terms of credibility (Davies, 1996). In general, children and adults have been shown to be much more vulnerable to suggestions regarding plausible but fictitious events from their own lives than implausible events (Pezdek & Hodge, 1999).

Another issue concerned the status and permanence of the misleading answers provided by the children. Ceci and Bruck (1995) followed Binet in distinguishing between *cognitive* and *social* effects of misleading suggestions. In order to explore the permanence or otherwise of the false memories provided by children, Huffman, Crossman, and Ceci (1997) re-interviewed the children who had participated in the study of Ceci *et al.* (1994a,b) 2 years previously. They reported a reduction in false assents from 22% to just 13%, but the children's accuracy for actual incidents from their lives remained high (77% recalled). This result might suggest that the majority of false allegations could be eliminated or reversed, given a supportive interview environment.

Finally, and perhaps most importantly, Ceci's work has generally involved memory for single isolated events but, sadly, those children who suffer sexual abuse frequently suffer repeated assaults by the same assailant which follow a similar pattern. Laboratory research has shown that children are more resistant to suggestions involving repeated involvement in stressful incidents than those arising from a single event. Repeated exposure gives rise to 'scripts' or expectations based on accumulated knowledge, which forms a bulwark against misleading questioning or suggestions that it never happened (Ornstein, Baker-Ward, Gordon, & Merritt, 1997; Roberts & Powell, 2001).

In their response to the critiques of Lyon and others, Ceci and Friedman (2000) defended the applicability and representativeness of their work, but emphasized that their purpose was not to provide a generalized dismissal of the evidence of children, but rather to establish a firm basis of research upon which professionals might base their practice.

Researchers who Practice: Expert Witnessing at Court

Ceci and Bruck moved from research into professional practice through their involvement as expert witnesses in a number of high-profile cases and as lead-authors of an *Amicus* (friend of the court) brief in the Kelly Michaels' case (Bruck & Ceci, 1995; *New Jersey v. Michaels* 1994). Ms. Michaels, a nursery school teacher, had been found guilty of multiple counts of sexual assault on the basis of a series of sometimes bizarre allegations which emerged from investigative interviews conducted by child protection professionals with children who had been in her care. Bruck and Ceci's *Amicus* brief highlighted the new research on the vulnerability to suggestion of pre-school children and the suggestive questioning procedures to which they had been exposed. Ms. Michaels' appeal was successful, and she was released after having served 5 years of a 47-year prison sentence.

This same path has now been trodden by memory researchers in the United Kingdom who see the forensic relevance of laboratory studies demonstrating how misleading questions and other suggestive procedures can produce false memories in children and adults (for a review see Wade & Laney, 2008). In 2008, a working party of the Research Board of the British Psychological Society published *Guidelines on Memory and the Law* which summarized research on false memory production and urged the courts to be cautious in evaluating the evidence of witnesses where this evidence was based on memory alone. They also urged the courts to rely exclusively upon expert testimony from what they termed 'memory experts' (defined as those with 'relevant outputs' such as peer-reviewed publications and presentations at professional meetings) rather than practitioners to assist them in evaluating such evidence.

Is a research background involving memory a necessary and sufficient condition to pass judgement on the reliability of children's testimony? In the Unites States, where expert testimony is more readily admitted, Ceci and Bruck (1993) quoted Mason's (1991, p. 20) view that 'courts are unconcerned about scientific knowledge, but are willing to accept the testimony of expert witnesses as long as they have clinical experience' and went on to argue, 'Experts rarely present a careful summary of the research because doing so would probably force them to attenuate their often strident claims' (Ceci & Bruck, 1993, p. 431).

Certainly, knowledge of current research on children's memory and suggestibility is necessary for any expert in a child abuse trial but, as has been argued, that research does not necessarily lend itself to one emphatic conclusion, and the incomplete nature of the evidence, whether from basic or applied studies, often leaves room for interpretation. But is knowledge of memory research alone sufficient for an expert witness in a case of alleged child sexual or physical abuse?

This was the view taken by the Professional Practice Board of the British Psychological Society in 2010, when it requested the withdrawal of the *Memory and the Law* document pending significant revisions, particularly in its definition of 'who is a memory expert witness?' This definition was perceived as simultaneously too broad and too narrow – too broad in the sense that the research of many memory experts would not be relevant in the courtroom (e.g., research on semantic or working memory) save in most unusual circumstances, and too narrow in that some specific knowledge of police evidence-gathering procedures, particularly interviewing and the often tangled motives which can lead to disclosure or retraction of allegations (the so-called 'disclosure wars'; see Pipe, Lamb, Orbach, & Cederborg, 2007), would seem essential to the expert witness if the court is to reach an informed decision. In a recent Court of Appeal decision, the testimony of an expert witness who amply fulfilled the criteria for being a 'memory expert' was rejected in part because of previous adverse legal comment on his lack of knowledge of police investigative procedures (in *R v. E* 2009).

At the time of writing, *Memory and the Law* has been withdrawn by the British Psychological Society, pending revisions. As this example illustrates, it is perhaps in the area of expert testimony, above all others, where the tensions between research and practice regarding the credibility of children's evidence remain strongest.

DEVELOPMENT OF LEGAL AND PROFESSIONAL GUIDELINES

The findings reviewed above on the strengths and vulnerabilities of children's memory led to a substantial international consensus as to how and how not forensic interviews should be conducted in order to elicit the most accurate and complete information (American Professional Society on the Abuse of Children, 1990, 1997; Home Office, 1992, 2007; Lamb, Hershkowitz, Orbach, & Esplin, 2008; Poole & Lamb, 1998). In 1992, the British Home Office published the *Memorandum of Good Practice*, providing evidence-based guidance on how to conduct interviews with child complainants for legal proceedings, which has influenced and shaped procedures not only in the United Kingdom but in many other countries (Bull, 1995; Davies & Pezdek, 2010).

The original *Memorandum* guidelines (1992) were drafted by a forensic psychologist (Ray Bull) and a lawyer (Diane Birch). The document sought to take account of both empirical research and best practice by practitioners and align these to the legal requirements of the revised laws of evidence, which for the first time, permitted pre-recorded videotaped interviews conducted by police officers or social workers to be submitted as evidence-in-chief by the prosecution. Although written and published some years before the appearance of Ceci *et al.*'s seminal work, Bull and Birch anticipated many of the problems uncovered by their research.

The *Memorandum* attempted to combat suggestibility by reducing the social distance between the interviewer and the child. Children were to be interviewed in interview suites in settings away from police stations and by interviewers wearing casual clothing. Interviews would begin with a rapport phase, where children and interviewers could discuss topics of mutual interest, such as football or television; only when rapport had been established would the interviewer raise the focus of the interview. The guidance encouraged eliciting an initial free narrative from the child, coupled with an injunction to use open questions and to refrain from specific or closed questions until free narrative was exhausted. The use of video recording also reduced the risk of contamination of the kind highlighted by Ceci *et al.* Video interviews could be conducted immediately following a complaint, ensuring that a contemporaneous account of what the child had said (and what questions were asked) was available to the court. Moreover, making this recording available to the defence and other agencies involved would help ensure that the child need only give a single interview, rather than be subjected to repeated interviews, as had occurred in some of the more notorious cases described by Ceci and Bruck (1995).

The *Memorandum* provided the basis for training courses for interviewers assigned to child protection duties in England and Wales. These were typically 1–2 week intensive courses, and research demonstrated that they were successful in teaching the main points of the guidance (Aldridge & Cameron, 1999; Powell & Wright, 2008; Warren *et al.*, 1999). However, the question remained: were trained interviewers putting these principles into practice in the field? The availability of videotapes enabled some assessment to be made of the extent to which interviewers were following the guidelines.

Sternberg, Lamb, Davies, and Westcott (2001) examined over 100 investigative interviews with children about alleged abuse conducted by officers in 12 representative police forces. Despite the *Memorandum*'s emphasis on the value of free narrative, just 52% of interviewer began with an open-ended invitation to say what had happened (in a further 11% of cases the child raised the topic spontaneously). Just 4% of all questions were classified as open: interviewers relied mainly on closed (20%) or specific (33%) questions, although training had served to minimize the number of blatantly leading questions (4%). Other surveys reported a similar failure to comply with the *Memorandum* requirements (Westcott & Kynan 2006; Westcott, Kynan, & Few, 2006).

Such findings raised questions about the effectiveness of guidelines that are not rigorously evaluated in the field and underscored the need for greater investment in ongoing training and supervision to bring about major changes in the quality of investigative interviewing (see Chapter 11; Lamb, Orbach, Hershkowitz, Esplin, & Horowitz, 2007). There is little doubt that interviewers sincerely believe that they are following best-practice guidelines (e.g., Aldridge & Cameron, 1999) despite the evidence to the contrary. Conducting a high quality investigative interview is no simple task: it demands a great deal of interviewers. Among other tasks, it requires accommodating children's limited language abilities and vocabulary, asking appropriate questions, obtaining detailed evidence about sensitive topics, and maintaining children's often limited attention. Moreover, the daily routines of investigative interviewers typically leave no time to access up-to-date research relevant to conducting interviews with children.

The gap between best-practice guidelines and interviewer performance led to a revision of the professional guidance in England

and Wales. *Achieving Best Evidence in Criminal Proceedings* (Home Office, 2002, 2007) reinforced the message concerning the value of free narrative and the importance of asking open-ended questions as the main form of interview prompt. It also encouraged interviewers to use scripted components to their interview in an effort to reduce inappropriate questioning styles. This was the path followed earlier by another interview schedule developed by the National Institute for Child Health and Human Development (NIHCD) in the United States (see Appendix 1). The NICHD Investigative Interview Protocol (Lamb *et al.*, 2008) is used by professionals in several countries and has been extensively validated in the laboratory and field.

Development of the NICHD Protocol

The NICHD Protocol was designed to guide interviewers to use prompts and techniques that maximize the amount of information elicited from free-recall memory (Lamb *et al.*, 2008; Orbach, Hershkowitz, Lamb, Esplin, & Horowitz, 2000). Importantly, the Protocol covers all phases of the investigative interview, taking into account research findings as well as practical needs and requirements. As with the *Memorandum* interview, in the introductory phase, the interviewer introduces him/herself, clarifies the child's task, and explains the ground rules and expectations (e.g., that the child can and should say 'I don't know' when appropriate). This phase was developed with sensitivity to the fact that children are usually unused to being the sole source of information and often fail to ask for clarification when they do not understand (e.g., Lamb, Sternberg, Orbach, Hershkowitz, & Esplin, 1999; Saywitz, Snyder, & Nathanson, 1999; Sternberg *et al.*, 1997 Waterman, Blades, & Spencer, 2000, 2004). As with the *Memorandum,* the introductory phase also includes questions designed to establish children's understanding of the difference between true and false statements.

Implementation Although the Protocol was based on decades of empirical evidence concerning children's eyewitness abilities, it was critical to determine its acceptability to practitioners and effectiveness in the field. The Protocol was introduced as a mandatory tool for interviewing youths in Israel in 1998. Implementation was sometimes difficult, with practitioners reluctant to abandon their own methods in favour of those advocated in the new protocol (Orbach *et al.*, 2000). It was necessary to build and maintain a constructive relationship based on mutual respect and good faith between researchers and practitioners in order to achieve successful adoption of the new methods.

Evaluation Independent field studies have now been conducted in four countries, all of which have demonstrated the Protocol's effectiveness in improving the quality of investigative interviews (Cyr & Lamb, 2009; Lamb *et al*, 2008; Orbach *et al.*, 2000; Sternberg, Lamb, Orbach, Esplin, & Mitchell, 2001). However, as with the *Memorandum*, evaluations of interviews conducted after the termination of training and feedback often showed poor compliance with the requirements of the Protocol. In fact, improvements derived from training and close monitoring and feedback from expert fellow interviewers diminished within 6 months of the cessation of regular feedback sessions (Lamb, Sternberg, Orbach, Hershlowitz, & Horowitz, 2002). To achieve lasting change, it was necessary to provide continuous support, guidance, and feedback for interviewers using the Protocol in the field. The adverse effects of termination of supervision and feedback have important, although somewhat sobering, implications for those attempting to apply information gleaned from research to practice in the real world. Clearly, it is possible to train professionals in different fields (law enforcement, social work) to improve the quality of information elicited from alleged victims of child abuse, but these benefits are only maintained through extensive efforts not just to train interviewers in recommended methods initially, but to monitor their practice as well (see Chapter 11).

Research and Practice: The Virtuous Circle

In response to practitioners' needs, which emerged during the course of implementation and practice, a version of the Protocol was developed for use with witnesses who are not victims (Lamb, Sternberg, Orbach, Hershkowitz, & Horowitz, 2003b) and another for use with youthful suspects (Hershkowitz, Horowitz, Lamb, Orbach, & Sternberg, 2004). Currently, Lamb and colleagues are field-testing a revision designed to provide support to children who are unusually reluctant to talk about their experiences (Hershkowitz, Horowitz, & Lamb, 2005; Pipe *et al.*, 2007). Recent work highlights the need for a variant of the Protocol for use with children with learning disabilities who are disproportionately more likely to be abused but may not have their statements taken seriously in legal contexts (see Chapter 13; Crosse, Kaye, & Ratnofsky, 1993; Hershkowitz, Lamb, & Horowitz, 2007; Sullivan & Knutson, 2000).

Practice developments have also had an impact on theory. For example, it was long believed that young children were incapable of providing narrative responses to invitational prompts (Bourg *et al.*, 1999; Hewitt, 1999; Kuehnle, 1996). However, research with the Protocol demonstrates that when invitations are carefully formulated and children appropriately prepared for their roles as informants, even children as young as 4 years of age can provide detailed narrative responses (Lamb *et al.*, 2003a).

The NICHD Protocol and its training model illustrates an influential relationship between academia and the field, with researchers and practitioners working together to generate solutions to the real-world issues involved in interviewing children in forensic settings (Lamb *et al.*, 2008). This model has been successful in improving the quality of interviews with alleged victims of child abuse in Israel, Canada, the United States, and parts of the United Kingdom. Continued evaluation of the Protocol, its components, and its implementations highlight the importance and informativeness of a continuous feedback loop between researchers (basic and applied) and practitioners. This virtuous circle has not only allowed for the evaluation and validation of the Protocol, but has also generated further research questions and problems for applied researchers to address.

SPECIAL MEASURES FOR CHILDREN: THE USE OF CCTV

In contrast to the studies on suggestibility, which were driven initially by a research agenda which then influenced practice, the initiative for facilitating children's evidence at court was fostered by practitioner concerns which in turn provoked research and innovation. Several studies had demonstrated that legal involvement was distressing to children and could lead to adverse short- and long-term consequences (Goodman *et al.*, 1992; Henry, 1997; Quas *et al.*, 2005; for review see Whitcomb, 2003). The facets of legal involvement that appear most distressing include providing testimony in open court, testifying while facing the defendant, and undergoing cross-examination (Davies & Noon, 1991, 1993). Research has demonstrated that these same factors are associated with poorer eyewitness memory performance (Goodman *et al.*, 1992; Saywitz & Nathanson, 1993). Children's statements may form a key piece of evidence at a trial. Giving evidence at court is a distressing experience for adults and children alike, but because children have more difficulty accessing memories under stress (Bjorklund, 2005; Fivush, 1993), this may inhibit children's ability to remember and communicate information to the detriment of the truth-seeking function of the court. Thus, special measures to assist children in giving their testimony are an advantage to the witness and court alike.

Both in the United Kingdom and the United States, child protection agencies have long campaigned for improvements to the conditions under which children give evidence at court. In the late 1980s, well-publicized incidents of cases collapsing as a result of the inability of children to 'come up to proof' in their evidence (Spencer & Flinn, 1993) led several legislatures, including England and Wales, to amend legal process to facilitate children's evidence. One of the first such innovations was the use of in-court closed-circuit television (CCTV) or the 'live link' as it is known in the United Kingdom.

The use of CCTV to enable a child witness to testify from outside the courtroom was first trialled in the United States but is not readily available to children there because of concerns over violation of the 6th amendment to the US Constitution, which enshrines the right of the accused to confront his/her accuser (Hill & Sales, 2008). In the US version of the link, the judge and the advocates are sequestered with the child and examination and cross-examination are broadcast to the jury in the courtroom. In England and Wales, the child alone is out of court, together with an usher or support worker and the cameras are interactive, allowing questions to be asked by the judge and advocates from court and the child's response to be relayed back to the courtroom. In terms of video image, the child sees whosoever is speaking from the court, while the court always sees the child. The main perceived advantage of the live link is that the child need not enter the alien and sometimes intimidating arena of the courtroom and, provided cameras are set up correctly, they need not see the accused during the taking of their evidence. Similar arrangements are used in Australia, New Zealand, and Scotland (Cashmore, 2002; Davies, 1999). In England and Wales, the use of the link is a mandatory requirement for all child witnesses giving evidence, although in other legislatures use of the link is at the discretion of the judge who may require that the child show fear of the accused (Hill & Sales, 2008).

The link was introduced on a trial basis into 14 Crown Courts in England and Wales in 1989 (Davies & Noon, 1991) with a requirement that its effectiveness for all court users should be properly evaluated. A few weeks before its introduction, the first author (G.M.D.) was approached by the government department responsible for implementation to conduct the evaluation. The history of the project provides an illuminating case study of some of the rewards and difficulties of conducting policy-led research.

Discussion with the department concerned revealed some serious constraints to a conventional field study. The researchers were allowed full access to the courts and legal personnel, and the judges and lawyers had signalled their willingness to cooperate and give their views. However, there were two major difficulties. First, and perhaps paradoxically, the one group who were unavailable for comment were the child witnesses themselves: there were concerns among lawyers that in the event of an appeal, any questioning by the researchers could contaminate their evidence. Secondly, the research project was to begin the day the court equipment became operational and, thus, there was no base level period when children could be assessed giving their evidence in the traditional way.

Most policy-driven research involves compromise. The response to the 'no contact' ruling pertaining to the child participants themselves was to rely exclusively on behavioural measures secured by trained observers sitting in court watching the children giving their evidence and rating the performance of child and legal counsel using scales developed for the US courts by Goodman (Goodman *et al.*, 1998). An added advantage of using Goodman's scales was that they were also being used in a second piece of research on child witnesses testifying in Scotland, where at that time evidence was still taken and tested in the traditional manner. With the kind cooperation of the researchers involved (Flin, Bull, Boon, & Knox, 1990), it became possible to secure enough comparable case material to be able to make comparisons between evidence given via the link and from the witness stand. Thus, in real world research, practical obstacles can provoke methodological innovations.

In addition to the quantitative data, the researchers were permitted to solicit qualitative impressions from three groups: judges, court officials, and lawyers, through the use of structured interviews. The results from these two very different data sets fortunately provided a good example of convergent validity. The observational data showed that children giving evidence via the link were rated as significantly less unhappy, more audible, more forthcoming, and more consistent in their evidence compared with Scottish children testifying in the traditional way. These findings complemented comments from judges, court officials, and lawyers with experience of both the traditional and new system: overall, the majority favoured its continuing employment in child witness trials.

However, other field studies that have accompanied the introduction of the live link in Scotland (Murray, 1995) and Australia (Cashmore & De Haas, 1992) failed to replicate these very positive findings: any differences favoured witnesses giving evidence in open court. The most likely explanation for the discrepancy lies in the rules on access to the link. In both Scotland and Australia at the time of the evaluations, use of the link was on application to the judge who had discretion based on his/her perceptions of the vulnerability of the witness. For instance, in the Scottish study, this discretion ensured that the link group comprised much younger witnesses, giving evidence in more serious cases, and who were more likely to be testifying against a parent (Murray,

1995). The Australian study found link users were rated as more relaxed than open-court witnesses, but no other differences emerged, except that those who had applied for the link and been refused were rated as significantly less competent and more stressed than any other group. Both the Australian and Scottish studies enjoyed greater access to the children involved. Murray reported that 73% of the link sample said they would have found difficulty in testifying in open court, and 92% were glad to have had the opportunity to testify in this novel way. Similar positive views from users emerged from the Australian study (Cashmore & De Haas, 1992). More recently, in England and Wales, Hamlyn, Phelps, Turtle, and Sattar (2004), who were permitted to talk to child users of the link, reported that 90% had found it useful in giving their evidence.

These field studies clearly demonstrate that children and court personnel value the link and the protection it provides from the courtroom environment and sight of the accused, with consequent positive effects on the child's demeanour. But what is the impact of video-mediated testimony received by the jury? And are jurors able to make informed decisions on the truth or otherwise of children's allegations on the basis of the more limited information available from the TV screen? Given the prohibition on questioning jurors that exists in England and Wales and other judiciaries, to answer these questions it is necessary to conduct complementary experimental studies to explore the relative impact of in-court and video-mediated testimony.

The most impressive experimental studies have been conducted by Goodman and colleagues (Goodman *et al.*, 1998; Orcutt, Goodman, Tobey, Batterman-Faunce & Thomas, 2001). Initially, children aged 5–9 years played games with a confederate in the course of which stickers were placed either on their clothes or exposed parts of their bodies. Several weeks later, individual children were asked to testify in mock trials conducted in a real courtroom, using actual courtroom personnel and volunteer jurors. They were examined and cross-examined by advocates either live in court or outside court with their testimony relayed via CCTV. Children in the 'defendant guilty' condition were required to tell the truth while those in the 'defendant innocent' condition were instructed to lie that the stickers were put on their bodies rather than their clothes.

Immediately following the children's testimony, jurors rated evidence given live more favourably than that given via CCTV. Children giving evidence on the witness stand were seen as more attractive, believable, and honest compared with those on CCTV, and jurors were less likely to convict when testimony was given via CCTV. However, the actual accuracy of judgements reached by jurors after deliberation was generally low and no more accurate when testimony was given live compared with via CCTV. This is consistent with the findings from a body of laboratory research demonstrating that participants perform at little better than chance levels when detecting deception from non-verbal cues: they frequently confuse signs of stress with indictors of deception (Vrij, 2008). Later research by Landstrom (2008) has confirmed Goodman *et al.*'s findings that jurors generally perceive evidence given by children in the courtroom more positively than video evidence, but that this advantage does not lead to any more accurate decisions, a result that holds for both the British and the US versions of the link.

In summary, there is now considerable evidence from experimental research that video-mediated evidence does lack some of the immediacy of evidence given from the stand and that in turn may influence juror perceptions of the witness – but no evidence that live testimony leads to any more accurate decisions or that conviction rates are higher in cases involving testimony given from the stand. Any loss of immediacy needs to be balanced against the advantages for the child witness, both in terms of the quality of their evidence and the reduced adverse impact on their future mental health (Davies, 1994; Quas *et al.*, 2005).

RESEARCH AND PRACTICE: THE WAY FORWARD?

It is critical for science to inform practice and vice versa. Researchers who perceive that their sole duty is to provide information and guidance to the field risk harming relations with practitioners and missing out on feedback that can enhance their research, including identifying novel research questions. When reviewing the research for guidance on important decisions, practitioners including investigative interviewers, policy makers, legal professionals, and expert witnesses, must consider the generalizability, representativeness, and ecological validity of the studies at hand.

Laboratory studies offer the advantages of testing children's memory for objectively verifiable, standardized events under controlled conditions. Researchers can manipulate key variables and test specific research hypotheses using carefully designed and ethically sound procedures. However, as we have illustrated, the target events may differ from actual abuse scenarios in critical features where ecological validity becomes a real concern. For instance, the pioneering studies of Goodman and colleagues on children and naturally occurring stressors (e.g., inoculations; Goodman, Hirschman, Hepps, & Rudy, 1991) broke new ground but lacked the embarrassment factor or the life-threatening features associated with some acts of child abuse. Now, researchers have interviewed children involved in painful and discomforting medical procedures, emergency room visits, and even natural disasters such as hurricanes (e.g., Fivush, Sales, Goldberg, Bahrick, & Parker, 2004; Peterson, 1999; Quas *et al.*, 1999).

In traditional studies of witness accuracy, it is possible to check the child's recollections and answers to questions against an objective record of what actually occurred. This is a luxury unavailable to practitioners in actual abuse investigations. They must start, often from a muttered confidence, an unexplained injury, or genital complaint, on the basis of which they must attempt to elicit a clear explanation from the child. It is not surprising that the types and styles of questioning in these two situations may be very different, and researchers are beginning to acknowledge this. For example, some researchers have questioned children about body touch (e.g., Quas, Davis, Goodman, & Myers, 2007) or examined children's event reports after they were coached to allege or deny events (e.g., Lyon, Malloy, Quas, & Talwar, 2008; Quas *et al.*, 2007). Others have designed or utilized paradigms that attempt to capture some of the socio-motivational aspects of children's testimony by, for example, questioning children about a forbidden act (e.g., playing with a forbidden toy; Talwar & Lee, 2008), implementing consequences of disclosure (e.g., Bottoms, Goodman, Schwartz-Kenney, & Thomas, 2002), or involving the child's parent as the perpetrator of wrongdoing (e.g., Talwar, Lee, Bala, & Lindsay, 2004; Tye, Amato, Honts, Devitt, & Peters, 1999). Such research is beginning to yield useful information which may assist practitioners in eliciting more reliable testimonies from young complainants. A good example of the reciprocal relationship that can exist between research and practice comes from a study that identified several questioning techniques taken from the interviews in the McMartin case and used them in interviews with children after a male adult made an innocuous visit to their classroom (Garven, Wood, Malpass, & Shaw, 1998). As Varendock (1911) had found many years previously, using identical questioning procedures to those used in the a legal case produced misleading responses among the children concerned.

Another area of research development that stems from practice considerations concerns the generalizability of findings from research studies. Most research concerning children's memory, suggestibility, and eyewitness testimony has been conducted on populations of Caucasian upper middle-class children. Maltreated children tend to be cognitively delayed and to be from lower socioeconomic backgrounds than nonmaltreated children. Thus, to ensure findings apply to actual child witnesses, it is imperative to study those children most often involved in the legal system – victims of maltreatment (e.g., Eisen, Goodman,

Qin, Davis, & Crayton, 2007; Howe, Cicchetti, Toth, & Cerrito, 2004; Lyon *et al.*, 2008).

Spreading the News: Translating Research into Practice

Such new research and findings need to reach those who practice in the field. Most academics who conduct research in the laboratory present it to other academics at conferences, and publish only in academic journals, which are inaccessible literally or figuratively to most non-psychologists. Sommer (2006) has argued that even cutting-edge findings will remain largely inaccessible unless psychologists reach out to professional audiences through what he terms a 'dual dissemination' strategy; writing articles for publication for more general audiences, rather than just focusing on specialized academic journals as a 'complementary' mode of dissemination. Publishing in more general outlets involves more than just reprinting articles elsewhere. Influential voices in the debate over children's evidence such as Goodman, Ceci, and Loftus, offer examples of dual dissemination in action, and Ceci has founded a journal, *Psychological Science in the Public Interest*, to encourage this process. Also, newsletters for relevant professional organizations can be important outlets for reaching and informing end-users. For example, the bulletin of the International Investigative Interviewing Research Group provides researchers and practitioners around the world with the latest research findings on investigative interviewing while creating a much-needed opportunity for dialogue between academia and the field.

Psychologists writing for other audiences must learn to write in a way very different from APA style. For instance, writing for judges, lawyers, and other legal practitioners may require special skills. Scholars have observed that those in the psychology and legal professions come from two different cultures (Bersoff, 1999; Saks, 1989), which may be, in part, responsible for the conflict, doubt, and even suspicion espoused on both sides. Some of these differences result from differences in organizational culture established from the earliest days of training in the respective fields. Summarizing the differences, Brigham wrote:

> Psychology tends to be creative, empirical, experimental, descriptive, theory driven, probabilistic, and academic. Law, in contrast, is more conservative, authoritative, adversarial, prescriptive, case-specific, and reactive. It emphasizes certainty and is less academic. Given these basic difference in approach, training, and philosophy, it is perhaps small wonder that psychologists and lawyers often have great difficulty respecting or even understanding each other. (Brigham, 1999, p. 283)

Some have argued that psychologists should be 'trilingual' – that is able to 'speak' the languages of psychology, the law, and their interface (Brigham, 1999). Learning to write for non-psychology audiences is critical: to the extent possible, publications should be kept brief, focused, and jargon-free.

CONCLUSIONS

On the Reciprocal Nature of Research and Practice

In this chapter, we have discussed the value of both basic and applied psychological research and the importance of the interaction between research and practice. Through a range of examples drawn from studies of the reliability of children's eyewitness memory, investigative interviewing, and the use of CCTV in the courtroom, we have demonstrated how research and practice can inform and complement each other. Research continues on areas of practice-based concern including the impact of stress and trauma on memory, styles of questioning, and the applicability of research findings to maltreated children and those with learning disabilities, among other key areas of concern. These new strands of research will test the validity and generalizability of findings from experimental research and, it is hoped, will spur researchers to create yet more ecologically valid paradigms. Researchers and practitioners can continue to work together toward creative and empirically based solutions to real-world problems, including those posed by the field of children's eyewitness testimony. However, it is important to recognize that, in many cases, simply publishing best-practice guidelines may not be enough to lead to lasting and effective change.

It is critical for science to inform practice and vice versa. Researchers must pay attention and respond to the feedback loop, rather than simply dispensing information to practitioners in the field. By making research more creative, applicable, and ecologically valid, while still maintaining ethical boundaries, researchers can obtain a clearer picture of children's capacities and limitations and be better able to inform practice.

Following the publication of the statement on recovered memories by the APA, each member of the original working party was interviewed by Jack Brigham. The words of one member provide a succinct coda for this chapter:

> We should stop teaching our students in this dichotomised [research versus practice] manner about psychology. All of us our doing variations of science and practice all the time with differing emphases.

That kind of polarised thinking is inculcated very young in our students and then we model it. We need to stop, now, and ask, rather, what can we each learn from the other? (Brigham, 1999, p. 289).

REFERENCES

Aldridge, J., & Cameron, S. (1999). Interviewing child witnesses: Questioning techniques and the role of training. *Applied Developmental Science, 3*, 136–147.

American Psychological Association Working Group on Investigation of Memories of Childhood Abuse. (1996). *Final Report*. Washington, DC: APA.

American Professional Society on the Abuse of Children (1990). *Guidelines for Psychosocial Evaluation of Suspected Sexual Abuse in Young Children.* Chicago, IL: APA.

American Professional Society on the Abuse of Children. (1997). *Guidelines for Psychosocial Evaluation of Suspected Sexual Abuse in Young Children (Revised)*. Chicago, IL: APA.

Banaji, M.R., & Crowder, R.G. (1989). The bankruptcy of everyday memory. *American Psychologist, 44*, 1185–1193.

Bersoff, D.N. (1999). Preparing for two cultures: Education and training in law and psychology. In R. Roesch, S.D. Hart, & J.R.P. Ogloff (Eds), *Psychology and Law: The State of the Discipline* (pp. 375–398). New York: Plenum.

Binet, A. (1900). *La suggestibilité* [Suggestibility]. Paris: Schleicher Freres.

Bjorklund, D. (2005). *Children's Thinking*. Belmont, CA: Wadsworth.

Bottoms, B.L., Goodman, G.S., Schwartz-Kenney, B.M., & Thomas, S.N. (2002). Understanding children's use of secrecy in the context of eyewitness reports. *Law and Human Behavior, 26*, 285–314.

Bourg, W., Broderick, R., Flagor, R., Kelly, D.M., Ervin, D.L., & Butler, J. (1999). *A Child Interviewer's Guidebook*. Thousand Oaks, CA: Sage.

Brigham, J. (1999). What is forensic psychology anyway? *Law and Human Behavior, 23*, 273–298.

Bruck, M., & Ceci, S.J. (1995). Amicus brief for the case of State of New Jersey v. Michaels presented by a committee of concerned social scientists. *Psychology, Public Policy, and Law, 1*, 272–322.

Bruck, M., Ceci, S.J., & Hembrooke, H. (1998). Reliability and credibility of young children's reports: From research to policy and practice. *American Psychologist, 53*, 136–151.

Bruck, M., Ceci, S.J., & Principe, G.F. (2006). The child and the law. In K.A. Renninger, I.E. Sigel, W. Damon, & R.M. Lerner (Eds), *Handbook of Child Psychology* (6th edn, Vol. 4, pp. 776–816). Hoboken, NJ: Wiley.

Bull, R. (1995). Interviewing children in legal contexts. In R. Bull, & D. Carson (Eds), *Handbook of Psychology in Legal Contexts* (pp. 235–246). Chichester: Wiley.

Butler, E.W., Fukurai, H., Dimitrius, J., & Krooth, R. (2001). *Anatomy of the McMartin Child Molestation Case.* Lanham, MD: United Press of America.

Butler-Sloss, E. (1988). *Report of the Inquiry into Child Abuse in Cleveland 1987*. London: Her Majesty's Stationary Office.

Cashmore, J. (2002). Innovative procedures for child witnesses. In H. Westcott, G.M. Davies, & R. Bull (Eds), *Children's Testimony: A Handbook of Psychological Research and Forensic Practice* (pp. 203–218). Chichester: Wiley.

Cashmore, J., & De Haas, N. (1992). *The Use of Closed-Circuit Television for Child Witnesses in the ACT.* Sydney: Australian Law Reform Commission Research Paper.
Ceci, S.J., & Bruck, M. (1993). Suggestibility of the child witness: A historical review and synthesis. *Psychological Bulletin, 113*, 403–439.
Ceci, S.J., & Bruck, M. (1995). *Jeopardy in the Courtroom: A Scientific Analysis of Children's Testimony*. Washington, DC: American Psychological Association.
Ceci, S.J., & Friedman, R.D. (2000). The suggestibility of children: Scientific research and legal implications. *Cornell Law Review, 86*, 33–108.
Ceci, S.J., Huffman, M.L.C., Smith, E., & Loftus, E.F. (1994a). Repeatedly thinking about a non-event: Source misattributions among preschoolers. *Consciousness and Cognition, 3*, 388–407.
Ceci, S.J., Loftus, E.F., Leichtman, M.D., & Bruck, M. (1994b). The possible role of source misattributions in the creation of false beliefs among preschoolers. *International Journal of Clinical and Experimental Hypnosis, 42*, 304–320.
Crosse, S.B., Kaye, E., & Ratnofsky, A.C. (1993). *A Report on the Maltreatment of Children with Disabilities*. Washington, DC: National Center of Child Abuse and Neglect.
Cyr, M., & Lamb, M.E. (2009). Assessing the effectiveness of the NICHD investigative interview protocol when interviewing French-speaking alleged victims of child sexual abuse in Quebec. *Child Abuse and Neglect, 33*, 257–268.
Davies, G.M. (1994). Editorial. Live Links: Understanding the message of the medium. *Journal of Forensic Psychiatry, 5*, 225–227.
Davies, G.M. (1996). Assessing the evidence of children. *Practitioner's Child Law Review, 9*, 80–82.
Davies, G.M. (1999). The impact of television on the presentation and reception of children's evidence. *International Journal of Law and Psychiatry, 22*, 241–256.
Davies, G.M. (2003). Psychology in the courtroom: In the footsteps of Varrendonck. In L. Kools, G. Vervaeke, M. Vanderhallen, & J. Goethals (Eds), *De waarheid en niets dan de waarheid: Over de verhouding tussen recht en psychologie* (pp. 2–17). Leuvan: die Keure.
Davies, G., & Noon, E. (1991). *An Evaluation of the Live Link for Child Witnesses*. London: Home Office.
Davies, G., & Noon, E. (1993). Video links: Their impact on child witness trials. *Issues in Criminological and Legal Psychology, 20*, 22–26.
Davies, G., & Pezdek, K. (2010). Children as witnesses. In G.J. Towl, & D.A. Crighton (Eds), *Forensic Psychology* (pp. 178–194). Oxford: BPS Blackwell.
Doris, J. (Ed.). (1991). *The Suggestibility of Children's Recollections*. Washington, DC: American Psychological Association.
Eisen, M.L., Goodman, G.S., Qin, J., Davis, S., & Crayton, J. (2007). Maltreated children's memory: Accuracy, suggestibility, and psychopathology. *Developmental Psychology, 43*, 1275–1294.
Fivush, R. (1993). Developmental perspectives on autobiographical recall. In G.S. Goodman & B.L. Bottoms (Eds), *Child Victims, Child Witnesses: Understanding and Improving Children's Testimony* (pp. 1–24). NY: Guilford.
Fivush, R., Sales, J.M., Goldberg, A., Bahrick, L., & Parker, J. (2004). Weathering the storm: Children's long-term recall of hurricane Andrew. *Memory, 12*, 104–118.

Flin, R., Bull, R. Boon, J., & Knox, A. (1990). *Child Witnesses in Scottish Criminal Prosecutions*. Edinburgh: Scottish Home and Health Department.

Garven, S., Wood, J.M., Malpass, R.S., & Shaw, J.S. III. (1998). More than suggestion: The effect of interviewing techniques from the McMartin preschool case. *Journal of Applied Psychology*, *83*, 347–359.

Gathercole, S.E., & Collins, A.F. (1992). Everyday memory research and its applications. *Applied Cognitive Psychology*, *6*, 461–465.

Goodman, G.S. (1984). Children's testimony in historical perspective. *Journal of Social Issues*, *40*, 9–31.

Goodman, G.S., Bottoms, B.L., Schwartz-Kenney, B.M., & Rudy, L. (1991). Children's testimony about a stressful event: Improving children's reports. *Journal of Narrative and Life History*, *1*, 69–99.

Goodman, G.S., Hirschman, J.E., Hepps, D., & Rudy, L. (1991). Children's memory for stressful events. *Merrill-Palmer Quarterly*, *37*, 109–157.

Goodman, G.S., Pyle-Taub, E., Jones, D.R.H, England, P., Port, L.P., Rudy, L, & Prado, L. (1992). Emotional effects of criminal court testimony on child sexual assault victims. *Monographs of the Society for Research in Child Development*, *57* (Serial No. 229).

Goodman, G.S., Quas, J.A., Batterman-Faunce, J.M., Riddlesberger, M.M., & Kuhn, J. (1997). Children's reactions to and memory for a stressful event: Influences of age, anatomical dolls, knowledge, and parental attachment. *Applied Developmental Science*, *1*, 54–75.

Goodman, G.S., Quas, J.A., & Redlich, A.D. (1998). The ethics of conducting 'false memory' research with children: A reply to Herrmann and Yoder. *Applied Cognitive Psychology*, *12*, 207–217.

Goodman, G.S., Rudy, L., Bottoms, B.L., & Aman, C. (1990). Children's concerns and memory: Issues of ecological validity in the study of children's eyewitness testimony. In R. Fivush, & J.A. Hudson (Eds), *Knowing and Remembering in Young Children: Emory Symposia in Cognition* (Vol. *3*., pp. 249–284). New York: Cambridge University Press.

Goodman, G.S., & Schaaf, J.M. (1997). Over a decade of research on children's eyewitness testimony: What have we learned? Where do we go from here? *Applied Cognitive Psychology*, *11*, S5–S20.

Goodman, G.S., & Schwartz-Kenney, B.M. (1992). Why knowing a child's age is not enough: Influences of cognitive, social, and emotional factors on children's testimony. In H. Dent, & R. Flin (Eds), *Children as Witnesses* (pp. 15–32). Chichester: Wiley.

Goodman, G.S., Toby, A.E., Batterman-Faunce, J.M., Orcutt, H., Thomas, S., Shapiro, C., & Sashsenmaier, T. (1998) Face to face confrontation: Effects of closed circuit technology on children's eyewitness testimony and juror s decision, *Law and Human Behavior*, *22*, 165–203.

Groark, C.J., & McCall, R.B. (2005). Integrating developmentsl scholarship into practice and policy. In M.H. Bornstein, & M.E. Lamb (Eds), *Developmental Science: An Advanced Textbook* (5th edn, pp. 557–601). Mahwah, NJ: Lawrence Erlbaum.

Hamlyn, B., Phelps, A., Turtle. J., & Sattar. G. (2004). *Are Special Measures Working? Evidence from Surveys of Vulnerable and Intimidated Witnesses*. Home Office Research Study No. 283. London: Home Office.

Hechler, D. (1988). *The Battle and the Backlash: The Child Sexual Abuse War*. Lexington, MA: Lexington Books.

Henry, J. (1997). System intervention trauma to child sexual abuse victims following disclosure. *Journal of Interpersonal Violence*, *12*, 499–512.

Herrmann, D., & Yoder, C. (1998). The potential effects of the implanted memory paradigm on child subjects. *Applied Cognitive Psychology*, *12*, 198–206.
Hershkowitz, I., Horowitz, D., & Lamb, M.E. (2005). Trends in children's disclosure of abuse in Israel: A national study. *Child Abuse and Neglect*, *29*, 1203–1214.
Hershkowitz, I., Horowitz, D., Lamb, M.E., Orbach, Y., & Sternberg, K.J. (2004). Interviewing youthful suspects in alleged sex crimes: A descriptive analysis. *Child Abuse and Neglect*, *28*, 423–438.
Hershkowitz, I., Lamb, M.E., & Horowitz, D. (2007). Victimization of children with disabilities. *American Journal of Orthopsychiatry*, *77*, 629–635.
Hewitt, S.D. (1999). *Assessing Allegations of Sexual Abuse in Preschool Children*. Thousand Oaks, CA: Sage.
Hill, S.R. & Sales, B.D. (2008). *Courtroom Modifications for Child Witnesses*. Washington DC: American Psychological Association.
Home Office. (1992). *Memorandum of Good Practice on Video Recorded Interviews with Child Witnesses for Criminal Proceedings*. London: Home Office.
Home Office. (2007). *Achieving Best Evidence in Criminal Proceedings: Guidance on Interviewing Victims and Witnesses, and Using Special Measures*. London: Home Office.
Howe, M.L., Cicchetti, D., Toth, S.L., & Cerrito, B.M. (2004). True and false memories in maltreated children. Child Development, *75*, 1402–1417.
Huffman, M.L., Crossman, A.M., & Ceci, S.J. (1997). 'Are false memories permanent?': An investigation of the long-term effects of source misattributions. *Consciousness and Cognition*, *6*, 482–490.
Johnston, M. (1997). *Spectral Evidence: The Ramona Case. Incest, Memory and Truth on Trial in Napa Valley*. Boulder, CO: Westview Press.
Kuehnle, K. (1996). *Assessing Allegations of Child Sexual Abuse*. Sarasota, FL: Professional Resource Press/Professional Resource Exchange.
Lamb, M.E., Hershkowitz, I., Orbach, Y., & Esplin, P.W. (2008). *Tell Me What Happened: Structured Investigative Interviews of Child Victims and Witnesses*. Hoboken, NJ: Wiley.
Lamb, M.E., Orbach, Y., Hershkowitz, I., Esplin, P.W., & Horowitz, D. (2007). A structured forensic interview protocol improves the quality and informativeness of investigative interviews with children: A review of the research using the NICHD Investigative Interview Protocol. *Child Abuse and Neglect*, *31*, 1201–1231.
Lamb, M.E., Sternberg, K.J., Orbach, Y., Esplin, P.W., & Mitchell, S. (2002). Is ongoing feedback necessary to maintain the quality of investigative interviews with allegedly abused children? *Applied Developmental Science*, *6*, 35–41.
Lamb, M.E., Sternberg, K.J., Orbach, Y., Esplin, P.W., Stewart, H., & Mitchell, S. (2003a). Age differences in young children's responses to open-ended invitations in the course of forensic interviews. *Journal of Consulting and Clinical Psychology*, *71*, 926–934.
Lamb, M.E., Sternberg, K.J., Orbach, Y., Hershkowitz, I., & Esplin, P.W. (1999). Forensic interviews of children. In R. Bull, & A. Memon (Eds), *The Psychology of Interviewing: A Handbook* (pp. 253–278). New York: Wiley.
Lamb, M.E., Sternberg, K.J., Orbach, Y., Hershkowitz, I., & Horowitz, D. (2003b). Diferences between accounts provided by witnesses and alleged victims of child sexual abuse. *Child Abuse and Neglect*, *27*, 1019–1031.

Landstrom, S. (2008). *CCTV, Live and Videotapes*. Gothenburg, Sweden: University of Gothenburg.
Leichtman, M.D., & Ceci, S.J. (1995). The effects of stereotypes and suggestions on preschoolers' reports. *Developmental Psychology*, *31*, 568–578.
Loftus, E.F. (1993). The reality of repressed memories. *American Psychologist*, *48*, 518–537.
Lyon, T.D. (1999). The new wave in children's suggestibility research: A critique. *Cornell Law Review*, *84*, 1004.
Lyon, T.D., Malloy, L.C., & Quas, J.A., & Talwar, V. (2008). Coaching, truth induction, and young maltreated children's false allegations and false denials. *Child Development*, *79*, 914–929.
Maclean, H.N. (1993). *Once Upon a Time: A True Story of Memory, Murder, and the Law*. New York: HarperCollins.
Mason, M.A. (1991). The McMartin case revisited: The conflict between social work and criminal justice. *Social Work*, *36*, 391–395.
McCall, R.B., & Green, B.L. (2004). Beyond the methodological gold standards of behavioral research: Considerations for practice and policy. *Society for Research in Child Development Social Policy Reports*, *18*, 1–19.
Miller, G.A. (2003). The cognitive revolution: A historical perspective. *Trends in Cognitive Sciences*, *7*, 141–144.
Murray, K. (1995). *Live Television Link: An Evaluation of its use by Child Witnesses in Scottish Criminal Trials*. Edinburgh: The Scottish Office.
New Jersey v. Michaels, 625 A.2d 579 aff'd 642 A.2d 1372 (1994).
Orbach, Y., Hershkowitz, I., Lamb, M.E., Esplin, P.W., & Horowitz, D. (2000). Assessing the value of structured protocols for forensic interviews of alleged child abuse victims. *Child Abuse and Neglect*, *24*, 733–752.
Orcutt, H.K., Goodman, G.S., Tobey, A.E., Batterman-Faunce, J.M., & Thomas, S. (2001). Detecting deception in children's testimony: Factfinders' abilities to reach the truth in open court and closed-circuit trials. *Law and Human Behavior*, *25*, 339–372.
Ornstein, P.A., & Davies, G. (Eds). (1997). Memory and suggestibility in child witnesses: The NATO conference [Special issue]. *Applied Cognitive Psychology*.
Ornstein, P.A., Baker-Ward, L., Gordon, B.N., & Merritt, K.A. (1997). Children's memory for medical experiences: Implications for testimony. *Applied Cognitive Psychology*, *11*, S87–S104.
Peterson, C. (1999). Children's memory for medical emergencies: 2 years later. *Developmental Psychology*, *35*, 1493–1506.
Pezdek, K., & Hodge, D. (1999). Planting false childhood memories in children: The role of event plausibility. *Child Development*, *70*, 887–895.
Pipe, M.E., Lamb, M.E., Orbach, Y., & Cederborg, A.C. (2007). *Child Sexual Abuse: Disclosure, Delay and Denial*. Mahwah, NJ: Lawrence Erlbaum.
Poole, D.A., & Lamb, M.E. (1998). *Investigative Interviews of Children: A Guide for Helping Professionals*. Washington, DC: American Psychological Association.
Powell, M.B., & Wright, R. (2008). Investigative interviewers' perceptions of the value of different training tasks on their adherence to open-ended questions with children. *Psychiatry, Psychology and Law*, *15*, 272–283.
Quas, J.A., Davis, E., Goodman, G.S., & Myers, J.E.B. (2007). Repeated questions, deceptions, and children's true and false reports of body touch. *Child Maltreatment*, *12*, 60–67.

Quas, J.A., Goodman, G.S., Bidrose, S., Pipe, M.E., Craw, S., & Ablin, D.S. (1999). Emotion and memory: Children's long-term remembering, forgetting, and suggestibility. *Journal of Experimental Child Psychology*, *72*, 235–270.

Quas, J.A., Goodman, G.S., Ghetti, S., Alexander, K.W., Edelstein, R., Redlich, A.D., Cordon, I.M., & Jones, D.P.H. (2005). Childhood sexual assault victims: Long-term outcomes after testifying in criminal court. *Monographs of the Society for Research in Child Development*, *70*, 1–145.

R v. E (2009). EWCA Crim 1370.

Roberts, K.P., & Powell, M.B. (2001). Describing individual incidents of sexual abuse: A review of research on the effects of multiple sources of information on children's reports. *Child Abuse and Neglect*, *25*, 1643–1659.

Saks, M.J. (1989). Legal policy analysis and evaluation. *American Psychologist*, *44*, 1110–1117.

Saywitz, K.J., & Nathanson, R. (1993). Children's testimony and their perceptions of stress in and out of the courtroom. *Child Abuse and Neglect*, *17*, 613–622.

Saywitz, K.J., Snyder, L., & Nathanson, R. (1999). Faciliating the communicative competence of the child witness. *Applied Developmental Science*, *3*, 58–68.

Sommer, R. (2006). Dual dissemination: Writing for colleagues and the public. *American Psychologist*, *61*, 955–958.

Spencer, J.R., & Flin, R.H. (1993). *The Evidence of Children: The Law and the Psychology* (2nd edn). London: Blackstone.

Stern, W. (1910). Abstracts of lectures on the psychology of testimony and on the study of individuality. *American Journal of Psychology*, *21*, 270–282.

Sternberg, K.J., Lamb, M.E., Davies, G.M., & Westcott, H.L. (2001). The Memorandum of Good Practice: Theory versus application. *Child Abuse and Neglect*, *25*, 669–681.

Sternberg, K.J., Lamb, M.E., Hershkowitz, I., Yudilevitch, L., Orbach, Y., Esplin, P.W., & Hovav, M. (1997). Effects of introductory style on children's abilities to describe experience of sexual abuse. *Child Abuse and Neglect*, *21*, 1133–1146.

Sternberg, K.J., Lamb, M.E., Orbach, Y., Esplin, P.W., & Mitchell, S. (2001). Use of a structured investigative protocol enhances young children's responses to free-recall prompts in the course of forensic interviews. *Journal of Applied Psychology*, *86*, 997–1005.

Sullivan, P.M., & Knutson, J.F. (2000). Maltreatment and disabilities: A population-based epidemiological study. *Child Abuse and Neglect*, *24*, 1257–1273.

Talwar, V., & Lee, K. (2008). Social and cognitive correlates of children's lying behavior. *Child Development*, *79*, 866–881.

Talwar, V., Lee, K., Bala, N., & Lindsay, R.C.L. (2004). Children's lie-telling to conceal a parent's transgression: Legal implications. *Law and Human Behavior*, *28*, 411–435.

Tye, M.C., Amato, S.L., Honts, C.R., Devitt, M.K., & Peters, D. (1999). The willingness of children to lie and the assessment of credibility in an ecologically relevant laboratory setting. *Applied Developmental Science*, *3*, 92–109.

Varendonck, J. (1911). Les temoignages d'enfants dans un proces retentissant [The testimony of children in a famous trial]. *Archives de Psycholgie*, *11*, 129–171.

Vrij, A. (2008). *Detecting Lies and Deceit: Pitfalls and Opportunities.* Chichester: Wiley.

Wade, K.A., & Laney, C. (2008). Time to rewrite your autobiography? *The Psychologist*, *7*, 588–592.

Warren, A.R., Woodall, C.E., Thomas, M., Nunno, M., Keeney, J.M., Larson, S.M., & Stadfeld, J.A. (1999). Assessing the effectiveness of a training program for interviewing child witnesses. *Applied Developmental Science*, *3*, 128–135.

Waterman, A.H., Blades, M., & Spencer, C.P. (2000). Do children try to answer nonsensical questions? *British Journal of Developmental Psychology*, *18*, 211–226.

Waterman, A.H., Blades, M., & Spencer, C.P. (2004). Indicating when you do not know the answer: The effect of question format and interviewer knowledge on children's 'don't know' responses. *British Journal of Developmental Psychology*, *22*, 335–348.

Westcott, H. (1998). Review of jeopardy in the courtroom. *British Journal of Psychology*, *89*, 525–527.

Westcott, H.L., & Kynan, S. (2006). Interviewer practice in investigative interviews for suspected child sexual abuse. *Psychology, Crime and Law*, *12*, 367–382.

Westcott, H.L., Kynan, S., & Few, C. (2006). Improving the quality of investigative interviews for suspected child abuse: A case study. *Psychology, Crime and Law*, *12*, 77–96.

Whitcomb, D. (2003). Legal interventions for child victims. *Journal of Traumatic Stress*, *16*, 149–157.

Zigler, E.F., & Finn-Stevenson, M. (1999). Applied developmental psychology. In M.H. Bornstein, & M.E. Lamb (Eds), *Developmental Science: An Advanced Textbook* (4th edn, pp. 555–598). Mahwah, NJ: Lawrence Erlbaum.

19

Child Protection Considerations in the United States

RICHARD J. GELLES AND REBECCA BRIGHAM

Key Points

- The core organizational task in child protection is decision making.
- In each decision, there is the risk of a false positive and a false negative.
- One cannot simultaneously reduce false positives and false negatives – therefore child protective services needs to decide which kind or error it can accept.
- The child protective service system in the United States operates as a series of gates, with gatekeepers who assess risk and safety and determine whether a case of child maltreatment is moved forward or closed.

A review of the mission statements in the policy manuals of almost every public child welfare[1] agency in the United States yields a consistent picture of the goals of public child welfare and child protective services.

[1]This chapter will use the terms 'child welfare' and 'child protective services' interchangeably. Some scholars and practitioners prefer to see the term 'child welfare' applied to the larger system that includes welfare, child protection, and juvenile delinquency. For stylistic sake, we use the terms interchangeably but use them to describe the system that responds to, and deals with, the abuse and neglect of children.

Children's Testimony: A Handbook of Psychological Research and Forensic Practice, Second Edition.
Edited by Michael E. Lamb, David J. La Rooy, Lindsay C. Malloy, and Carmit Katz.

The mission statements almost always state that the goal of the agency is to ensure the safety and well-being of children, preserve families, and ensure permanency for children. A typical example of such a mission statement appears on the home page of the New Jersey Department of Children and Families:

> The Division of Youth and Family Services (DYFS) is New Jersey's child protection and child welfare agency within the Department of Children and Families. Its mission is to ensure the safety, permanency and well-being of children and to support families. (http://www.state.nj.us/dcf/divisions/dyfs/)

Public agency mission statements are derived from the legal obligations of public child welfare agencies that are articulated in federal and state law. The most recent federal law that speaks to the primary mission of child welfare agencies is the Adoption and Safe Families Act of 1997 (PL 105-89); it states that our national goals for children in the child welfare system are safety and well-being:

> **15)** provides that—
>
> A. in determining reasonable efforts to be made with respect to a child, as described in this paragraph, and in making such reasonable efforts, the child's health and safety shall be the paramount concern;
> B. except as provided in subparagraph (D), reasonable efforts shall be made to preserve and reunify families— (42 U.S.C. Chapter 7, Subpart IV, Part E, Paragraph 671)

A cursory examination of the structure of public child welfare organizations with a focus on job titles and position descriptions would leave the impression that public child welfare's primary tasks are to deliver services for the purposes of supporting and preserving families and to ensure the safety and well-being of children. The front-line workers in public child welfare qualify for the position by possessing bachelor's degrees. Supervisors are most often required to hold Masters of Social Work (MSW) or master's degrees in related disciplines. The titles for the front line staff include 'social worker', 'case manager', or 'caseworker'. Overall, the formal and informal job titles and qualifications give the impression that the major task of child protection is to manage and/or deliver services for the purposes of fulfilling the goals of safety, well-being, and permanence.

THE MAIN ORGANIZATIONAL TASK IS DECISION MAKING

The mission statements and job titles are misleading. Child welfare practice is chiefly about making decisions (Rycus & Hughes, 2008). The challenging part of such a core task is that each decision has the risk of a false positive or a false negative – caseworkers can accurately assess a case; can assume a child is safe when in fact the child is at grave risk (a false negative); or assume that the child is at risk when the child is actually safe (a false positive). Although child welfare agency administrators often believe they can develop systems that can reduce both false positives and false negatives, the laws of probability theory are that one cannot reduce both false positives and false negatives at the same time.

The core task of decision making and the risk of false positives and false negatives is not unique to child protection work in the United States – decision making is a universal task in any nation's system of child protection. Thus, although our discussion here focuses on the situation in the United States, the conclusions are likely to apply to other developed countries with child welfare systems.

Child Protection in the United States

The structure of child welfare and child protection in the United States was established during the late 1960s through the mid 1970s with the enactment of laws that established procedures and protocols for the reporting of suspected child abuse and neglect. The child protection system in the United States is sometimes used as a model for the development of child protection systems in other nations (e.g. Australia), but most other nations have developed their own unique systems of child protection.

Through the efforts of advocates such as C. Henry Kempe and the actions of the United States Children's Bureau, by the late 1960s all states had some sort of procedure for mandatory reporting. The final incentive and structure was provided by the enactment of the federal Child Abuse Prevention and Treatment Act of 1974 (PL 93-247). The Child Abuse Prevention and Treatment Act of 1974 (CAPTA) provided funding to states provided that the states met specific conditions regarding state mandatory reporting laws, such as immunity of prosecution for anyone who makes a report in good faith, even when no maltreatment had actually happened.

Whatever child protective services were before the late 1960s, they changed dramatically after the implementation of CAPTA. There was an exponential growth in the number of reported cases of suspected child abuse. As a result, public child welfare agencies at the state and county levels developed structures that, metaphorically, created a series of 'gates' through which cases of suspected child abuse and neglect proceeded. Child protective service workers became 'gatekeepers' who manned the gates. The decisions of the workers determined what, if any, services or support children and families would receive.

This chapter identifies the key gates in the US child welfare system, examines the main policy and practice issues that influence the structure and function of the individual gates, and provides an overall assessment of the strengths and limitations of the child welfare system in the United States.

The 'Gates'

Prior to the enactment of mandatory reporting laws (and in nations that do not have laws requiring mandatory reporting of suspected child maltreatment), there were a variety of means by which child abuse and neglect would be identified. Physicians, nurses, teachers, counsellors, social workers, friends, neighbours, and strangers might observe a child who was dirty, inappropriately dressed, hungry, abandoned, or injured. The benchmark case that 'put a face' on the problem of child abuse and neglect was the case of Mary Ellen Wilson who was found in 1874 to be whipped and beaten by her caregivers (Gelles, 1996; Nelson, 1984). The child was discovered by Etta Wheeler who was a 'friendly visitor' working for Saint Luke's Methodist Mission in New York City.

While there were many means by which maltreated children could be identified, there was no well-developed infrastructure that could respond to cases of child maltreatment and organize and deliver appropriate services. In Mary Ellen's case, legend had it that she was represented in court by the American Society for the Prevention of Cruelty to Animals (ASPCA) after the New York City police refused to get involved. In reality, Mary Ellen was represented by an attorney who was a friend of the founder of the ASPCA. At the time, cases of maltreatment could be responded to by the police, physicians, hospitals, volunteers from private agencies, public agencies, or they could simply be ignored.

CAPTA, ensuing public awareness campaigns, and technological developments such as toll-free telephone numbers, increased the number of reports and funnelled those reports to a designated public agency – public child protective services. Figure 19.1 demonstrates that reports grew from 500 000 in 1976 to 1 million in 1979, 2 million in 1986, and 3 million in 1993 (Gelles & Spigner, 2008). The number of reports stabilized at between 2.5 and 3.4 million after 1993.

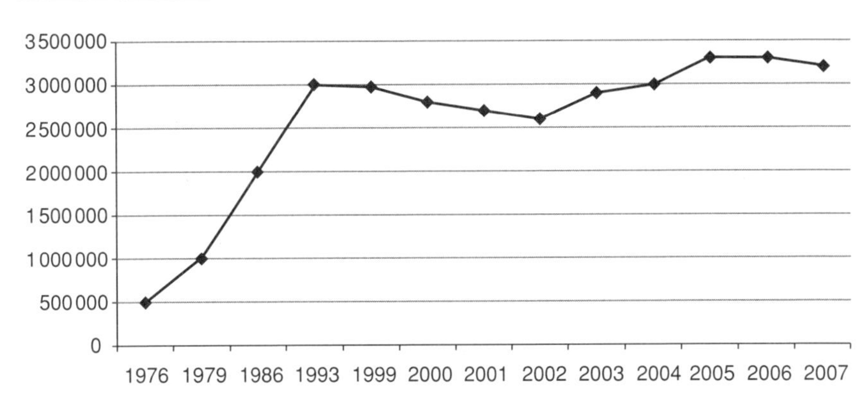

Figure 19.1 Estimated total reports received by the child protective service.

As a result of mandatory reporting laws, two gates were created to manage the reports. Gate 1 is what is generally referred to as 'screening'. Mandatory reporting laws require specific professionals, or in some states, all adults, to report suspected child maltreatment. Every state has some sort of 'hotline' that receives reports by telephone, fax, or in writing.[2] The task of the gatekeeper at the hotline gate is to screen reports and determine which should be investigated and the speed with which investigations should be mounted.

Gate 2 is the investigation. At this point a child protective service (CPS) worker begins the task of assembling information in order to determine whether there is a 'substantiated' or valid case of child maltreatment. Standard practice typically requires seeing the suspected victim(s), speaking with the caregivers and suspected perpetrators, and gathering relevant collateral information from schools, medical facilities, criminal justice agencies, and the child protective service agencies' own files. The result of the investigation is a decision whether to substantiate the report – in other words, determine that maltreatment has occurred or whether to 'unsubstantiate' a report, in other words to conclude either that maltreatment did not occur or that there is insufficient evidence to justify substantiation.[3]

Gate 3 and 4 are placed immediately after Gate 2. For those cases that are substantiated, the investigator must make an additional decision at Gate 3 – should the child remain in the household or should the child

[2]In some states there is a state-wide hotline, while other states have hotlines for each county or organizational geographical or administrative unit.

[3]The actual terms used vary from state to state – some states use the terms substantiated/unsubstantiated, while others use the terms founded/unfounded (Myers, 2006). Some states have three-part decision trees: substantiated, unsubstantiated, or indicated.

be removed? Gate 4 is the decision regarding children who remain in the home even after the report is substantiated. At Gate 4, the investigator or caseworker must decide whether the family should be provided services (required or voluntary) or whether the case should be closed. The time frame and personnel who are the gatekeepers vary. Typically, the Gate 3 decision is made in real time during the initial stage or hours of the investigation. Gate 4 decisions may be made by someone other than the investigator and are made in the course of, or at the end of, the investigations.

Subsequent gates include Gate 5: if the child is to be removed from the home, where should the child be placed? Gate 6 comes into play if a child must be moved from one out-of-home placement to another. Gate 7 is the point at which decision is made whether or not to return the child to the birth parents, and Gate 8 is the decision to terminate parental rights. One could conceivably identify sub-gates and other decisions that must be made by case managers, but the eight-gate system constitutes a reasonably accurate picture of the structure of child protective services in the United States.

This remainder of this chapter focuses on what is generally referred to as the 'front end' of the child welfare system – the travel of a report of suspected child maltreatment from Gate 1 (screening), through Gate 3 and 4 (placement or services).

GATE 1: SCREENING

The components of the child welfare system that receive reports of suspected child maltreatment constitute the portals of the child welfare system. In 2007, state and county child protective service agencies received an estimated 3.2 million referrals or reports of suspected child abuse and neglect involving approximately 5.2 million children (US Department of Health and Human Services, 2009).[4] This translates to a referral rate of approximately 43 referrals per 1000 children in the populations[5] in 2007 (see Figure 19.2; US Department of Health and Human Services, 2009).[6]

Professionals, individuals who encountered suspected child maltreatment in the course of their work, made 57% of the referrals.

[4]The numbers are estimated because only 48 of the 50 states reported data as part of the National Child Abuse and Neglect Data System.

[5]Note: the numerator for calculating the rate is 'referrals' not children, because a referral may include more than one child.

[6]The numbers are estimated because only 37 of the 50 states reported data as part of the National Child Abuse and Neglect Data System.

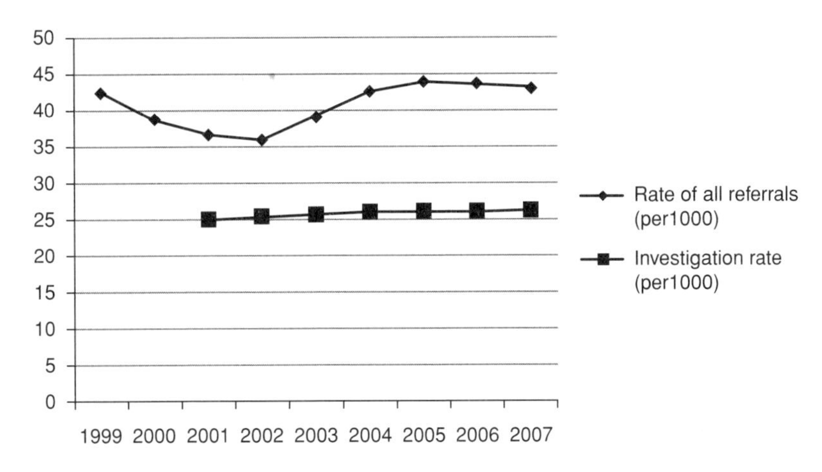

Figure 19.2 Investigation level rates (may be multiple children per investigation).

Professionals include teachers, legal staff, or police officers, social services staff, medical staff, mental health workers, child daycare workers, and foster care providers. The three largest sources of 2007 reports were from teachers (17.0%), lawyers or police officers (16.3%), and social services staff (10.2%). Non-professionals submitted 26.8% of the reports. These included parents, relatives, friends and neighbours, alleged victims, alleged perpetrators, and anonymous callers. The three largest groups of non-professional reporters were anonymous (7.6%), other relatives (7.3%), and parents (6.1%). Unknown or 'other' report sources submitted 15.7% of the reports (US Department of Health and Human Services, 2009).

The screening carried out at Gate 1 involves assessing information provided by a wide range of reporters, who provide varying details and information about the suspected incident of maltreatment. The main concern of the Gate 1 screener is whether the report meets the definition of child abuse and neglect as stated in state law (and agency policy), whether there is sufficient information to carry out an investigation, and whether the victim/child is the responsibility of some other entity – an Indian tribe or the military. If the victim is not a child – defined as under-18 years of age – the case will be screened out; in other words there will be no investigation of the allegations.

During FY 2007 (the 2007 Fiscal Year), CPS agencies screened in (i.e., decided to investigate further) 61.7% of referrals and screened out 38.3%. These proportions were identical in FY 2006 when 61.7% were screened in and 38.3% were screened out. There is considerable variation across states and agencies in terms of screening-in rates. In 2007, Arizona screened in 99.3% of 33 188 reports. Vermont, however, screened in only 20.8 of 2564 reports. Of the larger states, California, a county-administered system, screened in 68.5% of 232 297 reports while Texas screened in 82.5% of 166 584 reports. Overall, the investigation rate in 2007 reveal that there were approximately 26 investigations per 1000 children in the population (Figure 19.2; US Department of Health and Human Services, 2009).[7]

As will be seen in the following discussion of Gate 2 investigations, the national screen-in rate is considerably higher than the rate of investigations that result in 'substantiation'. It would be fair to say that at Gate 1, child welfare systems are 'false-negative' sensitive. The high rate of screening in seems to arise out of agency philosophies that it is best to investigate a case rather than miss a child who might later be seriously or fatally maltreated. Assuming the report includes adequate information to launch an investigation and the allegation meets the basic outlines of the state law, an investigation will be carried out. The probability of a screen in being followed by an investigation is likely related to the source of the report, with reports submitted by professionals more likely to be investigated (Gelles, 1992).[8]

The child welfare philosophy appears to be that, assuming there is enough information to initiate an investigation (names and addresses), the incident conforms to state definitions, and the report appears credible, an investigation will be initiated. The risk of not initiating an investigation is that the case will subsequently come to public attention as will the fact that the child welfare agency was alerted to suspected abuse or neglect and failed to respond.

Beyond taking in information and determining if the referral meets the standard of state law, there appears to be no scientific or systematic mechanism to aid the decision-making process regarding whether to screen in the case or not. Agencies do have screening protocols, but such protocols are limited in that, to date, no agency has real-time access to data that might be used in decision making, including educational records, medical records, juvenile records, and criminal justice records.[9] While the screener can access agency data on prior reports of

[7]When calculating the rate of investigations, the numerator is investigations and the denominator is number of children in the population.

[8]The National Child Abuse and Neglect Data System (NCANDS) public report does not provide data on rates of screening in by each category of reporter. However, there is a relationship between reporter status and rate of substantiation, so it seems logical that a similar relationship exists for screening (Gelles, 1982).

[9]Some agencies have access to some of these data, but at present no agency has full access across systems.

maltreatment, even these data are often incomplete or not accessible in real time. Thus, because of limited information, limited access to data, and agency fear of publicity surrounding false negatives, Gate 1 is relatively porous and an estimated 2 million investigations are initiated after cases are screened in at Gate 1. The cost of these investigations is borne entirely by the state or county, as there is no federal law or funding stream to support the functioning of Gate 1.

GATE 2: INVESTIGATIONS

The most recent National Child Abuse and Neglect Data System (NCANDS) data provide a breakdown of the results of 1.8 million investigations carried out in 2007. Of these investigations, 24.7% were either substantiated or indicated, while 61.3% were unsubstantiated (US Department of Health and Human Services, 2009). These statistics have remained relatively consistent over the past decade (Figure 19.3). In other words, child welfare agencies screen in more than 6 out of 10 referrals, while subsequent investigations confirm abuse and neglect in less than 1 in 4 of the households/children. Thus, the rate of children receiving an investigation ('child disposition rate') is about 26 children out of every 1000 children in the general population, and the rate of victimization (i.e., an investigation outcome of 'substantiated',

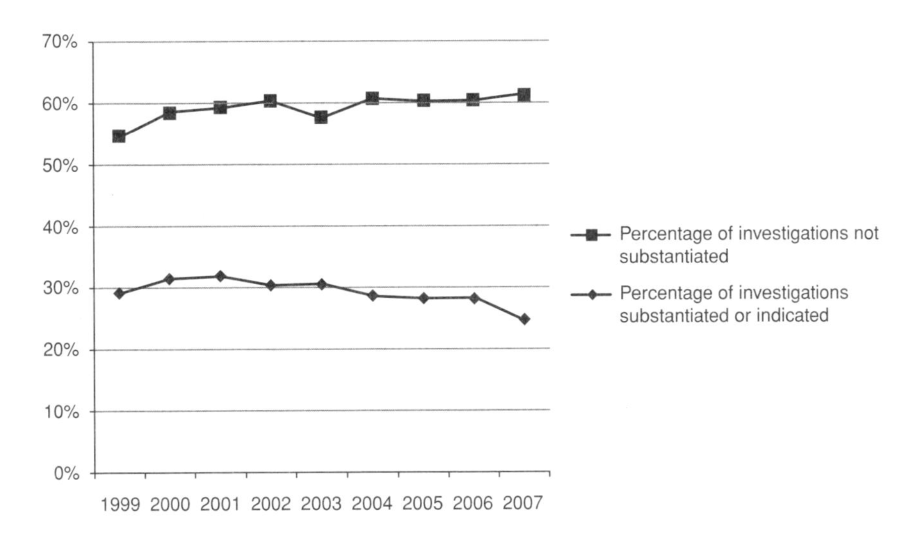

Figure 19.3 Outcome of investigations.

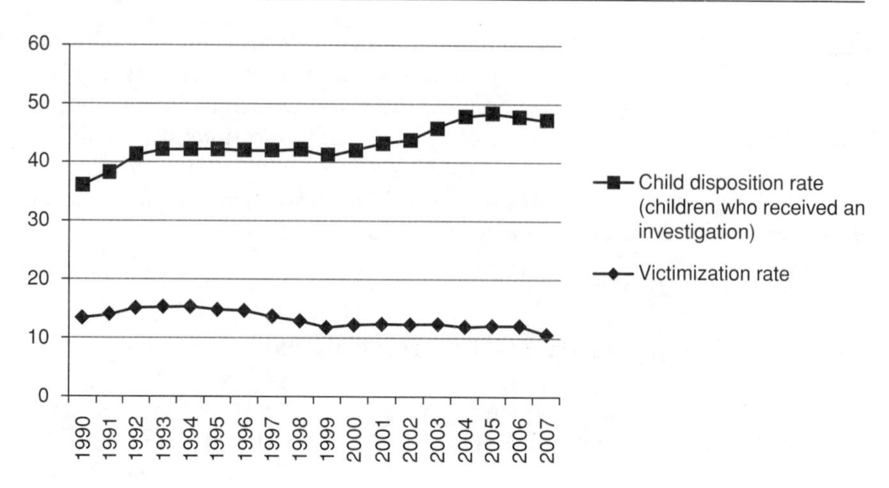

Figure 19.4 Rates of investigation and victimization (per 1000 children).

'indicated', or 'alternate response victim'[10]) is about 10 children per 1000 (Figure 19.4).

Compared with research on the process of screening reports, there is a much more substantial literature on decision-making during investigations. While the main goal of an investigation is to determine whether abuse or neglect have occurred, the purpose of investigations is to determine what level of risk exists in a household and whether there are safety concerns for the suspected victims of maltreatment. It is difficult to separate the decisions regarding substantiation, risk, and safety, so for the purposes of this section, we examine these components as part of the Gate 2 decision-making process.

The Basis of Decision Making

Clinical judgement A variety of processes or techniques are employed by child welfare agencies and workers in the decision making at Gate 2. Historically and up to the present, the most common form of decision making involves clinical judgement. When using clinical judgement, the CPS worker processes the information in his/her head and then makes a decision (Dawes, Faust, & Meehl, 1989). Generally, decisions

[10]This is an investigation disposition (outcome) that is reported by very few states – 2 in 2007 – and is used in only 0.5% of cases in those states to indicate that the child was deemed a victim despite the maltreatment being neither substantiated nor indicated.

are influenced by personal characteristics, biases, and experiences of the worker, which would lead to a variety of problems concerning the reliability and validity of the predicted risk (Gambrill & Shlonsky, 2000). The accuracy of clinical judgement is, according to research, minimal. For example, research comparing clinical judgement with actuarial methods (statistical) has shown actuarial methods to be superior in terms of reliability and accuracy. Clinical judgement, as a result of fatigue, recent experiences, or mood fluctuations, can produce random changes in judgement while actuarial methods always lead to the same conclusion for the given information (Dawes, Faust, & Meehl, 1989). When compared with statistical models, clinical judgements of experts do an inferior job of predicting behaviour as a result of low reliability (Gambrill & Shlonsky, 2000). Rossi, Schuerman, and Budde (1996) asked child welfare experts and CPS workers from three states to make decisions and write summaries about actual child abuse and neglect cases. The authors found that decision making in the child protection systems is inconsistent. 'Although there appeared to be some general principles used in making decisions, in the sense that certain characteristics of cases (especially prior complaint record) played roles in decisions, workers and experts varied widely in how each weighed those characteristics in making decisions' (Rossi *et al.*, 1996). The researchers concluded that decision making by way of clinical judgement in the child protection agencies may result in many false alarms and in many high risk cases being classified as low risk (Rossi *et al.*, 1996).

Consensus risk assessment A second common form of decision making is 'consensus risk assessment'. In consensus-based risk assessments, specific client characteristics are identified by the consensus judgement of experts in the context of child maltreatment (Baird, 2002). Generally, expert judges use knowledge from clinical experience and the research literature (Knoke & Trocme, 2005). Child welfare workers use the consensus from experts to guide decision making about child maltreatment while exercising their own clinical judgement about the case (Baird, 2002). The list of predictors or characteristics of child maltreatment is based on consensus, mainly by expert judges and accepted practice knowledge, and/or simple correlations found in research literature (Gambrill & Shlonsky, 2000). These instruments help organize the caseworkers' clinical assessment of child abuse risk, but are not based on research specific to the area that uses this instrument (Baird & Wagner, 2000). Some of the states using consensus-based risk assessments are Washington, Illinois, and California (Family Assessment Factor Analysis, the Fresno Model).

Actuarial risk assessment Actuarial risk assessment models are based on empirical research involving actual CPS cases. Empirical research is used to recognize a set of risk factors with a strong statistical relationship to the specified behavioural outcome. Actuarial-based instruments integrate client characteristics shown to be associated with future child maltreatment (Rycus & Hughes, 2003). These models are generally constructed by taking a sample of children and families in the child welfare system, examining their paths while in the system, and linking those paths to a set of characteristics or events related to each family in the sample (Gambrill & Shlonsky, 2000). The analysed characteristics and events are weighted and combined to form an assessment tool that categorizes families or individuals according to the 'risk' they may exhibit (Rycus & Hughes, 2003). Following this approach, workers use the actuarial instruments to score whether families are of low, medium, or high risk (Baird, 2002). The goal or purpose of actuarial instruments is to have the highest number of substantiations in the category of high-risk families and the lowest number in the low-risk category. Michigan, California (California Risk Assessment, not the Fresno model), Alaska, and New Jersey are some of the states currently using actuarial measures to assess the risk of child maltreatment.

A widely used actuarial risk assessment model is the Structured Decision Making System (SDM). SDM was developed and implemented by the National Council on Crime and Delinquency's Children Research Center (CRC). Space precludes a detailed discussion of the SDM approach to actuarial decision making.

Although actuarial risks assessments have been shown to be an improvement over clinical judgement and consensus-based tools, the predictive validity and reliability is still modest. Gambrill and Shlonsky (2000), who have compared the two risk assessments, state: 'although actuarial models tend to be the best predictors of future maltreatment, they are far from perfect' (Gambrill & Shlonsky, 2000, p. 826). The Michigan's SDM System Family Risk Assessment of Abuse and Neglect, is one of the most researched risk assessments demonstrating superiority over other tools, but still has a level of reliability lower than desired (Knoke & Trocme, 2005).

Data Mining: Neural Networks

Artificial Neural Networks (ANN), a type of data mining computing methodology, has the potential to be more reliable and efficient and to improve predictive accuracy in child maltreatment risk assessment (Flaherty & Patterson, 2003). As a computer-based learning system,

ANN is able to discover patterns in a set of data, especially concerning past behaviour (Zandi, 2000). According to Zandi:

> Artificial neural network (ANN) is a technology that is capable of discovering patterns in a set of data – if such patterns exist. ANN is a learning system that tacitly discovers the working mechanism of a system from examples of its past behavior. Thus, for complex systems that explanatory theories are lacking, but data regarding past behavior is available, ANN is a powerful tool of investigation. (Zandi, 2000, p. 5)

Schwartz, Kaufman, and Schwartz (2004) examined data gathered by the Third National Incidence Study of Child Abuse and Neglect. The researchers used ANN procedures to 'train' and test 1767 child abuse cases. The study showed that the trained network was able to categorize successfully 89.6% of the cases in the sample population, which resulted in a 10.4% predictive error. Most (about 75%) of the predictive errors resulted from the ANN's inability to classify some cases. Only 0.6% of the cases were false positives and 1.9% were false negatives (Schwartz *et al.,* 2004). Zandi (2000) replicated this study and was successfully able to train neural networks to classify child abuse and neglect cases as in the previous study. In one of the network experiments, 90% of the abused cases were correctly classified. Some 10% of the cases were false negatives and 13% were false positives (Zandi, 2000).

Research has also compared the effectiveness of ANN with linear or logistic multiple regression. Marshall and English (2000) applied neural network analysis to CPS data from the State of Washington's risk assessment model. The authors concluded that the neural network demonstrated better prediction and classification abilities than logistic regression models. This improvement can be explained by the ability of neural networks to represent non-linear relationships between highly interacting variables, which are generally characterized by risk assessment data (Marshall & English, 2000). Marshall and English suggest that neural networks can aid workers seeking to model complex relationships in child maltreatment risk assessments.

Contrary to the other research studies, Flaherty and Patterson (2003) did not find ANN superior to statistical models. The small number of actual case examples included in their study may explain the inferior performance of the ANN model in this study.

ANN appears to represent a promising advance in the assessment of risk for child maltreatment. Although CPS agencies collect a substantial amount of data on cases of suspected child maltreatment, these data are rarely subjected to rigorous analysis that could inform practice in the field of CPS. ANN provide a method for seeking interconnections between the many variables in CPS data sets. More importantly, because ANN is an 'artificial intelligence' technique, the ANN analysis can learn from new data inputted into the system. Other risk assessment instruments are 'static' and cannot be quickly revised in response to changing economic, social, or other circumstances that may be associated with the occurrence of child maltreatment.

GATES 3 AND 4: PLACEMENT AND SERVICES

Should a case of child maltreatment be substantiated, caseworkers and supervisors need to make two important decisions. First, is the risk to the child or children so substantial that the child(ren) should be removed from the residence and care of their caregivers? This decision – the Gate 3 decision – is often made in real time. State laws generally allow caseworkers to remove a child deemed at risk. In most cases, the CPS agency obtains an *ex parte* court order allowing the removal. In other instances, the decision to remove a child may occur during or at the end of an investigation or even during the process of providing services to a family. A court order may be issued *ex parte* or as a result of a dispositional hearing in which the agency and caregivers have legal representation.

By and large, the decision at Gate 3 is guided by clinical judgement and the perception of risk. In some instances, actuarial risk or safety assessment instruments may be used by caseworkers and supervisors, but it would be fair to say that risk or safety scores are typically used only to confirm clinical judgement-based assessments.

Of the nearly 1 000 000 cases of child maltreatment substantiated each year, only about 200 000 children are removed from their caregivers and placed in some form of out-of-home care, a percentage that has remained relatively stable over time (Figure 19.5). Some argue that a 20% rate of removal is too high (see Guggenheim, 2005), whereas we would argue that a system that removes 2 in 10 children who are victims of some form of child maltreatment leans toward keeping most children with their caregivers. Law and practice appear to tilt the decision making toward being 'false positive' sensitive. In other words, parents' rights are privileged in the decision making at Gate 3.

The major legal and policy precedents guiding the Gate 3 decision in the United States are two Supreme Court decisions and the provisions of the Adoption Assistance and Child Welfare Act of 1980 (PL 96-272). US law and tradition grant parents broad discretion as to how they rear their children. In *Smith v. Organization of Foster Families for*

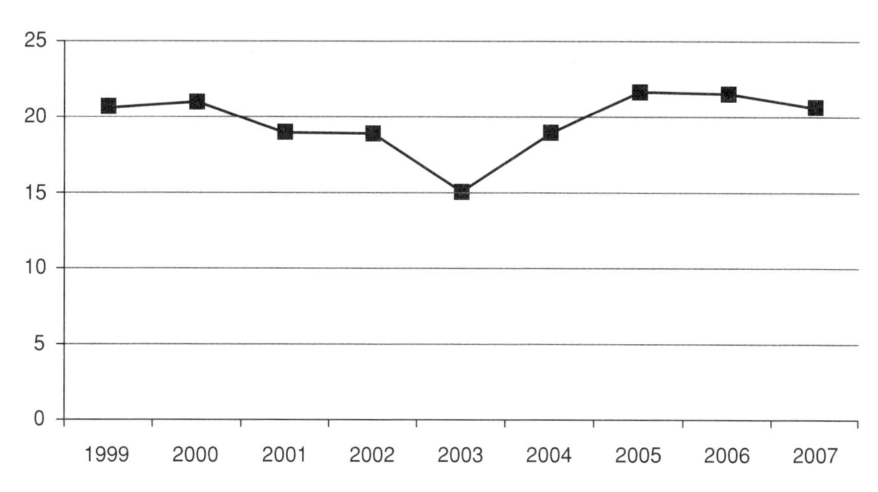

Figure 19.5 Percentage of children removed from home.

Equality and Reform (1977) the US Supreme Court held that the 14th amendment gave parents a 'constitutionally recognized liberty interest' in maintaining the custody of their children 'that derives from blood relationship, state law sanction, and basic human right'. This interest is not absolute, however, because of the state's power and authority to exercise *parens patriae* duties to protect citizens who cannot fend for themselves. The state may attempt to limit or end parent–child contact and make children eligible for temporary or permanent placement or adoption when parents:

1. Abuse, neglect, or abandon their children;
2. Become incapacitated in their ability to be a parent;
3. Refuse or are unable to remedy serious, identified problems in caring for their children; or
4. Experience an extraordinarily severe breakdown in their relationship with their children (e.g., owing to a long prison sentence).

Cognizant that severing the parent–child relationship is an extremely drastic measure, the US Supreme Court held in *Santosky v. Kramer* (1982) that a court may only terminate parental rights if the state can demonstrate with clear and convincing evidence that a parent has failed in one of the aforementioned four ways. Most state statutes also contain provisions for parents to voluntarily relinquish their rights. In addition, the state also has the authority to return a child to his/her parents. Ideally, this occurs once a determination is made that it would be safe to return a child to his/her home and that the child's parents would be able to provide appropriate care.

A second factor that emphasizes keeping maltreated children with their caregivers is the 'reasonable efforts' provision of the Adoption Assistance and Child Welfare Act of 1980. The 'reasonable efforts' provision stated that states must make 'reasonable efforts to maintain a family' before they remove a child from the child's birth parent(s) and 'reasonable efforts to reunify a family' before establishing a permanency plan of adoption. The reasonable efforts requirement mandated states to provide appropriate services prior to placement and/or services that would allow for a safe reunification of a child who had been removed.

Gate 4: Placement

The final gate of the front end of the CPS system is the decision about where to place a child or children to be removed from maltreating caregivers. The federal Adoption and Foster Care Analysis and Reporting System (AFCARS) indicates that as of 30 September 2009, of all children placed in out of home care, the modal placement was with a non-relative foster care provider (Table 19.1).

The major factors guiding the decisions made at Gate 4 are federal law and the availability of suitable (and safe) placements for children. Again, the guiding federal law is the Adoption Assistance and Child Welfare Act of 1980. This law stated that, as a requirement of receiving Federal Title IV-E matching funds, states are required to place a child in the least restrictive setting and, if the child will benefit, one that is close to the parent's home. Placement with a relative would be considered the 'least restrictive' placement while an institutional placement would be the 'most restrictive'.

In reality, the decision-making process for placement, while guided by federal and state law, is often more akin to 'any port in a storm'. CPS

Table 19.1 The placement settings of children in foster care

Pre-adoptive home	4%	17 485
Foster family home (relative)	24%	112 643
Foster family home (non-relative)	47%	217 243
Group home	6%	29 122
Institution	10%	47 165
Supervised independent living	1%	5217
Runaway	2%	9766
Trial home visit	5%	24 358

agency directors almost always claim that they have an insufficient number of licenced foster care providers available. A second limitation is the difficulty of fully vetting individuals and families seeking to be foster care providers. CPS agencies have limited access to the full range of criminal justice, child welfare, and other significant information regarding potential foster care providers. Here again, hard decisions are made based on incomplete data.

CONCLUSIONS

One of the paradoxical aspects of decision making in the CPS system is the consistent and persistent 'false negative sensitive' approach to screening reports and initiating an investigation that, upon carrying out the investigation, switches to a 'false positive sensitive' process. This paradox seems illogical on two grounds. First, the system itself is overall, by dint of federal law, false positive sensitive in that the bar for substantiating maltreatment and initiating a removal is so high. Secondly, the perceived advantage of being false negative sensitive in aggressively initiating investigations is immediately cancelled by the low rate of substantiations and low rate of removals. CPS agencies fear that abuse will be found among cases not investigated. The agencies also are subjected to condemnation when children whose cases were substantiated are abused and injured after they were allowed to remain or return to families substantiated for maltreatment. Placing children outside of the home carries risks because the rate of maltreatment in foster care is hardly trivial. So, in practice, agencies are subjected to withering criticism when false positives and false negatives occur. CPS agencies find themselves in what appears to be irresolvable dilemmas and the solution is to swing from one side (false positive sensitive) to the other (false negative sensitive) depending on the most recent public tragedy.

A more rational, theoretical, and empirical approach is needed. If the screening process were reformed to be less aggressively false negative sensitive, then resources currently devoted to carrying out investigations that yield non-substantiations could otherwise be spent on services, staff, or recruiting and vetting foster care providers. Secondly, given the number of important decisions that must be made at the front end of the child welfare system, it is surprising that so little energy is devoted to recognizing the importance of decision making as a key task of caseworkers and supervisors. Training, policy, and culture emphasize the service-providing functions of CPS agencies and fail to train caseworkers in decision making. More important, CPS agencies are currently unable to provide case workers and supervisors with accurate and timely information about the children and families. Workers also have little immediate access to information about children and families that might be contained in related systems, including educational, medical, and criminal records. This leaves caseworkers who initiate investigations with little information on exactly what they should expect to find when they arrive at the home of the suspected victim.

A refocusing of CPS on decisions, the process of decision making, and what critical information is needed to make sound, reliable, and accurate decisions at each gate of the system should be a priority for child welfare and child protective services.

REFERENCES

Baird, C. (2002). *Comparison Study of the Use and Effectiveness of Different Risk Assessment Models in CPS Decision Making Processes*. Ithaca, NY: National Data Archive on Child Abuse and Neglect.

Baird, C., & Wagner, D. (2000). The relative validity of actuarial – and consensus – based risk assessment systems. *Children and Youth Review Services*, *22*, 11–12.

Dawes, R., Faust, D., & Meehl, P. (1989). Clinical versus actuarial judgment. *Science*, *243*, 1668–1674.

Flaherty, C., & Patterson, D. (2003). Predicting child physical abuse recurrence: Comparison of neural network to logistic regression. *Journal of Technology in Human Services*, *4*, 93–112.

Gambrill, E., & Shlonksy, A. (2000). Risk assessment in context. *Children's Youth and Services Review*, *22*, 813–837.

Gelles, R.J. (1982). Problems in defining and labeling child abuse. In R.H. Starr Jr. (Ed.), *Child Abuse Prediction: Policy Implications* (pp. 1–30). Cambridge, MA: Ballinger.

Gelles, R.J. (1996). *The Book of David: How Preserving Families can Cost Children's Lives.* New York: Basic Books.

Gelles, R.J., & Spigner, C. (2008). Child welfare policy. In I.C. Colby, K.M. Sowers, & C.N. Dulmus (Eds), *Comprehensive Handbook of Social Work and Social Welfare: Volume 4, Social Policy and Policy Practice* (pp. 295–318). New York: John Wiley & Sons.

Guggenheim, M. (2005). *What's Wrong with Children's Rights?* Cambridge, MA: Harvard University Press.

Knoke, D., & Trocme, N. (2005). *Reviewing the Evidence on Risk Assessment*. Oxford University Press.

Marshall, D., & English, D. (2000). Neural network modeling of risk assessment in child protective services. *Psychological Methods*, *5*(1), 102–124.

Myers, J.E.B. (2006). *Child Protection in America: Past, Present, and Future*. New York: Oxford University Press.

Nelson, B.J. (1984). *Making an Issue of Child Abuse: Political Agenda Setting for Social Problems*. Chicago, IL: University Chicago Press.

Rossi, P., Schuerman, J., & Budde, S. (1996). *Understanding Child Maltreatment Decisions and Those Who Make Them*. Chicago, IL: University of Chicago, Chapin Hall Center for Children.

Rycus, J., & Hughes, R. (2003). *Issues in Risk Assessment in Child Protective Services*. Columbus, OH: North American Resource Center for Child Welfare.

Rycus, J., & Hughes, R. (2008). Assessing risk through the life of a child welfare case. In D. Lindsey, & A. Shlonsky (Eds), *Child Welfare Research* (pp. 201–213). New York: Oxford University Press.

Santovsky v. Kramer, 455 US 745 (1982).

Schwartz, D., Kaufman, A., & Schwartz, I. (2004). Computational intelligence techniques for risk assessment and decision support. *Children and Youth Services Review*, *26*, 1081–1095.

Smith v. Organization of Foster Families for Equality and Reform, 431 U.S. 816 (1977).

US Department of Health and Human Services. (2009). Child maltreatment 2007. Retrieved from http://www.acf.hhs.gov/programs/cb/pubs/cm07/table2_3.htm

Zandi, I. (2000). Use of artificial neural network as a risk assessment tool in preventing child abuse. Retrieved from http://www.acasa.upenn.edu.

20

Facilitating Effective Participation by Children in the Legal System

Lindsay C. Malloy, David J. La Rooy, and Michael E. Lamb

In the preceding chapters, professionals from around the world have provided clear and practical information summarizing what we currently know and what those working in the field *should* know about children's testimony. Since the first edition of this volume was published in 2002, our levels of understanding and knowledge have increased dramatically, making the time ripe for a completely new and fully up-to-date edition of *Children's Testimony* in which the scientific support underlying recommended practices is summarized and explained. Because all of the contributors have communicated relevant information in a straightforward manner, we hope that reading this book will increase adherence to and confidence in best practice. Certainly, readers who follow these recommendations will be well placed to defend their practices if challenged.

The contents of this volume make clear that the field of 'children's testimony' is a very broad one indeed. In fact, a diverse group of professionals – both researchers and practitioners – have worked together

Children's Testimony: A Handbook of Psychological Research and Forensic Practice, Second Edition.
Edited by Michael E. Lamb, David J. La Rooy, Lindsay C. Malloy, and Carmit Katz.

here to share and explain valuable expertise and advice. Although these professionals operate within the constraints of diverse legal systems with different rules and procedures, it is clear that professionals in these varied contexts face many common challenges and needs:

- What should I know about children's development (including the development of memory and language) before starting to interview child witnesses?
- How can I best build rapport and address motivational issues such as fear and reluctance?
- What is the best way to assess children's competency?
- Are there ways to make children more informative without being suggestive?
- What are the most effective and appropriate types of questions?
- How can I address children's emotional needs in both the short and long term?
- What is the best approach to training?

Forensic interviewers and other individuals working in the field of children's testimony have important roles in protecting children and innocent suspects alike. They must understand children's developmental characteristics, capacities, and limitations, including, for example, the development of memory and language in childhood. This foundational knowledge lays the groundwork for understanding children's testimony and for setting realistic expectations of children's performance in eyewitness contexts. An understanding of children's developmental capacities and limitations allows interviewers, lawyers, judges, and others to 'play to the strengths' of children involved in the legal system and to avoid compromising their evidence and testimony by asking them questions that require cognitive, linguistic, or social skills that have not yet been developed. For example, basic research by developmental psychologists tells us how children's testimonial competency might best be assessed. Specifically, rather than asking children to define 'truth' or 'lie', developmentally appropriate assessments call for asking young children to identify true and false statements and to promise to tell the truth. Children as young as 2–3 years of age can demonstrate their competency when assessed in this manner.

Of course, when it comes to eyewitness testimony, children are not the only ones whose capacities and limitations should be considered. For example, even adolescents struggle to be consistent and accurate during cross-examination, which is considered by witnesses to be one of the most stressful aspects of legal involvement. Furthermore, after many decades of research, experimental psychologists have come to understand the strengths, weaknesses, and features of memory very well. They have, in the process, come to realize that human memory has some limitations that must be recognized by the legal system regardless of the witnesses' age. For example, although there are major improvements in memory across childhood, memory is imperfect and reconstructive among children *and* adults even when stressful, traumatic, or 'highly memorable' events are involved. Furthermore, normal memory processes like forgetting, rehearsal, and reminiscence affect both children and adults. Legal and psychological professionals need to appreciate the complexities of human memory and avoid having unreasonable expectations regarding the amount, specificity, or type (e.g., temporal) of information that children can be expected to recall.

All professionals working in the field of children's testimony benefit when they understand normative development, and awareness of children's capacities and limitations is also critical when children with intellectual disabilities and developmental disorders need to be questioned. Such children are disproportionately likely to be involved in the legal system as victims/witnesses yet have greater difficulty participating effectively than do typically developing children. In their chapter, Henry and her colleagues describe the challenges associated with specific intellectual disabilities and developmental disorders (e.g., Down syndrome, autistic spectrum disorder) but also demonstrate convincingly that children with mild and moderate intellectual disabilities are capable of providing forensically relevant details about their experiences.

While young children are, on the whole, less communicatively competent and more suggestible than adults, it is vital to remember that even preschool children can provide coherent narratives about events if they are interviewed appropriately. Thus, building rapport, preparing interviewees for their roles as witnesses (e.g., via narrative practice), and asking open-ended, non-suggestive questions are crucial when children provide testimony. Before interviewers can begin these significant tasks, however, they must plan their interviews effectively. Interviewers and their managers must remember that planning is not a luxury and is an integral part of helping children's voices be heard. The idea that interviewers should be 'open-minded' and unbiased does not preclude careful planning and setting objectives for each interview. Knowledge of broader issues surrounding cross-examination, expert testimony, and the use of specialist techniques can help interviewers plan appropriately and thus avoid potential criticisms of their work further down the line. Planning can also help interviewers identify whether intellectual disabilities or emotional issues may influence children's testimony and plan accordingly (e.g., for an intermediary).

In addition to being planned, effective investigative interviews should include efforts to build rapport and give children opportunities to practice providing narrative responses. These techniques enhance children's reports for both cognitive and social reasons. For example, rapport building, which should be based on open-ended invitations prompting children to tell about personally meaningful experiences, may help children overcome any reluctance to discuss abuse by increasing their level of comfort with the interviewer. Prompting children to discuss recent events serves multiple purposes: it allows children to demonstrate their basic competency by way of their ability to 'perceive, remember, and communicate', builds rapport with interviewers, and provides 'training' in how to structure episodic narratives before substantive issues are discussed. This practice is beneficial for children *and* interviewers: interviewers who conduct practice narratives ask fewer questions and fewer of the less desirable types of questions later on in the substantive phase of investigative interviews.

The substantive phase of the interview should only commence when interviewers feel that rapport has been adequately established. The quality of this phase of the interview is crucial where the protection of both children and innocent suspects is concerned, because these protections are best achieved when forensically relevant information about suspected incidents is carefully obtained and evaluated. Investigators are encouraged to obtain this information as much as possible using open-ended prompts both because these are input-free and because they access free-recall rather than recognition memory. For both reasons, they are more likely to elicit accurate information than are closed questions. Interviewers should only use more focused questions if necessary, and only when open-ended prompts and techniques have been exhausted. Because countless researchers and notorious cases have highlighted the dangers associated with suggestive practices, these should be avoided completely.

Many interviewers often consider using supplementary techniques (e.g., props, toys, photographs, dolls, context reinstatement, drawing exercises, or truth induction strategies) to assist children in providing detailed reports of their experiences. Such aids are widely believed to help elicit information from children under some circumstances and for a variety of reasons (e.g., by increasing rapport, by assisting children with language difficulties). However, it is important to be cautious when using these aids. As Brown shows in Chapter 12, careful consideration must be given to 'the type of technique, the age of the child, how the technique is presented, when in the interview it is introduced, the level of interaction the child is allowed (e.g., with props), and most importantly, the verbal instructions that accompany them.' Whether such aids will be useful is a question to consider when interviews are being planned.

In addition to obtaining detailed eyewitness accounts from children, investigative interviewers are in a unique position to monitor children for signs of emotional stress resulting from the events in question or the legal processes that have ensued. From their unique vantage point on the front lines, interviewers can make a difference by recognizing when children may benefit from intervention and referring them for appropriate services accordingly.

Clearly, we ask a great deal of investigative interviewers – from building rapport with vulnerable children and addressing motivational issues, to asking developmentally sensitive and forensically relevant nonsuggestive questions, to monitoring children's emotional well-being. Their jobs are very demanding and can have a crucial impact on children's lives so it is vitally important that interviewers are trained extensively and appropriately in best-practice methods. Interviewers must be given the time to update their knowledge via continual training and to review their work regularly. Allowing time for interviewers to reflect on their behaviour – the strengths and weaknesses – with managers and peers is the only sure-fire way to ensure that high standards are maintained. When feedback and regular review are terminated, adherence to best practices often begins to decline.

Of course, the interview of possible child victims must be viewed as part of a larger investigation, and leads must be followed up and checked. The quality and quantity of information obtained must be assessed so that decisions about next steps can be made effectively. If cases are not ready to move forward, then a careful SWOT (strengths, weaknesses, opportunities and threats) analysis should make clearer what options might be pursued to ensure case progression. Case reviews also provide opportunities to anticipate concerns that may be raised by expert witnesses if the cases were to be prosecuted and the evidence challenged in court by experts hired by defendants. Such a critical evaluation – reflecting on the interview from another's perspective – provides another opportunity for interviewers to evaluate their performance in a particular case and perhaps to improve the skills they will bring to bear in their next case.

We hope that this volume has proven useful for investigative interviewers, their managers and trainers, lawyers, psychologists, expert witnesses, social workers, and public policy makers. Furthermore, we hope that the information conveyed in this handbook will help agencies, managers, and policy makers to update and improve guidelines concerning children's testimony regardless of their jurisdictions and legal traditions. This handbook reinforces many of the existing approaches while also drawing attention to new ideas, approaches, and insights, underscoring the fact that guidelines should be regularly reviewed and updated as new information comes to light.

When this volume was first published 10 years ago, most recommendations for interviewers came from psychologists who had conducted experiments on children's memory in school classrooms or university laboratories. This research greatly helped clarify children's strengths and weaknesses as eyewitnesses and has been supplemented in the last decade by increasing numbers of studies exploring children's memories not only in ecologically valid (i.e., forensically relevant) analogue situations but also in the real world. Together they have allowed considerable advances in our understanding of children's competencies and of how young witnesses should be interviewed about experienced or witnessed events. We have learned a great deal from the hundreds of studies conducted since the first edition of this book was published, although there is much we have yet to learn, as many of the contributors to this volume point out. Looking to the future – we face some very great challenges indeed.

Most importantly, the economic crisis of the last few years will mean service cutbacks in many countries, and this may reduce the emphasis on child welfare issues and effective child protection. All the contributors to this volume argue that empirically based best-practice methods are the only reasonable way forward and are cost effective in the long term. Well-validated structured interview protocols (like the NICHD Investigative Interview Protocol discussed throughout this volume) can easily be incorporated into existing training programmes because they are consistent with international consensus about best practices as well as with specific guidelines like those included in the British Home Office's manual, *Achieving Best Evidence* (2007). The Protocol should thus be viewed as an aid to help interviewers adhere to widely endorsed recommendations, not as a technique to replace current teaching. Moreover, the NICHD Protocol is widely and freely available because it is in the public domain, with versions translated into and being used in many languages, including English, French, Hebrew, Swedish, Finnish, Korean, and Japanese. Conducting interviews that are of higher quality will help investigators to make decisions more effectively and with greater confidence, thus saving time, money, and resources.

It may seem that human resources are so stretched that interviewers cannot afford the time to review their work and to reflect on their practice, but this is a flawed assumption. It is essential that interviewers be given the means and opportunities to develop and maintain their skills. Ensuring that interviewers can and do conduct interviews that adhere to best-practice guidelines is the foundation for better decision making throughout the investigative, legal, and welfare processes in which some children and families become involved.

The true social costs of failure in this regard are incalculable. By placing children in a context that allows them to 'tell what happened' in their own words, we give child victims/witnesses the best chance to be heard. It is important not to forget *why* we need to obtain reliable testimony from children – to ensure that as many children as possible live in safe and secure environments. This should be done in a way that is sensitive to their developmental capacities and limitations as well as to the potential consequences of legal involvement and aspects of the legal process that children find most stressful (e.g., cross-examination, lengthy delays and continuances). In the future, it is critical for researchers and practitioners to continue working together, building mutually beneficial and lasting relationships, protecting the children being interviewed today while ensuring that children and innocent suspects will be protected even better in the future. Science must inform practice and vice versa. In the past, difficult lessons have been learned, and it is important that these lessons not be repeated in the next decade. In order to develop good practice, it is imperative that new and up-to-date research findings reach those who practice in the field. We hope that we have promoted such an exchange with this volume.

APPENDIX

The National Institute of Child Health and Human Development (NICHD) Protocol: Interview Guide

I. INTRODUCTION

1. **'Hello, my name is ________ and I am a police officer.** [Introduce anyone else in the room; ideally, nobody else will be present.] **Today is _______ and it is now ______o'clock. I am interviewing ______ at ________.'**

   'As you can see, we have a video-camera and microphones here. They will record our conversation so I can remember everything you tell me. Sometimes I forget things and the recorder allows me to listen to you without having to write everything down.'

   'Part of my job is to talk to children [teenagers] **about things that have happened to them. I meet with lots of children** [teenagers] **so that they can tell me the truth about things that have happened to them. So, before we begin, I want to make sure that you understand how important it is to**

Children's Testimony: A Handbook of Psychological Research and Forensic Practice, Second Edition.
Edited by Michael E. Lamb, David J. La Rooy, Lindsay C. Malloy, and Carmit Katz.

tell the truth.' [For younger children, explain: **'What is true and what is not true'].**

'If I say that my shoes are red (or green) **is that true or not true?'**

[Wait for an answer, then say:]

2. **'That would not be true, because my shoes are really** [black/blue/etc.]. **And if I say that I am sitting down now, would that be true or not true** [right or not right]**?'**

   [Wait for an answer.]

3. **'It would be** [true/right], **because you can see I am really sitting down.'**

   'I see that you understand what telling the truth means. It is very important that you only tell me the truth today. You should only tell me about things that really happened to you.'

   [Pause.]

4. **'If I ask a question that you don't understand, just say, "I don't understand." Okay?'**

   [Pause]

   'If I don't understand what *you* say, I'll ask you to explain.'

   [Pause.]

5. **'If I ask a question, and you don't know the answer, just tell me, "I don't know".'**

   'So, if I ask you, 'What is my dog's name?" [Or "my son's name"] **what would you say?'**

   [Wait for an answer.]

   [If the child says, 'I don't know', say:]

6. **'Right. You don't know, do you?'**

   [If the child offers a GUESS, say:]

   'No, you don't know because you don't know me. When you don't know the answer, don't guess – say that you don't know.'

   [Pause.]

7. **'And if I say things that are wrong, you should tell me. Okay?'**

   [Wait for an answer.]

8. **'So if I said that you are a 2-year-old girl** [when interviewing a 5-year-old boy, etc.], **what would you say?'**

   [If the child denies and does not correct you, say:]

   'What would you say if I made a mistake and called you a 2-year-old girl [when interviewing a 5-year-old boy, etc.]?'

   [Wait for an answer.]

9. **'That's right. Now you know you should tell me if I make a mistake or say something that is not right.'**

   [Pause.]

10. **'So if I said you were standing up, what would you say?'**

    [Wait for an answer.]

    'OK.'

II. RAPPORT BUILDING

'Now I want to get to know you better.'

1. **'Tell me about things you like to do.'**

   [Wait for child to respond.]

   [If the child gives a fairly detailed response, skip to question 3.]

   [If the child does not answer, gives a short answer, or gets stuck, you can ask:]

2. **'I really want to know you better. I need you to tell me about the things you like to do.'**

   [Wait for an answer.]

3. **'Tell me more about** [activity the child has mentioned in his/her account. AVOID FOCUSING ON TV, VIDEOS, AND FANTASY].'

   [Wait for an answer.]

III. TRAINING IN EPISODIC MEMORY

Special Event

[NOTE: THIS SECTION CHANGES DEPENDING ON THE INCIDENT.]

[BEFORE THE INTERVIEW, IDENTIFY A RECENT EVENT THE CHILD EXPERIENCED – FIRST DAY OF SCHOOL, BIRTHDAY PARTY, HOLIDAY CELEBRATION, ETC. – THEN ASK THESE QUESTIONS ABOUT THAT EVENT. IF POSSIBLE, CHOOSE AN EVENT THAT TOOK PLACE AT ABOUT THE SAME TIME AS THE ALLEGED OR SUSPECTED ABUSE. IF THE ALLEGED ABUSE TOOK PLACE DURING A SPECIFIC DAY OR EVENT, ASK ABOUT A DIFFERENT EVENT.]

'I want to know more about you and the things you do.'

1. **'A few** [days/weeks] **ago was** [holiday/ birthday party/ the first day of school/ other event]. **Tell me everything that happened on** [your birthday, Easter, etc.].'

   [Wait for an answer.]

1a. **'Think hard about** [activity or event] **and tell me what happened on that day from the time you got up that morning until** [some portion of the event mentioned by the child in response to the previous question]**.'**

   [Wait for an answer.]

   [Note: Use this question as often as needed throughout this section.]

1b. **'And then what happened?'**

   [Wait for an answer.]

   [Note: Use this question as often as needed throughout this section.]

1c. **'Tell me everything that happened after** [some portion of the event mentioned by the child] **until you went to bed that night.'**

   [Wait for an answer.]

   [Note: Use this question as often as needed throughout this section.]

1d. **'Tell me more about** [activity mentioned by the child]**.'**

   [Wait for an answer.]

   [Note: Use this question as often as needed throughout this section.]

1e. **'Earlier you mentioned** [activity mentioned by the child]**. Tell me everything about that.'**

[Wait for an answer.]

[Note: Use this question as often as needed throughout this section.]

[If the child gives a poor description of the event, continue with questions 2–2e.]

[Note: If the child gives a detailed description of the event, say:

'*It is very important* that you tell me everything you remember about things that have happened to you. You can tell me both good things and bad things.'

Yesterday

2. **'I really want to know about things that happen to you. Tell me everything that happened yesterday, from the time you woke up until you went to bed.'**

   [Wait for an answer.]

2a. **'I don't want you to leave anything out. Tell me everything that happened from the time you woke up until** [some activity or portion of the event mentioned by the child in response to the previous question]**.'**

   [Wait for an answer.]

2b. **'Then what happened?'**

   [Wait for an answer.]

   [Note: Use this question *as often as needed* throughout this section.]

2c. **'Tell me everything that happened after** [some activity or portion of the event mentioned by the child] **until you went to bed.'**

   [Wait for an answer.]

2d. **'Tell me more about** [activity mentioned by the child]**.'**

   [Wait for an answer.]

   [Note: Use this question *as often as needed* throughout this section.]

2e. **'Earlier you mentioned** [activity mentioned by the child]**. Tell me everything about that.'**

   [Wait for an answer.]

[Note: Use this question *as often as needed* throughout this section.]

Today

IF THE CHILD DOES NOT PROVIDE AN ADEQUATELY DETAILED NARRATIVE ABOUT YESTERDAY, REPEAT QUESTIONS 2–2E ABOUT TODAY, USING 'THE TIME YOU CAME HERE' AS THE CLOSING EVENT.

'It is very important that you tell me everything about things that have *really* happened to you.'

THE SUBSTANTIVE PART OF THE INTERVIEW

IV. TRANSITION TO SUBSTANTIVE ISSUES

'Now that I know you a little better, I want to talk about why [you are here] **today.'**

[If the child starts to answer, wait.]
[If the child gives a summary of the allegation (e.g., 'David touched my wee-pee', or
'Daddy hit me'), go to question 10]
[If the child gives a detailed description, go to question 10a]
[If the child does not make an allegation, continue with question 1.]

1. **'I understand that something may have happened to you. Tell me everything that happened from the beginning to the end.'**

   [Wait for an answer.]

   [If the child makes an allegation, go to question 10.]

   [If the child gives a detailed description go to question 10a.]

   [If the child does not make an allegation, continue with question 2.]

2. **'As I told you, my job is to talk to kids about things that might have happened to them. It is very important that you tell me why** [you are here/ you came here/ I am here]**. Tell me why you think** [your mum, your dad, your grandmother] **brought you here today** [or 'why you think I came to talk to you today']**.'**

   [Wait for an answer.]

[If the child makes an allegation, go to question 10.]

[If the child gives a detailed description, go to question 10a.]

[If the child does not make an allegation and you do not know that there was previous contact with the authorities, go to question 4 or 5.]

[If the child does not make an allegation and you know that there was previous contact with the authorities, go to question 3.]

3. **'I've heard that you talked to** [a doctor/a teacher/a social worker/any other professional] **at** [time/location]**. Tell me what you talked about.'**

   [Wait for an answer.]

   [If the child makes an allegation, go to question 10.]

   [If the child gives a detailed description, go to question 10a.]

   [If the child does not make an allegation and there are no visible marks, proceed to question 5.]

   [When marks are visible, the investigator has been shown pictures of or told of marks, or the interview takes place in the hospital or right after the medical examination say:]

4. **'I see** [I heard] **that you have** [marks/ injuries/ bruises] **on your ______. Tell me everything about that.'**

   [Wait for an answer.]

   [If the child makes an allegation, go to question 10.]

   [If the child gives a detailed description, go to question 10a.]

   [If the child does not make an allegation, proceed with question 5.]

5. **'Has anybody been bothering you?'**

   [Wait for an answer.]

   [If the child confirms or makes an allegation, go to question 10.]

   [If the child gives a detailed description, go to question 10a.]

   [If the child does not confirm, and does not make an allegation, proceed with question 6.]

6. **'Has anything happened to you at** [location/time of alleged incident]**?'**

[Note: Do not mention the name of the suspect or any details of the allegation.]

[Wait for an answer.]

[If the child gives a detailed description, go to question 10a.]

[If the child confirms or makes an allegation, go to question 10.]

[If the child does not confirm or does not make an allegation, continue with question 7.]

7. **'Did someone do something to you that you don't think was right.'**

[Wait for an answer.]

[If the child confirms, or makes an allegation, go to question 10.]

[If the child gives a detailed description, go to question 10a.]

[If the child does not confirm or does not make an allegation, proceed to question 8.]

***PAUSE*. ARE YOU READY TO GO ON? WOULD IT BE BETTER TO TAKE A BREAK BEFORE GOING FURTHER?**

IN CASE YOU DECIDE TO GO AHEAD, YOU SHOULD HAVE FORMULATED SPECIFIC VERSIONS OF QUESTIONS 8 AND 9, USING THE FACTS AVAILABLE TO YOU, BEFORE THE INTERVIEW. BE SURE THAT THEY SUGGEST AS FEW DETAILS AS POSSIBLE TO THE CHILD. IF YOU HAVE NOT FORMULATED THESE QUESTIONS, TAKE A BREAK NOW TO FORMULATE THEM CAREFULLY BEFORE YOU PROCEED.

8a. **'Did somebody** [briefly summarize allegations or suspicions *without* specifying names of alleged perpetrator or providing too many details].' (For example, 'Did somebody hit you?' or 'Did somebody touch your wee-pee [private parts of your body]?')

[Wait for an answer.]

[If the child confirms or makes an allegation, go to question 10.]

[If the child gives a detailed description, go to question 10a.]

[If the child does not confirm or does not make an allegation, proceed to question 9.]

9a. **'Your teacher** [the doctor/psychologist/neighbour] **told me /showed me** ["that you touched other children's wee-pee"/"a picture that you drew"]**, and I want to find out if something may have happened to you. Did anybody** [briefly summarize allegations or suspicions *without* specifying the name of the alleged perpetrator or providing too many details].' [For example: 'Did somebody in your family hit you?' or 'Did somebody touch your wee-pee or other private parts of your body?')]

[Wait for an answer]

[If the child confirms or makes an allegation, go to question 10.]

[If the child gives a detailed description, go to question 10a.]

[If the child does not confirm or does not make an allegation, go to section XI.]

V. INVESTIGATING THE INCIDENTS

Open-Ended Questions

10. [If the child is *under the age of 6*, REPEAT THE ALLEGATION IN THE CHILD'S OWN WORDS without providing details or names that the child has not mentioned.]

[then say:]

'Tell me everything about that.'

[Wait for an answer.]

[If the child is *over the age of 6* simply say:]

'Tell me everything about that.'

[Wait for an answer.]

10a. **'Then what happened?'** or **'Tell me more about that.'**

[Wait for an answer.]

[Use this question as often as needed until you have a complete description of the alleged incident.]

[NOTE: IF THE CHILD'S DESCRIPTION IS GENERIC, GO TO QUESTION 12 (SEPARATION OF INCIDENTS). IF THE CHILD DESCRIBES A SPECIFIC INCIDENT, CONTINUE WITH QUESTION 10b.]

10b. **'Think back to that** [day/night] **and tell me everything that happened from** [some preceding event mentioned by the child] **until** [alleged abusive incident as described by the child].'

[Wait for an answer.]

[Note: Use this question as often as needed to ensure that all parts of the incident are elaborated.]

10c. **'Tell me more about** [person/object/ activity mentioned by the child]**.'**

[Wait for an answer.]

[Note: Use this question as often as needed throughout this section.]

10d. **'You mentioned** [person/ object/ activity mentioned by the child], **tell me everything about that.'**

[Wait for an answer.]

[Note: Use this question as often as needed throughout this section.]

[If you are confused about certain details (for example, about the sequence of events), it may help to say:]

'You've told me a lot, and that's really helpful, but I'm a little confused. To be sure I understand, please start at the beginning and tell me [how it all started/exactly what happened/how it all ended/etc].'

Focused Questions Relating to Information Mentioned by the Child

[If some central details of the allegation are still missing or unclear after exhausting the open-ended questions, use direct questions. It is important to pair open 'invitations' with direct questions whenever appropriate.]

[Note: First focus the child's attention on the detail mentioned, and then ask the direct question.]

Following is the General Format of Direct Questions:

11. **'You mentioned** [person/object/activity]**,** [Completion of the direct question.]**'**

Examples

1. **'You mentioned you were at the shops. Where exactly were you?'** [Pause for a response] **'Tell me about that shop.'**
2. **'Earlier you mentioned that your mother "hit you with this long thing". Tell me about that thing.'**
3. **'You mentioned a neighbour. Do you know his/her name?'** [Pause for a response] **'Tell me about that neighbour.'** [Do *not* ask for a description.]
4. **'You said that one of your classmates saw that. What was his/her name?'** [Pause for a response] **'Tell me what he/she was doing there.'**

Separation of Incidents

12. **'Did that happen one time or more than one time?'**

[If the incident happened one time, go to the *Break*].

[If the incident happened more than one time, continue to question 13. REMEMBER TO EXPLORE INDIVIDUAL REPORTED INCIDENTS IN DETAIL AS SHOWN HERE.]

Exploring Specific Incidents When There Were Several

Open-Ended Questioning

13. **'Tell me everything about the** *last time* [*the first time / the time in [some location] / the time [some specified activity / another time you remember well*] **something happened.'**

[Wait for an answer.]

13a. **'And then what happened?'** Or **'Tell me more about that.'**

[Wait for an answer.]

[Note: Use this question as often as needed throughout this section.]

13b. **'Think back to that** [day/night] **and tell me everything that happened, from** [preceding events mentioned by the child] **until** [alleged abusive incident as described by the child].**'**

[Wait for an answer.]

[Note: Use variants of this question as often as needed until all parts of the incident are elaborated.]

13c. **'Tell me more about** [person/object/activity mentioned by the child]**.'**

[Wait for an answer.]

[Note: Use this question as often as needed throughout this section.]

13d. **'You mentioned** [person/object/activity mentioned by the child]**. Tell me everything about that.'**

[Wait for an answer.]

[Note: Use this question as often as needed throughout this section.]

Focused Questions Relating to Information Mentioned by the Child

[If some central details of the allegation are still missing or unclear after exhausting the open-ended questions, use direct questions. It is important to pair open 'invitations' with direct questions, whenever appropriate.]

[Note: First focus the child's attention on the detail mentioned, and then ask the direct question.]

Following is the general format of direct questions:

14. **'You mentioned** [person/object/activity]**,** [how/when/where/who/which/what] [completion of the direct question]**.'**

Examples

1. **'You mentioned you were watching TV. Where exactly were you?'**

   [*Wait* for a response]

   'Tell me everything about that.'

2. **'Earlier you mentioned that your father 'whacked you'. Tell me exactly what he did.'**
3. **'You mentioned a friend was there. What is her/his name?'**

   [*Wait* for a response]

   'Tell me what he/she was doing.'

4. **'Earlier you said that your uncle "fingered you"** ["French kissed"/"had sex with you"/etc.]. **Tell me exactly what he did.'**

REPEAT THE ENTIRE SECTION FOR AS MANY OF THE INCIDENTS MENTIONED BY THE CHILD AS YOU WANT DESCRIBED. UNLESS THE CHILD HAS SPECIFIED ONLY TWO INCIDENTS, ASK ABOUT 'THE LAST', THEN 'THE FIRST', THEN 'ANOTHER TIME YOU REMEMBER WELL'.

VI. BREAK

[Tell the child:]

'Now I want to make sure I understood everything and see if there's anything else I need to ask. I will just [think about what you told me/go over my notes/go and check with?]'

[During the break time, review the information you received, fill out the Forensic Checklist, see if there is any missing information, and plan the rest of the interview. BE SURE TO FORMULATE FOCUSED QUESTIONS IN WRITING.]

After the Break

[To elicit additional important information that has not been mentioned by the child, ask additional direct and open-ended questions, as described above. Go back to open-ended questions ('Tell me more about that') after asking each direct question. After finishing these questions, proceed to section VII.]

VII. ELICITING INFORMATION THAT HAS *NOT* BEEN MENTIONED BY THE CHILD

[You should ask these focused questions only if you have already tried other approaches and you still feel that some forensically important information is missing. It is very important to *pair* open invitations ('Tell me all about that') whenever possible.]

[Note: In case of multiple incidents, you should direct the child to the relevant incidents in the child's own words, asking focused questions only after giving the child an opportunity to elaborate on central details.]

[BEFORE YOU MOVE TO THE NEXT INCIDENT, MAKE SURE YOU HAVE OBTAINED ALL THE MISSING DETAILS ABOUT EACH SPECIFIC INCIDENT.]

The General Format of Questions Focused on Information that has *not* been Mentioned by the Child

'When you told me about [specific incident identified by time or location] **you mentioned** [person/object/activity]**. Did/was** [focused questions]**?'**

[Wait for an answer.]

[Whenever appropriate, follow with an invitation; say:]

'Tell me all about that.'

Examples

1. **'When you told me about the time in the basement, you mentioned that he took off his trousers. Did something happen to your clothes?'**

   [Wait for an answer.]

   [After the child responds, say:]

   'Tell me all about that.'

   [Wait for an answer.]

2. **'When you told me about the last time, you mentioned that he touched you. Did he touch you over your clothes?'**

   [Wait for an answer.]

   [After the child responds, say:]

   'Tell me all about that.'

   [Wait for an answer.]

3. **'Did he touch you under your clothes?'**

   [Wait for an answer.]

   [After the child responds, say:]

   'Tell me all about that.'

4. **'You told me about something that happened on the playground. Did somebody see what happened?'**

[Wait for an answer.]

[When appropriate, say:]

'Tell me all about that.'

5. **'Do you know whether something like that happened to other children?'**

[Wait for an answer.]

[When appropriate, say:]

'Tell me all about that.'

6. **'You told me about something that happened in the barn. Do you know when that happened?'**

VIII. IF CHILD FAILS TO MENTION INFORMATION YOU EXPECTED

Use only the prompts that are relevant.

If you know of conversations in which the information was mentioned say:

1. **'I heard that you talked to [] at** [time/place]. **Tell me what you talked about.'**

[If child does not provide more information, ask question 2; If child does give some more information, say:]

'Tell me everything about that.'

[Follow up with other open-ended prompts, such as **'Tell me about that.'** If necessary.]

If you know details about prior disclosures and the information has not been disclosed to you, say:

2. **'I heard** [s/he told me] **you said** [summarize allegation, specifically but without mentioning incriminating details if possible]. **Tell me everything about that.'**

[Follow up with other open-ended prompts, such as **'Tell me about that.'** If necessary.]

3. If something was observed, say:

a. 'I heard that someone saw []. Tell me everything about that.'

[Follow up with other open-ended prompts, such as **'Tell me about that.'** If necessary.]

If child denies, go to 3b.

b. 'Has anything happened to you at [place/time]**? Tell me everything about that.'**

[Follow up with other open-ended prompts, such as **'Tell me about that.'** If necessary.]

If child has/had injuries or marks say:

4. **'I see** [I heard] **that you have** [marks/bruises] **on your [ ]. Tell me everything about that.'**

   [Follow up with other open-ended prompts, such as **'Tell me about that.'** If necessary.]

5. **'Did somebody** [summarize without naming the perpetrator (unless child already named her/him) or providing most incriminating details]**?'**

   If child denies, go to next section.

   If child acknowledges something say:

   'Tell me everything about that.'

   [Follow up with other open-ended prompts, such as **'Tell me about that'** if necessary.]

IX. INFORMATION ABOUT THE DISCLOSURE

'You've told me why you came to talk to me today. You've given me lots of information and that really helps me to understand what happened.'

[If child has mentioned telling someone about the incident(s), go to question 6. If child has not mentioned telling anyone, probe about possible immediate disclosure by saying:]

1. **'Tell me what happened after** [the last incident].'

   [Wait for an answer.]

2. **'And then what happened?'**

   [Note: Use this question as often as needed throughout this section.]

[If the child mentions a disclosure, go to question 6. If not, ask the following questions.]

3. **'Does anybody else know what happened?'**

[Wait for an answer. If the child identifies someone, go to Question 6.]

[If the child confirms but does not mention the name, ask:]

'Who?'

[Wait for an answer. If the child identifies someone, go to Question 6.]

4. **'Now I want to understand how other people found out about** [the last incident].'

[Wait for an answer. If the child identifies someone, go to Question 6.]

[If there is missing information, ask the following questions.]

5. **'Who was the first person besides you and** [the perpetrator] **to find out about** [alleged abuse as described by the child]**?'**

[Wait for an answer.]

6. **'Tell me everything you can about how** ["the first person mentioned by the child"] **found out.'**

[Wait for an answer.]

[Then say:]

'Tell me more about that.'

[Wait for an answer.]

[If the child describes a conversation, say:]

'Tell me everything you talked about.'

[Wait for an answer.]

7. **'Does anyone else know about** [alleged abuse as described by the child]?'

[Wait for an answer.]

[Then say:]

'Tell me more about that.'

[If the child described a conversation, say:]

'Tell me everything you talked about.'

[Wait for an answer.]

[If the child does not mention that he/she told somebody ask:]

REPEAT ENTIRE SECTION AS NECESSARY FOR EACH OF THE INCIDENTS DESCRIBED BY THE CHILD.

X. CLOSING

[Say:]

'You have told me lots of things today, and I want to thank you for helping me.'

1. **'Is there anything else you think I should know?'**

   [Wait for an answer.]

2. **'Is there anything you want to tell me?'**

   [Wait for an answer.]

3. **'Are there any questions you want to ask me?'**

   [Wait for an answer.]

4. **'If you want to talk to me again, you can call me at this phone number.'** [Hand the child a card with your name and phone number.]

XI. NEUTRAL TOPIC

'What are you going to do today after you leave here?'

[Talk to the child for a couple of minutes about a neutral topic.]

'It's [specify time] **and this interview is now complete.'**

Index

Note: Page numbers in italics refers to tables and figures

Children's Testimony: A Handbook of Psychological Research and Forensic Practice, Second Edition.
Edited by Michael E. Lamb, David J. La Rooy, Lindsay C. Malloy, and Carmit Katz.